MW01706662

Bound for Canaan

ALSO BY THE AUTHOR

My Mother's Ghost: A Courageous Woman, a Son's Love, and the Power of Memory

Killing the White Man's Indian: The Reinvention of Native Americans at the End of the 20th Century

Cathay: A Journey in Search of Old China

The Underground Railroad *and the* War *for the* Soul of America

Amistad *An Imprint of* HarperCollins*Publishers*

BOUND FOR
CANAAN

FERGUS M. BORDEWICH

For information, address HarperCollins Publishers Inc., 10 East 53rd Street, New York, NY 10022.

Designed by Judith Stagnitto Abbate

Maps by Nick Springer

ISBN 0-7394-5854-X

This book is dedicated to the countless thousands of men and women who fled the bonds of slavery but were recaptured or died at the hands of their pursuers before they reached the safe embrace of the Underground Railroad. They are not forgotten.

We were at times remarkably buoyant, singing hymns, and making joyous exclamations, almost as triumphant in their tone as if we had reached a land of freedom and safety. A keen observer might have detected in our repeated singing of

O Canaan, sweet Canaan
I am bound for the land of Canaan,

something more than a hope of reaching heaven. We meant to reach the *North*, and the North was our Canaan.

—FREDERICK DOUGLASS

CONTENTS

ACKNOWLEDGMENTS

Many people have contributed to this book, in large ways and small, and have helped to make *Bound for Canaan* better than it would otherwise have been. I am especially indebted to Christopher Densmore, curator of the Friends Historical Library of Swarthmore College; David Levering Lewis; Kate Clifford Larson; Milton C. Sernett of Syracuse University; Jill Jonnes; and Stanley Harrold of South Carolina State University at Orangeburg. They were unfailingly generous with their time and insights during the writing of *Bound for Canaan*, and offered many valuable suggestions. Judith Wellman's knowledge of the underground in upstate New York was a resource upon which I drew many times. As always, Jack Barschi's provocative questions prompted me to rethink and clarify more than a few half-rendered ideas. What flaws remain are of course my own.

In many parts of the country, historians and local researchers generously shared the wealth of Underground Railroad lore they have collected. Diane Perrine Coon unraveled for me the intricate web of underground activity around Madison, Indiana. Betty Campbell was a rich source of information about the abolitionists of Ripley, Ohio. Caroline Miller explained the interwoven worlds of slavery and abolitionism in

Bracken County, Kentucky. Randy Mills and Les and Mark Coomer were my guides in southwestern Indiana, an exceptionally interesting area for the study of the Underground Railroad. John Creighton led me expertly through Harriet Tubman country on the Eastern Shore of Maryland. Paul and Mary Liz Stewart made the Albany, New York, underground come alive. Steve Collins took me to the poignant site that was once the town of Quindaro and filled my ears with stories of the underground in eastern Kansas. George Nagle of the Afrolumens Project, Tracey Weis and Leroy Hopkins of Millersville State College, and Matthew Pinsker of Dickinson College helped me to understand the underground in south-central Pennsylvania. Jane Williamson, curator of the Rokeby Museum, in Ferrisburgh, Vermont, introduced me to the marvelous world of the Robinson family.

Bryan Prince, curator of the Buxton National Historic Site, in Ontario, was one of the first historians I interviewed in 1998, before *Bound for Canaan* was even a proposal. He spent another long and productive session with me in 2003, discussing the remarkable story of Reverend William King and the Elgin Settlement. Also in Canada, Gwen Robinson, director of the WISH Centre, in Chatham, was a bottomless mine of information on the fugitive community there, and on John Brown's activities north of the border. John MacLeod of the Fort Malden National Historic Site, and Elise Harding-Davis, curator of the North American Black Historical Museum, provided very useful background on the black community and the British military garrison at Amherstburg. Steven Cook, supervisor of the Uncle Tom's Cabin Site near Dresden, directed me toward material on Josiah Henson's life in Canada. Wilma Morrison of the Norval Johnson Heritage Library welcomed me graciously in Niagara Falls.

In Canada, my dear friend David Lipton of Toronto contributed his time, a historian's rigor, and best of all his company as a traveling companion. The Canadian sections of *Bound for Canaan* were sharpened and deepened thanks to him.

Many librarians lightened the weight of my work by adding their own expertise to my research. Among them were Alison Gibson of the Union Township Library, in Ripley, Ohio; Thomas D. Hamm, curator of the Friends Historical Collection at Earlham College; David Poremba, manager of the Burton Historical Collection of the Detroit Public Library;

Arden Phair, curator of collections at the St. Catharines Museum; and Judith Sweets of the Watkins County Museum, in Lawrence, Kansas. Elizabeth Moger; Walker Goller of Xavier University, in Cincinnati; Jae Breitweiser, director of the Eleutherian College Historic Site, in Lancaster, Indiana; Saundra Jackson, director of the Levi Coffin House Museum, in Fountain City, Indiana; Tom Calarco of Schenectady, New York; James A. McGowan, and Steve Strimer of Northampton, Massachusetts, also lent assistance or advice at important points in my research.

My mother-in-law, Marjorie Allen Parvin, first introduced me years ago to the fascinating history of the North Carolina Quakers. Barbara Wright; her mother, Marietta Wright; and Hal Sieber directed me to sources of material on the underground there. Gwen Gosney Erickson, archivist of the Friends Historical Collection at Guilford College, made my research on the North Carolina Quaker underground a real pleasure. Richard Parvin, Ed Parvin, and John Parvin provided valuable nautical information that enabled me to describe navigation along the Florida coast.

I owe much to Carl Westmoreland of the National Underground Railroad Freedom Center, who in the course of a day's drive along the Ohio River in 1999 convinced me that there was a real need for a new general history of the Underground Railroad. Carl's vast knowledge of the underground prompted many lines of inquiry that I would not otherwise have suspected.

Bound for Canaan might never have come into being at all without the unflagging enthusiasm of my literary agent, Elyse Cheney, and my ever-encouraging editor at Amistad Books, Dawn Davis, not to mention the support of my wife, Jean, and the forbearance of my daughter, Chloe, who has perhaps come to think of books as cosmic black holes into which her father periodically disappears.

CANADA
Lake Nipigon
CANADA EAST
St Lawrence R.
Lake Superior
Montreal
MAINE
CANADA WEST
Ferrisburg
North Elba
VERMONT
NEW HAMPSHIRE
Portland
MINNESOTA
Lake Huron
Rochester
Lake Ontario
Oswego
Syracuse
Utica
Albany
Hudson R.
Hudson
Boston
MASS.
Springfield
New Bedford
Nantucket
WISCONSIN
Mississippi R.
Toronto(York)
Hamilton
Erie Canal
St. Catharines
Buffalo
NEW YORK
Peterboro
Caanan
Norfolk
CONN.
Newport
RHODE ISLAND
MICHIGAN
Lake Michigan
Detroit
Chatham
Windsor
Lake Erie
Elmira
Delaware R.
New York
IOWA
Chicago
Cleveland
PENNSYLVANIA
NEW JERSEY
Sandusky
Oberlin
Hudson
Lancaster
Kennett
Philadelphia
Galesburg
Wabash R.
OHIO
Pittsburgh
Wilmington
INDIANA
Columbus
Ohio R.
Wheeling
DEL.
Quincy
Indianapolis
Newport
Marietta
Harpers Ferry
Baltimore
MARYLAND
Hannibal
ILLINOIS
Cincinnati
Gallipolis
Washington, D.C.
Cambridge
Madison
Lawrence
Missouri R.
St. Louis
Ripley
Kanawha R.
VIRGINIA
Richmond
Osawatomie
Corydon
Louisville
Evansville
Lexington
Norfolk
KANSAS TERRITORY
MISSOURI
KENTUCKY
Owensboro
Ohio R.
Smithland
Cumberland R.
New Garden Meeting
Edenton
Greensboro
UNITED STATES
Arkansas R.
Nashville
Mansker's Creek
NORTH CAROLINA
TENNESSEE
Memphis
Tennessee R.
INDIAN TERRITORY
ARKANSAS
Florence
SOUTH CAROLINA
Atlantic Ocean
Atlanta
Birmingham
Charleston
Macon
ALABAMA
MISSISSIPPI
GEORGIA
Savannah
Montgomery
Vicksburg
TEXAS
Tallahassee
LOUISIANA
Mississippi R.
New Orleans
Pensacola
Cape San Blas
Cedar Key
FLORIDA
Gulf of Mexico
Biscayne Bay
Nassau
Key West
THE BAHAMAS
Mountain areas over 1,800 feet
0
500 Miles
0
500 KM

Philadelphia and Its Surrounding Area

Black Settlements in Canada West

Cincinnati Area and the Ohio River Valley

Bound for Canaan

Introduction

The year is 1844 or 1845. The night air is acrid, as it always is in Madison, Indiana, with the smell of the slaughterhouses and tanneries that line the north shore of the Ohio River. It is almost ten o'clock, and in this era before electricity, the darkness is profound.

The barber has done what he was told. He is alone on the street corner. He waits with the nearly killing anxiety of a man who is about to commit a crime. He is a slave, and he is about to steal himself.

The barber had been working in Madison, and sending his earnings back to his master in Kentucky, a common enough arrangement in the border states. He could walk away from the corner, he knew. He could go home, abandon hope of escape, get along somehow as a slave, and stay safe, in a way. But he could not forget George DeBaptiste's words to him: "Aren't you ashamed—you, a man able to make money, and take care of yourself, with a good trade, young, strong, and a man all over, if you were only a mind to be—to be calling another man your master, like a dog, paying over to him your wages?"

At ten o'clock, steps approach, and a black man slips from the shadows. He tells the barber to walk to the roadbed where the new railway is to be laid north from Madison. When he gets to it, he is to walk north until he reaches the post that marks the second mile, and then whistle twice.

The barber follows the instructions. He is leaving an entire life behind, and walking into the unknown. He is attuned to every rustle, click, and murmur of life in the night, straining for the sounds of feet in pursuit. It is a hard place for blacks, this southern edge of Indiana. White vigilantes sometimes attack blacks in their homes, in Madison. Slave catchers prowl the back country, hunting runaways. The barber knows, as every fugitive knows, that at any moment his break for freedom may turn into a disaster.

At the two-mile marker the barber screws up his courage and whistles. Another black man slips from the woods, with a gun at the ready. Walk another two miles, he tells the barber, and falls into step behind him. At the next appointed spot, a second armed man appears, and orders him to walk two more miles, with the two gunmen now following behind him. The drill is repeated four times, until the barber is surrounded by eight armed men.

Sixteen miles beyond Madison, instead of another gunman, there is a wagon waiting. Into it the barber climbs, and for the first time during that long night, perhaps, he begins to breathe normally again. Ahead of him lie the welcoming farms of white Presbyterian and Quaker farmers, of free blacks who do not fear the writs and guns of slave hunters, and his own freedom.

George DeBaptiste, the man who prompted the barber's elaborate escape, who executed it, who ensured that even if the fugitive's party was discovered it was carrying enough firepower to defend itself, was also, as it happened, a barber. He was also the secret head of the local Underground Railroad. In some respects, DeBaptiste was a very ordinary man, about thirty years old at the time, well known to everyone in Madison as a respectable member of the town's small free-black middle class. Unknown to them, almost every day of his life, he tested the limits to which a black man would be allowed to go in the deeply racist America of the 1840s.

It was dangerous enough for radical white abolitionists to risk helping fugitive strangers, breaking federal law every time they did it. For a black man, who could never count on the law to be on his side, it was brave beyond imagining. For the underground, both opportunity and death were as close as the Kentucky shore. Madison stood on the invisible line that ran along the Ohio River, dividing the slave states from the free as absolutely as if they had been cut apart by a cleaver. During his eight years in Madison, DeBaptiste estimated that he personally assisted 108 fugitives to freedom, and several times that number indirectly. Failure at any point could easily have cost him his life.

The name of the barber who escaped that night more than a century and a half ago has long been forgotten. His story still exists only because it survived in the memory of George DeBaptiste, who recounted it to a reporter for a Detroit newspaper in 1870, a few years before he died. But the events of that night were epochal, in their way. Another chip had silently been knocked out of the edifice of slavery, and another victory gained for the clandestine army that was changing America.

At the start of the twenty-first century, Americans are in the midst of a contentious, often painful, national debate about slavery and its role in American history. At a time when earlier remedies for inequality have been discarded as politically and practically unacceptable, as the historian of American slavery Ira Berlin has put it, "slavery has become a language, a way to talk about race, in a society in which it seems that blacks and whites hardly talk to each other at all." Modern-day racism's roots lie in the slavery era, and any attempt to seriously address race today must also take into account not only the slavery of the past, but also the commitment and sacrifices of other Americans, both black and white, to bring slavery to an end. A better understanding of the Underground Railroad, and of men and women like George DeBaptiste, deserves to be part of that conversation.

The Underground Railroad occupies a romantic place in the American imagination that is shared by only a few episodes in the nation's history: the Lewis and Clark expedition, for instance, the California Gold Rush, the Indian wars, and a handful of others. It is a term that is so instantly recognizable that it is today automatically applied to clandestine routes of travel, whether of downed Allied airmen from Nazi-held France, or refugee Afghans making their way to Western Europe from their war-torn homeland. (During the Civil War, Southerners even used it to describe the passage of escaped Confederate prisoners southward from Yankee jails, with the help of proslavery sympathizers.) Yet its true history and its lasting significance are surprisingly little known. Because the Underground Railroad was secretive, and because much of its story has been forgotten, or deliberately suppressed, its memory has sheered away into myth and legend like no other piece of our history. To most Americans, perhaps, mention of the Underground Railroad evokes a thrilling but vague impression of tunnels, disguises, mysterious codes, midnight rides, and hairsbreadth escapes. And although residents of almost any town in the Northern states have heard about some old house or hidey-hole in which fugitive slaves were supposedly sheltered, few can name a single man or woman who was part of the Underground Railroad, apart from the inimitable Harriet Tubman.

The story of the Underground Railroad is an epic of high drama, moral courage, religious inspiration, and unexpected personal transformations played out by a cast of extraordinary personalities who often seem at the same time both startlingly modern and peculiarly archaic, combining then-radical ideas about race and political action with traditional notions of personal honor and sacred duty. For generations, Americans thought of the Underground Railroad as a mostly monochromatic narrative of high-minded white people condescending to assist terrified and helpless blacks. Only recently have African Americans begun to be restored to their rightful place at the center of the story. But the Underground Railroad is no more "black history" than it is "white history": it is *American* history, and it swept into its orbit courageous Americans of every hue. It was the country's first racially integrated civil rights movement, in which whites and blacks worked together for six decades before the Civil War, taking great risks together, saving tens of thousands of lives together, and ultimately succeeding together in one of the most ambitious political undertakings in American history. Their collective experience is, if anything, an even greater record of personal bravery and self-sacrifice than is generally known. In border areas, underground agents faced the constant danger of punitive litigation, personal violence, and possible death. In an era when emancipation seemed subversive and outlandish to most Americans, the men and women of the underground defied society's standards on a daily basis, inspired by a sense of spiritual imperative, moral conviction, and, especially on the part of African American activists, a fierce visceral passion for freedom.

Beginning with a handful of members around Philadelphia at the turn of the nineteenth century, by the 1850s the underground had developed into a diverse, flexible, and interlocking system with thousands of activists reaching from the upper South to Canada. In practice, the underground was a model of democracy in action, operating in most areas with a minimum of central direction and a maximum of grassroots involvement, and with only one strategic goal: to provide aid to any fugitive slave who asked for it. While the forwarding of fugitives was the central purpose of the underground, it also incorporated a broader infrastructure of itinerant preachers, teamsters, and peddlers who carried messages for the underground into the South, slaves who themselves never fled but provided information regarding escape routes to those who did, sailors and ships' stewards who concealed runaways on their vessels, lawyers who were willing to defend fugitives and those who were accused of harboring them, businessmen who provided needed funds, as well as an even wider pool of family members, friends, and fellow parishioners who although they might never engage personally in illegal activity, protected those who did and made it possible for them to continue their work. Although cell-like in structure, the underground resembled the Communist Party much less than it did the Internet. Where danger was immediate, and proslavery forces strong, few who were involved in the underground knew the names of collaborators farther away than the next town or two. In ardently abolitionist areas, however, it was less a secret movement than it was a public one that kept its activities secret only from its enemies. "The method of operating was not uniform but adapted to the requirements of each case," as Isaac Beck, an underground stationmaster in southern Ohio, put it. "There was no regular organization, no constitution, no officers, no laws or agreement or rule except the 'Golden Rule,' and every man did what seemed right in his own eyes."

The Underground Railroad's impact on the antebellum United States was profound. Apart from sporadic slave rebellions, only the Underground Railroad physically resisted the repressive laws that held slaves in bondage. The nation's first great movement of civil disobedience since the American Revolution, it engaged thousands of citizens in the active subversion of federal law and the prevailing mores of their communities, and for the first time asserted the principle of personal, active responsibility for others' human rights. By provoking fear and anger in the South, and prompting the enactment of draconian legislation that eroded the rights of *white* Americans, the Underground Railroad was a direct contributing cause of the Civil War. It also gave many African Americans their first experience in politics and organizational management. And in an era when proslavery ideologues stridently asserted that blacks were better off in slavery because they lacked the basic intelligence, and even the biological ability, to take care of themselves, the Underground Railroad offered repeated proof of their courage and initiative.

The Underground Railroad, and the broader abolition movement of which it was a part, were also a seedbed of American feminism. "Woman [is] more fully identified with the slave than man can possibly be," Elizabeth Cady Stanton, the first national leader of the women's movement, declared. "For while the man is born to do whatever he can, for the woman and the Negro there is no such privilege." In the underground, women were for the first time participants in a political movement on an equal plane with men, sheltering and clothing fugitive slaves, serving as guides, risking reprisals against their families, and publicly insisting that their voices be heard.

Like most Americans, probably, I first heard of the Underground Railroad in the form of legend. Near the community in suburban Westchester County, New York, where I was raised there was (and still is) a mainly African-American neighborhood which, a local story held, had been settled by fugitive slaves before the Civil War. Prosaic a place though it was in appearance—a few blocks of tar-shingled row houses and small, unadorned split-levels—it held a fascination for me as a symbol of a time of heroes long past. My mother, herself an activist as the national director of the Association on American Indian Affairs, more than once cited the neighborhood's supposed fugitive founders as proof of the power of individuals to defy injustice, and to shape the world they lived in for the better.

Over the years, I thought about the Underground Railroad from time to time. But the subject always had something impenetrable about it behind the hard sheen of myth: the stories often seemed too polished, the hideaways improbable, and the central protagonists, the fugitives themselves, frustratingly beyond reach. I knew something about Frederick Douglass and Harriet Tubman, who were among the tiny handful of

African Americans who turned up in school curriculums in the 1950s. But they seemed to exist in a virtual vacuum, at least as far as the Underground Railroad was concerned. In time, I came across other, totally unfamiliar names connected with the underground—Isaac Hopper, Levi Coffin, Jermain Loguen, and George DeBaptiste, to name just a few—whose stories, once I heard them, were astonishing in both their dramatic intensity and their political significance. How, I wondered, could they simply have been forgotten? Yet they remained almost completely unknown, outside a very small world of professional historians and researchers. I was intrigued, and began picking up pieces of underground history, like precious found objects, wherever I encountered them, in upstate New York hamlets, in North Carolina, in Ohio, and as far west as Kansas.

In June 1999, amid newly mown fields that stretched across the vast flat landscape of southern Ontario, I stood on the site of the school for fugitive slaves founded in 1841 by the remarkable Josiah Henson, himself a runaway who reached Canada after escaping from a plantation in Kentucky. Henson's Dawn colony was one of the terminals of the Underground Railroad, the ultimate safe haven for fugitives who had traveled hundreds of miles, mostly on foot, from Kentucky, Maryland, Virginia, and beyond. The site was marked by a small museum and Henson's preserved home. His gravestone, nearby, was topped with a carved stone crown, a symbol of the freedom that he found in Queen Victoria's dominions. I tried to picture the men and women who had found safety and hope there, and who had gone on to build new lives for themselves in freedom. Who were they? What had driven them to risk death and torture by taking flight? What had they left behind? How had they gotten here? Who had helped them across the blasted racial landscape of nineteenth-century America, through the war zone of antebellum politics, a field of battle within which fugitive slaves had no power, few rights, and little hope for protection? This book began with those questions.

I have not written an encyclopedic survey of the underground. I have not tried, for instance, to identify every agent and conductor, or to describe every "station" and "line." Nor have I attempted to chronicle the broader phenomenon of runaway slaves in general, some of whom found refuge in Spanish Florida and Mexico, and in "maroon" colonies within the South. These stories are important to the history of slavery, but are peripheral to that of the underground as it was known to its participants, who understood it as an organized system of free blacks, slaves, and radical white abolitionists allied in a common effort to help fugitive slaves reach safe havens in the free states and Canada. I have tried to show how the underground came into being, how it operated, and, more than anything else, what kinds of people—black and white, men and women—made it work. I have also tried to show that the Underground Railroad was much more than a picturesque legend, but a movement with far-reaching political and moral consequences that changed relations between the races in ways more radical than any that had been seen since the American Revolution, or would be seen again until the second half of the twentieth century.

PART ONE

Beginnings

1800 TO 1830

CHAPTER 1

AN EVIL WITHOUT REMEDY

> The Negro Business is a great object with us. It is to the Trade of the Country as the Soul to the Body.
>
> —JOSEPH CLAY, SLAVE OWNER

1

Josiah Henson's earliest memory was of the day that his father came home with his ear cut off. He, like his parents, had been born into slavery, and knew no other world beyond the small tract of tidewater Maryland where he was raised. He was five or six years old when the horrifying thing happened, probably sometime in 1795. "Father appeared one day covered in blood and in a state of great excitement," Henson would recall many years later. His head was bloody and his back lacerated, and "he was beside himself with mingled rage and suffering."

Henson was born on June 15, 1789, on the eastern shore of Chesapeake Bay, on a farm belonging to Francis Newman, about a mile from Port Tobacco. His mother was the property of a neighbor, Dr. Josiah McPherson, an amiable alcoholic who treated the infant Henson as something of a pet, bestowing upon him his own Christian name. In accordance with common practice, McPherson had hired out Henson's mother to Newman, to whom Henson's father belonged. Newman's overseer, a "rough, coarse man," had brutally assaulted Henson's mother. Whether this was an actual or attempted rape, or the more mundane brutality of daily life, Henson does not make clear. Perhaps he didn't know. Whatever the cause, Henson's father, normally a good-humored man, attacked the overseer with ferocity and would have killed him, had not Henson's mother intervened. For a slave to lift his hand "against the sacred temple of a white man's body," even in self-defense, was an act of rebellion. Slaves were sometimes executed, and occasionally even castrated, for such an act. Knowing that retribution would be swift, Henson's father fled. Like most runaways, however, he didn't go far, but hid in the surrounding woods, venturing at night to beg food at nearby cabins. Eventually, hunger compelled him to surrender. Slaves from surrounding plantations were ordered to witness his punishment for their "moral improvement." One hundred lashes were laid on by a local blacksmith, fifty lashes at a time. Bleeding and faint, the victim was then held up against the whipping post and his right ear fastened to it with a "tack." The blacksmith then sliced the ear off with a knife, to the sound of cheers from the crowd.

What the real sentiments of the slaves watching this punishment might have been no one can say. Perhaps they cheered in a desperate effort to reassure their masters that they, unlike Henson's father, were docile and trustworthy, and harbored no thoughts of rebellion. Or perhaps with relief, seeing a "troublemaker," whose deed had caused their masters to become more vigilant and harsh in an effort to forestall further rebellion, now getting his just deserts. Or perhaps, to people so brutalized by their own degradation, the cruelty may even have seemed a form of gruesome entertainment. Afterward, Henson's father became a different man, brooding and morose—"intractable," as slave owners typically described human property that no longer responded compliantly to command. Nothing could be done with him. "So off he was sent to Alabama. What was his after fate neither my mother nor I ever learned."

Following his father's disappearance, Henson and his mother returned to the McPherson estate. Even after years of freedom, Henson would remember the doctor as a "liberal, jovial" man of kind impulses, and he might well have lived out his life in passive oblivion as a slave had not it been for another stroke of fate that abruptly changed his life yet again. One morning, when Henson was still a small child, McPherson was found drowned in a stream, having apparently fallen from his horse the night before in a drunken stupor. McPherson's property was to be sold off, and the proceeds divided among his heirs. The slaves were frantic at the prospect of being sold away from Maryland to the Deep South, where it was well known that overwork, the grueling climate, and disease shortened lives. Even sparing that, an estate sale commonly meant that parents would be divided from children, and husbands from wives, lifelong friends separated from one another, a relatively benign master suddenly exchanged for a cruel one. For female slaves, the future might mean rape and permanent sexual exploitation. The only thing that those about to be sold did know was that the future was completely uncertain, and that they had not the slightest power to affect their fate.

In due course, all the remaining Hensons—Josiah's three sisters, two brothers, his mother, and himself—were put up at auction. The memory of this event remained engraved in Josiah's memory until the end of his life: the huddled group of anxious slaves, the crowd of bidders, the clinical examining of muscles and teeth, his mother's raw fear. His brothers and sisters were bid off one by one, while his mother, holding his hand, looked on in "an agony of grief," whose meaning only slowly dawned on the little boy as the sale proceeded. When his mother's turn came, she was bought by a farmer named Isaac Riley, of Montgomery County, just outside the site of the new national capital at Washington. Then young Henson himself was finally offered up for sale. In the midst of the bidding, as Josiah remembered it, his mother pushed through the crowd, flung herself at Riley's feet, and begged him to buy the boy as well. Instead, he shoved her away in disgust.

Henson was bought by Riley's neighbor Adam Robb, who kept a tavern at the site of present-day Rockville, then just a country crossroad. "He took me to his home, about forty miles distant, and put me into his negro quarters with about forty others, of all ages, colors, and conditions, all strangers to me," Henson recalled. "Of course nobody cared for me. The slaves were brutalized by this degradation, and had no sympathy for me. I soon fell sick, and lay for some days almost dead on the ground. Sometimes a slave would give me a piece of corn bread or a bit of herring." Robb, annoyed at being burdened with a useless slave, offered to sell the boy cut-rate to Riley. The planter agreed, although, as Henson would put it, he made clear that he didn't want to be stuck with "a dead nigger," and promised to pay Robb a small sum for him in horseshoeing only if Josiah lived.

Isaac Riley, who was to shape the remainder of Henson's life in slavery, was probably only about twenty years old when he took ownership of him. Isaac Riley's father, Hugh Riley, was one of the largest land and slave owners in Montgomery County. Isaac would inherit from him, and from his sisters, about four hundred acres of farmland mostly in present-day Bethesda, along with three tobacco houses, around twenty slaves, and at least one lot in George Town, as it was then written. "The natural tendency of slavery is to convert the master into a tyrant, and the slave into the cringing, treacherous, false, and thieving victim of tyranny," Henson opined. "Riley and his slaves were no exception to the general rule." Like most of Montgomery County at the turn of the nineteenth century, the gently rolling, lightly wooded hills of Isaac Riley's farm were planted mainly with wheat and other food crops, as well as tobacco, as the continuing presence of the drying sheds on the county tax rolls indicates. Nearly every farm in the county, probably including Riley's, also had a flock between six and twenty sheep, three or four dairy cows, and a dozen or so hogs. Farmers hauled grain to one of the local grist mills to get flour and corn meal custom ground, and shipped bushels of it to George Town; and to Washington, then still hardly more than a sprawling construction site; and even as far away as Baltimore.

Isaac Riley, according to Henson, was "vulgar in his habits, unprincipled and cruel in his general deportment." In the autobiography that he produced years later, with the assistance of a Boston abolitionist, for a primarily white, religious, Victorian audience, Henson was circumspect when referring to sex. But when he spoke of Riley's addiction to "the vice of licentiousness," he was probably referring to a propensity for sexually exploiting his female slaves. Henson's mother might well have been one of them. Henson never explicitly said so, but in spite of his evident attachment to his mother, she dropped completely out of his narrative after their purchase by Riley. Once again under her care, however, the boy, who was suffering as much from shock as from physical illness, rapidly recovered. His earliest jobs were carrying buckets of water to the older men at work in the fields, holding a horseplow for weeding between rows of corn and, when he grew taller, taking care of Riley's saddle horse. Eventually he was put to hoeing in the fields. Notwithstanding a staple diet mainly of corn meal and salt herring, he grew up to be an uncommonly robust boy, and a natural leader among Riley's slaves.

Henson would eventually become one of the most famous fugitive slaves of all, and one of the best-known African Americans of his time. He would become a conductor on the Underground Railroad, help found a community for refugee slaves in Canada, and travel to Europe, where he would even be introduced to Queen Victoria. But all that lay far in the future. Indeed, the small, terrified boy who stood transfixed by his father's torture and humiliation really had no future at all, to speak of. No future, that is, except the illiteracy, ignorance, and impotence that were the lot of the vast majority of slaves, unending days of toil, and the omnipresent threat of sudden, savage punishment. The lesson of loyalty was not lost on him. As he grew, Henson would craft himself into the ideal slave, a paradigm of loyalty, ever trusting and ever trusted, beyond reproach and therefore, he hoped, beyond punishment. He would never give a master cause for the kind of cruelty that his father had suffered, nor for selling him away to the unknown lands to the west, from which it was said that no slave returned.

2

North American slavery was born in the moist, flat tidewater country along Chesapeake Bay, and the lower Delaware, James, and Rappahannock rivers, where tobacco growing first made English settlement profitable. The first twenty African slaves were sold to the settlers at Jamestown, in 1619, by the captain of an errant Portuguese trading vessel. However, colonists continued to farm their ever-expanding plantations with an indiscriminate assortment of enslaved Indians from the dwindling coastal tribes, and indentured white laborers, as well as black Africans. The whites sold themselves (or were kidnapped) into what was, in effect, contract slavery in return for passage to America; although they were subject to the same restrictions and punishments as nonwhites, and could be resold during their term of servitude, they eventually had to be freed. The Indians died in staggering numbers from imported diseases that wiped out eighty percent or more of entire native communities. Gradually, the balance shifted toward the almost exclusive exploitation of black Africans. Slaves, unlike indentured whites, steadily continued to multiply their master's wealth, like well-invested money. And a slave, once "tamed" and trained to cultivate the crop that was the economic engine of the mid-Atlantic colonies, was a human tool that would last for decades. It was also, of course, harder for black slaves to slip away unnoticed and disappear into the free white population.

As tobacco production expanded from twenty thousand pounds in 1619 to thirty-eight million pounds in 1700, and then tripled again by the end of the eighteenth century, the demand for slave labor steadily grew. Between 1680 and 1750, the number of black slaves increased from about 7 percent to 44 percent of the population in Virginia and from 17 percent to 61 percent in South Carolina, where rice-growing in the coastal counties also lent itself to plantation economics. Slavery was by no means confined to the South. The number of black slaves in Connecticut grew from thirty in 1680 to fifteen hundred in 1715, and eventually to more than sixty-five hundred on the threshold of the Revolution. "The Negro Business is a great object with us," Joseph Clay of Savannah, Georgia, wrote, in 1784. "It is to the Trade of the Country as the Soul to the Body."

To be sure, commercial trade in all kinds of human beings was commonplace in seventeenth-century England. Bristol, London, and other ports exported large numbers of white indentured servants and prisoners of war. In 1652, for instance, 270 Scots who had been captured at the battle of Dunbar were put on the market and sold in Boston. Shipping kidnapped children and adults was also a thriving business. In 1617, a single agent, one William Thiene, exported 840 people, and in 1668 there were three ships at anchor in the Thames full of kidnapped children. By the end of the century, however, all other forms of the commerce in human flesh were dwarfed by the African trade. Between 1680 and 1700 alone, three hundred thousand slaves were shipped westward to the Americas in English vessels alone.

Slaves came in many varieties, and were marketed accordingly. Buyers in British America preferred sinewy and durable Fantis and Ashantis from the Gold Coast. The French, given a choice, tended to favor Dahomans. A reputed disposition to suicide undercut the export value of Ibos and Efiks.

Naturally "genteel and courteous" Senegambians were widely sought after for indoor work, while Mandingos were credited with exceptional skill at manual crafts, like barrel making and smithery. Angolans were alleged to be endemically lazy, and so commanded the lowest prices of all.

In Africa, slaves might be acquired in any one of several ways. Some were born into slavery, or sold into it by their own kings for imported commodities like weapons, factory-made textiles, and glassware. Some were captives of war, and others were kidnapped from their homes by roving bands of native slave hunters. Sometimes entire villages were surrounded and marched or carried by river to the coast. Still others were bred specifically for export by coastal traders. At the coast, slaves were processed for sale through established depots, or "factories," operated by one or another European trading company, or in some cases native Africans, or sold directly to foreign ships engaged in the trade. Olaudah Equiano, the son of a slave-owning tribal elder, was kidnapped as a child from his home in eastern Nigeria by slave hunters sometime in the 1750s. As the servant of a British naval officer, he eventually learned English and became one of the earliest slaves to recount his experiences in print, in his 1792 autobiography. His first sight of European slave traders aboard a ship terrified him beyond words. "I was immediately handled and tossed up to see if I was sound, by some of the crew; and I was now persuaded that I had got into a world of bad spirits, and that they were going to kill me."

The slave trade could be immensely profitable. One slave ship, the *Hawke*, carried three thousand British pounds of goods to West Africa in January 1779, where they were traded for an unspecified number of slaves, of whom 386 survived to be sold for more than seventeen thousand pounds in America, earning the owners a profit of more than seven thousand pounds. Massive profits from the slave trade fueled England's eighteenth-century Industrial Revolution. An early economist described the trade as "the first principle and foundation of all the rest, mainspring of the machine which sets every wheel in motion," generating capital that its wealthy investors in turn reinvested in mills, foundries, coal mines, quarries, canals, and other innovations, including James Watt's first steam engine.

By the time of the American Revolution, about two thousand American and British ships were engaged in transporting between forty thousand and fifty thousand Africans to the Americas every year. Although Thomas Jefferson, in an early draft of the Declaration of Independence, disingenuously blamed the slave trade on the king of England, the North American colonies were deeply implicated in it as well. Slave ships sailing from Charleston and Savannah, and from northern ports such as New York and Boston, generated huge profits trading cargoes of New England rum for slaves in Africa, typically at a rate of two hundred gallons per slave. Ships' captains were usually paid with a percentage of the cargo. "For every Hundred and four slaves In the West Indies or Where ever sold, you are to have four," one Yankee skipper was informed by his employers. Profits from sale of the slaves would be invested partly in West Indian molasses, which would be carried back to New England, to be distilled into more rum. When Parliament attempted to tax imported molasses in 1763, outraged Massachusetts merchants protested that it would ruin the slave trade. Such "taxation without representation" fanned already smoldering colonial resentment toward the Crown, contributing to revolution little more than a decade later.

No colony, or state, surpassed Rhode Island in its involvement in the transatlantic trade. Between 1725 and 1807, more than nine hundred Rhode Island ships sailed to the west coast of Africa, to bring an estimated 106,000 slaves back across the ocean to the Americas. Ships owned by merchants in just the three towns of Providence, Newport, and Bristol accounted for more than 60 percent of slaving voyages during that period, earning profits for investors from all levels of society, including the Brown family of Providence, the founders of Brown University. (Brown was not alone in benefiting from the slave trade: Harvard Law School's first endowed professorship, the Isaac Royall Chair, was financed with money from Royall's slave plantation on the island of Antigua, while Yale's first endowed professorship honored Philip Livingston, a slave trader.) Yankee merchants treated it as a trade like any other. "We left Anamaboe ye 8th of May, with most of our people and slaves sick," Captain George Scott wrote to his Newport investors, in 1740, from the coast of West Africa. "We have lost 29 slaves. Our purchase was 129. We have five that swell'd and how it will be with them I can't tell. We have one-third of dry cargo left and two hhds. rum. I have repented a hundred times ye buying of them dry goods. Had we laid out two thousand pound in rum, bread and flour, it would purchased more in value than all our dry goods."

On board ship, slaves were essentially stowed like any other commodity. Even in the better ships, conditions were horrific. Slaves were typically packed together so tightly in the hold that they could not move. In the "best regulated" ships, a grown person was allowed sixteen inches in width, thirty-two inches in height, and five feet eleven inches in length, or as was often said, "not so much room as a man has in a coffin." Men were generally confined two and two together either by the neck, leg, or arm, with iron fetters, sitting cross-legged in rows, back to back. In most ships, the slaves were crammed so tightly that it was impossible to walk among them without stepping on human flesh. The Reverend John Newton, a reformed slave captain—and composer of the hymn "Amazing Grace"—wrote that the slaves lay "close to each other, like books upon a shelf: I have known them so close that the shelf would not easily contain one more. The poor creatures, thus cramped, are likewise in irons for the most part which makes it difficult for them to turn or move or attempt to rise or lie down, without hurting themselves or each other." In the daytime, they were usually brought up at least briefly for air. It was not uncommon, at such moments, for despairing slaves to jump overboard to their deaths, in shackled pairs.

Olaudah Equiano, who was transported to the West Indies after his kidnapping in West Africa, remembered the voyage as a weeks-long nightmare of unremitting terror and excruciating discomfort. The stench of the hold was almost unbearable. "The closeness of the place, and the heat of the climate, added to the number in the ship, being so crowded that each had scarcely room to turn himself, almost suffocated us. This produced copious perspirations, so that the air soon became unfit for respiration, from a variety of loathsome smells, and brought on a sickness among the slaves, of which many died . . . This deplorable situation was aggravated by the galling of the chains, now become insupportable; and the filth of necessary tubs, into which the children often fell, and were almost suffocated. The shrieks of the women, and the groans of the dying, rendered it a scene of horror almost inconceivable."

Normal mortality during voyages was often as high as 25 percent. A similar proportion commonly died from illness, exposure, and shock before they were actually brought to sale, or during the so-called seasoning process, by which slaves were acclimated to their life and work in America, so that the total loss from any given voyage approached 50 percent. If there was an emergency at sea, slaves were simply "jettisoned" like any other cargo, that is, thrown alive into the sea to drown. In one case, in 1781, the British-owned *Zong* set sail with 440 slaves, and a crew of 17. After two and a half months at sea, during which both the slaves and crew were decimated by rampant dysentery, the captain explained that if the slaves died of thirst or illness, the loss would fall on the owners of the vessel, but if they were thrown into the sea, it would be a legal jettison, covered by insurance. One hundred and thirty-two slaves were deemed too sick and not likely to live and were simply swung into the sea by their handcuffs. The ship's owners later claimed thirty pounds of insurance money for each. (The underwriters refused to pay, and the suit went to court, where it went against the ship's owners; it was the first case in which an English court ruled that a cargo of slaves could not be treated simply as merchandise.)

During the entire span of the transatlantic slave trade, the vast majority of slaves, perhaps as much as 85 percent, were taken to Brazil, the various European colonies in the Caribbean, and Spanish South America. The British colonies of North America and the United States imported only about 6 percent of the between ten and eleven million slaves that were brought from Africa. More than 40 percent of all slaves sold in North America were imported through Charleston, South Carolina. New shipments were advertised like any other commodity. One poetically inclined auctioneer proclaimed in the *South Carolina State Gazette*, in September 1784:

Abraham Seixes,
All so gracious,
Once again does offer
His services pure
For to secure
Money in the coffer.

He has for sale
Some negroes, male,
Will suit full well grooms
He has likewise
Some of their wives
Can make-clean, dirty rooms.

For planting too,
He has a few
To sell, all for the cash,
Of various price,
To work the rice,
Or bring them to the lash.

Slave sales of course existed in every major city. William Wells Brown, who escaped to the North in 1834, worked for a time as an assistant to a slave speculator, or "soul driver," who made periodic trips down the Mississippi River with consignments of slaves to sell in the markets of New Orleans. Part of Brown's job was to prepare old slaves for market by shaving the men's whiskers off and plucking out their gray hairs, or else blacking them with dye, a process that took ten or fifteen years off the slaves' apparent age. Before the customers arrived, they were dressed and driven out into the yard, where, often in tears, some were set to dancing, some to jumping, some to singing, and some to playing cards. "This was done to make them appear cheerful and happy," Brown wrote.

When demand was high, buyers were sometimes swept with what planters called "Negro fever." Mobs descended on newly arrived ships, snatching at the ravaged and bewildered Africans, peering into mouths and grabbing at limbs, and buying what they wanted on the spot. In small communities, slave sales often took on an atmosphere resembling a country fair. One auction in rural North Carolina was described by a visiting Yankee ship's captain who attended it to entertain himself while his ship was being unloaded. The auction, the anonymous seaman wrote in his journal, brought crowds of the country people to town "and by the middle of the afternoon the streets and stores are pretty well speckled with drunkards."

3

For most people, as for the Yankee skipper, slavery was simply part of the American landscape, sometimes a pleasantly picturesque one. George Whitfield, an early Georgia religious leader, asserted in 1737 that to invite white settlers to the colony without making it possible for them to own slaves was "little better than tying their legs and bidding them to walk." One planter wrote, a few years later, "It is as clear as light itself, that negroes are as essentially necessary to the cultivation of Georgia as axes, hoes, or any other utensil of agriculture." The noted Philadelphia botanist William Bartram, who traveled through the Southern states in the 1770s, took what he saw of slavery at bemused face value. An unusually acute observer when it came to plants, he was charmed by the picturesque sight of a South Carolina timber crew "of a gigantic stature, fat and muscular," hewing great pine and cypress trees: "Contented and joyful, the sooty sons of Afric forgetting their bondage, in chorus sung the virtues and beneficence of their master in songs of their own composition." The sanitized image of simple, happy slaves would become a classic one in an ever-growing body of pro-slavery literature that would continue to flourish without interruption through the romantic twentieth-century hokum of *Gone With the Wind*.

The truth, of course, is that slavery never had any innocence to lose, and it was never simple except in the eye of the white beholder. In 1790, a year after Josiah Henson's birth, there were 697,647 slaves in the United States, about 17 percent of the total population of 3,929,827. Within the common denominator of lifetime bondage, their lives varied considerably. The vast majority, perhaps 90 percent, worked at some form of agricultural labor. Women as well as men were often assigned to the heaviest work, such as plowing. Many others were trained to specialized trades, as carpenters, coopers, blacksmiths, teamsters, grooms, and not infrequently as overseers. Slaves also worked as valets and maidservants, nurses, cooks, and laundresses, and as servants in hotels and taverns. They crewed trading vessels that ranged along the inland rivers and the Atlantic coast. In the estuaries of Chesapeake Bay and coastal North Carolina, slave watermen harvested shad, oysters, and crabs, and piloted oceangoing vessels around hidden shoals. In every major port, slave artisans worked at caulking and refitting, and slave draymen and stevedores moved cargoes of cotton and rice, molasses, rum, and Yankee textiles. Hired-out slaves worked in coal mines, foundries, textile mills, brickyards, and cigar factories. As far north as New England, slaves tilled fields and tended herds; in some rural areas of New York state, they reached 20 percent of the local population. While most slaves worked directly for their masters, many others were leased out like modern-day rental equipment. In the personal papers of slave owners, there are relatively few references to "negroes" or "slaves," apart from an occasional runaway, or the death of an especially trusted retainer. But then why should there be? Slaves were a form of real estate, or human furniture, so to speak, whose personal life had no more intimate meaning than that of a cow, or a settee. Where they were considered human, the law allowed them no claim on their own families. It has been estimated that in the Upper South forcible separations probably destroyed one out of every three first marriages by slaves, and that a similar proportion of enslaved children were taken away from one or both parents to be sold.

Slaves might be property, but they were costly property, especially at the dawn of the nineteenth century, when the burgeoning cotton industry dramatically increased the demand for labor just as public opinion was pressing for an end to the transatlantic slave trade. "The time has been," complained one planter, "that the farmer could kill up and wear out one Negro to buy another; but it is not so now. Negroes are too high in proportion to the price of cotton, and it behooves those who own them to make them last as long as possible." To return maximum value to their owners, slaves, like any expensive tools, had to be properly maintained. They had to be fed, clothed, housed, and kept in work.

When they failed to perform, they had to be punished. Disciplining slaves posed certain problems. In contrast to free laborers, slaves could not be fired, and they could not be jailed without losing the value of their work. Nor could they be fined, since they had no money. What remained was physical punishment, which at least in theory was carefully calibrated so that it wouldn't permanently damage the "property." In 1710 the Virginia planter William Byrd noted in his diary that "my wife against my will caused little Jenny to be burned with a hot iron, for which I quarreled with her." Boston King, a slave apprenticed to a Charleston carpenter in the 1770s, was beaten severely on the head when any of the men in the workshop misplaced one of the master's tools. Olaudah Equiano was terrified by the sight of a female slave, a cook, who, for unexplained reasons, "was cruelly loaded with various kinds of iron machines; she had one particularly on her head [an "iron muzzle"], which locked her mouth so fast that she could scarcely speak, and could not eat or drink." On a Georgia plantation, floggings were regulated so that field drivers could administer only twelve lashes, the head driver thirty-six, and the overseer no more than fifty, a number that would leave the victim's flesh in ribbons. In the late 1770s William Dunbar, a sophisticated Mississippi settler who corresponded with Thomas Jefferson, condemned two runaways to five hundred lashes each, spaced out over time, and to "carry a chain & log fixt to the ancle." Flogging, it should be said, was also widely practiced in white American families upon their own members. As a small boy in the first decade of the nineteenth century, John Brown, who would end his life as the most famous of abolitionist martyrs, was savagely thrashed by his father for stealing three pins, and as a father himself, he applied the rod to his own children in accordance with a strictly enforced regime: eight lashes for disobedience to their mother, eight for telling a lie, three for "unfaithfulness at work," and so on.

The punishment of slaves for serious infractions was at times obscene by modern standards, but less so in an age that believed in natural inequality, and utterly lacked contemporary ideas of human rights. As Josiah Henson cruelly learned, the amputation of ears, as well as toes and fingers, was standard, and castration and burning at the stake were not unknown. In 1736 a Methodist minister heard a South Carolina slave owner recommend that one "first nail up a Negro by the ears, then order him to be whipped in the severest manner, and then to have scalding water thrown over him." Moses Roper's owner punished him for attempting to escape by pouring tar on his head, rubbing it over his face, and setting it on fire, although he put the fire out, Roper noted, "before it did me very great injury." After another escape attempt, Roper's left hand was placed in a vise and squeezed until all his fingernails peeled off. In the 1830s William Wells Brown, another chronic runaway, was first whipped and then tied up in the smokehouse and subjected to a fire of tobacco stems, a technique referred to as a "decent smoking," by his innkeeper master. The harshest punishments of all were reserved for those who physically attacked whites. When a slave girl belonging to the comparatively enlightened William Dunbar was convicted of killing a white, her hand was first cut off, and she was then hanged.

A blow struck against one white man was considered a blow against all, an act of rebellion that was not to be tolerated in areas where slaves sometimes far outnumbered whites. The French-American farmer and author Hector St. John de Crèvecoeur learned this one evening in 1783, while walking to dinner in the suburbs of Charleston, when he came upon a scene that shocked his philosophical sensibility. "I perceived a negro, suspended in the cage, left there to expire!" he wrote. The cage hung from a tree alongside the path. Around it, birds of prey fluttered looking for a perch. "I shudder when I recollect that the birds had already picked out his eyes: his cheek bones were bare; his arms had been attacked in several places, and his body seemed covered with a multitude of wounds. From the edges of the hollow sockets, and from the lacerations with which he was disfigured, the blood slowly dropped, and tinged the ground beneath. No sooner were the birds flown, than swarms of insects covered the whole body of this unfortunate wretch eager to feed on his mangled flesh and to drink his blood." Crèvecoeur managed to give a little water to the man, who told him that he had been hanging in the cage for two days as punishment for killing the overseer of the plantation on which he had worked. Later, over dinner, Crèvecoeur's hosts explained that such executions were rendered necessary by the "laws of self-preservation."

4

At the end of the eighteenth century, slaves thus lived under a regime in which fear was woven into the fabric of life, the threat of savage punishment was horrifyingly explicit, and the obstacles to a general revolution were insurmountable. Slaves could run away, and often did. But the great majority didn't run far. Late eighteenth-century advertisements for runaways in the *Virginia Gazette* offer some idea of where they went. Peter, a slave "who speaks very broken" and "has a down look," was supposed to be lurking around his wife's dwelling "in the lower part of the county." Stepney Blue had acquired a forged pass as a free man and was supposed to be "hiring himself out somewhere in the region." Caesar, who escaped near Prince Edward Courthouse, may have gone to Cumberland County where he was raised, "and must have formed some connections." Gabriel, a weaver, had forged a pass and may be seeking to board a vessel to get out of the colony. An older couple, Toby and Betty, may have made off by water to North Carolina, where they originally came from. Of these fugitives, only Gabriel the weaver was striking out for complete freedom in some distant place. The rest, like the vast majority of runaways, had chosen to take their chances close to where they had been enslaved, apparently counting on poor communications to save them from recapture. But none of them could count on permanent safety.

From the earliest days of colonization, the law recognized runaway slaves as a problem. The United States Constitution explicitly required that fugitives from "service or labour" in any state be delivered up to their owner. To this was added, in 1793, the nation's first Fugitive Slave Act, which empowered a fugitive's master or a hired slave catcher to seize him and return him to the state from which he had fled, with the usually pro forma approval of a local magistrate. Both the law and public opinion so favored slave owners that as the new century approached, for fugitive slaves, there was no safe haven anywhere. Although there were growing numbers of men and women who opposed slavery for religious reasons, few believed that they had a *moral* right to break the law to help runaways. Slavery in some form was still legal in every Northern state except Vermont. In 1776 there were six and a half thousand black slaves in Connecticut, and fifteen thousand in New York state, only one thousand fewer than in Georgia as late as 1790. Fugitives managed to escape into wilderness regions, but by the late eighteenth century these were shrinking east of the Alleghenies. Moreover, most slaves were no better fitted to survive on their own than white men stripped of the accoutrements of civilization. Some slaves also escaped into Indian country, but they were as likely to be enslaved there or sold back to their masters, as they were to be welcomed as free men. Canada was still little known to slaves even in the Northeast, and in any case slavery was still legal there too, though no longer common.

The story of James Mars and his family suggests the prospects that fugitives faced, even where slavery was rare and whites sympathetic. Mars, who was born in 1790, his parents, a brother, and a sister belonged to a minister named Thompson, who lived in Canaan, Connecticut, in the rugged, thinly populated northwest corner of the state. Thompson, who was married to a Southern woman, had strong proslavery sentiments, and at a time when antislavery sentiment was spreading in New England, preached from the pulpit that God himself had sanctioned the institution.

Thompson had acquired property in Virginia, and in 1798 decided to move there permanently, taking along his slaves. Mars's father, however, was determined not to let his family be carried south, and carefully planned their escape on the eve of Thompson's departure. The elder Mars had learned that the inhabitants of the neighboring town of Norfolk were feuding with those in Canaan, for reasons unknown to him, and now lost to history. It is likely that he had already received encouragement from antislavery families in Canaan. In any event, as James Mars put it in a brief memoir later in life, the family threw itself on the mercy of people there. Initially, all went according to plan. As hoped, the Mars family was welcomed in Norfolk, eight miles to the east along the valley of the Blackberry River. There they were sheltered, fed, and protected for the next several weeks by an impressive number of townspeople, who included a number of Norfolk's most respected families. Their first host was none other than Giles Pettibone, the town's representative in the state assembly, as well as its treasurer and justice of the peace. For a time, the Marses were lent an empty house, and then, when Thompson was reported to be on their trail, they were led to a remote home occupied by "a very pleasant family." A visiting law student took Mars's older brother to his own home across the state line in Massachusetts. Meanwhile, Thompson somehow managed to make contact with the elder Marses and convinced them to return with him to Canaan to help him pack his belongings for the journey to Virginia. After a day or two, the Marses panicked and fled a second time to Norfolk, where they stayed at a popular tavern owned by Luther Lawrence, a Revolutionary War veteran. A human shell game now ensued. Whenever Lawrence heard that Thompson was in the area, he would send the Marses to hide in the surrounding woods. Sometimes the members of the family were separated. Eight-year-old James was sent to stay with Nathaniel Pease, a prosperous shoemaker, almost all the way back to Canaan, then with a man named Camp, then with someone named Akins, then a Foot family, then another Akins. This went on for weeks. The entire time, Thompson continued to propose deals: he would take the boys and give the parents their freedom; he would keep the parents and free the boys. Eventually the Marses became convinced that there was no safe place for them to live. Through intermediaries, a deal was made. Thompson proposed to sell the boys until they were twenty-five years of age (as permitted by Connecticut law) to somebody whom the elder

Marses would select. He would give the other members of the family their freedom. Buyers acceptable to the Mars parents were found in towns about fifteen miles apart, and the boys were sold to them for one hundred pounds each, in September 1798.

In this story, several important truths emerge. A surprising number of ordinary citizens were willing to ignore the law temporarily, and able to mobilize networks of family and friends—precisely what would later knit together the Underground Railroad—in an effort to keep the Mars family out of their master's hands. It is also clear that, especially in the person of Giles Pettibone, the local authorities were willing to turn a blind eye to activities that must have been obvious in a town as small as Norfolk. Indeed, several of the families who sheltered the Marses lived in homes only a few hundred feet apart, on or near the village green, the center of town. Mars never clarifies the motivation of the people who helped him and his family. The unspecified animosity between the inhabitants of the two towns may have played a part in the story, but it can hardly explain all the effort that the people of Norfolk undertook in the fugitives' behalf. Many of them must have helped the Marses because they believed it was the right thing to do. But it is also clear that there was no larger organization in place, no system for moving the fugitives far beyond the reach of the persistent parson. At no point during their odyssey were the Marses ever more than ten or fifteen miles from Thompson's home. In the end, there was no alternative to at least some of the family's reenslavement. In 1798, for the Mars family, despite a good plan, knowledge of the region and its people, great personal determination, and white friends, slavery was a fact from which there was still no escape.

CHAPTER 2

THE FATE OF MILLIONS UNBORN

I tremble for my country when I reflect that God is just: that his justice cannot sleep forever.

—THOMAS JEFFERSON

1

It is possible that the eleven-year-old Josiah Henson—now settled with his mother on Isaac Riley's farm, in Maryland—knew at least something about what was happening on March 4, 1801. Since he was illiterate, he could not read the *National Intelligencer*, the local newspaper, which in recent days had been carrying reports on the new president-elect Thomas Jefferson and his vice president Aaron Burr, the appointment of John Marshall as Chief Justice of the United States, and the gala inaugural gathering just a few miles away in Washington. But he surely heard whites talking about such things, along with news of the recent sale of public lots at Tunnicliff's Hotel, and the arrival of a shipment of wines for local sale. Even if news of the inauguration penetrated the slave quarters on the

George Town Road, it would have had little immediate significance to a boy who knew the young nation's ringing declarations of liberty and equality were intended to apply exclusively to white men.

A little before noon, Jefferson left Conrad and McMunn's boarding-house and, disdaining the pompous trappings of the state carriage that had been provided, democratically set out on foot toward the still-unfinished Capitol, where he was to take the oath of office. The new city, like the young nation itself, was still more an idea, more a hopeful plan than an established reality. Jefferson's walk that morning took him through what was essentially a worksite whose grandly named avenues were still troughs of red mud cluttered with alder trees and stumps, where only a relative handful of unimposing buildings lay scattered between patches of woods and the Potomac River. Even the president's official residence—not yet known as the White House—was still under construction. Cannon roared as Jefferson entered the north wing of the Capitol, the only concession to ceremony that the champion of the small farmers, and mechanics, and men of little property countenanced on this historic day, when power would pass, at least symbolically, into their hands and out of those of the Federalists.

When he raised his hand to take the oath from John Marshall, his cousin and political rival, the fifty-eight-year-old Jefferson was becoming president less of a stable union sharing a deep sense of common interest, than of a political confection that resembled the tacked-together Yugoslavia of the late twentieth century, a loose agglomeration of mini-states protective of their autonomy, and suspicious of encroachment by their weak central government. It was a simple, rural nation whose population was smaller than that of Ireland. Its largest city, Philadelphia, numbered seventy thousand inhabitants, and its constituent parts were linked by roads that were little more than rambling tracks sketched through the forest. The writ of the national government barely reached beyond the Appalachians, into lands that were still inhabited by powerful Indian nations who occupied most of the territory between the mountains and the Mississippi River. Indeed, only a few years earlier, the country had suffered the worst defeat ever to befall Americans at the hands of Indians, the loss of more than eight hundred men on the banks of the Wabash River, in present-day Indiana. Spaniards governed Florida; and the French, New Orleans and most of the Mississippi Valley. It was a country in which inequalities of class, gender, and race were ingrained and largely unquestioned.

The prospect of Jefferson's election had thrown fear into the hearts of many Americans. During the recent campaign, he had been denounced by his opponents as a "vulgar demagogue" and a "bold atheist," who would undertake "dangerous innovations." He owed his very election to the disproportionate power of the slave states in the Electoral College, a fact that infuriated legislators from New England. Now, however, his gracious demeanor, his acute intelligence, and more than anything else his conciliatory words reassured even Marshall, the leader of the Federalists, who had feared that Jefferson as president might prove to be an "absolute terrorist." When he began to speak, Jefferson's reedy voice barely reached the ears of his audience, who strained to catch every pregnant word. What he had to say was exquisite in its eloquence, fusing soaring idealism with the hard realities of politics.

The speech was Jefferson at his most seductive. "We are all Republicans—we are all Federalists," he declared, directly addressing his wary, not to say vengeful, opponents in the chamber. "If there be any among us who would wish to dissolve this Union or to change its republican form, let them stand undisturbed as monuments of the safety with which error of opinion may be tolerated where reason is left free to combat it. I know, indeed, that some honest men fear that a republican government cannot be strong; that this government is not strong enough. But would the honest patriot, in the full tide of successful experiment, abandon a government which has so far kept us free and firm, on the theoretic and visionary fear that this government, the world's best hope, may by possibility want energy to preserve itself? I trust not." He went on to describe his glowing vision of a rising nation, spread over a wide and fruitful land, traversing the seas with the rich productions of its industry, "advancing rapidly to destinies beyond the reach of mortal eye."

Jefferson never mentioned slavery. But the moral freight of his words could hardly be missed by anyone—they were still few, it is true, but their numbers were growing—who believed that simple justice demanded the emancipation of those in bondage. He promised "equal and exact justice to all men," the guarantee of equal rights for minorities, and a government "which shall restrain men from injuring one another, which shall leave them otherwise free to regulate their own pursuits of industry and improvement, and shall not take from the mouth of labor the bread that it has earned." Jefferson did not, of course, intend his words for Josiah Henson and the 896,848 other slaves in the sixteen states of the federal union. (Vermont had become a state in 1791, Kentucky in 1792, and Tennessee in 1796.) Although he passionately hated slavery, in the abstract, Jefferson had always accommodated himself to it in practice, and he had no wish to antagonize his many slave-owning supporters. Yet his words ringingly embodied beliefs about justice and equality that underscored the terrible contradictions in a nation that proclaimed its faith in individual liberty while continuing to hold seventeen percent of its inhabitants in bondage.

At fifty-eight, Jefferson's body was still slim and taut, and his "mild and pleasing countenance" radiated optimism. As he stood that day before his assembled countrymen, he embodied many of the deepest contradictions of his young nation. John Quincy Adams would describe him as "a rare mixture of infidel philosophy and epicurean morals, of burning ambition and of stoical self-control, of deep duplicity and of generous sensibility." He was an aristocrat, a product of the landed Southern gentry, who espoused a vision of the most radical democracy. An early and outspoken enemy of slavery, he was also one of the largest slave owners in Virginia. Slavery was woven inextricably into the fabric of his personal life and his political world. Like other planters, he measured his wealth largely in slaves and land. Slaves had served him since his birth. Nearly two hundred slaves tilled the fields of his estates. Slaves would attend him day in, day out in the president's house. A man who condemned racial mixing in the harshest terms, he carried on a liaison with one of his female slaves that lasted for decades.

Jefferson's enemies accused him of maintaining a sexual relationship with Sally Hemings, a light-skinned slave twenty-seven years his junior, the half-sister of his deceased wife, and said that he had fathered children by her. Jefferson vigorously denied the charge, although such relationships were extremely common. Gossip nonetheless took wing in the form of slanderous doggerel: "*Of all the damsels on the green / On mountain or in valley / A lass so luscious ne'er was seen / As Montecellan Sally*." Down to the present day, Hemings's descendants cited family tradition as evidence that the relationship had in fact existed, even as Jefferson's defenders dismissed such assertions as baseless, pointing to Jefferson's deep devotion to the memory of his wife, and to his oft expressed hatred of miscegenation to contradict them. Recent genetic research, though imperfect, has strengthened the Hemings claim and has gradually won over most modern scholars of Jefferson. Such a relationship, supremely private though it was, and ultimately as mysterious as any of the vagaries of the human heart, only deepens the profound ambiguity of Jefferson's professed, and deeply contradictory, attitudes about race.

2

Jefferson's racial dilemma, in all its dimensions—moral, psychological, emotional, political—was very much that of the nation itself in the early years of the nineteenth century. No American of his time examined his own ideas with more seriousness than Jefferson, a process that has been recounted with thoroughness by John Chester Miller, in *The Wolf by the Ears: Thomas Jefferson and Slavery*. In his struggle, and ultimate failure, to find a resolution to the problem of slavery, the uncertainties of the young nation can be seen as in no other single mind. From the grinding stress of that ambivalence would grow the inspiration for the abolitionist movement, and its activist cutting edge, the Underground Railroad, as well as the most bigoted defense of slavery, and the political philosophy of states' rights.

Jefferson embodied the very best in a nation that was increasingly struggling to find a painless way to end slavery, an effort that was doomed to failure from the start. He had, as much as any man living, created the United States, crafted the principles by which it strove to live, and been a part of the compromises that had been necessary to bring the country into being. More than most, he believed that slavery was morally incompatible with white men's freedom, and ultimately a reef upon which the nation might someday founder. In later years, his idealism, like that of many of his generation, would atrophy. Despite protestations to the contrary, he would eventually slip uncomfortably close to the camp of those who embraced slavery and states' rights as pillars of American stability. Yet his clarion appeals for liberty, which are most memorably enshrined in the immortal words of the Declaration of Independence, would have an impact far beyond his own ultimately class-bound intentions.

Jefferson held no illusions about the inherent cruelty of slavery: a "hideous evil," he called it. Intellectually, at least, he pitied the suffering of its victims. He also had little patience with the hypocrisy of the patriot "who can endure toil, famine, stripes, imprisonment, or death itself in vindication of his own liberty," but who could still wreak upon others a form of oppression "one hour of which is fraught with more misery than ages of that which he rose in rebellion to oppose." Perhaps most of all, he saw that its corrupting influence on those who owned slaves undermined the hardy self-reliance that he felt was crucial to the survival of democratic institutions. "The whole commerce between master and slave is a perpetual exercise of the most boisterous passions, the most unremitting despotism on the one part, and degrading submissions on the other," he wrote in "Notes on the State of Virginia," the fullest expression of his views on the subject. "Our children see this, and learn to imitate it . . . The parent storms, the child looks on, catches the lineaments of wrath, puts on the same airs in the circle of smaller slaves, gives a loose to his worst of passions, and thus nursed, educated, and daily exercised in tyranny, cannot but be stamped by it with odious particularity." He also feared that the continuation of slavery would inevitably lead to bloody rebellion and race war.

Coupled to Jefferson's hatred of slavery as an institution, however, was an ingrained repugnance toward blacks as human beings. He did not doubt that they were inferior to whites in both body and mind, and considered it to be at least possible that they were "different species of the same genus." He thought that it would be impossible for the races to live together in freedom, and miscegenation appalled him. As governor of Virginia, he had proposed a bill requiring a white woman who had given birth to a mulatto child to leave the state. Later, as part of a proposed plan for the emancipation of slaves, he suggested that black children be removed from their parents and reared at public expense, and trained either in farming or other trades, girls until the age of eighteen and boys to twenty-one, and then "colonized to such place as the circumstances of the time should render most proper." It was absolutely essential that they "be removed beyond the reach of mixture." Their parents, meanwhile, inured to the dependency of slavery, would eventually die off, and white immigrants would be invited to repopulate the land. For such a supremely rational man, it was a bizarre scheme, and would have required (he calculated) fifty ships per year to deport just the sixty thousand additional blacks who were born annually. "Why not retain and incorporate the blacks into the state, and thus save the expense of supplying, by importation of white settlers, the vacancies they will leave?" he asked, and then answered his own question: "Deep rooted prejudices entertained by the whites; ten thousand recollections, by the blacks, of the injuries they have sustained; new provocations; the real distinctions which nature has made; and many other circumstances, will divide us into parties, and produce convulsions which will probably never end but in the extermination of the one or the other race."

Blacks, Jefferson was convinced, were "in reason much inferior" to whites, being congenitally incapable of achievement in mathematics, arts, or science, and in their imagination "dull, tasteless and anomalous." He also found blacks physically repellent. They suffered from "a strong and disagreeable odor," while whites were endowed with "a more elegant symmetry of form," which kindled in blacks a sexual desire "as uniformly as is the preference of the Oranootan [Orangutan] for the black women over those of his own species." Even their emotions were inferior. They felt griefs less profoundly, and although they were "more ardent after their female," their love lacked the subtlety of expression that characterized romance among whites.

Jefferson was by no means alone in his prejudices. The eminent Philadelphia doctor Benjamin Rush, an early and sincere advocate of emancipation, wondered seriously if black skin might be a form of leprosy; once a cure for leprosy had been found, blackness would disappear, he reasoned. The intellectual ferment of the European Enlightenment that gave birth to liberating ideas about human rights also spawned a pseudoscientific approach to differences among the races that lent the authority of some of the most eminent thinkers to age-old bigotry. "The Negro exhibits the natural man in his completely wild and untamed state," asserted Friedrich Hegel. "We must lay aside all thought of reverence and morality—all that we call feeling—if we would rightly comprehend him; there is nothing harmonious with humanity to be found in this type of character." David Hume, the leading figure of the Scottish Enlightenment, declared, "There never was a civilized nation of any other complexion than white, or even any individual eminent either in action or speculation." Even John Locke, who formulated the theory of natural liberty, and who more than any other single individual provided the intellectual underpinnings of the American Revolution, was a staunch defender of slavery, not to mention an investor in the Royal African Company, which enjoyed the British monopoly of the African slave trade. In "An Essay Concerning Human Understanding," Locke wrote that "the child can demonstrate to you that *a negro is not a man*, because white colour was one of the constant simple *ideas* of the complex *idea* he calls *man*: and therefore he can demonstrate, by the principle, *it is impossible for the same thing to be and not to be*, that *a negro is not a man*."

What was remarkable about Jefferson and so many of the best men of his time was not that they held the prejudices they did, but that they managed to rise so far beyond them. Their reading of Locke, Rousseau, and other thinkers taught them that human beings were born with natural rights, which entailed inherent civil rights such as political liberty, freedom of religion, equality before the law, and the right to live one's life as one saw fit. Similarly, if human beings and societies alike were capable of limitless progress, to inhibit it was to commit a crime against Nature, if not against God. Such egalitarian ideas posed a problem for those who would defend slavery: if all men were created equal, how could some hold others in bondage? If all men were born free by law of nature, the Boston radical James Otis argued, "Does it follow that 'tis right to enslave a man because he is black? Will short curled hair like wool instead of Christian hair . . . help the argument? Can any logical inference in favor of slavery be drawn from a flat nose, a long or short face?" Tom Paine wrote that "every history of the creation" agreed on one point, "*the unity of man*; by which I mean that all men are of *one degree*, and consequently that all men are born equal, and with equal natural right, in the same manner as if posterity had been continued by *creation* rather than *generation* . . . and consequently, every child born into the world must be considered as deriving its existence from God." Alexander Hamilton, who as an officer during the Revolution saw black troops fight bravely on the battlefield, and knew their abilities, asserted, "Their natural faculties are as good as ours . . . The contempt we have been taught to entertain for the blacks, makes us fancy many things that are founded neither in reason nor in experience."

Americans' discomfort with slavery had a history. From the earliest days of settlement, at least some colonists had equivocal feelings about slavery. In 1641 Massachusetts forbade slavery in the colony "unless it be lawful Captives taken in just Warres, and such strangers as willingly sell themselves or are sold to us." By the eighteenth century, Quakers were beginning to argue that spiritual principles required Christians to take a personal stand against slaveholding. But thoughtful men of Jefferson's generation were more directly influenced by the movement toward emancipation in England. In 1772 Lord Chief Justice Mansfield, after determining that there was no law that stipulated that slavery existed in England, declared that slavery was so "odious" that no law could reasonably exist to support it. In effect, this meant that any slave who set foot on English soil became free. In 1787 British abolitionists, with strong support from the evangelicals and Quakers, including the famed potter Josiah Wedgwood, founded the Committee for Effecting the Abolition of the Slave Trade. The committee's most dynamic figure, Thomas Clarkson, memorably declaimed to the House of Commons that "this execrable traffic was as opposite to expediency as it was to the dictates of mercy, of religion, of equity, and of every principle that should actuate the breast." Even slaveholding Americans shared some of these sentiments. Patrick Henry regarded slavery as an "abominable practice," and Richard Henry Lee, an ancestor of Robert E. Lee, speaking in the Virginia House of Burgesses in 1772, condemned the slave trade as crueler than "the savage barbarity of a Saracen."

No man had been more consistent in arguing on behalf of individual rights than Jefferson. On the eve of the revolution, he had taken on the case of a mulatto who was suing for his freedom, arguing in a Virginia court that "under the law of nature, all men are born free, and everyone comes into the world with a right to his own person, which includes the liberty of moving and using it at his own will." And in a section of the Declaration of Independence that was deleted in deference to slave owners, he explicitly attacked the slave trade, asserting that King George III had "waged cruel war against human nature itself, violating the most sacred right of life and liberty in the persons of a distant people who never offended him, captivating and carrying them into distant slavery in another hemisphere, or to incur miserable death in their transportation thither." His Preamble, however, would be quoted in almost every important manifesto of the abolitionist movement, and cited countless times by the stationmasters and conductors of the Underground Railroad as an inspiration for the risks they undertook to help fugitive slaves on their way north: "We hold these truths to be self-evident: that all men are created equal; that they are endowed by their Creator with inherent and inalienable rights; that among these are life, liberty, and the pursuit of happiness; that to secure these rights, governments are instituted among men, deriving their just powers from the consent of the governed." From now on, as long as slavery lasted, the burden of proof would lie upon slaveholders to show why the blunt declaration that "all men are created equal" did not mean precisely what it said.

In 1784 Jefferson, then a member of the Continental Congress, was appointed to chair a committee charged with drafting a plan for the organization of the newly opened lands between the Appalachians and the Mississippi, which were destined soon to fill with settlers. Apart from dividing this vast territory into a grid of sixteen new states with fantastical Grecian names like Metropotamia, Pelisipia, and Cheronesus, the measure would have prohibited slavery in all the western territories of the United States, south as well as north. Had Jefferson's plan been adopted, slavery would never have been extended to the present states of Alabama, Mississippi, and Tennessee, or presumably to those west of the Mississippi. Congress failed to approve the plan by a single vote. "Thus," Jefferson wrote, "we see the fate of millions unborn hanging on the tongue of one man, and heaven was silent in that awful moment."

Three years later, representatives from every state gathered at Philadelphia to hammer out a plan for a national Constitution. Anxiety about slavery pervaded the convention, causing delegates, in the words of one Georgian, considerable "pain and difficulty." The resulting compromise pleased no one completely, granting slave states representation for three-fifths of their slave population, even though slaves of course could not vote, and requiring every state to lend assistance in putting down insurrections, and prohibiting any legislation to limit the slave trade for the next twenty years. Even so, many antislavery delegates considered the compromise a victory, naively believing that a stronger federal government would soon be able to exert its power to bring about general emancipation. "Yet the lapse of a few years, and Congress will have power to exterminate slavery from within our borders," exulted James Wilson of Pennsylvania. A like-minded delegate, William Dawes of Massachusetts, reported to his state's ratifying convention, "We may say, that although slavery is not smitten by apoplexy, yet it has received a mortal wound, and will die of a consumption." That same year, the Northwest Ordinance finally laid out a plan for the organization of the western territories, banning slavery north of the Ohio River after 1800, but permitting it in the states to the south. While the Ordinance represented another political compromise, it ensured that much of the West would be free territory forever and that the Ohio would in the dreams of countless slaves become the river Jordan, the threshold of Canaan, and the front line of battle in the moral conflict that would define America for the next three-quarters of a century.

Opposition to slavery among white Americans was, increasingly, not only philosophical but visceral. A Vermont judge named Theophilus Harrington declared in a written opinion that he would accept nothing less than "a bill of sale from God Almighty" as proof of one man's ownership of another. Before the Revolution, such intensely personal reactions were rare. By the last decade of the century, societies advocating emancipation existed in almost every state, North and South, and they attracted the support of many eminent figures. The Pennsylvania Society for Promoting the Abolition of Slavery was led by Benjamin Franklin, who earlier in life had bought and sold slaves himself. The president of Yale University, Reverend Ezra Stiles, chaired the "Connecticut Society for the Promotion of Freedom, and for the Relief of Persons Holden in Bondage," which claimed to reflect the sentiments of a large majority of the state's citizens. In New York, prominent men including Alexander Hamilton, Governor George Clinton, Mayor James Duane of New York City, future Chief Justice of the United States John Jay, and many Quakers, met at the Coffee House to organize the New York Manumission Society, naming Jay—who owned five slaves—its president. This was not unusual. In contrast to the abolitionists of a later day, such societies typically included slave owners and promoted only gradual emancipation, in the hopeful belief that masters could be persuaded to peacefully relinquish their human property.

Around the end of the century, a spate of state legislation made it appear that the momentum of history was on the side of emancipation. Delaware, Virginia, Maryland, the Carolinas, and Georgia all prohibited the importing of African slaves, a trend encouraged by those who believed that ending the transatlantic slave trade was virtually the same as terminating slavery itself. (South Carolina would reverse itself and import thirty-nine thousand more Africans before federal legislation finally put an end to the legal overseas slave trade, in 1808.) By the end of the century, most Northern states had enacted laws mandating gradual emancipation. State legislatures also revised their laws to make it easier for masters to free their slaves. Hundreds did so: between 1790 and 1810, Quaker and Methodist lobbying reduced Pennsylvania's slave population by more than half, from 8,887 to 4,177. In Delaware, the number of free blacks would grow from 30 percent of the state's black population to more than 75 percent between 1790 and 1810, and in Maryland from about 7 percent to more than 23 percent. Many who supported abolition in principle were less committed in actual practice, however. When one of George Washington's slaves fled to New Hampshire, the president wrote to the local authorities asking for his return, gracefully explaining, "However well disposed I might be to gradual abolition, or even to an entire emancipation of that description of people (if the latter was in itself practicable) at this moment it would neither be politic nor just to reward unfaithfulness with a premature preference, and thereby discontent beforehand the minds of all her fellow serv'ts, who, by their steady attachment, are far more deserving than herself of favor." Washington did, however, free his slaves upon his death, in his will, in 1799; Jefferson never did. But to Jefferson and others like him, the end of slavery seemed to be only a matter of time. "The spirit of the master is abating," he confidently asserted, "that of the slave rising from the dust, his condition mollifying, the way I hope preparing, under the auspices of heaven, for a total emancipation, and that this is disposed, in the order of events, to be with the consent of the masters, rather than by their extirpation."

3

The handiwork of a Yankee tinkerer in the summer of 1792 changed everything. Eli Whitney was a genius of a type who would become familiar in the course of the next century, like Robert Fulton, John Deere, Cyrus McCormick, Samuel F. B. Morse, and Thomas Edison, who fused native mechanical aptitude with the entrepreneurial instincts of the dawning industrial age. It was said that as a boy in Massachusetts during the Revolution, Whitney had set up his own small forge and made nails to sell to his neighbors, and then converted them to hairpins after the war. After graduating from Yale, he went south to take a position as a tutor. As a guest in the home of the widow of General Nathaniel Greene, in Georgia, Whitney overheard several of her neighbors discussing the problems of cotton cultivation.

Planters were well aware that a potentially vast market for American cotton was developing in England, where textile manufacture had been revolutionized by the factory system; thanks to new machinery operated by steam or water-powered engines, Britain's cotton imports had more than tripled, from nine million pounds to twenty-eight million pounds, between 1783 and 1790. American planters initially experimented with varieties of cotton imported from the Bahamas, which flourished on islands off the coast of Georgia and South Carolina, but they grew almost nowhere else. This so-called upland or short-staple cotton provided a much greater per-acre yield, but the seeds clung hard to the fiber and had to be pulled out by hand, a labor-intensive job that took one worker a full day to clean a single pound of seeds.

Whitney later wrote, "There were a number of very respectable gentlemen at Mrs. Greene's who all agreed that if a machine could be invented which would clean cotton with expedition, it would be a great thing both to the inventor and to the country. I involuntarily happened to be thinking on the subject and struck out a plan of a machine in my mind." It was the cotton gin, which would ultimately transform American slavery, project it into its boom time, and transform it into a pillar of the nineteenth-century American economy. Within ten days, Whitney had made a model, and soon after that a full-size machine, "with which one man will clean ten times as much cotton as he can in any other way before known," Whitney exulted. "It makes the labor fifty times less, without throwing any class of People out of business." The machine he created had an elegant simplicity. The cotton was picked up on a roller studded with metal teeth that carried it around to a metal grill; when the cotton was scraped off, the seeds dropped away. Simply by turning a hand crank, one slave could now do the work of a dozen. On large plantations, a water wheel could be used instead and the gin could do the work of hundreds.

On June 20, 1793, Whitney addressed his letter of application, along with a fee of thirty dollars, to Thomas Jefferson, then secretary of state, whose office was charged with issuing patents. "Mr. Jefferson," Whitney wrote to his father, "agreed to send the patent as soon as it could be made out." He established a factory in New Haven, and was soon shipping gins southward, where they would lead to a spectacular burgeoning of cotton cultivation, which would soon be matched by an exploding demand for slaves.

American cotton exports grew from almost nothing in the early 1790s to six million pounds in 1796, to twenty million pounds by 1801, and they would only continue to grow. Cotton was an ideal crop for the lands that were now being opened up in the Southeast, once the Indian inhabitants were removed, by either persuasion or force. It required only about two hundred frostless days, and twenty-four annual inches of rainfall, and was so simple to cultivate that even men and women fresh from Africa could quickly be taught the monotonous techniques of hoeing, planting, and picking. It was also a very efficient crop, in terms of the economics of slavery. Cotton kept slaves at work almost continuously, tilling fields, cleaning the crop, and preparing new land for the next year's planting. Mississippi's production alone would swell from 20,000 bales in 1821, to 962,006 in 1859, almost one-quarter of the nation's total output. And in each of the four decades before 1840 the slave population of Mississippi more than doubled.

The phenomenal expansion of the cotton economy carried slavery with it across the coastal states, through the still half-settled Mississippi Territory, and beyond, until the "Cotton Kingdom" stretched from the Atlantic coast to Texas. By 1800, when slavery in New York was on the brink of extinction, Georgia would tally more than fifty-nine thousand slaves, and they would reach almost half a million by the eve of the Civil War. Slave traders made fortunes buying up "surplus" slaves, and long, grim lines of them chained together in awkward lockstep became a familiar sight on the roads leading westward from Maryland, Virginia, and the Carolinas to the slave markets of the frontier Southeast. The new states wanted slaves, and more slaves. Lawyers, doctors, ministers, even the better class of "mechanics" dreamed of one day owning a plantation and slaves. "A plantation well stocked with hands, is the *ne plus ultra* of every man's ambition who resides at the south," one Northern traveler observed. "Young men who come to this country, 'to make money,' soon catch the mania, and nothing less than a broad plantation, waving with the snow white cotton bolls, can fill their mental vision."

Although the movement for voluntary manumission lingered on, deluding those who supported it into thinking that they were having a serious impact on slavery as a whole, it was becoming clearer that slavery was not going to disappear. Even as states passed legislation limiting the transatlantic slave trade, the actual number of slaves in the United States continued to grow steadily. Voluntary manumissions freed thousands, but they were merely a drop in the demographic bucket as the total number of slaves swelled due to natural increase from just under 900,000 in 1800, to about 1.2 million in 1810, to slightly more than 2 million in 1830, more than doubling in just thirty years. Their number would double again by the outbreak of the Civil War.

4

On the morning of Jefferson's inauguration in 1801, there were already signs that the optimism of the Revolutionary era was a spent force. As idealism collided with economic imperatives, southerners began to insist that the right to own slaves was their most important liberty, and that to deprive them of it would be to subject them to "slavery." The excesses of the French Revolution, followed soon afterward by the horrifying spectacle of successful slave insurrection against French rule on the island of Sante-Domingue (present-day Haiti), in 1791, raised slave owners' anxiety to the level of near panic. In the course of the decade, thousands of refugees fled to the United States, bearing tales of slaughter and rapine that fueled Americans' worst fears of what a slave rebellion might bring. George Washington's government advanced seven hundred thousand dollars to aid the embattled white planters, while rumors of an impending French invasion that would arm the slaves swept through the South. Jefferson predicted that the "revolutionary storm" would sweep through the United States, bringing massacres in its wake. He warned that if American slaves were not freed and deported, "we shall be the murderers of our own children." Southern suspicions of secret collaboration between abolitionists and slaves were further whetted by statements like those of a Presbyterian preacher named David Rice, who praised the rebels as "brave sons of Africa . . . sacrificing their lives on the altar of liberty," and by the president of Dickinson College in Pennsylvania, who proclaimed that a "Negro war" in the United States would benefit the antislavery cause.

Southerners' worst fears seemed about to be realized in the summer of 1800 when the plot for a supposed rebellion was uncovered in Virginia. The mastermind was a free blacksmith named Gabriel, who after his capture confessed that the rebels' plan had been "to subdue the whole of the country where slavery was permitted." All whites except Quakers, Methodists, and Frenchmen were to be massacred. The fury of rattled and vulnerable whites knew no bounds. "[W]here there is any reason to believe that any person is concerned, they ought immediately to be hanged, quartered, and hung upon trees on every road as a terror to the rest," one planter declared. A hunt for the conspirators resulted in the arrest of hundreds of blacks, usually with little or no evidence. Twenty-six eventually were executed, even though no white person suffered actual harm. In the aftermath, free blacks were particularly singled out, and their very freedom treated as a subversive threat to those still enslaved. New laws prohibited voluntary manumissions without prior official approval, and compelled newly freed blacks to leave the state or face reenslavement. In North Carolina, the law barred the manumission of any slave "under any pretense whatsoever" except for meritorious service, and then only by license from the county court, along with the posting of a two hundred pound bond to guarantee each freedman's "good behavior." Free blacks who traveled without authorization could be arrested, fined, and even sold into slavery, like William Hyden, a New York-born mulatto who en route to Washington, D.C., was arrested as an alleged runaway, and put up for sale in Virginia, even though potential buyers complained that he was "too white." They might also be reenslaved if they defaulted on a fine, or failed to pay their taxes, and they were barred from organizing schools, and from meeting together for almost any other activity that whites felt threatened by. White abolitionists, too, were increasingly treated as subversives. Members of abolition societies were prohibited from sitting on juries hearing suits brought by slaves, who claimed they had been manumitted by a will or other legal instrument, making it virtually impossible for a slave to win freedom in court, no matter how just his or her cause.

Meanwhile, free blacks now began to appear for the first time as a significant proportion of the population in Northern cities. Between 1765 and 1800, the number of free blacks in Philadelphia grew almost sixty-five times over, from 100 to 6,436, more than 9 percent of the city's population. A similar though less dramatic pattern occurred in other cities. In New York, the number of free blacks tripled between 1790 and 1800 to 3,500, when more than half the city's black residents were free. Some, of course, had been manumitted by local masters. Others had escaped to freedom in the chaos of the Revolutionary War, or won their independence by fighting in the ranks of the colonial forces. As Southern states made life more difficult for free blacks, expelling numbers of those who had been freed by their masters, many of them turned their eyes northward as well. Still others, growing numbers of them, were fugitives; advertisements in Southern papers began to mention that a fugitive had last been seen "on the Pennsylvania road."

For fugitive slaves, and eventually for the development of the Underground Railroad, the growth of Northern cities was crucial. There, fugitives could hope to disappear among friends, and former slaves learned the autonomy and self-reliance that were necessary to build lives in freedom. A free African American could even dare to defy a white, as an unnamed mulatto in New York did, in 1798, when confronted by a pursuing white man named Finch, who claimed that a black thief had fled into the mulatto's cellar. The mulatto "stood at the Door with some kind of weapon in his hands and Declared he would knock the said Finch's Brains out if Offered to come in." In cities, blacks also came into contact, often for the first time, with white people who treated them as near equals, and for whom slavery was a spiritual abomination. As Jefferson, the country's most graceful, if flawed, advocate of the Rights of Man ascended to its highest office on the steps of the Capitol, in the cobbled lanes of Philadelphia, fugitive slaves, free blacks, and white Quakers were discovering one another, and recognizing one another as allies in the struggle that was to come.

Chapter 3

A Gadfly in Philadelphia

> There is no use in trying to capture a runaway slave in Philadelphia. I believe the devil himself could not catch them when they once get here.
>
> —Anonymous Slave Master

1

A genial New Jersey farm boy named Isaac Tatum Hopper was just one among the many young men packed off by their parents in the hamlets surrounding Philadelphia in the years after the Revolution, in hope that he would make his fortune in the great city. By the end of his life, he would be a legend, a venerated figure who appeared on public platforms with William Lloyd Garrison, Lucretia Mott, and other abolitionist luminaries. But arriving in the nation's then-capital in 1787, the year of the Constitutional Convention, he was merely a sixteen-year-old tailor's apprentice new to city life, and hoping for adventure. Unusual for his time, even among abolitionists, he was unaffected by color prejudice. He traced his sympathy for blacks to an elderly African farmhand named Mingo who, when Hopper was a small child, had recounted to him in tears how he had been kidnapped from his home across the sea by slave traders. Soon after Hopper's arrival in Philadelphia, he encountered his first fugitive, an enslaved sailor who had jumped ship and was desperate to escape recapture. Wanting to help in some way, Hopper asked among his neighbors until he heard about a Quaker in rural Bucks County who was reputed to be "a good friend to colored people." He then found someone to provide the fugitive with a letter of introduction and directions to the man's house where, Hopper was later assured, the sailor was kindly received and provided with a job. The experience taught Hopper two simple but lasting lessons: that he could make the difference between slavery and freedom for a fellow human being, and that with imagination it was possible to hide a fugitive where no one could find him.

Nowhere in the United States was the atmosphere of democratic change more palpable than in Philadelphia. As Hopper wandered its cobbled lanes, he mingled with Quakers in their distinctive broad-brimmed hats, immigrants from Ireland and Germany, French refugees from the bloody revolution in Sainte-Domingue, indentured servants, free blacks, and slaves. He marveled at the templelike public buildings that self-consciously evoked the classical inspiration of the Founding Fathers, and at the flotillas of tall-masted brigs moored in the Delaware River, proclaiming that the city of seventy thousand was not just the nation's only metropolis, but one of the greatest ports in the world. Philadelphia's wealth was everywhere to be seen. At the same time, the capital also presented a panorama of appalling poverty, crime, and disorder of a magnitude never before encountered in North America. The poor and disenfranchised could be thrown into prison for minor transgressions without evidence or trial, while the constables charged with maintaining order were notoriously corrupt, "ready for any low business, provided it were profitable." Epidemics aided by inadequate sanitation carried people away by the scores and the hundreds. The French traveler C. F. Volney reported that the area around the docks, where many blacks lived, exceeded "in public and private nastiness anything ever beheld in Turkey." While thousands of men and women who had spent decades in bondage were experimenting with liberty for the first time in their lives, African Americans were excluded from most schools, denied the right to vote, barred from many public places, and relegated mostly to menial occupations, as chimney sweeps, wood cutters, casual laborers, and domestics.

Although slavery still existed in Pennsylvania as it did almost everywhere in the United States, nowhere else was the concept of freedom widening so rapidly for so many people. In 1780, more than eighty years before the Civil War, the state's emancipation law—the country's first—declared that while slaves born before that year were to remain in bondage, those born after that date would automatically become free when they reached their twenty-eighth birthday. The law also effectively ended slave trading locally by barring the purchase of new slaves within the state, and mandating that any personal slaves brought from out of state would automatically become free after six months' residence in Pennsylvania. By 1800, all but a few masters within the city had voluntarily manumitted their slaves, while in the surrounding region slave owners were discovering that their once docile property could walk away from them with comparative ease.

At a time when slavery was flourishing as never before in the South, and still widely tolerated in the North, word spread rapidly that Philadelphia was a haven for those who would be delivered from bondage. In 1800 a naval ship that captured two slave trading vessels off the coast of Delaware delivered 134 Africans to the city to be set free. Quaker planters in the West Indies, yielding to the abolitionist pressure of their co-religionists, sent their manumitted slaves to Philadelphia by the hundreds. Philadelphia courts also freed hundreds more French-speaking slaves who had been brought from Sante-Domingue by their fleeing masters. Fugitives walked off farms in New Jersey and Pennsylvania, and they made their way north by land and sea from Virginia and Maryland. For the city's African Americans, little was certain but uncertainty, however. Success in reaching Philadelphia was still no guarantee of safety. Because the state emancipation act did not apply to runaways, fugitives were detained in the county jail until their owner was notified. If no owner appeared, the law provided that a runaway could be sold or set free at the discretion of the local court. The outcome depended less on precedent than on the vagaries of individual magistrates, whose personal biases, particularly about slavery, were as much a factor in their decisions as their knowledge of the law, or lack of it. Runaways were numerous, vulnerable, and largely unprotected. Fugitives never knew which white person might direct them to a friendly magistrate, help find them a job, and transport them to a farm outside the city where they couldn't be found; or report them to the authorities, lock them up and send for their master, or kidnap them and sell them into slavery again across the Maryland state line.

Philadelphia was destined to become the country's first laboratory of abolition, but it would take a form much different from the orderly one envisioned but never brought to fruition by Thomas Jefferson. The Founding Fathers had provided the early abolition movement with a secular ideology by bestowing upon it the patriotic themes of natural rights and political empowerment. But their repeated efforts to legislate peaceful emancipation had tested the nation's commitment to its revolutionary ideals, and found it grievously wanting. The hard work of emancipation thus increasingly fell to Americans of a different type. They were not the aristocratic products of the Enlightenment, but men and women driven by a religious imperative that the rationalist Jefferson disdained, in league with the free blacks whom he feared with an almost skin-crawling disgust.

An engraving of Isaac Hopper made later in life shows a rather short, stout man, oval-faced and clean shaven, with a small, firmly set mouth, and long, wavy hair. (Hopper was friendly with the exiled Joseph Bonaparte, who lived near Philadelphia, and the former king of Italy enjoyed pointing the Quaker out to acquaintances as the nearest resemblance he had ever seen to his brother Napoleon, the deposed emperor of France.) Most of what is known about Hopper's early life is found in a biography written by his protégée, the abolitionist writer Lydia Maria Child in 1853, a year after his death. What comes through, along with an impression of unflappable self-possession and steely determination, is an impish delight in adventure that found its outlet in the hide-and-seek played by hunter and fugitive, and dramatic face-to-face confrontations with furious masters who, it was said, "had abundant reason to dread Isaac T. Hopper as they would a blister of Spanish flies."

Although not born a Quaker, Hopper was linked to the Society of Friends through his uncle, a tailor, to whom he was apprenticed, and in 1795, at the age of twenty-four, he was formally received into the sect. He embraced his new faith with the unflagging enthusiasm of a convert, shunning music and dancing as a "useless and frivolous pursuit," and as a matter of Quaker principle, refusing to pay taxes to maintain the state militia, compelling the authorities to collect the tax in kind by carrying off pieces of his furniture. A tenacious traditionalist, he continued to wear buckled shoes, high stockings, knee-length trousers, and broad-brimmed Quaker-style hat long after they had gone out of style. The Quakers soon recognized in Hopper's combination of stubbornness, conviction, and gentleness of manner a talent for what a much later age would call "social work."

In April 1796 Hopper was elected to membership in the Quaker-dominated Pennsylvania Abolition Society, the first organization in the United States to proclaim abolition as its explicit goal. He was appointed first to a charitable committee whose members visited the homes of the black poor, to collect information on their needs, to help find them jobs, and to arrange education for their children, an experience that greatly deepened his insight into the life of the city's African Americans, and provided him with innumerable contacts that would later prove invaluable in his underground work. In the meantime, he also served as an overseer for Philadelphia's first school for black children and as a teacher in a school for black adults, where he taught classes two or three evenings a week. In 1801 the Abolition Society handed him a new and far more challenging assignment: to investigate, and represent before the law, the claims of blacks who asserted that their liberty was being denied them illegally. Some of these were the victims of attempted kidnappings, and others of mistaken identity. Still others, though they dared not admit it publicly in a city where many in authority were ready to send them back to their masters, were really fugitive slaves.

In the first years of the new century, Hopper and his collaborators inside Philadelphia and in its surrounding countryside became what can fairly be described as the first operating cell of the abolitionist underground. Their numbers were few and their reach was limited, but the techniques that they developed eventually became a model of cooperation across racial and class lines, bringing together middle-class white tradesmen, Quaker farmers, black stevedores, and other African Americans in a collaborative effort that functioned with little or no central direction, and no distinctions of rank. Of course, they did not call their activities the "Underground Railroad": the invention of iron railways still lay a generation in the future. Hopper and his friends hardly thought of what they were doing as a system at all, but rather as the private actions of a handful of like-minded men—and apparently they were all men at this time, as far as can be known—doing what their individual consciences required them to do. Hopper, the most active of them, certainly had no grand national scheme in mind. He was no strategist. Rather, he led by example, bequeathing to the activists who followed him an ethic of unflinching personal responsibility, boldness, and quiet self-sacrifice.

In 1804 a black man in his mid-thirties appeared at the offices of the Abolition Society, and explained that he was a slave to Pierce Butler, a senator from South Carolina, but had lived most of the last eleven years with his master in Pennsylvania. Butler now intended to take him to Georgia. The black man, "Ben," was married to a free woman, and did not want to leave her. The society's governing committee agreed that since Ben had lived in Pennsylvania far longer than the six months stipulated by law, he was clearly entitled to his freedom. A writ of habeas corpus was obtained, and Isaac Hopper was chosen to serve it upon Butler at his Chestnut Street home. Butler, "a tall, lordly looking man, imperious in manner," ordered Hopper out, denouncing him as "a scoundrel." Said Butler, "I am a citizen of South Carolina. The laws of Pennsylvania have nothing to do with me." It was as if, in Butler's mind at least, the two men lived not just in different states but in different countries, which in a sense they did. Butler appeared in court to defend his property, as he saw it, maintaining that as a member of Congress, he was allowed to keep his slave in Pennsylvania as long as he pleased. A lawyer appointed by the society to represent Ben argued that the law to which Butler referred had only applied as long as Congress met in Philadelphia, but that it had become a dead letter once the government had moved to the new capital at Washington. To Butler's fury, his slave was declared a free man on the spot. As the pacifist Hopper continued to hustle about the waterfront on his missions of aid, he probably never imagined that the underground that he was inventing would eventually extend its reach across every Northern state, and that it would help bring the nation to the brink of Civil War.

2

The underground borrowed much from both the tightly disciplined organization and the self-contained style of the Society of Friends. Quakers had themselves been a persecuted minority both in England and in the North American colonies, and they knew that their survival depended on protecting the integrity of their community against outsiders, regardless of their internal disagreements. Moral opposition to slavery was a core Quaker tenet, although political activism was not. Even those who disliked Isaac Hopper's activities at least tolerated them. Many Quakers strongly opposed political engagement and law-breaking, and others, whatever their moral opposition to slavery, were deeply racist. But such internal struggles were almost never aired publicly. Turning in a fellow Quaker to secular authorities for practicing his religion as he saw it was virtually unthinkable. Thus it often would prove easy for fugitives to disappear in plain sight in Quaker communities, even where only a small minority might be directly involved in underground work.

Hopper's opponents—and there were many in a city where abolitionist sentiment was far from universal—attempted to dismiss him as a "meddlesome Quaker." At least once, a magistrate infuriated by Hopper's unyielding defense of a fugitive slave had him thrown bodily out of the courtroom. For years he lived with threats of assassination, attacks on his family, and arson against his house. But to Hopper none of this seemed to matter. Antislavery work was for him a profoundly religious act. "We may perform works of benevolence and kindness that are 'acceptable to God and approved of men,' which require but little self-denial," Hopper wrote, in one of the few documents in his own hand that still survives. "But when duty calls us to engage in such, that are unpopular, and in the discharge of which we risk the loss of friendship of those we love to be faithful therein, requires more devotion to principle and more firmness than many possess; and yet it is the path which leads to the enjoyment of that peace and consolation which the world can neither give nor take away."

Hopper and his allies were heirs to a spiritual revolution that had been gathering force for more than a century. By the early nineteenth century, this revolution was transforming more and more Americans' ideas about slavery and race on, at least arguably, a far deeper level than the lofty, intellectualizing pronouncements of Enlightenment *philosophes*. The earliest American critiques of slavery were rooted in powerful biblical injunctions. "It is most certain that all Men, as they are the Sons of *Adam*, are Coheirs; and have equal Right unto Liberty, and all their outward Comforts of Life," Samuel Sewall, a distinguished jurist in the Massachusetts Bay

Colony, wrote in 1700, citing Psalms 115:16. "God *hath given the Earth unto the Sons of Adam, And hath made of One Blood, all Nations of Men, for to dwell on the face of the Earth.*" He also cited Exodus 21:16: "And seeing GOD hath said, *He that Stealeth a man and Selleth him, or if he be found in his hand, he shall surely be put to Death.*" It was also held by the Puritans that blacks as well as whites could be among the spiritually "elect," a principle of profound importance, making clear as it did that the life and welfare of slaves could be sacred in the eyes of God. Puritan churches sometimes even admitted slaves to membership, a privilege that was denied to whites, the majority of them, in fact, who were deemed spiritually unworthy. Cotton Mather, best remembered for his religious bigotry, pressed vigorously for the education of slaves, asserting that "there might be some elected ones among the Negroes." He declared, in 1706, that "Who can tell, but that God may have sent this Poor Creature into My hands, so that One of the Elect may by my means be Called; by my Instruction be made Wise unto Salvation!"

Evangelical Methodists and Baptists also stressed the equality of all souls before God, and would produce many of the staunchest foot soldiers of the abolitionist underground. However, Quakers dominated the early phase of the antislavery movement well into the nineteenth century. Even after actual leadership had passed to other hands, traditions that were associated with Quaker thought and practice—especially the doctrine of nonresistance—continued to exercise significant influence among abolitionists. Beginning in the late 1600s the Quakers had steadily examined the moral consequences of slavery. They had come, by painful stages, to believe that they had an inescapable duty to combat it in every way possible, short of violating their doctrinal commitment to pacifism. As early as 1671, the Quakers' founder, George Fox, asked his followers to imagine themselves in the plight of the slave, and urged those who owned slaves to "train up their negroes in the fear of God, to use them mildly and gently, and after certain years of servitude to set them free." The first explicit protest against slavery in the North American colonies was articulated by the Quakers of Germantown, Pennsylvania, near Philadelphia, who stated, in 1688: "Now, tho' they are black, we cannot conceive that there is more liberty to have them as slaves, as there is to have other white ones . . . And those who steal or rob men, and those who buy or purchase them, are they not all alike?" By the middle of the next century, Quakers generally had come to believe that kind treatment alone was inadequate to address the fundamental evil that permeated the whole institution of slavery in all its ramifications.

The Quaker campaign against slavery was part of a broader spiritual reformation that was gathering force within the sect, calling upon members to return to a life of deeper simplicity, which also entailed educating their children apart from non-Quakers, avoiding marriage with outsiders, and shunning such "vain customs of the world" as music, theater, and art. In explaining their hostility to slavery, Quakers most often cited the Golden Rule, a potent principle that everyone in the intensely Christian nation could easily understand. More subtly, their opposition to slavery was rooted in their belief that a universal "divine light" was manifest in the soul of every person, female and male, black and white, and that to claim ownership of another human being was not only a moral but a spiritual travesty. In addition, slavery represented an inexcusable indulgence, a contradiction to the kind of plain life that was required by their faith.

Countless Quakers, including Isaac Hopper, were influenced by the widely quoted writings of John Woolman of New Jersey, who in the 1750s argued that emancipation of the slave was crucial to personal salvation. How, Woolman demanded, could a slaveholding Friend expect to gain salvation when he bore the sin of slavery on his soul? "The Colour of a Man avails nothing, in Matters of Right and Equity," he wrote. "*Negroes* are our fellow Creatures, and their present Condition amongst us requires our serious Consideration. We know not the Time when those Scales, in which Mountains are weighed, may turn . . . And whenever gain is preferred to Equity . . . there is real Cause for Sorrow to all such, whose Love of Mankind stands on a true Principle." The dawning recognition that slavery might entail real spiritual consequences provoked crisis for many, as it did for Samuel Nottingham, a Quaker who, as a result of marriage, was horrified to find himself the owner of hundreds of slaves, a spiritual and practical catastrophe that left him feeling "pierced through with very many sorrows."

Around the same time, Quakers began to press for the religious education of slaves, a cause championed most prominently by another Philadelphian, a French Huguenot convert to Quakerism named Anthony Benezet, who around 1750 began tutoring adult blacks at his home on

Chestnut Street. Benezet envisioned the eventual and complete integration of black and white Americans, but the prospect of sudden, mass emancipation was more than he—and for that matter almost any other white man of his time—could handle. "How would such a people be prevented from becoming a prey to their ignorance and passions, and a sad annoyance to their neighbors?" he worried. For Benezet, education was the answer. In the course of twenty years of teaching, Benezet helped convert Benjamin Franklin and others to abolitionism, by demonstrating that his students were capable of the same level of achievement as whites, thus undermining popular assumptions about black intellectual inferiority. Far ahead of his time, he also taught his black students that it was slavery rather than any inherent racial differences that bred ignorance and degradation among African Americans. The capstone of his life was the establishment, in 1773, of a school for free black and slave children, of which Isaac Hopper would later, in 1799, become an overseer.

As the century progressed, there was much preaching on the subject of slavery wherever Quakers gathered. In the 1770s, slaveholding was made a "disownable offense" by the Yearly Meetings of Philadelphia, New England, and New York. Other meetings soon followed suit. In eastern North Carolina, members who still held slaves were warned to "*be earnestly and affectionately advised to clear their hands of them as soon as they possibly can.*" In every Quaker community committees were appointed to "labor with such Friends as remain in the practice of holding their fellow men in a state of slavery, endeavoring to convince them of the iniquity of such practice." Even so, manumission was a process rather than a single event. Quakers belonging to the Nine Partners Meeting in Dutchess County, New York, later an important link in the Underground Railroad, took seven years to free all their slaves, completing the process in 1782. Quakers in Westbury, Long Island, did not succeed in freeing all their slaves until 1798.

Social pressure within the Quaker community was uniquely effective. Quakers were already segregated by dress, speech, religious services, opposition to taking oaths, and the marriage ceremony. Deviations from orthodoxy were punished with "disownment," a public and deliberately discomfiting proclamation that the individual concerned was in a state of spiritual disharmony with his, or her, fellow Friends. In the matter of slavery, as well as other doctrinal issues, the Quakers demanded total commitment. As one tract put it, "In the Christian warfare there must be no reservation."

3

Although the Quaker-led Pennsylvania Abolition Society did not regard itself as a subversive organization, it was a kind of culture dish that brought together men and, if indirectly, a few women who were uncompromising in their opposition to slavery, morally committed to emancipation, and pragmatic in their determination to put fugitives beyond the reach of their masters. No one was more pragmatic than Hopper. A man of instinct and action, he was a type that would often appear along the lines of the Underground Railroad. His home near the riverfront, at the corner of Dock and Walnut streets, was both a clearinghouse and a place of refuge for fugitives and kidnap victims. Hopper explained his motivation by citing biblical precepts that any American could understand, and that the underground would use to justify its defiantly illegal work for decades to come. Once when he was summoned to court as a witness in a slave case and was asked what course of action Quakers were expected to take when a fugitive came to them, he first replied, "I am not willing to answer for anyone but myself."

"Well," pressed the magistrate, a Mr. Ingersoll, "what would *you* do in such a case? Would you deliver him to his master?"

"Indeed I would not!" answered Hopper. "My conscience would not permit me to do it. It would be a great crime; because it would be disobedience to my own dearest convictions of right. I should never expect to enjoy an hour of peace afterward. I would do for a fugitive slave whatever I should like to have done for myself, under similar circumstances. If he asked my protection, I would extend it to him to the utmost of my power. If he was hungry, I would feed him. If he was naked, I would clothe him. If he needed advice, I would give him such as I thought would be most beneficial to him."

Hopper always preferred a legal attack to a physical one, and to manipulate the law rather than to break it. He was the first abolitionist to vigorously exploit the possibilities of the new, less stringent, state laws to help fugitives. His many successes suggest that his adversaries were still operating under an outdated idea of what was legal and possible, assuming as they always had that the law would continue to protect slaveholding when, in fact, it had decisively shifted, at least in Pennsylvania, in favor of abolition. As one judge told Hopper, when the evidence for and against freedom was evenly balanced, it was always a duty to decide in favor of liberty.

Hopper was unflagging in his search for loopholes. By employing clever tactics that befuddled professional lawyers and unfriendly magistrates alike, he sometimes managed to keep cases pending as long as three or four years, until a fugitive's claimants were worn out and ready to settle. Urged to become a professional lawyer, he declined, saying that he preferred to resist temptations that might lead him away from the simplicity of Quaker belief. On one occasion he agreed to help a young woman who had escaped from Virginia and had lived free in Philadelphia long enough to raise a family there. Tracked down by her former master, she begged Hopper for help. He knew that under the Fugitive Slave Law, the master was entirely within his rights to carry her back to Virginia. He offered to buy her from the Virginian, but was turned down. Undeterred, Hopper showed up with the woman in city court and promised to "be responsible to the United States" for seeing that she would return the following day for a ruling on her status. He also promised personally to pay a one-thousand-dollar bond if she failed to appear. This was deliberate double-talk on Hopper's part, since he knew quite well that the United States government had no claim of its own on the woman, and no jurisdiction in the case. (Nor, probably, did he have the money.) Nevertheless, this was agreed to as reasonable by the court and the slave owner, both of whom had missed Hopper's verbal sleight-of-hand. Next morning, all the parties were in court except the fugitive, who with her family had been sent away to safety during the night. When the magistrate stated that Hopper would have to forfeit the bond, the Quaker pointed out to the master's chagrin that since the federal government was not party to the case, there was no basis for a Philadelphia court collecting a fine in its name.

When the law failed, Hopper could call on a web of friends and collaborators. His network was primitive but efficient. Spies among black dock workers, laborers, and domestics alerted abolitionists when a kidnapping was taking place, or when a constable or a slave master was in the city stalking a fugitive. The story of a fugitive from Virginia named Ben Jackson makes it clear that when necessary Hopper was even able to call on friends in the constabulary and the courts. Jackson had been serving as coachman for a friend when he was caught and arrested by his former master. He was jailed, pending the issuance of a permit authorizing the master to take his property back to Virginia. He managed to get word of his predicament to Hopper, who arranged with the constable on duty at the jail, a man "who sympathized with the poor victim of oppression," to have the prisoner brought to court ahead of schedule. Almost certainly with Hopper's connivance, the justice before whom the case was heard—a man who "detested slavery, and was a sincere friend to the colored people"—declared that since the complainant, Jackson's master, was absent, the "presumptive evidence" indicated that Jackson was a free man, and ordered him released. By the time his master arrived, at the appointed time, Jackson was gone for good.

Hopper clearly relished the dramatic role that he played in more than a few rescues. Once Hopper sneaked up the stairs of a home and snatched a pistol from the hand of a partially blind man who was threatening to shoot anyone who interfered with his flogging of a slave girl. Another time, learning that a boat had left Philadelphia with a kidnapped boy on board, Hopper obtained a horse and raced alongside the Delaware River to the vessel's next landfall, arriving just in time to seize the boy and bring him home before he had been carried out of Pennsylvania waters. He also perfected ruses that were often used in later years by the Underground Railroad. Once, for example, when he was concealing a fugitive in his home and suspected that slave hunters were lurking about, he hired a black man to run out of the house after dark. As Hopper suspected, several men leaped from the shadows and seized the decoy, while the real fugitive escaped out the back door, and eventually to safety. Hopper even succeeded in having the decoy's assailants arrested for assault.

He also boldly came to the assistance of a free man named Samuel Johnson, who had married a slave belonging to a Delaware planter named George Black. The Johnsons, who had several children, fled to Philadelphia, where Samuel found work as a wood sawyer, and his wife took in washing. Two years later, Black learned of his slave's whereabouts and set off in pursuit. Learning that Black was in Philadelphia, Johnson sent his family into hiding while he remained at home, trusting that since he was legally free he could be in no danger. However, Black showed up at his door with two constables, and when they discovered that his wife had fled, they arrested Johnson himself. When he refused to reveal his family's whereabouts, they beat him and threatened to carry him to the South and sell him. They then tied his hands and dragged him to a tavern in Sassafras Street, where they left him under guard. By now, some of Johnson's black neighbors had contacted Isaac Hopper, who hurried to the tavern and, with a typical though distinctly un-Quakerly flourish, threatened to break down the door, accusing the guards and the landlord of false imprisonment. "Release that man immediately! Or thou wilt be made to repent of thy conduct," he reportedly cried. The landlord eventually yielded, and Hopper was allowed to leave with Johnson, who soon rejoined his family in an unspecified "place of safety."

Hopper and his collaborators pioneered the technique of passing fugitives from hand to hand among members of their extended family, personal friends, Abolition Society activists, and others whom Hopper decided should be asked to live up to their principles, until they reached a permanent haven, usually somewhere in the countryside outside Philadelphia. Their protectors, in effect the first stationmasters of the Underground Railroad, could be expected to provide temporary shelter, assistance in finding work, perhaps some rudimentary education, and advice in adjusting to life in a free but competitive society, where each man was expected to support his own family, and to fend for himself. Hopper's brother-in-law John Tatem often sheltered fugitives whom Hopper had forwarded to him at his farm in New Jersey, as did a friend named William Reeve, to whom he once sent a fugitive with a letter that concluded with a verse from the Bible: "Verily I say unto you, inasmuch as ye have done it unto the least of these my brethren, ye have done it unto me."

A kind of synergy was developing as local abolitionists evolved practices that would become standard procedure wherever the underground existed. Although fugitives generally seem to have been sent on by foot and unaccompanied, they were sometimes conducted on horseback across the countryside, or transported from place to place hidden in farmers' market wagons. Disguises were also used to confuse pursuers. As early as 1809, Philip Price of East Bradford, in Chester County, learning that slave hunters were in the vicinity, hurried three fugitives, two men and a woman, into a thicket near his farm. Disguising the woman as a man, he advised them to emerge at dark and to follow a certain rarely used road to a designated place where they would be met by a guide with horses. Price directed his son Benjamin to take one of the horses and lead another, along with some bags, as if intending to bring home a load of grist from the local mill. After collecting the fugitives, he led them to a prearranged "station" near the town of Darby. Chester County Quakers also received fugitives directly from Philadelphia, and settled them as safely as they could on farms in the vicinity. For fugitives, however, the danger of recapture never entirely disappeared. Only a few months after Isaac Hopper had settled the fugitive John Smith "in a very secluded situation" in the Philadelphia hinterland, he was betrayed by a false friend to whom he had confessed his life story. Smith received the tidings that his master was on his trail "with feelings of desperation amounting to phrensy," and appealed again to Hopper for help. On short notice, Hopper recruited a ship's captain to take Smith to Boston, illustrating the ability of Philadelphia abolitionists to respond creatively to pressing needs and, more importantly, suggesting that even at this early date they were beginning to conceive of a kind of national geography of freedom that extended far beyond the environs of their own city.

4

Never much of a businessman, Hopper had lived his life as if antislavery work were his only occupation. That, for Hopper, happy era ended abruptly in 1812. Financial problems forced him to devote himself single-mindedly to repaying personal debts that had soiled his reputation and caused his temporary suspension from the Society of Friends, which regarded solvency as a criterion of good character. Despite his efforts, he lost his home and much of his furniture to creditors, and was forced to move into a house owned by his father-in-law, in whose front parlor Sarah Hopper opened a grocery and tea shop to make ends meet. Hopper's enemies thought that he was silenced for good. But he would be heard from again, in another city and with new allies, and with an undimmed ferocity of faith.

In the meantime, like a kind of moral pollen, the spiritual imperative that motivated Hopper and his collaborators was also falling on other Quakers far from Philadelphia but bound to their coreligionists through the far-flung network of Yearly and Monthly Meetings, through family ties, and more than anything else, by a community of shared values that, for many, demanded personal action. Although no organized underground yet existed much beyond Philadelphia and its surrounding counties, the kind of men who had created it, and the ideas that drove them, were becoming visible wherever Quakers lived.

Reared in New York in the late 1700s, Timothy Rogers was a born pioneer, who founded the northwest Vermont towns of Ferrisburgh and Vergennes, in a region that would serve for decades as a terminus of the Underground Railroad. In 1797 Rogers recorded in his private diary an incident that vividly illustrates how the moral core of antislavery activism had begun to harden. It also hints at relationships that already had formed among antislavery Quakers in New York's Hudson Valley, which would in time become one of the trunk lines of the underground. While attending the Quaker Yearly Meeting in New York City, Rogers was approached by Isaac Leggatt, a Friend from Saratoga, in upstate New York, who broached the subject of slavery, offering the opinion that the law would soon free slaves in the state, and asking Rogers if he would be willing to hire a couple of black men in anticipation, even though they were fugitives. Rogers said that he would, on his friend's recommendation. Leggatt was already in touch with slaves who wished to escape, and was looking for somewhere safe to send them. En route home, Rogers was overtaken by two fugitives who identified themselves as Harry and Francis, and who told him that Leggatt had directed them to follow him to Ferrisburgh. "The next day as we went on, they was stopped with an advertisement," Rogers confided to his diary. Notices of the black men's escape had apparently already been distributed around the area, some thirty miles from Saratoga. Then, somewhere north of Danby, Vermont, the three were confronted by a local constable, who recognized the men as fugitives but agreed to allow the party to continue north to Ferrisburgh.

Rogers conscientiously wrote to the fugitives' owners, making it clear that no matter what the men's legal status, he did not intend to return them to bondage. Sometime later, presumably at Ferrisburgh, the men's owners arrived and demanded their property back. "Their masters came and attempted to run on them with rope, as supposed to bind them,"

Rogers recorded. "I being gone and they being frightened, they both ran to the woods. After three days I came home, heard what was done, went four miles to see the masters, found them very angry, threatened great things." Rogers does not describe in detail what must have been a dramatic and perhaps even violent confrontation at a public tavern, very likely in front of other citizens who may have taken sides in the affair. In any event, Rogers again refused to give up the men. The owners thereupon sued Rogers for five hundred dollars for each of the men under the terms of the Fugitive Slave Law, for the crime of "aiding and assisting" the fugitives' escape. In his diary, Rogers expressed some annoyance at his friend Leggatt for acting prematurely—"we had been too fast"—but admitted that deliverance of the fugitives took precedence over his personal feelings. "I thought it best to settle, for the black men was starving in the woods . . . But I had this satisfaction, that I had meant to do all the good I could toward freeing all slaves. So I concluded to not value interest with freedom, and bought them both for seven hundred dollars, that pinched me very much to pay, and then gave them their freedom." In return, Harry and Francis agreed to work for Rogers for the next six years, as employees.

The nation's fewer than one hundred thousand Quakers made up slightly less than 2 percent of the population at the turn of the century, but they exerted a moral influence far beyond their small number. Although their unfashionable dress and antique forms of speech sometimes attracted unfriendly attention, their almost universal literacy (among women as well as men) in an age when reading and writing were uncommon skills, their honesty in business, and their sober habits won them widespread respect. Quaker ideas about the immorality of slavery were carried throughout the country by itinerant preachers, who brought a personal, evangelical passion to their mission, warning those who continued to hold slaves that it would lead them to eternal damnation.

One of these men, Rogers's Vermont neighbor Joseph Hoag, carried the message of emancipation up and down the East Coast in the first decade of the new century. One day in 1803 Hoag had received an apocalyptic vision that became famous among Quakers. He was alone in a field when an ethereal mist eclipsed the sun's brightness, and his mind was "struck into a silence." A torrent of terrible, "volcanic" images followed, revealing a "dividing spirit" that ravaged first the churches, then the Free

Masons, then politics, not stopping "until it produced a civil war," in which "an abundance of blood was shed in the course of the combat; the Southern States lost their power, and slavery was annihilated from their borders." Traveling by carriage and horseback, over appalling roads, through the Carolinas and across the Appalachians into the frontier districts of Tennessee, often ill from nameless fevers and wretched food, Hoag preached with a terrific fervor wherever he went. "I was led to show that the Gospel, if complied with, led every true follower of Jesus Christ to endure every burden, break every yoke, and let the oppressed go free," he proclaimed, "and those who did not comply therewith, were not true Christians, but deceivers of themselves, and therefore, anti-christians." He preached to everyone he met, drilling away at complacency, sanctimony, and self-justification. He had only contempt for those who "chose to stop, and curl down on their fathers' sins, making that a couch of security," by condemning slavery in principle, but accommodating it in practice as a "burden" laid upon them by their ancestors and now impossible to change.

Hoag's path also took him through the much more receptive Quaker districts of the North Carolina Piedmont. Quakers had begun migrating into the area around present-day Greensboro since the middle years of the eighteenth century. The first wave arrived from Pennsylvania, followed in the 1770s by contingents of farmers from the overpopulated island of Nantucket, a bastion of abolitionist sentiment, a fact that was to do much to shape the peculiar vigor of abolitionist activity in their new home. Toward the end of the century, a third wave of migrants moved west from the coastal areas of the state as the political atmosphere there became increasingly unfriendly to Quakers. By the 1800s the North Carolina Quakers formed the only sizable abolitionist community south of the border states. Though isolated, an island in an ocean of slaveholders, they were numerous and well organized, and had close links with relatives, friends, and fellow Quakers in the free states. They were uniquely well situated to lay a foundation for the earliest long-distance route of the Underground Railroad.

CHAPTER 4

THE HAND OF GOD IN NORTH CAROLINA

The dictates of humanity came in opposition to the law of the land, and we ignored the law.

—LEVI COFFIN

1

As the nation steadily peeled back the western wilderness, shackled black men and women became an ever more familiar sight trudging southward toward the vast new lands that were being opened up beyond the Alleghenies. "A comfortable living can be found here by the most indolent," one enthusiastic young Virginian would write home from the Mississippi frontier, where he was carving a new plantation from what had only recently been Indian land. "Tis inferior to none for corn or cotton, and as for meat, it costs nothing, it grows without expense, and very little trouble." Wherever planters went, the demand for more slaves followed. By 1810 the price for slaves in Louisiana would be almost double what it was in Virginia, and almost four times the price in New Jersey and other

Northern states, where legal constraints on slavery were prompting masters to sell off their chattels at deep discount. Slaves were shipped by the thousands from East Coast ports to the markets of New Orleans. To avoid the difficult crossing of the Blue Ridge Mountains many others bound from the Tidewater country for the Deep South followed roads that led them through the Quaker counties of North Carolina. A tanner living near High Point, close to Greensboro, counted "at least five droves" of slaves passing his house to every one of cattle, horses or hogs.

The shuffling passage of one convoy sometime in 1805, an incident otherwise forgotten by history, was a seminal event in the development of the Underground Railroad. A Quaker boy of seven was standing in front of his father's farm three miles north of the New Garden meeting house, outside Greensboro, when a line of black men approached from the north, down the Salisbury Road. As his father chopped wood, the boy watched them with a sense of childish curiosity. Although on some of the neighboring farms slaves cut the wood, tended the livestock, planted the fields, and harvested the crops, the sight of men chained together puzzled him. "The coffle of slaves came first, chained in couples on each side of a long chain which extended between them; the driver was some distance behind, with the wagon of supplies," Levi Coffin recalled many decades later. "My father addressed the slaves pleasantly, and then asked: 'Well, boys, why do they chain you?' " One of the men, "whose countenance betrayed unusual intelligence and whose expression denoted the deepest sadness," replied: "They have taken us away from our wives and children, and they chain us lest we should make our escape and go back to them." After the black men had passed out of sight, the boy bombarded his father with questions. Why, he wanted to know, had the men been taken away from their families? "My father explained to me the meaning of slavery, and, as I listened, the thought arose in my mind, 'How terribly we should feel if father were taken away from us.' "

A second incident later brought home the inherent terror of slavery to Coffin in an even more visceral way. Near his home, Coffin encountered a party of westbound emigrants with their wagons. Half a mile behind them, a single black man trudged carrying a bundle. He asked Coffin how far ahead the travelers were, and then continued on his way. Coffin surmised that the man was a runaway slave, having heard of cases where, when slave families were broken up by a sale and the wife and children taken away, the father would slip off and trail the emigrants, hoping to find some way of remaining with them once they had reached their destination. In this instance, the man was soon arrested with a forged pass and jailed at Greensboro, where his master came to collect him. Coffin saw the slave again there at a blacksmith's shop, where a chain was being riveted around his neck, and handcuffs fastened to his wrists. He was deeply moved by the slave's expression of "piteous, despairing appeal" as the man's master told him, "*Now* you shall know what slavery is. Just wait till I get you back home!" What followed remained forever vivid and unnerving in Coffin's memory. "One end of the chain, riveted to the Negro's neck, was made fast to the axle of his master's buggy, then the master sprang in and drove off at a sweeping trot, compelling the slave to run at full speed or fall and be dragged by his neck. I watched them till they disappeared in the distance, and as long as I could see them, the slave was running."

It was an epiphany. Suddenly slavery came into sharp focus in the eyes of a boy for whom it was no longer just part of the landscape, like the familiar forests of oak, elm, and sassafras, but something utterly terrifying, the stuff of nightmare. Coffin and his father had talked to these men, had been admitted, if only for a brief time, into their private shame, desperation, and humanity. "*How terribly we should feel if father were taken away from us.*" The man running for his life behind the carriage was no longer a mere object, a "slave," like a horse or a cow, but a person like Levi himself, with a particular family, a lost home, lost freedom, and lost hope.

Like many of their Quaker neighbors, the Coffins had come to North Carolina in the 1770s from Nantucket, home to generations of seafaring men who were well known for both their advanced views on emancipation and their stoical independence. Levi Coffin's grandfather laid out his farm just west of present-day Greensboro. It was a fertile land, still dark and shadowy where the oak and hickory and elm trees stood in dense groves, and rolling in steep, rhythmic swells where industrious, mostly Quaker, farmers had chopped the foliage away. In the summer months, blackberries, dewberries, huckleberries, and strawberries grew plentifully in tangled thickets wherever the sunlight was strong. Settlements were still small and relatively primitive in the early years of the nineteenth century, and the few roads that traversed the land were no friends to travelers, becoming troughs of dust in dry weather, and canals of red gumbo when it rained. This was not tobacco country, and at least in the Quaker counties family farms on the Northern pattern were much more common than were plantations employing large numbers of slaves. The Coffins raised mainly corn and wheat, along with hogs that were allowed to forage in the thick underbrush that grew along Beale's Branch, a shallow stream that meandered along the eastern edge of their property. Levi's father, though primarily a farmer, also taught school, a profession which Levi himself would intermittently follow later on in life. Since Levi could not be spared from farm work, he was schooled at home, along with his sisters, in accordance with the Quaker commitment to equal education. Coffin's parents and grandparents on both sides were firmly opposed to slavery, and no one in either of the families had ever owned slaves: "All were friends of the oppressed."

Although North Carolina Quakers lived scattered through a society that was economically dependent on slavery, they set themselves firmly and somewhat precariously apart from it. In 1780 their representative body (Quakers having no permanent hierarchy), the North Carolina Yearly Meeting, which met at New Garden, had made it a disownable offense for a Quaker to persist in holding slaves. Manumission was simultaneously a divine injunction and an act of personal purification, "to be clear from the least stain of guilt in the blood shed on earth," and few dared lag behind in conforming to it. However, Quakers who freed their slaves were often publicly attacked outside their own community (and sometimes within it) for undermining public order, and even charged with responsibility for crimes that were supposed to have been committed by freed blacks. North Carolina's draconian state laws also made manumission a formidable ordeal, requiring any master who wished to free a slave to post a substantial bond for the freed person's good behavior, and permitted any propertied white man to take a freed slave to the sheriff's office, where he might be sold to the highest bidder. Others might simply be kidnapped with impunity, as John Howard, a former slave owner who had moved to Ohio, discovered, to his deep distress. Before leaving North Carolina, he had left his freed slaves, as he wrote to a fellow Quaker, "in the care of a man on whose land they lived, who appeared to be friendly to them and gave him the authority of an overseer to protect them in the enjoyment of their liberty til further orders from me; believing it to be the best thing I could do for them under such circumstances a few years after I received a letter . . . informing that William Phisioe had betrayed his trust and sold two of sd [*sic*] people to a Slave trader, who had taken them out of the state."

In 1808, Quakers attempted to solve their dilemma by making the Yearly Meeting itself the legal trustee of slaves whom its members wished to emancipate, until they could be freed or somehow gotten out of the state. Agents were appointed to oversee these slaves, hire them out, collect their wages, and apply them to community needs. Anyone who hired trusteeship slaves was admonished to use them in accordance with Quaker principles of kindness and respect. Ironically, Quakers thus found themselves the masters of hundreds of slaves, and engaged in an ongoing effort to acquire more, in the name of emancipation. Some slaves willed to the Yearly Meeting were either hurriedly sold off before the Quakers could take possession of them, or simply reenslaved by heirs who valued property more than they did Quaker ideas of spiritual redemption. Nevertheless, as the years passed, donations came by the score—thirty-six slaves from John Kennedy, eighteen from Joseph Borden, forty-nine from the estate of Thomas Outland—from Quakers and non-Quakers alike, and from all across the state, until the numbers became nearly unmanageable, and the cost of their support so expensive that financial assistance had to be sought from wealthy Friends in Pennsylvania and New York.

While the surviving records are inconclusive, it is likely that as early as the 1810s many of these trusteeship slaves were sent to the free Northwest with emigrant families. Small groups of Quaker "movers" from North Carolina had begun migrating north of the Ohio River around the turn of the century, bound for "the Miamis," as the western Ohio country was then called, a difficult journey of four hundred or more miles. There were three established roads, all of them difficult. The most popular route led through the Cumberland Gap and into Kentucky, eventually crossing the Ohio River at Cincinnati. A second route crossed the mountains through Flower Gap, and continued via Lexington, Kentucky, to the Ohio. The third, known as the Virginia route, was initially rough and steep, requiring emigrants to double up on teams for many miles until they reached the Kanawha River in what is now West Virginia, where they could transfer to flatboats for an easy voyage to the junction of the Ohio River at Gallipolis. As Ohio became more crowded in the second decade of the century, the migrants continued farther west and began settling in

Indiana, then known as the "Wabash country," where they provided the nucleus of a strong Quaker community that would become an important center of the abolitionist underground in the decades to come.

In the early years of the century, the public advocacy of gradual emancipation was still regarded as a respectable, if distinctly minority, opinion in the South. Emancipation societies existed in Delaware, Maryland, Virginia, North Carolina, Kentucky, and Tennessee, where a society was founded as early as 1797, and later included among its members the Presbyterian minister John Rankin, who would go on to become one of the most famous stationmasters on the Underground Railroad. To differing degrees, these organizations all looked to the Pennsylvania Abolition Society, the country's oldest and most experienced, for guidance. Beyond the border states, only in North Carolina, where Quakers provided the critical mass of support, would organized emancipationist sentiment survive on a significant scale, and produce men radical enough to break the law.

The first chapter of the North Carolina Manumission Society was established in 1814 at New Garden. Levi Coffin, still only a teenager, his older cousin and mentor Vestal Coffin, and several of their New Garden neighbors were among the society's founding members. "[T]he command of the great father of Mankind is, that we do unto others as we would be done by,—and that the human race however varied in color are Justly entitled to Freedom," the society's constitution proclaimed. The founders were respectable men, mostly farmers and middle-class craftsmen, including both uncompromising antislavery Quakers like the Coffins and "lenient" slaveholders who considered slavery a definite evil, but were unprepared to relinquish their own property. There was nothing radical about their agenda. They professed their commitment to gradual emancipation, and to legal reforms that would make it easier for those who wished to emancipate their slaves. In an appeal to whites' self-interest, the society also argued that slavery encouraged wasteful methods of farming that depleted the land, reinforced an extravagant way of life among the wealthier classes, and drove away home-grown "mechanical geniuses" who might otherwise have developed new local industries.

In 1818, after a rancorous internal debate, the North Carolina Manumission Society voted to amalgamate with the new American Colonization Society. To many, "repatriation" to Africa seemed to be the perfect solution to the national conundrum: what to do with the growing numbers of free blacks. The most optimistic, and there were many heartfelt abolitionists among them, believed that colonization would lead to the painless eradication of slavery. Gravely underestimating the South's insatiable demand for slaves, they naively believed that by means of an appeal to the Bible and the gentlest political push, masters could be persuaded to free their slaves. Newly minted freedmen would rejoice at the prospect of being shipped off to what whites insisted was their natural home, as if the grandchildren and great-grandchildren of the Efiks, and Mandingos, and Angolans had all hailed from some African counterpart of Cape Cod or Tidewater Virginia, and were not by now, willy nilly, Americans. Although colonization was rejected by the vast majority of African Americans, it was embraced by a few free blacks who were convinced that they would never be accepted on equal terms by whites, most notably by Paul Cuffe, a prosperous black sea captain and Quaker from New Bedford, Massachusetts, who promoted an abortive effort to settle black emigrants in Sierra Leone, which Britain had established as a haven for former slaves on the West African coast. Less idealistic members of the Colonization Society, and there were a great many of them too, worried that in the event of foreign invasion the country's slave population of nearly one and a half million would join the enemy, or launch a bloody rebellion as slaves had in Haiti. Behind a smokescreen of high-flown rhetoric—"Every emigrant to Africa is a missionary carrying with him credentials in the holy cause of civilization, religion, and free institutions," a longtime leader of the Colonization Society and perennial aspirant to the U.S. presidency, Senator Henry Clay, proclaimed—the society's real aim was much more cynical. Clay reassured slaveholders that colonization would actually help strengthen slavery, by removing from the country the most troublesome African Americans, a most "useless and pernicious" portion of the population: that is, free blacks. Colonization could never come close to keeping pace with the census returns. During its entire history, before its termination on the eve of the Civil War, the American Colonization Society transported fewer than fifteen thousand American blacks to Liberia, which the society acquired with federal assistance in 1818, and developed on the model of Sierra Leone. In its best year, 1832, the society would manage to send only 632 colonists to Africa.

The Coffins were already frustrated with the North Carolina Manumission Society's piecemeal approach. They were now affronted by its union with an organization dominated by slaveholders. Their disgust only grew when the society's convention that year was held on the estate of a large slaveholder. "Many of us were opposed to making colonization a condition of freedom," Levi Coffin would recall. "We had no objection to free Negroes going to Africa of their own will, but to compel them to go as a condition of freedom was a movement to which we were conscientiously opposed and against which we strongly contended." However, the proposal was carried by a small majority. The convention broke up in confusion, and the Coffins along with the rest of their New Garden branch quit the room. Wrote Coffin, "We felt that the slave power had got the ascendency in our society, and that we could no longer work in it."

Levi and Vestal Coffin were shortly to become the founders of the earliest known scheme to transport fugitives across hundreds of miles of unfriendly territory to safety in the free states. It is unclear whether their plan was organized in a formal way from the start, or if it initially reflected more of an unspoken understanding among the New Garden men, nearly all of them from the same Nantucket stock, all of them Quakers, all men who had worked side by side with one another for years, most of them tightly linked to one another by blood or marriage. In any event, Vestal Coffin's son Addison, himself later a conductor on the Underground Railroad, traced its formation in Guilford County specifically to a "long and exciting suit at law" which roiled the community between 1818 and 1820. It began when a free black man named Benjamin Benson was kidnapped from Delaware by one John Thompson, a slave trader, brought to the New Garden area, where he was sold to a wealthy farmer. A slave known locally as "Hamilton's Sol" learned what Thompson was about, and quickly got word to Vestal Coffin, clear indication that slaves and radical Quakers were already engaged in some form of communication. Coffin made contact with the authorities in Delaware, confirming the facts of the kidnapping. The state of Delaware, where Quaker influence was strong, appointed Coffin and two other Quakers to represent Benson, and they saw to it that a warrant was issued for Thompson's arrest in North Carolina. Forewarned, Thompson sent Benson to Georgia, where he was sold. Thompson then denied in court that Benson had ever existed, and was acquitted. "The result created much excitement," wrote Addison

Coffin. "It was the first open act of the slave spirit to override law and justice. [But] the three commissioners had Nantucket blood in them, and were not to be overawed, or frightened."

While the Benson case was sharpening the divisions between pro- and antislavery groups in Guilford County, a free black man named John Dimery became the first known fugitive to be spirited away from Guilford County to the free states. Dimery had been freed by his master in another part of the state, and had come to live at New Garden, with his wife. After the death of Dimery's old master, in 1819, two of his sons came to New Garden on the pretense of buying stock. Having located Dimery's house, they burst in upon him in the middle of the night. Dimery shouted to his daughter to run for "Mister Coffin" as fast as she could. "Father had just stepped outside to get wood to start a fire," Vestal Coffin's son Addison wrote. "Without stopping for coat or hat he ran at full speed, providentially meeting Isaac White, a special friend. He just said, 'Come,' and they both ran like the wind." Coffin and White caught up with the kidnappers at a neighbor's home nearby. The Quakers ordered them to release Dimery, or be taken before the nearest magistrate. While the kidnappers were debating what to do, the woman of the house had been quietly untying the rope that bound Dimery's hands. Suddenly he sprang from their grasp and through the door, and disappeared into the woods. Fearing arrest, the kidnappers mounted their horses and rode off. As for Dimery, Addison Coffin reports only that he "was started on the Underground Railroad that night and soon landed at Richmond, Indiana." Written some eighty years after the event, Coffin's casual reference to the Underground Railroad suggests a much more organized system than can possibly have existed in 1819. But it makes quite clear that the Quakers of Guilford County knew where they wanted to send a fugitive who needed their help, and how to do it.

Meanwhile, Vestal Coffin and his allies succeeded in proving that Benjamin Benson did in fact exist, and that he had been in the slave trader Thompson's possession. When Thompson was ordered to produce Benson in court, it "fell like a bombshell among the slave holders." It cost Thompson one hundred and sixty dollars, a great sum at the time, to bring Benson back to Greensboro where, to the outrage of local slave owners, he was restored to freedom.

2

No blueprint for the network that the Coffins and their associates created survives, no map showing routes of escape, no list of safe houses. Most likely, the first efforts were experimental, impulsive. Although no organizational link can be proved between the North Carolina underground and the Pennsylvania Abolition Society, the Coffins very probably modeled their activities on what they learned from their Northern brethren. The legal activities of Philadelphia Quakers on behalf of kidnapped blacks were well publicized, and their clandestine work was common knowledge. Ties between North Carolina and Pennsylvania Quakers were close: Quakers traveled to Philadelphia with some regularity, and they relied on Philadelphia money to help support and move to the West the slaves who were held in trusteeship by the North Carolina Yearly Meeting. And when their own underground work was exposed, it was to Philadelphia that they fled.

By 1820 the New Garden area was already well known for its friendliness to fugitive blacks. The Coffins and their friends now began to deliberately seek out fugitives, and hide them in the junglelike undergrowth that screened the stream behind the Coffin farms. "The [Benson] case naturally placed my father in the front rank of anti-slavery men," wrote Addison Coffin. Unfortunately, not much more is known about Vestal, who died prematurely at the age of thirty-four, in 1826, leaving behind little trace of himself except what may be gleaned from the autobiographies of his son and Levi Coffin. No picture of him survives, although perhaps there was something in his face of the cool, amiable self-possession, anchored by firm, narrow lips, and deeply chiseled lines about the mouth that may be seen in photographs of Addison. "Seemingly, without being conscious of how it came about," continued Addison, "he was expected to do all the dangerous work, to take all the responsibility and leadership; others were ready and willing to share the cost, do all the business, fetch and carry, if he would be the leader in the hours of trial." Young Levi Coffin, meanwhile, was responsible for supplying the fugitives with food and other necessities: "My sack of corn generally contained supplies of bacon and corn bread for the slaves, and many a time I sat in the thickets with them as they devoured my bounty, and listened to the stories they told of hard masters and cruel treatment." The streambed was, in places, only a few hundred feet from the Salisbury Road, and fugitives hidden there could sometimes hear the conversations of the patrols who were hunting them as they passed.

Levi would spend the next forty years putting into practice all that Vestal had taught him before he died, assisting fugitives with such single-minded ardor that he would come to be called by some the "president" of the Underground Railroad. As Addison Coffin put it, Levi "took his first lessons under my father, and many were the secret conferences they held after night, never meeting in the same place the second time, to prevent espionage or betrayal." They often met in a thicket where a fugitive was concealed, to lay plans for getting him started safely toward the North. Hamilton's Sol, a middle-aged slave belonging to one of the Coffins' neighbors, and known for his absolute trustworthiness, worked intimately with them. The Coffins recorded disappointingly few details about this remarkable man who was crucial to the establishment of the underground, but what they did say hints intriguingly at the role that slaves might play in the smooth functioning of the system. It was a relationship that prefigured many that followed and that was in many areas central to the success of the Underground Railroad.

Sol would examine every coffle of slaves to which he could gain access, to ascertain if there were any victims of kidnappings among them. When he found one, he would try to bring him or her at night to a rendezvous in the thickets to meet with the Coffins. One longs to hear Saul's version of these events. It was he, after all, who took the greatest chances, risking not only a fine and exile, but certain torture for assisting a fugitive. Why did this man, who might easily have escaped to a free state with the Coffins' help, choose to remain a slave? Was he held back by family ties, as so many would-be fugitives were? Or by loyalty to friends? Or by an altruistic determination to help others to freedom? It is impossible to say. But this extraordinary, highly efficient relationship continued for many years, with succeeding generations of the Coffin family, until in 1835 Saul himself was finally compelled, more by circumstances than by desire, to become a passenger on the route that he had pioneered.

At least in the beginning, the Coffins were careful only to offer help to kidnapped free men, like Benjamin Benson. In time, however, they became willing to take greater risks. As in Philadelphia and its surrounding area, activists relied almost entirely on other family members, and a few other close personal relationships. Clandestine activity that began on an ad hoc basis incrementally extended its reach, less by design than by circumstance, across hundreds of miles of territory to the free states. A story Levi Coffin recounted in his autobiography suggests both the limitations and the ingenuity of the budding underground. At the center of the story, which takes place in 1821, is a fugitive slave named Jack Barnes. This man, about whom little else is known, was freed by his master's will, but then seized by the dead man's heir as part of the estate. He fled to New Garden, having heard that the Quakers there "were opposed to slavery and friendly to colored people." He remained in the area, working on various Quaker farms, and earning general respect for his industriousness, intelligence, and "manly deportment." When advertisements for his capture appeared in the local newspaper, Barnes begged for help in getting to a free state. According to Levi Coffin, a council was held by "Jack's friends," by which he certainly meant the circle of New Garden abolitionists who had broken away from the Manumission Society. They arranged for him to travel to Indiana with yet another Coffin, Levi's cousin Bethuel, who was leaving immediately via the rugged Kanawha Road through western Virginia.

To confuse matters, another fugitive, known only as Sam, was hiding from his master, a harsh and unpopular man named Osborne, in the thickets behind the Coffin farm. Having learned that Bethuel Coffin's emigrant party had been seen in company with a black man, Osborne rushed to the conclusion that it must be Sam, and set off in pursuit. Learning of this, the Coffins feared that when Osborne caught up with the travelers, he would recognize Jack Barnes and have him arrested for the posted reward. It was decided that Levi would take a fast horse, overtake the emigrants, and somehow try to interfere with Osborne's plans. Levi, at twenty-three, had never before been more than twenty miles from home.

The country through which he would travel was still largely wilderness. Climbing up from the Piedmont, he was met by one of the most majestic panoramas in the eastern United States, the vast tidal sweep of the corrugated crests of the Blue Ridge Mountains receding westward like the waves of a frozen sea toward a horizon of hypnotic blue haze. Along the way, Coffin ran into Osborne himself. This was not such a remarkable coincidence as it might seem. There was only one road and travelers were few. Picking his words carefully to avoid entangling himself in an un-

Quakerly lie, Coffin told Osborne misleadingly that he had an uncle whose farm lay over the mountains, and that he planned to travel by the same road that he supposed Osborne would be following. "I had certainly deceived him, but told no untruth," Coffin wrote. Delighted, Osborne asked Coffin to join him, saying, "See here, young man, I want you to go with me, and help capture the nigger." Coffin agreed. "I was all excitement," wrote Coffin, "for I felt that the crisis was near. Now was the time to act." He obviously relished the play acting, entertaining the slave owner as they rode, telling him stories and recounting jokes that kept him constantly laughing.

Somewhere deep in the mountains, Osborne and Coffin stopped for the night at a tavern. Coffin, showing himself already a shrewd judge of men, took aside the innkeeper, a man named Howells, who was also a local magistrate, and explained the situation to him. He told Howells that Osborne had such a reputation for cruelty that even slaveholders who knew him would not aid him in capturing the fugitive. When he finished, Howells declared, "If it is the Negro you describe, he ought to be free; I would not detain him a moment, but would much rather help him on his way." He agreed to go along with Coffin and Osborne, and to collect a crew of reliable men who would provide whatever assistance was needed. (Forty years later, mountaineers such as these would refuse to fight for slavery and the Confederacy, and break away to form the new state of West Virginia.) Bethuel Coffin was of course startled to find his young cousin suddenly appearing at the crack of dawn, along with a party of armed strangers. In the event, Osborne failed to recognize the fugitive Barnes, and acknowledged grudgingly that it was not his man. After some time spent talking, joking, and partaking of Bethuel's peach brandy, Osborne, Howells, and the rest of the party departed, while Levi remained with the emigrants, and explained the entire series of events that had brought him there. Barnes continued on safely with Bethuel's group, while Levi later rejoined Osborne and headed back toward North Carolina. Afterward, Coffin reflected on the meaning of what had transpired. "In looking back over the work of the past few days, I felt that the hand of God was in it. He had blessed my efforts; he had guided my steps; he had strengthened my judgment. My heart was full of thankfulness to my Heavenly Father for his great mercy and favor; my eyes filled with tears, and I wept for joy."

In Coffin's account, it is possible to glimpse the Underground Railroad literally come into being. What happened in the mountains had also transformed Coffin from a boy into a man. It was his first great adventure, his first journey on his own in behalf of a fugitive, and it reveals much about his character and the steely self-control that he would bring to clandestine work in later years. He had discovered in himself an unexpected capacity for physical endurance—he had traveled 120 miles through rough country, virtually without sleep or rest—and spur-of-the-moment ingenuity, as well as a priceless knack for gaining the trust of strangers. He also learned that he could manipulate men much older and harder than himself, a skill that he would masterfully put to use during a lifetime of involvement with fugitive slaves who would seek his help in Indiana and Ohio. Coffin's narrow face, high forehead, and tightly compressed, rather humorless lips lent him a solemn air, an impression that in later life must have been accentuated by the plain black broadcloth clothing that he always wore. But behind this sober exterior, there lay coiled a bold and venturesome mind. Although as a pious Quaker Coffin would never have admitted it, there was not only something of the actor in him, but also something of the con man. Perhaps too he recalled the biblical verse in Matthew 10:16: "Behold, I send you forth as sheep in the midst of wolves: be ye therefore wise as serpents, and harmless as doves."

For Osborne's slave Sam, the outcome was not so fortunate. All this time, he had been living in the thickets behind the Coffin farm, surviving on food supplied by the Coffins. Upon Levi's return, he and Vestal Coffin arranged to send Sam west with another Quaker emigrant named David Grose—"a kind-hearted, benevolent man, of anti-slavery sentiments"—who was also heading for Indiana. The plan was for Sam to travel at night, on foot, and make his way to the Groses' campsite before daylight, to get breakfast and provisions to last him through the day. Where the road forked, Grose was to leave a green bush or some other sign in the road that he had taken to guide Sam. At river fords, he would wait for Sam to come up, then conceal him in the wagon for the crossing.

The Coffins' plan again revealed close collaboration with local blacks, both slave and free. According to Levi Coffin, "Some shrewd young men [probably Levi and Vestal Coffin themselves], not overly conscious about violating the slave laws of the State, believing that every man was entitled to liberty who had not forfeited that God-given right by crime, managed to get hold of free papers belonging to a free colored man in the neighborhood, and copied them, counterfeiting the names of the signers as well as they could, not stopping to consider the severe penalty attached to such violations of the law. It was so managed that the papers were given to Sam by a slave, and he was instructed not to use them unless he should get into a tight place." The papers were stowed safely in his bundle of clothes, in the Groses' wagon.

One night, frightened by wolves, Sam panicked and lost his way. He begged for help at the cabin of a poor white family, who invited him to come inside and rest. The consequences of this seemingly kind reception epitomized the terrible randomness that fugitives faced in a strange country, when hunger, fear, or sheer loneliness compelled them to risk throwing themselves on the mercy of white strangers. Sam might have found a friendly face. Instead, his hosts sent a boy running for the neighbors, who seized him and tied him up, surmising that he was a runaway for whom there might be a large reward. Sam's forged papers were, of course, beyond his reach with the Groses. He never saw them or the Groses again. As was customary, notices describing Sam were placed in various newspapers. Osborne saw one of them and soon afterward arrived in Wytheville, Virginia, where Sam was being held in the local jail, to collect his property. He set out for home with Sam in chains. But Sam never arrived. Osborne claimed that he had sold Sam along the way. Levi Coffin reported that many believed that he had whipped Sam to death, and had left his body in the mountains.

Despite the torture that he may well have suffered at Osborne's hands, Sam never implicated any of the men who had helped him in his flight. However, Osborne later learned that Sam had once been seen driving the carriage of Jesse Stanley, a Coffin cousin, and sought to have Stanley arrested for "Negro stealing," a crime that at least in principle was punishable by death. The danger to Stanley was serious enough that he hurriedly left the state for Philadelphia. Osborne also ascertained that Sam had been seen on the property of Abel Stanley, Jesse's uncle. Abel Stanley had already sold his farm, in preparation for emigrating to Indiana. However, hearing that Osborne was seeking to have him arrested, he too fled to Pennsylvania, leaving his family to complete the arrangements for their departure.

3

As the story of Jack Barnes shows, in 1821 there were no designated "station-masters" posted along the emigrant trail that connected North Carolina with the Northwest. Although Addison Coffin suggests that by 1830 (when he was still a boy) stations had been established, it is quite possible that the routes across the mountains always depended mainly on the discretion of emigrants who agreed to carry fugitives along with them. Slaves belonging to the Yearly Meeting had been traveling to the Northwest that way for years, more than four hundred in 1823, and nearly twice that number in 1824, and by 1826 regular "convoys" were being sent west under the auspices of the "African Committee" of the Quakers already established there. In one typical instance, an Indiana man was hired, for thirty dollars plus expenses, to conduct a company of twenty blacks from Guilford County across the Ohio, furnishing his own horse to draw the wagon.

But even with white assistance, fugitives were in danger every mile of the way to the Ohio River. "A gang of ruffians, moved by the prospect of the large reward generally offered in such cases, frequently stopped emigrant wagons and searched them for runaway Negroes," Levi Coffin wrote, a clear indication that slave owners knew that the emigrant trails were being used to move fugitives. Every month, fresh arrivals in Indiana halted their weary teams at one or another of the frontier settlements that were being cut from the wilderness beyond Cincinnati. For many of them, the trek out of North Carolina had a Manichaean quality; it was not merely a geographical journey, but a spiritual one from the darkness of moral depravity into the light of redemption. One Quaker, Borden Stanton, recalled how he had first heard from traveling Friends about the Ohio country: "It seemed as if they were messengers sent to call us out, as it were from Egyptian darkness (for indeed it seemed as if the land groaned under oppression) into the marvelous light of the glory of God." Entire meetings picked up and moved en masse, leaving whole regions of the Carolinas empty of Quakers.

There were of course other factors that propelled Quaker emigrants to the free states. Quaker farmers found it increasingly hard to compete with slave owners. As pacifists, Quakers were harassed and fined for refusing to muster with local militias. They were also mocked by other whites for performing manual labor—"nigger work"—that ought to have been done by slaves. "Gradually the idea prevailed everywhere that labor was not respectable, and he, or she who labored with their hands had to take second rank," wrote Addison Coffin. In 1825 Levi Coffin's parents emigrated west to a new Quaker colony that was forming near Richmond, Indiana. He followed them himself the next year, the last in his family to go. In their search for better land and wider opportunity they were like hundreds of thousands of other Americans who were simultaneously migrating westward along rough tracks through the forests, on the steamboats that were now proliferating on the western rivers, and on the horse-drawn boats that plied the new Erie Canal. But for nearly every Quaker, not only family, friends, and played-out fields would be left behind, but the taint of living evil. "If the question is asked," Addison Coffin declared, "why did the Friends emigrate from North Carolina? It can be answered by one dark, fearful word SLAVERY, than which a darker is not known."

4

In this second decade of the nineteenth century, there was a gathering sense in the nation that something important was changing. Indelible lines were being drawn across the map of the states, and in the hearts of their citizens, demarcating slave states and free, pushing apart those who only a few years before had found common cause in societies of manumission and colonization, dreams that were by no means dead, but that from now on would increasingly give way to political warfare. For a time, in 1820, it had even looked as if the country might split apart over the admission of Missouri to the Union as a slave state, as the halls of Congress rang with the passionate defense of slavery, and dire warnings of civil war. North Carolina's Senator Nathaniel Macon spoke with contempt of the Declaration of Independence's assertion that all men were created equal. "Follow that sentiment and does it not lead to universal emancipation?" he demanded of his colleagues. To impose restrictions on slavery, Macon and other Southerners argued, could only lead to a national catastrophe.

His voice thundering through the circular domed chamber of the House of Representatives, the Kentucky statesman Henry Clay proclaimed that the spread of slavery into the western territories would actually benefit the slaves themselves, while reducing whites' fear of free blacks by thinning out their numbers in the more densely populated East. The Union, he warned, must not be put at risk by political assaults on an institution that he alleged was destined eventually to fade away from natural causes.

Earlier in the century it had by no means been a foregone conclusion that Missouri would become a slave state. Its soil was generally inhospitable to large-scale cotton cultivation. But most of its settlers came from the South, and they brought their slaves with them, fanning out from the frontier ports that sprang up alongside the muddy surge of the Missouri River. The three thousand slaves in Missouri in 1810 had grown to ten thousand a decade later, in a total population of sixty-six thousand. The heart of the matter, however, was a constitutional question with far-reaching implications: Did Congress have the power to restrict slavery when it admitted a new state to the Union? Missouri was the first state that would be formed out of the lands acquired by the Louisiana Purchase. If slavery was excluded from Missouri, then it was likely that future trans-Mississippi states would come into the Union on the same terms, a prospect that mortified Southerners, who could see as well as everyone else that the steady piling up of new free states must inexorably undermine the disproportionate power that the South wielded over the federal government. Because the Constitution provided that three-fifths of a state's slave population be counted as citizens in apportioning seats to the House of Representatives, the slave states collectively were able to elect twenty more congressmen than they would have been entitled to on the basis of their white population alone; put another way, every Southerner who owned one hundred slaves enjoyed an additional sixty votes. A far-reaching compromise was finally reached, averting the drift toward secession. Missouri would be admitted to the Union as a slave state. In return, Southerners grudgingly agreed to the exclusion of slavery in the territories north of thirty-six degrees thirty minutes north latitude west of Missouri, in effect extending the Mason-Dixon line westward across the continent. At the same time, Maine was admitted to the Union as a free state, thus adding two more free-state senators to balance Missouri's.

The settlement distressed no one more than the aged lion of American radicalism, Thomas Jefferson. The former president's once fiery idealism had hardened into a chilly crust of disillusionment. He was paralyzed by the contradictions that had always infected his thinking about slavery. In 1814, when Edward Coles, a neighbor and the former secretary to President James Madison, had approached him, begging him to lend his prestige to a national campaign against slavery, Jefferson first pleaded the limitations of age. He could do nothing, he told Coles. To undertake such "arduous work" at the age of seventy-eight was "like bidding old Priam to buckle the armor of Hector." He added, "This enterprise is for the young." He regretted that more could not be done for the cause of the slaves. Someday emancipation would come, he assured Coles. But, morally desirable though it might be, it was not a happy prospect. The "idleness" of free blacks, and their "depredations," already made them pests to society. Worse yet, "Their amalgamation with the other color produces a degradation to which no lover of his country, no lover of excellence in the human character can innocently consent." (This from a man who had fathered several children by his slave Sally Hemings.) In the end, he urged Coles to do nothing extreme, but to treat his slaves kindly, and to lend a calming voice to public debate. Instead, Coles freed his slaves and moved to the free territory of Illinois, as far as he could get from the land of slavery.

Although he didn't admit it to Coles, Jefferson had traded his sunny optimism for a regional chauvinism that foreshadowed the bigoted and self-serving arguments that would lead to the South's secession forty years hence. He never abandoned his professed desire to end slavery in principle, but he was now less concerned with the rights of man than with the rights of the slave owners whom he had once scathingly condemned. He declined to endorse the Missouri Compromise. Reversing his position of 1784, when he argued that slavery ought to be barred from the new lands of the South as well as the North, he now asserted that Congress had no power at all over slavery in the territories. The Union, as Jefferson conceived it, was a confederation based on a compact between "independent nations." The federal government was a creature of the states' will, existing only by their sufferance, and with strictly limited authority, which did not include the power to legislate on slavery. As slavery became increasingly profitable, Jefferson had come to see that it was impossible to oppose it without undermining the agricultural system that he believed with an almost mystical passion formed the natural moral and cultural foundation of the American republic. He wrote to a friend from his aerie at Monticello, "A geographical line, coinciding with a marked principle, moral and political, once conceived and held up to the angry passions of men, will never be obliterated; and every new irritation will mark it deeper and deeper." Then, speaking directly of slavery itself, he added, "We have the wolf by the ears, and we can neither hold him, nor safely let him go. Justice is in one scale, and self-preservation in the other."

The Missouri Compromise made antislavery men seethe too. "Hell is about to enlarge her borders and tyranny her domain," declared the Quaker editor Elihu Embree. To Embree, and to men like Vestal and Levi Coffin, the slaveholders' victory in Congress made it clear that the institution that they regarded as the most evil on the face of the earth was continuing to metastasize, and that if it was to be thwarted, they would have to undertake risks, personal risks, of an entirely new kind: to do nothing was to court damnation.

CHAPTER 5

THE SPREADING STAIN

It is quite easy to imagine, then, what was the state of my mind, having been reared in total moral midnight.

—JAMES PENNINGTON, FORMER SLAVE

1

Despite his early sickliness, Josiah Henson grew into a vigorous and self-reliant young man. He was passionately competitive, and proud of his physical strength, claiming that he "could run faster, wrestle better, and jump higher than anybody about me." His master Isaac Riley looked upon him as "a wonderfully smart fellow" from whom great things were to be expected, Henson says in his "autobiography," a work originally published in 1849 and revised several times under Henson's supervision, though actually penned by his Boston abolitionist friend Samuel A. Eliot. "My vanity became vastly inflamed, and I fully coincided in their opinion," Henson goes on. "Julius Caesar never aspired and plotted for the imperial crown more ambitiously than I did to out-hoe, out-reap, out-husk, out dance, out-everything every competitor; and from all I can learn he never enjoyed his triumph half as much. One word of commendation from the petty despot who ruled over us would set me up for a month." Pride and naive optimism at least mitigated, if they could never erase, the inherent humiliation of slavery. Henson enjoyed "jolly Christmas times," "midnight visits to apple orchards," and occasionally poaching a neighbor's pig or sheep to provide a feast for his fellow slaves, exploits that won him gratitude and friends. One can already see in the brash teenager the qualities that Riley must have prized: the pride in work well done, loyalty to authority, and a remarkable ability to harness his determination and ambition within the slave system. Put another way, Henson was destined for great success as a slave.

Henson's intricate relationship with Isaac Riley embodied the basic problem of slavery. Henson was not just an ordinary field hand, but prized property, like a finely bred piece of livestock, that had to be nurtured, well maintained, and used only in ways that would enhance his value. Indeed, if there is any story that shows that autonomy, even upward mobility, was possible under the constraints of slavery, it is Henson's. He was a man who believed in the system, one that had raised, favored, and on the whole protected him, and given him limited power in the world he knew. He knew quite well that his lot was far better than that of the average agricultural laborer. Yet he would finally risk everything—high status, his family's safety, not to mention his life—to flee north. In the end, even Henson was compelled to face the fact that no amount of favoritism could hide slavery's fundamental nature and its terrifying insecurity. With that recognition, Henson's story became the story of thousands. Once there was someplace to go where fugitives had some real hope of keeping the fruits of their own labor and enjoying the comfort of their family without fear of it being ripped apart, they would flee there, no matter how distant, no matter how low the odds of successful escape.

Before that, however, he would suffer. His life, like so many, both black and white, slave and free, would move from the confines of the eastern hamlet where it had begun and into the larger world of the young nation, a nation that was just awakening to its power, and searching for its geographical limits, and pushing beyond them. Both slavery and abolitionism would grow now with the country, would move west with it, cut through the wilderness, push away the Indians who had lived there before, and transform the land. Westward expansion carried slavery with it into the new territories, and then states, of Alabama and Mississippi, Tennessee and Kentucky, Florida and Louisiana, Arkansas, Missouri, and Texas. It traveled westward like a spreading epidemic, crossing the Appalachians in ox carts and Conestoga wagons, traveling on hardened feet, carried on the steamboats that nosed their way down the Ohio, the Tennessee, the Cumberland, and the Mississippi. It would, in these early years of the century, even insinuate itself into states that were nominally free, where slavery was supposedly barred for all time, into the southern edges of Illinois and Indiana. But abolitionism was on the road too, less visible certainly, still mostly concealed in the hearts and minds of men and women who did not yet know that they were part of a movement that would soon begin to change the country as surely as a million woodsmen's axes would make the forests of the new states vanish.

The seed of Josiah Henson's self-liberation was sown inadvertently when he was eighteen years old, in 1807 or 1808. Something utterly unexpected happened to him in that year. Henson, who had never expressed particular interest in religion, underwent a profound experience that left him burning with an inner sense of divine purpose. Until now, he had never heard a sermon, and his spiritual life, if he had any, probably amounted to little more than the Lord's Prayer. Henson's mother, a devout woman, urged him to go and hear John McKenney, a George Town baker by trade and a Methodist by conviction, who preached to slaves as well as to whites. When Henson arrived, McKenney was discoursing on what Henson (presumably later) learned was Hebrews 2:9: "That he, by the grace of God, should taste of death for every man," words that would indelibly remain printed in his memory. Henson stood rapt as McKenney's words opened a door onto the previously unimagined realm of Christian myth. Embedded in the preacher's story of crucifixion and ascension, compassion and redemption, was the extraordinary idea—Henson repeated it over and over in his mind—that Christ's salvation was for everyone, not just white men, even for a cocky field hand in the hills of Maryland. He imagined "a glorious being" smiling down at him from high above, welcoming him to the skies, and he felt a "sweetness of feeling" pouring through him, an onrush of divine love. "Nothing will seem so hard after this," Henson thought. He was so excited that on the way home he flung himself down in the woods outside George Town and prayed to God for further enlightenment. As his religious feelings grew, he began to pray with his fellow slaves, to "exhort" them, and to share with them "those little glimmerings of light from another world, which had reached my own eye."

While his conversion to Methodism unlocked in Henson a powerful sense of his own humanity and his spiritual worth, it also strengthened his loyalty to Isaac Riley. When they were a small, evangelical minority within the Church of England, the Methodists had vigorously denounced slavery as a travesty of divine, human, and natural justice. In 1780 Methodist leaders gathered in Baltimore had directed ministers to set free any slaves that they possessed. A second conference a few years later explicitly prohibited Methodists from "buying or selling the bodies or souls of men, women, or children, with an intention to enslave them." In spite of such views rather than because of them, the next two decades were a time of explosive growth for the Methodists. Having cut their link with the British church, they now offered themselves as a home-grown sect served by itinerant ministers who could turn a field, forest, or tent into a temple of God. The message of individual redemption that they delivered, in language that even the most lowly could understand, resonated deeply with Americans in an era when the secularist passions of the Revolutionary generation had grown stale. In a single generation, Methodists would grow *twenty-five fold*, to include 172,000 whites, most of them in the South, and some 42,000 blacks, by 1816.

Once they were no longer subversive outcasts, however, the church's leaders recognized that opposition to slavery would hamper their growth and their steady elevation to respectability as long as Southerners perceived them as "firebrands of discord." Instead of insisting that their members separate themselves from slavery as Quakers had, Methodist clerics began apologizing for their former opposition to it. By 1808 the Methodist establishment had abandoned scalding polemics, softening its criticism of slavery—when they made it at all—to mild formulations that even slave owners could tolerate. Preachers now assured Southerners that their slaves were better off than European peasants and many American whites. And to slaves, they piously emphasized prayer, sobriety, kindness, and of course obedience. A similar, cynical process also took place in the Presbyterian church, which as late as 1818 had declared, through its General Assembly: "We consider the voluntary enslaving of one part of the human race by another as a gross violation of the most precious and sacred rights of human nature, as utterly inconsistent with the law of God, which requires us to love our neighbor as ourselves and as totally irreconcilable with the spirit and principles of the gospel of Christ which enjoin that all things whatsoever ye would that men should do to you do ye even so to them."

Not all masters were as accommodating as Isaac Riley. Many barred their slaves from receiving any religious training at all. The fugitive William Wells Brown wrote: "In Missouri, and as far as I have any knowledge of slavery in other states, the religious teaching consists in teaching the slave that he must never strike a white man; that God made him for a slave; and that, when whipped, he must not find fault,—for the Bible says, 'He that knoweth his master's will, and doeth it not, shall be beaten with many stripes!' " In the summer of 1821 Levi and Vestal Coffin had started a Sunday school for "the colored people," mostly slaves, at the Quaker schoolhouse near the New Garden meeting house. But hostile slave owners threatened to prosecute both the Coffins and those masters who permitted their slaves to attend the school, and it was forced to close. Coffin wrote, "They said that it made their slaves discontented and uneasy, and created a desire for the privileges that others had."

Henson's status was significantly enhanced when he exposed some sort of fraud on the part of the farm's white overseer. Riley thereupon dismissed the man, and replaced him with Henson. Black overseers were hardly typical, but they were not uncommon either. Henson may already have been serving as a driver, or assistant overseer, drivers typically being chosen from among slaves who, like Henson, stood out in physical strength, intelligence, loyalty, and managerial ability. He supervised the raising of crops that included wheat, oats, barley, potatoes, corn, and tobacco, and was entrusted with carting them to the markets in George Town and Washington, where he negotiated their sale on Riley's behalf. Even after nearly half a century of freedom, Henson would still be proud that he had more than doubled the farm's yield, and inspired his fellow slaves to "more cheerful and willing labor" than Riley had ever seen. Although, in his autobiography, Henson was careful to avoid the subject, he also must have been responsible for their punishment. As a slave himself, he was under much greater pressure than a white overseer to show that he would not tolerate slacking or misbehavior. William Grimes, a contemporary of Henson, who was a slave on plantations in Virginia and Georgia before escaping to Connecticut, feared black overseers more than white ones: "My master gave me many severe floggings; but I had rather be whipped by him than the overseer, and especially the black overseers," Grimes related in his 1824 autobiography. Charles Ball, another contemporary, also served as a plantation superintendent in Georgia. "I not infrequently found it proper to punish [my fellow slaves] with stripes to compel them to perform their work," Ball admitted. "At first I felt much repugnance against the use of the hickory, the only instrument with which I punished offenders, but the longer I was accustomed to this practice, the more familiar and less offensive it became to me; and I believe that a few years of perseverance and experience would have made me as inveterate a negro-driver as any in Georgia."

The relationship between Riley and Henson was a curiously codependent one. Henson portrayed his master as a swaggering drunk given to fits of depression and rage, but to whom he was nevertheless sincerely devoted. "I had no reason to think highly of his moral character; but it was my duty to be faithful to him in the position in which he placed me; and I can boldly declare, before God and man, that I was so. I forgave him the causeless blows and injuries he had inflicted on me in childhood and youth, and was proud of the favor he now showed me, and of the character and reputation I had earned by strenuous and persevering efforts." Like many farmers, Riley was "slave rich" but cash poor, a problem that was probably exacerbated by the tight credit that afflicted many eastern planters after the Panic of 1819, as well as a costly lawsuit with his brother-in-law. Henson painted a picture of the master sunk in boozy despair, and the born-again slave full of solicitous, even condescending compassion: each man both helpless and powerful in his own way, one with the prerogatives of skin color, tradition, and the law, but crippled by incompetence and alcohol; the other a slave, but swollen with self-certitude and evangelical fervor. "Partly through pride, partly through that divine spirit of love I had learned to worship in Jesus, I entered with interest into all his perplexities," Henson recalled. "The poor drinking, furious, moaning creature was incapable of managing his affairs. Shiftlessness, licentiousness and drink had complicated them as much as actual dishonesty." Henson chose his adjectives deliberately, one must assume, damning his master with the same language—"shiftlessness," "licentiousness," "dishonesty"—that Southern apologists traditionally used to justify the enslavement of blacks.

Isaac Riley's financial crisis set in motion a series of events that would change Henson's life. Showing the extraordinary confidence that he placed in his slave, Riley ordered Henson to "slip away" to the plantation of his brother, Amos Riley, in Kentucky, taking with him eighteen slaves to prevent them from falling into his creditors' hands. Among these were Henson's wife, Charlotte, "a very efficient, and, for a slave, a very well-taught girl," whom he had met at a revival meeting, and four young sons. "[My] heart and soul became identified with my master's project of running off his negroes," recalled Henson, who was placed in charge of a one-horse wagon, stocked with oats, meal, bacon, and feed for the animal. Everything depended on the other slaves' willingness to obey him. "Fortunately for the success of the undertaking, these people had been long under my direction, and were devotedly attached to me in return for the many alleviations I had afforded to their miserable condition, the comforts I had procured them, and the consideration I had always manifested for them . . . The dread of being separated, and sold away down south, should they remain on the old estate, united them as one man, and kept them patient and alert."

Henson's party followed the new National Road across Virginia, via Culpepper and Harpers Ferry, and then through the mountains of western Virginia, to Wheeling. It must have seemed to Henson as if the entire country was bound for the Ohio Valley. Declared one federal official, "No poor man in the Eastern states, who has feet and legs, and can use them has any excuse for remaining poor where he is, a day or even an hour." He and his charges would have passed whole convoys of middle-class "movers" driving ox-drawn wagons and "one-horse tumbrils" piled high with stacks of bedding, furniture, spinning wheels, pots, and tools, as well as ragged families who trudged along with two or three half-naked children, a limping, lantern-ribbed pony and, as one traveler put it, a pathetic "bag of old plunder" containing their meager belongings. Isaac Riley's unshackled bondsmen no doubt looked with compassion upon the coffles of slaves shuffling westward toward the markets and plantations of Kentucky and the Mississippi Valley. The Quaker abolitionist Benjamin Lundy, who had lived in Wheeling a few years before Henson's party passed through, described its streets filled with "droves of a dozen or twenty ragged men bound for the West, chained together and driven through the streets, *bare-headed* and *bare-footed, in mud and snow*," by men armed with whips and bludgeons.

At Wheeling, Henson sold the horse and wagon and with the proceeds bought "a large boat, called in that region a yawl," for the long journey down the Ohio River. So far, Henson had little cause to worry about discipline among his charges. But now they were sailing just yards from the shore of a free state. "On passing along the Ohio shore, we were repeatedly told by persons conversing with us, that we were no longer slaves, but free men, if we chose to be so," he says. At Cincinnati, crowds of free blacks gathered around Henson's party, urging them to remain in Ohio, telling them that they were fools for continuing on to Kentucky, and surrendering themselves again to slavery. All they had to do was to walk away and disappear into the city. They could easily have found work along the booming riverfront, or in the hinterland, where new towns were being raised, farms carved from the forest, timber cut, and roads laid. There was nothing to stop them but the will of Josiah Henson, and even he felt his resolution giving way. "The duties of the slave to his master as appointed over him in the Lord, I had ever heard urged by ministers and religious men," he wrote. To run away seemed to him like outright stealing. "And now I felt the devil was getting the upper hand of me." But he had given Riley his word. "Pride, too, came in to confirm me. I had undertaken a great thing; my vanity had been flattered all along the road by hearing myself praised; I thought it would be a feather in my cap to carry it through thoroughly."

Henson determined to act, before he changed his mind. It was, in its way, a pivotal moment in the history of slavery. All the powerful machinery of the slave power was turning in Henson's heart, and against it the unnatural, troubling prospect of freedom: unexamined, largely unknown, insecure, alluring yet frightening, and problematic. And yet, here were men and women like themselves shouting to them from the riverbank, free. "I sternly assumed the captain, and ordered the boat to be pushed off into the stream," Henson recalled. "A shower of curses followed me from the shore; but the negroes under me, accustomed to obey, and, alas! too degraded and ignorant of the advantages of liberty to know what they were forfeiting, offered no resistance to my command."

2

A few months after Josiah Henson passed westward on his journey down the Ohio, Levi Coffin crossed the river northward en route to his new home in Indiana. Coffin had made an earlier, exploratory trip there in 1822, in the company of his future brother-in-law Benjamin White. "Town booming," as it was called, was taking place just about anywhere that buildings could be erected. One unhappy European traveler reported that the Westerners seemed determined to plant their settlements in the dirtiest puddles they could find. To newcomers the atmosphere seemed semibarbarous. Respectable farmers from New England, New York, and the Mid-Atlantic states, along with a smattering of young lawyers and "mechanics" (as skilled working men were called), lived alongside shaggy frontiersmen who wore buckskins and tomahawks or foot-long knives stuck in their belts. Although the rich, black prairie earth was capable of producing forty bushels of wheat or a hundred of corn to the acre, tilling it was "jerking, wracking, shin-cracking labor," in soil so tangled with roots and grubs that chains broke and plows stuck fast.

There were very few African Americans in Indiana at this time, perhaps fewer than three thousand, and they were not made to feel welcome. Before statehood, Governor William Henry Harrison had proposed legalizing slavery in the territory, and in later years there were repeated attempts to exclude blacks entirely. A typical memorial to the territorial authorities from settlers in Harrison County stated: "We are opposed to the introduction of slaves or free Negroes in any shape. Our corn Houses, Kitchens, Smoke Houses . . . may no doubt be robbed and our wives, children and daughters may and no doubt will be insulted and abused by those Africans. We do not wish to be saddled with them in any way." Although immigration was not in fact restricted, the laws did discriminate harshly against blacks. Voting was limited to white males. Blacks were barred from testifying in court cases involving whites, and their children excluded from public schools. After 1831 blacks wishing to settle in Indiana would be required to register with the local authorities and to post a bond as a guarantee of good behavior.

On the whole, though, Coffin approved of Indiana. As a Quaker he was pleased by the leveling aspect of frontier society. Equality among whites, or at least white men, was not just a theory but a basic fact, so ingrained in the way life was lived that it was scarcely remarked upon by anyone. Settlers, no matter what their origins, all lived in the same small cabins made of rough bark logs, with a floor made of "puncheons," or split timber, and a fireplace made of the same construction, plastered with mud. They ate the same stewed pumpkin, cabbage, salt pork, and hominy. And they endured the same abominable trails that turned into morasses of mud every time it rained. At the same time as the sheer difficulty of frontier life tended to strengthen cooperative relationships, the absence of firm government encouraged an aggressive individualism that was rare in more densely populated areas back East. Both tendencies were to play a role in the Underground Railroad, where success and safety depended on both absolute trust in one's friends and neighbors, and a sometimes self-righteous willingness to take the law into one's own hands.

Coffin spent several weeks traveling among the Quaker settlements visiting relatives, and then settled down for the winter teaching school at several locations in the vicinity of Richmond. The next spring, a cousin, Allen Hiatt, asked Coffin to join him in crossing what was then known as the Grand Prairie, to rendezvous with family members who had settled on the Sangamon River, in western Illinois, or "Kaskaskia." In spite of the Northwest Ordinance, de facto slavery continued to exist in Illinois with little interference from the authorities. Indeed, the state's first governor, Shadrach Bond, owned thirteen slaves, and his lieutenant governor, twelve. Slaves could freely be brought into the state as long as they were registered at a county clerk's office. Typically, they were registered as "indentured servants," whose "contracts" could be freely bought and sold. Whipping was permitted by law, including twenty-five lashes in front of a magistrate if a "servant" was found more than ten miles from his home. Those who refused to work could be sold back into the slave states. Even as Coffin was making his way across the empty heart of the state, proslavery settlers from the South were vigorously agitating for a constitutional vote that would convert Illinois officially into a slave state. The proslavery forces eventually were defeated at the polls, in 1824, but only by a comparatively narrow margin of 6,640 to 4,972. That the antislavery forces were successful at all was due mainly to the passionate advocacy of Governor Edward Coles, the Virginian who as a young man a decade earlier had begged Thomas Jefferson to speak out for abolition.

If Indiana was primitive, most of Illinois was still raw wilderness, confusing and forbidding by turns. There were barely seventy thousand settlers in the entire state, most of them along the Mississippi River; Chicago was a hamlet with more Indian wigwams in it than houses. Much of the state was scarcely known at all, except to hunters and trappers. After crossing the Wabash, Coffin and Hiatt followed an Indian trail that wound from northwest to southwest across a limitless prairie, empty but for occasional native villages, and scaffolds that the Indians had built to dry their venison. They wandered over the prairie for six days, at one point, without seeing a single human being. Trails abruptly vanished in swamp and tall grass. Wolves howled in the distance. "Starvation seemed to stare us in the face," Coffin remembered. At last, having almost abandoned hope, they saw smoke rising from a log cabin, and were overjoyed to discover that it was inhabited by white people, who directed them to the settlement they were searching for. Hiatt's relatives were preparing to move on still farther west, however. At this point, Levi Coffin might well have passed out of history. The man who was to become, arguably, the Underground Railroad's most effective single organizer might have become yet another itchy-footed pioneer, drawn ever westward by the lure of better and cheaper land and freedom from the entanglements of society. Hiatt's relatives "asked me to go too, but I told them that ever since I had come to the West I had heard of a better place a little further on, and now that I had got within forty miles of it, I thought I would turn back," Coffin would dryly recall. He rejected the frontier and the open spaces, and returned home, choosing commitment, obligation, duty, and a more complex and problematic future darkened by the spreading stain of slavery.

Back in North Carolina in 1824, Coffin alternated between periods of farming and teaching at various schools in Guilford County. He also married Benjamin White's sister Catherine, an "amiable and attractive young woman of lively, buoyant spirits," who would cheerfully share his work on behalf of fugitive slaves. Two years later, they would leave North Carolina for good. About this time, Vestal Coffin unexpectedly died at the age of thirty-four. It is not clear whether these events caused a serious interruption in the dispatch of fugitive slaves northward. However, a few years later the slave known as "Hamilton's Saul" would still be working clandestinely with Vestal's young son Addison, so it seems probable that the system that the elder Coffins created continued to operate, with Levi soon to be positioned to receive fugitives at the Indiana end of the line.

In September 1826 Levi and his wife headed west via the Kanawha Road. They settled in Newport, today known as Fountain City, in eastern Indiana, a village of about twenty families where they would live for more than two decades, and which they would make into one of the most important centers of underground activity in the West. Many Quakers had settled in the surrounding area, as had free blacks, including many sent there by the North Carolina Yearly Meeting. So many of the Quakers were from Guilford County that they named their local meeting New Garden after their former one in North Carolina. Coffin bought property and, seeing the need for a mercantile business, he purchased goods from Cincinnati and opened a store, the first in the town.

Coffin observed that runaway slaves often passed through Newport, probably drawn by the presence of a black community into which they might hope to blend. They "were often pursued and captured, the colored people not being very skillful in concealing them, or shrewd in making arrangements to forward them to Canada," Coffin wrote. Simply reaching the nominally free soil of Indiana was by no means a guarantee of safety. Slave hunters operated freely under the provisions of the Fugitive Slave Law. Nor were Quakers all of one mind when it came to harboring fugitives. Many felt that they had done all that their religion required of them by emancipating their own bondsmen and immigrating to a free state. Indeed, the Quaker committee charged with resettling free blacks in Indiana had to beg Quakers to overcome their personal prejudices and "yield to the interests and happiness of our fellow human beings," by accepting African Americans as neighbors.

Coffin was not among those Quakers who left their convictions behind in North Carolina. When he asked fellow Quakers why they did not help fugitives on their way, they typically temporized, saying that they were afraid of the law. "I told them that I read in the Bible when I was a boy that it was right to take in the stranger and administer to those in distress, and that I thought it was always safe to do right," Coffin would answer, adding pointedly that he was "willing to receive and aid as many fugitives as were disposed to come to my house." According to Coffin, the first fugitives arrived at his home in the winter of 1826–27. "Friends in the neighborhood, who had formerly stood aloof from the work . . . were encouraged to engage in it when they saw the fearless manner in which I acted, and the success that attended my efforts. . . . They would contribute to clothe the fugitives, and would aid in forwarding them on their way, but were timid about sheltering them under their roof; so that part of the work devolved on us." Some seemed genuinely happy to see the work go on, as long as the Coffins took the risk, while others actively tried to discourage them. "They manifested great concern for my safety and pecuniary interests, telling me that such a course of action would injure my business and perhaps ruin me; that I ought to consider the welfare of my family; and warning me that my life was in danger, as there were many threats made against me by the slave-hunters and those who sympathized with them." To such arguments, Coffin replied, "If by doing my duty and endeavoring to fulfill the injunctions of the Bible, I injured my business, then let my business go. As to my safety, my life was in the hands of my Divine Master, and I felt that I had his approval."

3

In the middle of April 1825, Josiah Henson's party arrived at the plantation of Amos Riley, which extended across a wide tract of rolling, lightly wooded hills on Big Blackford's Creek, near Owensboro, Kentucky. In contrast to Indiana and Ohio, whose embryonic towns were already increasingly dominated by middle-class farmers and tradesmen, Kentucky was a volatile region with a tradition of violence that frightened many visitors from more civilized places. A European who traveled widely in North America in 1823 and 1824, Karl Anton Postl (like a sort of early nineteenth-century John Gunther, having written *Austria As It Is*, he was now at work on *The Americans As They Are*) compared Kentucky's climate favorably to the South of France, praising its undulating hills and valleys, and the "inexhaustible fertility" of its soil. The people, on the other hand, frankly repelled him. The Kentuckian was a frontiersman, not a Tidewater aristocrat, and his home was more likely to be a rude and battered cabin than it was a mansion, strewn with guns and saddles, whips and farm implements. The state's fifty-seven thousand inhabitants, of whom some fifteen thousand were slaves, were mainly emigrants from Virginia and the Carolinas, in Postl's words, "a proud, fierce, and overbearing set of people," who "established themselves under a state of continual warfare with the Indians, who took their revenge by communicating to their vanquishers their cruel and implacable spirit." Postl complained further about Kentucky's epidemic of insecure land titles, ferocious hostilities between the state's different courts of law, a governor who was "a disgrace to his station" along with a son who ought to "be hung in chains," the country's worst paper currency, and the utter disregard of religious principles.

Henson's life in Kentucky began auspiciously enough. Amos Riley was a very rich man by Kentucky standards, owning between eighty and one hundred slaves, and occupying a large and fertile plantation five miles from the Ohio River, the most important interstate highway of its day. On Isaac Riley's recommendation, Henson was appointed a "manager," which probably meant that he oversaw one or more large teams of field slaves. At the age of thirty-six he had risen higher than most slaves could ever hope to. His family probably enjoyed somewhat better housing and diet than the hands that he supervised, as well as a certain amount of freedom to move about the plantation unmolested. He was also able to attend camp meetings in the area, since he soon began to preach in a more or less formal way, "speaking from the fullness of a heart deeply impressed with its own sinfulness and imperfection."

Nehemiah Adams, a Northern minister who was recuperating from an illness in the South, attended numerous Methodist prayer meetings that probably resembled those that Henson frequented. Typically, Adams reported, a white brother presided and read a portion of Scripture, but the slaves conducted the meeting. Each worshipper, after prostrating himself in prayer, stood up and repeated a hymn, two lines at a time, and then began again to pray, as the spirit moved him, with intense "earnestness of manner," expressing gratitude to Christ for his love, a "touching sense" of unworthiness, supplications for mercy, and the desire to be kept free from sin. The unemotional Adams was nearly overwhelmed by the "involuntary shoutings from the whole meeting, in which I almost wished to join, for the thoughts expressed were so awakening and elevating." He was especially moved to hear one slave say, "Bless our dear masters and brothers, who come here to read the Bible to us, and pay so much attention to us."

In the spring of 1828 the Hensons' security was suddenly shaken. An agent arrived from Maryland with directions from Isaac Riley to liquidate the slaves that Henson had brought out three years earlier. Only Henson's own family was to be spared, a striking measure of the close ties between master and slave. Henson was ordered to return to Rockville to manage what remained of Isaac Riley's estate, leaving his wife and family behind in Kentucky. In modern terms, Henson was retraumatized by the impending sale: intense emotional flashbacks reawakened the grief that as a child he had seen in his mother's eyes when she was separated from her children, opening him up, in turn, to the enormity of what he had done to these same slaves when he had forced the yawl away from the docks at Cincinnati. As he listened now to their "groans and cries" he was overwhelmed by guilt, finally realizing how he had been responsible for keeping in slavery men and women who might otherwise have gone free, and for now bringing about the same rending of husband from wife and mother from child that had wrecked his own family thirty years before. "And now," he admitted, "through me, were they doomed to wear out life miserably in the hot and pestilential climate of the far south." Henson seems for the first time to have fully grasped that loyalty, no matter how profound, could never guarantee security for any slave. With something akin to panic, he longed "to get away with my wife and children, to some spot where I could feel that they were indeed *mine*." He began to think seriously about obtaining his own freedom.

Sometime before his departure for the East, in September 1828, Henson met "a most excellent white man" who, "in a confidential manner," told him that he had "too much capacity to be confined to the limited life of a slave," and that he deserved to be free. If Henson had ever had such a conversation before, it left no impression on him. But now he listened intently. Although Henson never revealed the man's identity, he was probably an itinerant preacher. While the leadership of the evangelical churches had by the 1820s shifted decisively toward tolerance for slavery, if not outright support, many individual preachers, Presbyterian and Baptist as well as Methodist, continued to espouse an antislavery message, especially in the western states where political attitudes about slavery had not yet hardened. The Methodists' Tennessee Conference, which also oversaw preachers active in Kentucky, in particular stood out for its continuing hostility to slavery, still refusing to ordain unrepentant slaveholders as late as 1820, while a Presbyterian clergyman, John Finley Crowe, published the weekly *Abolition Intelligencer and Missionary Magazine* in Shelbyville, barely a day's journey from Amos Riley's plantation. Henson's new friend, whoever he was, did not urge him to flee outright or, at least at this stage, say much if anything about an underground network, but he did promise to help him earn the money to buy his freedom, by putting him in contact with a "brother preacher" in Cincinnati.

The Cincinnati that Josiah Henson found en route back to Maryland was "a bright, beautiful and flourishing little city" whose feverish bustle epitomized a region that was inventing and reinventing itself almost literally from day to day. Steamboats swarmed along the riverfront, hooting their arrivals and departures, columns of smoke churning in white clouds from their lofty flutes. Pillared Greek Revival homes graced the finer blocks. Business houses and banks, hotels, churches, even a university, a museum, a theater, and a hospital proclaimed the city's aspirations to culture. Local newspapers advertised the latest fashions from London and New York, furs from the Pacific, and oysters from Philadelphia. Since 1810 its population had quadrupled to more than sixteen thousand, four thousand of whom had arrived in the last two years alone. Almost three thousand city residents were black, many of them fugitives who had rowed or swum across the Ohio, walked across its frozen surface in the winter, or simply jumped off riverboats moored at the docks. Virtually the only jobs open to them were as laborers, barbers, and menials, and competition with immigrants, mostly Irish, for even those jobs would soon erupt into ugly riots, leaving many blacks dead, and hundreds more homeless. Lamented John Malvin, a black visitor to Cincinnati, in 1827, "I found every door was closed against the colored man in a free state, excepting the jails and penitentiaries."

With the introduction that Henson received from "the excellent white man," he was able to meet a number of "invaluable friends who entered heart and soul" into his plans. They arranged for him to preach in several of the city's churches, probably to both white and black congregations, where he appealed directly for donations to purchase his freedom. In a few days he had earned 160 dollars, a substantial sum. He continued eastward, traveling from town to town, preaching as he went. He was deeply moved by the courtesy that he encountered, probably never before having addressed all-white audiences, much less ones that listened to him with the pious respect that they would grant to a white man. By the time he left Ohio, he had 275 dollars, plus new clothes and a horse, very likely the first valuable personal property that he had ever owned.

Isaac Riley was delighted to see Henson after his long absence in Kentucky. However, he took away the pass that for a few weeks had given Henson the fleeting illusion that he could travel as freely as a white man. Henson was also sent to sleep in the slave quarters over the kitchen, a rude shock after what must have been fairly comfortable accommodations that he had enjoyed in Ohio. All night he lay awake, physically sick from the stench of the place, feeling humiliated and bitter, and more determined than ever to obtain his freedom. Riley seemed amenable to his proposition, agreeing to allow Henson to purchase himself for 350 dollars in cash, plus a promissory note for 100 dollars more. This was an increasingly common practice in Maryland, where slave owners resorted to such negotiations in an effort to stem the flight of their chattels across the state line to Pennsylvania, or into the free black neighborhoods of Baltimore. Henson was ecstatic. His savings and his horse enabled him to pay the cash portion on the spot. In March 1829 he received his manumission papers. He was now, he believed, a free man. This, he was soon to find out, was only an illusion.

Riley agreed to allow Henson to return to Kentucky, but insisted on putting Henson's manumission papers under a personal seal for his brother Amos to open, and told Henson to travel with his slave pass instead. This made a kind of sense. Paradoxically, it was much safer to travel as a slave than as a free black. Henson knew that free blacks were often kidnapped and sold into slavery, with no hope of redress from the law. Kidnapping a slave, however, was outright theft, and whites were sometimes executed for it; molesting a free black man was no crime at all.

Back in Kentucky, Henson found that news of his negotiations and his fund raising had traveled ahead of him. His wife, Charlotte—here he betrays a rare insight into what may have been a less than perfect marriage—revealed that she suspected that he had earned the money not by preaching, which her plantation-bound experience apparently could not grasp, but by stealing it. "But how are you going to raise the rest of the thousand dollars?" she asked Josiah, shocking him. He believed, of course, that he had already paid everything except the one-hundred-dollar promissory note. Pressed to explain what she meant, Charlotte explained that Amos Riley had said that Henson had put 350 dollars down, and that when he had paid the remaining *650 dollars* he would have his freedom—and his papers, which he had so trustingly delivered to Amos under his brother's seal.

Henson realized that a cruel trick had been played on him, and fell into "a frenzy of grief." To whom could he appeal? Who would believe that he had been cheated? Not a magistrate, certainly. No black man's word was admissible in a Kentucky court against a white man, certainly not against his own master. Amos Riley told Henson, with cruel sarcasm, "Want to be free, eh! I think your master treats you pretty hard, though. Six hundred and fifty dollars don't come so easy in old Kentuck. How does he ever expect you to raise all that? It's too much, boy, it's too much."

(Isaac Riley's widow, Matilda, who lived until 1890, told a different story of these events. In an 1883 interview in the *Rockville Sentinel*, she claimed that she was still holding a promissory note for *five* hundred dollars that Henson had negotiated, which she asserted Henson had never paid. "Uncle Si," she said, using the family's nickname for Henson, had negotiated with Riley for the purchase of his whole family, promising to return together with them to Maryland, and to remain there until he had paid off the note. Armed with a document from Isaac Riley ordering his brother Amos to "let Si Have his wife and children," Matilda said, " 'Uncle Si' returned to Kentucky, obtained possession of his family, and when he reached Cincinnati made for Canada." Denying that Riley had been duplicitous, the article portrayed Henson as an ungrateful "pet servant," who craftily took advantage of his indulgent master, whose confidence in Henson's honesty "remained unshaken until he had deceived him in obtaining the order for his family.")

So long the model slave, Henson had now branded himself as unreliable. Not long after his return from Maryland, Amos Riley ordered him to accompany his twenty-one-year-old son, also named Amos, to New Orleans with a flatboat loaded with produce. As the miles grew between Henson and his family back in Kentucky, he fell into a deep depression, sensing that the Rileys had decided to sell him along with the rest of the cargo. Sure that he could survive no more than a few years in the cotton fields of the Deep South, he thought first of suicide. Then he seriously considered murdering young Amos and the three crewmen while they slept, taking what money he could find, and trying to make his way north. Only his religious scruples held him back. "I was about to lose the fruit of all my efforts at self-improvement, the character I had acquired, and the peace of mind that had never deserted me." Afterward, alone on the deck in the night, with the dark landscape of the Mississippi slipping by in the wet blackness, he was filled with shame and remorse. "Nothing brought composure to my mind but the solemn resolution I then made, to resign myself to the will of God, and take with thankfulness, if I could, but with submission, at all events, whatever he might decide should be my lot."

In New Orleans, young Amos confirmed Henson's worst fear. Once the cargo was gone, Henson wrote, "Nothing was left but to dispose of me, and to break up the boat." Several potential buyers came to size Henson up. He recalled, "My points were canvassed as those of a horse would have been." Henson was saved by a stroke of sheer luck when young Amos fell ill from "river fever," possibly cholera or typhoid, and abruptly ordered Henson to accompany him back to Kentucky, by the earliest steamboat. Although the immediate crisis had passed, it was inescapably clear to Henson that the Rileys were determined to get rid of him. "[Isaac Riley's] attempt to kidnap me again, after having pocketed three-fourths of my market value, in my opinion absolved me from all obligation to pay him any more, or to continue in a position which exposed me to his machinations."

In short, Henson had at last decided to make his escape. He had been as much a man of the system as any slave could be. He had believed that it would protect him, and that it would reward him for good behavior and for achievement. And the system had taken care of him, giving him security, status, a source of pride, power over his fellow slaves, even a sense of superiority over many white men. When Henson at last broke free, it was with the disillusionment and rage of a man whose whole world had betrayed him.

PART TWO

CONNECTIONS

THE 1830s

CHAPTER 6

FREE AS SURE AS THE DEVIL

The more we knew of freedom, the more we desired it.

—AUSTIN STEWARD, FORMER SLAVE

1

In the summer of 1831 a seismic shift took place beneath the racial landscape of the United States. That August a charismatic Virginia slave named Nat Turner, believing that he was guided by a divine hand, led a band of followers in the nation's bloodiest slave revolt ever. Before it was suppressed, less than three days after it had begun, at least sixty white men, women, and children had been killed, many of them brutally hacked to death in their beds or while they begged for mercy. " '[T] was my object to carry terror and devastation wherever we went," Turner would confess before his own execution. Between one hundred and two hundred African Americans would also be executed in retribution, most of them guilty of no wrongdoing. Near Southampton, an innocent black traveler was shot to death and decapitated, and his head stuck on a pole at a county crossroads. In Dupin County, North Carolina, more than ten blacks were summarily executed because of an alleged conspiracy, and in nearby Murfreesboro, a black man was beheaded for having predicted that there would someday be a war between the black and white peoples. Harriet Jacobs, a slave in Edenton, North Carolina, hid in terror from an orgy of white-on-black rape and savagery in which men, women, and children were randomly whipped "till the blood stood in puddles at their feet," and "no two people that had the slightest tinge of color in their faces dared to be seen talking together." Another woman who was enslaved near the Virginia–North Carolina border recalled that in the months after Turner's rebellion "the brightest and best men were killed."

Fulfilling the worst fears of race war that had beset Southern whites since the slaughter in Haiti in the early years of the century, Turner's insurrection effectively put an end to what lingering support for emancipation remained in the South, and led directly to ever more stringent restrictions on blacks, as well as on whites who dared to publicly challenge the institution of slavery. Rumors of insurrection raced through the South. In Raleigh, North Carolina, every free black in the city was put under arrest. Virginians debated how they could expel the fifty thousand free blacks who resided in the state, while the state legislature enacted a "police bill" that denied free blacks the right to trial by jury, allowed for their sale and transportation if they were convicted of a crime, and barred all blacks from preaching or attending religious meetings unless they were escorted by whites. Where schools for slaves existed, they were suppressed. The Virginia House of Delegates declared, in 1832, "We have, as far as possible, closed every avenue by which light can enter . . . [their] minds. If we could extinguish the capacity to see the light, our work would be completed; they would then be on a level with the beasts of the field, and we should be safe."

Earlier in the year—Southerners saw the coincidence in timing as irrefutable evidence of an unholy conspiracy linking antislavery Northerners to rebellious slaves—the Boston abolitionist William Lloyd Garrison had proclaimed a new doctrine of uncompromising radicalism in the national debate over slavery. Garrison's doctrine would soon reshape the way countless white Americans in the free states thought about slavery, as well as what they were personally prepared to do to bring it to an end. Calling for a "revolution in public sentiment," he proclaimed, in the first issue of the *Liberator*, the nation's first newspaper dedicated to immediate abolition: "I *will be* as harsh as truth, and as uncompromising as justice. On this subject, I do not wish to think, or speak, or write with moderation. Tell a man whose house is on fire, to give a moderate alarm; tell him to moderately rescue his wife from the hands of a ravisher; tell the mother to gradually extricate her babe from the fire into which it has fallen;—but urge me not to use moderation in a cause like the present. I am in earnest—I will not equivocate—I will not excuse—I will not retreat a single inch—AND I WILL BE HEARD."

Less visibly, but no less significant for the enslaved, scattered numbers of Americans who hated slavery enough to risk their reputations and their property to lend assistance to fugitive slaves were slowly beginning to discover one another. This process would soon accelerate dynamically as like-minded people, white and black, reached the point of critical mass that would transform a multitude of charitable personal acts into a movement guided by a shared idea of moral action transcending racial, class, and geographical differences, and that found its ultimate expression in the Underground Railroad. But all this was happening far beyond the narrowly circumscribed awareness of slaves isolated on Southern plantations. Except for the fragile hope of assistance from "benevolent men" of the type Josiah Henson had met during his visit to Cincinnati in 1829, fugitive slaves were largely on their own.

2

Tens of thousands of slaves ran away from their owners every year. Jarm Logue, a slave in Tennessee, decided to flee after his drunken master rammed a wooden wedge into his mouth and pounded it in with his fist, badly mangling him. Moses Roper was driven to flee from his Georgia master by a combination of harsh punishment, poor food, and a desire to see his mother, from whom he had been taken away as a child. William Wells Brown, who would one day become the country's first African-American novelist, ran when he learned that his financially hard-pressed master had sold Brown's mother and all the rest of her children, and that he was soon to be sold as well. Slaves ran because they had been beaten too often, because they were terrified of a sadistic overseer, because they couldn't bear to be sold away from family and friends one more time, because they had come to believe that their labor was worth a salary. Many, like the father whom the young Levi Coffin saw skulking behind the wagon that was carrying his enslaved family west, fled with a desperate hope of reuniting with wives, children, or parents who had been taken away from them. Christmas was the most popular time for slaves to escape. Typically, they could expect several days off and a travel pass to attend a prayer meeting, or to visit friends or relatives in distant communities, and they might not be missed for days. (Underground Railroad operatives in Chester County, Pennsylvania, just north of the Maryland state line, always prepared for an influx of fugitives immediately after the holidays.)

The very fact that slaves wanted to run away at all often confounded their masters, who believed—this was constantly affirmed by the ideologues who shaped the South's thinking about slavery—that bondage was ordained in the natural and God-given order of things. In this, they shared the conviction of twentieth-century totalitarians that dissent from a regime of pervasive and relentless control was a psychiatric problem rather than an elemental human desire for freedom. Newspaper notices for fugitive slaves subtly reflected slave owners' self-delusion: while fugitives were sometimes advertised as "incorrigible" or "defiant," far more were described by their owners as "inoffensive," "cheerful," and "well-disposed," as if flight itself were proof of blacks' childish inability to adapt to their ordained condition. One overseer explained with perplexed annoyance in a message to his employer that a slave had run off "for no other cause than that he did not feel disposed to be governed, by the same rules and regulations that the other Negroes . . . are governed by." Occasionally whites enticed slaves to escape for criminal motives. In *Life on the Mississippi*, Mark Twain recounted the terrible story of a gang of con men who would promise a slave that if he ran away and allowed them to sell him, they would give him a portion of the profit, and that upon his return to them a second time they would send him safely to a free state. Sometimes the gang would sell a man three or four times over, earning thousands of dollars in the process. Then, when they felt that they had used him up, they would murder him, toss his body in the Mississippi, and start over with a new victim.

Most runaways did not run very far. In the parlance of the time, most "lurked," or "lay out," near towns and cities, or the slave quarters of neighboring plantations, where they had friends who could provide them with food and occasional shelter, until they were either caught or returned voluntarily to their master. The Tennessee slave Jarm Logue, for instance, hid out in a cave for a week after a fistfight with his drunken master, getting food and news from his friends, and trying to learn what was in store for him if he went home. Logue, as his biographer would put it, now found himself in a situation that "greatly disappointed and embarrassed both parties." Logue was not in a position to escape, and his master was in no economic condition to dispense with his abilities. Logue returned to his home when word got to him that his master would ignore what had happened between them. For the average master, coping with "absentees" was essentially just one more headache of managing a plantation. In 1826 a Mississippi planter named John Nevitt recorded in his diary a steady, workaday pattern of slaves disappearing and returning. The slave Peter, who went off on February 2 was "brought home" by a neighbor on April 24, and "whipped and ironed" as punishment. The following year Bill ran away on February 28 and came back on March 3. Maria ran away on April 21, and was caught a week later by two other slaves who were dispatched to find her. John was gone from July 1 to July 20. Rubin ran away on October 1, but returned the next day.

In a region that operated under a system of police control that was specifically designed to terrorize blacks into helpless submission, few succeeded in remaining free for long. Steamboats were searched systematically for stowaways, and in ports throughout the South black travelers and workers were subject to immediate arrest if they could not prove their status. Each slaveholding community supported a force of "patrollers," legally sanctioned vigilante squads that were charged with monitoring the movements of blacks and punishing any who broke the rigid system of rules that governed the lives of all, both slave and free. In 1830 a single South Carolina community, Georgetown, spent more than three hundred dollars in salaries—a substantial sum, at that time—for the local guards. John Capeheart, a Norfolk constable and freelance slave hunter from the 1830s to the 1850s, reported, "It was part of my business to arrest all slaves and free persons of color, who were collected in crowds at night, and lock them up. It was also part of my business to take them before the Mayor. I did this without any warrant, and at my own discretion. Next day they are examined and punished. The punishment is flogging. I am one of the men who flog them. They get not exceeding thirty-nine lashes. I am paid fifty cents for every Negro I flog. The price used to be sixty-two and half cents. I am paid fifty cents for every Negro I arrest, and fifty cents more if I flog him. I have flogged hundreds. I am often employed by private persons to pursue fugitive slaves. I never refuse a good job of that kind."

Patrollers typically had the legal authority to ride onto anyone's property, search any home, and to shoot any black who did not surrender on command. Where African Americans were barred from testifying against whites in court, patrollers terrorized black families with complete impunity. "If a slave don't open his door to them at any time of night they break it down," the fugitive Lewis Clarke told a Northern audience. "They steal his money if they can find it, and act just as they please with his wives and daughters. If a husband dares to say a word, or even look as if he wasn't quite satisfied, they tie him up and give him thirty-nine lashes." Even where laws discouraged the use of excessive force against runaways, they were often ignored. Patrollers gathered in a tavern in southern Virginia told a Northern traveler that they had just returned from an unsuccessful expedition to kill a fugitive slave who had been lurking for the past year in the neighborhood of a nearby plantation. When he asked if it was not against the law to shoot an unarmed man, the visitor was matter-of-factly informed "that the laws of that state were as pointedly against it, as they were in any state, but the damned Negroes were so bad that nobody took notice of it—that it was a common thing to shoot them there . . . and it was not common in those cases to make any inquiry—a hole was dug, the Negro thrown in, covered up, and that was an end of it."

Fear of the patrollers, sometimes called "paddy rollers," or "patter-rollers," even infiltrated black folk culture. The suggestive lyrics of one tune might have been sung as a warning to fugitives that danger was near:

As I was goin cross de field
A black snake bit me on my heel
Run nigger run, de Patrol catch you
Run nigger run, tis almost day
When I run, I run my best
Run my head in a hornet's nest
Run nigger run, de Patrol catch you
Run nigger run, tis almost day.

Particularly in the Deep South, fugitives who sought more than a temporary respite from bondage tended to run in any direction that seemed to offer a hope of escape. Some followed river valleys eastward to one or another of the Atlantic coast ports, in hope of escaping the South by sea. Some tried to lose themselves in the free black populations of New Orleans, Charleston, and Savannah. Others fled to remote areas within the South, like Virginia's Great Dismal Swamp and the Florida wilderness, where they might form "maroon" communities of their own, where children were born and lived out their entire lives without ever emerging. Still others joined multiracial societies that managed to exist beyond the rim of white control, such as the stew of fragmented Indian tribes, fugitive slaves, and renegade whites who inhabited the marshes of Robeson County, North Carolina. Drives to flush out runaways from forests and swamps were popular sporting events in some parts of the South. In West Feliciana Parish, Louisiana, for instance, professional slave hunters would arrive in the morning, and along with local slave owners they would gallop through the countryside behind packs of dogs, running down fugitives as if they were rabbits.

Some fugitives sought refuge with Native Americans. Before the acquisition of Spanish-ruled Florida by the United States, numbers of them settled among the Seminoles there. Indeed, the First Seminole War, in 1816, climaxed with the bloody capture of "Fort Negro," a mixed black and Indian community on the Apalachicola River, by American and Creek Indian troops led by Andrew Jackson. (Nearly three hundred were killed outright, many of them when the fort's ammunition dump exploded; the survivors were marched back into slavery.) Native Americans offered no sure promise of protection, however, since slaveholding was not uncommon among them, and they might be as likely to enslave fugitives for their own use, or to sell them back to their masters, as to welcome them as freemen. One youngster, a free black named Samuel Scomp, who had been kidnapped from his home in Philadelphia, escaped from a slave driver in Alabama in 1825, hoping to find refuge with the Choctaw, but the first Indian he met handed him back to his captor, who beat him savagely for running off. When the Choctaw sold their lands in Mississippi to the United States in 1830, their chief, Greenwood Leflore, remained behind with his nearly four hundred slaves, making him one of the largest slave owners in the state. The Cherokee in particular, who occupied large parts of Georgia, Tennessee, and North Carolina until their expulsion by federal forces in the late 1830s, treated the adoption of black slavery as a part of their process of "civilization," akin to their establishment of modern courts and schools, the transition to European-style architecture, and the creation of a written language.

In the early 1830s, the free states of the North offered fugitive slaves the opportunity to live an autonomous life on the margin of society, and personal freedom that was protected only erratically by law. William Grimes, in his 1825 memoir, expressed with trenchant sarcasm the bitterness of freedom seekers like himself who had endured the racism of the North: "I do think there is no inducement for a slave to leave his master, and be set free in the northern states. I have had to work hard; I have been often cheated, insulted, abused, and injured; yet a black man, if he will be industrious and honest, he can get along here as well as any one who is poor, and in a situation to be imposed on." Fugitives could count on little or no organized help from antislavery whites, even if they could find them. While their numbers were growing, such men and women were still few and far between even in the Quaker communities of Pennsylvania. Ohio, Indiana, and Illinois all discouraged even the entry of free blacks. Only a few years earlier, the state supreme court of New Jersey had declared it "a settled rule . . . that black color is the proof of slavery," a principle that facilitated the work of Southern slave catchers. In most Northern states slave hunters were able to operate with little official interference, although as a practical matter the pursuit of fugitives was often a costly and time-consuming proposition. As one frustrated slave hunter complained, obviously expecting sympathy from his Southern friends, Ohioans who opposed slavery were "disposed to throw objections in the way of retaking slaves," and even when he managed to track one down "it was very difficult to get him." Even so, African Americans living as far north as Detroit, New York, and Boston went in constant fear of recapture. As if the real dangers of flight were not daunting enough, many fugitives carried the added burden that whites who appeared to offer them help might really be slave hunters in disguise.

Would-be fugitives were for the most part woefully ignorant of what lay to the north. Discontented slaves in northern Kentucky, Virginia, or Maryland might be only a few days' or even just a few hours' walk from the border of a free state. But few had ever seen a map, and in any event the psychological distance from freedom was often a far greater deterrent than the merely physical. To the young Frederick Douglass, who was destined to become the most eminent African American of his era, living as a slave on the western shore of Maryland less than seventy-five miles from the Pennsylvania state line, the prospect of flight was both alluring and intensely terrifying. "The real distance was great enough, but the imagined distance was, to our ignorance, much greater," Douglass would write. Slave masters who mentioned Canada at all commonly told their slaves that it had bad soil, was frozen all year, and was infested with wild beasts and with geese that would scratch a man's eyes out. "Slave holders sought to impress their slaves with a belief in the boundlessness of slave territory, and of their own limitless power," wrote Douglass. "Our notions of the geography of the country were very vague and indistinct . . . Then, too, we knew that merely reaching a free state did not free us, that wherever caught we could be returned to slavery. We knew of no spot this side of the ocean where we could be safe. We had heard of Canada, then the only real Canaan of the American bondman, simply as a country to which the wild goose and the swan repaired at the end of winter to escape the heat of summer, but not as the home of man." Douglass had heard of Pennsylvania, Delaware, and New Jersey, and remotely, New York City, but he did not know that there was a State of New York or Massachusetts. "The case sometimes, to our excited visions, stood thus: at every gate through which we had to pass we saw a watchman; at every ferry a guard; on every bridge, a sentinel, and in every wood a patrol or slave hunter. We were hemmed in on every side. The good to be sought and the evil to be shunned were flung in the balance and weighed against each other." By comparison, freedom seemed a phantom. "On the other hand," wrote Douglass, "far away, back in the hazy distance where all forms seemed but shadows under the flickering light of the north star, behind some craggy hill or snow-capped mountain, stood a doubtful freedom, half frozen, and beckoning us to her icy domain."

Canada in the 1830s was not yet a nation. It was still a congeries of six separate British colonies whose total population of fewer than three million people was clustered in a narrow belt along the edge of the Great Lakes, the St. Lawrence River, and the Atlantic Coast. Although plantation slavery had never developed in Canada, slaves had continued to be legally bought and sold until the appointment of John Graves Simcoe, a passionate abolitionist, as the first lieutenant governor of Upper Canada (modern Ontario), in 1791. Of the fourteen thousand inhabitants of the province at that time, perhaps one thousand were blacks, some of them the descendants of slaves who had escaped from rebel masters during the American Revolution, and others of slaves brought north by retreating Tory masters. Simcoe's blunt declaration that he would never support any law that "discriminates by dishonest policy between the Natives of Africa, America or Europe" was followed by a series of laws and high court rulings over the next decade that made slavery a dead letter more than a generation before it was formally abolished in the British Empire, in 1833.

Word slowly spread that fugitives were safe from recapture in the King's dominions. American veterans returning from service in the War of 1812 brought home the first detailed information about the routes north. After the war, Canada openly welcomed runaways, especially those who were willing to settle in the strategically vulnerable region near the Michigan Territory, on the assumption that former slaves could be counted on to vigorously resist another invasion by the United States. They were granted land and citizenship on the same terms as other immigrants, as well as the right to vote, a privilege that was enjoyed by free blacks in only a handful of Northern states. By the 1820s fugitives were starting to appear in noticeable numbers around St. Catharines opposite Buffalo, and on the Canadian side of the Detroit River, in the townships that would become the northern terminals of the Underground Railroad. In 1832 the first avowedly abolitionist report on Canada would appear in Benjamin Lundy's *Genius of Universal Emancipation*, in the form of a travel diary, transforming what had until now been largely a myth into a real place that was not only a refuge for the desperate but a land of opportunity. Lundy described a landscape rich beyond all expectation with extensive stands of timber, large corn stalks, and stacks of fine timothy hay by the roadside. It was also a country, he affirmed, where blacks were truly "*free and equal.*"

3

The odds against reaching a safe haven in either Canada or the Northern states were slim indeed. No one really knows just how many succeeded. Many fugitives left no trace at all of their movements, and what limited records were kept by those who assisted them have, with a handful of exceptions, almost entirely been lost. Very few successful freedom seekers were from the Deep South. The Canadian census of 1861, encompassing the more populous areas of present-day Ontario, where most blacks settled, found that about 80 percent of the Southern-born blacks then living there came from just three states, Virginia, Maryland, and Kentucky, all of which shared long borders with the free North. A slave running from northern Kentucky or Maryland might at least hope to be in a free state within a few days, or even hours, while a fugitive from, say, Alabama, Georgia, or the Carolinas would have to spend weeks or months on the road.

Although many fugitives fled in family groups, a majority were men traveling alone, or with a single male companion. Most were in their twenties and teens. To attempt to flee slavery with a wife and children in tow was an act of harrowing risk and heroism whose difficulty can scarcely be imagined. Children, especially, hampered movement, made noise, needed to be fed and to have rest. If he traveled alone, Josiah Henson's chances would have been better than average. Resourceful and experienced, he could expect to move quickly across country. With five more people to conceal, and five more mouths to feed, the odds would be strongly against them. It was the terrible alternative that almost every fugitive slave faced at some point, and that few other Americans have ever been required to make: to choose between freedom or family, to leave behind wife, children, parents, brothers and sisters, or to risk losing everything.

Henson determined to take the risk. The plan terrified Charlotte. She begged Josiah to stay at home on the Riley plantation in Kentucky, reminding him of possible outcomes that were all too real to slaves. "She knew nothing of the wide world beyond, and her imagination peopled it with unseen horrors," he would recall. "We should die in the wilderness,—we should be hunted down with bloodhounds,—we should be brought back and whipped to death." Finally, rather cruelly accusing her of being "a poor, ignorant, unreasoning slave-woman," he warned her that he would run away no matter what she did. "Exhausted and maddened, I left her, in the morning, to go to my work for the day. Before I had gone far, I heard her voice calling me, and waiting till I came up, she said, at last, she would go with me."

Henson organized their flight with his customary attention to detail. He had Charlotte make a knapsack large enough to hold his two youngest sons, and practiced carrying them in it for several nights until he was confident that he could endure their weight over long distances. For defense, at considerable risk, he bought a pair of pistols and a knife from a poor white man, a transaction that hints at a degree of ambiguity in relations between the races, and classes, that the conventional history of slavery often misses. In Kentucky, as in other Southern states, the possession of firearms by a slave was a crime punishable by death. However, similar transactions in other fugitives' reports of their escapes show that it was not uncommon for nonabolitionist whites to ignore race laws when they stood to gain by it.

Henson judged that the most auspicious time to leave the Riley plantation would be on a Saturday night. Sunday was a holiday, and the following two days he was expected to be working at farms distant from the main house. Thus, with luck, they might not be missed until Wednesday, when they should be across the Ohio River and well on their way. Dangerous as their proposed journey was, the Hensons did have a few things in their favor. The Riley plantation was close to the river, so they did not face a trek through unfamiliar territory before they reached it. And thanks to Josiah's trip East the previous year, he also had at least some knowledge of the northern bank of the river.

He had arranged with a fellow slave to row them across the Ohio. "We sat still as death," Henson recalled. As they skimmed across the water, the Indiana shore must have seemed both beckoning and fraught with danger, a free but nonetheless forbidding land with their unknown fate hidden deep in the dark, shapeless mass of forest that loomed closer with each stroke of the boatman's oars.

In the middle of the river, the boatman whispered ominously, "It will be the end of me if this is ever found out; but you won't be brought back alive, will you?"

"Not if I can help it," Henson replied.

"And if they're too many for you and you get seized, you'll never tell my part in the business?"

"Not if I'm shot through like a sieve."

" 'That's all,' " the boatman said. "And God help you."

The Hensons' luck held, and they crossed without incident. They probably landed somewhere near the present-day town of Grandview, Indiana. Henson did not record his emotions as they stood alone on the riverbank and listened to the rising and falling of the oars as the skiff disappeared into the night. But Charlotte now grew distraught and pleaded with him to return with them to Kentucky and the Riley plantation before they were missed. The product of a time and culture, both slave and free, that demanded stoic fortitude as a proof of "manliness," and condemned as "womanish" any admission of fear, Henson rarely revealed feelings that would show him in a weak light, usually preferring at moments of crisis to attribute natural reactions of terror and panic to his wife. It is hard to believe, however, that beneath the pose of icy fortitude Josiah was not as frightened as Charlotte was at what might lie in store. Escape from the Riley plantation had been imperative: had they not run away, they would have been sold and separated from each other. But flight was a psychological as well as a geographical odyssey, a journey of self-discovery and self-realization. The Hensons, profoundly devout people, of course believed that their lives ultimately lay in the hands of God. In the act of flight, however, they would discover if they could become the agents of their own fate. After a lifetime spent in the fragile security of the plantation, they were now suddenly more completely alone, and in charge of their own destiny, than they had ever been in their lives. Now even the simplest decision, a moment's lack of attention—a fork in the road, the problem of finding food, whether to trust a stranger, how long the children could keep going—was heavy with potentially catastrophic consequences.

From the moment they stepped ashore, their fears ceased to be abstract. Many of the settlers in that part of Indiana had come from the South and were notoriously hostile to fugitive slaves. The Hensons' destination was Cincinnati, 150 miles to the east along confusing and unmarked roads, where Josiah hoped for help from the "benevolent men" who had befriended him in 1829. Until they reached Cincinnati, they could not safely trust anyone, white or black. Even free blacks were known to turn runaways in for the reward, and sometimes to serve as decoys for slave catchers. Henson, who had traveled north of the river before, could have no illusions that their passage would be easy, or their safe arrival assured.

The Hensons probably stayed close to the Ohio, passing the river ports of Troy, Leavenworth, New Albany, and Madison, an area that was then very lightly populated. Had they turned north at Madison, through Versailles and Connorsville, they would have found a ready welcome in the Quaker settlements around Richmond; the fact that they did not suggests that they were probably unaware of any source of assistance outside Cincinnati. Instead, they continued eastward along the river, resting in the forest during the day and walking by night, and dodging for cover whenever they heard someone approaching. After about twelve days on the road, they ran out of food. "All night long the children cried with hunger, and my poor wife loaded me with reproaches for bringing them into such misery," Henson recalled. "It was a bitter thing to hear them cry, and God knows I needed encouragement myself. My limbs were weary, and my back and shoulders raw with the burden I carried. A fearful dread of detection ever pursued me, and I would start out of my sleep in terror, my heart beating against my ribs, and expecting to find the dogs and slave-hunters after me." Desperate, Henson ventured into a settlement in search of food, apparently their first contact with other people in the two weeks since they had left Kentucky. He went up to the first cabin he saw and asked if he might buy some bread and meat. "No, I have nothing for niggers," the owner replied. At the next farm, Henson was initially turned away too. However, the woman of the house called him back, telling her husband, "How can you treat any human being so? If a dog was hungry I would give him something to eat." Laughing, the man told her that she might "take care of niggers," if she wished, though he wouldn't. To Henson's surprise, the woman quietly gave him some venison and bread, which he wrapped in his handkerchief and carried back to his family in the woods.

4

Apart from the sheer physical and mental strain of finding their way through unfamiliar territory, without map, compass, or road signs, fugitives had to run a gauntlet of local constables, slave catchers, informers, and often an unfriendly populace that despised blacks, both free and enslaved. The most dangerous of these were the professional slave hunters who operated throughout both the South and the North. Most were hired for a flat fee by slave owners who could not afford the time to track fugitives themselves. Others worked on a contingency basis, buying discounted fugitives on the run, and then selling those they managed to catch, for a profit. Rewards for the recapture of fugitives ranged from between twenty dollars or less in the South, to fifty dollars for those who were captured in the free border states, to one hundred and twenty-five dollars, plus travel allowance, for fugitives caught as far north as New England and New York. Recaptures were almost everyday events in the border areas of Pennsylvania, Ohio, and Indiana. However, no fugitives, no matter how far they ran, or how long they had lived in freedom, could feel entirely safe anywhere south of the Canadian border. In 1832 a North Carolina jailer advertised a man he had captured who had been a fugitive for twenty-five years. William Wells Brown and his mother were apprehended 150 miles into Illinois just as they were congratulating themselves on their daring escape from St. Louis. Alexander Hemsley had lived peacefully for years in Northampton, New Jersey, when a band of Southerners suddenly appeared at his door. As far north as Wisconsin, the fugitive William A. Hall was warned that "there are men here now, even where you are living, who would betray you for half a dollar if they knew where your master is." Hall fled to Canada.

There was no single prototype for the successful fugitive. Some planned for months or years, painstakingly saving money, hoarding extra clothes, and collecting information about river crossings and back roads. Others simply walked away, and hoped for the best. Jim Pembroke carried only a half pound of cornmeal bread for a week-long odyssey from Maryland to Pennsylvania, and nearly starved. William A. Hall, who fled impulsively after a savage beating, carried no provisions or extra clothes at all, but still managed to reach Chicago from Tennessee in three months. Many fugitives carried false documents, which appear to have been surprisingly easy to acquire. Alfred T. Jones, a semiliterate slave in Madison County, Kentucky, wrote himself a pass that enabled him to travel from Lexington, Kentucky, to Cincinnati. "I could scarcely put two syllables together grammatically, but in fact, one half the white men there were not much better," Jones related.

In the end, most fugitives relied on pluck, physical stamina, and the north star, the single reliable guide for fugitives who, with only the rarest exceptions, were incapable of reading road signs, where they existed. Charles Ball carefully furnished himself with a "fire-box" containing flints, steel, and tinder; a greatcoat given him by his master; a needle and thread; a linen bag filled with parched corn; and a stolen sword for protection. He guided himself as best he could by the north star during a grueling nine-month odyssey that took him from Georgia to Maryland. Although he started out with a sense of the approximate route that he had to travel, he frequently found roads that he thought were carrying him north were in fact leading him in another direction entirely. Sometimes, when clouds obscured the stars, he discovered to his grief that he had been walking for hours or days in a circle, or zigzag. One night he wandered directionless for hours in pitch darkness, in a bog with the mud and water over his knees, totally lost. Another time, nearly discovered by a party of patrollers, he became so confused that the stars seemed "out of their places," and he remained for three days concealed in a thicket, for fear that any direction he set off in would prove to be the wrong one. On still another occasion, upon coming to a crossroads, he spent eleven days hidden in the woods, waiting for a clear night so that he could take his bearings by the stars before choosing which fork to take. It took him two months just to reach the vicinity of Columbia, South Carolina, "so near the place from which I had first departed, that I could easily have walked to it in a week, by daylight."

Jim Pembroke, who lived only a short distance below the Mason and Dixon Line, in Hagerstown, Maryland, knew only that Pennsylvania was a free state. "But I know not where its soil begins, or where that of Maryland ends," wrote Pembroke, who became known in freedom as Reverend James Pennington. "My only guide was the *north star*, by this I knew my general course northward, but at what point I should strike Penn, or when and where I should find a friend, I knew not." Pembroke had been born on the Eastern Shore of Maryland in 1807, and was given along with his mother and an older brother as a wedding gift to a son of his master, a wheat farmer. Trained as a mason and blacksmith, by adulthood he had become a valued craftsman within the limited cosmos of plantation life. Like Josiah Henson, Pembroke viewed his work as a moral endeavor. "I had always aimed to be trustworthy; and feeling I had aimed to do my work with dispatch and skill, my blacksmith's pride and taste was one thing that had reconciled me so long to remain a slave." He endured the daily insults of slavery until, one day, his master savagely caned him simply for looking him straight in the eye. "After this," Pembroke wrote, "I found that my mechanic's pleasure and pride were gone," and he decided to run for Pennsylvania. The thought of fleeing threw him into a confusing tumult of "hope, fear, dread, terror, love, sorrow," and deep depression. He knew the risks. Other slaves in the neighborhood who had run away and been caught had been punished with severe flogging and exile to the Deep South. But he also felt that if he did not make his attempt now, driven by shame and rage, he might never make it at all.

Pembroke's first sensation of freedom was sheer terror. He spent his first day of it squatting fearfully behind a corn shock, very hungry, and almost more depressed than he could bear, "chilled to the heart," and unnerved by fears of utter destitution. He passed the second day hiding under a bridge, eating sour apples that gave him diarrhea. The third night, he discovered that the road he had been following led southward toward Baltimore rather than north to Pennsylvania, and that he had been walking most of the time in the wrong direction. Impulsively, he now decided to continue on to Baltimore, in hope of sneaking aboard a boat that would carry him north. He soon encountered a young white man with a load of hay, who instantly recognized that Pembroke was a runaway and warned him that there were slave patrols nearby, directing Pembroke to a certain house, where an "old gentleman" would "further advise" him. Pembroke was so confused by having lost his direction, however, that he forgot what the young man told him and, worrying that he might become even more lost, decided to stay on the road that he was following. After he traveled only a short distance, the boy's warning was proved apt when Pembroke was stopped and seized by several white men when he was unable to produce free papers.

Pembroke's captors held him in a nearby tavern and immediately identified him as a "runaway nigger." Knowing that if he told them the truth, he would receive a hundred lashes from his master, and as likely as not be sold away to the Deep South, he continued to maintain that he was a free man until his captors decided that he would go with one of them and remain at his house until they learned if there was a reward for his capture. Left under the observation of the owner's small son, Pembroke managed to make his escape after dark, fleeing into nearby woods, and eluding his pursuers after a desperate race. Unable to see the north star through the rain, Pembroke zigzagged all night through tangles of vines and briars, utterly terrified of recapture. At one point he even heard horsemen nearby, discussing their search for him. "Every nerve in my system quivered, so that not a particle of my flesh was at rest," he recalled. Too frightened to travel by road, Pembroke continued across country. He was almost starving now, having eaten nothing for days except raw dry corn that he painstakingly chewed kernel by kernel. In desperation he decided to risk traveling by daylight, and to find out where he was. Shortly after dawn on the sixth day, he arrived at a toll gate that was operated by an elderly woman. She informed him, to his immense relief, that he was already in Pennsylvania. When Pembroke asked her where he might find work, she directed him to the farm of a Quaker "who lived about three miles away, whom I would find to take an interest in me."

The Quaker, William Wright, later the leader of the Underground Railroad in the Gettysburg area, provided the fugitive blacksmith with room and board in return for chopping wood. In the course of his six months' sojourn with the Wrights, they taught him to read and write, and introduced him to arithmetic, astronomy, and the Bible. They eventually decided that the danger of recapture made it imperative for Pembroke to move farther away from the state line. After reluctantly leaving the security of his benefactors, Pembroke made his way "in deep sorrow and melancholy" toward Philadelphia, where, probably with an introduction from Wright, he found shelter in the home of another Quaker farmer, where he spent the next seven months, more or less taking charge of the farm. Then, passing through Philadelphia, he made his way to New York, where he would eventually achieve a prominent career in the ministry and, in 1838, play a small but poignant role in the northward flight of Frederick Douglass. He would also become a stationmaster on the Underground Railroad.

5

The Hensons, too, like Pembroke, would find people to "take an interest" in them. Josiah left his family hidden in the woods outside Cincinnati while he went into the city in search of the "benevolent men" he had met the previous year. Since Henson's last visit, the "bright, beautiful" little city had been torn by dreadful racial strife. City officials had directed all the city's three thousand blacks to register with the authorities, post a crippingly expensive five-hundred-dollar bond for good behavior, or identify themselves publicly as slaves. Those who failed to do so would have thirty days to leave the city. Blacks reacted initially with despair. If the laws were enforced, they protested, "we, the poor sons of Ethiopia, must take shelter where we can find it. If not in America, we must beg elsewhere . . . where Heaven only knows." When they continued to protest, white dockworkers raided the shanty towns, assaulting black families and demolishing their homes. In the aftermath, more than half of Cincinnati's black residents left the city, mostly for Canada. Henson's friends nevertheless welcomed him warmly, and just after dusk he brought his wife and children safely in. "We found ourselves hospitably cheered and refreshed," Henson recalled. "Carefully they provided for our welfare until our strength was recruited, and then they set us thirty miles on our way by wagon."

On their own once again, Henson and his family continued northward, heading for Lake Erie, about 150 miles farther north. Their friends in Cincinnati do not seem to have prepared them very well for what lay ahead. The interior of the state then was still largely unsettled. The Hensons traveled for days along the old military road that was cut for the War of 1812 and ran from Dayton to Detroit, through vast hardwood forests of oaks, poplars, and walnuts, clambering over fallen trees, picking their way through banks of briars, and racked with anxiety about being recaptured, attacked by wild animals, or murdered by Indians. Josiah's many talents do not seem to have included wilderness survival skills. Although they were surrounded by abundant wildlife—flocks of five hundred wild turkeys were not uncommon in the region at that time, and shoals of fish in some rivers were known to cover half an acre—the Hensons again ran out of food. They were saved by a chance encounter with a band of unexpectedly friendly Indians, probably a last remnant of the Wyandot or Shawnee. The Indians, who had never seen black people before, surprised the terrified Hensons by feeding them "bountifully," and providing them with a "comfortable wigwam" for the night.

Henson was not exaggerating the dangers of the trek. Two years later, the peripatetic abolitionist editor Benjamin Lundy walked south from Michigan Territory through the same part of northern Ohio. "The worst traveling ever experienced," he wrote in his journal; "but one house in 20 miles . . . swale & swamp. Had to wade from half leg to knee deep more than 20 times while snow falling fast & it was *freezing* rapidly!! . . . cloak, coat, pantaloons, stockings, all a glare of ice. Feet benumbed!!—nothing to strike a fire!!!"

Buoyed by the help they received from the Indians, the Hensons set off the next day, guided by several tribesmen who accompanied them to ensure that they didn't get lost again. They got their first sight of Lake Erie near Sandusky, then called Portland, a town of about five hundred inhabitants. Henson hid his family in the bushes and made his way to the shore, where he could see a small ship with gangs of men loading cargo. "Promptly deciding to approach them, I drew near, and scarcely had I come within hailing distance, when the captain of the schooner cried out, 'Hollo there, man! You want to work?' 'Yes, sir!' shouted I . . . In a minute I had hold of a bag of corn, and followed the gang in emptying it into the hold. I took my place in the line of laborers next to a colored man, and soon got into conversation with him. 'How far is it to Canada?' He gave me a peculiar look, and in a minute I saw he knew all. 'Want to go to Canada? Come along with us, then. Our captain's a fine fellow. We're going to Buffalo.' 'Buffalo; how far is that from Canada?' 'Don't you know, man? Just across the river.' I now opened my mind frankly to him, and told him about my wife and children. 'I'll speak to the captain,' said he. He did so, and in a moment the captain took me aside, and said, 'The Doctor says you want to go to Buffalo with your family.' 'Yes, sir.' 'Where do you stop?' 'About a mile back.' 'How long have you been here?' 'No time,' I answered, after a moment's hesitation. 'Come, my good fellow, tell us all about it. You're running away, ain't you?' I saw he was a friend, and opened my heart to him."

The captain promised that once the grain was loaded, he would pull off from shore, and then send a boat back to pick up Henson and his family, telling him, "There's a lot of regular nigger-catchers in the town below, and they might suspect if you brought your party out of the bush by daylight." That night, Henson watched with his heart in his throat as the boat left its moorings and, sails unfurled, cruised out into the lake, leaving him behind, so he thought. "Suddenly, however, as I gazed with weary heart, the vessel swung round into the wind, the sails flapped, and she stood motionless. A moment more, and a boat was lowered from her stern, and with steady stroke made for the point at which I stood." In a few minutes, the boat was on the beach, and he recognized his black friend among the sailors.

"Three hearty cheers welcomed us as we reached the schooner," Henson recalled, "and never till my dying day shall I forget the shout of the captain—he was a Scotchman—'Coom up on deck, and clop your wings and craw like a rooster; you're a free nigger as sure as the devil.' " Henson "wept like a child," feeling God's presence wash through him, and a happiness so powerful that it was indistinguishable from pain.

The next evening, they reached Buffalo. In the morning the captain pointed across the water to a copse of trees. He told Henson, "They grow on free soil, and as soon as your feet touch that you're a *mon*. I want to see you go and be a free man. I'm poor myself and have nothing to give you; I only sail the boat for wages; but I'll see you across." He arranged with a ferryman to take Henson and his family across. Then, with the mingled warmth and condescension common to many abolitionists, he put his hand on Henson's head, and said, "Be a good fellow, won't you?" Promising the captain to use his freedom well, Henson and his family pushed off for the opposite shore.

It was the twenty-eighth of October, 1830, in the morning, when Henson's feet first touched Canadian soil. "I threw myself on the ground, rolled in the sand, seized handfuls of it and kissed them, and danced round till, in the eyes of several who were present, I passed for a madman." Henson had not just completed a successful escape. He had also begun the birth of a man who for the first time in his life was truly autonomous, not just legally free but also psychically free, a man who now knew with absolute certainty that he could survive without a master. "He's some crazy fellow," said a Colonel Warren, who happened to be there. "O, no, master!" exclaimed Henson, whose language was instinctively still that of slavery. "Don't you know? I'm free!" The white man burst into a shout of laughter. "Still I could not control myself. I hugged and kissed my wife and children, and, until the first exuberant burst of feeling was over, went on as before."

CHAPTER 7

FANATICS, DISORGANIZERS, AND DISTURBERS OF THE PEACE

> My God helping me, there shall be a perpetual war between me and human slavery.
>
> —ADAM LOWRY RANKIN, ABOLITIONIST

1

Jarm Logue's mouth never completely healed from the damage it suffered when his master pounded a block of wood into it in a fit of drunken rage. The wound left him with a speech impediment that, years afterward, when he would be admired as a preacher of uncommon power, would serve as a badge of honor, a survivor's memento of the unequal war of master against slave. Jarm, a young man of exceptional intelligence and grit, was, like Josiah Henson, a natural leader. However, in contrast to Henson, whose ethics were rooted in a belief in spiritual elevation through physical submission, Logue was deeply defiant: he was, in short, a revolutionary in the making. Born around 1813 and raised on a small plantation on Mansker's Creek, near Nashville, Tennessee, he was the son of a slave mother, named Cherry, and the youngest of the three slave-owning Logue brothers who operated a whiskey distillery. His childhood experiences combined sometimes savage and unpredictable violence with a degree of love that may have been rare for slaves in such an environment. Although he would describe the brothers as "drunken, passionate, brutal, and cruel," he remembered with affection his father, Dave Logue, who treated him as a "pet," bestowing on him "many little favors and kindnesses." What trust Jarm had in his father was shattered, however, when after promising never to sell Cherry or her four children, Dave Logue did just that, initially to his brother Manasseth, who in turn sold two of the children to a slave trader. Cherry was left emotionally shattered, and Jarm now understood that in spite of his blood relationship with the Logues, his own future could never be secure.

At first, Jarm merely fantasized a place where he owned his own farm and could "go and come as he pleased." His first inkling of a world that lay beyond the immediate vicinity of the plantation where he lived came in his late teens, when he met a young white boy whose family had returned from a failed attempt to immigrate to Illinois. As his 1859 biographer reconstructed the conversation, Logue scoffed, "There ain't any place such as Illinois."

"I say there is such a place!" the boy retorted. "Don't you think I know?"

"What kind of place is it then?"

"All the negroes are free in Illinois—they don't have any slaves there."

The boy also provided Logue with his first geography lesson, telling him that a traveler to Illinois had to cross many rivers, the biggest of them called the Ohio, which horses and sleighs could pass over when it froze in winter. "Illinois" came to encompass all of Logue's fuzzy ideas of freedom, and it was for there, in 1834, that he struck out after Manasseth's alcoholic assault on him.

He enlisted as partners in his escape two close friends, John Farney and Jerry Wilks, who lived on neighboring plantations. Critical to their success was the assistance of a white man named Ross. In addition to forged free papers, Ross procured for them a pair of pistols, a crime that could have resulted in Ross's execution if it were found out. The slaves each paid him ten dollars' cash plus a quantity of bacon, flour, and other staples that had been stolen from the slaves' masters. Ross also gave the friends valuable advice. He advised them, surprisingly, to be bold, and to stop at the best houses while still in the slave states, "to act as freemen act." The big houses were the most willing and able to entertain travelers in what was still an only half-settled frontier region, he explained, and they were also the last place that a fugitive slave would be expected to be found. "If you go dodging and shying through the country, you will be suspected, seized, imprisoned and advertised—but if you ride boldly through, like freemen, you will get through unmolested."

On Christmas Eve, at two o'clock in the night, Jarm and his friend John Farney set off on horses taken from their masters' stables, leaving behind their third partner, Wilks, who at the last minute could not overcome his loyalty to his master and chose to stay behind. Clad in overcoats, and wrapped against the midwinter cold, they rode through Nashville "at a traveler's trot . . . like wise freemen, turning neither to the right nor left, carefully avoiding any matters not their own." That evening they put Ross's advice to the test by asking for a night's lodging at a "baronial mansion." All went as Ross had predicted. Their host behaved with discomforting politeness, charging them a shilling apiece for a place to lie down. They spent the next night, tense but unmolested, at an ordinary tavern among rough-cut white men "in all stages of intoxication." The third night, they again put up at a private mansion, whose owner sneered at them as "black rascals," but nonetheless provided them with shelter.

Logue and Farney twice ran into patrollers. On both occasions they were forced to fight for their passage, once leaving one of the patrollers unconscious on the road. Shaken, they now hastened to get out of the slave states as fast as possible. They rode hard, following back roads and sleeping among haystacks, finally reaching the Ohio River somewhere in the vicinity of West Point or Brandenburg, Kentucky. The river was frozen solid. Following the tracks of horsemen who had gone before, the two fugitives walked their mounts across the ice into what they learned was "Indiana," a free state of which they had never heard.

A "colored man" who had been watching them as they crossed told them, to their dismay, that they were barely any safer now than they were in Kentucky. He urged the two men to continue on to Canada, another totally unfamiliar place. He added that in the free states there were people who "will do what they can" for fugitive slaves, and pointed the way to the village of "Corridon"—actually Corydon, in Harrison County—where they should ask for a certain man, an "abolitionist," who would tell them what to do next. In Corydon, Logue and Farney found the man to whom they had been directed, "a true hearted colored man ready to advise and assist them to the best of his means." (This may have been a laborer named Oswell Wright, who was born a slave in Maryland and traveled to Indiana with one of his former owners, and was later sentenced to five years in the Kentucky State Penitentiary for guiding a fugitive across the Ohio River.) He too urged them to continue on to Canada. He gave them the name of a James Overrals in Indianapolis, about two hundred miles away, "as he supposed, in a north-westerly direction—but he could say nothing of the intervening country and the inhabitants."

Unfortunately, almost as soon as they left Corydon, the fugitives lost their way in a vast forest. They stopped to ask for food at a log cabin whose occupant, a friendly white man, recognized them as fugitive slaves in spite of their denials. He warned them that not only were they in a region inhabited by proslavery squatters from the South, but they had taken the wrong road and were actually heading toward Kentucky. He directed them to the road to Indianapolis, adding that in the next village, probably Salem, they would see a brick tavern whose landlord—"your friend," he told them—would direct them further. The innkeeper welcomed them warmly and directed them to a settlement of African Americans a day's ride in the direction of Indianapolis, probably the "Hut and Patch" area at New Farmington, where fifteen or twenty black farming families lived under the protection of neighboring Quakers. There, he assured them, people would "be glad to receive them."

In early February, after three weeks' rest in the black settlement, the fugitives set off again across a sodden, drizzly landscape, most likely along the current route of Interstate 65. They arrived a few days later in Indianapolis, where they found Mr. Overrals, who "though colored, was an educated man," and respected among both whites and blacks for his "large character" and good sense. Overrals sent them on to a Quaker settlement in Hamilton County, about forty miles from Indianapolis, where the two fugitives were received hospitably. The Quakers advised them to head directly north or northwest, so that they would be among immigrants from the Northern states. Logue and Farney traveled now through a snowswept desolation. With considerable difficulty, they managed to ford the flooded and ice-choked Wabash and St. Joseph rivers. The region was still inhabited by Indians, who sometimes offered the fugitives food and shelter, and other times refused them entirely. Eventually they arrived once again among white settlers, who "treated them as equals under the law, though not always with respect." At Logansport, north of Kokomo, Logue traded his horse for "boot money," offered him by a "benevolent looking Quaker," who in fact took advantage of his ignorance to cheat him. Heading north again, they lost their way once more in another "howling wilderness," finally arriving at their destination, Detroit, starving and in a state of near destitution, having ridden, Logue estimated, hundreds of miles out of their way. On the morning of their third day in Detroit, the two men at last crossed the Detroit River to Windsor, Canada, penniless, knowing no one. "Nature and humanity surrounded them like a globe of ice," Logue's biographer exquisitely wrote, "but they rejoiced and thanked God with warm hearts."

2

In the course of Logue's flight it is possible to see the early stirrings of organized assistance to the fugitive, a system in the process of creation. Logue and Farney receive help from all sorts of people, yet many of them are barely, if at all, aware of one another's existence. Ross, who supplies them with weapons and advice, is an isolated loner. The "colored man" whom Logue meets on the bank of the Ohio River knows that the "abolitionist" in Corydon will lend help to fugitives. But he has no nearby collaborator to send the fugitives to closer than Indianapolis, and he is not entirely clear about where the city lies. Meanwhile, the friendly white homesteader seems completely unaware of the black abolitionist in Corydon. However, the homesteader's confidence in the innkeeper at Salem, and the innkeeper's corresponding certainty that the fugitives will find a refuge at the Hut and Patch settlement, hint at an ongoing link among at least those three locations: an Underground Railroad line in embryo, as it were. Similarly, Overrals, in Indianapolis, has links with an incipient network of trustworthy Quakers. The Quakers advise the travelers to make their way north through a wilderness inhabited by Indians, suggesting that they had little or no contact with the abolitionists to their east until the formation of broad-based antislavery societies later in the decade.

Other fugitives during this period had similar experiences. Josiah Henson, like Logue, received assistance from a wide variety of people who had little or no connection with one another. It is unclear, for example, if the "benevolent men" who assisted the Henson family in Cincinnati were an organized group devoted to facilitating the escape of fugitives, or if their aid to the Hensons was a rare case. The allusion to his primary contact, the "brother preacher" he had met on his first visit, suggests that his protectors were a church group of some kind. Like the Quakers whom Logue encountered in Indiana, however, the "benevolent men" were working in a vacuum. Their assistance extended only thirty miles outside Cincinnati, and they failed to provide the Hensons with even the most elementary information about the difficulties his family would face traversing the wilderness that lay between the interior of Ohio and Lake Erie.

By 1834, however, the year of Jarm Logue's escape, Cincinnati abolitionists began to lay a foundation for later, more organized, underground operations by breaching the color line in a city which, until now, had been distinguished for its pro-southern sentiments. In that year, students at Lane Seminary, a training school for evangelical ministers financed by the philanthropic Tappan brothers of New York, staged nine days of widely publicized debates over slavery. "Like men whose pole star was fact and truth, whose needle was conscience, whose chart was the Bible," one energized attendee wrote, the participants wound up converting virtually the entire student body, including several sons of slave owners, to immediate abolition. Many were inspired to set up schools and undertake social work in the city's black neighborhoods on a basis of racial equality, shocking the seminary's more conservative trustees. When the trustees ordered all discussion of slavery to cease immediately, scores of students abandoned Lane, and enrolled at Oberlin College, in northern Ohio, where they formed the nucleus of one of the most ardent Underground Railroad communities west of the Appalachians.

Many fugitives still never encountered any white person they felt they could trust. The only help that William A. Hall, for instance, received during his trek to freedom from Tennessee to Chicago, and eventually to Wisconsin, came from other African Americans, one of whom sheltered him for three days. Another nursed him when he was ill, having "carried him ten miles on his own beast." William Wells Brown, starving and suffering from frostbite, hoped desperately but without luck to encounter a "colored person" as he trudged northward into Ohio. Only as a last resort did he finally stop an elderly white man dressed in a broad-brimmed hat and a long coat, which Brown perhaps recognized as distinctively Quaker dress. Brown recuperated for two weeks with the Quakers, who gave him clothing, boots and pocket money, and sent him on his way north. He walked the rest of the way to Cleveland with no other assistance except for food that he managed to beg along the way. The warmth with which the Quakers received Brown caused him to suffer paralyzing anxiety, an experience that was shared by many fugitives when they first encountered courteous whites. "I had never had a white man to treat me as an equal, and the idea of a white lady waiting on me at the table was still worse!" Brown wrote. "Though the table was loaded with the good things of this life, I could not eat." Only when the lady of the home, a "Thompsonian," provided him with a cup of "composition" did he begin to relax. (William Thompson, a New England farmer with no medical training, had acquired a large following by asserting that illness was the result of "clogging the system," a state that could be remedied by the application of an assortment of powerful herbal emetics: Brown delicately spared his readers further details.)

Soon there would be widening webs of committed antislavery activists in most of the free states. There would be hundreds of men and women, white and black, who saw the succor of fugitives as a personal mission, and their homes as oases of hope for the desperate. They would be able to move fugitives hundreds of miles, carrying them, where necessary, from farm to farm and town to town, and directing them to havens in distant states, or Canada. But as the new decade of the 1830s dawned, assistance was still almost entirely a matter of luck. Most fugitives had never even heard of abolitionists. Jim Pembroke, who escaped from Maryland to Gettysburg, Pennsylvania, in 1828, spoke for countless others: "There was no Anti-Slavery Society then—there was no Vigilance Committee. I had, therefore, to select a course of action, without counsel or advice from any who professed to sympathize with the slave."

3

Through the 1820s, only in southeastern Pennsylvania was there anything resembling the Underground Railroad as it came to be understood in later years. In Philadelphia, the Quaker abolitionist Isaac Hopper had long been at the center of a web of black and white collaborators—in effect, an underground cell—who at short notice could move fugitives around from home to home with relative ease, like chess pieces, or quickly spirit them away into the countryside, or into the anonymity of the city's expanding African-American community. Picaresque though they sound, Hopper's exploits were in deadly earnest. In one of his last cases in Philadelphia, he was informed that a fugitive slave and her son were hidden in a closet, terrified and in immediate danger of recapture. They had been enslaved in New Jersey, which although nominally a free state would still hold some African Americans in bondage as late as the 1860s. Their master traced them to Philadelphia, where he procured a constable and went to the house where they were holed up. Leaving a guard at the door, he went off to obtain a search warrant. While he was thus engaged, a crowd of African Americans gathered. Whether by prearrangement or on impulse, they seized the guard—a remarkable illustration of blacks' growing self-confidence in what was very much a white men's city—and held him fast while the fugitives fled to the home of a black family on Locust Street. The slaves' master, still mindful of Pennsylvania's stringent laws, departed again to obtain a new warrant to search the second house. It was at this point that someone sent for Hopper. In accordance with a plan that he presumably worked out with his black friends on the spot, the door was opened, allowing the crowd outside to rush in. With a characteristically theatrical flourish, Hopper ordered the crowd to leave. As they did so, the two fugitives slipped out unnoticed among them, and hurried to the home of Hopper's son. Hopper himself remained at the Locust Street house as a decoy, correctly surmising that as long as he was there, the watchman would assume that the fugitives were still in the house. As soon as he could, Hopper returned home and sent the fugitives "to a place of greater safety." Significantly, for it shows a technique that would become standard as the Underground Railroad became increasingly systematized, he also dispatched his son to the home of a farmer thirty miles outside the city, to forewarn him of the fugitives' arrival.

Apart from his invigorating work in the underground, the decade of the 1820s was a sad time for the usually ebullient Hopper. His beloved wife died in June 1822, and a year later his fifteen-year-old son, Isaac, followed. Hopper was also drawn into the deepening rift that split Quakers into two factions, the Hicksites and the Orthodox. The fissure was rooted in doctrinal differences that seem obscure today, but it destroyed lifelong friendships, tormented the spiritual lives of thousands of Quakers, and tore apart meetings, which battled with un-Quakerly rancor over the ownership of community property, including schools and meeting houses. Elias Hicks, a charismatic Long Island farmer who won over most of the Quakers in the Northeast to his views, insisted that the crucifixion and the resurrection of Jesus must be understood mainly in spiritual terms and as models of the death of self-will within each person, rather than as historical events. His opponents attacked his teachings as doctrinally unsound. Within these arguments, feelings about slavery formed a strong undertow, with the Hicksites more frequently urging that personal spiritual growth demanded a wholehearted commitment to the struggle, and the Orthodox more often urging restraint. "Friends generally seem to deplore the present excitement," Hopper's close friend and associate in the underground, Charles Marriott, would write to a fellow Hicksite. "For my share I hope it will never subside until slavery be abolished. There is tenfold more to be dreaded from our own relapsing into our former sleep of death." Because of Hopper's Hicksite leanings, many of his Orthodox customers dropped away, and his tailoring business suffered. Finally, in 1829, he was forced to abandon Philadelphia and relocate to New York, where he opened a bookstore that specialized in Hicksite tracts and antislavery literature.

By the time of Hopper's departure, the sedate Philadelphia of his youth had grown into an industrial metropolis of more than 164,000 inhabitants, whose air was gritty with the smoke of factories and forges, textile mills and ironworks. Twelve thousand or more African Americans (many may not have dared to allow their presence to be recorded) dwelled in the tumbledown shanties and grimy lanes of Moyamensing and Southwark. There was also a small but vibrant middle class of self-employed black barbers, carters, restaurateurs, and oystermen, as well as a handful of wealthy men like the sailmaker James Forten, whose property was valued at the fabulous sum of forty thousand dollars. African Americans' sense of community and of autonomy within the larger city was steadily deepening, and it was made manifest by scores of benevolent associations, schools, and churches, foremost among them the mother church of the African Methodist Episcopal denomination, many of whose locations would eventually serve as stations on the underground.

At the same time, as waves of immigrants swelled the city's white population, blacks were increasingly being crowded out of skilled jobs, including dockwork, long a mainstay of the African-American economy. New measures had been proposed to restrict blacks' mobility, to impose special taxes on them, and to allow townships to auction off black felons for a term of years as contract labor. Color prejudice was ingrained even among many who professed opposition to slavery. Quakers rarely invited blacks to join the Society of Friends, and Isaac Hopper was considered remarkable for his willingness to sit down with them at dinner. The new, combustible politics of the street introduced an era that was to be rent by bitter class and racial conflict. In 1828 a white mob gathered outside a dance hall where a fancy-dress African-American ball was taking place and assaulted elegantly dressed women as they stepped from coaches, throwing some of them into the gutter. The following year, a full-scale race riot occurred in Cedar Ward, leaving many blacks dead and causing terrible damage to the homes and property of black families who could ill afford the losses.

Under the Fugitive Slave Act of 1793, local magistrates had been empowered to issue warrants for the "removal" of any Negro or mulatto claimed to be a fugitive from labor, enabling slave hunters from Maryland to operate with impunity in the border regions of Pennsylvania. Free blacks were often arrested in broad daylight and hurried out of the state with no more than the most perfunctory formalities. In 1806 even the eminent founder of the first African Methodist Episcopal Church, Richard Allen, had been seized by a Southerner with a sheriff's warrant, although he succeeded in winning his release. Then, in 1825, Philadelphians were shocked to learn that a kidnapping ring had operated in the city for years, luring black children as young as nine and ten onto sloops moored in the Delaware River, and shipping them into the Deep South, where they were sold. (This kind of trade was by no means restricted to Philadelphia. Jarm Logue's mother, born free, had been kidnapped by itinerant slave traders from a free black settlement in Ohio along with several other children; the kidnappers traveled south through Kentucky and Tennessee, selling the children out of the back of their wagon to less affluent whites, for whom a slave was an important status symbol, but who couldn't afford the prices of the open market.)

Popular repugnance at the kidnapping of free blacks prompted the passage of new laws in the 1820s that had gradually made it easier for abolitionists who wished to aid fugitives to do so with less risk to themselves, and creating a legal umbrella that sheltered the early phases of underground activity. In March 1820 the Pennsylvania legislature passed the first law in United States history that was deliberately intended to interfere with the Fugitive Slave Act. The legislature's action was rooted in the then nearly universal belief that any state had the constitutional authority to ignore, or nullify, federal laws of which it did not approve. The law made kidnapping any Negro or mulatto a felony punishable by a fine of up to two thousand dollars and up to twenty-one years' imprisonment at hard labor. More critically for those who dared to assist fugitive slaves, it also barred local magistrates from recognizing any matter arising from the national fugitive slave law, under penalty of a substantial fine. The law was tested in 1821 when a judge ruled that a fugitive slave who had killed his former master in the act of attempting to recapture him on Pennsylvania soil was guilty of no crime, since he had acted in both self-defense and to prevent a felony—his own kidnapping.

In 1826, under pressure from the Quaker lobby, the legislature passed a stronger law that made it even more difficult for a master to recover a fugitive slave from Pennsylvania. This law declared that the seizure of a runaway by anyone, including his presumed master, except by a constable with a properly executed warrant, constituted kidnapping. The arresting officer was required to bring the alleged runaway before a court, where, the law stipulated, "the oath of the owner or owners shall in no case be received in evidence, before the judge on the hearing of the case." This meant that a master could only prove his claim by importing, at his own expense, impartial witnesses to testify on his behalf. Although the federal Fugitive Slave Law remained in force, authorizing any master to seize a fugitive, Pennsylvania law made him liable to indictment as a kidnapper and made public officials who cooperated with it subject to a heavy fine. Men and women who had shied away from breaking United States law could now claim that their activities were protected by Pennsylvania's.

Underground activity steadily continued to grow in the farm country outside Philadelphia. A particularly strong node of activism was developing at Columbia, in Lancaster County, where the Quaker William Wright, a respected descendant of the town's pioneer founder, had established a welcoming atmosphere for African Americans who settled near his home on the Susquehanna. As early as the turn of the century, several Southern masters who wished to emancipate their slaves had brought them to Columbia to be freed, fifty-six in a single batch in 1804, a hundred in another group the following year. Slave catchers and kidnappers followed. Wright is locally credited with hitting on the idea of passing fugitives along from one home to another at intervals of ten or twenty miles, with other friends designated to pilot them in between. He sent them first to his brother-in-law and fellow Quaker Daniel Gibbons, who lived in the quaintly named town of Bird-in-Hand, twenty miles to the east. Gibbons, who was said to have aided as many as two hundred fugitives by 1824, usually hid them overnight in his barn and in the morning assigned each one a new "freedom name" on the spot, a rite that while perhaps liberating to some, burdened as they often were by slave names not of their own choosing, may well have been disturbing to others.

If the fugitives were in no immediate danger of recapture, Gibbons distributed them among the farms in the surrounding area, where many found jobs and put down permanent roots, often helping other fugitives in their turn. If their masters were in pursuit, they were hurried eastward into neighboring Chester County. Gibbons forwarded some to the Quaker farmer Abraham Bonsall and dispatched others to the home of Thomas Vickers, a prosperous Quaker manufacturer of pottery, who lived twenty miles to the east near Caln Meeting, in Chester County. Vickers, a key link between Philadelphia abolitionists and those in the counties to the west, also received fugitives from Isaac Hopper. In short, a kind of synergy was developing in a region that would become perhaps the most supportive of the underground in the United States, absorbing fugitives from the east, the west, and the south, and sharing them out around this Pennsylvanian foreshadowing of Canada. Thomas Vickers's son John, also a potter, would become one of the most active managers in the underground, and his home at Lionville one of its great central stations. Fugitives were recorded there as early as 1818, when he hid two men in his attic. When their masters suddenly showed up, Vickers managed to delay them until the two men escaped. One of the masters was heard to remark, "We might as well look for a needle in a haystack as for a nigger among Quakers."

African-American abolitionists played a vital, even aggressive, role in the rural districts of Lancaster and Chester counties, as they did in Philadelphia, sometimes alone and sometimes in partnership with friendly whites. Robert Loney, a freed slave, ferried many fugitives across the Susquehanna River to Columbia, while the white Quaker Daniel Gibbons sent many fugitives to the farm of his collaborator Jeremiah Moore, at Christiana, where they were kept safe until they could be taken in a furniture wagon, in care of "a trusty colored man," to Ercildoun, eight miles away. Blacks were also much less constrained than pacifist Quakers in their use of force. One day in 1825 a master who was taking two recaptured slaves back to Maryland stopped at York for the night, and came out in the morning to find that his carriage had been cut to pieces by outraged African Americans; the fate of the fugitives went unrecorded. A few years later, in an incident that vividly illustrates the ad hoc quality of much Underground Railroad activity, white witnesses to the abduction of a fugitive in Sadsbury, in eastern Lancaster County, immediately notified blacks in the vicinity, "who assembled under arms after dark, and surrounded the house in ambush." While the slave owners were at dinner, the landlady at the inn where they put up secretly loosened the slave's handcuffs, enabling him to flee with the help of his protectors outside.

By the 1820s, sparks of deliberate underground activity were becoming evident in other parts of the United States as well. Radical Presbyterians were assisting fugitives in southern Ohio as early as 1822, while the tanner Owen Brown, father of the charismatic abolitionist John Brown, was harboring fugitives in his home in Hudson, Ohio by the middle of the decade, as was David Hudson, the town's founder and its wealthiest resident. On January 5, 1826, Hudson's son matter-of-factly recorded in his diary what was evidently a fairly commonplace occurrence: "Two men came this evening in a sleigh, bringing a negro woman, a runaway slave, and her two children." A few years later, James Adams, the mulatto son of an overseer on a plantation near the Virginia shore of the Ohio River, along with a male cousin, a woman, and her four children, stumbled onto what appears to have been a prototype underground cell near the river port of Marietta, Ohio. Once across the river, Adams and his band passed three nights "at the house of a white friend." This unidentified man concealed the fugitives on a rocky hill and told them to keep their eyes on a pole visible near his house on which a white cloth had been attached. If the pole was lowered, it meant danger. Later that day, several armed white abolitionists guided Adams and his companions to a cave which had a wide view of the surrounding country. Three days later, they brought the fugitives knapsacks full of cakes, dried venison, and other provisions, as well as flints and steel to strike it against. They also gave them a compass, which the fugitives had never seen before. One walked with them half a day to show them how to use it, and before he left them he notched the compass and told them to steer north by northwest until they reached Cleveland, six days' march away. During that time, they had no assistance of any kind. Just outside Cleveland, they by chance met a white preacher who recognized them as runaways. He declared himself to be a "friend of all who travel from the South to the North," and directed them to the home of a shoemaker, who sheltered them for two days. The shoemaker found them a berth on a schooner bound for Canada, free of charge.

The Massachusetts whaling port of Nantucket, with its large population of Quakers, had also welcomed fugitives for years. In 1822, local citizens had systematically thwarted the efforts of a Virginia slave catcher named Camillus Griffith to recover George and Lucy Cooper, who had escaped north on a Yankee ship a few years before. "We are not in Virginia now but in Yankee town, and we want those colored people to man our whale ships and will not suffer them to be carried back to bondage," a defiant islander told Griffith. A magistrate then warned Griffith that *he* would be arrested if he attempted to carry the Coopers off. Griffith moved on to New Bedford to seize a third fugitive, John Randolph, but the magistrate there refused even to hear the case. Two New Bedford men then pursued Griffith all the way to Boston, where they had him arrested for assaulting Randolph, who meanwhile had been put safely on a ship bound for New York.

Who were these first pioneers of the underground? Many, especially in Pennsylvania, were of course Quakers. Others, increasingly, were evangelical Methodists and Presbyterians, Scotch Covenanters, and New England Congregationalists. Some, like David Hudson, were colonizationists by conviction, but coming to believe in immediate emancipation. Many were racist by present-day standards: William Jay, one of the most eloquent antislavery men in New York, was shocked when some abolitionists began to call for black suffrage. Yet no matter how they felt personally about African Americans, white abolitionists were exhilarated by the conviction that they were doing what faith demanded of them. They were, after all, assuring their own salvation in a deeply pious era when Judgment Day was an event as real as the annual spring planting and autumn harvest. That they would be judged for their actions, and for their sins, was beyond doubt or debate. "Those who do remain partakers with murderers and man stealers will be involved in their guilt," the Quakers' North Carolina Yearly Meeting informed its members. However, having done their duty with the divine assistance that they did not doubt was guiding them, they would be purified, ready for salvation when the moment came. At the same time, accurate information about the realities of slavery steadily percolated through the free states from travelers, immigrants, and fugitives themselves. Many formed their lasting impression of slavery in church, from the terrifying stories of floggings, torture, and rapes delivered by an abolitionist preacher, or even from the lips of a fugitive passing through en route to a safer place farther north. The future underground conductor Calvin Fairbank, who grew up in rural New York, was converted to passionate abolitionism as a child in just such a setting. One night, while attending a Methodist revival, Fairbank's family was billeted in the home of two escaped slaves, who told their story at the fireside that night. "My heart wept, my anger was kindled, and antagonism to slavery was fixed upon me," Fairbank wrote in his 1890 autobiography. " 'Father,' I said, on going to our room, 'When I get bigger they shall not do that'; and the resolve waxed stronger with my growth." Fairbank would later serve the longest prison sentence on record for assisting a fugitive slave.

Abolitionists throughout the free states were increasingly discovering in themselves the same kind of imperative to oppose slavery in the most personal way possible. They were getting regular abolitionist news from the roving journalist Benjamin Lundy, who carried the printing cuts, column rules, and subscription book for his newspaper *The Genius of Universal Emancipation* in a pack on his back as he trudged the border states collecting damning evidence of slavery's iniquity. After 1831 William Lloyd Garrison's fierce Boston-based paper the *Liberator* would shape a whole generation's antislavery thinking. They were also reading the same books, often by evangelical ministers who drew damning contradictions between the corrupting sin of slavery and the proclaimed political ideals of the American republic. In *The Book and Slavery Irreconcilable*, a jeremiad first published in 1816 and kept in print for decades, Reverend George Bourne, a Virginian who was forced to flee to Pennsylvania because of his views, had called for the "immediate and total abolition" of slavery, warning that its perpetuation must ultimately endanger the Union. "For a gradual emancipation," Bourne wrote, "is a virtual recognition of the right, and establishes the rectitude of the practice. If it be for just one moment, it is hallowed forever; and if it be inequitable, not a day should it be tolerated."

Among such works, the most influential of all was a collection of letters that Reverend John Rankin of Ohio wrote to his brother, who had become a slave owner in Virginia. These powerfully reasoned essays first appeared in Ripley's newspaper the *Castigator* in 1824 and 1825, were reprinted by William Lloyd Garrison in the *Liberator* in 1832, and later gained still wider readership in book form. In them, Rankin—who was soon to become one of the most effective underground men in the Ohio River Valley—dissected every argument that was commonly used to rationalize slavery. It was not the inherent nature of Africans, he wrote in one letter, but the hand of oppression that had "pressed them down from the rank of men to that of beasts," preventing in them "that expansion of soul which dignifies man, and ornaments civilized life." Africans, having originally sprung from the same common parent as whites, also possessed the same aspirations, the same powers of mind, the same profound human feelings. In another, he asked his brother to imagine his own wife in the grip of slavery: "how could you have endured to see her tender frame bleed beneath the lacerating whip! Could you have witnessed her innocent tears and cries, without being overwhelmed with the mingled floods of compassion, resentment, and grief!" Attacking the common assertion that blacks must have been designed by God for slavery, Rankin declared, "Every man desires to be free, and this desire the Creator himself has implanted in the bosoms of all our race, and is certainly a conclusive proof that all were designed for freedom; else man was created for disappointment and misery. All the feelings of humanity are strongly opposed to being enslaved, and nothing but the strong arm of power can make man submit to the yoke of bondage."

Adam Lowry Rankin, John Rankin's eldest son, initially wished to live a more normal life than was possible in the ferociously evangelical Rankin home. Having settled on a career as a draftsman for a shipbuilding firm, he made a habit of visiting steamboats that stopped at the Ripley wharf in order to examine their construction. One day, as he wandered over a new boat, an unexpected scene met his eyes belowdecks. Two groups of slaves, twenty-five in each, were chained to the sides of the boat, men on one side and women on the other. At one end of the chain was a young woman with long, fine, wavy hair, who "was as white as any woman of my acquaintance, requiring the closest scrutiny to detect the least touch of African blood," Rankin wrote in later years. He grasped a stanchion for support. He was quite conscious that he was attracted to her, and horrified that a woman as white as himself was destined for the auction block. Then a sudden insight overwhelmed him. "I asked myself why let all my sympathies be expended upon that one woman? Were the women, her companions in slavery, though they be of darker hue than she, any less the daughters of the Lord Almighty? Were they not as well as their white sisters the objects of Christ's redeeming love?" Rankin might have gone away with a heightened, if still passive, opposition to slavery had not he chanced to overhear conversation between two approaching men, one apparently a slave trader, carrying a small rawhide cane, and the other a prospective client, a tall, well-dressed young man, who turned out to be the unmarried son of a planter on his way to New Orleans to transact some business. The words "Ain't she a beauty?" caught Rankin's ear.

The trader was proposing to sell the woman to his prospective client as a mistress for twenty-five hundred dollars, swearing that he could get three thousand dollars for her in New Orleans. As Rankin watched transfixed, the woman burst into tears and covered her face with her hands. Swearing at her, the trader struck her on the shoulder with his cane and ordered her to stop crying or he would half-kill her. After a little more discussion, the young man offered two thousand dollars. The trader rejected this, but invited the young man to try her out en route to New Orleans. He would have the girl delivered to his stateroom. "You can have a splendid time," the trader told him. "It will cost you nothing. I have paid her passage and bond." The trader then ordered the girl to unfasten her dress, striking her on the shoulder with his cane when she hesitated. He invited the young man to feel her breast, and then her thighs. "By this time the young man was carried to the point of yielding and the money paid, the woman relieved of her chain, followed by her new master to his stateroom." Recalled Rankin, "As I left the boat my indignation reached the boiling point over the wicked transaction and, lifting my right hand toward the heavens, I said aloud, 'My God helping me there shall be a perpetual war between me and human slavery in this nation of which I am a member and I pray God I may never be persuaded to give up the fight until slavery is dead or the Lord calls me home.' "

On reaching his uncle's house, where dinner had been held up for forty-five minutes awaiting his return, he said that he had no appetite and felt unwell. "I have seen enough to make a strong man sick, much less a boy," he said. Asked what he meant, Rankin replied that he had seen "fifty chained slaves, borne like hogs to the market, and I am angry." Replied his uncle, "Let not the sun go down on your anger, my boy." Young Rankin went up to his room and sat down before his drafting board. He tried to work, but couldn't. Pacing the floor, he finally told himself, "Young man, you made today a most solemn vow before God. Now what are you going to do about it? Will you settle down and drift with the popular current and be satisfied with an expression of your abhorrence of slavery in idle words?" After an internal struggle, he decided to abandon his drafting work and "fight slavery as a minister of Christ." It was not an idle commitment. He would soon be leading fugitive slaves toward safety through the hills behind his father's farm.

4

Abolitionists, though increasing in number, were still almost everywhere fragmented and isolated in lone outposts or in small groups of like-minded friends or family. But this was about to change. In the last days of December 1833, delegates began arriving in Philadelphia for the first national conference of abolitionists in the country's history. The conference was William Lloyd Garrison's idea. Garrison had founded the Boston-based New England Anti-Slavery Society the previous year, and it already had several thousand members, a dozen local branches, and three full-time grassroots organizers in the field. In October the wealthy Manhattan dry goods merchants Lewis and Arthur Tappan had established a sister organization in New York. Intensely religious, the Tappans were among the most generous and steadfast contributors to the abolitionist and other evangelical causes. The sixty-three delegates from ten states planned to form a national society powerful enough to mount a sustained spiritual crusade to sway the hearts and minds of America against slavery and, they fervently hoped, to eventually inspire slave owners themselves to voluntarily yield up the two million souls that they held in bondage.

The atmosphere in the city was tense. The delegates were denounced in local newspapers and from hostile pulpits as "fanatics, amalgamationists, disorganizers, disturbers of the peace, and dangerous enemies of the country." One delegate, the Unitarian minister Samuel J. May, who nearly two decades later would become Jarm Logue's closest partner in the clandestine work of the Underground Railroad, dryly wrote, "we learnt that a goodly number were already there; and the newspapers of the day were seeking to make our coming a formidable affair, worthy the especial attention of those patriotic conservators of the peace who dealt in brickbats, rotten eggs, and tar and feathers."

The police warned that they could not guarantee anyone's safety after dark. Denied other facilities for fear of mob violence, they finally met at the small Adelphi Building, which was owned by a black benevolent association.

The delegates were mostly young, and came mainly from New York, New England, and Pennsylvania, although a hardy few had made the arduous journey from as far away as the Western Reserve of Ohio. Most were evangelical Christians. About one-third were Quaker. A handful were African Americans, most notably Robert Purvis and James McCrummel, who before the decade was out would form the Philadelphia Vigilance Committee, one of the most efficient underground operations in the country. There were also "a number of excellent women," including the Quaker Lucretia Mott. Her participation was a revolutionary event in itself, the first time that most of the men there, except her fellow Quakers, had ever heard a woman speak in public. Although she made only minor suggestions, they were the first seeds of the increasingly important women's wing of the antislavery movement, and of its mighty offshoot, the women's rights crusade. Beriah Green, the strident, sandy-haired president of the country's first racially integrated college, the Oneida Institute in upstate New York, was chosen as the convention's presiding officer, and the Quaker poet John Greenleaf Whittier and Lewis Tappan were elected as secretaries. On December 3 Green's clarion voice opened the convention with words from Isaiah: "Cry aloud, spare not, lift up thy voice like a trumpet, and show my people their transgression, and the house of Jacob their sins." For the next three days, the assembly met almost continuously, declining to break even for meals, and pausing only long enough for the hungry to gulp down crackers and cold water.

On the penultimate day of the convention, Garrison, "our Coryphaeus" May called him, was assigned to write the draft text of a declaration. May left him at ten o'clock at night, at the home of the grocer James McCrummel. When he returned at eight in the morning, Garrison was polishing the last paragraph of one of the most momentous documents in American history. Garrison dramatically entered the Adelphi Building with the "Declaration of Sentiments" in his hand. It was a ringing proclamation of the principles that would guide the core of the abolition movement until the Civil War, and that would codify concisely the values that would inspire most of the conductors and stationmasters on the Underground Railroad. Its language was not political but religious, an appeal to men and women whose hearts had already been tilled by evangelical proselytizing. Its message was one of urgent moral regeneration, and it uncompromisingly insisted that each individual squarely face his duty to take immediate action against the overarching sin of the age. The declaration called unambiguously for immediate emancipation, stating "that all those laws which are now in force, admitting the right of slavery, are therefore before God utterly null and void; being an audacious usurpation of Divine prerogative, a daring infringement on the law of nature, a base overthrow of the very foundations of the social compact . . . and a presumptuous transgression of all the holy commandments." Contemptuously rejecting slaveholders' protestations that slavery had been an accepted practice since the dawn of civilization, it asserted "that if [slaves] had lived from the time of Pharaoh down to the present period, and had been entailed through successive generations, their right to be free could never have been alienated, but their claims would have constantly risen in solemnity."

All persons of color, the declaration went on to say, ought to be immediately granted the same privileges as other Americans, and "the paths of preferment, of wealth, and of intelligence" opened to them as widely as to any white. Freedom must be unconditional. Schemes of colonization were "delusive, cruel, and dangerous." The payment of compensation to slave owners was also unacceptable. "Because the holders of slaves are not the just proprietors of what they claim; freeing the slaves is not depriving them of property, but restoring it to the right owner; it is not wronging the master, but righting the slave—restoring him to himself." Compensation, if it was to be given at all, ought to be given to the slave "not to those who have plundered and abused them." Crucially, the statement asserted that all Americans, not just slave-owning Southerners, were entangled in the sin of slavery. Northerners too were guilty of fastening "the galling fetters of tyranny" upon the enslaved millions, by tolerating the Constitution's provision that allowed a slave owner to vote for three-fifths of his slaves as property, by supporting a standing army to help protect Southern oppressors, and by silently permitting slave hunters or public officials to seize a fugitive "who has escaped into their territories, and send him back to be tortured by an enraged master or a brutal driver." The "highest obligations" thus rested upon the people of the free states "to remove slavery by moral and political action."

Two short years after Nat Turner's rebellion, when fears of slave uprisings in the South remained pervasive and raw, the delegates explicitly renounced violence, or "carnal means" of bringing about a general emancipation, as the pacifist Garrison put it. Slavery must be overcome only by persuasion. Asserting that "we shall spare no exertions nor means to bring the whole nation to speedy repentance," the delegates promised to organize antislavery societies "in every city, town and village" in the nation. Building on Garrison's model, which itself drew on an evangelical style borrowed from the religious revivals that had swept the country in recent years, a new national organization, to be named the American Anti-Slavery Society, would send out trained agents to carry the abolitionist message, to disseminate antislavery materials nationally, and to "aim at a purification of the churches from all participation in the guilt of slavery."

The declaration did not call for a specific effort to assist fugitive slaves. Nor did it contain any language that could be construed as ordering Americans to disobey the law. But the logic of the declaration was inescapable: slavery must be terminated without delay, and every individual, North and South, had a duty to do what he—or as Lucretia Mott's presence testified, *she*—could to end it. In the coming years, many thousands of Northerners would come face to face with that duty, and with laws that they could not in conscience obey, in the living form of fugitive slaves. As they gathered to put their names to the document, it seemed to Samuel May that a "holy enthusiasm" lighted up every face. "It seemed to me that every man's heart was in his hand,—as if every one felt that he was about to offer himself a living sacrifice in the cause of *freedom*, and to do it cheerfully."

CHAPTER 8

The Grandest Revolution the World Has Ever Seen

The sword, which is now drawn, will never be returned to its scabbard.

—Gerrit Smith

1

As Gerrit Smith drove at a brisk trot toward Utica over the steep hills of central New York with their freight of stubbled fields in the early morning hours of October 21, 1835, thoughts of sin and slavery intruded on his generous mind. That evening, he intended to see his elderly and difficult father at Schenectady, where he lived in retirement. Smith would catch a canal boat at Utica for the trip east along the Erie Canal. But first he would stop at the Bleecker Street Presbyterian Church, where delegates from around the state were meeting that day to form a New York affiliate of the American Anti-Slavery Society. Smith was a man who made a powerful impression on people. William Goodell, an associate of William Lloyd Garrison who knew him well, particularly praised Smith's "strong discriminating mind" and polished manners, and compared his eloquence to that of Daniel Webster, the most famous orator of the age.

Though only thirty-eight years old, the manic-depressive, hulking Smith—he was six feet tall and weighed two hundred pounds—was heir to a huge fortune and vast holdings of land in three states. Even now, with his father, Peter, slipping into an old age of increasing instability, there was little affection between them. The elder Smith was a rough-cut, self-made man, and emotionally cold, who had come to what was then Oneida Indian territory in 1794, and had made his fortune trading in furs with his partner John Jacob Astor, and later by speculating in Indian lands. He had forced his sons to work alongside his slaves as boys, a humiliating experience that inspired the sensitive Gerrit with an instinctive empathy for the victims of slavery. Although Gerrit had adored the poetry of Byron, and for a time even aspired to a literary career, after graduation from Hamilton College he agreed to take over his father's business instead. Smith was already a potent force in many of the reform movements that were sweeping through the country. "Boundless was his faith in moral powers," sighed his first, adoring biographer, Octavius Frothingham. Smith's moral sensibility was a product of the passionate religious revivalism that had flared across central New York in the 1820s with such frequency and fury that the region became known as the Burned Over District, conjuring a vivid image indeed in an era when memories of charred landscapes cleared for settlement were still fresh across the interior of the state.

Smith had thought deeply about slavery. He dismissed as hypocrisy the argument that if slavery were simply left alone it would die a natural death. True Christians tolerated no other sins with such complacency: did they supinely expect intemperance or adultery to disappear on their own? Hardly. Even were it "indisputably evident" that if slavery survived another century the slaves would be "better prepared than they now are for the boon of freedom," he wrote in 1834, it was still immoral to prolong their bondage. "By such a concession, I might be sanctioning the abhorrent doctrine of doing evil, that good may come." As early as 1826, Smith lent support to the establishment of a seminary to educate blacks for missionary work in Africa, and he had recently decided to refuse any commodity that derived from slavery—no small sacrifice at a time when nearly all the cotton and sugar sold in the United States were produced by slave labor. But he was not an abolitionist. He was, in fact, a major contributor to the American Colonization Society, which envisioned the deportation of blacks back to Africa as the only acceptable alternative to slavery. He hated slavery because it was a sin, and fear of sin burned so deeply and unquenchably in his capacious heart that he would devote his life to the eradication of it from the American soul.

The atmosphere in Utica was very tense. A few days before the antislavery convention, a public protest meeting chaired by the mayor had declared the abolitionists to be "enemies of the most valued institutions of their own country; of her happy experiment of free government; emphatically, of the slave population of the South; and the human race." One speaker, to wild cheers, had declared, "Whenever a servile insurrection shall commence at the South, the best blood of the North will be spilt in her defense. Is there a man here who would not buckle on his armor and go?" The area's demagogic and well-connected Democratic congressman, Samuel Beardsley, threatened violence, saying that "it would be better to have Utica razed to its foundations, or to have it destroyed like Sodom and Gomorrah, than to have the convention meet here."

The Democratic hostility to abolitionism was in part unembarrassed racism, and in part political hardball. New York Democrats regarded African Americans as tools of the Whig opposition. In 1800 the vote of a single black-dominated ward had won control of New York City for the Federalists, and again in 1813 the votes of three hundred free blacks in New York City swept the Federalists into power, and gave them control of the state legislature. The Democrats took their revenge in 1821, when the new state constitution effectively disenfranchised almost every black voter in New York by requiring that they prove that they owned at least two hundred and fifty dollars' worth of property, a restriction not imposed on whites. In 1821 the triumphant Democrats changed the New York State constitution to enfranchise all white males, while erecting barriers to black male voters, so that by 1825 fewer than three hundred blacks out of a total state population of almost thirty thousand, and only *sixteen* of New York City's more than twelve thousand blacks, could actually vote.

In the teeth of savage local opposition, more than six hundred antislavery delegates turned up in Utica. The organizers of the convention had pressed Smith to lend his prestige to the event to help "call out the moral energies of this region." He had agreed, though only as an observer. But what was about to happen to Smith that morning would have a profound impact on the antislavery movement in America. It would turn the wealthiest man in New York state into one of the most subversive, and a stationmaster for the Underground Railroad.

The convention got under way at 10 A.M. Alvan Stewart, a Utica lawyer and a leading abolitionist, spoke first. "We have been proclaimed traitors to our own dear native land, because we love its inhabitants," he declared, with feeling. "Our humanity is treason, our philanthropy is incendiarism, our pity for the convulsive yearnings of downtrodden man is fanaticism." This was not empty rhetoric. Even as he spoke, a mob of at least several hundred milled menacingly outside the church. Stewart warned his listeners that their own liberties would be in immediate danger were they to allow themselves to be silenced by intimidation. "My countrymen, ye sons of the Pilgrims, the *tyrant* is at your doors, liberty is dying, slavery has robbed you of the liberty of discussion, of conscience and the press." Afterward, while the evangelical New York City dry goods merchant Lewis Tappan was reading a declaration of sentiments, a crowd led by Congressman Beardsley pushed and shoved its way down the aisle, shouting, "Open the way! Damn the fanatics! Stop your damn stuff!" There were roughnecks and riffraff among the mob, but it was leavened with the town's respectable elite, its businessmen and lawyers, all of them howling in an effort to drown out Tappan. James Caleb Jackson, a young delegate from Oswego who was sitting halfway between the pulpit and the door, feared that any kind of violence was possible. But he was inspired to a state of religious exaltation by the feeling of willing martyrdom that he sensed among the abolitionists around him: "I have no doubt that they would have consented to stay there and be massacred, before they would have left the church, if it had not been for two or three members in the meeting, who knowing how outraged the moral sense of the citizens of Utica was held counsel of nonresistance." Among the many delegates who clamored to be heard the chairman recognized Gerrit Smith. To the excited Jackson, it seemed that "his face was clothed with a glory that was more than human." Declaring that he was "no abolitionist," but that he loved fair play, Smith's clarion voice shouted above the uproar, "It seems from what appears here this morning that it is a crime not only to be black, but to be a friend of the black man." He spontaneously invited the entire convention to reconvene at his own home in Peterboro, where, he promised, he could guarantee "a peaceful meeting."

The delegates made their way out through an even larger mob screaming insults at them, and that pursued them to their hotels and lodgings. Meanwhile, hooligans raided the office of the local antislavery newspaper and threw its type into the street. Beardsley's followers even pursued the carriages of delegates for miles along the road to Peterboro, hurling curses and stones until they were out of sight. James Caleb Jackson had an easier journey. Along with a large group of delegates, he hailed a freight boat passing through Utica along the Erie Canal. Singing, and praying, and swearing eternal hostility to slavery as they traveled through the night, Jackson thought of the early, persecuted Christians at prayer in the catacombs of Rome and the martyred Albigensians of medieval France. At 3 A.M. the boat arrived in Canastota, and in a drizzling rain Jackson's party, more than a hundred strong, set off on foot for Peterboro ten miles away, still "singing and shouting, and laughing and praying" as they marched, startling farmers milking their cows, and shoemakers and carpenters on their way to work. To Jackson, the scene of marching men was a vision in flesh and blood of the power of Christian righteousness, an unstoppable, divinely inspired force. "When asked, 'What is the matter, has war been declared?' our answer was, 'Yes, war to the death against slavery. We have been mobbed out of the city of Utica, and we are going to Peterboro to hold a convention. We have begun the grandest revolution the world has ever seen; and if we do not die, we mean to see that revolution accomplished, and our land freed from the tread and fetter of the slave.' "

The events in Utica were part of a coordinated crackdown on abolitionists across the North. On the same day, mobs led by men affiliated with the Democratic Party also attacked abolitionist speakers in Newport, Rhode Island; Montpelier, Vermont; and Boston, where William Lloyd Garrison was physically seized and led through the streets with a noose around his neck. The spread of democracy in the Jacksonian era had done nothing to help the cause of the slave. The Northern men whom the Jacksonians brought into office had close ties to the South, and their prospects depended on the proslavery party leaders. Samuel Beardsley was, in fact, vice president Martin Van Buren's closest associate in the House of Representatives. Van Buren, a wealthy landowner from New

York's Hudson Valley whose family had been slave owners, was himself under heavy pressure to appease the South by suppressing abolitionist activity, especially in what amounted to his own political backyard. Charging a politician with being "soft" on abolitionism in the 1830s was much like accusing one of being "soft" on Communism in the 1950s, and Van Buren, who expected to run for president in 1836, knew that he could not win his party's nomination without the South's support. Not long after the Utica riot Beardsley was rewarded for his rabble rousing with appointment as the attorney general of New York state.

Meanwhile, abandoning his trip to see his father in Schenectady, Gerrit Smith raced back to Peterboro and awakened his household. Inside the white Greek Revival mansion, servants spent all night mixing bread, grinding coffee, paring apples for pies, and baking rolls for the abolitionists who straggled in through the early morning hours. The day dawned with what must have seemed to be the blessing of God himself, the rain having blown past to reveal the austere hamlet in all its Yankee plainness in the crisp, clear light of an autumn morning. Later the three hundred remaining delegates met at the ample, three-story Presbyterian church across the village green from Smith's pillared home. Smith, no pacifist, had posted armed men around the church to fend off a new attack by the mob. In the course of the day, the delegates agreed to call for "universal and immediate emancipation." They further resolved—and this was the argument that more than any other would eventually win the abolitionists tens of thousands of allies in the North—"that the time has come to settle the great question, whether the North shall give up its liberty to preserve slavery to the south, or the South shall give up its slavery to preserve liberty to the whole nation."

After this, Smith himself rose to speak. His words, penned in the course of a sleepless night, articulated the inner thoughts of countless men and women who were coming to the conclusion that civil power must be challenged by moral law. He spoke of the outrage that had been committed upon young Amos Dresser, a divinity student from Cincinnati, who while traveling in Tennessee selling religious literature to earn money for his tuition, had been publicly stripped and flogged in Nashville simply because abolitionist tracts had been found in his luggage. The suppression of free speech was a crime not only against treasured American values, but against the laws of God, Smith boomed. "Take from the men who compose the church of Christ on earth, the right of free discussion, and you disable them for His service. They are now the lame and the dumb and the blind. If God made me to be one of his instruments for carrying forward the salvation of the world, then is the right of free discussion among my inherent rights; then may I, must I speak of sin, any sin, every sin, that comes in my way—any sin, every sin, which it is my duty to search out and assail." Northern men were being asked to lie down in front of the menacing slaveholders "like whipped and trembling spaniels." To stand up for the slave was therefore a matter now not only of spiritual and patriotic imperative, but a matter of simple manhood. "The sword, which is now drawn, will never be returned to its scabbard, until victory, entire, decisive victory is ours or theirs," he concluded.

The events of the past day had transformed Smith from an intellectual bystander to the drama of slavery into a committed activist, a patrician revolutionary who would not rest until the sinful national compact was overthrown. By the end of the day, he made clear that he would commit his property, his reputation, and his life if necessary, to the struggle. A month after the Peterboro convention, Smith resigned from the American Colonization Society, pronouncing himself cured of the "colonization delusion." In 1836 he would be elected to the first of four terms as president of the New York Anti-Slavery Society. By mid-1837 he would be secretly shipping abolitionist tracts into the South. By the next year he would be harboring slaves, and the mansion in Peterboro would be a station on the Underground Railroad.

2

In the middle years of the 1830s, abolitionism was transformed from a sentiment, a set of beliefs held by a small number of men and women in the Northern states, and upon which even fewer were prepared to act, into an organized national movement, an expanding array of antislavery societies whose members would provide the white rank and file of the Underground Railroad, linking them together with isolated cells and African-American communities into a system that, in time, would spread across more than a dozen states. It was not by coincidence that, apart from the Quaker settlements, abolitionism flourished most vigorously where evangelical revivalism was most active, or found its most ardent foot soldiers in Americans like Gerrit Smith, for whom religion infused politics and politics religion in a seamless transcendental web. At a time when the old Calvinist doctrine of divine predestination was rapidly fading and the nation's secular ideology treated individual enterprise as a sacred duty, abolitionism—especially in its ultimate form, the Underground Railroad—offered the chance to live out prayer in action, to put faith to *practical* effect. "This is the carrying out of practical Christianity; and there is no other," William Goodell declared in the *Friend of Man* on September 6, 1837. "Christianity is *practical* in its very nature and essence. It is a life, springing out of a soul imbued with its spirit . . . Come, then, and help us to restore to these millions, whose eyes have been bored out by slavery, their sight, that they may see to read the Bible. Do you love God whom you have not seen? Then manifest that love, by restoring to your brother whom you have seen, his rightful inheritance, of which he has been so wrong and so cruelly deprived."

Northerners were torn. Decent citizens hardly knew what they feared more, the troublemaking abolitionists, or the threat of mob violence. Most dearly wished that the abolitionists would simply shut up and go away. When they failed to, no one quite knew what to do. "The abolitionists are wrong in forcing upon the world measures so decidedly in the face of public opinion," the *Poughkeepsie (NY) Journal* editorialized, after a mob drove an abolitionist speaker from the pulpit of the local Presbyterian church. "That they possess the abstract right to discuss the subject of slavery no man denies, and 'tis unfortunate that they are not permitted to do so, but still more unfortunate that in defense of an abstract right, the exercise of which can do no good, men will jeopardize the supremacy of the laws and hazard the existence of the Union. On the other hand, it is to be regretted that the abolitionists were not let alone."

Debate grew intense and bitter across the Northern states, rending families, church congregations, and entire towns. "I well remember hearing conversations, arguments, and often very bitter words between the elder members of our large connection, when they would meet *en famille* at our home, and what had always been a pleasure to me as a child became a source of dread," recalled Mary Ellen Graydon Sharpe, whose father, Alexander Graydon, an elder of the Presbyterian church, became a central figure in the Harrisburg, Pennsylvania underground. "My parents and one uncle stood firm for the slave and the duty of abolition; while all the others considered them fanatics and hurled abuse upon them in no very gentle manner. My grandfather once said to my father, in my presence, 'I can not see, Alexander, *why* you have taken up such wild ideas! Why do you attempt to force public opinion? Why not let well enough alone?' and I can even now hear my father's firm reply: 'If the old society should work a hundred years it could not lift more than a few hundreds of poor slaves out of bondage a year, while this system is piling up its tens of thousands of agonized men, women, and children every year of its existence. No, we will work until slavery is wiped out and is no longer a foul blot on our escutcheon.' From that time our home was thrown open for all whose sympathies were with the slave, and became the *central station of the underground railroad.*"

Since its founding in 1833, the American Anti-Slavery Society had undertaken a massive national effort to carry out what a later generation would term "consciousness raising," to convert white Americans to immediate emancipation. At different points, this would involve the shipment of quantities of abolitionist literature into the South, the lobbying of state governments for legislation to strengthen the rights of African Americans, and persistent local agitation. In the middle of the decade, the society undertook a massive petition campaign calling upon Congress to abolish slavery in the District of Columbia, the one part of the country over which the national government had undisputed authority. Petitions on other slavery-related questions soon followed. But year after year, the House of Representatives by overwhelming majorities adopted a "gag rule," in the process originating the term, stating that all petitions that related to slavery must be tabled without discussion or referral to committee. Abolitionists knew this would be the outcome, but they kept the petitions coming. By March 1838 Congress had received so many petitions that they filled to the ceiling a room twenty feet wide by thirty feet square. The petitions had no impact on federal legislation, but the refusal of Congress to even consider them helped to radicalize Northern public opinion by vividly illustrating the grip that proslavery interests held upon the national government. Abolitionist rhetoric would henceforth be stippled with evocative descriptions of the nation "fettered and gagged" like a slave.

The core of the society's efforts, however, centered on a brigade of militant traveling agents who were selected to carry out a vast systematic grassroots campaign, one of the first in the nation's history. (Many agents built on experience gained organizing for the temperance movement in the 1820s.) Most were young clergymen, and they were expected to treat their duties as an extension of their spiritual vocation. "Jesus Christ has a right to *any* man whom he pleases to call," Elizur Wright, an official of the society, wrote to one candidate, "and we trust that you will regard this as *His* call." Agents traveled for months on end through assigned territories, speaking once or twice daily, often for hours at a time, on the sinfulness of slavery, building local affiliates, gathering names on petitions, and collecting donations. They focused mainly on rural areas. "Let the great cities *alone*," advised Theodore Dwight Weld, one of the most successful of all the agents. "They must be burned down by *back fires*." (Like many Christian reformers of the time, white abolitionists often exhibited an almost pathological fear of cities, which by the 1830s were evolving into recognizably modern conglomerations of diverse ethnic and religious groups, who had a penchant for ignoring evangelical recipes for proper behavior. "Reformations commence and flourish most where the moral atmosphere is clearest," one correspondent wrote to the *Friend of Man*, in August 1836. "They do not commence in crowded and morally pestilential cities, but in the country . . . where the mockery of human art has not shut God out.")

While the traveling agents did not carry an explicit mandate to develop routes for the Underground Railroad, by holding rallies and organizing local abolition societies, they often brought newly converted abolitionists into contact with those who were already engaged in clandestine activity. Agents sometimes took personal responsibility for forwarding fugitives. For example, on January 27, 1837, Oliver Johnson wrote from Jenner Township, in Somerset County in western Pennsylvania, where he was doing organizational work, to an ally in Vermont, asking permission to dispatch a fugitive to him at his home near Burlington. Johnson's remarkable letters concerning a man whom he identified only as "Simon" are among the few documents from this period that explicitly describe the Underground Railroad in operation. Johnson, a rather somber twenty-eight-year-old from Peacham, Vermont, was a founder of the New England Anti-Slavery Society, and sometimes edited the *Liberator* during Garrison's absences. His contact in Vermont was Rowland T. Robinson, a deeply devout Quaker with hollow eyes and a beard that jutted out like a fist from his gaunt face. Johnson knew his man. Robinson was a founder of the Vermont Anti-Slavery Society, and he was always willing to find a place for a fugitive on the large farm where he raised merino sheep, within sight of Lake Champlain and the blue silhouette of the Adirondack Mountains. Fugitives were already being sent with some regularity from downstate New York to Robinson or one of the other abolitionist farmers in the neighborhood, whose families spanned several generations of anti-slavery activism. Robinson's extensive network of correspondents included other radical Quakers, among them Isaac Hopper, as well as William Lloyd Garrison, Theodore Weld, and C. C. Burleigh.

Fugitives commonly would work for Robinson for up to several months until they had saved money to move on to Canada, or elsewhere in New England, or New York. Rokeby, Robinson's farm, was thus less a way station on the Underground Railroad than a terminus, a place beyond the reach of slave catchers, in a state that had explicitly stated as early as 1786 that any attempt to take a fugitive slave out of the state would be "in open violation of the laws of the land." While the underground was as secret as its participants could keep it in the border counties of Delaware, Pennsylvania, Ohio, and Indiana, there was nothing clandestine about it at all in northern Vermont. One of Robinson's closest associates was the Vermont secretary of state, Chauncey Knapp, and in the spring of 1837, Robinson would actually correspond with a North Carolina farmer, making it quite clear that the man's former slave was living at Rokeby, and that he hoped to purchase his freedom for a hundred and fifty dollars. This the master rejected as inadequate, but he confessed with chagrin that "he at this time is entirely out of my reach." Robinson harbored scores, if not hundreds, of fugitives during his long Underground Railroad career. In writing to him, Johnson supposed that he could take one more.

Read with care, Johnson's letter provides a window onto the operation and the reach of the Underground Railroad at the end of the 1830s. In addition to a detailed physical description of the man he was sending, Johnson supplied Robinson with a personal testimonial. "I was so well-pleased with his appearance, and with the account given of him by Griffith [a local Baptist], that I could not help thinking that he would be a good man for you to hire," he wrote. "Mr. Griffith says he is of a kind disposition, and knows how to do all most all kinds of farm work. He is used to teaming, and is very good to manage horses. He says that he could beat any man in the neighborhood where he lived, in Maryland, at mowing, cradling, or pitching . . . Would you not like to have him go to you in the spring?" Simon would have to walk all the way to Philadelphia, but he would be furnished with the names of abolitionists on whom to call upon the way. "If you say, 'let him come' I will endeavor to make the best possible arrangements in regard to the journey," Johnson concluded. Robinson replied in the affirmative, and on April 3 Johnson wrote back that he'd given Simon directions to Philadelphia, "where he will put himself under the direction of our friends, who will give him all needful information concerning the route to New York, at which place he will be befriended by the 'Committee of Vigilance,' or by members of the [Executive] Committee."

3

In the aftermath of the Utica riot, upstate New York state became a primary target of the abolitionist organizing effort. "Half the moral power of the nation lies within 24 hours easy ride (mostly steam boat) of New York City," Henry B. Stanton, a secretary of the American Anti-Slavery Society, declared. "There the fulcrum must be placed by which we are to overturn the nation." In a similar vein, Theodore Weld wrote to Rowland T. Robinson in June, 1836, "New York is the *Empire State*. Its extent of territory, its position with reference to the South—its numerous population, its vast political sway—its commercial relations with the South, &. &. All make it a matter of immediate moment that it should be *abolitionised* as speedily as possible . . . No state in the Union is now so ripe for lecturers as *this*."

Dozens of traveling agents were deployed across New York. In January and February 1836, Theodore Weld spoke sixteen times at Utica's Bleecker Street Presbyterian Church, from which the abolitionists had been expelled only three months before. To the dismay of the Democrats who had counted on mob violence to put an end to abolitionism, crowds jammed Weld's lectures, and no fewer than 600 enrolled in the Utica Anti-Slavery Society, making it the largest in the state. In Rochester, Weld increased membership in local antislavery societies more than five-fold, from 150 to 850. In Lockport, he was almost shouted down by hostile demonstrators, but after a marathon four-hour speech, 440 people signed the new constitution of the Niagara County Anti-Slavery Society; a year later, the society would have 21,000 members, with branches in nine of the county's twelve townships. Although Weld was forced out of Troy by mobs throwing stones and rotten eggs and forbidden by the mayor to speak in the city again, he moved on to Greenwich in Washington County, where he spoke for five successive evenings, and signed up 118 members for the local affiliate. He then added 90 more new members at the nearby towns of Fort Ann and West Granville. Other agents reported equally stunning successes, often in spite of mob opposition. J. M. Blakesley formed an 85-member antislavery society in Sardinia, in the far western part of the state, and recruited another 200 in the town of Colden, which had a total population of only 1,000 people. Lumond Wilcox signed up more than 300 in the towns of Delaware County, which had never heard of immediate emancipation before. In July William Chaplin signed up more than 100 members in Auburn after just a single lecture. Genesee County was thoroughly "abolitionized" by L. Q. Curtis, who boasted that twenty of its twenty-four towns now had antislavery societies with memberships ranging between 40 and 300. All told, the agents' success was astonishing.

In 1838 Gerrit Smith himself undertook several lecture tours on behalf of the New York Anti-Slavery Society. One of them took him to the handsome lakeside village of Cooperstown, where he debated the novelist James Fenimore Cooper, a hardcore Jacksonian Democrat, who spoke for almost five hours straight in defense of slavery to a hall so crowded that hundreds failed to gain admittance and milled around on the streets outside. Although the debate, between the greatest American writer of his age and the "second Webster," was not recorded, Cooper recounted his views on slavery in *The American Democrat*, published the same year. Slavery was as old as time, he asserted, and it was "no more sinful, by the christian code, than it is sinful to wear a whole coat, while another is in tatters." There was nothing that made it impossible to be an excellent Christian and a slaveholder at the same time. Indeed, slavery had distinct virtues. For instance, it enabled the master to exhibit toward his slave some of the mildest graces of human character, such as between king and subject.

Moreover, North American slaves were no worse off than the average European peasant. "In one sense," Cooper proposed, "slavery may actually benefit a man, there being no doubt that the African is, in nearly all respects, better off in servitude in this country, than when living in a state of barbarism at home." Although American slavery was generally mild, and therefore "physical suffering cannot properly be enumerated among its evils," the question was really moot since blacks were essentially brutes. Their ignorance was a positive blessing. "Neither is it just to lay too heavy stress on the personal restraints of the system," he concluded, "as it is a question whether men feel very keenly, if at all, privations of the amount of which they knew nothing."

Cooper was far from alone in his hostility to abolition. Abolitionist speakers were greeted with rocks, eggs, mob attacks, and public calls for repression. When it was learned that a traveling agent was to speak at Poughkeepsie, in the Hudson Valley, handbills entitled "OUTRAGE" suddenly appeared all over the city, warning that a "seditious lecture" was to be delivered at the Presbyterian church, and calling upon citizens to "unite in putting down and silencing by peaceable means this tool of evil and fanaticism." Henry B. Stanton claimed to have been mobbed 150 times before 1840. Major antiabolition riots occurred in Newark, New Jersey; Concord, New Hampshire; New Britain and Norwich, Connecticut, and New York City, where rioters burned to the ground the home of the wealthy abolitionist Lewis Tappan, the president of the American Anti-Slavery Society. In Ohio, antislavery lecturers were tarred and feathered, pelted with broken glass, and attacked by club-wielding thugs. And in November 1837 abolitionism acquired its first white martyr, when the newspaper editor Elijah P. Lovejoy was shot to death while defending his press—his fourth, after three previous ones had been destroyed—from an attacking mob at Alton, Illinois.

If Northerners regarded abolitionists as deluded and sanctimonious troublemakers, Southerners saw them as a mortal enemy determined to destroy both the foundation of their economy and their way of life, by means of agitation that could only lead to a national bloodbath. In the aftermath of Nat Turner's rebellion, the South increasingly moved in the direction of authoritarian controls that affected not only (as always) blacks, both slave and free, but also whites whose actions or utterances in any way might be deemed to threaten, however obliquely, the institution of slavery. New laws, vigilante activity, and public pressure increasingly shackled the press, censored literature, and coerced individuals who dared speak out against the prevailing proslavery opinions. Rights commonly taken for granted by other Americans—the right of free speech, free press, and assembly—were increasingly curtailed. With the open acquiescence of federal authorities, mail coming from the North was searched and local postmasters were empowered to destroy anything that they judged subversive. In Charleston, mobs seized mailbags containing antislavery literature and burned them at the post office. The monitoring of free blacks and the movements of slaves sharply increased, while suspicious travelers were interrogated by local vigilante committees, and their belongings investigated by force. Laws in several states provided up to twenty years in prison for the publication or circulation of materials "tending to incite insurrection." The Vigilance Association of Columbia, South Carolina, offered a fifteen-hundred-dollar reward for the arrest and conviction of any white person circulating "publications of a seditious tendency." In 1835 Georgia imposed the death penalty for anyone publishing materials that could be construed as inciting slaves to rebellion. A Virginia law of 1836 barred members of abolition societies from even entering the state. Louisiana laws made it a crime to write, publish, or speak anything in court, stage, or pulpit that tended to "destroy that line of distinction which the law has established between the several classes of this community." All over the South, public figures openly threatened to kill any abolitionist they could lay their hands on, and watchdog committees put bounties of tens of thousands of dollars on the heads of abolitionist leaders. President Jackson bluntly demanded that the Northern states outlaw the activities of the abolitionists, while in 1838 South Carolina congressman Robert B. Rhett published a letter to his constituents in which he declared that either the Constitution should be amended to limit freedom of speech on the subject of slavery, or else the Union must be dissolved.

Southerners confused—and would continue until the Civil War to confuse—the abolitionist movement as a whole with the Underground Railroad. The two were never completely congruent. The American Anti-Slavery Society never advocated breaking the law, although it refused to censure any of its members who assisted slaves in their escape. There were active members of the underground, including at least some Democrats, who never joined any formal organization, just as there were countless abolitionists who refused to break federal law. To use a modern analogy, membership in an antislavery society was no more proof of participation in Underground Railroad than belonging to the Sierra Club means that one would personally sabotage lumber company equipment in the forests of the Pacific Northwest. The two networks existed, however, in a symbiotic relationship, with the societies serving as a fertile recruiting ground for clandestine activists, and the Underground Railroad in turn supplying abolitionist lecture halls and fund-raisers with a steady stream of flesh-and-blood fugitives who, like figments come to life from the nation's collective nightmare, were living proof of slavery's inhumanity.

Structurally, the aboveground abolitionist movement was a layered pyramid whose national leadership exerted little overall control, and whose center of gravity lay solidly within its sprawling popular base. Wherever they went, antislavery agents preached that success depended on the local units, and specifically on their members' personal commitment to the cause. Local societies could have no more strength "than is possessed by the INDIVIDUALS of which they are composed and can *exist* only by the INDIVIDUALS' self-denial and labor," the New York Anti-Slavery Society stressed in its annual report for 1837. Every community was advised to appoint two agents, a man and a woman, to canvass each school district in the town, conversing with individuals, from house to house, from shop to shop, in the counting room, in the harvest field, and by the family fireside," talking to them about slavery and selling them an antislavery almanac; if they couldn't sell the almanac, they were to give it away free. Another tactic was to go from door to door, carrying petitions calling for the federal government to abolish slavery in the western territories and in the District of Columbia, to reject the annexation of Texas as a slave state, to halt interstate traffic in slaves, and so on. "Nothing is easier than for them in one short year to have every village and neighborhood within their limits reading, thinking and talking on the stirring topic of 'human rights,' " the executive committee of the state society proclaimed. "And for people to read, think, and talk on that subject is to become thorough converts to the great doctrines of impartial liberty." Children were not forgotten either. Each school district was urged to purchase a library of antislavery literature. The American Anti-Slavery Society also produced a periodical called *The Slave's Friend*, which explained abolition in easy-to-read fashion, accompanied by woodcuts. The pitch was not subtle. One article profiled Henry Wright, who oversaw the society's juvenile auxiliaries: "He will try to get every little boy and girl to take hold of the great work of pulling slavery up by the roots," the piece opined. "I think they will all like to take hold, and pull as hard as they can."

The executive bureau of the American Anti-Slavery Society limited itself mainly to lobbying Congress, hiring agents to organize states that had not yet formed local groups, and publishing antislavery propaganda, while local antislavery groups typically functioned as divisions of their state and county societies. The state societies appointed their own traveling agents, and sponsored regional conventions as well as an annual meeting to which all abolitionists were invited. County societies were expected to hold their own conventions several times a year. Local meetings served as a forum for educating both new members and the general public. Whatever other purpose they served, at every level these gatherings also enabled underground activists to network with like-minded men and women from different parts of their state or county, to whom a fugitive might safely be sent.

For example, one day in the autumn of 1837, an abolitionist in the town of Mexico, New York, was looking out his window when he saw a "colored man" enter the tavern across the street. "Someone asked if that was not one of *our* people," the abolitionist—probably a local tinsmith named Starr Clark—wrote in the *Friend of Man*, on February 28, 1838. He went on to describe what happened next: "I went over to the tavern, and saw the colored man sitting by the fire. After waiting till all had left the bar-room, I stepped carelessly toward him, and asked him if he was going to Oswego. No was the answer. Which way are you traveling?—No answer. Do you know what an abolitionist is?—No answer. I took a chair and sat down close to him; told him that I did not wish to intrude upon him, but that I was an abolitionist and friendly towards the colored people. The only answer he gave was that there was a difference in abolitionists. This was all I could get him to say, and I was about to give him up, when I observed to him that if he wanted any assistance, my store was directly opposite, and he could call over. For once he looked up and said, 'Sir what may I call your name?' I told him, and now came the change in his countenance. He thrust his hand into his pocket, and drew out two letters directed to me. . . . The letters were from brethren in the south part of the county, recommending him to me as a fugitive and a Christian; and so we found him to be." The abolitionist later learned that George had escaped by sea from somewhere in the South and had walked all the way from Pennsylvania to Onondaga County, where he had encountered a chain of abolitionists who passed him northward from friend to friend. On December 5 the local abolitionists helped him on his way to Canada.

By the late 1830s, thanks mainly to the dynamic effect of the proliferating antislavery societies, the Underground Railroad had taken recognizable form. Where apathy had ruled only a few years earlier, fugitives were now forwarded smoothly from town to town, county to county, and state to state. Oliver Johnson could confidently arrange for "Simon" to travel from western Pennsylvania to northern Vermont, a distance of six hundred miles. Starr Clark of Mexico could expect his collaborators elsewhere in Onondaga County to send fugitives to him as a matter of course, and knew that others in Oswego and Canada were standing by to receive them when he was ready to move them on. The fact that Clark felt free to report his own role in a newspaper also makes quite clear that the transit of fugitives was not only an open secret but also virtually risk free through large parts of the North. So secure did he feel that he even mentioned by name two other abolitionists—Hiram Gilbery of Schroepell, and a Deacon Gilbert, who had given the man a pair of boots—who assisted the fugitive along the way.

The fourth annual meeting of the New York Anti-Slavery Society in 1838 was, with good reason, an optimistic affair. From a despised fringe group, abolitionists had become a political force to be reckoned with. In 1837 alone, 161 new local societies had been formed in New York, more than any other state, and the state's abolitionists were contributing more than half the funds necessary to operate the national office in Manhattan. There were forty thousand committed abolitionists in the state, enough to deter the election of proslavery candidates to state office. The once-hostile state assembly had recently passed several resolutions favoring antislavery principles. Thirty-seven of the state's fifty-seven counties had antislavery societies, and five of them had placed antislavery libraries in every village. New York was not alone. After three years of intensive grassroots effort, public opinion had significantly shifted in other parts of the North as well. Between 1835 and 1836, the number of antislavery societies in the nation grew to more than five hundred, and then doubled again by 1837. That year the American Anti-Slavery Society claimed more than one hundred thousand members, and listed more than a thousand affiliates across the country.

And Gerrit Smith, who only three years earlier had regarded abolitionism as little more than a sideshow in the gallery of American reform, was now entering his third term as president of the New York Anti-Slavery Society. In years to come, his home in Peterboro would become a mecca for the most radical reformers in the nation. Among them would come William Lloyd Garrison, Lincoln's future Secretary of the Treasury Salmon P. Chase, the black abolitionists Henry Highland Garnett and Samuel Ringgold Ward, Susan B. Anthony and Elizabeth Cady Stanton, Harriet Tubman, John Brown (to whom Smith would sell a farm, and later provide money for his attack on Harpers Ferry), and an untold number of fugitive slaves.

On December 1, 1838, Smith wrote with graceful irony an open letter to newspapers about two guests who had recently enjoyed his hospitality, and in return had exposed their whip-scarred backs to his family and a number of his neighbors: "My Dear Sir, You will be happy to hear, that the two fugitive slaves, to whom in the brotherly love of your heart you gave the use of your horse, and are still making undisturbed progress toward the monarchical land whither republican slaves escape for the enjoyment of liberty. They had eaten their breakfast, and were seated in my wagon, before day-dawn, this morning. Fugitive slaves have before taken my house in their way, but never any, whose lips and persons made so forcible an appeal to my sensibilities and kindled in me so much abhorrence of the hell-concocted system of American slavery."

CHAPTER 9

A WHOLE-SOULED MAN

Colored people should mark the signs of the times, and be warned!

—DAVID RUGGLES

1

David Ruggles soared like a meteorite into the boiling human nebula of mid-1830s New York City, flaming red hot with outrage, creating in his own image a model for the Underground Railroad in the urban North, then burning out with a tragic suddenness that has left his name, indeed his very presence, all but forgotten today. A period sketch of Ruggles shows a man with small features, a narrow mustache, his head encased in a massive stovepipe hat, and rather weak, deep-set eyes framed by narrow wire-rimmed glasses, hinting at the threat of blindness that would plague him throughout his life. Ruggles was born to free parents in Norwich, Connecticut, in 1810, the oldest of five children. At seventeen he moved to Manhattan, and at nineteen owned a grocery store—how he acquired the capital for it is not known—specializing in "fresh Goshen butter" which he offered "for sale by the Firkin, Tub, or single Pound," as well as superior "Canton and Porto Rico Sugars," cheese, rum, gin, porter, and cider. In 1833 he gave up his store to become an agent for an antislavery newspaper, the *Emancipator*. Ruggles traveled at least as far as Pennsylvania selling subscriptions, delivering antislavery lectures that "excited the liveliest emotions in every heart," and making contacts that would prove valuable to the underground. He had been comparatively well educated, probably at a local sabbath school, an experience that had endowed him with a passion for learning and intellectual self-confidence, but that had hardly prepared him for the ruthless racial battlefield of New York.

As recently as the 1810s, New Yorkers had complained that their new city hall, a quarter mile north of Wall Street, lay inconveniently far out of town. Twenty years later, the city had raced far beyond city hall, every year bursting its limits anew, building and rebuilding, tearing down only to build itself up again in a different way. Manhattan's population had swelled from 120,350 in 1820 to 188,613, and by the late 1830s was approaching 300,000. It was still a low city, and along the waterfront, which defined its image for the outer world, the masts of sailing ships stood higher than anything else erected by man. Public services were primitive. There was no restriction on the number of people who could be packed into a single dwelling, no sewage system, and precious little police protection for the law-abiding in a society that seemed to grow more violent by the day. But in the dusty, churning air that stank of sewage, pigs, charcoal, and unwashed bodies, there was also a pervasive sense of opportunity not to be missed, of fast money to be made. The mood could be felt in the quickened pace of the high-stepping horses that pulled the green and red omnibuses, in the impatient cries of the men who sold fresh oysters and the girls who hawked hot corn, the fast foods of the day, in the fizz of the popular theaters that were sprouting along the old country road known as the Bowery, in the architectural pomp of the grand buildings that proclaimed the city's growing sense of power: the spectacular dome of the Mercantile Exchange with its fifteen-foot-high statue of Alexander Hamilton in its grand rotunda, the elegant facade of the New Centre Market, the new city prison, designed to resemble an Egyptian temple and known to all as "The Tombs," and the colonnaded splendor of city hall, with its confident allusions to imperial power.

The great shaping force of the city's life was its ever-widening commercial orbit. Workshops near the waterfront manufactured everything from mustard and playing cards, to furniture and locomotives. New canals, the Erie Canal foremost among them, drew commodities of all kinds toward the city from the innermost reaches of the agricultural heartland, and the more distant frontier, while its vast port welcomed both immigrants and ships from every corner of the world. On a single day, no fewer than 921 cargo ships lined the East River waterfront alone, and another 330 lay moored along the bank of the Hudson. The city's shipyards, the most productive in the country in 1833, that year turned out twenty-six ships and barks, seven brigs, thirty-six schooners, and five steamboats. The port also maintained a lucrative trade outfitting ships, including slavers, even though such business was technically barred by federal law. Nearly five hundred commercial houses specialized in foreign trade, and more than twice that number in domestic.

New York's prosperity was wedded to the South. The city formed the hinge of the so-called Cotton Triangle. New York ships carried consignments of cotton from New Orleans, Mobile, and Charleston to Liverpool, in England, and the French port of LeHavre, returned to New York with cargoes of manufactured goods, and then worked their way southward along the eastern seaboard, selling their goods and buying more cotton. (At least one-fourth of the cotton reaching Liverpool from the United States came through the East River waterfront.) In addition, hundreds of coastal trading ships brought Southern cargoes directly to New York, where the city's expanse of wharves and warehouses facilitated the transshipment of cotton directly to European mills, in the process enriching local middlemen, shipowners, insurers, and warehousemen. Southern planters, having virtually no commercial banks in their own region, depended grudgingly on New York agents to convert their profits from cotton into cash, and to speculate on their behalf in other commodities on the New York market; up to forty cents of every dollar paid for Southern cotton wound up in the hands of New York merchants. Many wealthy Southerners also kept second homes in New York, or vacationed in the city's luxurious hotels. When they came, they brought their black servants with them, knowing that New York law allowed them to maintain their slaves in the state for up to nine months, and confident that the city's accommodating magistrates would not trouble them unduly if they overstayed the deadline.

Racism was virulent. New York state's constitution unfairly applied property qualifications to disqualify all but a handful of black voters. African Americans were almost completely excluded from colleges and public schools, and segregated in theaters, eating places, and accommodations. They were compelled to cling to the outsides of the omnibuses that traveled the city's avenues and barred from going indoors on the steamboats that plied the city's waters. Even menial professions were hard for them to break into. When William S. Hewlett sought a cartman's license in 1836, the mayor turned him down, despite his having provided *forty* character references, "on the grounds of public opinion." Some people trained their parrots to curse every black who passed.

The city's political culture was also friendly to slavery. Slave hunters openly advertised their services in the newspapers. F. H. Pettis, a Virginian practicing law in New York, placed an ad—its title in bold caps: "IMPORTANT TO THE SOUTH"—announcing "to his friends and the public in general, that he has been engaged as Counsel and Adviser in General for a party whose business it is in the northern cities to arrest and secure runaway slaves. He has thus been engaged for several years, and as the act of Congress alone governs now in this city, in business of this sort, which renders it easy for the recovery of such property, he invites, post paid, communications to him, enclosing a fee of $20 in each case, and a power of Attorney minutely descriptive of the party absconded, and if in the northern region, he or she will soon be had. NB. New York City is estimated to contain 5,000 Runaway Slaves."

Fugitives were at the mercy of an informal and shifting ring that was known to abolitionists as the "New York Kidnapping Club." It included professional slave hunters, city constables, local lawyers, and allegedly the city recorder, Richard Riker, a power in the Democratic Party, and a former slave owner, who had declared that emancipation was a curse rather than a blessing for blacks, blaming it for the "prevalence of crime among free people of color." In practice, it was usually necessary for a man claiming to be the slave's owner only to appear before a magistrate and submit an affidavit in order to be permitted to take the slave back to his home state. It was not an uncommon sight for recaptured slaves to be seen being marched down Broadway in chains to a waiting steamer bound for the South. Seven-year-old Henry Scott, for instance, was physically snatched from his classroom by a city policeman and a Virginia planter who claimed him as his slave. Peter Martin, a fugitive who had lived in New York for four years, was assaulted by police and, when he tried to defend himself, clubbed to the ground and savagely beaten by a mob who came to the aid of the police. Francis Smith, a waiter, was preparing to leave for New Haven to be married when he was caught by slave hunters. Smith's fiancée tried to purchase his freedom, without success. After months in jail, he was sent back to slavery in Virginia. Other fugitives were jailed on trumped-up criminal charges, and then deported to the South before their lawyers were informed of what happened.

Most of the city's fifteen thousand or so black inhabitants lived packed alongside immigrant Irish around the Five Points, so named because of the five narrow streets that intersected there. For most of the nineteenth century, the area was a national by-word for squalor and mayhem, described by the *New York Mirror*, in one typical report, as a "loathsome den of murderers, thieves, abandoned women, ruined children, filth, drunkenness, and broils [brawls]." George Catlin, an artist best known for his portraits of Indians on the Great Plains, painted the Five Points, depicting a riotous scene of battling drunks, leering prostitutes, and intermingled races, which to most Americans of the time by itself suggested unspeakable wickedness and sin. Tenements had names such as "The Gates of Hell" and "Brickbat Mansion"; the most notorious of all was an abandoned brewery where as many as one thousand of the poorest Irish and African Americans lived crammed together, prostitutes plied their trade openly, and the dead were often interred beneath the basement's earthen floor. Everywhere in the neighborhood, lanes ran thick with a soup of rotting garbage and human waste, and pigs and other animals foraged in the fetid byways. "Saturate your handkerchief with camphor, so that you can endure the horrid stench," visitors to the area were advised by a Temperance worker.

Fueled by poverty, ethnic rivalries, and social dislocation, violence slithered restlessly through the city's life, without pattern or remedy. Mob violence was endemic. Only some of it was racial. White gangs like the Bowery Boys, the True Blue Americans, and the Atlantic Guards waged street battles over turf. Elections were an extension of street warfare, with hired gangsters blackjacking their opponents and serving as repeat voters at the polls. In 1833 the homes of prominent abolitionists were attacked by stone-throwing gangs, and on July 4 of the following year, mobs provoked by Democratic politicians and Southern sympathizers laid siege to the Chatham Street Chapel, a popular site for abolitionist meetings. The rioters then moved to City Hall Park, reported the *Sun*, "to act out their patriotism in knocking down the blacks." In the days that followed, mobs ranged through the Five Points, terrorizing African Americans, burning down black churches, groceries, and saloons, and sacking brothels. The violence was not limited to blacks, however: an Englishman who was caught had his eyes gouged out and both ears torn off by the rioters.

In November 1835 a mostly African-American group calling itself the Friends of Human Rights met "to ascertain, if possible, the extent to which the cruel practice of kidnaping men, women, and children is carried on in this city." The result was the formation of the Vigilance Committee of New York, the first organized effort on the part of African Americans to defend themselves against the city's racial lawlessness. David Ruggles was selected to serve as secretary, the committee's executive officer. He was already well-known among the city's small community of politically active African Americans. In 1833 he had called for "a union amongst our people without regard to sects or sectarian principles and one that will encourage schools for children and foster the arts and sciences." Convinced that "moral virtue" could only be acquired by observation, reading, and reflection, he opened a bookshop in his home on Lispenard Street, where he circulated antislavery publications and did job printing. When the bookstore was damaged by arsonists, unfazed, he opened a reading room for young blacks, who were excluded from the city's cultural institutions. Without "some centre of literary attraction for all young men whose mental appetites thirst for food," he warned, "many are in danger of being led into idle and licentious habits by the allurements of vice which surround them on every side." Some of his views pointed toward the black nationalism of the future. He envisioned racial separation by mutual consent, approvingly citing the example of the Jews, who were "standing proof that nations and people can live together in the same country, enjoy the same political and domestic equality, and never intermarry." When colonizationists accused the abolition movement of promoting racial "amalgamation" that would turn the nation into one of "mulattoes and mongrels," Ruggles retorted, "Amalgamation of the races! Now I for one detest the idea of amalgamation. I do not wish it, nor does any colored man or woman of my acquaintance, nor can instances be adduced where a desire was manifested by any colored person; but I deny that 'intermarriages' between the 'whites and blacks are unnatural.' "

Under Ruggles's leadership, the Vigilance Committee publicized descriptions of missing people, raised money for fugitives, hiring lawyers for them when necessary, and took legal action against ships' captains who trafficked in slaves. The committee also became the hinge upon which the Underground Railroad's operations turned in New York, with links that extended southward to Philadelphia, and north to central New York state, New England, and Canada. The needy came in many guises. Some were fleeing areas where laws had been enacted against free blacks, others were kidnap victims found aboard ships in New York harbor, and others were free persons abducted by kidnappers and sold into the cotton states. The committee also helped those recently arrived from the South who desperately needed immediate food, shelter, and transportation north. All this, Ruggles undertook to provide. "This business was almost wholly neglected previous to the organization of this committee," he wrote in the *Emancipator*. This, he added, was "*practical* abolition."

2

The Vigilance Committee consisted of about one hundred members, headed by a steering committee of five or six men led by Ruggles. Members financed the committee almost entirely with collections taken up among blacks. Each member carried a small book and entered in it the names of ten or twelve of his or her friends, and solicited from each a donation of one penny each week. In its first year the committee raised a total of $839.52, and disbursed $1228.71. The difference was probably made up from lump-sum contributions by wealthy whites, including the Tappans and Gerrit Smith, whom Ruggles had already approached for aid in establishing a school for African Americans.

Beyond its organizational structure, the committee was something new as a variant of the Underground Railroad. It was confrontational and street smart, and it was run almost entirely by African Americans. For the most part, it dispensed with the spiritualizing sanctimony that characterized white abolitionist organizations. Blacks did not have to explain to themselves, or to anyone else, why they thought slavery was wrong, and why something must be done about it, and immediately. Ruggles was not a pacifist. He wrote, "We cannot recommend non-resistance to persons who are denied the protection of equitable law, when their liberty is invaded and their lives endangered by avaricious kidnappers." Northern blacks had grown up in what were legally slave states only a few years earlier, and nearly all were just one or at most two generations removed from slavery themselves. Fugitive slaves were an integral part of their daily lives; they worked with them, they lived with them, they were married to them. Freeborn and fugitive alike knew that at any time they could be kidnapped and taken away to the South. Fugitives' fear of recapture was part of their own fear, emancipation an imperative that all could share.

While Ruggles accepted whites as allies—his closest was the elderly Isaac Hopper—he by no means regarded them as superiors, or as the natural leaders of the abolition movement. "The American Anti-Slavery Society has nothing to do 'officially' with concealing, abducting, or rescuing fugitive slaves," he stated. "The only 'combination organized' for any purpose relative to refugees is the New York Committee of Vigilance, which is an organization deriving no power, authority or instruction from the American Anti-Slavery Society, and having no connection with it at all." Initial expectations for the committee were not high. Even many of its supporters considered its plans both hazardous and hopeless. Ruggles, however, acted with a boldness that New Yorkers had never witnessed before on the part of a politically engaged black man. For the next three years he would yield ground to no one, even in the face of physical violence and withering prejudice. He also gave some of the men who appointed him more than they bargained for.

The committee's highest priority was the epidemic of kidnappings. "Let parents, and guardians, and children take warning. Our city is infested with a gang of kidnappers—Let every man look to his safety," the committee warned. "Colored people should mark the signs of the times, and be warned!" In particular, black sailors who signed on board southbound vessels were in danger of being sold there as slaves. The case of young Edward Watson illustrates all too sadly the official inertia against which Ruggles had to struggle. Watson was apprenticed to a man named Ayres, who arranged with the captain of the brig *Buenos Aires* to use him as a sailor and then sell him into slavery when the ship reached South Carolina. Learning of this beforehand, Ruggles applied for a writ of habeas corpus to one Judge Irving, but the magistrate refused on the ground that he felt ill and wanted to go to bed. A second judge refused to issue the writ because he was preparing to eat dinner, and ordered Ruggles out of his house. By the time Ruggles had obtained the writ, the next day, the boy had already been shipped south.

Among his admirers, Ruggles acquired something of a romantic aura as "a General Marion sort of man," renowned for "sleepless activity, sagacity, and talent," as one put it, evoking the exploits of a legendary Revolutionary War guerrilla. He boarded incoming ships to see whether slaves were being smuggled in, and boldly pushed his way into homes in fashionable neighborhoods to investigate the status of black domestics whom he suspected might be held in involuntary servitude. "Procuring the escape of a slave from bondage to liberty is a violation of no law of the land," he declared. "I may, I *must*, suffer the laws of the government under which I live, but I must not *obey* them if they are contrary to the laws of God . . . I would show, clearly, by the example of Paul and other Apostles, that wicked and unjust laws *must* be *resisted* even unto *death*."

In June 1838 Ruggles reported in detail how he had entered the house of D. K. Dodge, a slaveholder from South Carolina who maintained a home on Henry Street, in Brooklyn Heights, where he kept three slaves, one of them for four years, far longer than the nine months permitted to out-of-state slave owners by New York law. At least one of the slaves, a maidservant named Charity, had made contact with the Vigilance Committee and asked for help. Once admitted to the Dodge house, Ruggles simply refused to leave. Dodge's wife maintained that they had brought the slaves north specifically to set them free.

"Haven't I told you that you are free?" she asked Charity.

"You told me to *say so* if anybody ask me," Charity replied, emboldened by Ruggles's presence, "but you beat me here as much as ever, missee."

"Why, if Mrs. Dodge brought you here to be free, she would not treat you ill; but on the contrary, she would be kind to you and pay you wages," said Ruggles.

"Wages!" exclaimed Charity.

"Oh, no," said Dodge. "But I take good care of you."

At this point a neighbor, a Dr. McClennan, "a little fellow with a pair of stiff whiskers," suddenly appeared, apparently intending to evict Ruggles, whom he charged with being an intruder. Ruggles retorted that it was the doctor who was the true intruder, with no right to interfere "against liberty and the laws of the state."

"I am here to remove a disorderly person," McClennan declared.

"Find such a person here, and I will aid you in his removal," replied Ruggles. "I was invited here to relieve humanity."

"I wish you would *leave*, sir," McClennan repeated.

"I wish *you* would leave, sir," said Ruggles.

"You aggravate me," said the doctor.

"You don't aggravate me," replied Ruggles.

The doctor, looking over and under his spectacles, as though getting ready to use his rattan cane, visibly came to the conclusion, Ruggles supposed, that since the abolitionist was some inches taller and heavier, he would not attempt it. After further irritable debate over the consequences of bringing slaves into New York, the doctor at last begged Ruggles to wait until the man of the house returned before attempting to "carry off" any of the slaves.

"They are perfectly free to do as they please," said Ruggles blandly. "If they choose to remain, they can; I employ no force to remove them; if they go with me, I will protect them."

"I is free as a rat, and am going," Charity proclaimed. "If I was to stop here I should find myself dead tomorrow morning. I know you, missee."

Concluded Ruggles, "As I was then ready to leave, Charity took a bundle of rags, which were an apology for clothes, and with the editor, left her kind and affectionate mistress to take care of herself, and is now doing well."

The postscript to this story was not a happy one, and it grimly underscores the extreme precariousness of existence for the city's black poor. The Vigilance Committee found Charity a place to live, but she slipped into prostitution, became pregnant, and was abandoned by the father of the child. The committee finally washed its hands of her, and she returned to Brooklyn, where she begged support from the Dodge family. However, they never employed her again.

During the Vigilance Committee's first year of operation, Ruggles and his associates protected and gave aid to 335 men and women. But their tactics did not go unremarked. Proslavery newspapers viciously attacked him as a "sooty scoundrel" and as "the official ourang outang of the Anti-Slavery Society." More than once he was thrown into prison as an accessory to a case. An attempt to kidnap Ruggles himself was made in the early morning of December 28, 1835, when several notorious slave catchers, including two New York constables and a sailor from a suspected Portuguese slave ship, invaded his home as he made a hasty exit through the back door. The next morning Ruggles went to a city magistrate to complain, but he was seized and jailed by a constable named Boudinot, who had previously posed as an abolitionist to spy on the committee's activities. Boudinot, it turned out, held an open warrant empowering him to arrest any black person claimed by a certain Georgia slave catcher who was then active in New York. Ruggles gained his release, but he remained convinced that the slave catchers' plan had been to ship him south on the Portuguese brig.

Ruggles's aggressive leadership made the New York committee a model for vigilance committees in other cities, most notably Philadelphia. The Philadelphia committee, founded in August 1837, under the leadership of the prominent dentist James McCrummel (who had hosted William Lloyd Garrison in 1833), and Robert Purvis, a wealthy Charleston-born mulatto, was soon handling about one hundred fugitives a year. Among them was James Lindsey Smith, a lame eighteen-year-old shoemaker, whose experience offers an unusually detailed picture of how the underground operated. Smith, with two friends Lorenzo and Zip, stole a boat on the Cone River in Virginia and sailed as far as they could up Chesapeake Bay, then abandoned the boat and set off on foot in the direction of Pennsylvania. Smith's physical limitation slowed down the others, and they left him behind, in tears. Later that night, Smith was almost run over and killed by the first train that he had ever seen. (He was sure that it was some demonic creature transporting souls to hell, but felt heartened when he noticed that its only passengers were white people.) In despair, he was about to give himself up to the local authorities, when he reminded himself that he had already traveled 250 miles, and could at least try to go a little farther. It was a lucky decision. Reaching New Castle, Delaware, he ran into Lorenzo and Zip again, and the three of them boarded a ship bound for Philadelphia, nonplussed at their luck in succeeding in buying tickets without being questioned. Once in Philadelphia, Lorenzo and Zip took ship for Europe, leaving Smith to wander the streets looking for work. Confused and again despairing, he approached a black minister and asked for lodging for the night, but the man curtly refused, telling him to go to a tavern. Almost as an afterthought, the minister asked him if he was free. "Here I was in a great dilemma, not knowing what to do or say," Smith wrote. "He told me that if I was a fugitive I would find friends. I told him frankly that I was from the South and that I was a runaway." After interrogating Smith briefly, the minister arranged for Smith to stay with a black cobbler who was apparently a member of the underground. "After giving me a good supper, they secreted me in a little room called the fugitive's room, to sleep." The following day, the fifth after Smith had left Virginia, he was handed over to a group of abolitionists, including white Quakers, who decided on the spot, without explanation, to send him to Springfield, Massachusetts. The next morning, the cobbler took Smith to the dock and placed him on a steamboat for New York, with a letter addressed to David Ruggles. Ruggles then personally put him on a steamer for Hartford, Connecticut. Left to his own devices and having been given no pocket money, Smith slept on the deck amid heaps of cotton bales, and was fed only thanks to a waiter who took pity on him. At Hartford, he was met on the dock by an African American, who had been notified ahead of time by Ruggles. This man took Smith to his own house and introduced him to local abolitionists, from whom he solicited contributions (a total of three dollars) to send him on up the Connecticut River valley to Springfield.

Other fugitives, probably the majority, were forwarded to abolitionist settlements in upstate New York, or to Canada. By the late 1830s, many of these were dispatched by steamboat from New York City up the Hudson River to Albany or Troy, a ten-hour trip. From there they might be forwarded either via the Erie Canal to Oswego, or farther west to Rochester or Buffalo, and on to Canada. With luck, a fugitive could expect to be in Canada within a week after leaving the dock at the foot of Barclay Street, in Manhattan. Some fugitives traveled the much slower land route through the chain of Quaker farming communities along the eastern edge of New York state, either settling somewhere along the way, or continuing on ultimately to Vermont. In November 1838 Charles Marriott, a gentleman farmer and close friend of Isaac Hopper, wrote matter-of-factly from his home near the small city of Hudson to their mutual friend Rowland T.

Robinson, in Vermont: "Many fugitives from the South effect their escape. 3 passed through my hands last week."

3

It is often unclear why the underground chose to send fugitives by certain routes, or to particular destinations. Sometimes destinations were selected in accordance with the fugitives' own preferences, and other times on the basis of the forwarding agent's own biases, or the availability of work. Oliver Johnson, whose connections were mainly in New England, for instance, sent "Simon" all the way to Vermont because he knew that Rowland T. Robinson would give him work, and because he feared that he would sink into indolence in Canada; "Simon" would have been spared an arduous overland trek had Burleigh passed him on to abolitionists in nearby Ohio. Fugitives with experience in the maritime trades were often sent to the whaling port and abolitionist stronghold of New Bedford, Massachusetts. One of them was an intense, well-built young man with an exceptionally penetrating gaze, named Frederick Bailey, who appeared at David Ruggles's door in September 1838. Of the thousand or so persons whom Ruggles helped during his three-year tenure, none had anywhere near as much impact on history as the frightened and bedraggled Bailey, who had spent his few previous days of freedom as a vagabond on the streets of Manhattan.

The twenty-year-old Bailey had grown up on plantations on the Eastern Shore of Maryland. Three years earlier, he had planned an escape by boat, similar to the lame James Smith's, but had been betrayed at the last minute by a black informer. Luckier than many would-be fugitives, he was brought by his master to Baltimore, where he was put to work learning caulking. (He helped build three ships for the slave trade, the *Delorez*, the *Teayer*, and the *Eagle*.) In Baltimore, perhaps the freest city in the South for blacks, he had lived in a state of negotiated slavery, eventually hiring out his own labor and paying his master a fee of three dollars at the end of each week, and providing for his own board and lodging. By the time he decided to flee northward, he had already acquired a common-law wife, a free woman named Anna Murray. Although he was living a life far more autonomous than that of a field hand, even relative freedom proved infectious. "I could see no reason why I should, at the end of each week, pour the reward of my toil into the purse of my master," he wrote in later life. "When I carried to him my weekly wages, he would, after counting the money, look me in the face with a robber-like fierceness, and ask, 'Is this all?' " Bailey's discontent grew, and it took all the self-control that he could muster to suppress the rage that threatened always to get the better of him.

Sometime in the summer of 1838, he and Anna worked out a plan for his escape. Bailey had saved some money from his work on the docks. Anna sold a featherbed and added the proceeds to his nest egg. On September 3, dressed in a sailor's red shirt and flat, broad-brimmed hat, carrying seaman's papers lent to him by a friend, and feeling as terrified as "a murderer fleeing from justice," Bailey stepped aboard a train for Wilmington, Delaware. Three times along the way he saw men who knew him, two of them white. Bailey was sure that one of the whites, a German blacksmith, recognized him too, but to the fugitive's immense relief the man apparently hadn't the heart to betray him. At Wilmington Bailey boarded a steamboat for Philadelphia, and by that afternoon he was riding northward on a train to New York. Less than twenty-four hours after he left Baltimore, Manhattan's teeming waterfront came into view.

The "unspeakable joy" that Bailey felt upon his arrival in New York was subverted by raw fear. Soon after landing, he encountered another fugitive slave whom he had once known in Maryland, who warned him forcefully that no one in New York could be trusted. The city, he said, was full of Southerners and hired men on the lookout for fugitives, and even blacks would betray him for a few dollars. The man was even frightened of Bailey, for fear that he too might be a spy. Afraid to ask for work, Bailey roamed the streets day and night, he recalled years later, "without home, without acquaintance, without money, without credit, without work, and without any definite knowledge as to what course to take or where to look for succor." Finally, with trepidation, he took the risk of divulging his plight to a friendly black sailor named Stewart, who approached him near the Five Points, in front of "The Tombs." After providing him with some refreshment at his own house nearby, the seaman led Bailey the few blocks to David Ruggles's home, on Lispenard Street. Bailey remained hidden there for several days while Ruggles arranged for Anna Murray to come to

New York from Baltimore. "Notwithstanding my hopeless, houseless, and helpless condition," Bailey would write, the two were formally married in Ruggles's home, by the Reverend James W. C. Pennington of the Congregational church, who nine years earlier had himself escaped from slavery in Maryland, as the fugitive blacksmith Jim Pembroke.

As was the case for so many others, physical escape had been only the first step in Pembroke's liberation, a process that was to take years, before he had achieved what he regarded as true independence of mind and soul. After leaving William Wright's farm, near Gettysburg, in 1829, Pembroke had spent seven months working for another Quaker family near Philadelphia, and then made his way to New York, where he settled in a small town in the present-day borough of Queens. There, having adopted the name Pennington, he began attending school, and for the first time learned how many slaves there actually were in the United States. "The question completely staggered my mind," he later wrote, "and finding myself more and more borne down with it, until I was in an agony; I thought I would make it a subject of prayer to God, although prayer had not been my habit, having never attempted it but once." For three weeks he prayed and fasted, asking himself over and over, "What shall I do for the slave?" He resolved to train for the ministry. After mastering "logic, rhetoric, and the Greek testament, without a master," and—an even harder task—at last "throwing off the crouching aspect of slavery," he had recently been licensed to preach.

As Jim Pembroke had done, Frederick Bailey now selected for himself a new name, which both concealed his old identity and symbolized his rebirth as a free man: Frederick Johnson. He had been intending to go to Canada, but Ruggles argued against it. Having learned that the fugitive was an experienced ship's caulker, Ruggles decided to send him to New Bedford instead, telling him that he should easily be able to get work there. After the wedding, Ruggles presented the "Johnsons" with a five-dollar bill and their marriage certificate, proof of a sacrament that was all but denied to slaves in the South. Johnson then hoisted one part of their baggage onto his shoulder and Anna the rest, and with Ruggles in the lead they set out for the waterfront, where Ruggles personally placed them aboard the steamboat *John W. Richmond* bound for Newport, Rhode Island.

The Johnsons were taken in hand at Newport by two friendly

Quakers, who kept them company in the overland stagecoach to New Bedford. Ruggles had provided them with a letter of introduction to Nathan Johnson, a confectioner and one of the most prominent blacks in a city that was home to more than one thousand African Americans out of a total population of some twelve thousand. Frederick Johnson was amazed by what he saw. Having been taught to believe that slavery was the only basis of real wealth, he had expected to find New Englanders as impoverished as "white trash" in the South. But instead he found the houses even of New Bedford's laboring classes more abundantly supplied with conveniences and comforts than were the homes of many slave owners in Maryland. A man endowed with a physical love of work that was matched only by his intellectual energy, he was also impressed by the countless ingenious "contrivances" that here took the place of slave labor, as well as the sheer "earnestness" with which free men attacked their jobs. He knew that he was going to like life in New Bedford. But there was the unexpected problem of his name. Nathan Johnson informed him that there were so many African Americans in New Bedford by the name of Johnson that they already had a hard time being distinguished from one another. Nathan Johnson had recently been enjoying Sir Walter Scott's epic poem "Lady of the Lake," and had taken a particular fancy to one of its heroic Scottish characters. With the fugitive's willing consent, Nathan Johnson renamed him once again. Henceforth, he would be known—to his future collaborators on the Underground Railroad, and around the world—as Frederick Douglass. As Ruggles's name seeped out of public consciousness, Douglass would become the most famous African American of his generation.

4

While the newly minted Douglasses were settling into life in New Bedford, Ruggles was struggling with ebbing success to keep body and mind together. As early as the summer of 1837, his chronically poor health had compelled him to leave the city for a time and take refuge in the country. By early 1838 he was threatened with total blindness. That November he announced that he would have "to retire from the exciting conflict," in hope of regaining his health, particularly his rapidly diminishing eyesight through "the practice of some skillful Oculist." His illness was also nurtured "by reasons of great mental anxiety, occasioned by frequent causes which are unavoidable in the field in which I labor." He was on the brink of a nervous breakdown.

The troubling case of a fugitive named Tom Hughes finally pushed him over the edge. One evening in August 1838 there was a knock at the door of Isaac Hopper's home on Eldridge Street, in lower Manhattan. Henry Clark, a waiter from Contoit's on Broadway, was standing outside with another black man. (Hopper's address, like Ruggles's, was well known, and easily found by anyone seeking help from the underground.) The stranger's hair was bushy and full, and he had on a black beaver hat, a white coat, light-colored trousers, and a neckcloth. Clark introduced the man as Tom Hughes, and mentioned that he needed a place to stay the night. Hopper assumed that the twenty-two-year-old Hughes was a fugitive. It was a common enough occurrence for Hopper. "When fugitive slaves have called upon me and asked my protection, I could not take any steps to return them into bondage," Hopper wrote. "In me, it would be a crime to do so."

Hopper, at sixty-seven, was quite old by the standards of his time. He clung quaintly to idiosyncratic customs, such as ringing a farmer's cow bell when it was time for dinner, saying that it reminded him of his boyhood in rural New Jersey. A fastidious man, he took a cold bath every day and allowed no particle of mud or dust to remain on the knee breeches, long stockings, and buckled shoes that he continued to wear long after they had fallen out of fashion. He was something of an elder statesman for younger members of the abolition movement, who gathered at his bookstore on Broadway to hear how he had once helped to liberate the slave of South Carolina Senator Pierce Butler and other colorful anecdotes of his years in Philadelphia. A living anachronism though he may have been in some respects, his resolve remained undulled after forty years of antislavery work. On at least one occasion he was threatened on the street by a gang of slave hunters armed with bowie knives and pistols, and on another he was knocked down from behind and beaten savagely on Chatham Street, in an incident that left him incapacitated for days. Warned by friends to put up his shutters and flee during the 1834 riots, he replied, "I'll do no such thing. Dost thou think I am such a coward as to forsake my principles, or conceal them, at the bidding of a mob?" Deterred by his calm demeanor, the mob left him in peace, and went off to pillage Lewis Tappan's home instead. As his loathing for slavery deepened, Hopper had come to feel, as had William Lloyd Garrison, that the Northern states might have to secede from the Union lest they be corrupted beyond redemption by the political undertow of Southern slavery. "Far better, in my view, that this should take place, if it can be effected without violence, than to remain as we are; when a peaceable citizen cannot enter your territory on his own lawful business, without the risk of being murdered by a ruthless mob." This was no mere polemic. In January 1837 his son John, a lawyer, had been dragged from his hotel room in Savannah, Georgia and nearly lynched by a drunken mob after he was recognized by a proslavery constable from New York.

The morning after Tom Hughes's appearance, Hopper, who knew that his own home might be under surveillance, sent the black man to a safer location in the neighborhood. The day after that, an advertisement appeared in the *Sun*, offering a reward for the apprehension of a "mulatto man" who had stolen more than seven thousand dollars from a house on Varick Street. Hopper intuited that Hughes might be the person the ad referred to. When Hopper questioned him, Hughes claimed that although he was the man in question, he was guilty of nothing, saying that it was a common slaveholder's ploy to advertise for a fugitive as an alleged thief rather than as a runaway slave. While Hopper was meeting with Hughes, a fellow Quaker abolitionist named Barney Corse and David Ruggles were calling on the editor of the *Sun*. They learned that the robbery had really taken place, and that Hughes was in fact the culprit.

The money had been stolen from an india rubber belt that Hughes's owner, John P. Darg, had left in his trunk, to which Hughes, until then a trusted servant, had the key. Hughes had been born the bastard son of a wealthy Virginian, and at the age of thirteen was taken to Kentucky by his master's legitimate son, his own half-brother, and sold along with a consignment of five hundred slaves bound for Louisiana. He was purchased by a gambler, and eventually by Darg, who was also a gambler as well as a casual speculator in slaves. Darg, now a resident of Arkansas, was originally from New York, and had come to town to visit his parents. Hughes later claimed, not too plausibly, that he had stolen the money only to bargain for his freedom.

What now followed entangled Hopper, Ruggles, and Corse in a byzantine plot crafted by shadowy proslavery figures in the police department that was intended, it seems, to destroy the city's most prominent underground figures in one decisive sweep. Hopper quickly realized that to lend assistance to a thief could fatally injure the antislavery cause. Confronted with the truth, Hughes confessed to Hopper that he had given portions of the money to Clark, and to another man named Jackson, who had in turn sent part of it to a third man in Albany. Meanwhile, Ruggles, Corse, and Hopper's son-in-law James S. Gibbons called on Darg and offered to help recover the money, if Darg agreed to manumit Hughes. This Darg readily agreed to do. When Darg asked if they knew where Hughes was, Ruggles replied boldly, if untruthfully, "He's on his way to Canada." In fact, Hughes was holed up in a boardinghouse around the corner from Hopper's home. Corse, meanwhile, was sent to Albany for the money that Jackson had sent there. Upon his return, Corse and Gibbons brought the recovered money to Darg's home. They were in the process of handing it to him when two constables rushed into the room, snatched up the money, and arrested Corse on the spot for "compounding a felony." Ruggles, who was not even present, was charged as an accomplice and eventually thrown into "a filthy cell, among several individuals of the most abandoned character." Hughes was taken into custody, and offered his freedom in return for testifying against the Quakers.

In October Hughes was indicted for grand larceny. Corse, Ruggles, Hopper, and Gibbons were charged with harboring Hughes and helping him avoid prosecution. Antiabolitionist newspapers reacted with their customary venom, accusing the Quakers and Ruggles of "abducting" Hughes, and abetting the theft itself. During the trials that ensued, the authorities resorted to gross intimidation in an attempt to make their case. Corse was warned that if he did not cooperate, "it will create a riot, and your house may be pulled down." The police also tried, unsuccessfully, to force Clark's wife (Clark, the waiter, had himself fled the city), to manipulate Hopper into confessing that he had been a partner to the theft. The district attorney openly urged the jury to "appease the South" by convicting Corse, and in the jury room, one of the jurors freely admitted that he would never acquit an abolitionist. On the stand, Hopper declared that he never intended to yield up Hughes to his master, but that he had never taken any measures to keep Hughes from his master either. Ruggles defiantly stated that if it was true that Hughes was a slave to Darg, and the advertisement was true, it only meant that the slave had manumitted himself, and collected what was due him in the process.

In the end, Hughes's deal with the prosecutors fell through, and he was sentenced to two years in prison. His testimony was so transparently unreliable that the case against Hopper and Gibbons was soon abandoned, as eventually was the one against Corse. Although the threat of legal action hung over Ruggles for more than a year, no evidence against him was ever produced, and the charges against him were finally dropped in November 1839. But by then Ruggles was seriously ill. He had always been a high-strung, emotionally vulnerable man who concealed his sensitivity beneath fierce self-control, a man who deliberately sought out confrontation but suffered inwardly from its emotional impact. It required superhuman self-control of a black man to live as risky a public life as Ruggles had chosen. "At all times," he wrote, "it behooves us to place the most careful watch over our own demeanor, living down, by consistent and virtuous conduct, every charge which may be brought against us." But the years of worry, fatigue, and stress were finally exacting their toll.

Unfortunately, Ruggles had also managed to irritate Lewis Tappan, the most influential, and the wealthiest, antislavery man in the city. "Like most every colored man I have ever known, he was untrustworthy about money matters," snapped Tappan, who in spite of his abolitionist principles declined to employ black clerks in his store. "I do not accuse him or others as deficient in integrity, but no regular account appears to be kept of money received or paid." As if this were not enough, Ruggles had become enmeshed in a debilitating libel suit with his former friend Reverend Samuel E. Cornish, one of the founders of the Vigilance Committee, who now attacked him mercilessly in the pages of the *Colored American*. The conservative Cornish may already have resented Ruggles's impulsive and confrontational style. But the feud turned vicious when Cornish blamed Ruggles for a costly libel suit that was lodged against the newspaper by an alleged kidnapper, whose name Ruggles had mentioned in a published report of the Vigilance Committee. "Great in promises and in performances nothing," one of Cornish's broadsides cruelly snarled. Another charged him with being "reckless of principle," his brain "distempered," his imagination "heated." The internecine strife saddened Ruggles deeply. His sense of personal defeat was palpable. "There is too much personal quarreling among us," he wrote. "But for the sake of the cause, I bleed in silence." The black abolitionist William Whipper, a key underground figure in Pennsylvania, begged publicly for a cessation of the attacks. He wrote in his own newspaper, the *National Reformer*, "Let not a faithful public servant that has lost his eyesight in the cause of liberty, suffer a worse infliction by having his character assailed because he is now too poor to defend it."

Ruggles's reputation was tottering, and his sight was indeed rapidly failing. He was also broke. After years of working without salary, he was compelled to plead for back pay from the Vigilance Committee, and was awarded four hundred dollars. Ruggles had already sold the "last scrap" of his property to raise funds "to seek treatment for the opacity which affects our eyes." But he now had to spend virtually every penny of it on his defense in the Darg case. For a man as proud as Ruggles, it must have felt deeply humiliating when he even had to beg friends and distant acquaintances for money. Gerrit Smith gave twenty dollars, the largest single donation.

In January 1839 Ruggles resigned as secretary of the Vigilance Committee. Destitute and almost blind now, he fell back on the charity of friends in New Rochelle. For the next several years, he was "repeatedly bled, leeched, cupped, plastered, blistered, salivated, dosed with arsenic, nux-vomica, iodine, strychnine and other poisonous drugs" which caused an "enlargement of his liver, the worst kind of dyspepsia, irritation of the lungs, chronic inflammation of the bowels, piles, nervous and mental debility" and a numb "state of the skin." Astonishingly enough, he survived all this. He would live on until 1849, and would even manage to reinvent himself as the proprietor of a health spa in New England. But at the age of twenty-eight, his most important antislavery work was effectively over. Under his leadership, the Vigilance Committee helped or rescued something in excess of one thousand men and women. After his departure, the committee went into decline, but other less flamboyant men would eventually pick up the work that he had left off. Frederick Douglass never forgot what Ruggles had done for him. "He was a whole-souled man," he wrote of his benefactor, "fully imbued with the love of his afflicted and hunted people, and took pleasure in being to me, as was his wont, 'Eyes to the blind, and legs to the lame.' "

PART THREE

CONFRONTATION

THE 1840s

CHAPTER 10

ACROSS THE OHIO

A good man lives in that house, go to it and go in, and you will be safe.

—ANONYMOUS KENTUCKIAN,
TO A FUGITIVE SLAVE

1

In August 1844 Calvin Fairbank, a young seminarian from Oberlin College, was scouting out a route by which he might guide a family of fugitives from Lexington, Kentucky into Ohio. Fairbank had been bringing slaves across the Ohio River since he was twenty-one. He had rescued a total of forty-three over the last seven years, working independently or with one or two partners, often on his summer vacations from college. He had just completed an exploratory trip to Lexington, and was now crossing the river on the ferry to the Ohio town of Ripley, where he had been told that "friends of the fugitives" could be found. He intended to make contact with them, and he wanted their help when he brought his runaways north.

From the ferry Fairbank noticed a man crossing in a skiff. He hailed him.

"Mister, are you a Kentuckian?"

The man replied that he was.

Indicating Ripley, Fairbank asked, "Well, what kind of place is this?"

"It is a black, dirty, Abolition hole, sir."

Inquiring further, Fairbank got the man to point out the homes of several well-known abolitionists. "And Dr. Rankin occupies the one on the hill," the man concluded, indicating a red brick farmhouse that stood by itself on a steep bluff overlooking the town.

John Rankin was arguably the most formidable antislavery man on this stretch of the river. Fairbank probably had read the immensely influential public letters attacking slavery that Rankin had written to his brother in 1824 and 1825, which were widely reprinted in the *Liberator* and the publications of the American Anti-Slavery Society. Rankin had recruited hundreds of Ohioans to the abolitionist cause, and thanks to his indefatigable efforts the Underground Railroad was as firmly rooted in Ripley as the mighty oak trees that lent their deep and concealing shade to the precincts of his farm, across which as many as two thousand fugitives eventually would pass. In spite of his notoriety, Rankin and his brood of stalwart children—there were nine sons and four daughters—continued to dwell on their exposed hilltop, their home a beckoning symbol of freedom that could be seen for many miles along the river.

Pictures of John Rankin show a rather flinty-looking man: high white forehead towering over a long nose, uncompromising eyes, and thin, compressed lips, a face of sharp delineations, without softening half-tones. It is not a misleading image. Rankin's life was exclusively organized around a fierce, outspoken, and evangelical opposition to slavery. He was born in Jefferson County, Tennessee, in 1793, into a family of Scotch Presbyterians who had come to America from the North of Ireland. His father, a Revolutionary War veteran who had personally witnessed the surrender of Cornwallis at Yorktown, "was remarkable for the purity of his morals," Rankin wrote, taking his offspring to revival meetings whenever he could, and drilling them in the writings of obscure Scottish clerics. His mother, a gentler figure, had pronounced antislavery views, which impressed themselves on him at an early age.

As a child, he was tortured by spiritual anxieties. After church on

Sundays, while other young people skylarked, he felt obsessed with death, judgment, and eternity. The doctrine of election and foreordination in particular filled him with "anguish of spirit." He tried to explain them away, "but it was a vain effort." He also brooded over slavery, which he saw as a living sin oozing through the deep valleys of Tennessee. He was fortunate to attend Washington College in Jonesboro, which was run by an eminent Princeton University graduate, Dr. Samuel Doak. Himself a slaveholder, Doak taught his students that slavery was morally wrong, although like most Southern Christians he justified it with the argument that the danger of servile revolution was too great to risk actually setting slaves free. For Rankin there would be no such compromise.

Once ordained as a minister, Rankin ran into trouble immediately. He resigned from his first congregation because it would not tolerate his antislavery views. He then settled in eastern Kentucky, where antislavery men lived interspersed with slave owners, and he believed that he would be permitted to preach to the local slaves. Since it was a criminal offense to teach slaves to read, Rankin started a Sunday school in which only oral instruction was given, and only slaves who had written permission from their masters were accepted. One day, however, a mob of whites armed with clubs drove the slaves off. Rankin then gathered them in a friend's kitchen, but the slaves were ambushed and beaten on the way home. Disgusted by the behavior of his fellow whites, Rankin sold his property at a sacrifice, and on New Year's Day 1822 moved his family across the Ohio River to Ripley, Ohio, where the local Presbyterian church had invited him to serve as its pastor, at a salary of five hundred dollars per year.

Ripley was then in its commercial heyday, a bustling town of about three thousand, its economy fueled by river traffic and the businesses that sustained it, including a small ship-building industry. It was also one of the most important pork-butchering and packing towns in the West. Rankin's son John Jr. estimated that, as a boy, he had "fired the kettles that had scalded sixty thousand hogs one year and sixty-two thousand another year." Steamboats linked Ripley with ports from Pittsburgh to St. Louis, and in the spring flatboats came down the creeks and rivers by the hundreds with cargoes of corn, tobacco, beef, whiskey, lumber, lime, and poultry destined for markets as far away as New Orleans. Rankin initially found Ripley an "exceedingly immoral" place "badly infested with infidelity, Universalism and whiskey," where the Presbyterians were heavily outnumbered by "infidels," and swearing, frolicking, and dancing were openly tolerated. He went to work with Old Testament ferocity, forming Bible classes and Sunday schools, organizing satellite churches in the surrounding towns, denouncing saloons, and fulminating against farmers who celebrated their harvest with whiskey. He apparently had an impact, for in 1837 a traveler from New York declared Ripley to be "very pleasantly situated and the most moral place I was ever in."

In his preaching, Rankin tirelessly reiterated three basic principles: that all men were created equal, that God had "made of one blood all nations of men," and that every man ought either to do his own work or pay the man who does it for him. He thundered with his East Tennessee twang, "Let us be willing to go down and do the lowest service in Christ's kingdom, and labor to elevate the lowest of our race, that they may become the sons and daughters of the Almighty." For Rankin, each suffering slave embodied a mortal vision of the sacred. The loss of a fugitive to slave catchers was thus not just a tactical defeat but a spiritual catastrophe. When Rankin learned that a fugitive who had been safe in the North had returned to Kentucky to rescue his family and had, along with them, been captured and reenslaved, he "was seized with such anguish of spirit that it seemed as if there were nothing in creation that could cheer me."

Rankin can be seen as an emblematic figure among white radicals in much the way that David Ruggles can among blacks—a bridge from the pacifist style of the early nineteenth century to the confrontational activism of mid-century. Both men's writings and public utterances ran equally hot with moral outrage, but their styles differed considerably. Where Ruggles was impetuous to the point of rashness, Rankin avoided unnecessary risks. And while Ruggles pursued his work in often painful, underfinanced isolation, Rankin could rely on a disciplined phalanx of collaborators. He had another advantage that Ruggles could never have: he was a white man in a society that with rare exceptions treated even a brilliant black man like Ruggles with barely concealed contempt. Ruggles had burned himself out in less than five years. Rankin would serve their cause in Ripley without interruption for more than thirty.

The Northwest had changed since Josiah Henson and Jarm Logue had made their way north through the wilderness. Where Indians had roamed, new fields were everywhere being cleared, new houses built, barns erected, orchards planted, and roads pushed through the forest (although in much of the region they were still so poorly maintained that people referred to them as "mud roads" even when the dust was thickest). In the north, livestock was plentiful, and in the southwest, including the area around Ripley, hogs were raised in such profusion that several towns that lived on the slaughtering trade proudly claimed the sobriquet "Porkopolis." But it was still a rough land, full of proud, self-confident men who were in a hurry to acquire land and get rich fast, men who wore their clothes caked with mud, their hair long, and spoke a language that blended the idioms of the Carolinas and Kentucky, New York and New England. As the 1840s dawned they were increasingly "tetchous" over the issue of slavery, "contrarious" if challenged, and ready to engage in violent "ructions" if pressed too hard.

Throughout the region, color prejudice against blacks was entangled with the pragmatic bigotry of businessmen and farmers whose economic interests were interwoven with those of the South. In 1832, a committee of the Ohio House of Representatives had menacingly reported that free blacks represented "a serious political and moral evil" that threatened white citizens of the state. Five years later Caleb Atwater, an influential Cincinnatian, declared, "As a state it is [in] our interest . . . to have slavery continued in the slave holding states, for a century yet, otherwise our growth will be checked." In September 1841 organized mobs had once again attacked blacks in Cincinnati, dragging barbers and waiters out of their places of employment, threatening the homes of abolitionists, and at one point even turning a cannon on a black neighborhood near Sixth Street and Broadway. Large majorities continued to support laws that barred blacks from testifying against whites in court and from service on juries, as well as from the public schools, asylums, and poorhouses, even as abolitionist agitation reached fever pitch. "The whole country was like a huge pot in a furious state of boiling over," recalled Levi Coffin's nephew Addison Coffin, who followed his uncle to Indiana in 1842. The twenty-year-old North Carolinian was overwhelmed by "the contending, declaiming, denouncing, vilifying, swearing and vulgarity" that filled the community. "It was almost universal for ministers of the gospel to run into the subject in all their sermons; neighbors would stop and argue pro and con across the fence; people traveling along the road would stop and argue the point; at mills, stores, shops, everywhere it was abolition, proslavery, niggers, amalgamation, nigger wives, and all other such."

The new decade was a time of transformation for abolitionism. The American Anti-Slavery Society was, in a sense, a victim of its success. It had grown with astonishing speed since its founding in Philadelphia barely a decade before. But serious cracks soon began to show. By the end of the 1830s, William Lloyd Garrison had adopted a cluster of radical positions that were unacceptable to more conventional abolitionists. He rejected the Constitution because it incorporated tolerance of slavery, and advocated the secession of the North in order to separate it from the sins of the South. He declared in the *Liberator*, "*My hope for the millennium begins where Dr. Beecher's expires—viz.*, AT THE OVERTHROW OF THIS NATION." He scandalized evangelicals—who made up almost the entire rank and file of the movement—by suggesting that not everything in the Bible was divinely inspired, and by disparaging clergymen as "blind leaders of the blind, dumb dogs that cannot bark, spiritual popes—that . . . love the fleece better than the flock." Garrison's opponents feared, with some cause, that antislavery would be submerged in Garrison's wider reformist agenda. Lewis Tappan, for instance, regarded the Protestant churches as the most effective agencies for advancing the abolitionist cause, and felt deep suspicion of anyone who was not a professed evangelical. "I sometimes fear we have greatly erred in associating with ungodly men in the Anti S. Enterprise," he wrote to Gerrit Smith, who tried his best to remain on good terms with both factions. The last straw, at least for Tappan and the powerful circle of evangelicals based in New York, was Garrison's embrace of women's rights, including the participation of women in antislavery organizations on an equal basis with men. In 1839 Tappan's supporters, who represented the great majority of the movement's membership, as it proved, walked out of the American Anti-Slavery Society, leaving its rump to Garrison. They then met to form an entirely new organization, the American and Foreign Anti-Slavery Society, singing at the top of their lungs, "*Lo! What an entertaining sight/Are brethren who agree.*"

Many white abolitionists had also given up hope that gentle admonition would convince slaveholders to relinquish their human property. Despite decades of appeals to Christian morality, the number of slaves in the United States had steadily increased to just under two and a half million by 1840, more than double the figure at the beginning of the century. The political landscape offered only unpalatable alternatives. Neither of the major parties showed the least sign of being willing to challenge slavery's overwhelming power in Washington. Abolitionists had only contempt for President Martin Van Buren. As Andrew Jackson's vice president, Van Buren had provided the tie-breaking vote in the Senate that prohibited postmasters from delivering any abolitionist literature where it was prohibited by state law, and in his own 1837 inaugural address he had blamed mob violence on abolitionists' "reckless disregard for the consequences of their actions." Van Buren's Whig opponent in 1840, William Henry Harrison, as a member of Congress had voted to introduce slavery into Illinois, and he had publicly asserted that in his opinion the constitutional guarantees of freedom of speech and the press did not apply to abolitionists. Into this vacuum Gerrit Smith and his upstate New York supporters that year launched the Liberty Party, the first political party in American history to advocate the immediate abolition of slavery, its only platform. Its nominee for president was James G. Birney, a former Kentucky slave owner who had become converted to abolitionism. As befitted its origins in the Burned Over District of central New York, the party spoke with a distinctly evangelical voice, calling upon all abolitionists to "Vote as you pray, and pray as you vote." Although the Liberty Party won only about 7 percent of the vote that year, and would never win much more than that, it would serve as the main national channel of political action for abolitionists throughout the 1840s. It also represented the first crucial step in forcing slavery onto the nation's agenda, a process that would finally be complete with the founding of the Republican Party in 1856. Those who dared to vote for Birney did so at their peril. In Cincinnati, for example, one Samuel Ogden cast his vote at the Cheviot Hotel, and was instantly attacked by proslavery men who beat him senseless and trampled him in the mud.

Although John Rankin would later join the Liberty Party, he voted as a staunch Whig that year. He had met Harrison personally, "and admired the manly stand he had publicly taken in favor of the use of the Bible in the public schools." (In contrast to many abolitionists, who advocated emancipation without condition, Rankin believed that the only peaceful way to free the slaves was through their outright purchase and emancipation by the national government; he estimated the total cost at one billion dollars.) Gerrit Smith, even more of an absolutist than Rankin, took his defection at the polls as a personal affront. In an open letter in the

Philanthropist he called Rankin's support for Harrison "wicked presumption" and a "tempting of God": "What—that dear old pioneer of the Anti-Slavery cause, contribute to make those rulers of the nation, who are in favor of protracting the bondage of the slave? Impossible! I repeat, Impossible!" Rankin replied graciously, "I offer no excuses. If I am in error, it is [a] matter of deep regret, and I hope you will not cease your efforts to lead me into truth."

2

Disillusionment with the national parties fostered the growth of the Underground Railroad as more and more Americans became willing to break laws that they believed to be sinful but impossible to change by political means. As Gerrit Smith put it in an article in the *Friend of Man*, the organ of the New York Anti-Slavery Society, "If there be human enactments against our entertaining the stricken stranger—against our opening our door to our poor, guiltless, and unaccused colored brother pursued by bloodthirsty kidnappers—we must, nevertheless, say with the apostle: 'We must obey God rather than man.' "

The underground was expanding nowhere more rapidly than in the Ohio River valley. Once across the river, fugitives who managed to make contact with the underground could, with some confidence, hope to be passed in safety from town to town and from farm to farm all the way to the Great Lakes. Although their total can never be known, probably more northbound fugitives crossed the region that extended from eastern Ohio to central Indiana than any other part of the free states. In contrast to Pennsylvania, whose steeply corrugated and thinly populated landscape of southwest-to-northeast ridges funneled most fugitives into the narrow Philadelphia–to–New York corridor, Ohio and Indiana formed a wide, comparatively flat expanse that was webbed with roads leading north to Lake Erie, and peopled with the two kinds of communities that were most valuable for underground transit: free black settlements and well-organized white abolitionists. The geographical distance from the slave states to Canada was also short. No place in the Ohio River valley between Marietta, Ohio, and Cincinnati was more than two hundred miles from

Lake Erie, and from Wellsville, Ohio, across the river from the northernmost point in Virginia, the distance was only ninety miles. The speed of travel along the underground lines varied considerably. "Our aim was safety not speed, for it made little difference to the fugitive whether he was a week or a month in getting to Canada, so that he got there safely and was fed on the way," Isaac Beck, a longtime conductor in Sardinia, Ohio, near Ripley, told a newspaper reporter later in his life.

In all the Southern border states, blacks both slave and free lent assistance to the underground by directing fugitives to the best places to cross the river, and where to go once they had gotten to the northern bank. In some places, black agents worked directly with contacts in the Free States, at extreme risk to their own safety. According to John Rankin, several slaves belonging to a Kentucky patroller named Peter Driscol surreptitiously assisted fugitives for several years, even as Driscol boasted to whoever would listen that "no abolitionists, not even 'Uncle Johnny' [Rankin] whom all niggers like, could persuade my niggers to leave me." (Flee they did, however, having heard a rumor that they were to be sold southward; Driscol pursued his slaves as far as Cleveland, where, so it was said, he arrived at the wharf just in time to see his former property climbing the sides of a schooner bound for Canada.) An elderly female slave living in Virginia opposite Gallipolis, Ohio was known to have ferried many runaways across the river there, and in Worthington, Ohio, white abolitionists periodically collected money for "Old Man Clark" to travel into Kentucky to lead out fugitives. George DeBaptiste and his underground cell in Madison, Indiana had contacts as deep into Kentucky as Frankfort and Lexington. Occasionally, daring rescuers ventured across the river to bring out slaves, as Calvin Fairbank proposed to do when he landed in Ripley on that August day in 1844.

But it was for the most part in the river towns of Ohio, Indiana, and to a much lesser extent Illinois, where the Underground Railroad's main western lines began. Although fugitives might land in Ohio at almost any point, there were about fifteen key crossings where the narrowness of the river, the convergence of roads, and the presence of strong abolitionist cells combined to attract them in significant numbers. Some distance north of the main crossings, the underground routes generally converged into "trunk lines," which, although they might zigzag to the east or west, tended always northward, with lines from Ripley and other points in western and central Ohio terminating at Toledo or Sandusky, and those farther east at Lorain, Cleveland, or Ashtabula. Some routes in far eastern Ohio had links in western Pennsylvania, and fugitives traveling in that region were as likely to find themselves carried to Erie, Pennsylvania, or Fredonia or Buffalo, New York, as they were to an Ohio port. Fugitives crossing into Indiana most often were forwarded to Detroit.

John Rankin was not the first abolitionist in Ripley, or the first to offer help to a fugitive slave. Rather, he was a kind of moral entrepreneur who brilliantly mined the hearts and minds that were at hand, and molded them into an underground army. The underground had three interlocking elements in the area around Ripley. The first consisted of antislavery Presbyterian ministers, many of them former Southerners who, like Rankin, had come north to escape the claustrophobic climate of slavery. United through the administrative body known as the Chillicothe Presbytery, they formed a ready-made web of relationships that linked Ripley with Red Oak, Sardinia, Russellville, and a galaxy of other towns in southern Ohio. According to Isaac Beck, one of Rankin's collaborators in Sardinia, when William Lloyd Garrison founded the *Liberator*, these like-minded men collectively embraced the abolitionist cause "with increased zeal," and "every Presbyterian church became a center of Abolitionism, increased by the intelligent and pious of the churches and [by] non-church members. Here was where the U.G.R.R. workers originated."

The second component included politicized white abolitionists. In 1835 Rankin personally reorganized Ripley's antislavery society and linked it with the statewide body. The following year he undertook a hair-raising but ultimately successful organizing campaign through the southwestern counties as a traveling agent of the Ohio Anti-Slavery Society. In the course of six months, he was attacked no fewer than twenty times. At Putnam, he wrote, "We were surrounded by a large mob which threw stones at the building," and as they left the hall, Rankin and a companion were pelted with goose eggs, and "the small gravel of the street fell around us like hail." On his way home, in Chillicothe, Rankin "preached morning and night for the colored people," while "a few fellows of the baser sort" threw stones into the church, injuring members of the audience. At Felicity, where one of Rankin's brothers was the pastor, he enrolled sixty members in an antislavery society. A classmate from Samuel Doak's school in Tennessee helped him to form another large antislavery society at

Goshen. Although the pastor at Williamsburg warned him that his activities would lead to bloodshed and war, Rankin ignored him and called a meeting anyway, and soon, Rankin wrote, "Abolitionism was so deeply implanted in Williamsburg, that it could not be uprooted." At Winchester, a mob assembled and beat drums so that nothing could be heard, nevertheless, sixteen new names were added to the rolls of the local antislavery group. At Batavia, despite another egging, he enrolled, among others, Henry Ward Beecher's son and county prosecutor John Jolliffe, who would for decades lend his legal skills to the defense of fugitive slaves. Arriving at the church in Williamstown where he was to speak, Rankin found waiting for him only a crowd of wild-looking young men. "I fixed my eyes upon the rudest looking fellows to awe them down, just as I would a biting dog, and so long as I could look them in the eyes they were quiet but they turned their backs to me and began to behave badly; but I talked to them and stilled them down until I got through. When I closed they rose up and used the most filthy and indecent language of which they were capable, and when we left they gathered up the fire brands and followed us, throwing at us. They first hit the man with whom we lodged, next they hit me on the shoulder but I was so far off it did no injury." The experience left the usually imperturbable Rankin momentarily rattled: "After all the argument I had just used to prove that all men should be free, it did seem as if some men were not fit for freedom." He went on to lecture at Sardinia, New Gilead, Beach Grove, Bethel, Monroe, Springdale, and Grassyrun, leaving newly formed or expanded societies behind him in each place. "In Clermont County," Rankin wrote in a letter to the *Ripley Bee*, "the cause is going on delightfully. I formed the last three societies in three days."

Along with the Presbyterians and members of antislavery societies, African Americans formed the third pillar of the underground. Blacks were statistically negligible in all the Free States that bordered the Ohio River. They numbered just over half of one percent of the population in Illinois, by far the least welcoming of the three, slightly more than one percent in Indiana, and about one and a quarter percent in Ohio. In Ohio and Indiana, much of the black population was distributed in the river counties, which positioned them well to offer assistance to fugitives crossing from Kentucky precisely where their role was absolutely critical. Blacks worked as underground conductors and agents, and black hamlets scattered through the region served as key holding areas, or way stations, where fugitives could rest and recuperate before being moved farther north. In the Sardinia area, north of Ripley, reputedly the most reliable conductor for many years was a freed slave named John D. Hudson, "a man of good intellect and powerful physique and when enraged of no more fear than a mad bull," as Beck described him.

African American hamlets such as the Gist settlement near Sardinia, however, offered little security to fugitives, who often sought them out in hope of linking up or settling in with relatives or friends. But prejudice and the unreliability of law and order made them very unsafe, since they were a favorite hunting ground for slave catchers, who were also far more apt to use violence against blacks than against whites. These communities often owed their existence to the charitable impulses, or the guilt, of reformed Southern slave owners who emancipated their slaves and resettled them in free territory. The Gist settlement was just such an example. In 1819 several hundred slaves belonging to a wealthy Virginia merchant named Samuel Gist were settled by the executors of his will on two parcels of land north of Ripley. Whites more crudely referred to these as the "Nigger Camps," and regarded them as sumps of vice and intemperance. "We feel no prejudice against the black man on account of color, or for mere degradation; but at the same time, we are unwilling that we should be morally infected by contact with an inferior race, the result of which contact is in no way beneficial to the black, and highly injurious to the white," the *Xenia News* sneeringly editorialized.

Isolated and largely unprotected, blacks defended themselves against slave catchers in whatever ways they could. Where they were numerous enough, they might resort to physical violence as they did in Detroit, in July 1833, when they rioted against the recapture of a fugitive couple from Kentucky, Ruth and Thornton Blackburn, by slave hunters. Blacks armed with clubs, stones, and pistols surrounded the jail where the Blackburns were being held, and refused to obey the local authorities' order to disband. Mrs. Blackburn was liberated through a ruse and quickly spirited to Canada, which lay barely ten minutes' sailing time away across the Detroit River. The following day, armed protesters seized the cart that was carrying Thornton Blackburn to the waterfront, where he was to be placed on a steamboat in the custody of his captors. In the fracas, the Detroit sheriff was fatally injured, and Thornton was hurried across the river to Canada, where he rejoined his wife.

But in vulnerable black settlements close to the Ohio River, such defiance was rarely possible. Instead, when they could, blacks often improvised a kind of inspired street theater. Isaac Beck recounted the story of a slave named Ike who escaped from Mason County, Kentucky and by some means reached the Gist settlement. There someone informed on him in hope of claiming a reward for his capture. A message was sent to Ike's master, a man named Taylor, who arrived in the settlement and seized the fugitive. That evening, Taylor, Ike, and his captors were sitting on the unnamed informer's porch while a number of "camp negroes," as Beck recounted it, were "loafing" nearby. Among them was the underground operative John D. Hudson. When Taylor and his men went in to supper, Ike went in with them, acting as if he expected to be welcomed inside as well, but Taylor ordered him out again. According to Beck, Ike obeyed and left the room "but forgot to stop on the porch." He ran for the woods where, apparently by arrangement, he was taken in hand by a guide and disappeared. When Taylor realized what had happened he and his posse set off in pursuit, tailed by several of the other "loafers" including Hudson, who was carrying a conch shell that he continued to blow throughout the pursuit. Ike's guide led him to a certain cabin, where he hid him in the loft. When Taylor and his men in time came to the same cabin, two men idling nearby suddenly "commenced a game of fisticuffs," and were soon locked in a clinch and rolling down a hill, surrounded by a crowd of shouting neighbors. The fugitive's pursuers became so engrossed in the excitement that they followed the mayhem away from the cabin. Ike, meanwile, escaped from the loft and ran out the back door. There another guide stood waiting, and led him to another cabin in a dense wood two miles away, owned by a white abolitionist named Pettijohn, who cared for him until the danger eased, then sent him on his way via the Underground Railroad. When Hudson was later asked if he was not afraid to follow the hunters blowing his conch shell he replied, "No, the knots on the shell would hurt a fellow's head very bad."

3

In many of the river communities, underground work was carried out almost entirely by African Americans. One of the most effective networks of all was based in the port of Madison, Indiana, about eighty miles downriver from Cincinnati. With a few exceptions, it is difficult to form a sharp picture of the men who formed this cell. None of them left memoirs or diaries. Their activities remain visible at all only as they have been refracted through the anecdotes of white abolitionists, often long after the fact, and in a handful of nineteenth-century newspaper articles that omit more than they reveal. It is clear that the man at the cell's center in the early 1840s was the freeborn Virginian George DeBaptiste, whose picaresque career suggests that he had much more than the average share of charm and nerve. A natural mole, he would not have been out of place in the shadowy world of twentieth-century espionage. The only picture of him, an engraving made later in his life when he had become a successful businessman in Detroit, is unrevealing: it shows a rather heavy-featured man, with beetling brows and deep-set, grave eyes, and a short, dense beard that enfolds his square jaw like a baseball glove. Born in Fredericksburg, Virginia, in 1814, he was trained as a barber, and by the age of eighteen became the body servant of a professional gambler, with whom he traveled widely around the country, including the Deep South. In 1838 DeBaptiste had settled in Madison, and his barbershop at the corner of Second and Walnut soon became the underground's local headquarters.

As late as 1840, Madison was the second largest city in the state, with almost ten thousand inhabitants, two hundred of them African American. Like Ripley, Madison owed its prosperity to the confluence of the Ohio River with the staple commodity of the mid-century western diet: pork. More than a dozen firms dealt in pork-related products: lard, bristle, hides, barrels, as well as meat. Their brick warehouses lined the mile-and-a-half-long riverfront, where flatboats, keelboats, steamboats, and fishing boats jostled for space along the wharfs amid floating clouds of flimsy skiffs. Little more than a couple of planks hammered crudely together, these had so little value that they were left lying everywhere along the river's shores, where they were pressed into service as many a fugitive's express to freedom. Poised here in a political no man's land between slavery and freedom, the lives of Madison's blacks—sailors, stevedores, waiters, and casual laborers, for the most part—were intertwined with those of proslavery and antislavery whites in an unstable equilibrium that both favored the clandestine work of the underground and accentuated its danger.

DeBaptiste and most of his collaborators were part of Madison's tiny black middle class, self-employed businessmen or artisans who possessed economic independence, freedom of action, and the kind of organizational sense that was essential to make the mechanisms of the Underground Railroad work. They were well-known to everyone in town, and thus always exposed to the scrutiny of whites, few of whom they could trust with their secret. In essence, they hid their underground work in plain sight. Less than a block from DeBaptiste's barbershop, where he trimmed the hair of abolitionists and slave owners alike, stood the businesses of his fellow African Americans: John Carter's stall in the public farmers' market, Stepney Stafford's laundry, and Elijah Anderson's blacksmith shop, at Third and Walnut. Slaves who brought produce in from Kentucky farms passed on to Carter information about fugitives who were waiting to cross the river. Stafford's employees served as the cell's eyes and ears as they made their daily rounds to homes that included those of proslavery families, who might let slip information about the movements of local slave catchers. Anderson, one of several conductors, personally took fugitives as far north as Levi Coffin's home in Newport. At least two white men were also part of DeBaptiste's circle: John Todd, who lived just west of Madison, and his brother who lived in Kentucky, who would beat on an old brass pot and then wave lanterns when it was safe for a fugitive to cross the river. For blacks, who were vulnerable in ways that whites were not, secrecy was potentially a matter of life and death. Although he was widely suspected of helping to run off slaves, DeBaptiste succeeded for years in brushing off suspicion with disarming innocence. He always declared, with what one imagines must have been a carefully calibrated chuckle and a servile smile, that he only wished that he was "smart enough to steal the niggers, and he would steal all there was in Old Kentuck."

DeBaptiste estimated that in the course of eight years in Madison, he personally assisted 108 fugitives to freedom, and several times that number indirectly. He sometimes crossed into Kentucky himself to make arrangements for their escape. When a fugitive was ready to cross the river, a message of this sort might be sent to DeBaptiste: "There is a chance to purchase a horse that will suit your purpose. He is a mahogany bay, young, well broken, large, and is just the thing for a minister. You can see him on Tuesday afternoon. Price $100." DeBaptiste would understand from this that a large mulatto, a church member, needed his help; that he would be in, say, Louisville on Tuesday night, and that he had one hundred dollars to pay his expenses. If the message had described a "light brown filly," he would have known that the fugitive was a light-skinned girl. If it was said that the price would be cheap, he would know that the fugitive had no money, and had to be provided for. If it stated that the animals would be sent across the river, on the night mentioned, DeBaptiste and one or two friends, would go down to an agreed-upon point on the river after dark and lie at the water's edge, sometimes for half the night, listening for the sound of muffled oars. Most often, DeBaptiste, Anderson, or one of the others took fugitives to Lancaster, twelve miles north of Madison, a town inhabited by fiercely abolitionist immigrants from Vermont and Maine, who in 1839 had formed the first antislavery society in southern Indiana.

With good reason, DeBaptiste was wary of traps. One of the leaders of the Lancaster cell, Daniel Nelson, a veteran of the War of 1812, was twice arrested and jailed for aiding fugitives. When a fellow barber first approached DeBaptiste in 1844 or 1845, asking for help in escaping from his Kentucky master, DeBaptiste correctly suspected that he had been recruited to entrap him. DeBaptiste initially denied knowledge of any illicit activity. Not long afterward, however, DeBaptiste met the same man on the street in Cincinnati. The conversation that ensued suggests the kind of reasoning that DeBaptiste and other black agents in the border country may have used to penetrate the servile resignation of slaves they hoped to entice out of bondage. After castigating the barber for having been willing to betray "a man of his own race," DeBaptiste repeatedly challenged him where it must have hurt the most, in his manhood: "Why, aren't you ashamed—you, a man able to make money, and take care of yourself, with a good trade, young, strong, and a man all over, if you were only a mind to be—to be calling another man your master, like a dog, paying over to him your wages, which you earn here on the north side of the river? Don't you feel low-down to be setting such an example to the colored people? You will marry, and raise children to be sold down South as slaves. Aren't you ashamed?" According to DeBaptiste, the barber replied, "Now, George,

I've been thinking of that, too; and I don't mean it. I will be a man. I'll leave massa right off, if I can only get away." And with the help of DeBaptiste's friends in the underground, he did just that.

There was a dramatic postscript to the barber's story, however. A reward of three hundred dollars was soon posted for the runaway, whose name unfortunately has gone unrecorded. Slave hunters traced him to White Pigeon, Michigan, an abolitionist stronghold more than two hundred miles north of Madison, where they found him working in a barber shop. Cornered, the barber fought his way out with an axe, nearly cutting off the hand of one of his assailants. White citizens of the town held back the pursuers until the barber could be gotten out of town, and placed once more on the Underground Railroad, which speedily forwarded him to Detroit, and on to the more certain safety of Canada.

In 1846 Kentucky slave owners and their local allies launched an effort to destroy the underground in Madison. White mobs invaded the homes of blacks and nearly beat to death those who dared to resist. One of DeBaptiste's conductors, Griffin Booth, was almost drowned by proslavery men in the Ohio River. Elijah Anderson abruptly moved upriver to Lawrenceburg before something similar happened to him. DeBaptiste himself fled to Detroit, fearing exposure and arrest. Outside Madison, gangs of proslavery hoodlums terrorized white abolitionists. The stress on underground families was extreme. The son of Lyman Hoyt, a white farmer, remembered how he had slept on a trundle bed in his parents' room and was frequently wakened at night by his mother sobbing and his father stealthily slipping out of the room: "My curiosity, then awakened, was not wholly satisfied for a year or more, during which time the, to me, mysterious events recurred. My parents were devout Baptists, members of the church nearby, and I attended regularly the meetings and Sunday school. I heard much of wicked men, thieves, robbers, and murderers, and began to fear that my father must be engaged in some such wicked work, and I used to cry to myself when I heard poor mother crying and because, I thought, she was grieving over my father's wickedness." Finally, one morning, after a year of this, the boy discovered that his father was hiding fugitives in the hayloft, where he found three men, a woman, and a baby hidden concealed in the hay. "Father then explained the whole history, cautioning secrecy. Thus warning that some of the pro-slavery men might kill him, or burn his barn and other outbuildings."

The system that DeBaptiste and his collaborators built continued to flourish, despite attacks by white vigilantes and the flight of several key leaders. New men continued to step forward to fill the breach. The kind of repression that a generation earlier would have been sufficient to destroy the underground had little lasting effect. If anything, it stiffened resistance to intimidation. The Yankee farmers in Lancaster made it known to all that if they were attacked by proslavery forces they would fight back, even on Sunday. Remembrance Williams, a member of the Baptist congregation to which nearly all of them belonged, recalled, "Firearms were carried into the church, revolvers sometimes falling from the coat pockets as Deacons rose from prayer."

4

By the late 1830s, the Rankins could count on the support of between 150 and 200 abolitionists in Ripley. Many were people of some social standing, like Thomas McCague, a wealthy Ripley pork packer who was probably the primary financier of the local underground. As the white abolitionists increased in number, they provided an ever firmer cushion of security for those, like the Rankins, who undertook the most dangerous work. Only a small group including the Rankins and members of the Campbell, Collins, and McCoy families, and a few others worked directly or regularly with fugitives. These relationships have been explored in detail by Ann Hagedorn in *Beyond the River*, a history of the Underground Railroad in and around Ripley. The larger antislavery community provided money when it was needed, intelligence about the activities of slave hunters, and armed protection when the core activists were under attack.

The underground network, in Ripley and elsewhere, was built on a cellular structure consisting mainly of discrete, family-based units that were linked to one another only at their outer edges, and whose members typically did not know the names of fellow members who lived more than two or three towns away. For families who occupied a particularly critical location, like the Rankins, clandestine work was a full-time vocation. Jean Rankin, the reverend's wife, was responsible for seeing that a fire was always burning and food was on the table for unexpected visitors who came in the night, and for providing dry clothes and a place for them to rest. By the 1840s, at least, John Rankin focused his efforts primarily on political debate and antislavery work within the Presbyterian church. He did little if any conducting of fugitives himself. That was the responsibility of his sons, most of whom were now in their teens and twenties: slim Samuel, the handsomest of them, with his father's piercing eyes and high, chiseled cheekbones; Calvin, with his mother's broad face and high-domed forehead; John Jr., a copy of Calvin, but shorter and wirier; sad-eyed, weak-chinned Adam Lowry (who was known always by his middle name), the eldest, with his flyaway hair. All would follow their father into the ministry, though Lowry only reluctantly, even grudgingly, for he had dreamed of becoming a draftsman and escaping the relentless single-mindedness of the Rankin home, but he too had finally surrendered to the reverend's wishes when he saw a slave girl sold away in front of him one day in the bowels of a steamship at the Ripley wharf.

At least one of the Rankin boys was expected to be on call at any given moment to saddle up and hasten his charges to the next friendly home. "The mode of travel was sometimes afoot, sometimes on horses, sometimes in wagons and the route chosen was governed by the circumstances of each case as was thought would be most safe and the guide preferred," the underground veteran Isaac Beck recalled. Whenever possible, a runner was sent on ahead to alert the next station to be ready for an arrival. Stations were commonly between fifteen and twenty miles apart, the maximum distance for mounted riders or a wagon to travel at night and return before dawn. The Rankins' main route initially ran a long twenty-one miles north through rolling, lightly forested hills to Sardinia. Later, when volunteers became more abundant, the legs were shortened considerably and linked up with alternative routes to other nearby towns. By the late 1830s the Rankins most often carried fugitives four and a half miles to the village of Red Oak. There the route split, with one branch continuing north via Russellville to Sardinia, and the other via Decatur to West Union, in Adams County. At a Quaker settlement near Clinton, the Sardinia line joined a different route that originated at the river port of Moscow, west of Ripley, and passed northward through Felicity, Bethel, and Williamsburg. In times of unusual danger, none of these routes might be used, and fugitives might be sent west toward Cincinnati, and from there into Indiana.

The Rankins' operation was no secret—every Kentuckian in the neighborhood seemed to suspect them, and their house was often the first searched when a slave was missed. Fugitives could not be kept long in Ripley, where there were plenty of roughnecks, proslavery Democrats, and footloose Kentuckians in town always ready to hunt fugitive slaves if the pay was good. (Within hours, a master in pursuit of his runaway property could easily command a posse with the promise of whiskey and a dollar a day, at a time when a good farm hand could at best earn only three bits for a long day's work.) The Rankins tried to ensure that as few people as possible knew when a fugitive was passing through. "It was the custom with us not to talk among ourselves about the fugitives lest inadvertently a clue should be obtained of our *modus operandi*," Lowry Rankin wrote. " 'Another runaway went through at night' was all that would be said." While John Rankin must have had a wide knowledge of the larger network, he kept it to himself. His sons, who left much more detailed memoirs than his, rarely mention any stations except those in Red Oak and Sardinia, the two to which they most often conveyed fugitives. Judicious ignorance guaranteed safety: a man could not inadvertently give away knowledge that he did not have.

The success of the arrangement depended on an equilibrium of boldness and discretion. Courageous as their nightly trips were, the Rankins refused to cross the river into Kentucky, where the penalty for such activity was up to twenty-one years in the penitentiary. The Rankins also disliked freelancers from out of town who threatened to upset that equilibrium. When, for instance, a Canadian stranger showed up unexpectedly at the Rankins' home with a former fugitive and claimed that he intended to go into Kentucky to rescue the man's enslaved wife and four children, they urged him to give up the attempt and go home. Ignoring their advice, the stranger obtained work in Kentucky as a woodcutter and set about making contact with the fugitive's family. Over the next few weeks, he succeeded in bringing out not just the family but no fewer than twenty other slaves in the course of several trips back across the river, before he was arrested on suspicion of slave stealing. Fortunately, he managed to break jail and make his way back to Ohio. The Rankins sent the fugitives north on the Underground Railroad, but they were glad to see the last of the Canadian. Wrote Lowry Rankin, a little sourly, "His experience in jail on bread and water had satisfied his ambition and he went back to Canada with his last load and we were thankful he did for we were afraid he would make us trouble."

When Calvin Fairbank landed in Ripley, hoping to secure a route by which he could escort a family of fugitives from Lexington, Kentucky, he expected the local underground to readily tender the help he needed. He didn't know what he was in for. The Rankins were so standoffish, he decided their house was not really an Underground Railroad station at all. He met an equally chilly reaction from the other abolitionists in Ripley, who even accused him of being a spy or a slave hunter in disguise. "It was altogether an unpleasant experience," Fairbank wrote. He left Ripley frustrated but undissuaded. He too had been raised on the stubborn verities of evangelical antislavery, in western New York, and he was as single-mindedly committed to battling sin in his way as the Rankins were in theirs. The object of his efforts was a slightly built waiter named Lewis Hayden, who worked at Lexington's fashionable Phoenix Hotel. Hayden had once been the property, oddly enough, of a distant relative of John Rankin, also a Presbyterian minister, who had declaimed from his pulpit that there was no more harm in separating a family of slaves than a litter of pigs, and swapped him for a pair of carriage horses. In 1825, when Hayden was fourteen, the Marquis de Lafayette on his last visit to the United States happened to glance directly at him and, apparently, bow to him during the welcoming parade in Lexington. For Hayden, it was a transformative and liberating moment. "You can imagine how I felt, a slave boy to be favored with [Lafayette's] recognition," Hayden wrote. "I date my hatred of slavery to that day."

Fairbank's collaborator was a transplanted Yankee schoolmistress named Delia Webster. An adventurous Vermonter with elfin eyes and high, handsome cheekbones, she had been raised in the town of Vergennes, not far from the home of the stalwart abolitionist Rowland T. Robinson, whose sheep farm served as a terminus of the Underground Railroad. She had become acquainted with Hayden and his hope of escaping to the free states, and was his link to Fairbank. In the guise of a Methodist itinerant, Fairbank preached several times in Lexington and the surrounding area while exploring routes of escape. Since Hayden lived with his own family and apart from his masters, who leased him to the hotel, it was not difficult for them to leave the city in Fairbank's rented carriage without attracting attention. Webster fancied herself in the role of a secret agent and willingly agreed to go along, knowing that the presence of a white woman would do much to allay suspicion. Unfortunately, Fairbank and Webster complicated things by adopting several contradictory cover stories. Fairbank hinted to the man from whom he rented the carriage that he was taking his fiancée to Maysville, on the Ohio River, to get married. Webster told people at the rooming house where she lived that they were traveling into the countryside on church business. Once under way, with the Haydens' skin daubed with flour to make them look white, and their son Jo hidden under the seat, they told people they encountered that they were helping a pair of friends to elope to Ohio.

The party headed north along the Maysville turnpike, modern Route 68. Fairbank had chosen their path carefully. The turnpike was the first stone-paved road west of the Alleghenies, enabling a well-handled coach to maintain a steady speed of eight miles an hour. They made good time through Paris, but then at Millersburg things began to go wrong. One of the horses fell ill and had to be exchanged, causing a dangerous delay. While there, Fairbank and Webster were recognized by two slaves from Lexington, who on their return unwittingly divulged information that helped connect the disappearance of the Haydens with the rented coach. The rest of the journey was uneventful, and at nine o'clock the next morning the party crossed the Ohio at Maysville, Kentucky, where the river sweeps northward between low bluffs in a great westward arcing bend. They passed through Ripley, where Fairbank temporarily left Webster, while he went on to Red Oak, having managed to win the confidence of an underground man there named Hopkins. Unfortunately, Webster insisted on driving back to Lexington, where she intended to resume her teaching the following day. By the time the two abolitionists reached Washington, Kentucky, four miles south of the river, they already started seeing handbills announcing the disappearance of the Haydens. On the outskirts of Lexington, the owner of the carriage met them on the road, seized the vehicle, and drove it to the seedy Megowan Hotel, which served variously as slave jail and public prison. A mob almost instantly surrounded the two Yankees, and Fairbank was tied and dragged into the barroom. Webster was allowed to return to her boardinghouse. However, in her absence, her landlady had rifled through her trunk and found a fatally incriminating letter from Fairbank, offering to help in running off slaves.

Fairbank was tried and convicted of slave stealing, and wound up serving four and a half years in the Kentucky State Penitentiary. Webster was pardoned after serving five months, and returned home to Vermont. During her imprisonment, her modesty and grace won her the sympathy of many Kentuckians, who were embarrassed at the presence of such an obviously fine-toned woman in their penitentiary. After her release, to the dismay of Fairbank's supporters, however, she wrote a book exculpating herself, and suggesting that she had renounced abolitionism forever. Yet she remains an enigmatic figure. Despite her published apologia, she would later return to the Ohio Valley with an even bolder scheme to run off slaves. Nor had the underground heard its last from Calvin Fairbank.

Having been deposited with the abolitionist in Red Oak, Ohio, Lewis Hayden and his family were carried northward without further incident to Sandusky, and thence to Canada. They eventually settled in Boston, where Hayden would help found that city's Vigilance Committee, and become a leading figure in the Underground Railroad. In Hayden, the Rankin family had missed meeting one of the most remarkable African Americans of the era. Further, had they lent Calvin Fairbank the experience that they had gleaned from years of eluding Kentucky slave catchers, they might have saved him and Delia Webster from capture. But caution was the adhesive that held the Ripley network together. This close to the Ohio River, any misstep might easily lead to arrest, mob violence, or death. In 1839 Sally Hudson, a black woman who went to the aid of a fugitive who had been recaptured in the Gist settlement, was shot in the back and killed by a slave catcher. Although there were many witnesses, the murderer was never convicted. One of the Rankins' white collaborators, Reverend Dyer Burgess, a member of the Chillicothe Presbytery, was nearly lynched while traveling on an Ohio River steamboat, being saved only by the timely intervention of friends. John B. Mahan, a Methodist minister, was arrested at his home in Sardinia and carried back to Kentucky, where after sixteen months in jail and a prolonged trial, he was subjected to a ruinous fine that impoverished his family and contributed to his premature death. Then in the summer of 1841 the Rankins' own hilltop stronghold was the target of an armed assault.

One Sunday evening, Calvin Rankin was seeing a young lady home, and noticed several suspicious-looking men in town whom he took to be Kentuckians. There was nothing unusual about this, and the Rankins took no special precautions. However, Calvin and a teenage nephew named John P. Rankin, who was living with them, lay awake listening for sounds in the night. At about two-thirty in the morning, they heard a low whistle. Taking pistols, they immediately slipped downstairs and out the back door, waking Lowry Rankin in the process. Once outside, Calvin edged toward the northern end of the house, and John toward the south. Both boys were barefoot, and moved silently across the grass. At the front corner of the house, Calvin came suddenly face to face with a strange man, who stared back at him in astonishment. When Calvin demanded to know what he wanted, the man abruptly raised a pistol and fired point-blank. The shot passed over Calvin's shoulder, though so close that it set his shirt on fire. Another intruder posted at the south end of the house fired at John as soon as he came around the corner, but he also missed, and began to run. John fired his own pistol at the disappearing figure, and then heard "an unearthly scream," but the man disappeared into the darkness. Several more men now appeared coming up the hill from the direction of the town, firing as they approached.

Inside the house, a wild scene was taking place. After the first two shots, Lowry jumped out of bed, pulled on his clothes, and started for the door. But his wife flung her arms around his neck "like a vise," begging him not to go out. At the same time, their mother, Jean Rankin, ran in her nightclothes to the door, which the boys had left open, and locked it. With a decisiveness that suggests a well-practiced routine, she also seized the keys from the other doors, and was standing with her back against the front door when Lowry reached it, and refused to let him out. Lowry and the other brothers pleaded with her to clear the way, but she asserted with grim self-possession that Calvin and John must already have been killed, and that the murderers would be watching the doors, waiting to shoot whoever appeared in them. She would have no more killed, she declared. The boys' father agreed. "She added that we could do the dead no good, and our duty was now to preserve our own lives," Lowry recalled. Lowry, however, slipped to the back of the house and forced open a window that had been nailed down. He jumped out the window followed by his brother

Samuel, when firing began again in the orchard a little distance to the east. Lowry was relieved to hear the voices of Calvin and John demanding the intruders' surrender. He and Samuel went to assist them when they discovered that a fire had been set against the barn. Picking up a pail at the cistern, Lowry ran to the barn and threw water on the blaze, and stamped out what remained of it. Had he been only a few minutes later, the fire would have reached the unthreshed crops in the barn. The family would have lost its entire store of wheat, oats, and hay, and the fire might well have spread, as probably it was intended, to the Rankin house itself.

Realizing that Lowry and Samuel had managed to get outside, Reverend Rankin now ordered the other boys out as well. A running battle was meanwhile taking place in the orchard, where Calvin and his cousin were in pursuit of the intruders. Barefooted, however, they made slow progress across the stubbly ground, and their quarry eluded them. By now, people in the town below had heard the shooting, and hundreds of them swarmed up the hill to the Rankins' aid. The Kentuckians managed to reach their boats and escape, taking their wounded with them. The man that John shot, a cobbler named Smith, later died, the only known white fatality in the Rankins' long war with slavery.

That week, Reverend Rankin published a warning in the *Ripley Bee.* Until now, he had prohibited his family from attacking any strangers seen on their property, unless they were seen actually committing a crime. In the course of that violent night, however, something had changed crucially. It represented an abrupt moral shift that foreshadowed the coming evolution of the entire abolitionist movement away from pacifism toward a willingness to fight, a course that would inexorably lead toward open warfare in Kansas in the next decade, and to the apotheosis of John Brown at Harpers Ferry. Rankin stated in his blunt Presbyterian way that although he was a man of peace he felt it was as much a duty to shoot down the midnight assassin as to pray. Strangers thereafter on his property after bedtime came at their own risk, for they certainly would be shot. Never was a man seen prowling about the Rankin land after that.

5

Still the fugitives came, night after night, having seen the Rankins' ever-glowing light from the Kentucky bluffs. Sometimes they swam. More often they rowed across the river in skiffs "borrowed" from the Kentucky shore. Sometimes, in the hottest weather, when the Ohio was so dry that steamboats were stranded, they could walk most of the way across. (The river was narrower then, about 150 yards across at Ripley; today, after much dredging and banking, it is about 600 yards wide.) But escapes were most common in winter, when the dense vegetation on the Kentucky side was easier to move through, the snakes that infested the hills were dormant, and the ice on the river froze as much as eighteen inches thick.

Unfortunately, John Rankin never wrote about these people until he reached old age, and in the brief account of his life that he did record, they are rarely more than tantalizing shadows. One young woman is "beautiful and accomplished in her manners and but slightly colored," a seamstress who "had intercourse with the highest class of ladies, from whom she gained much knowledge and learned politeness." Another, a pious Presbyterian nurse, was fifty years old, and about to be sold away from her home in Kentucky when she was brought across the river by "a free colored girl of Ohio." Another was a young man who "said that in Kentucky there were twenty men after him in a wheat field and they were so near him he thought they would hear his heart beat." These heroic men and women remain elusive in the first hours of their freedom, seen only for a moment in the Rankins' accounts as if in the sudden glare of a flash in a darkened room, only to mutely recede again into the darkness of the past as abruptly as they appeared.

The most famous single fugitive to pass through the Rankin home was also the most enigmatic of all. On a bitter night in the winter of 1838, a heavy-set black woman picked her way furtively down Tuckahoe Ridge toward the frozen river. She followed the familiar track from the plantation where she was enslaved, careful to keep herself out of sight when she reached the snow-covered floodplain, moving close to the ground. In her arms, she carried an infant whom she had wrapped in a shawl against the cold air. She was leaving her other children and a husband behind, hoping that if she was not caught, and if she did not die, she might be able to return for them someday. She had fled abruptly for the same reason as so many other fugitives: a day or two earlier a slave trader had appeared at her master's estate to negotiate her price or that of her child. She knew that she might die crossing the river, but if she did nothing she would die a different kind of death, to be sold away south, and away from her family forever.

In some accounts, the woman begged help from an elderly Scotsman or Englishman who lived near the shore, and who sheltered her until she heard the baying of dogs on her trail. As she ran from his house she grabbed hold of a plank and raced to the river's edge. When the ice was solid, teams of horses could cross it. But there had been a thaw and the ice was rotten, full of air holes and cracks, and the water was running over it, and it was ready to break up. No one had ventured onto it for the past two days, but she had no choice. Her first step broke through. For a moment she stood paralyzed in freezing water. Then she plunged forward, carrying her baby in one hand and the plank in the other. The ice seemed firmer as she ran toward the Ohio shore, but then without warning she broke through again, this time up to her armpits. She pushed the baby ahead of her onto the ice, then levered herself up with the aid of the plank. Laying the plank across the broken ice, she crept along it until she fell through once more. Again she managed to throw the infant ahead of her before she sank. Crawling back onto the ice, she continued her progress in this fashion until the ice disintegrated beneath her again. This time she sank in only to her knees, and she knew that she was close to the Ohio shore. When she finally touched solid land she collapsed, physically spent.

She was safe for the moment, she thought. But she was not alone. A white man had come up out of the darkness and loomed over her. Had she known who he was she would have recognized him as her worst nightmare. He was a Ripley man named Chancey Shaw, a sometime slave catcher who often prowled the northern bank of the river on the lookout for fugitives. He had watched attentively as the woman made her way across the ice, and he was preparing to seize her when, he later admitted to a local abolitionist, he heard her baby whimper and something unexpectedly moved inside him. Surprising himself, he heard himself tell her, "Woman, you have won your freedom." Instead of arresting her, he led her, soaked and freezing, to the edge of the village. There he pointed to a long flight of steps that ascended a bare hill, at the top of which the rectangle of a farmhouse and a light were visible. He told her to make for the light, saying, "No nigger has ever been got back from that house."

The first that the Rankins knew of the fugitive woman's presence was when Jean Rankin heard her poking at the fire. (The door to the Rankin home was always unlocked in anticipation of fugitives.) Immediately falling to the indispensable work that was everywhere performed by the women of the Underground Railroad, she soon had the mother and her baby fed and out of their wet clothes. Upstairs Lowry Rankin was awakened by the voice of his father. "I had answered that night call too many times not to know what it meant," Lowry recalled many years later. "Fugitive slaves were downstairs. Ahead of us was a long walk across the hills in the dead of night under a cold winter sky. Then the long cold walk back home, which must be made before daybreak."

Still sleepy, Lowry came downstairs with his brothers Calvin and John Jr. to see a short, stout mulatto woman dressed in one of their mother's old linsey-woolsey dresses and a pair of their father's socks, seated before the fire with her baby in her arms and a pile of clothes drying before the fire. The Rankins massed around her as she told them her story. "She seemed so simple as she looked up in our faces," Lowry recalled. "How little did we know that this courageous mother, who was though now unknown, was to stir the heart of a great nation." More than a decade later, she would be transformed in the imagination of the novelist Harriet Beecher Stowe into the fictional slave "Eliza," and her perilous crossing of the frozen Ohio River would achieve the dimensions of myth as the most famous rendering of a fugitive's escape ever written. But in the shivering figure before their fire, the Rankins simply saw a fugitive slave who had to be moved on quickly and safely to the home of another friend who would house and feed her, and then guide her on her lonely way to freedom.

Three horses were brought around to the back door, and using an old chair as an "upping block," the fugitive hoisted herself up onto Jean Rankin's horse. Calvin was assigned to carry the baby, and John Jr. fell in behind him, as the boys wound down the thickly wooded bank of Red Oak Creek. At Red Oak, they handed off the woman and her child to James Gilliland, the local Presbyterian minister, who would in turn see that they were forwarded to the next station north. "So far as we were concerned, it was only another incident of many of similar character," John Rankin Jr. told an interviewer long afterward. The Rankins never even knew her real name.

CHAPTER 11

THE CAR OF FREEDOM

Let us render the tyrant no aid; let us not hold the light by which he can trace the footprints of our flying brother.

—FREDERICK DOUGLASS

1

"Eliza" and her child spent the winter with abolitionists in Greenfield, Ohio. In the spring, to put slave hunters off their trail, they were sent west to one of the most secure underground bastions west of the Appalachians, the home of Levi and Catherine Coffin, in Newport, Indiana. She would soon make another entrance onto the stage of history almost as dramatic as her first, but for the Coffins, as for the Rankins, "Eliza" was now but a fleeting presence. She remained with them for several days, told them her remarkable story, one of the multitude they heard every year, and then made way for other fugitives, who were appearing at the Coffin home in a steady stream. Rarely did a week pass when the Coffins were not awakened in the night at least once by a tap at the side door of their house. "Outside in the cold or the rain, there would be a two-horse wagon loaded with fugitives," Levi wrote in his autobiography. "I would invite them, in a low tone, to come in, and they would follow me into the darkened house without a word, for we knew not who might be watching and listening. When we were all inside, I would cover the windows, strike a light and build a good fire. By this time, my wife would be up and preparing victuals for them."

The sensitive, lantern-jawed farmboy who had wept at the sight of a flogged slave, and who had ridden over the mountains of western Virginia to foil the pursuit of a fugitive, was now well-advanced into middle age and, to all appearances, a respectable burgher, a pillar of the local establishment, an impression that was accentuated by the solemnity of his customary conservative costume of black broadcloth coat, immaculate white neckcloth, and high-crowned Quaker hat. Age had deepened the furrows in his gaunt cheeks, thinned his hair, and infused his hazel-colored eyes with a tired gravity. In spite of the recent national depression, his businesses had grown along with Newport. In addition to his thriving dry goods store, he had "commenced cutting pork," two hundred thousand pounds of it in 1841. He also owned a mill that manufactured linseed oil. Robert Burrel, a fugitive slave, operated it around the clock when there was water, and at night neighbors fell asleep listening to the fall of the weight on the wedge that pressed out the oil. Recently Coffin had built a fine new two-story red brick home, one of the best in Newport, on what everyone now called the "Coffin corner," near Pleasant Unthank's boardinghouse, Charles Comfort's shoe store, and a blacksmith shop belonging to a man named Sigafoos, who kept as a pet a large timber wolf that bared its teeth to anyone who stopped to look at it. Appearances aside, Coffin presided over what may well have been the busiest center of illegal activity in the state of Indiana.

Outside of certain river towns like Madison and the Quaker counties in the eastern part of the state, the underground was less ubiquitous in Indiana than it was in Ohio. (It was weaker yet in Illinois, which was still thinly populated, and whose southern tier was inhabited mainly by intensely proslavery immigrants from the South; the most significant underground routes in Illinois ran from west to east, from the Missouri state line to Chicago.) As it was elsewhere, the underground in Indiana was a fluid web whose component strands were never static or unchangeable. Broadly speaking, however, three main routes traversed the state from south to north. The first ran from Cincinnati and Lawrenceburg, via

Newport and Wayne County, through Fort Wayne, and into Michigan. The second originated from separate branches that crossed the Ohio River at Madison, New Albany, and Leavenworth. The first two of these joined at Salem, merged with a third near Columbus, and continued northward through Indianapolis and South Bend. The westernmost route began at Evansville and followed the Wabash River north through Terre Haute and Lafayette to South Bend, where it joined the middle route from Indianapolis. The Coffins received fugitives from at least three directions—from Cincinnati, Madison, and Jeffersonville, and sometimes Indianapolis—and usually forwarded them northward either toward the lake port of Sandusky, Ohio, or toward Battle Creek, Michigan, where the line from eastern Indiana linked up with routes from Illinois, and from central and western Indiana, and continued on across southern Michigan to Detroit.

Like George DeBaptiste in Madison, Coffin represented a new, pivotal kind of figure in the clandestine network, sometimes called a "general manager," who exerted a combination of managerial efficiency and moral suasion to rationalize the operation of what had formerly been a fairly haphazard system. These men, and there would be more and more of them as the system continued to grow, were products of it's growing maturity and reach. As the underground spread, it required more sophisticated coordination. Someone had to be able, often on very short notice, to muster and allocate resources, and to deal simultaneously with traumatized and suspicious refugees, law enforcement officials, slave hunters, and willing but not always effective abolitionists. Money had to be raised to buy shoes and cloth to make clothing for fugitives who arrived destitute, and often barefooted, in rags, and footsore. Food had to be collected and kept ready. Wagons had to be hired, horses procured, feed purchased, drivers paid, messengers dispatched, guards arranged for, medical care provided.

Coffin was one of those men, unusual in any age, with the strength of character and knowledge of his own heart to know what his role on earth truly was. This produced a self-confidence that enabled him to withstand both physical danger and extraordinary social pressure during his early years in Newport. He also owed his effectiveness, in part, to his prominence in the community. In addition to running his own enterprises, he was a director of the Richmond branch of the state bank. When anyone wished to do business with the bank, as Coffin put it, "much depended on the director from the district where the applicant lived," a fact that restrained many of the proslavery men of the area, who declined to challenge his clandestine activity as they might otherwise have done. He did not hide his beliefs. "I expressed my anti-slavery sentiments with boldness on every occasion," he wrote. "I told the sympathizers with slave-hunters that I intended to shelter as many runaway slaves as came to my house, and aid them on their way; and advised them to be careful how they interfered with my work."

Coffin's personal feelings about color were ambiguous. He frequently cited the danger of racial miscegenation as an argument on behalf of abolition and *against* slavery, because, as he often pointed out, bondage led to the sexual exploitation of black slaves by their white masters. Only free blacks, in other words, could be kept out of white people's bedrooms. However, his misgivings about racial mixing were mitigated by a deep and undoubtedly genuine sense of charity. "We were not in favor of amalgamation and did not encourage the intermarriage or mixing of the races, but we were in favor of justice and right-dealing with all colors," Coffin wrote of his antislavery friends in Newport.

However, his commitment to emancipation was unalloyed. Slave hunters often passed through Newport, and Coffin made it bluntly clear to them that he had the local authorities on his side. How effectively Coffin's power could be deployed when he wished is shown by the experience of two slave-owning brothers from Maryland, named Dawes, who bought a tanyard at Winchester, in neighboring Randolph County. They had a pair of enslaved girls with them when they arrived, whom they decided to sell before permanently settling in Indiana. The brothers had originally intended to continue on to Missouri. Although Indiana law permitted the passage of slaves through the state, it did not allow the importation of slaves by state residents. When the Daweses purchased the tanyard, they fell under the provisions of the state's personal liberty law. En route to Kentucky, where they planned to sell the girls and buy a stock of hides with the proceeds, the brothers passed through Newport. An abolitionist from Winchester, realizing that the girls were being taken south, galloped ahead to Newport in an attempt to have the Daweses arrested as kidnappers. Levi Coffin recalled, "We at once called a meeting in our schoolhouse, and by ringing the bell and sending out runners, we soon had most of the citizens convened." Knowing that the masters would soon be out of the state, they had no time for delay. Coffin filed an affidavit with the town magistrate, Jonathan Unthank, an active member of the underground, who presided over the meeting. Unthank, in turn, issued a writ and gave it to the town constable, John Hunt, who, significantly, was also in attendance. Hunt collected a ten-man posse, and with Coffin they set off through a torrential rain in pursuit of the Daweses. They found the brothers two hours' ride south, sheltering in a farmhouse. Hunt arrested them on the spot. Coffin informed the two girls that under Indiana law they were now free. Hunt then ordered the brothers to return with him to Newport, and told them that they would be charged with kidnapping, and that the penalty was five hundred dollars' fine and two years' imprisonment. A trial was organized within days. An hour before it was to begin, the brothers panicked and offered to abandon their claim to the girls if Coffin would not testify against them. Coffin agreed only on condition that they make out papers of emancipation for the girls on the spot. The papers were written, and signed by Coffin's attorney and the Newport magistrate. The girls were then turned over to Coffin and sent north via the underground lines. The Daweses later attempted to sue Coffin for his part in the affair, but they were unable to find a lawyer anywhere in the area who was willing to take their case.

On another occasion, when Coffin was summoned to appear before a grand jury at the county seat for harboring fugitive slaves, he found that he was personally acquainted with a majority of the jurors, and knew several of them to be active abolitionists. Asked if he knew that harboring fugitives was against Indiana law, Coffin replied opaquely, "Persons often travel out our way and stop at our house who *say* they are slaves, but I know nothing about it from their statements, for our law does not presume that such people can tell the truth, since the laws of our state do not admit colored evidence." Coffin's close collaborator Dr. Henry H. Way was then called to the stand. He was asked if he knew where in Newport a certain band of fugitives had stopped. "At Levi Coffin's," Way replied blandly, adding that he had helped to dress the wounds of some of them. Asked if he knew that they were fugitives, Way replied, "They said they were slaves from Kentucky, but their evidence is worthless in this state." Several other witnesses testified in much the same fashion, all agreeing that the fugitives had been lodged at Coffin's house, and that anyone who wished to meet them had been allowed to do so. In the end, the jury declined to indict either Coffin or Way for any crime.

Almost everyone in Newport seemed to be involved in the underground in one way or another. Their boldness is sometimes astonishing. Once when a slave owner pursuing a fugitive with a warrant demanded to investigate the home of the Coffins' friend Daniel Hough, Hough led him through the house with a lantern and then, opening the attic door, bluntly told him, "Here is where we keep our runaway darkies, but there are none in there tonight." As time went on, the Coffins openly kept fugitives at their house with little fear of being molested. Many years later, a Newport man named Jesse Way would remember how one day in his youth he had been passing the Coffin home and noticed a crowd of people standing in the street around the door. "What is the matter?" he asked his uncle Henry, who was coming out of the house. "Is somebody dead?" His uncle replied matter-of-factly, "Only a fresh load of negroes come to town." Newport's abolitionist sewing society met regularly at the Coffin house to make clothes for the fugitives. And the Coffins' door was always open to visiting antislavery lecturers, including, in 1843, Frederick Douglass, who was just beginning to make a name for himself as a newly minted abolitionist orator, on his first western tour as a speaker for the American Anti-Slavery Society.

2

Once Frederick and Anna Douglass were certain that they were safe in New Bedford, they settled into a domestic life that was unremarkable for free people, but must have seemed wondrous and exotic for a man who had been enslaved all his life, until only a few months before. Douglass put on the "habiliments of a common laborer," as he expressed it, and set off in search of work. He sawed wood, dug cellars, shoveled coal, swept chimneys, loaded and unloaded sailing vessels, and stoked furnaces. Once in a while he managed to work at what he had been trained to do, caulking ships, when white caulkers did not warn him off, for even in the "Gibraltar of the fugitive," as abolitionists called it, there was discrimination. Nevertheless, blacks, who numbered 10 percent of the population, were better off in New Bedford than anywhere else in the North. Protected by white abolitionists and a legal system that would defend them, they were safe from slave catchers, and they worked at a wide variety of professions. Some were even wealthy. But their position was only relative. Douglass was furious when he discovered that the Methodist church that he had joined, and most of the other white churches in New Bedford, did not permit black congregants to take the sacrament of bread and wine until the whites had been served first. Prejudice against color, he would write, "hangs around my neck like a heavy weight. It presses me out from among my fellow men." His face glares out from daguerreotypes taken around this time with the intensity of a Byzantine saint. It is a face—the chiseled planes of his cheeks, the firm chin, the brow curled into that fierce wrinkle above the bridge of his aquiline nose, and more than anything else that unnervingly, unforgivingly direct gaze—that perhaps more than any other of his era radiates a jarring fusion of intellectual brilliance and rage. He eventually joined an all-black congregation, where he began to talk about his life in slavery, in the process gradually discovering the first stirrings of the mesmerizing voice that would become one of the most famous of the nineteenth century.

Four or five months after he arrived in New Bedford, a young man tried to sell him a subscription to the *Liberator*. When Douglass explained that he was himself an escaped slave and was too poor to pay, the young man put him on the subscription list at no charge. Douglass was then working at a brass foundry that made fittings for ships. His job was to blow the bellows and empty the flasks in which the castings were made. It was hot, difficult work. He would nail the newspaper onto a wall and read it as he worked. "I already had the spirit of the movement, and only needed to understand its principles and measures," he wrote. "These I got from the *Liberator*." The newspaper immediately took its place next to his Bible. Douglass began to feel, for the first time, reading Garrison's inspired screeds, that the complete liberation of his race might actually be possible, and that it could be brought about through concerted human action. He threw himself into the local abolitionist movement "from a sense of delight, as well as duty," attending antislavery meetings, speaking out in his church against colonization, and beginning to "whisper in private, among the white laborers on the wharves, and elsewhere, the truths which burned in my breast."

In the summer of 1841, an antislavery convention was held on the island of Nantucket, the capital of the American whaling industry, and a Quaker stronghold. William C. Coffin, a prominent banker and abolitionist, knew Douglass from New Bedford, and invited him to tell the convention something about his life. Douglass, who had never spoken before a white audience, was nearly paralyzed with anxiety. "It was with the utmost difficulty that I could stand erect, or that I could command and articulate two words without hesitation and stammering," he later recalled. "I trembled in every limb." Haltingly, he spoke of how he had been taken from his mother in infancy, "a common custom in the part of Maryland from which I ran away," and then later, traumatically, from the beloved grandmother who had raised him; of the coarse blankets upon which he had slept in a common bed with other slaves; of being awakened at dawn by the shrieks of an aunt stripped, and tied to a joist, and whipped until she bled; of his life as a slave in Baltimore, where he was taught to read by a kind mistress, and taught the trade of caulking; of the craving for death that overtook him as he grew old enough to understand the hopelessness of his plight; of his first, failed, attempt to flee to the North by canoe up the Chesapeake, and his betrayal by another slave; and, circumspectly, of his escape to New York three years before. Garrison followed Douglass at the podium, and by repeatedly referring to the story that the Nantucketers had just heard magnified its power with his own eloquence. "Here was one 'every inch a man,' ay, a man of no common power, who yet had been held at the South as a piece of property, a chattel, and treated as if he were a domesticated brute," Garrison thundered. Douglass, though he remembered little of what he had said, must have had a powerful effect, for after the meeting John A. Collins, an agent of the Massachusetts Anti-Slavery Society, offered him a job as a traveling speaker. Douglass, with a shyness that would very soon evaporate, at first demurred, but eventually surrendered to Collins's pleas.

Douglass set out with a naive enthusiasm, traveling initially with a supercilious white agent named George Foster through the eastern counties of Massachusetts. (During one trip, in April 1842, he visited a community of radical reformers near the town of Florence, where he encountered the pathetic spectacle of his benefactor David Ruggles, now blind and dependent on the charity of friends, undergoing a water cure at a nearby spa.) Douglass's job was simply to tell the story of his enslavement and escape, to present himself as a living artifact, as it were, of the "peculiar institution," flesh and blood proof of its cruelty and sinfulness. He was usually introduced dramatically as a "*chattel*," a "*thing*," a "piece of southern *property*," an effective rhetorical flourish with middle-class Yankee audiences for whom the degradations of slavery were a kind of pornography. Douglass soon began to recognize in this language a form of condescension, a verbal dehumanization that left him feeling ashamed and angry. While he understood the propaganda punch that this kind of pitch delivered, he also realized that he simply did not think of himself as a "thing." He was in his own mind a man, and he wished to be presented as one. He also grew tired of repeating his life story over and over. But when he deviated from the script to express his own *ideas* about slavery, Foster would whisper insistently, to just "tell your story, Frederick."

Douglass was not alone in his resentment. Many blacks were becoming frustrated with white leadership of the abolitionist movement. With some notable exceptions, blacks had less interest than whites in the era's gallimaufry of general moral reform, which encompassed everything from temperance and women's rights to communal living, fad diets, and spiritualism. There was also a growing recognition that the abolitionist movement itself was infected with racism. Samuel Ringgold Ward, a former slave and a powerful orator in his own right, chided abolitionists "who love the colored man at a distance." It was a glaring fact that although blacks' donations provided about 15 percent of the budget of the American Anti-Slavery Society, its leadership was almost completely white, and African-American traveling agents received only about half the salary of their white counterparts. "This northern freedom is nothing but a nickname for northern slavery," Peter Paul Simons, a porter, caustically told a black abolitionist gathering in New York, in 1839. "Our friends tell us we must not fill low stations, for it degrades us the more, but they take good care not to adopt the means that some of our talented men might fill respectable stations."

Douglass knew what Ward and Simons were talking about. Collins and Foster kept telling him, "Give us the facts, we will take care of the philosophy." They also advised him to "have a *little* of the plantation manner of speech than not; 'tis not best that you seem too learned." Douglass could not deny the realism of their advice, for when he expressed himself in his own terms, with correct grammar and moral judgment, he could hear audiences, who expected someone raw from the lash and crude in speech, grumbling, "He's never been a slave, I'll warrant ye." But Douglass would not, and could not, conform. Not only a talent for oratory, but a sense of dignity, of integrity, was coming to life in him. He told Foster, "I must speak just the word that seemed to *me* the word to be spoken *by* me."

Douglass was one of the most charismatic members of an emerging generation of black intellectuals who were beginning to give African Americans a national voice through antislavery lecturing, journalism, and the ministry. More than anything else, however, it was the steady growth of independent black churches that provided the African American with what John Mercer Langston, the founder of the Ohio State Anti-Slavery Society, a black organization, called the "opportunity to be himself, to think his own thoughts, express his convictions, make his own utterances, test his own powers." Between 1836 and 1846, African Methodist Episcopal congregations grew from eighty-six to nearly three hundred, and spread from the church's original base in Philadelphia as far west as Indiana. Black Baptist churches, meanwhile, had grown from just ten in 1830 to thirty-four in 1844. Not surprisingly, black churches were usually outspoken in their denunciation of slavery, and many of them were woven into the web of the abolitionist underground, like the Bethel AME church in Indianapolis, a key station on the Underground Railroad, and Cincinnati's Zion Baptist Church, which regularly sheltered fugitives in its basement. Not all black churches were so engaged. Many shied away from politics altogether. Douglass withdrew from his own church because it was insufficiently antislavery. Also, few black ministers met his demanding intellectual standards. Most, he once rather nastily asserted, "have not the mental qualifications to instruct and improve their congregations."

At the same time, black newspapers, self-improvement societies, debating societies, schools, and reading rooms were also proliferating. Black abolitionists were usually in the forefront of this movement. At a typical meeting, in December 1842, the black Philomathian Society of Albany, New York, debated the proposition "Is the human mind limited," under the supervision of the abolitionist William H. Topp. In Philadelphia, a library intended for blacks who were excluded from the city's white institutions was founded by Robert Purvis, who also headed the local Vigilance Committee. David Ruggles had organized a similar library in New York.

In several states, committees organized by blacks led petition campaigns for black suffrage, fought discrimination on public transportation and in schools, and demanded the passage of personal liberty laws that would help protect fugitives once they reached the North. In contrast to white abolitionism, with its evangelical overtones, the antislavery passion of black Americans came out of the personal experience of bondage and of the ingrained racism that governed their daily lives. As one former slave put it, it was "more than a figure of speech to say that we, as a people, are chained together." Some blacks openly advocated armed rebellion against slavery, citing as an example the successful mutiny of slaves aboard the *Amistad*, in 1839, as proof that the slave masters could be overthrown. It was the slaves' "solemn and imperative duty to use every means, both moral, intellectual, and physical that promises success," Henry Highland Garnet declared in 1843, at a national convention of black leaders. Douglass, still deeply influenced by the pacifism of his mentor, William Lloyd Garrison, had not yet reached this point. But he would.

The antislavery movement provided Douglass and a host of his fellow speakers with a forum for their views and life experience that African Americans had never enjoyed before. The stories that they told of floggings, sadistic overseers, shattered families, and prostituted mothers and sisters overwhelmed skeptical Yankees for whom slavery was an unpleasant but abstract national problem, and turned thousands of them into active abolitionists. Douglass soon became one of the movement's most popular lecturers. "All the other speakers seemed tame after Frederick Douglass," Elizabeth Cady Stanton wrote, after a convention at Boston's Faneuil Hall. His immensely popular autobiography, first published in 1845, made his name close to a household word.

The Douglasses, who now had three children, two daughters and a son, had moved to Lynn, Massachusetts, to give Frederick easier access to the railroad. Leaving Anna and the children at home, he lectured widely in Massachusetts, Rhode Island, Connecticut, and New Hampshire. When he could not find a church or hall that would allow him to speak, he would take his stand in the street and keep talking for as long as people paid attention to him. Mobbing had dropped off in New England by 1840, but discrimination was still rife. Douglass was several times dragged off trains for refusing to ride in the "Jim Crow" car that was reserved for blacks. On one occasion, on the line between Boston and Portland, a conductor sent six men to remove him from the first-class carriage for which he had paid his fare, finally lifting him out of the train while he still clung to part of his wooden seat.

In the spring of 1843, the New England Anti-Slavery Society resolved to hold a series of one hundred conventions, beginning in Vermont and New Hampshire, and ending in Ohio and Indiana. Douglass was selected as one of the corps of traveling speakers who would cross the country. He was thrilled. This was his breakthrough, his opportunity to carry his message to a national audience. "I never entered upon any work with more heart and hope," Douglass wrote. "All that the American people needed, I thought, was light. Could they know slavery as I knew it, they would hasten to the work of its extinction." Beginning in Vermont, where he lectured in the old abolitionist stronghold of Ferrisburgh, near the home of Rowland T. Robinson, he and his fellow speakers moved on to central and western New York state, and then by steamer to Cleveland, Ohio, where he joined in a convention with some of the most prominent African-American speakers of the time, including Charles L. Remond, Henry Highland Garnet, Amos Beaman, Charles M. Ray, and others. "From Ohio," he wrote, "we divided our forces and went into Indiana."

The final leg of the tour proved to be an unexpected ordeal. Douglass was used to the racism of the East Coast, but he was unprepared for the savagery that he met with in Indiana. Richmond, only seven miles south of Levi Coffin's Newport, was a hotbed of proslavery sentiment. When Quakers arrived there with six wagonloads of legally freed slaves from North Carolina, a local newspaper denounced this addition to what it called "a worse than useless population," asserting, "This town is one of the great headquarters for these blacks, that the semi-abolitionists of the South, who are horror-struck by the idea of colonization, are continually throwing off their own hands and sending here to steal their living from the hospitable citizens of our place. It is a disgrace upon our town, and a dead weight to its improvement." In neighboring Jackson County, Indiana every African American who came into a certain store was "seized and tied up and held until it could be ascertained whether or not a reward was offered for him among the notices of runaway slaves displayed at the local post office." When a white mob rampaged through black neighborhoods in Dayton, Ohio a short distance across the state line, in 1841, the *Richmond Palladium* sneeringly blamed it on abolitionists, who it alleged had "excited all the latent passions of mobocracy." There was even racism among Quakers. Many were repelled by the aggressive polemics of the abolitionist movement, and by 1840 some Yearly Meetings were urging their members to withdraw from all antislavery activity. One Henry County, Indiana Quaker was quoted as saying that she would faint if a black man ever appeared at her door, while another announced that she would be afraid to step outside to visit a neighbor's house if the slaves were freed.

In the fall of 1842, the conservatives who controlled the Indiana Yearly Meeting formally disowned Levi Coffin and seven other Quaker activists because of their alleged divisiveness on the subject of slavery. "We were proscribed for simply adhering to what we believed to be our Christian duty," Coffin responded. "We asked only liberty of conscience—freedom to act according to one's conscientious convictions." Some of the conservatives were colonizationists by conviction, while others supported only gradual emancipation, but many believed viscerally, as so many Americans still did, that there was something inherently disgraceful about abolitionism itself. They were shocked when hundreds, and ultimately about two thousand of their fellow Quakers, about 10 percent of the Yearly Meeting, seceded in support of Coffin's group to form their own Anti-Slavery Yearly Meeting, based in Newport.

Such was the state of affairs in eastern Indiana when Frederick Douglass arrived at the Coffin home to begin his local tour. At Richmond, he was smothered by a hail of "evil-smelling" eggs when he tried to speak. Worse was in store. A few days later, at Pendleton, in Madison County, he barely escaped with his life. No building could be found for the speakers, so local abolitionists had erected a platform in the woods. As soon as Douglass began to speak, a mob led by a man in a coonskin cap emerged from "a miserable, rum-drinking place," shouting at him to be silent. Douglass refused, with unconcealed contempt. At this, the mob began to hurl stones and rotten eggs at him and his fellow speakers. When Douglass grabbed hold of a stick, the mob, made furious by the sight of a black man actually preparing to defend himself, began shrieking, "Kill the nigger! Kill the damn nigger!" Douglass was hit with a club that broke his hand, and might have been killed where he fell, thus abruptly ending the career of the century's most influential black American, had not his friend, a white antislavery agent named William A.

White, a nephew of the Coffins, broken the blow. Douglass was for a time left prostrate on the ground, where the attackers continued to pummel him. Although seriously injured, Douglass and William White, whose scalp had been laid open in the melee, managed to escape with the help of local Quakers. Later, when a member of the mob was arrested by the local authorities, two hundred antiabolitionists descended on the jail and set him free.

3

The Underground Railroad is often visualized as a fixed system that, once established, was rarely altered. In actuality, routes were always in flux. Even as new routes were opened, old ones became too dangerous, or no longer practical, and were abandoned. Participants died, moved, dropped out, or were driven out of the business by threats. Isaac Beck described an ongoing effort to shorten and simplify routes near Sardinia, Ohio, reducing one section, for example, from forty miles—"too long for a night's travel"—to three comfortable stages, first by recruiting new Quaker agents in one nearby town, and then a pair of Wesleyan Methodists further along the line. When a line from Columbus, Ohio, to Oberlin via the town of Delaware was compromised by a spy, another one was created via the town of Reynoldsburg. In some areas, participants changed their mind about abolition, or simply lost interest. Bushrod Johnson, who was raised a Quaker in Ohio and aided fugitives with his uncle, moved to the South and eventually became a general in the Confederate army. In Henry County, Indiana, the antislavery spirit faded when several of its key participants became involved in spiritualism.

The operation of the Coffins' Newport "station" provides a window into the underground at its most efficient. At a reunion of underground veterans in Newport, in 1874, Levi Coffin stated that during his lifetime he had directly and indirectly aided about thirty-three hundred fugitives to escape from slavery. Of these, he estimated that the annual average of fugitives passing through Newport was "more than one hundred," or about one every three or four days, a figure that is supported by a contemporary, Daniel Huff, who stated that about two thousand fugitives were assisted at Newport during the twenty years that Coffin lived there. Of course, the refugee flow was never regular. The total differed from year to year, and probably grew steadily as the underground became more effective.

By comparison, Elijah Anderson, an African American who conducted fugitives on a busy route north of Madison, Indiana, claimed to have handled eight hundred between about 1839 and 1848, an average of eighty-nine a year. The Miller family of Medina County, Ohio, who lived on a more lightly traveled route, assisted about one thousand fugitives during almost three decades of service, or about thirty-three per year. In some areas, there were willing conductors but virtually no fugitives at all. (Or at least none who was willing to trust his safety to whites.) Milton Kennedy, a white man who worked on a steamboat based at Portsmouth, Ohio, openly proclaimed himself an abolitionist, but was disappointed to encounter just two fugitive slaves during his years on the river.

Particularly after the passage of the draconian Fugitive Slave Law of 1850, agents and conductors destroyed what records they may have kept of the fugitives they assisted. One of the rare surviving examples belonged to David Putnam, an underground man based at Point Harmar, near Marietta, Ohio. The cryptic notations in his diary for August 1843 only hint at a galaxy of individual dramas whose details and protagonists have been lost to history:

Aug.	*13/43*	*Sunday Morn.*	*2 o'clock*		*arrived*	
		Sunday Eve.	*81/2*	"	*dep. For B.*	
	16	*Wednesday Morn.*	*2*	"	*arrived*	
	20	*Sunday eve.*	*10*	"		*dep. For N.*
Wife & Children	*21*	*Monday morn.*	*2*	"	*arr. From B.*	
		" *eve.*	*10*	"		*left for Mr. H.*
	22	*Tuesday eve.*	*11*	"		*left for W.*
A.L.&S.J.	*28*	*Monday morn.*	*1*	"	*arr.*	*left 2 o'clock*

Putnam and his friends used the call of a hoot owl to signal arrivals. When practical, they also employed explicit written messages, like this one from his friend John Stone, also dating from August 1843:

Belpre Friday Morning

David Putnam
Business is arranged for Saturday night be on the lookout and if practicable let a carriage come and meet the cariwan

J.S.

Fugitives remained with stationmasters for varying lengths of time, usually ranging from a few hours to a few days. When slave hunters were near, they might be kept much longer. The most employable, like Robert Burrel, who ran Levi Coffin's linseed oil mill, might be given work immediately and remain for years. Where the danger of recapture was unusually high, a stationmaster might go to some lengths to create a secure hideout. For instance, John Todd, who lived on the bank of the Ohio River near Madison, built a soundproof double fireplace that was entered from the top, next to the real chimney. And a miller who lived a few miles from the Maryland state line outside Gettysburg, Pennsylvania, sometimes placed his charges in a tiny room that he had constructed behind the water wheel, which completely concealed the hiding place when the wheel was set in motion. But exotic hiding places were rare. Fugitives were more typically hidden in spare rooms, attics, basements, barns, sheds, hay mows, cornfields, thickets, or creek bottoms. The Coffins simply invited fugitives into their house and put them to sleep in an upstairs bedroom.

Although railroads, steamships, and canals were being used more and more by the underground in the eastern states, in the West transportation was still almost exclusively by wagon or horse, or on foot. Unaccompanied fugitives posed the most serious security concern. Between Lawrenceburg and Madison, Indiana, and in other parts of the country, fugitives were handed a coin with a hole drilled in it, as a token of trustworthiness, and told to hand it over to the agent in the next town. At Logansport, Indiana, local African Americans were assigned to interview fugitives who arrived in town on their own, to ensure that they were not imposters, and then to report to white collaborators who supplied them with provisions and, if necessary, money. Generally, one of the Logansport men would then travel ahead to the next town to arrange for the arrival of the fugitives.

At Newport, Levi Coffin tried to keep a team harnessed and a wagon ready at all times. When additional teams were needed, his friends generally did not need to be told what to do. "The people at the livery stable seemed to understand what the teams were wanted for, and they asked no questions," Coffin recalled. If the fugitives were concealed at all, it was most often inside a covered wagon or beneath a load of hay, or among boxes. When necessary, they might be carried in a hearse, or a false-bottomed wagon fitted with a shallow compartment that could hold four or five people in very cramped conditions. More than once, a female fugitive was dressed in men's clothes and hustled through the streets in broad daylight, while a man dressed in her garments was left as a decoy for the pursuers. Quakers sometimes disguised both male and female fugitives in skirts and deep bonnets to transport them through proslavery neighborhoods. Levi Coffin availed himself of this stratagem on at least one occasion, when he sent a fugitive in Quaker disguise along with a committee of Quakers who had been delegated to represent Newport at a meeting to be held in Michigan. "They were very willing to engage in Underground Railroad work, though the Quarterly Meeting had not appointed them to that service," Coffin wrote, with his characteristic, wispy irony.

Providing for fugitives could be expensive, particularly for large groups. While the initial costs of feeding and transporting them were usually borne by the local agent, money was also raised from among local sympathizers. "It often became necessary to obtain, on a sudden emergency, a considerable amount of funds in order to place large parties of fugitives beyond the power of the slave hunters," wrote Eber Pettit, a longtime stationmaster based in Fredonia, New York, near Buffalo. "For that purpose certain individuals called on ladies and gentlemen, and stated the case without ever giving such information as could possibly betray the fugitives into any danger, and at such time men of all parties were solicited for aid." No records survive describing Coffin's fundraising in Newport. However, in his autobiography, writing of his years at Cincinnati, after 1847, he often tells of visiting fellow merchants to ask for ad hoc contributions to feed and forward newly arrived fugitives. In some towns, stationmasters paid conductors set fees. Isaac Beck of Sardinia, Ohio, paid John Hudson, an African-American teamster, twenty-five cents for each trip he made, while Charles Huber, a Williamsburg, Ohio, tanner, paid a mulatto named Mark Sims to drive fugitives to Quaker settlements in

Highland and Clinton counties. Huber also paid a white man, Samuel Peterson, to carry food to runaways hiding on his farm, and to provide them with paregoric to keep their infants quiet if slave hunters were near.

Fugitives usually were forwarded singly or in pairs, though sometimes in much larger groups. John H. Bond of Randolph County, Indiana, once received twenty-five, some riding in a wagon and the others walking beside it. The largest company the Coffins received, seventeen men and women, had all lived in the same part of Kentucky, about twenty miles south of the Ohio River, and had organized their own escape. Their experience makes clear that the underground was sufficiently well-organized to move a party of that size the length of Indiana without mishap, and that it had both the resources and the flexibility to respond to an unexpected crisis. "It was an interesting company," Coffin thought, all in the prime of life and "of different complexions, varying from light mulatto to coal black, and had bright and intelligent expressions." They had "for a liberal sum" hired a poor white man to ferry them across the river near Madison. Apparently they had not been in contact with the Madison stationmaster, George DeBaptiste, and had no idea how to find help once they were in Indiana. They spent their first night of freedom wandering without direction across cornfields and farms. In the morning they were spotted by slave hunters, and scattered into the broken, densely wooded hills north of the town. When they emerged, in ones and twos, they were found by local blacks who finally directed them to white abolitionists linked with the underground. Miraculously, none of the fugitives was captured.

White conductors transported the group in two wagons to the next station, and they continued on in this way, traveling at night, until they reached a Quarker settlement in Union County. There a new pair of conductors undertook to carry them thirty miles on into Newport. They arrived early in the morning. Catherine Coffin opened the door and immediately recognized the drivers from Union County. Writing years later, Levi Coffin reconstructed the scene with a hint of humor.

"What have you got there?" Catherine asked.

"All Kentucky," one of the men replied.

"Well, bring all Kentucky in," she answered.

Levi, hearing the noise below, quickly came downstairs to find the fugitives seated in the main room.

"Well," he said, "seventeen full-grown darkies and two able-bodied

Hoosiers are about as many as the cars can bear at one time. Now you may switch off and put your locomotives in my stable and let them blow off steam, and we will water and feed them."

The Coffins sheltered the group for two days, and then arranged for teams and conductors to take them onward to the log-cabin home of John H. Bond, another expatriate North Carolina Quaker who lived near the black settlement of Cabin Creek, about twenty miles north. Bond was also a founder of the Union Literary Institute, a biracial school where many fugitive slaves were given their first lessons in literacy before being sent farther north. The group should have been safe by now, but early the next day Coffin learned that fifteen Kentuckians in search of fugitives had entered Richmond. He immediately dispatched a galloper to Bond, to warn him to get the seventeen out of sight as quickly as possible. However, Bond had already sent them on toward another Quaker community in Grant County, to the northwest. With Coffin's message in hand, Bond mounted his horse and raced after them. He found the party still on the road, and turned them around and led them back in broad daylight to Cabin Creek.

While the Kentuckians searched known abolitionist settlements in the vicinity of Newport, Bond was arranging for the fugitives to be scattered in homes around Cabin Creek. There they remained for several weeks, until the Kentuckians gave up their pursuit, and the fugitives could be sent on to Detroit. In the meantime, the slave hunters publicly blamed Levi Coffin, the best known abolitionist in the area, for their disappearance. In the taverns of Richmond, they loudly swore that Coffin must be the "president" of the underground, and threatened to hang him or burn him out of his home. The remark was widely repeated by Coffin's friends and enemies alike, and he frequently received letters addressed simply to "Levi Coffin, President of the Underground Railroad." The story gave birth to a tenacious legend that Coffin was in fact the overall director of the abolitionist underground. No such title or position ever existed, of course, in a system where stationmasters and "general managers" were usually regarded by their collaborators as only the first among equals. While Coffin took considerable pride in his new nickname, with Quaker modesty he announced that he would accept any position at all on the Underground Railroad—"conductor, engineer, fireman, or brakeman"—that anyone cared to give him.

4

When Levi Coffin told the men from Union County to "switch off your locomotives," and "let them blow off steam," remarking that seventeen passengers were as many as "the cars" could bear at one time, he was using a brand-new language that, to Americans of the 1840s, was as fresh as the language of the Internet was to wired Americans at the end of the twentieth century. Until now, there had never been any agreed-upon way of describing how the underground actually worked. In the 1830s, members of the underground sometimes spoke of a "line of posts," or of a "chain of friends." Tightly knit family groups, like the Rankins, probably never used special terminology at all. Others invented their own codes. At Tanner's Creek in Indiana, one cell of underground agents, all emigrants from northern England, simply communicated with one another in their native Yorkshire dialect, which was incomprehensible to everyone else around them. Others spoke cryptically about "packages" and "parcels," or about deliveries of "black ink," "indigo," and "finest coal." Joseph Mayo, a black well digger who was the principal local conductor in Marysville, Ohio, would receive word that fugitives were waiting to be picked up when someone would come to him, perhaps in a crowd, and say, "Joe, I have two black steers and a brown heifer at my house," or "three bucks and two ewes," and ask that they be driven into town. Mayo would pick them up, take them on foot to his own house, where he would feed them, and then carry them on the same day to the home of a white abolitionist at New Dover.

The growth of the underground network was almost precisely contemporaneous with the expansion of iron railroads, which were transforming the physical and psychological landscape of America as dramatically as the abolitionist movement was changing the country's moral landscape. Smoke-belching locomotives, shining steel rails, and spiffily uniformed conductors were all new and exciting, and travel by rail a thrilling adventure that compressed time and space in ways that thrilled Americans who were born in the era of Jefferson and Jackson, when most traffic moved at the pace of an ox-drawn wagon. The country's first practical railroad had begun service on a mile-and-a-half-long track near Baltimore, in 1830. Five open cars were pulled by a horse at a fare of nine

Isaac Tatum Hopper embodied the Quaker commitment to emancipation. His collaboration with free blacks in early-nineteenth-century Philadelphia set a pattern for the Underground Railroad. (FRIENDS HISTORICAL LIBRARY OF SWARTHMORE COLLEGE)

David Ruggles. He led the New York Vigilance Committee, the cutting edge of the city's underground in the late 1830s.

Gerrit Smith. He was a friend and patron to many of the most radical activists in the abolitionist underground. His home in Peterboro, New York, was also a refuge for fugitive slaves. (BOYD B. STUTLER COLLECTION, WEST VIRGINIA STATE ARCHIVES)

ANTI-SLAVERY RECORD.

VOL. I. FEBRUARY, 1835. NO. 2.

HOW SLAVERY HONORS OUR COUNTRY'S FLAG.

"Coffles" of slaves on the march were familiar sights on southern roads. A North Carolina Quaker counted "at least five droves" of slaves passing his house to every one of cattle, horses, or hogs. (FRIENDS HISTORICAL LIBRARY OF SWARTHMORE COLLEGE)

William Lloyd Garrison in the 1830s. The *Liberator*, founded in 1831, won countless readers to the principle of immediate emancipation. (COURTESY OF THE BOSTON PUBLIC LIBRARY/ RARE BOOKS DEPARTMENT)

LIBERTY LINE.

NEW ARRANGEMENT---NIGHT AND DAY.

The improved and splendid Locomotives, Clarkson and Lundy, with their trains fitted up in the best style of accommodation for passengers, will run their regular trips during the present season, between the borders of the Patriarchal Dominion and Libertyville, Upper Canada. Gentlemen and Ladies, who may wish to improve their health or circumstances, by a northern tour, are respectfully invited to give us their patronage.

SEATS FREE, *irrespective of color.*

Necessary Clothing furnished gratuitously to such as have "*fallen among thieves.*"

"Hide the outcasts—let the oppressed go free."—*Bible.*

☞For seats apply at any of the trap doors, or to the conductor of the train.

J. CROSS, *Proprietor.*

N. B. For the special benefit of Pro-Slavery Police Officers, an extra heavy wagon for Texas, will be furnished, whenever it may be necessary, in which they will be forwarded as dead freight, to the "Valley of Rascals," always at the risk of the owners.

☞Extra Overcoats provided for such of them as are afflicted with protracted *chilly-phobia.*

By the 1840s, the existence of the Underground Railroad was common knowledge. Virtually any American would understand the point of this ironic—and iconic—image, one of the earliest to illustrate the clandestine system as an actual train disappearing into the earth.

False-bottomed wagon: This technique was sometimes used to transport fugitives in insecure border areas, and in the Quaker region of North Carolina. (COURTESY OF THE LEVI COFFIN HOUSE MUSEUM, FOUNTAIN CITY, INDIANA)

Jonathan Walker. His epic journey by sea in a whaleboat with a party of fugitive slaves ended in disaster.

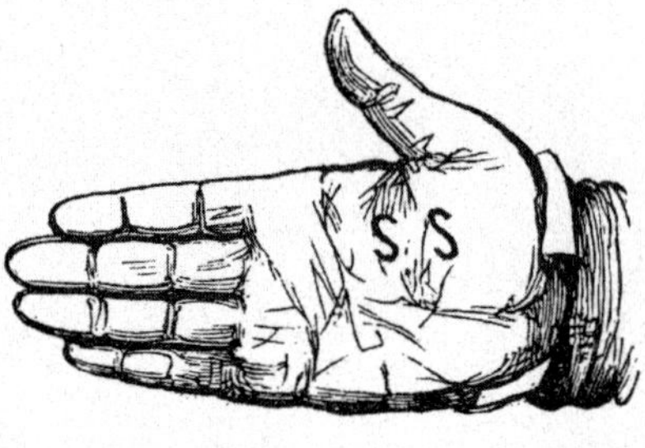

"All things whatsoever ye would that men should do unto you, do ye even so unto them. For this is the law and the prophets."

Walker's "Branded Hand." John Greenleaf Whittier's poem was memorized by generations of New England schoolchildren:

Then lift that manly right hand, bold
ploughman of the wave!
Its branded palm shall prophecy
'SALVATION TO THE SLAVE.'

William Parker's home near Christiana, Pennsylvania. In 1851 it became the site of a bloody confrontation when Maryland slaveowner Edward Gorsuch and an armed party attempted to capture fugitives who were protected by members of the underground.
(FRIENDS HISTORICAL LIBRARY OF SWARTHMORE COLLEGE)

A nineteenth-century artist's rendering of the "Christiana Tragedy."

Jermain Loguen. Born Jarm Logue, he began life as a slave in Tennessee. By the 1850s, he was one of the leaders of the underground in Syracuse, New York. He defiantly advertised his home in newspapers as a refuge for fugitives from slavery. (ONONDAGA HISTORICAL SOCIETY)

Quakers Isaac and Dinah Mendenhall were key members of the underground in Chester County, Pennsylvania. They sheltered hundreds of fugitive slaves during decades of service, including William Parker during his successful escape from Christiana. (FRIENDS HISTORICAL LIBRARY OF SWARTHMORE COLLEGE)

Harriet Tubman. A modest, mystical woman who possessed remarkable physical courage, her exploits would reach the dimensions of myth. (BOYD B. STUTLER COLLECTION, WEST VIRGINIA STATE ARCHIVES)

Thomas Garrett. He served the underground for forty years, in Wilmington, Delaware. Tried and convicted of assisting fugitives, he publicly promised to add another story to his house to accommodate more. (FRIENDS HISTORICAL LIBRARY OF SWARTHMORE COLLEGE)

William Still managed the Philadelphia Anti-Slavery Office in the 1850s. He received hundreds of fugitives direct from the South, and was linked to underground activity as least as far south as Norfolk,Virginia. (FRIENDS HISTORICAL LIBRARY OF SWARTHMORE COLLEGE)

William Still (SECOND FROM RIGHT, STANDING) was on hand to help open the box that contained Henry "Box" Brown, in 1848.

Robert Purvis, (FIRST ROW, THIRD FROM RIGHT) the mulatto son of a South Carolina slave owner, was a founder of the Philadelphia Vigilance Committee and provided shelter for fugitives in his home outside the city. In the 1850s he was chairman of the executive committee of the Pennsylvania Anti-Slavery Society. On Purvis's left is Lucretia Mott.
(FRIENDS HISTORICAL LIBRARY OF SWARTHMORE COLLEGE)

JAMES AND LUCRETIA MOTT.

From a Daguerreotype by Langenheim about 1842.

The Quaker Lucretia Mott was one of the first American women to claim a political role for herself, in the antislavery movement, and was an important influence on Elizabeth Cady Stanton. Her husband, James, chaired the first women's rights convention, in Seneca Falls, New York. (FRIENDS HISTORICAL LIBRARY OF SWARTHMORE COLLEGE)

In Detroit, William Lambert (LEFT) and George DeBaptiste (BELOW) headed one of the most effective underground groups in the United States. DeBaptiste had previously led the underground in Madison, Indiana, until he was forced to flee for his life. (BURTON HISTORICAL COLLECTION, DETROIT PUBLIC LIBRARY)

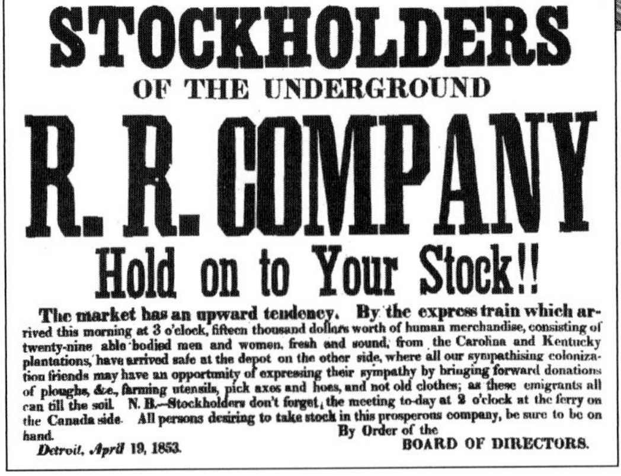

STOCKHOLDERS
OF THE UNDERGROUND
R. R. COMPANY
Hold on to Your Stock!!

The market has an upward tendency. By the express train which arrived this morning at 3 o'clock, fifteen thousand dollars worth of human merchandise, consisting of twenty-nine able bodied men and women, fresh and sound, from the Carolina and Kentucky plantations, have arrived safe at the depot on the other side, where all our sympathising colonization friends may have an opportunity of expressing their sympathy by bringing forward donations of ploughs, &c., farming utensils, pick axes and hoes, and not old clothes; as these emigrants all can till the soil. N. B.—Stockholders don't forget, the meeting to-day at 2 o'clock at the ferry on the Canada side. All persons desiring to take stock in this prosperous company, be sure to be on hand.

By Order of the
BOARD OF DIRECTORS.

Detroit, April 19, 1853.

Underground Railroad poster, Detroit, 1853. By the mid-1850s, the "underground" was an open secret in many parts of the North. (BURTON HISTORICAL COLLECTION, DETROIT PUBLIC LIBRARY)

Josiah Henson as patriarch. His life as a slave, the well-known story of his escape to Canada, his founding of the British-American Institute, and his role as a supposed model for Harriet Beecher Stowe's "Uncle Tom" had made him a legend.
(TORONTO PUBLIC LIBRARY)

Henry Bibb was a veteran of the Detroit underground. His meteoric career as a journalist and community leader in Canada ended with his premature death in 1854.
(TORONTO PUBLIC LIBRARY)

Mary Ann Shadd. She was Henry Bibb's bitter rival, and the first black woman to publish a newspaper in North America.
(TORONTO PUBLIC LIBRARY)

John Brown. He dreamed of a "Subterranean Pass Way" that would penetrate deep into the heart of the South, protected by outposts of armed abolitionists and liberated slaves. (BOYD B. STUTLER COLLECTION, WEST VIRGINIA STATE ARCHIVES)

Shields Green. He was the only fugitive slave among the men who joined John Brown's raid on Harpers Ferry. He chose to remain with Brown rather than flee when he had a chance. (BOYD B. STUTLER COLLECTION, WEST VIRGINIA STATE ARCHIVES)

cents for a round-trip excursion. It was an immediate success, and by the end of the year thirteen miles were in operation, the beginning of what became the Baltimore & Ohio. The following year, an engine that resembled an upended boiler and a smokestack stuck on a wagon bed towed a half-dozen flatcars the seventeen miles between Albany and Schenectady, New York, terrifying horses, setting fire to the clothes of spectators, and completing its run in the mind-boggling time of just thirty-eight minutes. Early trains were by turns mesmerizing, terrifying, and inspiring. "I saw today for the first time a Rail Way Car," one man wrote in 1835, scarcely able to contain his excitement. "What an object of wonder! How marvelous it is in every particular. It appears like a thing of life . . . I cannot describe the strange sensation produced on seeing the train of cars come up. And when I started in them . . . it seemed like a dream."

The first use of railroad metaphor to describe underground work is unknown. A persistent but almost certainly apocryphal legend credits its genesis to an irate slave master who after failing to catch a runaway in Ripley, Ohio, is alleged to have exclaimed, "He must have gone off on an underground road!" Quite possibly, the terminology was more deliberately coined by two early Pennsylvania abolitionists, Emmor Kimber and Elijah Pennypacker, who in the early 1830s were engaged simultaneously in helping fugitives and in developing plans for some of the first railroads around Philadelphia. (Kimber invented a device that kept early, weakly powered engines from rolling backward down steep hills.) Whatever the origin of the lingo, the underground readily lent itself to railroad imagery as the iron roads, with their exotic new idiom of "trains," "engines," "lines," "stations," and "stationmasters," spread rapidly across the Northern states in the 1830s and 1840s.

By 1840, about 3,000 miles of railroad had been completed, virtually all of it in the East. Indiana had only 20 miles of track, and Ohio just 39. (New York, by comparison, had 453, and Pennsylvania, 576.) Almost immediately, western businessmen began agitating for the extension of railroads to the West. Boosters were certain that these wondrous contraptions would make their isolated towns wealthy overnight, by opening them to the vast markets of the East and South. "Rouse! Fellow citizens, Rouse!" exclaimed the *Richmond Palladium* in 1832, begging for immediate investment in the iron roads. "Let your energies lie no longer dormant—let us not be the last to engage in the good cause . . . So soon as this cheap and rapid means of transportation is in operation . . . large capitalists will be induced to settle amongst us—the price of property will be doubled—the farmer will find a market for his products."

The imaginative link between railroads and the work of the abolitionist underground ran far in advance of the actual tracks. Underground men from New York to Illinois who had never even seen an actual railroad soon began to describe themselves as "conductors," and to speak of their wagons as "cars," and of the fugitives they carried as "passengers." Slave hunters stymied by defiant African Americans at the Cabin Creek settlement, years before the first mile of track had been laid in Indiana, were sarcastically advised "to look around and see if there was not a hole in the ground where the girls had been let down to the Underground Railroad." In 1844, George Washington Clark, of Rochester, New York, the "liberty singer," as he billed himself, was traveling across the northern states singing a song titled "Get off the Track," to the tune of "Old Dan Tucker":

Let the ministers and churches
Leave the sectarian lurches
Jump on board the car of freedom
Ere it be too late to need 'em
Sound the alarm, Pulpits, thunder
Ere too late you see your blunder.

Although his song was aimed at recalcitrant churchmen, Clark's audience could hardly help being reminded of the Underground Railroad.

Frederick Douglass, for one, condemned the increasingly open discussion of the Underground Railroad. Loose talk, he warned, only alerted Southerners to its existence, and undermined the hopes of slaves who wanted to escape. "I have never approved of the public manner in which some of our western friends have conducted what they call the *underground railroad*, but which, I think, by their open declarations, has been made most emphatically the *upperground railroad*," he wrote in 1845, in his autobiography. "I honor those good men and women for their noble daring, and applaud them for willingly subjecting themselves to bloody persecution, by openly avowing their participation in the escape of slaves . . . while, upon the other hand, I see and feel assured that those open declarations are a positive evil to the slaves remaining, who are seeking to escape. They do nothing toward enlightening the slave, whilst they do much toward enlightening the master. They stimulate him to greater watchfulness, and enhance his power to capture his slave. I would keep the merciless slave holder profoundly ignorant of the means of flight adopted by the slave . . . Let us render the tyrant no aid; let us not hold the light by which he can trace the footprints of our flying brother."

The consolidation of the underground in the 1840s reflected an evolving American ethos that increasingly emphasized predictability, speed, and efficiency. Elsewhere in the North, this same kind of thinking was creating the modern factory system, rationalizing the production of commodities that until now had been made locally and often by hand, and developing patterns of long-distance distribution that could as reliably deliver a fugitive slave from an Ohio River crossing to Canada as they could a consignment of boots, broom handles, or Colt pistols from Connecticut to the western frontier. By the 1850s, railroad terminology would become the lingua franca of abolitionists, slaveholders, politicians, and other Americans alike, as they argued, with heightening violence, about the hemorrhaging of fugitive slaves toward Canada.

5

In 1844 Levi Coffin made his first trip to Canada, in the company of William Beard, a fellow Quaker who had forwarded many fugitives to Coffin from his home in Union County, Indiana. The two had been delegated by their respective meetings to survey the condition of refugees in the queen's dominions. They set out in mid-September, on horseback, stopping along the way at several black settlements in Ohio and Michigan, where they were warmly greeted by fugitives whom they had sent north earlier. In Detroit, the Quakers visited schools that had recently been established for the city's small but growing black population. The next day, their tenth after leaving Newport, they crossed the Detroit River to Windsor, in Canada West. At Sandwich, they attended a court session, where they had the satisfaction of watching a white man tried and convicted for decoying a fugitive back across the river to the United States, and into the hands of his master. They then made their way down the river to Amherstburg, where Coffin was pleased to discover that the best tavern in town was kept by William Hamilton, a black man.

In the course of their two months' stay in Canada, the travelers met many former fugitives who had settled in the surrounding towns. Coffin, in particular, was often greeted with cries of "Bless the Lord! I know you!" and he would find himself face to face with someone who had spent a night in his Newport home ten or even fifteen years earlier. Their emotion both flattered him and discomfited his Quaker reserve. "Some would cling to our garments as if they thought they would impart some virtue," he wrote, with embarrassment. Although he saw some destitution among the refugees, Coffin was happy to learn many of them owned their own farms, and that some were now even worth more than their former masters. At Dawn Mills, near Dresden, eighty miles east of Windsor, they visited the British-American Manual Labor Institute for Colored Children, a model community that had recently been established to help train former slaves for self-sufficiency, with an emphasis on literacy and learning useful trades. Unfortunately, they missed meeting the institute's guiding spirit, himself an escaped slave, and a man who like Coffin was destined to become one of the mythic figures of the antislavery movement: Josiah Henson.

Chapter 12

Our Watchword Is Onward

I hear that Queen Victoria says
if we will all forsake our land of chains and slavery
and come across the lake,
She will be standing on the shore
with arms extended wide

—Abolitionist ballad

1

When Josiah Henson and his family landed in Canada, within sight of the walls of Fort Erie, with their British cannon protectively pointed across the Niagara River at the United States, they were strangers in an alien land, without family, friends, or money, except for the dollar that they were given by the Scottish captain who had carried them from Sandusky to Buffalo. They spent that on lodgings for the night. The next morning, Josiah began looking for work. Someone told him about a farmer named Hibbard, who lived six or seven miles inland, and whose reputation, as

Henson delicately put it, "was not, by any means, unexceptionably good," but who needed a man used to hard labor. Modesty was never one of Henson's limitations, and he quickly convinced the man to take him on. When Henson asked Hibbard if there was a place for his family to live, he "led the way to an old two-story sort of shanty, into the lower story of which the pigs had broken, and had apparently made it their resting place for some time. Still it was a house, and I forthwith expelled the pigs, and set about cleaning it for the occupancy of a better sort of tenants."

If Henson felt disappointment—had he really risked the lives of family just to wind up in a pig sty?—there was no trace of it in his memory of that wondrous day. He scrubbed, scraped, and mopped far into the night to clean the pigs' filth from the floor. He recalled his family's arrival the following day with italicized pride: "I brought the rest of the Hensons to *my house*, and though there was nothing there but bare walls and floors, we were all in a state of great delight, and my wife acknowledged that it was worthwhile, and that it was better than a log cabin with an earth floor." For the first time in his forty-one years, he now had the right to shut their door against the world of white men. The Hensons remained on Hibbard's farm for three years. A prodigiously hard worker as always, Josiah soon managed to acquire some pigs, a cow, even a horse, the nineteenth-century counterpart of a private automobile, the first conspicuous accoutrements of economic independence. In 1833, Henson went to work for another farmer in the area, named Riseley, "who was a man of more elevation of mind than Mr. Hibbard."

As a man of property, however modest, Henson now felt sufficiently self-confident to measure himself against other refugees from the South, several hundred of whom lived scattered in the vicinity of his home. What he saw troubled him deeply. Most of them were working as casual farm laborers, and making little effort to improve their situation. "The mere delight the slave took in his freedom, rendered him, at first, contented with a lot far inferior to that which he might have attained," Henson gloomily observed. Ignorance of contracts, leases, and the most elementary rules of commerce led the refugees repeatedly to make "unprofitable bargains" that prevented them from saving money or acquiring property of their own. "They were content to have the proceeds of their labor at their own command, and had not the ambition for, or the perception of what was within their easy reach, if they did but know it." Henson was entrepreneurial by nature, and intensely ambitious. They were the qualities that had made him valuable to his former masters. They now combined with his compulsion to teach and lead as he began to discover a far wider field of action in the American gospel of self-improvement, self-discovery, and economic achievement.

Henson began meeting with some of the more successful black farmers and tenants. Ten or twelve of them eventually agreed to pool their savings, and to purchase land together for a settlement where they would, he wrote, "be, in short, our own masters." In the autumn of 1834, he set off on foot, eventually trekking almost three hundred miles in search of a suitable site. Vast tracts of densely forested government land were constantly being opened up for settlement all across the broad, flat peninsula that extends across the southern part of present-day Ontario from Lake Erie to the Detroit River. The colonial authorities, still smarting from American invasion during the War of 1812, were eager, even desperately so, to see the region settled with any men loyal to the Crown, white or black. Land was cheap: fifty-acre lots could be purchased for two dollars per acre, with ten years to pay. Henson found what he wanted at Colchester, a short distance inland from the reassuring earthen ramparts of Fort Malden, overlooking the Detroit River where it debouched into Lake Ontario. For seventy-five miles along the shore of Lake Ontario, the only crop he had seen was the one he knew best, tobacco, which had been brought north by refugees like himself. A few of them had even made small fortunes. Everywhere around Colchester, he saw black faces, and heard the familiar drawl of Kentucky. Also at Colchester he met a white man named McCormick, who had already cleared a tract of land that he was happy to lease to Henson and his friends. They could begin sowing crops immediately. It was a more fortuitous decision than Henson expected. It turned out that McCormick had failed to meet the terms of his grant, and lost his claim to it, enabling Henson's group to live there rent-free for the next seven years, raising crops and accumulating savings with which they could later purchase land of their own.

Henson thrived at Colchester. However, he noticed how ignorance of the elementary principles of practical economics undermined the efforts of even the most hard-working refugees. They would often lease a tract of wilderness land, and contract to clear a fixed number of acres. By the time the land was clear—a backbreaking job, involving felling trees, and dragging out stumps, root systems, and rocks—the lease had run out, and the owner of the land would reoccupy it, and begin raising crops to which the refugee had no claim. The same refugee would then take up another, identical lease, with the same results, so that after years of labor he still had neither land nor savings. Henson similarly noticed how refugee farmers were ruining the profitable monopoly on the cultivation of tobacco that they had once enjoyed. They were flooding the market with needless overproduction, thus depressing the price, and putting themselves out of business. Henson's experience as a farm manager for the Rileys gave him a grasp of the larger dimensions of the problem that almost all his neighbors lacked. He began lecturing them about wages and profits, urging independent farmers to diversify, and renters to raise their own crops and to save their wages. It was all basic economics, but revolutionary to men and women who had never before had to plan for the future. There was so much that they had to learn.

As he plowed, and sowed, and harvested, a grander dream was taking shape in Henson's mind. He began to envision a community far more ambitious than the simple group of friends gathered at Colchester, a place where refugees from slavery would not only support themselves economically, but would also remake themselves as independent men and women, learning to read and write, to acquire mechanical skills, to become responsible for their own decisions, to develop the magical spirit of enterprise: in short, to think like white men. "It was precisely the Yankee spirit that I wished to instill into my fellow-slaves, if possible." What he had in mind was destined to become one of the Canadian terminals of the Underground Railroad.

The Underground Railroad was not the end of the journey from slavery to freedom, but the beginning. Paradoxically, it was in Canada that blacks became real Americans. Only there were they completely free to pursue the American dream of personal liberty, the acquisition of property, self-improvement, and the unfettered pursuit of happiness. By and large, what former slaves wanted was legal protection, physical security for themselves and their families, honest wages, recognition of the marriage bond, freedom to worship when and how they pleased, protection for their homes and property, education for themselves and their children, the power of the vote, and personal respect. Many shared feelings similar to those of Alexander Hemsley, once a slave in Maryland who had escaped to New Jersey, where he had lived for years before being captured by slave hunters. Except for the intervention of Quakers, he would have been sent back to bondage by a local proslavery judge. Even so, the court had stripped him of everything he owned, and, terrified of further harassment, he fled to Canada. "I had been in comfortable circumstances, but all my little property was *lawed* away," he told a visiting journalist, with deep bitterness. "When I reached English territory, I had a comfort in the law,—that my shackles were struck off, and that a man was a man by law."

Nowhere in the Northern "free states" was freedom for African Americans fully guaranteed or protected. In 1840, more than ninety percent of Northern free blacks lived in states that either partially or completely disenfranchised them. Only in Maine, Vermont, Massachusetts, and New Hampshire did blacks vote freely. Only Massachusetts allowed blacks to serve as jurors. In Illinois, Ohio, Indiana, and Iowa, testimony by blacks was forbidden in cases involving whites. Several Northern states limited or barred black immigration. Ohio, in particular, required a certificate of freedom from each black resident, barred blacks without such certificates from employment, fined anyone caught harboring a fugitive slave, and required every black entering the state to post a five-hundred-dollar bond, signed by two white men, as security. In some states, blacks were not allowed to be clerks or typesetters, to buy or sell alcohol, to trade farm products without a license, or to inherit property. Even in the New England states, personal discrimination was widespread in education, transportation, public facilities, and eating places. In Canada, freedom was protected by laws that were enforced by a government that supported abolition in both principle and fact. When a group of potential settlers from Ohio met with Upper Canada's Lieutenant General, Sir John Colborne, in 1829, he pointedly declared: "Tell the Republicans on your side of the line that we Royalists do not know men by their color. Should you come to us, you will be entitled to all the privileges of the rest of His Majesty's subjects." It is impossible to imagine a public official of equal stature in the United States holding such a meeting with blacks for any reason at all.

Refugees in Canada were crossing a cultural watershed that in some ways was more challenging even than the physical ordeal of flight through hundreds of miles of hostile or indifferent territory. In the world of slavery, no matter how hard men and women worked, it made no difference to their condition. Rarely was there any reward for intelligence, initiative, or ambition. Enterprise was as likely to lead to punishment as it was to profit. For all but a small handful of privileged slaves, the concept of choice barely existed, while a master's caprice, insolvency, or death might without warning lead at any time to traumatic separations, or worse. For the slave, poverty was foreordained.

In Canada, for the first time, former slaves could anticipate prosperity. Life became predictable in the best sense of the term. A man or woman who worked hard could expect to be paid. Families could expect to spend their lives together. A woman could expect to live her life without being raped. Children could expect to receive an education. Although racism certainly existed, a man could nonetheless expect to be treated in public with politeness. If he managed to save money, he could invest it and expect to enlarge his fortune. And if he made a bad business deal, he had as much hope as any white immigrant did of recovering and starting over. Wilson Ruffin Abbott, a free immigrant and businessman from Alabama, became one of the most prominent real estate developers in Toronto. And he was not alone.

The black press promoted Canada as a safe and welcoming destination for blacks, both fugitive and free, who wished to escape from the bigotry of "mock republicans," contrasting it with the "barbarous and pestilential" shores of Africa. "Is not Upper Canada as salubrious and fertile as any other country under the sun?" the *Colored American* posed in 1839. "Instead of sharks, alligators and tiger, there are wild turkey, and deer, and buffalo. Instead of savages and traders in human flesh, there is civilization, refinement, and religion. A colored man of good character and information and some means, may live in Canada without the least social or civil proscription." Although in Canada there was in fact color prejudice, the law was color-blind. Blacks had property rights. They could sue. They served on juries. They testified in trials. And they could vote. In 1849, when Colchester blacks (who by then made up one-third of the population) insisted upon their right to vote for the election of local officials, which was opposed by the white office holders, the town chairman was prosecuted and severely fined. A bigoted British immigrant wrote home with astonishment to relatives in England, "Here by the way, I may mention as illustration of the state of society, that everyone is called, it matters not in what position or occupation they stand, as Mr. or Mrs., or this Gentleman, or that Lady, even the Niggers." A black man even carried the Union Jack at the head of an "Orange Tory procession" in London in the summer of 1836. And in 1843, black residents of Toronto successfully petitioned the mayor and the city council to bar a traveling circus from performing blackface acts that ridiculed Afro Canadians.

In the 1820s, Canada had for all practical purposes ceased to sanction the return of fugitive slaves to the United States. In 1826, after months of fruitless negotiations, Albert Gallatin, the American minister to the Court of St. James, wrote resignedly to Secretary of State Henry Clay that Britain refused to depart from "the principle recognized by the British courts that every man is free who reaches British ground." A series of fugitive slave cases in the mid-1830s hardened the Crown's resolve. In the first of these, in 1833, Canadian officials refused to extradite Thornton and Ruth Blackburn, who were the center of an uproar in Detroit when a crowd of angry blacks had torn them out of the hands of the authorities and spirited them off to Canada. Four years later, the governor of Kentucky demanded the return of a fugitive named Jesse Happy, claiming that since he had escaped on his master's horse he should be treated as a simple thief. In response, Lieutenant Governor Francis Head wrote that "it may be argued that a slave escaping from bondage on his master's horse is a vicious struggle between two parties of which the slave owner is not only the aggressor, but the blackest criminal of the two—it is the case of the dealer in human flesh versus the stealer of horse flesh." Happy was allowed to remain in Canada undisturbed.

Blacks returned the Canadians' welcome with extravagant loyalty. They were staunch supporters of the most conservative Tories, believing with some reason that continuing rule by royalists best ensured that Canada would remain under the British flag. Blacks took a particular pride in bearing arms and wearing the uniform of colonial militia. For men who had been chattels only a few years or even months before, who would have been executed in the South for daring to carry guns, and flogged just for daring to protect their wives and daughters, or for that matter their own lives, the ability to defend themselves may have been the single most liberating experience of all. Strikingly, black militia companies had the lowest rate of desertion in the colonial forces.

Their mettle was tested in the winter of 1837, when the colonial authorities faced rebellion by reformers who demanded a republic, and an end to rule by local oligarchies. The rebels recruited volunteers—"fillibusters," as they were then called—in New York state, and moved to invade Canada with small forces across the Niagara and Detroit River frontiers. The Crown recruited heavily in the black townships of Canada West. Nearly a thousand blacks volunteered for service in a single month, including almost every black man in the town of Hamilton. Lieutenant Governor Head wrote that "they hastened as volunteers in wagon loads to the Niagara frontier to beg from me permission" to fight. Among them was Josiah Henson, who joined a company that helped defend Fort Malden. When the rebel schooner *Anne* sailed down the Detroit River firing its guns into the town of Sandwich, a memorable incident in the brief war, Henson was among the men who waded into the river and helped to take the ship's crew prisoner after it ran aground on a sandbar. The rebels were easily defeated, with little loss of life. For years afterward, Canadians remembered how the refugees had rallied to the Union Jack, and black military companies enjoyed something of a patriotic vogue. The Chatham militia, in particular, was a local tourist attraction, impressive in its scarlet uniforms. A British visitor wrote, "They are all runaway slaves (barring the officers); they look fierce and pompous enough; I daresay they would fight like devils with the Yankees." Blacks remembered the war as a glorious victory, not just over rebels who they feared would carry the spirit of repression north into Canada along with their American-style politics, but also over the scorn of whites who maintained as an article of racist faith that black men lacked the courage to fight. Freedom created its own rituals, in which pride, self-confidence, and defiance increasingly replaced the servile habits of slavery. In 1842 Chatham's black community celebrated the ninth anniversary of emancipation throughout the British Empire with an appropriately martial flourish, as black, red-coated militiamen fired twenty-one rounds from a cannon stationed on the parade ground, a sight that must have chilled the heart of any Southerner there, had one been present.

2

While living as a farmer, first at Fort Erie and then at Colchester, Henson was also living a kind of double life as a conductor for the Underground Railroad. He claimed in his autobiography to have led a total of 118 fugitives out of Kentucky, in the course of several rescue missions. Unfortunately, his account of these exploits is sketchy, possibly because money was involved and the exchange of cash for assistance did not fit the template of the selfless abolitionist motivated only by idealism and self-sacrifice. His involvement with the underground began with a sermon. One Sunday, he preached on the duty of former slaves who were safe in Canada to bring about the freedom of those still in servitude. Afterward, he was approached by a refugee named James Lightfoot, who had escaped from Kentucky several years earlier. Lightfoot explained that he had left behind his parents, three sisters, and four brothers on a plantation near Maysville, on the Ohio River. The sermon had left him feeling guilty for having done nothing to help them get to Canada. He was willing to pay someone to go to Kentucky to bring them north. The two men met together several times after that. Henson, in his own words, was moved by "seeing the agony of his heart in behalf of his kindred." He was also struggling to survive in a land where every man was on his own, and he needed money. There is no reason to doubt Henson's sympathy, but it is likely that the meetings included negotiations over the price that Henson would charge for undertaking such a dangerous venture.

They evidently came to an agreement, for Henson says that he traveled southward on foot through New York, Pennsylvania, and Ohio. Whether he was in contact with the underground during the trip he does not say, but it seems clear from later events that he knew where to find it when he wanted it. Once in Kentucky, he succeeded in making contact with Lightfoot's family. But the result was disappointing. Lightfoot's parents were too frail to travel, and his sisters were unwilling to risk the lives of their small children. The four brothers and a nephew were willing, but they were reluctant to abandon their parents and sisters at such short notice. The brothers promised Henson that if he returned for them in a year, they would be ready to go. Meanwhile, Henson had heard of a party of slaves fifty miles deeper into Kentucky, in Bourbon County, who wanted to escape, but needed a guide. After a week spent working out a plan of escape, he led the group across the Ohio River, and arrived in Cincinnati the third night after their departure, where they "procured assistance," an allusion, certainly, to the Underground Railroad. The following year, Henson says, he returned to Kentucky and brought away the Lightfoot brothers, as he had promised.

How much Henson was paid for this and for similar jobs that he undertook is unknown. But his profits from such clandestine work may well have helped him to save enough money to lease his share of the land at Colchester, and later to purchase two hundred acres near Dresden. That a man like Henson—secure with his family in Canada, and nothing if not acute at assessing risks and rewards—would undertake such dangerous work was less unusual than it might seem. It was not uncommon for fugitives to hire agents, white or black, to go south on their behalf, to rescue enslaved members of their family. As Levi Coffin bluntly expressed it, the underground operated on different terms in the South: "It was done for money." A certain free black man living in Buffalo, who "was well paid for his work," made a business out of going to the South after the wives of slaves who had found a home in Canada or the northern states. M. C. Buswell, whose family was part of the underground in northern Illinois, remembered a black man known to them only as "Charlie," a former slave from Missouri, "a bright and determined fellow," who for several years led fugitives on foot from Missouri across northern Illinois, and ultimately to Canada where, according to Buswell, who encountered him many times, "he succeeded in planting quite a large colony of his people." How another Canadian, this one a white man, carried out one of the most memorable rescues in the Ohio River valley gives some idea of how Henson may have gone about his clandestine work.

One day in June 1841, Reverend John Rankin was picking raspberries in the garden behind his hilltop home at Ripley, Ohio when he looked up to see standing before him a white stranger dressed in a homespun jacket buttoned to the top of his pants, an outfit common enough in parts of Canada, but outlandish in the Ohio Valley. Even more startling to Rankin was the stranger's companion, the squat black woman "Eliza," who had fled across the ice-bound Ohio three years earlier, and whom Rankin hadn't expected to see again.

"Oh, master Rankin, I want my daughter," she said.

The man with her was a French Canadian. The two had walked to Ripley from Cleveland, almost three hundred miles away. They intended to cross the river and bring away Eliza's grown daughter and her four children. She explained that the Canadian, whose name has gone unrecorded, was a rugged fellow who had worked as sailor, fisherman, and farmer, and understood the risks if he was caught. She had promised to pay him well. How she acquired the money Rankin does not say, but it is possible that she raised it by recounting the story of her escape to white church congregations and asking for donations, a common practice.

Without a country, without rights, without scope for their ambitions, without respect, without security, family was all that most slaves had, and its very precariousness made its bonds all the more precious. Eliza's own freedom was the only real capital she possessed, and she had decided to invest it in the salvation of her family. Since communication between slaves and relatives in the North, especially those in Canada, was all but impossible, Eliza's daughter of course knew nothing of this plan.

"Nonsense!" Rankin exclaimed when he had heard them out. He was consistently opposed to gambling the life of a free person who was safe on the uncertain chance of liberating any number of enslaved ones, even family. He looked the Canadian up and down, and then said to Eliza, "As sure as you and that man go over there, they will catch you and sell you down the river, and they will hang him. Now do not try it."

Eliza made it clear that they would go ahead with or without his help. Resigning himself, Rankin found Eliza temporary work with an abolitionist family near Ripley, and togged out the Canadian in a suit of less conspicuous clothes.

The Canadian found work chopping wood for steamboats and clearing land at the Thomas Davis farm, in Kentucky, where Eliza's daughter was enslaved, two and a half miles from the river. He found accommodations in the river port of Dover, opposite Ripley, which allowed him to observe the habits of the local slave patrols, which, he carefully noted, retired for the night between three-thirty and four A.M. Certain that he could bring off the rescue, he returned to Ripley for a final conference with Rankin, and to pick up Eliza, who was essential to the plan, since the daughter might not agree to leave without the assurances of her mother.

Rankin arranged to have Eliza and the Canadian rowed across the Ohio on Friday evening, and to have them brought back again with the daughter and her children the following night. He also arranged for a wagon to be ready in Ripley to take the whole party north into Highland County as soon as they landed. Eliza was disguised—rather comically, to the younger Rankins—in a man's brown shad-bellied coat and wide-brimmed hat, with her voluminous skirts stuffed inside in a way that made her look even more rotund than usual. Lowry and Samuel Rankin went across the river with them in a skiff belonging to the Rankins' close collaborator, John Collins, whose house faced the river in Ripley. When the boys shoved off to return to Ripley, Eliza and the Canadian were left alone and as vulnerable as any human beings on earth could be.

Saturday night passed with no trace of Eliza's family. The wagon that was supposed to carry them north departed without them. At last, on Sunday, the Canadian returned alone, and holed up at the Collins house. Collins sent a report up the hill to Rankin with a small boy who had not yet learned to read, and thus could never accidentally betray the contents. In substance, the Rankins were informed Eliza and the Canadian had reached the Davis farm before dawn on Saturday, and hid behind a haystack until Eliza's daughter appeared, on her way to milk the cows. When Eliza rose up before her, the shocked daughter "began to squall and hollow," until the Canadian "caught her by the neck and said that if she didn't stop he would choke her to death." When she had calmed down, Eliza returned with her to her cabin, and settled herself beneath the cabin's floor while the daughter explained the situation to her children. The Canadian remained out of sight in the woods.

After nightfall, the Canadian slipped into the cabin, as planned. He discovered that Eliza's daughter now had six children in all, two more having been born since Eliza's escape. Also, the daughter was pregnant. Moreover, she had collected "two or three hundred pounds of stuff in bundles, piled up," and flatly refused to leave without every piece of it. He and Eliza finally agreed to carry the bundles in relays, hiding them in the woods, then going back for another load. The children toted what they could, the older ones moving faster, the smaller ones straggling behind with an armful of clothing, a pot, or some other trifle. The details hint at a trauma that eluded the white abolitionists: a home suddenly disrupted, the wrenching disorientation of leaving fathers and husbands behind (they weren't even mentioned in the Rankins' accounts), perhaps even ambivalence about flight itself on the part of a young woman who had been abruptly torn from her home by a fiercely strong-willed mother who, it must have seemed, had suddenly risen from the dead.

By the time they reached the river, it was too late to cross before daylight. The Canadian settled Eliza's family in a cornfield and then left them, promising to return on Sunday, after the patrols had bedded down for the night. Eliza was charged with keeping the children quiet until he returned. The Canadian had stolen a skiff to cross back to Ripley. Probably on Rankin's advice, he pulled it up onto the Ohio bank, where it could plainly be seen by anyone looking across from Kentucky. When the Davises awoke on Sunday morning, they soon discovered that seven of their slaves had disappeared. Thomas Davis hurried into Dover to alert the patrol and set to scouring the riverbank to see if any skiffs were gone. Mike Sullivan, a flatboat builder, recognized his skiff on the shore at Ripley. As John P. Rankin recorded the story, Sullivan told the slave owner and his party, "Them niggers are right over in that town, they sure are up there in some of them holes that old John Rankin has to hide niggers in." In fact, Eliza's family was at that very moment lying just a short distance away in Sullivan's own cornfield.

Davis and a posse of Kentuckians took the Dover ferry across to Ripley, where he spent the rest of the morning stalking around town, offering a reward of four hundred dollars to any man "that would only point his finger at the house they were in." From their perch above the town, the Rankins could see both the tumult in town, as the Kentuckians hurried through the streets, searching for the fugitives, and the cornfield across the river where they were actually hidden. Knowing that their home would be searched, they made an ostentatious show of descending the hundred stone steps down the hill to town to attend church, leaving the door to their house open behind them.

That night, after the patrols had retired, the Canadian rowed silently back across the river to Kentucky in Collins's skiff. He beached it under a clump of trees just below the fence that was the Mason and Bracken county line. Eliza herself had kept watch all day and night, never having shut her eyes. Just before dawn on Monday morning, they shook awake Eliza's daughter and her children, and hurried them to the river so quickly that—by the Canadian's design, surely—almost all the luggage they had packed the day before was left behind before the daughter realized what was happening. There on the riverbank, Eliza handed a wallet of gold to the Canadian. He took it without looking inside, and pulled for Ohio.

They were met on the Ohio shore by Collins and "Jolly Bob" Patton, a deacon of the Reform Church, who had arranged with one of the elders, Thomas McCague, one of the wealthiest men on the river, for the fugitives to be hidden in McCague's sedate brick home. McCague's slaughterhouse at that time was killing more hogs than all Cincinnati, and he was never suspected as a member of the underground. His house was used only in an emergency like this, when slave hunters were expected to be in close pursuit. The gate had been left unlatched. As they entered, the Canadian took his adieu, and headed back to Canada on foot. He was never seen in Ripley again.

The fugitives were taken upstairs to a large room on the third floor. Now the problem was to get them up to the Rankin house somehow without being seen. Six black children with a pregnant woman, accompanied by known abolitionists, climbing the steps to the Rankin farm, could hardly be missed. They would obviously have to be split up. The smallest children were carried unsuspected up the hill in the McCagues' elegant carriage. Others were led by different guides by roundabout routes, avoiding freshly tilled fields where they would leave tracks. Once the party was reassembled in the Rankins' kitchen, they were placed in a wagon belonging to a cooperative traveling salesman. With John P. Rankin and the sons of two other underground men as guards, the triumphant Eliza and her family, utterly numb by now with exhaustion and fear, set off for Hillsboro, thirty-five miles north on the road to Columbus, and thus passed out of recorded history, although she would live on for generations to come as a fictional construct born from the imagination of Harriet Beecher Stowe.

John P. Rankin and his friends returned to Ripley just before dawn. "In the morning mother had us up to regular breakfast, and soon it was school time," he recalled. "We hustled ourselves down and were at school just as gay and lively as any other boys there, and never whispered a word to each other."

3

In March 1841 the *Free Labor Advocate and Anti-Slavery Standard* of Newport, Indiana, reported to its readers, "We have no means of ascertaining the exact number of fugitives who have passed over Lake Erie this season, but we are confident it is greater than it was the last, when eight hundred was the estimated number. They have gone singly and in pairs; in tens and twenties, and even in larger companies." The *Advocate* was talking, as it made clear, only about refugees who had crossed Lake Erie, and only those who were known to the organized underground. Unknown numbers also crossed the St. Lawrence from northern New York and Vermont, and coasted the rocky shores of New England from Boston to Nova Scotia. But the underground lines funneled the largest proportion of Canada-bound fugitives into the lake ports between Oswego, New York and Detroit, and from there by water directly to Canada. (In winter, underground men from Buffalo, New York, drove fugitives in their farm wagons to Canada across the frozen Niagara River, and Sandusky, Ohio, conductors carried them in speeding sleighs across the ice on Lake Erie.)

Conductors who were in a hurry, or desperate, sometimes literally flung fugitives onto a passing ship, and hoped for the best. In one such instance, a steamboat captain named Chapman, en route from Cleveland to Buffalo, was hailed about three miles offshore by four men in a small boat, two of them merchants with whom he had done business the day before, and the others black strangers. One of the whites threw on board a purse containing fifteen dollars in silver, and asked Chapman to land the black men in Canada, telling him to take his pay out of it, and to give the passengers what was left. The sight of the new passengers didn't please the captain, who, imbued with the racial prejudices of his time and place, found them "very black, coarse in feature and build, stupid in expression, and apparently incapable of any mental excitement except fear." Fortunately, however, Chapman was a man with a heart, and he ran in near the Canadian shore, and landed the men on a beach, where they were met by the agents of the underground, "though," Chapman recalled years later, "at the time I had never heard of that institution, and my vessel was pressed into service, and constituted an 'extension of the track' without my knowing it." Chapman handed the men the entire fifteen dollars, and told them they were free. What he then witnessed startled the captain. "They seemed to be transformed; a new light shone in their eyes, their tongues were loosed, they laughed and cried, prayed and sang praises, fell upon the ground and kissed it over and over. I thought to myself, 'My God! Is it possible that human beings are kept in such a condition that they are made perfectly happy by being landed and left alone in a strange land with no human beings or habitations in sight, with the prospect of never seeing a friend or relative?' Before I stepped upon my deck I had determined to never again be identified with any party that sustained the system of slavery."

For the most part, however, the underground relied on trusted captains and crews. In the 1840s the *Mayflower* transported fugitives from Sandusky, Ohio, to Amherstburg, in Canada, with such regularity that it became known as the "abolition boat." (The *Mayflower* was the venue of a memorable incident in August 1854, when, as it was nearing the dock at Buffalo, the ship's barber, a fugitive slave named Hoover, recognized his former master in the company of several police officers; Hoover ran to the bow of the *Mayflower*, and leaped from it onto the stern of the nearest ship—named the *Plymouth Rock*, no less—and then climbed up from it onto the ferry bound across the Niagara River to Canada, thus making his escape.) Samuel B. Cuyler of Pultneyville, New York boldly led fugitives to the town landing in broad daylight to meet the *Ontarian*, whose captain was a cousin by marriage, and paid their fares with funds donated by local abolitionists. Horace Ford delivered fugitives to a black barber named John Bell, in Cleveland, who in the evening would put them aboard a certain Canadian passenger boat captained by an Englishman, "who would wink at our enterprise and say nothing about it though he must have understood the situation." Captains bound for Detroit often put fugitives in small boats as they passed beneath the British guns of Fort Malden, and had crewmen row them ashore.

For many fugitives, the lake crossing must have had a weirdly theatrical quality, after weeks or months of furtive flight. Few had ever seen such a vast expanse of water as the Great Lakes, or traveled on anything as grand as a mid-century steamboat. Shallow and turbulent Lake Erie was the center of steamship activity on the lakes, and giant craft like the twenty-two-hundred-ton *City of Buffalo* with their deep hulls and low superstructure rivaled in size and elegance anything on the Atlantic at that time. Fugitives, naturally, were much more likely to travel on deck, or with the cargo, but they could not help being dazzled by these floating palaces, which were luxurious beyond the experience even of the common white man, opulent with gilded fretwork, dazzlingly illuminated crystal chandeliers, ornamental paintings, acres of luxurious red plush, and furniture of mahogany or rosewood. They were also harrowingly dangerous. Nearly 30 percent of all the steamboats built before 1849 were lost to accidents. Boilers exploded, scalding passengers to death by the score. Boats were blown apart by storms, collided with other boats, and caught fire and burned like tinder. (On steamboats that plied the rivers of the South, the owners typically preferred Irishmen to slaves as firemen, because if the boiler exploded and killed them their deaths would bring no financial loss to the management.)

Of all the underground gateways to Canada, the busiest was Detroit. By 1837 forty-two regularly scheduled steamers touched at its port. (Many fugitives, of course, also arrived in Detroit by overland routes from Indiana and Illinois.) The opening of the Erie Canal, in 1825, helped make Detroit a natural hub for westbound emigrants, and the fastest growing city in the region. Between 1830 and 1840 its population tripled from three thousand to more than nine thousand, and it would more than double again by 1850, to twenty-one thousand. Arriving fugitives found a city that was inventing itself literally day by day. Against a backdrop of church steeples framed against the majestic western sky, enormous steamers, sidewheelers, brigs, sloops, small three-sailed *chaloupes*, ten-oared *bateaux* laden with cargoes for the frontier hinterland, and flitting canoes crowded the noisy waterfront. Everywhere, new streets were being laid out, big new brick houses were under construction, and the plank sidewalks were crowded with emigrants from the East and Europe pouring through on their way to the frontier. Fugitives also found one of the best organized underground operations in the country.

By the 1840s most fugitives were forwarded across the Detroit River by the city's Vigilance Committee, founded by the redoubtable black abolitionist William Lambert, a Quaker-educated tailor from New Jersey, who had come to Detroit to seek his fortune in 1838. Lambert was also a superb businessman, and would amass a fortune before his death in 1891.

In 1840 he had addressed the Michigan State Legislature, calling forcefully but unsuccessfully for the franchise to be extended to blacks. Three years later, he organized and chaired the state's first convention of black citizens, whose final statement, a radical one by the standards of the era, boldly declared that the people "have the right at all times, to alter or reform [their government], and to abolish one form of government and establish another, whenever the public good requires it." It was, in essence, an open call for slave rebellion. Lambert's closest collaborator in clandestine work was William C. Munroe, minister at Detroit's first black religious institution, the Second Baptist Church, whose handsome new neo-gothic building on Beaubien Street was an ornament of Detroit's increasingly sophisticated cityscape. Messages from conductors in his congregation often had a quaintly biblical flavor. "Pastor, tomorrow night at our 8:00 meeting, let's read Exodus 10:8," one might read, meaning that a conductor would be arriving at 8 P.M. with ten fugitives, eight men and two women. From the church, it was but a five-minute walk to the waterfront, and then a ten-minute ferry ride across the mile of water that separated the United States and Canada.

Detroit was nothing if not cosmopolitan, and few passengers took any special note of the black faces among the melange of French Canadians, brisk Americans, "sad-eyed Indians folded in their blankets," and "long-waisted damsels of the city" who packed aboard what a British visitor described as the "pretty little steamer, gaily painted, with streamers flying," that shuttled back and forth between Detroit and Windsor. For countless fugitives, the brief trip on what some called "freedom's ferry" was the final stage of the journey that had taken them from somewhere deep inside Kentucky, western Virginia, or Tennessee, across the Ohio River, and northward for hundreds of miles through the hostile or indifferent countryside of the Northern states, often no more than a few days, or even hours, ahead of pursuers bent on carrying them back to slavery. Few fugitives cared that their landfall in Canada was a scrubby, somnolent hamlet where, in sharp contrast to booming Detroit, a handful of small boats idled among yawping seagulls, and bobbing flotillas of mallards. Unpromising though the town of Windsor seemed, as fugitives stepped ashore they became transformed into refugees, impoverished perhaps, but safe and free, in the words of one abolitionist, "where the deep gloom of a worse than Egyptian night departed, and gave place to the bright sun of British liberty."

4

Most refugees discovered upon their arrival in Canada that they had traded one kind of insecurity for another. Most arrived penniless. Fortunate ones found work quickly. Others wandered for days, weeks, even months before settling down. Jarm Logue's experience was typical of many. Having left behind his beloved mother, Cherry, and several siblings still enslaved to the whiskey-brewing (and whiskey-swilling) Logue family, he and a single companion had ridden on an epic journey northward from Tennessee, fighting their way through two bands of patrollers, crossing the frozen Ohio River, and trekking through the desolate wilderness of northern Indiana, before reaching Detroit. When he crossed the Detroit River to Canada in the winter of 1835, Logue was alone and desperate for work. He swapped his mare for a broken-down nag and a few shillings and continued overland to the town of London, where he traded the nag to a farmer for board and another handful of coins. Still unable to find work, and now horseless, he hitched a ride to the port of Hamilton, on Lake Ontario. As he gazed across the iron gray sheet of water—a vista of surpassing bleakness beneath the overcast skies of winter—he felt overwhelmed by despair. "There I stood," he wrote years later to Frederick Douglass, "a boy of twenty-one years of age (as near as I know my age) the tempest howling over my head, and my toes touching the snow beneath my worn-out shoes—with the assurance that I was at the end of my journey—knowing nobody, and nobody knowing me or noticing me, only as attracted by the then supposed mark of Cain on my sorrow-stricken face. I stood there the personification of helpless courage and finited love." Like refugees of all times and places, he had never imagined that freedom could feel so painful.

But at last, in Hamilton, Logue's luck turned. He found work splitting rails, and was accepted into the local sabbath school, where before the winter was over he had learned the rudiments of reading and writing, and was introduced for the first time to the Bible, an encounter that would eventually change his life, and help propel him to the front rank of black abolitionists. From that time on, he never failed to find work at good wages.

It was here that the Underground Railroad, in a literal sense, finally came to an end, in Hamilton, St. Catharines, and Fort Erie near the Niagara frontier, in the inland towns of Chatham and London, in Amherstburg, Sandwich, and Colchester at the head of Lake Erie, in bustling York, later to be called Toronto, and to the north in frontier hamlets on Owen Sound. By the early 1840s, there may have been as many as twelve thousand former slaves living in Canada, the great majority of them in communities scattered across southern Canada West, present-day Ontario.* Without immigration agents to register newcomers, however, it was impossible to reliably quantify new arrivals, or departures. The refugee population was in constant flux: like many, Jarm Logue eventually moved back to the United States, where he would one day play a central role in one of the most dramatic events in the underground's history.

Some refugees, like Logue and Josiah Henson, were remarkably successful. Three years after his inauspicious arrival, Logue was leasing a two-hundred-acre farm and had saved several hundred dollars, more than many white immigrants. In Amherstburg, where it was said that four hundred thousand dollars' worth of Southern slaves were walking the streets, former refugees owned successful farms, a livery stable, a gravel pit, and the best hotel in town. Throughout Canada, refugees commonly found work in the skilled construction trades, and as shoemakers, tailors, barbers, cooks, and agricultural laborers. Others worked as waiters in the tourist hotels at Niagara Falls, and they were among the first guides who took visitors under the falls.

Many others, however, remained destitute, or trapped in the kind of

* Josiah Henson estimated the total number of blacks in Canada at twenty thousand, but his guess was probably high. Among these, Colchester had the largest proportion of blacks, about 30 percent. Blacks were about 23 percent in Malden township, 16 percent in adjoining Amherstburg township, and 11 percent in Amherstburg village, the civilian settlement that grew up outside Fort Malden.

marginal existence that worried Henson. Even Jarm Logue, who was exceptionally acute, but who had no business experience, lost almost all his property when he took on a partner who was encumbered with debts; as soon as they had harvested their first crops, not only the crop itself, but their implements and livestock too were seized by creditors. Visitors to some settlements reported refugees living in utter destitution, and reduced to beggary. In the late 1830s their plight began to attract the attention of missionaries. Isaac J. Rice in 1838 abandoned a comfortable ministry in Ohio for a shack on a back street in the black section of Amherstburg, where he opened a dispensary and a school, and issued mournful appeals to abolitionists who, he begged to remind them, had not finished their work just because the victims of slavery had crossed the Canadian border. Levi Coffin, who visited Rice in 1844, regarded his home as the "main terminus" of the Underground Railroad in the West. Two years before that, Rice claimed to have provided clothes to three hundred refugees in the course of twelve months, a very plausible figure, and to be schooling ninety students. He and his wife were sometimes reduced to living on nothing but bread and beans, and at one point sold even their beds to buy food for the refugees who showed up in a daily stream at their door. Even those who admired his work found him personally off-putting, a man whose sense of Christian martyrdom, and identification with the suffering victims of slavery, ran so deep that he seemed to relish his own poverty, and to exhibit his hollow eyes, rotting teeth, and tattered clothes as badges of honor.

Rice competed for donations with another, almost equally unappealing American missionary, a peripatetic young graduate of the Oneida Institute named Hiram Wilson. One of the American Anti-Slavery Society's first contingent of lecturers, known as The Seventy, Wilson was also a veteran of underground work, having personally conducted at least one fugitive, and probably many more, across Lake Erie from Ohio to Canada. Since 1836 he had traveled on foot through Canada West, preaching the gospel to refugees, and establishing schools among them wherever he could. Even more than Rice, he had a gift for the self-pitying touch. "I am a stranger in my own house," he wrote morosely to the *Colored American*, after one journey during which he had founded no fewer than ten schools, and had recruited fourteen teachers, all of them "ardently pious," before setting out on yet another odyssey of three hundred miles "with but a shilling in my pocket." He added, "So urgent was my errand that neither the piercing cold, nor heavy storms, nor snowdrifts breast high, impeded my progress, nor prevented my walking 40 miles in a day." A few months later, he wrote again, with an almost audible sigh, "How long I shall continue to labor thus without means of support, the Lord only knows." (He would in fact manage to do so for more than twenty years, never flagging in either his commitment to the fugitive, or in his talent for irritating potential supporters.)

Wilson's peregrinations took him to every black community between York and Windsor. It was inevitable that he would eventually meet the rising leader of Colchester's more ambitious settlers, Josiah Henson. The two men immediately recognized in each other kindred souls, or at least an equally fervent belief that the ultimate liberation of the former slaves, the inner continuation of the Underground Railroad as it were, lay in the transformative power of education. Henson understood this in a painfully visceral way. When the Hensons were living at Fort Erie, Josiah's employer, the farmer Hibbard, had paid for the schooling of their eldest son, Tom. On Sundays, Henson would ask the boy to read something from the Bible to him before going to preach. He was apparently able to memorize long passages after a single hearing, a skill that concealed his own illiteracy. One Sunday, when he asked Tom to read to him, the boy asked where he should start. Henson told him to begin anywhere, not knowing how to direct him.

The boy happened to open the book to Psalm 103. When he read, "Bless the Lord, O my soul and all that is within me, bless his holy name," Josiah's heart inexplicably seemed to melt in a wave of gratitude, as images from his slave life tumbled pell-mell through his mind: the wrenching loss of his mother, his betrayal by Isaac Riley, the dreadful flatboat journey to New Orleans, when he had nearly murdered Riley's young nephew. He began to weep with gratitude for his family's survival, which he believed with a devouring intensity of faith had flowed not from his own courage and physical strength—he had, after all, carried the two smallest children in a pack on his back for hundreds of miles—but from the profuse and mysterious grace of God.

When Tom got to the end of the passage, he turned to his father, and asked an unexpectedly devastating question, "Who was David? He writes pretty, don't he?"

Henson had never heard of David. He could not bear confessing his ignorance, and so replied vaguely, "He was a man of God."

"Where did he live?" Tom persisted. "What did he do?"

Unable to escape his son's barrage of questions, Henson finally gave up and confessed that he had no idea who David was.

Tom looked at him in astonishment, perhaps with sudden disillusionment. This father who seemed omnipotent, who boasted of his physical strength and of his influence, could not even read. Henson's sense of identity hinged on maintaining the image of a man who, although a slave, was smarter even than the whites who gave him orders, a man who controlled the immediate world around him, in short, a hero even in his own eyes. But for this challenge he had been utterly unprepared.

"Why, father," Tom asked, "can't you read?"

Henson admitted that he couldn't. The truth left him feeling devastated. Whatever else he might be, he was ignorant of everything that existed in books, including most of the Bible.

"Well, you can learn now, father," Tom piped up.

"No, my son, I am too old, and have not enough time. I must work all day, or you would not have enough to eat."

"Then you must do it at night."

"But still there is nobody to teach me."

"Why, father, *I'll teach you*," Tom replied.

Henson was now torn by conflicting emotions. The perceptiveness with which he described them was acute, revealing not just his own confusion—shame mingled with hope, bitterness with resignation, rage with gratitude—but that which tormented countless black refugees in Canada. "I was delighted with the conviction that my children would have advantages I had never enjoyed," Henson recalled, "but it was no slight mortification to think of being instructed by a child of twelve years old. Yet ambition, and a true desire to learn, for the good it would do my own mind, conquered the shame, and I agreed to try."

The two studied each evening by the light of a pine knot or burning hickory bark. Henson's progress was so slow that Tom's initial enthusiasm began to flag. Sometimes he fell asleep during their lessons, and sometimes would "whine a little over my dullness, and talk to me very much as a schoolmaster talks to a stupid boy." Josiah was close to despair. The letters that he wrote seemed no more than pathetic "little scratches." He had finally encountered an obstacle that he could not surmount, and it shamed him mightily. However, by dint of Herculean effort, by the end of winter he had managed to learn to read enough to keep his hope alive. How much literacy he ultimately achieved remains an open question.

"It has made me comprehend better the terrible abyss of ignorance in which I had been plunged all my previous life," he would later say. "It made me also feel more deeply and bitterly the oppression under which I had toiled and groaned; but the crushing and cruel nature of which I had not appreciated, till I found out, in some slight degree, from what I had been debarred. At the same time it made me more anxious than before to do something for the rescue and elevation of those who were suffering the same evils I had endured, and who did not know how degraded and ignorant they really were."

Hiram Wilson would play a larger role in Henson's life than any white man since Isaac Riley. Allying his own connections to potential donors with Henson's determination and charisma would, in turn, provide Wilson with an opportunity to play out his pedagogical ambitions on a far grander scale than ever before. Just where they met, and how they spoke with each other, is not recorded. But they both agreed that only through education and self-sufficiency would blacks ever become independent of the white man. They envisioned an institution like none that existed in Canada, where in addition to the customary grammar school subjects, boys would also be trained in the mechanical arts, and girls, as Henson, who was no revolutionary in the sphere of women's roles, put it, "in those domestic arts which are the proper occupation and ornament of their sex." The school's graduates would, in turn, become teachers themselves, spreading out to bring both basic literacy, practical knowledge, and the gospel of self-sufficiency to refugees throughout Canada.

Dawn, as they decided to call it, was not the first planned black settlement in Canada. In 1829, a company of immigrants seeking to escape from the coruscating racism of Cincinnati had purchased eight hundred acres of land near London, naming their new home Wilberforce, in honor of the great British parliamentary advocate of emancipation. Like the plan for Dawn, Wilberforce promoted an idealistic vision of private ownership and cooperative activity. However, in spite of support from both William Lloyd Garrison and the Tappan brothers, the colony was an embarrassing failure. Its first leader, Israel Lewis, proved to be a rogue who absconded with most of the money that had been raised, and when Hiram Wilson visited in 1838, he was dismayed to find Wilberforce "a miserable concern" inhabited by only eighteen or twenty families, many of them wretchedly poor, all that remained of hundreds who originally had set out from Cincinnati.

Dawn's beginnings were more auspicious. Wilson excitedly wrote to a Quaker friend named James Canning Fuller, a gentleman farmer who had immigrated to the United States from England, and who had become very active in abolitionist work, harboring fugitives in his home at Skaneateles, New York, and serving as secretary of his local antislavery society. Wilson knew that if Fuller's interest was aroused, his resources were virtually limitless. On one occasion, Fuller was personally escorting an emancipated family back with him from the South when he was informed that the public coach they planned to take would not carry blacks; Fuller bought the vehicle on the spot, and continued north in style with his charges.

Fuller liked what Wilson told him about Dawn. During the summer of 1840, he easily raised sixteen hundred and fifty dollars for the colony from antislavery philanthropists, in the course of a trip to England. At an open meeting of black settlers in Canada, six trustees for the new school were elected, three of them black, and three white, including Fuller. Although the settlement as a whole continued to be known as Dawn, in deference to the source of Fuller's donation, the school was formally named the British-American Manual Training Institute. With Fuller's money, Henson and Wilson purchased two hundred acres of fertile, gently undulating land well wooded with black walnut, white oak, ash, hickory, and maple trees on the Sydenham River, one hundred miles east of Detroit.

On November 28, 1841, a delegation of settlers and well-wishers, both black and white, stood together in a semicircle on the snow-whitened banks of the Sydenham, beneath the branches of a great oak tree. To Wilson, the winter-bare branches seemed to symbolize the arms of God spread protectively over their endeavor. Kneeling in four or five inches of snow, they raised their voices in "a refreshing season of prayer." Wilson set to work on the house in which he planned to live, on the site of an old Indian wigwam. He pulled up the wigwam's stakes with his own hands. Triumphantly he wrote, "I shouldered an axe, called a few colored men to my aid, cut away the brush, cleared off a beautiful building spot, chopped the logs, and in three days got my house up as high as the [joist], 26 by 20 feet."

Little more than a year after the groundbreaking, on December 12, 1842, the British-American Institute opened with twelve students. Wilson mainly taught academics, while Henson, ever the preacher, "expounded spiritual truths." As enrollment grew, Wilson recruited teachers from among his friends from Oberlin. Students both lived and had their classes in the school building, a long, low structure of hewn logs in a small clearing near the riverbank. They spent a half day in the classroom and the rest of the day at "practical" activities, cutting timber and cordwood, or carrying on farming operations on the institute's two hundred acres of cleared land. (An additional hundred acres would be acquired in 1844.) By the latter half of the decade, the settlement stretched for nearly half a mile along both sides of the Sydenham. Between sixty and eighty students were usually enrolled in the institute at any given time, ranging in age from five to twenty-five, and older, in its two divisions, junior and adult. Initially, the institute's endeavors flourished. Two "enterprising men of color" from North Carolina and Virginia were manufacturing rope from locally grown hemp. A black millwright from South Carolina was building a steam-driven grist mill, while two machinists were at work making the boilers and furnaces, using bricks that were also being made on the site. Henson traveled to Boston where he raised one thousand dollars to build a sawmill, and to develop markets for the export of the colony's fine hardwoods. All the profits from these several enterprises were to be "sacredly devoted to the cause of education," and within a few years, Henson hoped, would pay off the colony's debts—between four and five thousand dollars in the mid-1840s—and eliminate the need for begging and borrowing from abroad. Attracted by the opportunity for education and work, refugees continued to arrive, turning the surrounding area into what was, in effect, a swarming terminal of the Underground Railroad.

The colony's reputation spread widely. Before the decade was out, there were five hundred black settlers in the immediate vicinity of the institute, occupying fifteen hundred acres of their own land, apart from the school's holdings. By Henson's estimate, another thirty-five hundred settlers lived within one day's travel from Dawn. They were, he asserted, "with few exceptions refugees from slavery." One of them was a fugitive named John Brown, who had escaped from bondage in Mississippi a few years earlier, and had arrived at Dawn after living for a time with abolitionists in Michigan, and then working with a crew of Cornish miners in the copper mines on Lake Superior, where he had heard about the thriving new colony. Given work at the sawmill, he helped to cut the walnut planks that Henson would personally escort to the Crystal Palace Exhibition, the first world's fair, in London, England, in 1851.

As a slave in Maryland and Kentucky, Henson had dreamed as perhaps all slaves did of having land that belonged to him alone. Now, at the age of fifty-three, apart from managing the institute, he held two hundred acres of prime farmland in his own name, in a true community of men like himself for whom such dreams had once seemed impossible and pathetic, men who understood the mysteries of money and deeds, profit and loss, leases and percentages, the magic of the written word, and the majestic truths of the Bible. An even rosier future was undoubtedly in store. In November 1847, he proclaimed, "Trusting in the God of Heaven, and not in an arm of flesh, our watchword is ONWARD."

CHAPTER 13

THE SALTWATER UNDERGROUND

Then lift that manly right hand, bold ploughman of the wave!
Its branded palm shall prophecy "SALVATION TO THE SLAVE."

—JOHN GREENLEAF WHITTIER

1

It's easy to imagine how it must have begun, on the beach at Pensacola, one steaming day in the middle of June, 1844. The strapping seaman Jonathan Walker is at work on his whaleboat, where he has pulled it up on sand that is so blindingly white that it is painful to look straight at it in the sun's glare. Walker's friend, the slave Charles Johnson, has come by. Although he is young and fit, his body is marred by ugly "scrofulous risings" on his chest, as the wanted poster would later put it. Perhaps Walker has hired his labor, rented him, so to speak, so that they work together hour after hour, brushing dark green paint onto the overturned hull, talking and laboring. Perhaps the plan begins with a seemingly casual question. Johnson wonders aloud if Walker has ever heard of sailors helping slaves to get to the North, and what he thinks about it, and if he ever knew any sailors like that. Or maybe it is Walker himself, with his Yankee twang, asking Johnson if he ever thought of running away from his master, if he ever wanted to be free.

Florida resembled the Texas frontier more than it did the interior of the cotton-growing South. Ceded to the United States by Spain only in 1821 and still governed as a territory—it would become a state in 1845—Florida had a population more Spanish and African than Anglo-Saxon. Almost half the territory's fifty thousand inhabitants were black, all but a handful of them slaves. Pensacola occupied a scant two dozen city blocks. Life focused on the port, one of the best on the Gulf Coast, and on the several military posts in the vicinity, most prominent among them the massive red brick bastions of Fort Pickens, whose heavy guns commanded the approaches to the harbor. The writ of law did not carry far beyond the city's thinly populated outskirts, however. Since the days of Spanish rule, the swamps that surrounded Pensacola had been home to bandits and renegades of every stripe. Although Florida had been a comparatively tolerant place under Spanish rule, in keeping with the policies of the slave states to its north, the territorial government had begun to enact more racially repressive laws that limited the movements and opportunities of free blacks, and forced many of them back into slavery as punishment for offenses as minor as the failure to pay fines.

Johnson soon learned, if he had not known it all along, that Walker was an abolitionist who believed that slavery was an "awful depravity," a "national poison" that "ranked with the highest wrongs and crimes that ever were invented by the enemy of man." Unlike many abolitionists, Walker was genuinely comfortable in the company of African Americans. Probably he had served with black seamen, who were numerous in the merchant marine. He also viscerally identified with slaves in ways that intellectual, middle-class abolitionists rarely could. He knew from painful experience what it was like to be helpless, vulnerable, and dependent on strangers for his survival. Indeed, he saw slaves and sailors fundamentally as comrades in suffering. "I think that next to the slave, the sailor is thrown most shamefully into the scale of oppression, wrong, and neglect," he later wrote. Shipowners, like slave owners, he believed, were only interested in profit, and cared nothing for the privation that sailors suffered for their benefit, while the captains under whom they served were often as abusive as overseers. Any sailor who stood up to them was treated as a mutineer, and just as liable as a slave to be punished by a whip laid across his bare back.

As Walker's biographer, Alvin F. Oickle, has shown, Walker grew up about as poor as anyone could, on a hardscrabble farm that clung precariously to the played out, sandy soil of Cape Cod. He went to sea as a boy, and by the time he was first seen striding the dusty streets of Pensacola with his rolling nautical gait, he had traveled the world from Russia to the South Seas. His life at sea was a litany of hairsbreadth escapes. In 1817, at the age of eighteen, he survived a nearly fatal bout of tropical fever in the East Indies. At twenty-one he was blown overboard from the yardarm of a ship into the frigid North Atlantic. He survived a yellow fever epidemic in Havana. In 1835 he and one of his sons were attacked by Mexican bandits who seized their boat and shot the elder Walker in the abdomen and the wrist. Walker and his son survived by swimming out to sea and treading water until night, and then hiking, stark naked, for twenty-four hours without fresh water until they reached help. He had been an abolitionist for more than a decade, after being converted by Reverend Samuel J. May, an ally of William Lloyd Garrison, in 1831, and he may have assisted fugitive slaves passing through Cape Cod as early as 1832.

Walker first appeared in Pensacola in 1836, piloting a sloop laden with potatoes, beets, bricks, and "other notions," which he offered for sale. Compared to a bleak existence on Cape Cod, he found Florida's "soft and genial climate" positively luxurious, and he decided to stay on. His family joined him in 1837, and for the next five years he worked as a carpenter, boatwright, and caretaker for the property of a railroad, planned but never built, that was intended to link Pensacola with the plantation country in Alabama. He was known as a Bible-reading man, always a badge of respect in that evangelical age. But his outspoken interest in blacks attracted unfavorable attention. People thought him merely eccentric for tending a sick black man who was being held in the city jail as a runaway, and repeatedly praying with another prisoner, a slave who was falsely accused of raping a white woman. Although things like this could fairly be construed as Christian acts, Walker was known, more disturbingly, to consort with blacks "on terms of equality and intimacy," the *Pensacola Gazette* later reported, even allowing them to eat with his family, and to be served by his own daughters. He had twice been called in by the mayor "in consequence of the reports in circulation that I was on good terms with the colored people." Both times, he was warned that he might be the victim of violence if he did not respect local "rules and customs." In 1842 Walker moved his family back to Massachusetts, but he came south again in the fall of 1843, to work as a shipbuilder in Mobile, Alabama. Then, just days before the meeting with Charles Johnson, he showed up in Pensacola, this time with a twenty-five-foot schooner-rigged whale-boat, with the idea of salvaging copper from a wreck at the bottom of the harbor. But the prospect of human salvage soon engaged his interest.

Johnson told Walker that he and three other slaves wanted him to take them to the free states. Walker was willing, but he knew that they could not travel far north along the Atlantic seaboard without being discovered. Instead, he proposed a daring plan. He volunteered to take Johnson and his friends to the British-ruled Bahamas, where slavery had been abolished eleven years earlier. They knew that fugitives could expect a welcome there. Both men would have remembered how less than three years earlier 135 slaves had mutinied on the brig *Creole*, en route to New Orleans, and sailed it to freedom in the Bahamas. Walker knew that the risks were immense. They would have to traverse almost one thousand miles in an open boat, without shelter from the weather, and unable to conceal themselves from passing ships. Walker told Johnson that if they made good, they could pay him whatever they thought his help had been worth. He asked for nothing else.

Escape by land from the Deep South was close to impossible. It is clear from interviews carried out among fugitives in Canada in the 1850s and 1860s that only a very small proportion of them came from anywhere south of Kentucky and Virginia. To reach the nearest free state overland, which was Ohio, Johnson and his friends would have had to travel seven hundred miles due north, through the slave states of Alabama, Tennessee, and Kentucky, all of them hostile to fugitives, and closely patrolled by slave catchers and local constables. Nowhere along the way could a fugitive count on finding assistance. (There was the rare exception: one celebrated fugitive would travel all the way from Huntsville, Alabama, to Ohio clinging to the tops of railway cars.) A handful made their way across Texas and over the border into Mexico. The only other direction left open to them was the sea.

The sea was, in a sense, a commercial extension of the Northern states, and every Yankee ship that touched at a Southern port like a piece of free territory that suddenly came within the physical reach of restive slaves. Merchants based in New York and Boston dominated commerce everywhere along the coast, while New Englanders, New Yorkers, and free black sailors crewed the thousand-ton brigs and low-slung coasters that shipped cargoes of plantation-grown tobacco and cotton, New Jersey bricks, Georgia turpentine, Pennsylvania coal, and Hudson River ice among the hundreds of Southern ports between Norfolk and Galveston. Ashore, they mingled with enslaved as well as free black stevedores, carters, fishermen, pilots, and caulkers, blurring the edges of segregation and providing potential fugitives with access to inside information about friendly captains, abolitionism, and life in the free states. Southern ports were also entry points for subversive material. As early as 1809, several hundred pamphlets "of an insurrectionary character" were carried into Charleston by the black steward of a New York ship. Twenty years later, the black radical David Walker recruited sailors to smuggle his *Appeal to the Colored Citizens of the World*, with its call to arms, into Southern ports.

Escape by sea held an obvious appeal. A land journey that could take months, and was unlikely to succeed, might by sea take only a week or two, and from some ports just days. One of the more remarkable seaborne escapes took place in September 1832, when a band of eighteen enslaved men sailed a stolen boat directly from Northampton County, Virginia, to New York City. More commonly, fugitives slipped aboard Yankee ships as stowaways, or tried to negotiate their passage with a member of the crew. Slaves in coastal regions were alert to the arrival of any Northern ship. "No sooner, indeed, does a vessel, known to be from the North, anchor in any of these waters—and the slaves are pretty adroit at ascertaining from what state a vessel comes—than she is boarded, if she remains any length of time, and especially overnight, by more or less of them, in hopes of obtaining a passage in her to a land of freedom," wrote Daniel Drayton, a New Jersey skipper whose notoriety as an abolitionist ultimately eclipsed Jonathan Walker's. Moses Roper, a very light-skinned man who could pass for white, succeeded in enlisting as a steward on a schooner bound for

New York. William Grimes, a slave in Savannah, was invited aboard a Boston-based brig by members of the racially mixed crew and kept hidden from the ship's officers until it arrived in the North. Charles Ball was permitted to board a ship, also at Savannah, with the help of a black sailor, and lay concealed in the hold among bales of cotton until it reached Philadelphia. These men were among the lucky few.

So far from the free states, assistance was almost always indispensable to a successful escape. Many, if not most, fugitives initially depended on ad hoc networks of family and friends who came together only temporarily to help them on their way to a coastal port. Long distance travel out of the port cities was an inverted image of the underground system as it existed in the North: while the web of agents willing to assist fugitives was steadily consolidating and expanding in the 1840s, in the South help from whites remained fragmented and driven more by the market value of slaves' desire to escape bondage than it was by idealism. Increasingly dangerous as the decade wore on, underground work usually hinged on the mercenary motives and the mercurial moods of captains and crews. Broaching the subject of flight, especially to a white man, was the riskiest step of all, since it would expose everyone involved to arrest. Contact had to be made so delicately that even the fugitive's target might not really understand what he was up to. Very few captains were willing to risk their commands on behalf of fugitive slaves: departures of suspect ships were vulnerable to expensive delays; sailors could be jailed indefinitely; captains themselves could be fined, threatened with trial, and barred completely from Southern ports. A North Carolina law mandated hanging for taking a fugitive out of the state, while captains outbound from Louisiana faced up to ten years in prison if they were caught aiding a fugitive. Such draconian legislation had the intended effect. Sea captains all along the coast understood that there would be consequences for becoming involved with a fugitive. In September 1846, in a case that would attract considerable attention in both the North and the South, the skipper of the Yankee brig *Ottoman* panicked when he discovered a stowaway slave en route to Boston from New Orleans. After failing to find a New Orleans–bound ship onto which he could off-load the fugitive, the captain handed him over to the pilot boat in Boston harbor, until the owners of the *Ottoman* arranged to ship him out on the outward-bound *Niagara*. After the *Niagara* ran aground, the fugitive stole a boat, but was recaptured, and shipped out again on the *Vision*. Upon his return to New Orleans, the officers of the *Vision* were arrested for "possession" of a runaway.

Captains who did knowingly take fugitives on board expected to be paid well for it, by the fugitives. During the peak period of underground activity, in the 1850s, several captains worked closely with the Philadelphia Anti-Slavery office, ferrying fugitives north from Norfolk and the Chesapeake region. One of these regularly carried away at least two slaves on each voyage, and once took an astonishing total of twenty-one. Fugitives embarking in this manner from Norfolk, Virginia, where they could count on assistance from a cell of black underground agents, were expected to pay up to twenty-five dollars each for arranging passage, bribing harbor guards and officials, and obtaining forged passes, apart from the fees demanded by the captains themselves, which varied considerably. One captain took one hundred dollars from the fugitive John Hall for passage to Philadelphia, and 240 dollars from a separate party of four, consisting of a man, his wife, their son, and a friend. In another instance, four adult fugitives with a child paid a North Carolina skipper a total of 125 dollars to carry them from Norfolk to Philadelphia.

Only around Norfolk, Virginia, and in coastal North Carolina did the saltwater underground resemble, at times, the networks that existed along the land border between the slave states and the free. In the 1830s, for instance, the abolitionist son of a slaveholder with links to Robert Purvis and the Philadelphia Vigilance Committee concealed fugitives in timber vessels bound for Philadelphia from the port of New Bern. North Carolina's web of tidal estuaries drew fugitives from inland plantations to the coastal lowlands, where there were good hiding places in the swamps as well as a large population of black watermen, slave and free, who might help in making contact with Yankee sailors. Wilmington had a particular reputation as a haven for fugitives. In October 1849 a letter to the *Wilmington Journal* complained that "it is almost an every day occurrence for our negro slaves to take passage and go North." This was surely an exaggeration, but it nonetheless suggested the existence of activity that slave owners were aware of, but unable to completely stop.

2

Even for fugitives able to pay their way, finding passage on a vessel bound for the free states could take months or years. Henry Gorham, a fugitive carpenter, remained in hiding for eleven months before managing to get aboard a schooner. Another, Ben Dickinson, waited for three years. For Harriet Jacobs, a nineteenth-century Anne Frank who lived entombed in an attic crawlspace and was given up as if for dead by almost everyone she knew, it took seven years. Jacobs's account of her life in slavery, published in 1861 under the deceptively innocuous title *Incidents in the Life of a Slave Girl*, harrowed Victorian readers with its blunt sexuality. It also revealed, like no other slave narrative, how one black family invented an underground cell dedicated to the survival and escape of a single, beloved human being.

Jacobs spent her entire life as a slave in Edenton, North Carolina, a small port on Albermarle Sound, near the mouth of the Chowan River. Jacobs's extended family stood poised unsteadily on the fault line between slave and free. Born in 1813 and orphaned early, she was raised by the family matriarch, her grandmother, Molly Horniblow, a woman so highly esteemed for her probity and piety that she could even count white people among her personal friends. One of them, by agreement, using Horniblow's own savings, bought her out of slavery and emancipated her. The same woman also bought Horniblow's son Mark Ramsey, Harriet's uncle, and deeded him as a slave to his own mother. (North Carolina law required that free blacks prove they owned sufficient property so as not to become dependent on public charity, a condition that was fulfilled by Horniblow's ownership of her son, who was valued at four hundred dollars.) Horniblow's daughter Betty remained a slave, but married informally to a free black sailor, known to Harriet Jacobs simply as Stephen. Another of Horniblow's sons, Joseph, was sent to New Orleans to be sold, but had escaped on a ship to the North a few years before. Harriet, of course, was a slave, like her brother John, both of them the property of James Norcom, a prominent middle-aged medical doctor whose large and predatory sexual appetite would eventually drive her to flight.

As a child, Jacobs was treated well by the Norcoms. She was trained for household service as a ladies' maid and seamstress, and could look forward, in slavery's terms, to a life of relative privilege. A photograph taken of her in later life shows a light-skinned, placid-looking woman with a broad oval face, and a small mouth that might well have been pert and humorous in the flush of youth. She obviously had charm and spunk, as well as intelligence, having learned to read and write at an early age. Then, when she was fifteen, "a sad epoch in the life of a slave girl," Norcom began to "whisper foul words" into her ear. "He tried his utmost to corrupt the pure principles my grandmother had instilled," she would write. "He peopled my young mind with unclean images, such as only a vile monster could think of. I turned from him with disgust and hatred. But he was my master."

It is hard to understand what restrained Norcom from simply raping her. He was already reputed to have fathered eleven children by other slaves. The rape of a slave woman by her master was not a crime. Jacobs sometimes suggests that he wanted her as a willing partner, and at others that outright rape was beneath his dignity as a prominent member of the community. Norcom was also, she wrote, "hard pushed for house servants, and rather than lose me he had restrained his malice." But she knew that it would be only a matter of time before she had to submit to him.

Ashamed and frightened—Norcom said that if she breathed a word about his demands, he would kill her—she chose the single expedient that seemed open to her: she became another white man's mistress. Samuel T. Sawyer was young, politically ambitious, and as a graduate of the College of William and Mary, and a descendant of a colonial governor, considerably higher in social status than Norcom. Jacobs seems to have cared for him, but her involvement with him was also an act of calculated self-interest. She was counting on him to purchase her and the two children that she had by him, and counting on him, too, to emancipate them, to open for them the gateway out of slavery that she could never open on her own. "Seeing no other way of escaping the doom I so much dreaded, I made a headlong plunge," she would write. Not surprisingly, Norcom resented this liaison. That he allowed it to continue reflected the mannered relations among white men of his own class more than it did sensitivity for Jacobs's feelings. She was still his slave, and the sexual pressure with which he surrounded her continued unabated. Despite the ambiguous alliance with Sawyer, preservation of her self-respect in the Norcom household was a daily, if not hourly, struggle. She worried constantly about her own fate, and about her children growing up in slavery. Sawyer repeatedly offered to purchase Jacobs, but the doctor refused to sell. When Norcom removed her from his house in Edenton, to his isolated plantation outside town, and away from Sawyer, she decided to flee.

On a June night in 1835, Jacobs climbed out a window of Norcom's home, slipped to the ground, and began to run. She ran all the way to Edenton, five miles away, to the home of a woman friend, and begged to be taken in. She planned to stay there until Norcom stopped searching for her, and then somehow find a way onto a ship bound for the free states. Her uncle Mark and her aunt Betty's husband Stephen both worked on ships. One of them would be able to stow her away, she felt sure.

When Norcom discovered that Jacobs was missing, he immediately assumed that she would try to escape by sea. Advertisements distributed by Norcom described her as "corpulent," curly-haired, and probably "tricked out in gay and fashionable finery." He had every northbound vessel in the harbor searched, and the state law against harboring fugitives read aloud to every crew. His men then searched every place in town where he thought Jacobs might be, including Molly Horniblow's home on King Street, a few doors away from his own office. Until then, Horniblow had no idea that Harriet was even gone. When Harriet made contact with her, her first reaction—the kind of thing that must have won Horniblow the affection of so many Edenton whites—was to urge her granddaughter to do her duty and return to Norcom. However, when she understood that Harriet would never go back of her own volition, no matter what the consequences, she mobilized the family on her behalf.

Jacobs never suggested that the Horniblow clan was part of any organized underground network that extended beyond Edenton. Yet they knew immediately what had to be done to put Jacobs beyond her master's reach, probably because they knew from observation and experience what had worked for other local fugitives, and what had not. They knew that her friend's house was sure to be searched. Therefore they arranged for her to hide temporarily in the last place that Norcom would ever think to look: the home of a slave-owning but sympathetic white woman, Martha Blount, who had an affection for the Horniblows that overrode her loyalty to her own caste. One day, while Jacobs was there, Norcom himself came to the house on a visit, and she had to be hurriedly concealed under a plank in the kitchen floor, where she listened in a state of nervous collapse as the familiar voice resonated terrifyingly over her head.

It was becoming clear that escape from Edenton would not be as easy as Jacobs had thought. Mark Ramsey, Harriet's brother John, and even her two small children had been locked up in jail, in an unsuccessful effort to flush her out. Even after their release, thanks to Sawyer, the men were watched so closely that they abandoned the idea of trying to slip Jacobs aboard a boat. A more permanent hiding place would have to be found for her. In the meantime, she had to be moved. One night, a former apprentice to her father, whom Jacobs identified only by the pseudonym "Peter," brought her a set of sailor's clothes and a "tarpaulin hat," and in this disguise escorted her to the harbor. There they were met by her aunt Betty's husband Stephen, who rowed them three miles down the bay to a forbidding place known as Cabarrus Pocosin, a dense cypress swamp known to be a resort of bandits and runaways. There was a reason it was rarely searched by slave catchers. "As the light increased," Jacobs wrote, "I saw snake after snake crawling round us. I had been accustomed to the sight of snakes all my life, but these were larger than I had ever seen. As evening approached, the number of snakes increased so much that we were continually obliged to thrash them with sticks to keep them from crawling over us."

While Harriet and Peter fended off water moccasins, Mark Ramsey constructed a hiding place in the attic of the Horniblow house, where she would be able to remain indefinitely. This was actually little more than a crawl space about four feet high at its peak, over a storage shed that stood against one side of the house. Ramsey had built a cupboard in a corner beneath the attic, and cut a trap door into its ceiling, so that food and whatever else Harriet needed could be passed up to her. When Peter escorted her back to the Horniblow house and up to the attic the next day, she never imagined that she would not stand again in the open air, or feel the damp Carolina earth again under her feet, until 1842, seven years later. General opinion in Edenton held that she had succeeded in slipping away to the North. Only Molly Horniblow, Mark Ramsey, Aunt Betty and her husband Stephen, and Peter knew where she was. It was not thought safe to tell even her children. When asked where their mother might be, they were taught to say, "in New York."

As she waited for a boat to carry her north, through weeks that turned into months, and then into years, the "dismal little hole" in which she dwelled became her entire world, a prison in which she could neither stand upright nor crawl more than a few feet in any direction, but which was paradoxically the only place on earth where she was truly free. Her physical discomfort was extreme. At night, mice ran over her bed. In summer, the heat was intense. When it rained, water tainted with turpentine poured through the flimsy roof, soaking her bedding and clothes. Her limbs grew numb from disuse. Occasionally, her only luxury, Harriet's grandmother would close the shutters in the storeroom and allow her to come down and walk in circles, stretched to her full height. At first she lived in total darkness. This was so unendurable that she was finally given an auger to drill a "loophole," as she called it, about one inch across, in the wall, to let in a pencil of daylight and a trickle of fresh air. During the day she read the Bible by holding it at a certain angle in front of the hole and sewed garments that her grandmother would give as presents to Harriet's children. With her eye pressed to the hole, she watched the people of Edenton pass by. Sometimes she saw Norcom on the way to his office, and she saw her own children, as far beyond her reach as if they lived on a star, and friends going about their normal lives, utterly oblivious to her presence nearby. Her isolation tested her faith to its limits. "Sometimes I thought God was a compassionate Father, who would forgive my sins for the sake of my sufferings," she would write. "At other times, it seemed to me there was no justice or mercy in the divine government. I asked why the curse of slavery was permitted to exist, and why I had been so persecuted and wronged from youth upward. These things took the shape of mystery, which is to this day not so clear to my soul as I trust it will be hereafter."

During her years in the attic, the nation grew by two more states, Arkansas and Michigan, Andrew Jackson retired from the presidency, to be followed by Martin Van Buren, and William Henry Harrison, who would drop dead after just three months in office, and then another slave owner, the seventh to hold the country's highest office, John Tyler of Virginia. Texans would fight a war of independence and establish slaveholding in what had been a free province of Mexico. A national depression would ravage the nation's economy. Railroads would be transformed from a novelty into a necessity. And abolitionism, an eccentricity at the country's political margins in 1835, would surge with messianic fervor from lecture halls to become a national movement. But none of this would touch Harriet Jacobs. In Edenton, the smaller gears of history turned too. Aunt Betty's husband Stephen sailed north and never returned, choosing freedom over family. Aunt Betty herself died sometime later. Norcom finally decided to disencumber himself of Jacobs's brother and children, and sold them, unwittingly, through an intermediary, to his archrival Sawyer, who took on John as his personal manservant. In 1838 Sawyer was elected to Congress, as a Whig, and took John with him to Washington, and afterward to New York. One day John walked out of the Astor House hotel and into the Manhattan traffic, and never looked back. The note he left for Sawyer said: "Sir—I have left you, not to return; when I have got settled, I will give you further satisfaction. No longer yours."

Now only Molly Horniblow, Mark Ramsey, and Peter knew that Jacobs was still in Edenton. They were constantly looking for a way to get her on board a ship, but none seemed realistic, or safe. Stowing away was both difficult and very dangerous. Slave catchers were always on the lookout for fugitives. Specially appointed inspectors searched seagoing vessels, and fumigated their holds to drive fugitives up on deck. A fugitive from Georgia who stowed away on a sloop carrying a cargo of turpentine was killed by the fumes when the hatches were sealed, trapping him in the hold. Another lashed himself beneath the bowsprit of a deepwater steamer. He lasted through twenty-four hours of drenching by bone-chilling water before begging for help. The captain gave him a suit of dry clothes, but turned him over to the authorities in Newcastle, Delaware. (A Philadelphia newspaper cruelly made light of this tragic incident, commenting that the shipowner should only charge the man half-fare, since the fugitive had "come half the way as a fish.") In fact, it was typical for frightened or angry captains to dump stowaways with the authorities at the nearest Southern port. In December 1844 Captain Gilbert Ricketson, the nephew of one of New Bedford's most prominent abolitionists, would go out of his way to surrender not only a fugitive who had come aboard the *Cornelia* at Portsmouth, Virginia, but also the ship's black steward, who had brought him aboard and concealed him. Two years after that, when a slave who escaped from New Orleans in a merchant vessel landed in Boston, Frederick Douglass reported bitterly in the *North Star*, "He was hunted like a partridge on the mountain, secured and sent back to hopeless bondage."

It was harder than it had ever been to find seamen willing to take a fugitive on board. Free blacks, in particular, were blamed for conniving at the disappearance of any slave who disappeared near a Southern port, and laws designed to keep them apart were growing increasingly harsh. A Charleston, South Carolina, law that was later copied in other ports mandated that free black sailors be jailed until their ships' departure, and that if a captain failed to pay the cost of their incarceration, they were to be "taken as absolute slaves, and sold." Some ports tried to bar free blacks entirely. Although such laws may not have been fully enforced, they still had a devastating impact. In the 1820s blacks had constituted about 15 percent of sailors working out of Savannah, Georgia; by the 1830s they were only 2 percent. Similar legislation in Louisiana caused the proportion of black seamen working from New Orleans, the biggest port in the South, to plunge from 10 percent to 1 percent. Even where free blacks were permitted to land, slave patrols flogged and jailed them at will. In several cities, black dockworkers were required to wear badges to show whether they were enslaved or free. Slave owners near the North Carolina coast demanded with only limited success that black oystermen and fishermen be prohibited from sailing after dark, a restriction that would have reduced everyone's food supply. Authorities in Wilmington, however, succeeded in banning slaves from piloting or stevedoring on seagoing vessels manned by free blacks.

In June 1842 Harriet Jacobs's friend Peter reported that he had finally found a ship willing to carry her to Philadelphia. "The accommodation had been purchased at a price that would pay for a voyage to England," Jacobs wrote. "But when one proposes to go to find old England, they stop to calculate whether they can afford the cost of the pleasure; while in making a bargain to escape from slavery, the trembling victim is ready to say, 'Take all I have, only don't betray me!' " Plans were laid to sneak Jacobs to the harbor. But on the eve of the boat's departure, she panicked. She became obsessed with the idea that she was about to be betrayed. Having spent a quarter of her life in the attic, perhaps she was really terrified that she was no longer capable of surviving in the outside world. At the last minute, another fugitive who had been hiding for several weeks in a house nearby was substituted for her. Although Jacobs was not aware of this woman, Fanny, her friends obviously were, suggesting that information about fugitives and compliant ships' captains circulated freely among Edenton's blacks.

While Fanny was en route to the ship, Jacobs abruptly changed her mind again and decided that she wanted to leave after all. Peter was sent racing through Edenton to catch the boat before it departed. "The captain agreed to wait at a certain place till evening, being handsomely paid for his detention," Jacobs wrote. "Faint in body, but strong of purpose," she was taken to the point of rendezvous by Mark Ramsey, where she found a rowboat waiting for her on the shore.

Once aboard the ship that was to take them north, Jacobs and Fanny were told to keep below whenever there was a sail in sight, but at other times they were allowed to remain on deck. As the ship eased down the bay, past the snake-infested swamp where she had hidden seven years before, and out finally into the deep blue waters of the open Atlantic, revealing a vastness that must have made Jacobs's head spin, all the anxiety that she had somehow managed to suppress during her years in the attic now came flooding out in a torrent. First she became obsessed with the fear that constables would come on board and arrest her, then that the sailors might do her harm, then that the captain himself, a Southerner who had lived most of his life in the slave states, was planning to turn her in. Terrifying as it was, this was freedom.

Ten days after leaving Edenton, the ship arrived at Philadelphia. Jacobs stepped onto the wharf dazed with culture shock, into a maelstrom of jostling draymen, bustling sailors, and stevedores shouting to one another like mountaineers amid alps of barrels and crates. Nothing had prepared her for this city charged with a teeming humanity beyond her imagining. No arrangements had been made for her arrival. She knew no one in Philadelphia, and had no plans except a fixed determination to get to New York, a city she had of course never seen, but where she knew there were people from Edenton. The captain touched her shoulder and pointed out "a respectable-looking colored man," saying, "I will speak to him about the New York trains, and tell him you wish to go directly on." By good fortune, this man turned out to be Jeremiah Durham, a minister of the African Methodist Episcopal church, a cartman by trade, and an agent of the antislavery Vigilance Committee, who had been deputed to keep a lookout for possible fugitives arriving on the docks. Durham found Fanny a place to stay, and took Harriet to his own home, on Barclay Street. There, later that day, an "anti-slavery friend" interviewed Harriet, and promised to help her on her way. When the Anti-Slavery Society offered to pay both women's train fare to New York, "I declined to accept it, telling them that my grandmother had given me sufficient [funds] to pay my expenses at the end of my journey," Jacobs rather primly replied, evincing the same tenacious pride that sustained her integrity under Norcom's assaults, and her sanity through her years of hiding. One of Mrs. Durham's friends escorted her to New York, the only point in her strange odyssey when she might be said to have been traveling in the company of the abolitionist underground.

Jacobs's life in the North would not be without pain, but it would be free. Although she lived until 1897, she would never marry. She would eventually be reunited with her brother John, now a sailor himself, with her daughter, Louisa, who had been sent north by Sawyer to serve as maid in the home of a relative, and with her son, Joseph. But she would never have the family life that she craved. She would find work as a nursemaid, and she would have kind employers who protected her when, after the passage of the 1850 Fugitive Slave Law, she feared recapture. Eventually, she would move to Rochester, New York, where she would oversee the local antislavery reading room, just above the editorial office of Frederick Douglass's paper the *North Star*. In 1861, she would publish an account of her years in Molly Horniblow's attic, a book that she could proudly proclaim was written by none but her own hand, and that offered perhaps the ultimate metaphor for the spiritual claustrophobia of American slavery.

3

Jonathan Walker had expected only four passengers aboard his boat in Pensacola. But on the night of June 19, eluding the eyes of suspicious whites, and of the armed patrols who were supposed to monitor the movements of slaves after dark, seven dark forms made their separate ways to the beach, and one by one slipped onto Jonathan Walker's whaleboat. There was Charles Johnson and his fast-talking brother Moses, plus two more Johnson brothers, and bowlegged Silas Scott, a brother of Silas, and their friend Anthony Catlett. Each of the men, Walker would later learn, was valued at six hundred dollars. Taken together, they were worth forty-two hundred dollars, a very substantial sum. Silas Scott and Moses Johnson were the property of a transplanted Ohioan, Robert C. Caldwell, who had once studied for the ministry, and was now a second lieutenant in the navy. The others belonged to George Willis, a federal marshal, and to his brother Byrd C. Willis. Walker turned none of them away.

In the light of what happened later, it seems likely that Walker was already ill before the trip began. But the plans had been made, he had given his word, and he was confident—this man who had survived shipwreck, shooting, and tropical fevers—that he was up to the task. In silence, he steered the boat into the harbor, out past the anchored ships with their masts suggesting a forlorn forest of naked trees in the dark, out past the hidden shoals that edged the coast, out beneath the looming battlements of Fort Pickens, toward the barrier islands that sheltered the bay from the open sea. Just before daylight there was a sudden scare. Their voyage was almost terminated before they had even left the bay. The whaleboat was hailed by a pair of fishermen off the low hump of Santa Rosa Island. Asked where he was bound, Walker shouted, "To Mobile!" Then he heaved about and set off up the bay, in the opposite direction. Although they must have been puzzled by this odd behavior, the fishermen let it pass. In this saltwater no-man's-land traveled by smugglers and outlaws, it was unwise to ask too many questions of strange boats in the night.

Walker did not describe his boat in detail, but it was probably a typical New England whaleboat made of light half-inch-thick cedar planks, with the buoyancy to ride over rather than through the waves. Walker did not underestimate the challenge of the journey ahead. But he had reason for confidence. Small though his boat was, barely more than twenty-five feet in length, it was a sturdy craft with fore and main spritsails, and very likely also with a rope-operated device that enabled him to raise the top of the mainsail a few feet higher on the mast, to capture additional wind. Such boats were designed to be sailed in the open ocean, and to withstand almost any kind of weather. In 1821 shipwrecked sailors from the Nantucket whaler *Essex* had managed to sail six thousand miles in almost one hundred days in just such a boat, from the central Pacific to the coast of South America. Walker had laid in several barrels of bread, a hundred and twenty pounds of pork and bacon, a keg of molasses, cheese, and a barrel of fresh water. It would have been plenty for five men. It was not enough for eight.

The first three days were an ordeal. Headwinds pressed them back toward Pensacola. Repeated squalls lashed the craft as it tacked painstakingly eastward. There was no shelter, no way to keep dry. Sleep must have been virtually impossible, certainly for the already weakened Walker, whose navigational skill was in constant demand. On June 26, the stormy weather finally broke, and the party made its first landfall at St. Andre's harbor, near present-day Panama City, barely one hundred miles east of Pensacola. They had averaged about fifteen miles a day, far less than Walker had hoped for. For the first time in a week, however, the men at least were able to dry their clothes, cook food, and replenish their water supply. Restored, they put to sea again that evening. The following day, they at first made better time, but Walker then made a misjudgment that cost them precious hours. Hoping to avoid having to tack around Cape San Blas, he steered into St. George's Sound, in the vicinity of present-day Port St. Joe, intending to manhandle the whaleboat across the neck of the peninsula at the southern end of the sound. But when they reached it, they found the distance over the sand was too great. They were forced to retrace their course around the peninsula, and to fight their way around Cape San Blas after all. In the midst of these maneuvers, they were spotted by another boat, the first that had approached them since they left Pensacola Bay. Several of the fugitives were sent ashore to hide in the spiky grass, as a precaution. But their luck held, and the strangers turned away before the fugitives were noticed.

On July 1 Walker and his party reached Cedar Key, nearly four hundred miles from Pensacola. Things were far from well in the whaleboat. On top of his original illness, Walker was now felled by sunstroke, which typically produces crippling headaches, fever, distorted vision, and, if untreated, delirium. He needed shelter and rest. Neither was possible. For days on end, Walker lost track of time. He would later recall, "I remember looking at the red horizon in the West, soon after sundown, as I thought for the last time in this world, not expecting to behold that glorious luminary shedding its scorching rays on me more." When he was lucid, he offered what direction he could, but the fugitives' freedom now depended as much on the strength of their backs at the oars as it did on

Walker's impaired navigational skill. They were desperately short of water. They made several landfalls, hoping to replenish their supply, but without any luck.

Walker's laconic account of the voyage conveys little of what the mood was like, but especially during those first rain-soaked days when their progress was so agonizingly slow, it must have been grim. For the seven fugitives, the whaleboat had become as claustrophobic as the attic of Harriet Jacobs, a strange illusion of freedom hemmed in on every side by a prison of sea and sky. With them traveled seven lifetimes of slavery, of thwarted lives, broken families, fragile hopes. Their physical discomfort was extreme. They were crusted with salt, wet most of the time, and in constant danger of dehydration. There was never enough water. There was no room to lie down. Men slept where they sat, when they could sleep at all. But there was no way to turn back now, for either the fugitives or for Walker.

Fortunately, the weather held good. In spite of Walker's infirmity, they made fairly good headway down the west coast of the peninsula, sailing when there was breeze and rowing when there was none, past long miles of some of the world's most spectacular sand beaches, gleaming white off the port side. They were now averaging something like fifty miles a day. As long as they avoided being seen, and found water, they would be safe. The odds were now on their side. Nearly everyone in the Territory lived either along its northern edge, or in Key West, at the far end of the chain of islets that curled westward into the Gulf like a monkey's tail. The rest of the peninsula was virtually empty of people, apart from the mysterious Seminoles and Miccosukees who lived unseen in the trackless interior. For days on end, mile after mile, the coastline had been a bright ribbon of white sand on the eastern horizon. Now, as the whaleboat neared the peninsula's tip, the sand disappeared, to be replaced by the deep, vast gloom of mangrove swamps.

Walker's discomfort was extreme. In addition to the effects of sunstroke, his entire face was blistered from sunburn. As he lay numbly in the rocking whaleboat, parched and half-mad from the sun, he could not help asking himself why he was here, so far from the windscoured but familiar fields of Cape Cod, among fugitive strangers, facing sure and swift punishment if he was caught. The implacable answer was always the same, and it kept him going, struggling for consciousness when nothing else could:

slavery, "the most heinous, unjust, oppressive, and God-provoking system that ever cursed the dwellers of earth." Calmly, he concluded that what he was doing must "secure approbation of that great 'Judge of all earth, who doeth right,' and before whose presence I soon expected to appear."

Meanwhile, Pensacola was in an uproar. On June 29, a week after Walker's party had sailed, the *Pensacola Gazette* reported that "the most impudent and daring outrage" had been perpetrated on the peace of the territory by the "abduction" of seven Negroes. The paper complained, "Where is our police? Where is our patrol? How is it that numbers of Negroes can prowl unmolested the limits of the Corporation and from our very dwellings, while persons are in the pay of the Corporation to see that no Negro is at large after the bell rings?" Speculation quickly centered on the abolitionist sailor who had suspiciously left town the same night that the slaves disappeared. Fortunately for the fugitives in the whaleboat, a report that Walker had been seen in Mobile sent pursuers off in the wrong direction. Once that rumor had been dispelled, there was still no way to speed news of the slaves' escape to authorities elsewhere in Florida. No railroad tracks had yet been laid anywhere in the territory, while the first telegraph line in the country had been strung just a month earlier, between Washington and Baltimore. Even had the telegraph been available, there still would have been almost nowhere to send such a message. Florida's emptiness was the fugitives' greatest asset.

Passing through the keys posed the greatest challenge of all for Walker's seamanship. Larger boats detoured seventy-five miles to the south, via Key West, before turning northward again on the Atlantic side of the keys. This option was closed to Walker and his companions. Key West was one of the busiest ports on the Gulf. There was no way to pass it without being noticed. Closer to the Everglades, however, the water was in many places only a foot or two deep, and the bottom so muddy that if a man climbed out to push a beached boat forward he would be sucked under. Channels through the upper keys were shallow and hard to find. Walker likely relied on high tide to pull the whaleboat safely through the pass between Sandy and Clive keys, and on the evening of July 7 they emerged into the turquoise waters of Biscayne Bay.

Their immediate destination was Cape Florida, the southernmost point on Key Biscayne, just below present-day Miami. Walker knew that they would find water there. He dared not set out across open sea without a fresh supply, even though they were, if the weather held, less than twenty-four hours from Nassau. They had already sailed and rowed some seven hundred miles in fourteen days. They had every reason to feel confident. Their ordeal would soon be at an end, Walker thought. The seven fugitives would be free men within the day, and Walker, though not a prideful man, could truthfully claim to have accomplished one of the most epic journeys in the history of the abolitionist underground.

But the night fell away to reveal two large sloops, too close to be avoided. They were salvage vessels out of Key West, and each carried a crew of fifteen or more men, outnumbering Walker's parched and bedraggled party by two to one.

Richard Roberts, the skipper of the nearer sloop, the *Eliza Catherine*, shouted to Walker, who as the only white man in the whaleboat he naturally took to be in command, "Where are you from, and where are you bound?"

"From St. Joseph's, bound to Cape Florida," Walker answered hopefully.

"I am going that way, and will give you a tow," Roberts replied, running the *Eliza Catherine* alongside the whaleboat and making fast to it with a rope.

Perhaps Walker gazed across the dark sea toward the Bahamas, just beyond the horizon. After nineteen days at sea, he knew how tantalizingly close they were to their destination. He knew that, had they arrived an hour earlier or an hour later, the sloops would have missed them.

There was not much he could do. He bluffed anyway. He first told Roberts that the men in the boat were slaves, and that he was under contract to their owners to open up land on the Miami River. When the fugitives were questioned separately, however, they claimed that Walker himself was their owner. Walker finally admitted that he was an abolitionist, and asserted that he had talked the men into running away. This may not have been true, but by taking the blame onto himself he was giving the men the last thing that it was in his power to give.

After several days under guard in Key West, Walker was taken back to Pensacola in chains for trial. He arrived on the eighteenth of July, just under a month after he left. Until September, he remained in the *calabozo*, as the old Spanish jail was still called, shackled to the wall of the single cell with a twenty-two-pound chain. Although he was so wasted from illness that he could encircle his shrunken leg with his thumb and finger, Walker was given no bedding for the first month, and chained at night to the other prisoners. The sheer filth of the place tested even his heroic powers of endurance. On one side of the room, the floor remained stained for days with the blood of a slave who had committed suicide by slicing open his belly and throat with a razor.

Walker's first trial, for his involvement in the escape of four of the seven slaves, took place on the morning of November 11. (The three remaining cases were deferred until spring.) The charges against him included every crime of which a slave owner dreamed an abolitionist ought to be accused. The indictment claimed that he had *assisted* Silas Scott in running away, *enticed* Charles Johnson, and *stolen* Catlett and Moses Johnson. They, of course, were never brought to court at all. No black man's testimony was admissible in a case against a white man. Like any sort of lost property, they had been restored immediately to their owners, who were left to punish them however they saw fit. The three slaves belonging to the naval lieutenant Robert Caldwell were apparently not punished at all. The four others were each given fifty blows with a wooden paddle. Walker pleaded not guilty on the grounds that assisting men to escape slavery was not a crime. Not surprisingly, the court treated this as no defense at all. The judge directed the jury to find Walker guilty, and urged them not to allow sympathy to sway them from imposing the severest justice. They took only half an hour to reach a verdict. No one expected them to find Walker innocent. But the sentence they laid upon him shocked even many who loathed everything that Walker stood for. He was first to be exposed for public exhibition in the pillory on the steps of the courthouse, and then to be branded like an animal with the letters "SS," for "slave-stealer."

The sentence was carried out on November 16 by Marshal Ebenezer Dorr, a transplanted Maine Yankee, by strange coincidence, and the son of a hero of the American Revolution who had ridden with Paul Revere. The younger Dorr was now, as Walker tersely put it, a "practical slave owner, and a strong advocate of the system." He led Walker out the door of the courthouse and locked his head and hands into the pillory. For precisely an hour, he was left to the taunts of the mob and to the marksmanship of George Willis, the owner of several of the fugitive slaves, who hurled rotten eggs at Walker's face, a misdemeanor for which the court later fined

Willis the sum of six and a quarter cents. When the prescribed time was up, Dorr brought Walker back inside and placed him in the prisoner's box. He tied Walker's right hand to the wooden railing. Taking a branding-iron "of a slight red heat," he pressed it into the ball of Walker's hand, and held it there firmly for fifteen or twenty seconds. "It made a spattering noise, like handful of salt in the fire," Walker stoically recalled. "The pain was severe." Walker was then sent back to his cell. Dorr soon returned with three writs in hand for trespass and damage to the property of Caldwell and the Willises, to the staggering amount of one hundred and six thousand dollars, a sum so great, in 1844, as to be scarcely imaginable. (Of this sum, the vindictive federal marshal George Willis demanded all but six thousand dollars.) Walker had already surrendered his only possession of any value, his boat, to Caldwell. He was now penniless.

The first notice of Walker's plight appeared in abolitionist newspapers in mid-July. In November, news of his branding sped across the country. Northerners were horrified. Southerners had actually branded a *white man*. Protest meetings were held throughout New England. On December 6, 1844, the *Liberator* published a boldfaced headline: "**Jonathan Walker Sentenced, and Branded!!**—Horrible, horrible beyond all description." The *Christian Citizen* proclaimed Walker to be one of a "new order of knighthood," and that his tortured hand was now "daguerreotyped in the chancery of heaven." Everywhere, abolitionist speakers declared that the burned-in letters truly stood for "Slave Savior." A "martyr's fund" was established for Walker's defense. Contributions and letters of support came from as far away as England. Gerrit Smith and Lewis Tappan, the wealthy New York patrons of the abolitionist movement, both made donations. James C. Fuller, the financier of Josiah Henson's Dawn colony, sent twenty-four dollars. Frederick Douglass undertook a speaking tour on Walker's behalf. William Lloyd Garrison cited "the afflicting and hopeless case of the unfortunate Walker" at every opportunity. Lawyers were hired and dispatched to Pensacola.

The notoriety of Walker's punishment proved to be an embarrassment greater than Pensacolans were prepared to bear. Willis's ludicrous demand for damages was finally dropped, and when Walker was again brought to trial in May 1845, for assisting in the escape of the remaining three slaves, the jury—"men untrammeled by prejudice or revenge," as Walker rather generously described them—found him guilty, but fined him only fifteen dollars. He was released from jail on June 16, 1845, almost exactly a year from the day that he set sail. Northern abolitionists and Walker's friends on Cape Cod paid his fines and the costs of his prosecution, a total of five hundred ninety-six dollars and five and a half cents, including, among other charges, twenty-five dollars to the city of Pensacola for the "use" of the jail, and eighty-seven and a half cents for the cost of a new lock.

Although Walker probably had no formal connection with the abolitionist underground while he lived in Pensacola, slaveholders had no doubt at all that Walker was a knowing part of a vast and powerful international conspiracy to undermine the institutions of the South. The reaction of the territorial government was paranoid. "It can no longer be denied that systematic and powerful influences are at work throughout a large portion of Europe and many parts of our own country, the direct tendency of which is to impair our rights of property and to involve ourselves and the unconscious objects of this false philanthropy in one common ruin," the official report of Florida's Legislative Council on the affair stated. "A vicious fanaticism clothed in the garb of religion, is prowling around our borders . . . whose direct purposes, scarcely concealed, are to deluge our very hearthstones in blood, and to rear an altar to its false principles upon the ruin of all that is precious to us as freemen and dear to us as men." The report called for harsh punishment of anyone who dared to help slaves to escape. "Henceforward we are compelled to regard negro-stealing, by the instruments of the abolitionists, as a crime of a different character. It is no longer a mere larceny, but a species of treason against the State—a direct assault upon the very existence of our institutions." The crimes of Negro stealing, and of aiding and abetting Negro stealing—the very work of the Underground Railroad—were to be made punishable by death.

Walker was hailed in the North as a martyr. He was immediately taken up by New York abolitionists when he arrived there on July 11, and was soon drafted for the lecture circuit, where he was billed as the "hero of Pensacola." In effect, he became the first media star of the abolitionist movement, a figure of talismanic power who had but to hold up his wounded hand to electrify audiences. Although he was not articulate as a speaker, through 1846 he was in constant demand at abolitionist gatherings, and continued touring for several years after that. He appeared throughout New England and central New York state, recounting his own sufferings in the cause, and exhorting others to follow his example. At the close of every lecture, members of the audience were invited to personally inspect the famous hand itself, which Walker styled the "coat of arms of the United States."

Images of the hand were printed in dozens of newspapers throughout the United States. The abolitionist poet John Greenleaf Whittier wrote a paean to it that was recited for decades in New England schools:

Then lift that manly right hand, bold ploughman of the wave!
*Its branded palm shall prophecy "*SALVATION TO THE SLAVE*"*
Hold up its fire-wrought language, that whoso reads may feel
His heart swell strong within him, his sinews change to steel.
Hold it up before our sunshine, up against our Northern air—
Ho! Men of Massachusetts, for the love of God look there!
Take it henceforth for your standard—like Bruce's heart of yore.
In the dark strife closing round ye, let that hand be seen before!

Universally known as "The Branded Hand," Walker's callused seaman's palm became an emblem of the entire abolitionist movement and, perhaps inevitably, of the Underground Railroad, the most riveting symbol both of the sacrifice that was demanded of men who dared to assist fugitive slaves, and of the punishment that awaited them if they were caught. It was physical proof of slavery's barbarism, bringing home to middle-class white audiences with lurid violence as nothing else yet had done how fatally their freedoms—*white men's freedoms*—were even now being violated by Southern slavery.

PART FOUR

VICTORY

THE 1850s

CHAPTER 14

A DISEASE OF THE BODY POLITIC

Wo to all the just and merciful in the land.

—FREDERICK DOUGLASS

1

In February 1848 William Chaplin and Daniel Drayton met each other for the first time, in Washington, D.C. This was the Underground Railroad as Southerners imagined it: a clandestine meeting, a sinister organization reaching across state lines, a plot to run off slaves. Chaplin, a polished and strikingly handsome, if slightly balding, man of fifty-two, was the agent of radical New York abolitionists who regarded the existence of slavery in the nation's capital as an intolerable affront to its democratic ideals. Like his predecessor Charles Torrey, who had died two years earlier in a Baltimore prison after being convicted for aiding the escape of fugitives, Chaplin was a believer in direct action. Drayton was of a rougher cut, with a large cleft chin, gloomy eyes, and brows that knotted over the bridge of his nose: it was a sad face, wrinkled and scored by more than two decades at sea. Strictly speaking, he was not really an underground man, at least not in the way that Chaplin was. He was a Philadelphia ship's captain who desperately needed money. What they were planning was the biggest organized break-out of slaves in underground history thus far.

Chaplin told Drayton that he wanted a boat to transport "a family or two," who were technically free but tied up in litigation, and were afraid of being sold south before their case was resolved. Drayton would be undertaking a great Christian service to carry them north. That was well and good, Drayton replied. He did not lack sympathy for the enslaved. But he would need to be paid.

Drayton's life was one long hard-luck story. He was born in poverty, in 1802, in New Jersey, not far from the mouth of the Delaware River. Taking to sea as a cook at the age of nineteen, after several miserable years as a shoemaker, he eventually saved enough money to buy a half-interest in a sloop working the mid-Atlantic coast. On its second voyage, the sloop struck a snag near the mouth of the Susquehanna and sank in five minutes, its uninsured cargo a total loss. His next vessel sank off North Carolina with a cargo of coal and several of its crew. Another was blown ashore on Long Island, with a hundred tons of plaster. Still another was lost in a freak snowstorm, in Chesapeake Bay.

He would be well paid for his work, Chaplin assured him. It was, Drayton would say, in his ghostwritten memoir, "an offer which the low state of my pecuniary affairs, and the necessity of supporting my family, did not allow me to decline."

Much, if not most, of the actual planning was done by a slave named Thomas Ducket and by Daniel Bell, a free black iron-monger who worked at the Washington Navy Yard, who feared that his enslaved family was about to be sold. They alerted slaves not only in Washington, but also in outlying Georgetown, and across the Potomac in Alexandria, that a Yankee boat would soon be available to take anyone who wanted to leave. Chaplin had not been entirely honest with Drayton: three weeks before the planned departure, he wrote his close friend Gerrit Smith that he expected as many as seventy-five fugitives to join in the escape, not a family or two.

Back in Philadelphia, Drayton recruited another down-on-his-luck skipper named Edward Sayres, who owned a small coaster called the *Pearl.*

Drayton offered him one hundred dollars to sail from Washington to Frenchtown, New Jersey, on the Delaware River, where the fugitives were to be set ashore. This was far more than Sayres could expect to earn for any ordinary cargo. The third member of the crew was a naive boy named Chester English, who had never been more than thirty miles from home, and had a craving to see the tourist sights of Washington.

On the evening of Thursday, April 13, 1848, the *Pearl* docked at the foot of Seventh Street on the Anacostia River, within the present grounds of the Washington Navy Yard, but then comparatively isolated beyond open fields and sheltered by a steep earthen bank. That night, the city was in a tumult over news of the republican revolution that had recently taken place in France. It seemed to patriotic Washingtonians that the fulsome spirit of their own democracy was finally cresting, as they always dreamed that it would, on the far side of the Atlantic. In Congress, Senator Henry Foote of Mississippi declared, unconscious of the irony of his words, "that the age of tyrants and of slavery was rapidly drawing to a close, and that the happy period to be signalized by the universal emancipation of man from the fetters of civic oppression . . . was at this moment visibly commencing." As bonfires roared and impromptu processions wound through the streets, the news of Drayton's arrival crackled through the underground.

Soon after dark, small groups of shadowy figures began to arrive over the fields. English, who had been told that they were going to load a cargo of ship timber, was now posted at the hatch, and ordered to close it after each passenger. In all, seventy-seven fugitives boarded the *Pearl.* At ten o'clock, Drayton ordered Sayres and English to cast off. There was no wind at all, and they made little headway as the night slipped past. The sun was already rising when they passed Alexandria. Then, for the first time, Drayton went into the hold, where he counted thirty-eight men and boys, twenty-six women and girls, and thirteen children, "pretty thickly stowed." One belonged to a congressman from South Carolina. Another was a coachman for the secretary of the treasury. Two were slaves owned by a local black hackman. Fifteen-year-old Mary Ellen Steward was the property of Dolley Madison, the widow of President James Madison.

The wind now rose at last, and once past Fort Washington, the *Pearl* ran steadily southward past George Washington's Mount Vernon, past Quantico, past Robert E. Lee's birthplace at Stratford Hall, past St. George's

Island. But as they approached Point Lookout at the mouth of the Potomac, the winds shifted unfavorably. Drayton's plan was to sail north up Chesapeake Bay, and then cross the northern portion of the Delmarva peninsula through the Chesapeake and Delaware Canal, to the Delaware River. He and Sayres agreed to anchor until the winds changed in a small cove known as Cornfield harbor. Exhausted after a night and a day without rest, they and English flung themselves onto their bunks and went to sleep.

Consternation had swept Washington when it was learned that slaves belonging to no fewer than forty-one different masters had disappeared in the night. In spite of the *Pearl*'s agonizingly slow passage down the Potomac, the plan might still have worked, but Drayton's ill-luck won out yet again. The scheme was betrayed by an informer. A black hackman named Judson Diggs, who had driven two fugitives to the boat, went to the authorities in hope of collecting a reward. A waterborne posse of thirty armed men hurriedly set off in the *Salem*, a small steamboat belonging to one of the slave owners. After searching the river all Sunday afternoon and most of the night, they were about to return to Washington when they arrived at Cornfield harbor.

The screech of a steamer's whistle blasted Drayton from his sleep. He heard a voice shout, "Niggers, by God!" and the banging of gun butts on the deck. As Drayton emerged from his cabin, he was seized and hauled onto the *Salem*, along with Sayres and the hapless English. The fugitives were kept under guard aboard the *Pearl*, as it was towed back upriver to Washington.

Just after dawn on February 18, the posse marched its captives into the city in an antebellum version of a Roman triumph. Drayton and Sayres were driven ahead in the lead, lashed together, and guarded by a man on each side. The fugitives trudged behind them, also tied in pairs. Several women carried babies in their arms. The first scattered onlookers swelled into a howling mob by the time they approached the center of town. As they passed Gannon's slave pen, one of Washington's largest, a man rushed at the two Yankees, waving a knife in their faces. At Pennsylvania Avenue, thousands were yelling, "Lynch them! Lynch them! The damned villains!" Only when they reached the "Blue Jug," the three-story city jail at the corner of Fourth and G Streets, did Drayton begin to believe that he would come through the ordeal alive.

In the course of the day, proslavery men fired by rumors of the capture of the "slave-stealers" flooded into Washington from the outlying districts and laid siege to the most prominent symbol of abolitionism in the city, the office of the antislavery newspaper the *National Era*. They milled in the streets threatening to wreck the building and to burn down the home of its editor, Gamalial Bailey. Both Bailey and his newspaper were saved only by a freezing rain, which dissipated the mob. The next morning, shaken by the demonstrations, President James K. Polk, a Tennessee slave owner, ordered federal employees into the streets to restore order. Order, of course, meant not just the immediate suppression of potentially uncontrollable mob violence, but the lasting protection of slavery in the capital of the only nation in the world dedicated, on paper at least, to the proposition that all men were created equal.

Washington, although it was now a city of forty thousand, was still groping for a shape. Rows of one-story structures straggled alongside frowsy patches of waste ground, muddy streams, and spacious avenues that seemed to begin in nothing and lead nowhere. Charles Dickens, who visited Washington early in the decade, hated the place, calling it "the headquarters of tobacco-tinctured saliva." He wrote disgustedly, "put green blinds outside all the private houses, with a red curtain and a white one in every window; plough up all the roads; plant a great deal of coarse turf in every place where it ought *not* to be; erect three handsome buildings in stone and marble, anywhere, but the more entirely out of anybody's way the better . . . leave a brick-field without the bricks, in all central places where a street may naturally be expected: and that's Washington." Manners were remarkably informal. Anyone could visit the president at the Executive Mansion, and White House levees were open to the respectable public, although they were rather glum affairs and not popular, since the straitlaced Polks disdained dancing and served no liquor or food. The grand monuments that would impress future visitors existed, when at all, mainly in the minds of architects. South of the White House, the cornerstone of the Washington Monument had just been laid, and on a low eminence to the east, the ambitious Corinthian facade of the Capitol terminated anticlimactically in a frail wooden dome.

Slavery was seamlessly woven into the fabric of life in the capital, although abolitionists had tried for years without success to legislate it out of existence. A free African American active in the underground, dryly wrote, "I knew that I was in the midst of a slaveholding community, in which, even the white man, who had more liberty and freedom than I, dare not raise his voice in favor of freedom for the African's descendants in Christian America, although he might raise it as high as he pleased for the Greeks and Poles." Like a foul, persistent odor, the harsh fact of slavery intruded everywhere. In 1849 slave hunters would even force their way into Mrs. Ann Sprigg's popular boardinghouse near the Capitol, and arrest one of the black waiters in front of the guests, who included a first-term Whig congressman from Illinois named Abraham Lincoln. The waiter had been working to purchase his freedom and had paid off all but sixty dollars of the price when his master changed his mind, and ordered him to be collected and readied for sale. Some of the largest slave-trading establishments in the United States stood within sight of the Capitol building, advertising their trade with signboards that unabashedly proclaimed: "*Cash! Cash! Cash! And Negroes Wanted.*" Although the number of permanent resident slaves was small—somewhat more than two thousand out of the city's eight thousand black inhabitants—interstate traders used it as a convenient transshipment point for slaves who were gathered annually in northeastern Virginia and Maryland, and sent by steamboat or on foot, chained in coffles, to the plantation states of the Deep South. The owner of one establishment told the Quaker traveler Joseph Sturge that he shipped between fifteen hundred and two thousand slaves south from Washington each year.

As Stanley Harrold has shown in *Subversives*, a masterful history of abolition in the District of Columbia, nowhere did underground activity provoke slaveholders more than in the nation's capital, the city which to all the world symbolized, for better or worse, the true nature of the United States: a beacon of freedom for all, or a government criminally complicit in the tyranny of man over man. The *Pearl* incident, with its mass escape of more than seventy slaves, was only the latest provocation. Earlier in the decade, a secret ring operated by Charles T. Torrey, a flamboyant young Congregationalist minister from Albany, New York, and a former slave named Thomas Smallwood had systematically run off hundreds of slaves from the area under the very nose of Congress. Torrey and Smallwood relied more on daring and luck than on technique. Lacking the kind of extensive family- and church-based networks enjoyed by, say,

John Rankin or Levi Coffin, they were reduced to the risky expedient of hiring local men to drive rented wagons and carriages as they needed them, often at short notice and, apparently, with little planning. "We had to pay teamsters a very high price in order to induce them to risk themselves and teams in so dangerous an enterprise," Smallwood would write, paying up to fifteen dollars per person to carry a passenger just to the first underground station, thirty-seven miles from Washington. Unfortunately, several of their mercenary collaborators revealed themselves to be swindlers and spies, demanding fees from fugitives in Smallwood's name, and then betraying some of them to their masters for the reward. Smallwood, more circumspect than the doomed Torrey, sensed danger, and moved his family to Canada.

For the first months of 1844, the Byronic Torrey worked on alone, personally collecting fugitives from as far away as Winchester, in the Shenandoah Valley of Virginia, and making plans—grandiose ones in light of what happened—to mount rescue expeditions in distant North Carolina and Louisiana. There was a certain compulsive quality to his behavior, as if each success bred a need for another, still greater risk. Not alone among evangelical abolitionists, he was also hooked on the frisson of imagined crucifixion. "Did you ever hear of a Torrey that suffered martyrdom?" he once asked his father. "I hope among our good old Puritan ancestors there were some who had the martyr spirit." That June, Torrey was identified by a Washington slave dealer, who named him as the man who had carried off slaves from Winchester. Once in custody, he was also convicted for enticing three other slaves away from a Baltimore tavern owner, and sentenced to six years' hard labor. It was a death sentence. Torrey did not have the constitution of the hardy seaman Jonathan Walker, and prison proved an agony for him. He was racked by "bilious fever," and his moods swung wildly between depression and Christian exaltation. Then the tuberculosis from which he had suffered early in life crept inexorably and fatally through his lungs. On the night of May 7 he suffered a severe hemorrhage, and on the eighth he died. With Smallwood, he had helped an estimated four hundred slaves to freedom.

Both proslavery forces and abolitionists regarded the trial of the *Pearl* prisoners Drayton and Sayres as a case of national significance. The prosecutor, District Attorney Philip Barton Key, was a slave owner and a lion of Washington society, as well as the son of Francis Scott Key, the composer of the "Star-Spangled Banner." Against each of the Yankee captains Key lodged forty-one indictments for slave stealing, one for each of the masters whose slaves were found aboard the *Pearl*, and seventy-four indictments for transporting slaves out of the District of Columbia. (Three of the seventy-seven passengers were free blacks traveling with family members.) But Key was after bigger game than the two unfortunate seamen. At the time of his capture, Drayton had half-admitted that he had been hired by abolitionists. Key hoped to force Drayton to implicate William Chaplin, the suspected head of the underground in Washington, and his patron, the New York philanthropist Gerrit Smith. Although Smith was not, in fact, directly involved in the *Pearl* affair, Chaplin kept him well-informed of his activities, and regularly solicited money from him to purchase the freedom of slaves. To catch Smith would deal a death blow to what Key considered the slave-stealing underground conspiracy. For their own part, the abolitionists had two goals: to turn Drayton into a martyr like Charles Torrey and, at all costs, to protect Chaplin. Were he to be indicted, it would expose not only his local collaborators, but also his support network of well-connected whites, including several senators and congressmen.

Drayton's trial began on July 27. His lead attorney, Massachusetts congressman Horace Mann, contended implausibly that the *Pearl* fugitives had spontaneously decided to escape on the same day, and had coincidentally managed to find their own way to the ship. Slyly, he further suggested that they might have been inspired to escape by the patriotic speech of Senator Foote of Mississippi the previous night, in honor of the French uprising against Louis Philippe. At the mere mention of slavery, the judge abruptly stopped Mann, warning that he would not permit any "harangue against slavery" to be heard in the courtroom, another unpleasant reminder to Americans, who were following the trial avidly in their newspapers, that the right of free speech did not exist when it came to the subject of slavery.

Key maintained that Drayton was a liar and a thief. He easily demonstrated that Drayton knew that his passengers were runaway slaves, that he knew that he was committing a crime when he allowed them aboard, and that he had deliberately hidden them in the *Pearl*'s hold. Likening the fugitives to machinery, he added, "Suppose a man had taken it into his head that the northern factories were very bad things for the health of the factory-girls, and were to go with a schooner for the purpose of liberating those poor devils by stealing the spindles, would he not be served as this prisoner is served here?"

Despite transparently false testimony by "witnesses" introduced by Key, Drayton was found guilty. To Key's chagrin, however, nothing could be proved against Chaplin. Neither Sayres nor English had ever met him. Indeed, English was so obviously ignorant of the whole business that he was released without trial. Under intense pressure from the prosecution, Drayton continued to refuse to implicate anyone else. His silence did not come free of charge. Drayton was no Jonathan Walker, motivated solely by moral commitment to the cause of the slave. He had undertaken Chaplin's commission for money, not as an exercise in self-sacrifice. Chaplin had promised Drayton that if he were arrested, his wife and six children would be taken care of. Now Drayton was reassured that the abolitionists would continue to work for his release, and to pay his fines if he continued to keep silent.

Sayres was convicted of assisting in the escape of slaves, and sentenced to a fine of one hundred and fifty dollars on each count. Initially, the uncooperative Drayton received an unprecedented twenty years' imprisonment, for theft. But the prosecution's conduct had been so grossly and obviously improper that the sentence was overturned on appeal by a panel of federal judges who actually included a slave master who owned two of the fugitives who had been aboard the *Pearl*. In the spring of 1849, Drayton was resentenced to more than ten thousand dollars in fines and costs and, like Sayres, to remain incarcerated until that amount was paid. Since both men were penniless, they still faced years in prison, a pointed warning to anyone who served the underground of the punishment they faced if caught.

In the most human sense, the *Pearl* incident was a tragic failure: more than forty of the fugitives captured on the sloop were eventually shipped off to the slave markets of New Orleans. But it also represented something more far-reaching. The case broke upon the nation's capital in the midst of one of American history's great political realignments. The tectonic plates of public opinion were shifting as Americans by the hundreds of thousands were questioning their received beliefs about slavery and individual rights, and searching for new, firm terrain upon which to root their convictions. On the nation's most visible battlefield, in Congress, positions were hardening. Defenders of slavery portrayed the *Pearl* incident as just the latest naked outrage in a coordinated abolitionist assault against the South. Some talked of civil war. South Carolina's cadaverous John C. Calhoun, the elder statesmen of states' rights radicals, for whom abolitionism was not politics at all but a kind of illness—"a disease of the body politic"—the fugitive slave problem was "the gravest and most vital of all questions to us and the whole Union."

2

Throughout the South, anxiety about abolitionism insinuated itself like a virus into every community, marking every stranger as a potential carrier, curling up inside every relationship where a person's sentiments about race were in doubt. Antislavery societies, once respectable, had melted away. Mail from the North was routinely opened by local post offices, and anything that could be remotely construed as challenging slavery was confiscated and destroyed. Families who opposed slavery left for the free states, or learned to keep silent. "It just seems like I can't stand it; and we don't dare to let anybody know it but our good friends," Susan B. Hubbard, the daughter of a North Carolina Quaker accused of harboring a fugitive, confided to a friend. "Trouble, trouble; oh, just for me to think of leaving, and I can't take time to tell my friends farewell; it seems like it would break my heart." In Smyrna, South Carolina, a Presbyterian minister was tarred and thrown out of the town by the Vigilance Committee simply for reading in church a copy of the Baltimore Synod's official letter on slavery, even though it contained nothing contrary to South Carolina law. When a cache of abolitionist material was discovered in Mark Twain's hometown of Hannibal, Missouri, its owners were driven out of town, and the literature itself was publicly burned. "In that day for a man to speak out openly and proclaim himself an enemy of Negro slavery was simply to proclaim himself a madman," Twain wrote. "For he was blaspheming against the holiest thing known to a Missourian, and could *not* be in his right mind."

Loyalty to the South increasingly came to mean conformity to the interests of slave owners. In the Deep South especially, defenders of slavery no longer sighed with embarrassment that it was a necessary evil, as they did years before, but now praised it, as Calhoun did, as "a good—a positive good," adding, "We see it now in its true light, and regard it as the most stable and safe basis for free institutions in the world." Calhoun firmly believed that God and nature alike had set limits beyond which blacks were incapable of improvement, and that efforts to emancipate them were not only immoral but irrational. He maintained that no truly civilized society could exist unless its more valuable members were supported by the labor of the lesser, thus relieving masters from manual labor and enabling them to reach the intellectual and spiritual heights for which they were destined. To upset this arrangement was to tamper with the divine order, he believed. "To destroy the existing relation between the free and servile races at the South would lead to consequences unparalleled in history," he asserted, in 1849. "They cannot be separated, and cannot live together in peace or harmony or to their mutual advantage except in their present relation. Under any other, wretchedness and misery and desolation would overspread the whole South."

The hardening ideology of the South rested on the axiom that African Americans were doomed to slavery not only by the economic interests of the South, but also by sacred doctrine and biology. "God has made the Negro an inferior being, not in most cases, but in all cases, for there are no accidents or exceptions in His works," wrote Dr. J. H. Van Evrie, a popular scholar of racial theory. In an era that had scant knowledge of archaeology or anthropology, and that almost universally believed mankind to be only about six thousand years old, Africans were typically conflated with the biblical descendants of Ham, or Canaan, the Bible's supposed progenitor of the black "race." Slaveholders pointed triumphantly to Genesis, in which it was written, supposedly for all time: "And He said, Cursed be Canaan; a servant of servants shall he be unto his brethren." They further pointed out that the Patriarchs from Abraham through Moses were large slaveholders, and that God had clearly sanctioned slavery when his angel commanded the runaway slave Hagar to return to her mistress. More pertinent still, in Leviticus the Bible had explicitly authorized the enslavement of nonbelievers. And that was just the Old Testament. Christ himself had obviously approved of slavery, its apologists triumphantly asserted, since he had nowhere specifically condemned it.

Cogent as the biblical arguments were, they were no longer entirely convincing by themselves. As the abolitionists tirelessly reminded Americans, the Bible also asserted the sanctity of universal brotherhood. If there was such a thing as a common human race, then the logic of abolitionism was incontrovertible. But if the African could be shown to have a different biological nature from whites, moral appeals for emancipation were irrelevant. A developing school of racial thinkers was also now lending the weight of up-to-date "science" to proslavery politics. Some, led by the immensely influential Dr. Josiah C. Nott of Alabama, theorized that there must have been separate Creations, and that Africans, like American Indians, Malays, and others, were therefore not human beings at all, but different species entirely. Even internationally respected scholars such as Louis Agassiz, the father of modern anthropology, maintained that "the brain of the Negro is that of the imperfect brain of a 7 month's infant in the womb of the white." Differences in physical appearance among the races, he theorized, reflected innate differences in moral character and intelligence.

S. A. Cartwright, a prominent Southern doctor who lectured on the physiology of Africans, asserted that when punished blacks did not feel physical pain as whites did, "[nor] any unusual resentment more than stupid sulkiness." He also concluded that the disposition of slaves to run away was also a disease, a form of dementia that he labeled "drapetomania." "Like children," he wrote, "they are constrained by unalterable physiological laws, to love those in authority over them." Similarly, James D. B. DeBow, a widely respected economist and editor, solemnly (if bizarrely) assured readers of his book *The Industrial Resources of the Southern and Western States* that the physiology of the Negro was entirely different from that of whites: "The great development of the nervous system, and the profuse distribution of nervous matter to the stomach, liver, and genital organs, would make the Ethiopian race entirely unmanageable, if it were not that this excessive nervous development is associated with a deficiency of red blood in the pulmonary and arterial systems, from a defective atmospherization or arteriolization of the blood in the lungs."

Meanwhile, the plantation economy continued to expand. Although there were about 350,000 slaveholders in the South, the wealth of the cotton states was concentrated in the hands of just three or four thousand families, who received three-quarters of the returns from the yearly exports, and owned two-thirds of the region's slaves. "Niggers and cotton—cotton and niggers; these are the law and the prophets to the men of the South," a Scottish traveler wrote home from Mississippi. By 1850, cotton flourished across a four-hundred-thousand-square-mile swath of America from South Carolina to Texas. Production spiraled ever upward, doubling between 1815 and 1820, from 150,000 to 300,000 bales, doubling again by 1826, and yet again between 1830 and 1837. By 1859, it would reach nearly five million bales, to make up more than half of the nation's total exports. As always, more cotton demanded more slaves. Between 1820 and 1850, the number of slaves in Alabama grew from 41,879 to 342,844, in Mississippi from 32,814 to 309,878, and in Louisiana from 69,064 to 244,809. (The state with the largest number of people in bondage in 1850, however, was still slave-exporting Virginia, with 472,528, up from 425,148 in 1820.) As the price of slaves continued to rise, buyers clamored for relief, pressuring their representatives in Washington to reopen the international slave trade to bring down prices. A Georgia planter, one of the many who equated slavery with progress, complained that the state of Virginia was more immoral than the slave trade, and more "unchristian" too, because when he went there to "buy a few darkies," he had to pay between one thousand and two thousand dollars apiece. Had federal law been reasonable and allowed it, he said, he could easily have gone to Africa and bought better stock for fifty dollars a head. To such entrepreneurs, as to ideologues like John C. Calhoun, slavery was not a vestige of the medieval past, it was the future.

Slave owners who considered themselves honest and God-fearing were infuriated by the seeming impunity with which the Underground Railroad allegedly enticed away their valuable property. In truth, they credited the underground with a ubiquitousness and a reach that it did not have. But there were just enough traces of abolitionist activity where it was least expected to fuel fears of a far-flung conspiracy that had penetrated the innermost recesses of the South. There was the black headwaiter in Grenada, Mississippi, who was caught hiding a runaway in the garret of the hotel where he worked, and the Connecticut abolitionist posing as a preacher who was captured at Vicksburg in the very act of smuggling three slaves on board a steamboat bound for Cincinnati, and the Yankee lumbermen who camped along the Mississippi River and sold cut wood to passing steamboats and, people said, secretly gave refuge to fugitives in return for work.

But the only place in the inner South where organized underground clearly went on without interruption was in the Quaker counties of North Carolina, centering on the New Garden Meeting, near Greensboro, Levi Coffin's home until his departure for Indiana, in the 1820s. Fugitives trickled into the Quaker hamlets from other parts of the state and, it is said, even from as far away as South Carolina, using specially notched coins to enable stationmasters to identify them. For the handful of abolitionists who dared help them, the pressure was close to debilitating. "The life of anxiety and extreme danger I was leading was rendering me nervous, excitable and suspicious of all my surroundings," recalled Levi Coffin's cousin Addison Coffin, who became an underground conductor at the age of thirteen. "There was a constant sense of danger resting on my heart, a presentiment of impending peril." After weeks or months concealed on local farms, fugitives were sent on foot or hidden in false-bottomed wagons to the Quaker colonies in Indiana, along the trans-Appalachian route the Coffin family had pioneered decades before. One Indiana-bound emigrant, Joshua Murrow, carried several fugitives all the way in such a wagon, from which he blithely sold off pottery and cornmeal to pay expenses along the way.

Addison Coffin left a vividly detailed account of the ingenious local techniques that were used to mark the way through the confusing tangle of back roads that meandered through rural North Carolina. At each fork, the fugitive was shown how to find a nail driven into a tree precisely three and a half feet from the ground, halfway around the tree. If the right-hand road was to be taken the nail was driven on the right-hand side; if the left, the nail was to the left. Where there were fences but no trees, the nail was driven in the middle of the second rail from the top, on the inside of the fence, and pointing either to the left or right. When nothing else was available, the nail was driven into a stake, or else a stone was so set as to be unnoticeable by day, but easily found at night. "When a fugitive was started on the road they were instructed into the *mystery*," Coffin wrote. "When they came to a fork in the road, they would go to the nearest tree, put their arms around and rub downward, whichever arm struck the nail, right or left, that was the road, and they walked right on with no mistake, so with fences, but the stakes or stones had to be found with their feet, which was tolerably easily done. Those who were doubtful as to their ability to remember details, would take a *string* and tie *short* pieces of string to the long one to represent the fork and cross roads, and then by tying knots which they understood make a complete but simple way that was almost unerring in its simplicity."

The conductor's main duty was to keep the road well-marked, and when necessary to change and relocate the nails as emergencies required. "Coupled with the extreme personal danger, the strain on brain and nerve was so great that few conductors could stand it more than ten years without rest, and for that rest they generally went west, and took service on the lines in the free states, where it seemed like mere child's play, compared with the South," wrote Coffin, who was close to a nervous breakdown when he left North Carolina in 1842, to settle near Levi and Catherine Coffin, in Indiana. Addison's brother Alfred continued working for the underground in North Carolina until 1853, when he was exposed, and fled for his life.

One of the most daring escapes of all from the Deep South was the flight of Ellen and William Craft, who, in December 1848, succeeded in traveling by train and steamship from Macon, Georgia, to Philadelphia in just three days, with the light-skinned Ellen disguised in man's clothes as an invalid young planter, and William posing as a loyal servant and interlocutor. Once in Philadelphia, the Crafts were taken under the wing of the Anti-Slavery Office, and they soon became among the most popular attractions on the abolitionist speakers' circuit. While the Crafts' dazzling escapade had little to do with the ongoing operation of the underground, it exerted a powerful effect on public opinion by portraying African Americans as bold, resourceful, and independent men and women, rather than the barely tamed savages or docile livestock that proslavery propaganda claimed. Northern imaginations were thrilled even more by the daring exploit of a Virginia slave named Henry Brown, whose incredible escape in March 1849 has lost nothing of its edge-of-the-seat suspense after a hundred and fifty years.

A skilled tobacco worker who, by his own account, up to then had been generally well treated and "escaped the lash almost entirely," Brown was smoldering with resentment, his wife and child having recently been sold away from him, in spite of his efforts to save enough money to buy their freedom. He had become friendly with a white merchant, Samuel Smith, who one day hinted to him, in the cryptic way that such conversations had to take place in the slave states, that as a man with a valuable trade he might be better off free. Making sure that no one else was near, Brown confessed that he had been "meditating" his escape. Could Smith give him any advice? Warily, Smith asked Brown if he were not afraid to speak to him of such things. Brown replied that, no, he wasn't, because he supposed that Smith "believed that every man had a right to liberty." He was quite right, Smith assured him. After discussing and discarding several possible options for escape, Brown would write, "The idea suddenly flashed across my mind of shutting myself *up in a box*, and getting myself conveyed as dry goods to a free state." A deeply religious man, he regarded the idea as a revelation direct from God.

Smith managed to send a message to the Philadelphia Anti-Slavery Office, advising it to watch for a crate that would be arriving on a certain date, and to open it immediately. Meanwhile, a free black friend of Brown's arranged for a carpenter to build a box three feet long, two feet wide, and two feet, six inches deep, to be lined with baize cloth. The fit would be tight, allowing the two-hundred-pound, five-foot-eight-inch-tall Brown no space to turn himself around. At about 4 A.M. on March 29, Brown climbed into the box. Three gimlet holes were drilled opposite his face for air. He was handed a few biscuits and a cow's bladder filled with water. After the top was hammered on, the box was addressed to a contact in Philadelphia, and plainly marked "THIS SIDE UP." Smith had the box delivered to the railway express office, where it was then put on a wagon and driven to the station. By the route that the box would have to follow, Philadelphia lay three hundred and fifty miles away.

The journey north from Richmond was a harrowing ordeal. At Potomac Creek, where the tracks then ended, baggage had to be offloaded and put aboard a steamer. Despite the instructions on the box, Brown was placed upside down, in a "dreadful position" where he remained for an hour and a half, "which from the sufferings I had thus to endure, seemed like an age to me," he would write. "I felt my eyes swelling as if they would burst from their sockets; and the veins on my temples were dreadfully distended with pressure of blood upon my head." Brown tried painfully to move his hand to his face, but couldn't do it. He felt a cold sweat coming over him, and feared that he was close to death. He began fervently to pray. Soon afterward—miraculously, he believed—he heard a passenger complain that he had been standing for two hours and wanted something to sit on, and then threw down Brown's box so that it landed right side up, and sat on it with a friend. "I could now listen to the men talking, and heard one of them asking the other what he supposed *the box contained*," Brown would recall. "His companion replied that he guessed it as 'THE MAIL.' " At Washington, the box was taken off the steamboat, placed on a wagon and carried to the railroad depot. There, when the driver called for someone to help unload it, another voice replied that he should just throw it off, it didn't matter if whatever was in it broke, the railway company would pay for it anyway. "No sooner were these words spoken than I began to tumble from the wagon, and falling on the end where my head was, I could hear my neck give a crack, as if it had been snapped asunder and I was knocked completely insensible." Next he heard someone saying that there was no room left for the box, and that it would have to wait for the next day's shipment on the "luggage train." Another voice, belonging to some unknown clerk whose devotion to regulations probably saved Brown's life, replied that since the box had come with the express, it must be sent on with the express. The box was loaded on, and Brown was thrown once again on his head, though when the baggage was later shifted, he was finally placed upright for the rest of the trip to Philadelphia.

The next morning, twenty-seven hours after Brown left Richmond, several members of the Philadelphia Vigilance Committee stood nervously around the crate, where it had been deposited by an Irish cartman on the floor of the Anti-Slavery Office on North Fifth Street. When the lid was pried off, Brown rose to his feet, extended his hand, and asked, "How do you do, gentlemen?" He then promptly fainted. When he came to, it seemed to him like nothing less than "a resurrection from the grave of slavery," and he burst spontaneously into song:

I waited patiently, I waited patiently for the Lord, for the Lord;
And he inclined unto me, and heard my calling;
I waited patiently, I waited patiently for the Lord

As he sang, smiling men surrounded him, each more anxious than the other to offer help, he would write, and "bidding me a hearty welcome to the possession of my natural rights."

Appeals to "natural rights" were the last thing that the proslavery lobby in Washington wished to hear. As the decade progressed, that very concept had increasingly been enshrined in personal liberty laws enacted by many Northern states. Such laws discouraged public officials from cooperating in the recapture of fugitives, and for the first time, in some states, extended to runaway slaves the right to a fair trial; although they were never uniformly enforced, the damage they did to Southerners' trust in the good faith of Northern state governments was severe. The underground, of course, continued to enrage Southerners by acting as if there was no federal fugitive slave law at all. In 1847 an astonishing forty-five fugitives had been fed, sheltered, and paraded through Battle Creek, Michigan, in a single day. "Everybody heard of their coming and every man, woman and child in town was out to see them," Erastus Hussey, a local underground man-recalled. "It looked like a circus." And in Delaware, a slave state no less, the underground stationmaster in Wilmington, Thomas Garrett, convicted in May 1848 for facilitating the escape of fugitives, dared to announce to the court that he considered the penalty imposed on him as a license to help fugitive slaves for the rest of his life. "If any of you know a slave who needs assistance, send him to me," he declared proudly. Admitting that he had always feared to lose what little property he possessed, Garrett added, "But now that you have relieved me, I will go home and put another story on my house, so that I can accommodate more of God's poor."

3

The single event that would do the most to shape both the nation's sectional politics for a decade to come, as well as the growth of the Underground Railroad, had nothing at all to do with slavery, and took place nearly three thousand miles away from Washington. On January 24, 1848, perhaps on the very day that William Chaplin was meeting secretly with Daniel Drayton in Baltimore to plan the *Pearl* escape, a workman noticed several sparkling flakes of metallic ore in the mill-race that he was digging in the Sierra Mountains of California. Three weeks later, a Mormon merchant strode through the sleepy Mexican hamlet of San Francisco brandishing a bottle full of gold dust, shouting, "They've found gold in the American River!" In ways that no one could possibly foresee, the shock waves of the discovery would resonate through every town and city in America, through the marble halls of Congress, through the hardening ideological positions of the North and South, and along the distant lines of the Underground Railroad. Within weeks, news of the strike raced across the continent, around Cape Horn, and over the Pacific Ocean. San Francisco quickly mushroomed into a raucous, half-born city of fifteen thousand where eggs sold for ten dollars a dozen, and canvas tents were rented to gamblers at forty thousand dollars annually, payable in gold dust. By the autumn of the following year, at least ninety thousand gold seekers had poured into California. The vast majority were from the Northern states, and they brought their politics in their knapsacks. (William Lloyd Garrison's *Liberator* recorded its first California subscriber on February 17, 1849.) Ignoring tradition and counsels of patience, they declared themselves a state and ratified, by an overwhelming vote of twelve thousand to eight hundred, a constitution barring slavery from what abolitionists and proslavery forces alike recognized was the most valuable prize won by the United States in its recent war with Mexico. Southerners were apoplectic at this apparent fait accompli, which would upset the delicate balance of power that had existed since the Missouri Compromise of 1820, by reopening the question of slavery in the western territories. The crisis had been foreshadowed six years earlier, in the debate over the admission of Texas, which some proponents had wanted to see divided up into half a dozen or more slave states. The admission of California would tilt the Senate in favor of the free states. Angry talk of secession boiled through the South. John C. Calhoun wrote menacingly, "We have borne the wrongs and insults of the North long enough."

The debate that began in February 1850 over the admission of California was among the most memorable ever to take place on the floor of the Senate. In the course of the next eight months, the fate of the nation hinged on the ability of three aging statesmen—the Kentucky Whig Henry Clay, the consumptive South Carolinian John C. Calhoun, and the silver-tongued, profoundly conservative Massachusetts orator Daniel Webster—to strike a compromise between the sectional interests of the North and the South. But at the core of the crisis lay the question of whether Congress had the moral duty to extend freedom westward as the nation grew, or rather a duty to protect slavery there. Calhoun and his allies were threatening secession if slavery were not permitted everywhere in the vast territory that the United States had seized from Mexico. Antislavery Northerners wanted not only the admission of California, but an explicit prohibition of slavery in the new lands.

Clay opened the debate on February 6. A slave owner himself, he professed distaste for slavery in principle, and regret for it in practice. His admirers flatteringly called him "the Great Pacificator" for his skill at winning the confidence of men who loathed each other's principles. Tall, stooped now with age, he ranged his sardonic eye across the panorama of his colleagues, their faces swollen with plugs of tobacco packed in their cheeks. He gazed at the other titans of his own generation, and at new men such as Jefferson Davis, master of one of the largest plantations in Mississippi, and William Seward, Lincoln's future secretary of state, who hid fugitive slaves in his home in Auburn, New York, and beyond them toward the nation itself, "so oppressed, so appalled, and so anxious." To reassure Southerners of his true loyalties, Clay belittled the moral aspect of slavery: "In the one scale, then, we behold sentiment, sentiment, sentiment alone, and in the other, property, the social fabric, life, and all that makes life desirable and happy." He then revealed his pragmatic intent. He bluntly told them that rash talk of secession made little sense. How would the South be better off if it seceded? Then there would be no remedy at all for the fugitive slave problem. Within the Union, the South at least had a means of redress. He warned that if the South became a separate nation, "There would be no right of extradition; no right to demand your slaves; no right to appeal to the courts of justice to demand your slaves which escape, or the penalties for decoying them. Where one slave escapes now, by running from his owner, hundreds and thousands would escape if the Union were severed in parts." He asked Northerners to be realistic, too. In practical terms, slavery would never flourish in the arid wastes of New Mexico, no matter what the letter of the law. Banning slavery in Washington, as the abolitionists asked, could not happen without the consent of Maryland and Virginia, and that would never be forthcoming. But the slave trade within the city itself was an embarrassment to all Americans. Ending it was possible, and would do no damage to slavery elsewhere. But this was to be a compromise, after all. In return, the fugitive slave law must be strengthened. Clay would go with "the furthest senator from the South to impose the heaviest sanctions on the recovery of fugitive slaves."

On March 4, John C. Calhoun rose to speak, wrapped up in a black cloak, his face ashen, and his body corroded by the tuberculosis that would kill him less than three weeks later. Coughing uncontrollably, he passed his speech to a fire-eater of the younger generation, James Mason of Virginia, to read. But the tone was vintage Calhoun, seething with his passionate conviction that slavery was an ideal worth fighting for. The Union was endangered by nothing except "the many aggressions" which the North had perpetrated against the South, he asserted. The "equilibrium" between the two sections that was intended by the Founding Fathers had already been destroyed. The South and slavery had been unfairly shut out of the territories since the enactment of the Northwest Ordinance in 1787. Too much federal spending also went to the North, while import duties fell unjustly on the cotton-exporting states.

Calhoun's complaints were deeply felt, but disingenuous. The Louisiana Purchase, the War of 1812, the protection of native manufactures and its later repeal, the annexation of Texas, the War with Mexico, the removal of Indians from the Deep South, all had served the interests of the South. Slave states chose 30 of the 62 members of the Senate, 90 of the 233 members of the House of Representatives, and 105 of the 295 electors of the president. Even these numbers understated Southern power, since Democratic and proslavery politics were virtually synonymous, and Democrats overwhelmingly controlled both houses of Congress. Seven of the eleven presidents, and similarly disproportionate numbers of senior cabinet officers, House speakers, and presidents of the Senate were Southerners. At the end of the 1840s, the chairmen of all the important committees of Congress were owners of slaves, while seven of the nine members of the Supreme Court were either slave owners or proslavery in attitude. But Calhoun and every other Southerner could see that broader demographic trends favored the North, and that the North led the South in commerce, industry, railroad building, overall wealth, and population, while the South remained almost completely agricultural, with its planters cash-starved, and chronically in debt to Northern creditors. He foresaw five new states being developed, all of them aligned with the North, eventually giving the North an overwhelming majority of forty senators to the South's twenty-eight. It was imperative, he demanded, that the South be conceded "an equal right in the acquired territory," and for the North to "do her duty" by enforcing fugitive slave laws. Unless "something decisive" was done to stop abolitionist agitation, it would snap every cord that bound the sections together.

Abolitionists had expected nothing different from Calhoun or Clay. But Daniel Webster's speech produced shock and disbelief. Although he was a thoroughgoing creature of the establishment, backed by the Boston and New York business elites, who had extensive investment in the South, he was still considered an antislavery man. Thirty years earlier, had he not stood upon the sacred altar of Plymouth Rock and evoked the spirit of his Puritan forefathers in a scathing denunciation of slavery as an "odious and abominable trade" that disgraced Christianity, and against which every feeling of humanity must revolt? But he too called for compromise. Many considered Webster the finest orator of the age, of whom it was ambiguously said that his "every sentence weighed a pound." Craggy and "mastiff-mouthed," priming his famous voice like a long-range cannon, he began to speak, and kept on for three hours, sweating like a gunner in battle, attacking abolitionism and secessionist sentiment with equal brio. Booming, "I speak for the preservation of the Union," he attacked the abolitionist societies, which he said had "excited feelings," and "whose operations for the last twenty years have produced nothing good or valuable." He also agreed with Clay and Calhoun that the North had fallen short in its constitutional duty to restore runaway slaves to their masters. No public officials had a right to flout the law, he roared, "None at all; none at all." Calling upon his fellow senators to enact a strong fugitive slave law that would give the South what it wanted, he cried, "Let us not be pigmies in a case that calls for men!"

The South loved Webster's speech. The opponents of slavery were appalled. William Lloyd Garrison likened Webster to Benedict Arnold, while Ralph Waldo Emerson wrote: "The word *liberty* in the mouth of Mr. Webster sounds like the word *love* in the mouth of a courtezan."

The debate continued through the summer. When the muggy heat became insupportable, the tobacco-stained red carpet was taken up, and the draperies removed from the chamber, in an ineffectual effort to cool the room. Members stretched their legs in the ninety-six-foot-high rotunda, ornamented by historical pictures painted by Trumbull, or sprawled back with their feet on their desks, cutting fresh plugs of tobacco with their penknives, and shooting the old ones from their mouths at spittoons placed strategically around the chamber. Meanwhile, as Congress discussed putting a stop to the local slave trade, sales in the area soared. "Scarcely a day passed that gangs of chained slaves did not pass through the city," the underground agent William Chaplin gloomily observed.

Chaplin was busy that summer. Following the capture of the *Pearl*, he had actually increased his work with fugitives. Then, on August 9, as he was driving a closed carriage with two fugitive slaves north out of Washington, he was ambushed at the Maryland state line by a detachment of militia, who had been alerted in advance by a spy. Chaplin drew a pistol from his coat and fired at a man who tried to seize the reins. The fugitives, who were also armed, then began blazing away from inside the carriage. Twenty-seven shots were fired before the three men realized that they were trapped, and surrendered. The confrontation was no more than a skirmish, if measured by the numbers involved. But like the first shots fired at Concord Green in 1775, they signaled a fundamental sea change in the underground's willingness to fight back.

Chaplin was taken to the nearest jail, at Rockville, Maryland, not far from the farm where Josiah Henson had toiled for Isaac Riley a quarter of a century earlier. There he was charged with larceny and assault with intent to kill. (The two fugitives were returned to their owners, both Southern members of Congress, and quickly sold.) Gerrit Smith wrote reassuringly to his old friend to remind him that he was still endowed with "a freedom of soul, a freedom in Christ Jesus—which not men, nor Devils, can take from you." More practically, he immediately dispatched a delegation of New York abolitionists to Washington to try to get Chaplin out of jail.

While Chaplin was awaiting trial, on August 21, abolitionists held an extraordinary two-day convention of fifty fugitive slaves and two thousand white supporters in Cazenovia, New York, near Smith's Peterboro home. Frederick Douglass presided. In addition to Smith, of course, among those in attendance were the veteran abolitionist Samuel J. May, Charles M. Ray, the most active underground man in New York City, and Reverend Jermain Loguen, who as the slave Jarm Logue had escaped from slavery in an epic ride from Tennessee to Canada in 1834. (Logue had paid for his education at the interracial Oneida Institute by working as a hotel porter, and was now a minister famous throughout the Burned Over District for his fiery antislavery preaching.) A photograph taken at the convention shows a still youthful-looking Gerrit Smith, arm upraised with an oratorical flourish, standing between the teenaged Edmonson sisters, primly dressed in plain frocks and deep bonnets. They had been passengers on the *Pearl* and were bought out of slavery by Chaplin, on behalf of Reverend Henry Ward Beecher, of Plymouth Church in Brooklyn, who then "sold" them publicly in a mock auction to raise public consciousness about slavery, a charade that reportedly sent the titillated reverend into "extacies" of excitement. Following denunciations of the debate taking place in Washington, the convention provocatively nominated William Chaplin for president of the United States on the Liberty Party ticket, threatening "revolution" if he was not released. Another resolution, which sent shock waves through the South, openly urged slaves to escape from their masters, to carry arms when they did so, and to kill masters who pursued them. A Tennessee newspaper likened the convention to the witches' cauldron in *Macbeth*: "Can any scene be found more disgusting? Can any movement be found more alarming than this? Treason, murder, and robbery are openly proclaimed and advised. If patriots tremble for the safety of our glorious Union . . . let them look to the madness of these wild fanatics." Rockville slaveholders, citing the proceedings of the convention, pressured the local magistrate to set Chaplin's bail at an astronomical nineteen thousand dollars. Gerrit Smith, brandishing his preferred weapon, the cashbox, pledged twelve thousand dollars. Freed on bond, Chaplin fled north with the help of his abolitionist friends, and never stood trial.

On August 26 the new Fugitive Slave Act was voted into law. It was comprehensive and draconian. Anyone who hindered a slave catcher, attempted the rescue of a recaptured fugitive, "directly or indirectly" assisted a fugitive to escape, or harbored a fugitive, was liable to a fine of up to one thousand dollars and six months' imprisonment, plus damages of one thousand dollars to the owner of each slave that was lost. Commissioners were to be appointed by the federal circuit courts specifically to act on fugitive slave cases, and provided with financial incentives—"bribes," abolitionists charged—to facilitate the recovery of runaways: the commissioner would receive a fee of ten dollars each time he remanded a fugitive to the claimant, but only five dollars if he found for the alleged slave. Commissioners could be fined one thousand dollars for refusing to issue a writ when requested, and they were personally liable for the value of any slave who escaped from their custody. Contravening new liberty laws in some Northern states, testimony by an accused slave was disallowed, and there was no right to trial by jury. The provision that outraged most Northerners, and not only abolitionists, gave commissioners the authority to compel any bystander, no matter what his beliefs, to help them seize any alleged fugitive. The Columbus, Ohio, *Standard* announced with disgust, "Now we are all slave catchers."

Webster, with visions of himself in the White House, pronounced the compromise "a providential escape," confidently adding, "Whatever party may prevail, hereafter, the Union stands firm." Clay was also ecstatic. "I believe from the bottom of my soul that this measure is the reunion of this Union," he bloviated. "I believe it is the dove of peace, which, taking its aerial flight from the dome of the Capitol, carries the glad tidings of . . . harmony to all the remotest extremities of this distracted land."

Although conservative Northerners praised the compromise for putting an end to "agitation of the slave question," the gusts of anger at Webster blew into a cyclone. Meetings of condemnation were reported from Maine to Iowa. In a typical such convention, held in Canandaigua, New York, abolitionists resolved: "Compromise or no Compromise—constitution or no constitution; whether the escaping fugitive from slavery shall have his trial for freedom before a jury, or pro-slavery post-master, or whatsoever tribunal—'that no testimony short of a Bill of sale from God Almighty,' can establish the title of the master to his slave, or induce us to lift a finger to aid in his return to the house of bondage." Frederick Douglass wrote furiously, in the *North Star*, "Wo to the poor panting fugitive! Wo to all that dare be his friends! Wo to all that refuse to help hunt him down, hold him fast and send him back to his bloody prison-house. Wo to all the just and merciful in the land."

CHAPTER 15

DO WE CALL THIS THE LAND OF THE FREE?

> Must the citizen ever for a moment, or in the least degree, resign his conscience to the legislator? Why has every man a conscience then?
>
> —HENRY DAVID THOREAU

1

At about 2 P.M. on the afternoon of February 15, 1851, a phalanx of twenty or more black men with their collars turned high and sou'westers camouflaging their faces shoved their way through the doors of Boston's lofty Doric courthouse. Pushing aside federal deputy marshal Patrick Riley and his constables, they took hold of Shadrach Minkins and carried him out into the rain-slick streets of the city to the cheers of what may have been the largest gathering of African Americans in the city's history. Over his head, one of Minkins's rescuers brandished the city's official Sword of Justice, which he had plucked from the courtroom's wall. Picking up more supporters with every step, the rescuers streamed like a squall in a shouting procession north along Court Street, past the Paul Revere house, whose symbolism could not have been lost on the crowd, whose leaders knew full well that they were part of a second, abolitionist American revolution, into Cambridge Street, and on into the black neighborhood that tumbled down the back of Beacon Hill toward the Charles River. And there Minkins disappeared.

That morning, Marshal Riley and his men had arrested Minkins at Taft's Cornhill Coffee House, where he worked as a waiter. Minkins had been in Boston only a few months, having escaped by sea from Norfolk, Virginia, in May 1850. His arrest in the heart of Boston, headquarters of the American Anti-Slavery Society and the home of William Lloyd Garrison, whose office at the *Liberator* stood only a few doors away from Taft's, was no coincidence. It was meant to demonstrate not just to abolitionists, but also to the slaveholding South that the federal government was serious about enforcing the new Fugitive Slave Law. However, with a rapidity that the lawmen were completely unprepared for, the city's Vigilance Committee had mobilized its members, both black and white, and in less than two and a half hours after Minkins's arrest they had organized a rescue plan, and successfully brought it off, under the direction of the indefatigable and courageous Lewis Hayden, the fugitive slave whom the unfortunate Calvin Fairbank and his companion Delia Webster had driven out of Kentucky beneath the seat of a carriage six years before. Police searched frantically for the missing fugitive, while news of his escape raced in every direction along the country's newly strung telegraph wires. In Washington, outraged Senator Henry Clay demanded to know whether "a government of white men was to be yielded to a government by blacks," and a distressed President Fillmore called a special cabinet meeting, after which he issued a proclamation describing Minkins's rescue as "a scandalous outrage," and ordered civil and military officials of all ranks to cooperate in recapturing the fugitive.

Minkins, meanwhile, was as safe as any man in his position could hope to be, in Hayden's capable hands. A natural entrepreneur, since his arrival in Boston the forty-year-old Hayden had built up a clothing business to become one of the wealthiest black men in the city, as well as the leading black member of the Vigilance Committee. (He had also raised six hundred and fifty dollars to pay for Fairbank's release, in August 1849.) Most of the fugitives who found their way to Boston were sheltered initially in his three-story brick home on Southac Street. But Minkins was too hot a property to hide in such an obvious place. After a circuitous trip through Cambridge to throw off pursuers, Hayden personally drove Minkins to Concord, eighteen miles west of Boston, to the home of Francis Bigelow, a white blacksmith and a core member of the local underground. Once Minkins had been fed, Bigelow gave him new clothes and drove him on to Leominster, where he was switched to another carriage, in which he was driven to West Fitchburg, where he was put on a train for Vermont, and ultimately Canada. Four days after leaving Boston, Minkins was safe in Montreal.

"Do we call this the land of the free?" a reflective young Concord man "of taut mind and wound-up muscles" wrote in his diary the day after Minkins passed through. "What is it to be free of King Geo[rge] the IV and continue the slaves of prejudice? What is it [to] be born free & equal & not to live?" The writer, the son of a local pencil maker, was Henry David Thoreau, an operative in the Concord underground, although he would become far more famous for his affinity for a pleasant bit of local landscape known as Walden Pond. Thoreau or Bigelow usually received the late-night arrivals. Thoreau's mother, Cynthia, was one of the founding members of the town's Female Anti-Slavery Society, and in 1846 Thoreau himself had elected to go to jail rather than pay his poll tax, as a protest against slavery. In 1848 Thoreau had lectured in the town's public meeting hall on "the relation of the individual to the state," the genesis of what was to become one of the most famous essays ever written by an American, "Civil Disobedience," and the inspiration for countless radical challenges to the tyranny of the majority in generations to come.

The enactment of the Fugitive Slave Law hardened ideas that had begun to gestate during the Mexican War of the late 1840s, which Thoreau and most abolitionists passionately opposed. Before Thoreau, Quakers and some evangelicals had argued that civil disobedience was a principled religious response to slavery and war. Thoreau proposed for the first time that a man's individual conscience was reason enough to defy a law in which he did not believe. The state, he argued, had no more truth or intelligence than the average man, only greater physical strength: "I was not born to be forced. I will breathe after my own fashion. Let us see who is the strongest. They can only force me who obey a higher law than I." How could a moral man bring himself to obey immoral laws? he asked himself. "The only obligation which I have a right to assume is to do at any time what I think right. Law never made men a whit more just; and, by means of their respect for it, even the well-disposed are daily made the agents of injustice."

The Fugitive Slave Law instantly transformed philosophical reflections into questions of practical immediacy. "We must trample this infamous law underfoot, be the consequences what they may," Unitarian Samuel J. May told his Syracuse congregation. "It is not for you to choose whether you will or not obey such a law as this. You are as much under obligation not to obey it, as you are not to lie, steal, or commit murder." Similar thoughts were coursing even more starkly through the agitated minds of many other Northerners. "This so-called Fugitive Slave Law, what is it, that I am called upon to obey it and assist in its execution?" demanded Rodney French, a Yankee ship's captain who was denied landing rights in the South because he was rumored to be an abolitionist. "It is the most disgraceful, atrocious, unjust, detestable, heathenish, barbarous, diabolical, tyrannical, man-degrading, woman-murdering, demon-pleasing, Heaven-defying act ever perpetrated in any age of the world, by persons claiming to have consciences and a belief in a just God. In one word, it is the sum of all villainies."

The arrest of Shadrach Minkins was not the first attack on a fugitive in the North, under the new law. That sad honor went to James Hamlet, who was literally snatched off the street in New York City in October 1850, eight days after the act's passage. Antislavery newspapers brought almost daily reports of fugitives being handed over to federal authorities somewhere in the free states. There were captures in New York, Ohio, Illinois, Pennsylvania, Massachusetts. By the time of the "Shadrach Rescue," as it became universally known, there had been at least sixty (and possibly many more) attempted arrests in the North, involving a total of more than one hundred different fugitives. In February 1851, in a speech to Syracuse businessmen, the administration's favorite Yankee shill for the Fugitive Slave Law, Daniel Webster, promised that the law "will be executed in all the great cities," even "in the midst of the next Anti-Slavery Convention." Those who dared to oppose the law, he warned menacingly, "are traitors! traitors! traitors!"

Fugitive slaves who had lived in comparative safety for years in Northern states, who had painstakingly acquired nest eggs and bought homes for themselves, suddenly fled, as Frederick Douglass memorably put it, "as from an enemy's land—a doomed city," to begin over again farther north or in Canada, impoverished and among strangers. To one missionary, it seemed that panicked black refugees were appearing in the queen's dominions "by fifties every day, like frogs in Egypt." Desperate calls were put out to antislavery societies in the free states for fresh shipments of food and clothing. As many as three thousand fugitives crossed into Canada within three months after the enactment of the new law. In western New York, where the panic was extreme, about one-third of the 600 blacks living in and around Syracuse fled north. It was reported that of the 114 members of a Baptist church in Rochester, all but 2 left the country, and that in Buffalo, 130 left from another black Baptist church. More than 40 fled Boston within three days after the signing of the Fugitive Slave Law, followed by another hundred after the Minkins incident. Their fears were vindicated when, six weeks after Minkins's rescue, Thomas Sims was arrested in Boston and marched to the port surrounded by an armed guard of three hundred policemen and citizen volunteers. (With cruel though probably unintended irony, he was embarked from the same wharf where radicals dressed as Indians had dumped British tea into the harbor in the prelude to the American Revolution.) An estimated 300 blacks fled from Pittsburgh, including nearly all the waiters in the city's hotels. Columbia, Pennsylvania, one of the largest African-American communities in the North, was particularly hard hit as slave hunters and outright kidnappers targeted the town: in January 1851 constables snatched a black man named Baker, who had lived in town for years, and who was negotiating to purchase his freedom. Two months later, a woman and her twelve-year-old son were carried off to Philadelphia. And in April a man and his wife and child were dragged from their sleep and taken to the office of the federal commissioner in Harrisburg, leaving the couple's ten-month-old baby behind. Columbia's black population of 873 abruptly dropped by 40 percent.

Others stayed. Reverend Jermain Loguen of Syracuse, formerly the slave Jarm Logue, was one who would not be moved. When urged by his wife and friends to flee to Canada, he refused, just as he had always rejected friends' offers to buy his freedom for him. With the same boldness with which he had fought his way through two separate bands of armed patrollers on his galloping flight north from Tennessee, he now proclaimed his defiance of the law from pulpits all over central New York, daring his former owner, Manasseth Logue, and the United States government to come after him. He was a fugitive slave, he declared to anyone who cared to listen, and he had made up his mind to stand his ground at his home in Syracuse. "What is life to me if I am to be a slave in Tennessee?" he thundered. "I have received my freedom from Heaven, and with it came the command to defend my title to it. The question is with you," he told Syracusans at a rally that resulted in the formation of a local Vigilance Committee. "If you will give us up, say so, and we will shake the dust from our feet and leave you. But we believe better things. Whatever may be your decision, my ground is taken. I have declared it everywhere. I don't respect this law—I don't fear it—I won't obey it! It outlaws me, and I outlaw it. I will not live a slave, and if force is employed to reenslave me, I shall make preparations to meet the crisis as becomes a man."

2

Edward Gorsuch was also an angry man. He had, by his lights, been kind to the four prime field hands who had run away from him on the night of November 6, 1849. He had even promised them freedom when they reached the age of twenty-eight. That was an economically sensible decision in the border country of Maryland, where slavery had been in decline for decades, and the steady hemorrhaging of slaves north into Pennsylvania made human livestock a poor long-term investment. But it was also magnanimous, the sixty-three-year-old Gorsuch thought. After all, he had every right to sell unwanted slaves southward, if he preferred. But he was a Methodist, and a Sunday school teacher, and a man of principle. He was also a deeply proud man, and by the spring of 1851 his failure to find the men—Noah Buley, Nelson Ford, and George and Joshua Hammond—embarrassed him in front of his fellow slave owners, and set a worrisome precedent for his seven remaining slaves. Then, in September 1851, he received an encouraging message from an itinerant clock mender in Lancaster County, Pennsylvania, who earned extra income by serving as a spy for local slave catchers. Nelson Ford and Joshua Hammond had been spotted living near the town of Christiana, a nexus of Underground Railroad routes, which lay just fifteen miles north of the Maryland state line.

Gorsuch did not imagine that recovering the men would be easy. But at least the law was now firmly and unequivocally on his side. He started for Pennsylvania with a well-armed party that included his son Dickinson, nephews Joshua Gorsuch and Thomas Pearce, and two other Marylanders. They traveled first to Philadelphia, where Gorsuch, appealing for assistance under the terms of the Fugitive Slave Law, acquired the services of the bewhiskered U.S. deputy marshal Henry H. Kline, who was well-known as an ardent slave hunter, and two city constables. Unknown to Gorsuch, however, he was being tracked by Philadelphia abolitionists, who closely monitored the arrivals of slave-catching parties from the South. En route to Christiana, an underground spy named Samuel Williams managed to gain Gorsuch's confidence by ostensibly offering him advice about fellow blacks in Lancaster County. Having learned the slave owner's plans, Williams hurried ahead to Christiana, where he spread news of the expedition's imminent arrival among the many fugitives living in the area.

Gorsuch was traveling into one of the richest farming counties in the United States, an expanse of gently rolling fields, red-brick villages, and prosperous farms, centering on the small, handsome city of Lancaster, with its stately ensemble of harmonious Federal Era homes. The northern part of the county was occupied largely by conservative Germans, including many Amish and Mennonites, and its southern tier, the heart of the county's underground, by a substantial minority of Quakers. Interspersed among them were hundreds of blacks, many of them fugitives who on their way north had acquired work and made homes for themselves in tiny rural hamlets that existed just beyond the perimeter of white attention and control. Not surprisingly, they were also magnets for slave hunters. In 1851 Lancaster's blacks lived in a state of permanent high alert against gangs of night-riding kidnappers who broke into cabins without warning, seized men and women in their sleep, and carried away entire families.

The county's underground was diverse, complex, and superbly organized. In addition to as many as fifty permanent stations, divided more or less equally among the homes of blacks and whites, some of whom had been hiding runaway slaves since the turn of the century, it could draw on the support of a constellation of black churches and their traveling ministers, plus several outstanding local public figures, including at least two state senators, a former president of the American Anti-Slavery Society, and the county's fierce abolitionist congressman, Thaddeus Stevens. After the Civil War, Stevens would become the architect of the most radical plan of congressional reconstruction of the South, as well as the father of the Fourteenth and Fifteenth Amendments, which would guarantee former slaves equal protection under the law, and the right to vote. Beginning in the 1840s, he personally paid a spy to infiltrate the "manstealing" counter-underground of slave catchers, and passed on what he learned to fugitives. (Recent archaeological excavations strongly suggest that he also concealed fugitives in a dry cistern next to his own home in the heart of Lancaster city.)

Slave hunters also had to contend with a secret black militia led by William Parker, which mobilized on short notice to fend off slave hunters, and recovered kidnap victims, by force if necessary. Parker, twenty-nine years old in 1851, was born a slave in Anne Arundel County, Maryland, and had escaped to Pennsylvania in 1842 by following the railway tracks from Baltimore to York. He had spent the intervening years working on farms in Lancaster County. In 1843, he underwent a transformative experience at an abolitionist rally where he listened raptly to an oration by Frederick Douglass, whom he had known years earlier in Maryland as the simple slave Frederick Bailey. "I was therefore not prepared for the progress he then showed," Parker later wrote. "I listened with the intense satisfaction that only a refugee could feel." Parker became a fighter in the tradition of Denmark Vesey and Nat Turner, although unlike them he operated in a free state and was supported by an interracial underground that recognized both his personal courage and his strategic skill. He acknowledged no federal law. When a Quaker neighbor urged him and the other fugitives to quietly head for Canada, he replied that if the laws protected black men as they did whites, he too would be a pacifist. "If a fight occurs, I want the whites to keep away," he told her. "They have a country and may obey the laws. But we have no country."

Parker's fortresslike, two-story fieldstone house two miles outside Christiana was the cockpit of black resistance in eastern Lancaster County, and lay close to the homes of several of the oldest underground stations in the region. Secluded on the slope of a forest-rimmed hill, yet situated so that anyone inside could keep watch over a broad expanse of countryside below, the house was well-situated for defense. At least two of Gorsuch's slaves plus Parker, his equally warlike wife Eliza, and several other armed men were holed up on the second floor of the house when the Marylanders and Marshal Kline appeared in the narrow lane outside before dawn on the morning of September 11.

Kline deployed four of his men to cover the back of the house. Then, with Edward Gorsuch, he entered the house. Kline announced that he was a U.S. marshal and that he had come to arrest Ford and Hammond. A voice shouted down that there were no such men there. Kline next heard the sound of guns being loaded. He ordered everyone in the house to come downstairs. When no one did, Kline and Gorsuch attempted to go up the narrow stairs, but someone thrust a blunt-pronged pitchfork at them. An axe was next thrown down, but hit no one. Parker's men then made a sudden rush down the stairs, and crowded the surprised whites out of the house.

The two groups, both armed and implacable, now faced each other in the yard. Looking up toward the several blacks who were visible in the second-floor windows, Kline read the arrest warrants aloud three times. He told Parker that he had fifteen minutes to turn over Ford and Hammond.

Parker replied that he cared nothing for him or for the United States government.

"I've heard a negro talk as big as you, and then have taken him, and I'll take you," Kline retorted.

"You can burn us, but you can't take us," replied Parker. "Before I give up, you will see my ashes scattered on the earth."

"I want my property, and I shall have it," Gorsuch shouted.

A bizarre dialogue next took place, reflecting the dense religiosity of the age, when slaves, their masters, and abolitionists all looked to the literal words of the Bible to sanction their actions.

"Does not the Bible say, 'Servants, obey your masters?' " Gorsuch challenged, as if the fatal drama that was unfolding concerned merely a fine point of theology.

The same Bible, Parker retorted, also said, "Give unto your servants that which is just and equal." He added, "Where do you see it in Scripture that a man should traffic in his brother's blood?"

"Do you call a nigger my brother?" Gorsuch demanded.

"Yes," replied Parker.

The tension mounted on both sides as dawn began to break. Although Gorsuch didn't know it, several of the men in the garret were panicking and urging surrender. Eliza, who, William wrote, had endured a slavery "far more bitter" than his own, grabbed a corn cutter and declared that she would cut off the head of anyone who attempted to give up.

The Parkers kept a horn that was to be used in times of emergency. Eliza now asked William if it was time to call for help. He told her to go ahead. Standing at one of the garret windows, she raised the horn and blew a squalling note that friends anywhere within hearing would instantly understand. One or more of the whites began firing at her, and she fell to her knees, unhurt, and, crouching beneath the sill, she continued to blow blast after blast into the brightening air.

Men and women dropped what they were doing and began to run toward the sound. They came from every direction, some on horseback, others on foot, armed with guns, clubs, barrel staves, and razor-edged corn cutters, until there were several dozen blacks gathered at the house. Some began to pace menacingly up and down the lane. Others pointed guns at Kline's increasingly nervous posse.

At this moment, two white men on horseback arrived on the scene, Elijah Lewis, a Quaker shopkeeper, and a mild-mannered miller named Castner Hanway, both of them well-known locally as sympathetic to blacks. Neither was active in the underground, but they were apparently part of the larger support network of individuals who, although they would not personally risk harboring fugitives, protected those who did, and helped to insulate the most radical activists against exposure. Kline peremptorily ordered the two whites to assist in arresting the fugitives. Both refused. Kline angrily warned them that by refusing they were committing a federal crime under the new Fugitive Slave Law. They, in turn, warned the marshal that unless he left the scene immediately there was certain to be bloodshed. As the two Lancaster men backed away, Hanway raised his arm, apparently to urge Parker's men back, although members of the posse later claimed (betraying the slave hunters' assumption that blacks could not act on their own) that he was signaling them to attack.

The standoff lasted almost an hour. The air fairly quivered with two and a half centuries of rage distilled into the figures that faced each other, no more than ten paces apart. Pride would not let Gorsuch walk away from a mob of blacks. Contempt seemed to seep from his very pores like sweat. Parker's men were ex-slaves who were filled with lifetimes of abuse from the men who once owned them, men like Gorsuch. They also knew that any one of them might be the next target of a slave-hunting posse.

By this point, there may have been as many as fifty blacks versus the posse's nine men, some of whom were still guarding the back of the house to prevent the fugitives' escape. Gorsuch was exhausted, furious, and hungry, an unfortunate combination. "I have come a long way this morning, and I want my breakfast," he declared. "I'll have my property, or I'll breakfast in hell."

"Old man, you had better go home to Maryland," someone told Gorsuch.

"Father, will you take all this from a nigger?" Gorsuch's son Dickinson exclaimed.

Parker threatened to knock Dickinson's teeth down his throat.

At this, young Gorsuch ran forward and fired his revolver at Parker but failed to hit him. Parker's brother-in-law fired back point-blank with a double-barreled shotgun. Dickinson fell, staggered to his feet, and went down again.

The tension broke like a dam, and Parker's men flooded forward with a shout. The yard in front of the house dissolved into chaos. All the white men in the lane then fired. At least two blacks were hit. Shots flew in every direction. Someone struck Edward Gorsuch with a rifle and clubbed him to the ground. As long as he could, he clung to his pistols—"he was the bravest of his party," Parker grudgingly recalled—fighting three men at the same time, until he finally went down for good under a hail of blows from clubs and corn cutters. Others caught Joshua Gorsuch and clubbed him until the blood ran out of his ears. Pearce, too, was caught and beaten senseless. Kline and the constables, the only members of the posse who escaped unharmed, leaped the fence and ran for their lives. Apart from the two men hit by the whites' first volley, no blacks were seriously injured. It was said afterward by veterans of the fight that "the Lord shook the balls out of their clothes."

Most of the whites didn't stop running until they reached Chester County. Several survived further injury only because they were escorted to safety by Castner Hanway and Elijah Lewis. Dickinson Gorsuch, although initially left behind in a pool of blood, eventually recovered.

Edward Gorsuch was the only fatality; his death sent waves of shock radiating through Washington, and across the South.

William Parker had no illusions about what fate lay in store for him if he remained in Lancaster County. He was determined not to be taken alive. While most of his men scattered among the homes of white and black supporters in the surrounding area, he and two of his closest friends, Abraham Johnson and Alexander Pinckney, quickly disappeared into the maze of underground lines that extended eastward into Chester County. Before the day was out, they had raced through Parksburg, Downington, and Kennett to the home of Isaac Mendenhall, one of the busiest underground stations in the region, which lay tucked in a narrow fold of hills just north of the Delaware state line. Dinah Mendenhall, normally a woman of steely resolve, later admitted that she was terrified as long as Parker's party was there, knowing that they were wanted for murder. "I had scarce strength to get into the house," she recalled. "But I held to my faith in an Overruling Providence. These were the times which tried men's souls, and women's too." The Mendenhalls passed the party on to portly Dr. Bartholemew Fussell, who carried them to the home of his niece, Graceanna Lewis. The next day, they were driven in a closed carriage, "throwing some old carpet over them, just as they would cover a butter-tub," to Phoenixville, and from there to Norristown, where they were hidden beneath a pile of shavings in a carpenter's shop. Judging the usual underground route via Philadelphia and New York City to be too dangerous, in order to deflect pursuers Dr. Jacob Paxson arranged for five wagons to be hired for that evening. He sent four of them off in different directions as decoys. After they had departed, Parker and his men were disguised, given ten dollars, hidden in the fifth wagon, and driven north by a black teamster.

From here on, the three fugitives would be on their own until they reached Rochester, New York. There, if they were not caught first, they had been directed to contact Parker's old friend Frederick Douglass, who had moved there from Boston in 1847, to establish his newspaper the *North Star.* Speed was critical. For all Parker knew, the sheriff in every town they passed through might be on the lookout for them. Traveling in rented wagons, they passed through the thinly populated mountains of northeastern Pennsylvania, through Friendsville, Tannersville, and Homersville, and finally crossing the Delaware River into New York at Big Eddy. From there they "took the cars" to Jefferson, where at 4 A.M. on September 20 they changed trains, arriving in Rochester five hours later, exhausted and dust-drenched. They had traveled five hundred miles in less than five days. During this last leg of the journey, a newsboy had passed through the car hawking New York City papers that carried the first reports about the events at Christiana. Parker was shaken, if not surprised, to learn that a reward of one thousand dollars had been placed on his head.

After leaving the train station, they walked the streets until they found a black man who could direct them to Douglass's home. The orator, and now journalist, greeted them enthusiastically. These were the kind of black men of whom he had dreamed: fearless and self-confident, "heroic defenders of the just rights of man against manstealers and murderers." But there were also no more dangerous men in the United States to have in one's home than these. There was no time to lose. When the three had eaten and rested, Douglass sent one of his collaborators, a white woman named Julia Griffiths, to the nearest landing, three miles away on the Genesee River, to learn when the next steamer was leaving for Canada. She returned a few hours later to breathlessly report that a Toronto-bound steamer was leaving that very night at 8 P.M. There was barely time to catch it. Douglass hurried the three men into what he facetiously called his "Democrat carriage" and raced for the landing, arriving just fifteen minutes before the boat's departure. He escorted them on board, and remained with them in a state of tortured anxiety, knowing that if they were arrested now, he too would be charged with abetting murder and treason. His entire career would be ruined. He might well find himself condemned to prison, and quite possibly to death. When they at last heard the order to lift the gangplank, Douglass felt a gust of relief. He shook each man's hand and prepared to disembark. Parker stopped him and handed him Edward Gorsuch's revolver, as a memento. The gun was a symbol, both men knew, that the war against slavery had taken a new and deadly turn, and that more, perhaps much more, violence lay ahead. It was one of the great moments in the history of the Underground Railroad.

If Parker's resistance had seriously damaged the Fugitive Slave Law, as Douglass passionately wished, the wound was not readily evident. Unconfirmed rumors later spread through the South that black women had castrated the fallen Edward Gorsuch and cut his body to pieces. The night after the Christiana "tragedy," as newspapers quickly dubbed it, a fifty-man posse was mustered at Lancaster. It was joined by gangs of proslavery hoodlums from Maryland, crews of Irish laborers, and eventually by contingents of United States marines and Philadelphia policemen to comb the countryside around Christiana in search of anyone who was implicated in the confrontation. They spread out across the autumn countryside, forcing their way into the homes of blacks and whites alike, threatening anyone who was thought to have anything to do with the Underground Railroad, arresting scores of men on suspicion, with little concern for constitutional niceties. As one eyewitness put it, "blacks were hunted like partridges."

3

Humiliated in Boston and again at Christiana, the federal government was now determined to break the back of Yankee opposition to the Fugitive Slave Law, this time in the abolitionist heartland. As vigilante gangs continued to storm across Lancaster County, another confrontation was about to begin in the antislavery citadel of Syracuse, New York, where on October 1 radical abolitionists were gathering for the Liberty Party's national convention. No one had forgotten that back in February, Daniel Webster had pointedly warned that the federal government was prepared to enforce the Fugitive Slave Law even "here in Syracuse, in the midst of the next Anti-Slavery Convention."

Nevertheless, William Henry, who was known to everyone for some reason as "Jerry," had reason to feel secure as he went about his work at Morrell's barrel-making shop. An athletic, squarely built mulatto with a striking head of red hair, the forty-year-old Henry was a skilled cooper who had come to Syracuse a year or two earlier, after escaping from slavery in Missouri. If a fugitive could expect to feel safe anywhere in the United States, it was in Syracuse, a bustling and progressive city of twenty-two thousand located in the heart of the Burned Over District. The local black population was small but militant. White antislavery forces were well-organized, and the most powerful abolitionist in the country, Gerrit Smith, lived just a few miles away in Peterboro. For years the city had been a key switching point for the Underground Railroad, receiving hundreds of northbound passengers via Elmira and Albany, and routing them, depending on the season, either directly to ports on Lake Ontario, or westward to Buffalo. The previous autumn, a public meeting chaired by the mayor himself had actually proclaimed Syracuse an "open city" for fugitive slaves. Henry had no way of knowing, as September turned into October, that a Missourian named James Lear had arrived in town, and that the United States commissioner had already sent a posse of federal marshals to arrest him.

Henry was at work on a barrel when the deputies burst in on him. Taking him from behind, they threw him onto the floor, and had shackles around his feet and hands before he realized what was happening. They then sped him in a hired carriage to the office of U.S. Commissioner Joseph F. Sabine. As it did for countless Northerners, the Fugitive Slave Law put Sabine in a complex and morally uncomfortable position. He regarded himself as an abolitionist in principle, but he also believed firmly in obedience to the law. Unlike most other abolitionists, however, the fate of fugitives actually hinged on what he did. His solution may, in its own private way, have been the single most subversive event of the day. He issued the writ for Henry's arrest without demur, but then informed his wife, who immediately reported the news to Charles Wheaton, a member of the city's antislavery Vigilance Committee. Wheaton, in turn, raced to the Congregational church, where the Liberty Party convention was under way. "A slave has been arrested!" Wheaton breathlessly announced.

An "impulsive citizen" raced from the convention to the Presbyterian church and began tolling the bell, a signal that danger was at hand. Soon every church bell in the city, except that of the conservative Episcopalians, was ringing. En masse, furious convention delegates, blacks and whites, local politicians, and the merely curious flooded into the street and streamed toward Sabine's office, in the Townsend Block, a large brick building that opened onto the Erie Canal. The canal was the commercial spine of the city, having more or less brought Syracuse into being when it was cut through to nearby Lake Onondaga, in the 1820s, and it continued to carry a steady traffic of packets and freight boats through the very center of town. Among the first to reach Sabine's second floor office were Jermain Loguen and Gerrit Smith, who immediately declared himself ready to serve as Henry's counsel. From the very start, Loguen and Smith were thinking of a rescue. But the atmosphere was chaotic. So many people had pushed into the cramped office that Smith and Loguen were physically pressed up against the commissioners' deputies. Every time that Lear, the Missourian—who wore a pair of pistols stuck prominently in his trousers—attempted to speak, Henry's supporters began to jeer. Sabine tried unsuccessfully to keep some kind of order, then after an hour simply gave up and adjourned for lunch, leaving the abolitionists in the courtroom with the prisoner and the virtually immobilized deputies.

Seizing the moment, Henry impulsively hurled himself across the table, scattering papers and pistols in every direction. The crowd instantly opened a path for him. When Marshal Henry Allen tried to follow, someone grabbed him by the throat as the crowd closed again behind the fugitive. Still shackled at the wrists, Henry stumbled down the stairs and into the street, and set off running. Friends and enemies alike took up the chase. A black barber named Prince Jackson kept pace with him, trying to fend off anyone who tried to grab him. For half a mile Henry managed to stay ahead of his pursuers. Two constables finally tackled him on the Lock Street Bridge, where it crossed the canal. When more constables came up a cart was commandeered, and the lawmen heaved the spent man into it. Two of them sat on his bloody and battered body, one across his legs and the other on his back, to hold him down as they jogged triumphantly back the way they had come. The sight sent waves of revulsion through men and women who only minutes before had gazed upon Henry's desperate flight as passively as if they were witnessing a piece of theater rather than a man running for his life. "I have just witnessed a scene (Heaven save me from a repetition) that has frozen my heart's blood," one eyewitness wrote the next day. "I have seen the perdition of slavery enacted in Syracuse, in the heart of New York . . . I have heard his frantic wail, his scream of despair. O such a look! O such a wail!"

Instead of returning to Sabine's office, Henry was taken to the more secure police station on Clinton Square, also alongside the canal. Marshal Allen, deciding that a show of force was necessary to deter any attack by the abolitionists, called on the county sheriff, a Democratic Party hack named William Gardner, for help. Gardner, evading the proper channel of command, thereupon went to his fellow Democrat, Lieutenant Prendergast of the National Guard, who took it upon himself to muster the local militia, as well as the guard and a company of artillery. When the tireless Charles Wheaton of the Vigilance Committee learned what was happening, he appealed in person to Colonel Origen Vandenburgh, the commander of the Fifty-first National Guard Regiment, and a man of presumed abolitionist sympathies. The two men hurried together to the armory, where Prendergast was already in the process of arming the troops. Vandenburgh ordered the guard to disarm and disband immediately. "My soldiers will never be kidnappers with my consent," he angrily declared. At this, the militia and the artillery also stood down, forestalling what might have turned into a street battle that would have dwarfed the skirmish at Christiana, and which no one wanted, except perhaps the deflated Prendergast.

While these events were taking place, in a doctor's office a few blocks away between twenty and thirty underground men and other abolitionists, including Jermain Loguen and Gerrit Smith, were laying out a plan of rescue. The great majority were white men of business, craftsmen, ministers, by no means the city's elite (who were no friends to abolitionism, for the most part), but solid and respectable, and thoroughly radicalized by what they had already seen. Some counseled restraint. Jerry might possibly be saved by legal argument, some said. Sabine might even free him after the hearing. The pacifist Reverend Samuel J. May, whose home was the main Underground Railway station in Syracuse, abhorred the prospect of violence. Smith, however, argued with his usual vigor for "bold and forcible" action that would serve as an example of resistance for abolitionists everywhere. Loguen too wanted to fight no matter what the consequences. The others listened with deep respect. They all knew that Loguen could have gotten away to Canada, but had stayed at the risk of his own freedom to preach against the Fugitive Slave Law. Good men must stand their ground against federal tyranny, Loguen insisted. They were engaged in a war whether they realized it or not, and they must win it. "If white men won't fight," he told them, "let fugitives and black men smite down marshals and commissioners—anybody who holds Jerry—and rescue him or perish." Loguen's eloquence won the day. It was decided that Henry had to be taken away from his captors without delay. The plan was as simple as a sledgehammer: a company of picked men would rush the police station, break in the doors and windows, and overwhelm the deputies inside. With this decided, men were dispatched immediately to obtain a swift horse, a strong buggy, and a bold driver, and to collect the necessary tools from

Wheaton's hardware store. As they left the meeting, Reverend May, who finally embraced the plan wholeheartedly, was heard to pray, "If anyone is to be injured, let it be against us, and not by us."

The police station was on the ground floor of an ordinary brick office building. The comparatively large courtroom could be entered directly from the street, and was packed with agitated abolitionists when Henry's hearing resumed at about 5:30 P.M. Behind the courtroom lay an inner office, and beyond that a still smaller chamber with barred windows, where Henry was being held, shackled at the feet this time, under heavy guard. Outside, between twenty-five hundred and three thousand people—more than 10 percent of the city's population—filled Clinton Square and spilled across the nearby bridges over the canal. The mood was fervid and expectant, though for exactly what, not many in the crowd yet knew, except for the few dozen men, perhaps fifty in all, who slipped toward the police station with Wheaton's tools under their coats. A minister named Johnson began orating from a window on the third floor of the police station itself. When the sheriff tried to silence him, Johnson roared so that everyone could hear, "As you command me to stop, I shall begin again, to test the liberty of speech!" As other antislavery orators harangued the crowd, voices by the hundreds chanted, "Let him go! Let him out!"

Shortly before 8 P.M., a voice from somewhere in the crowd shouted, "Bring him out!" It was the signal. A moment later, a stone smashed through a window, showering glass over the lawyers, marshals, and constables. More stones began to fly, so many of them rocketing through the courtroom's windows that Sabine abruptly turned Henry over to Marshal Allen and declared the court adjourned. The band of chosen men, blacks mingled together with whites, some of them with cork smeared on their faces, began rushing toward the building, pulling clubs, axes, and iron bars from beneath their coats as they ran. Loguen was probably somewhere among them, and possibly in the lead, although he later denied it. "Don't leave without the Negro!" supporters shouted.

Within minutes, the rescuers forced their way into the courtroom. Doors and windows were smashed, furniture splintered. The marshals and their deputies, perhaps twenty in all, retreated into the inner office and barred the door. Almost immediately, a miller from Oswego named William Salmon appeared with a party of men carrying a thick, fourteen-foot plank. Using it as a battering ram, they charged at the door, with the burly Salmon shouting, "Go ahead boys! Oswego is here and will stand by you!" The door soon gave way beneath their charge, and the rescuers poured through, sweeping the vastly outnumbered constables in a stumbling tangle before them. Marshal Allen, deciding for himself that the battle was already lost, borrowed an overcoat and fled ignominiously through the crowd to a nearby hotel.

Another door remained between Henry and his rescuers. This was defended by Henry Fitch, a tough U.S. deputy marshal from Rochester, and several very frightened constables. Fitch opened the door slightly and pointed his pistol at one of the rescuers. Someone struck him hard with one of Wheaton's iron bars, breaking the marshal's arm, and knocking the gun out of his hand. In agony, and terrified for his life, Fitch leaped out of the north window of the room, a drop of nine or ten feet, and, landing on the tow path of the canal, disappeared into the night. Inside the office, most of the remaining lawmen had covered themselves with boxes or crowded into the closet, leaving the shackled Henry alone on the floor, shouting to anyone who could hear, "Here I am, don't hurt me!" Suddenly all the gas lights went out, and the entire office was plunged into darkness. Shots rang out. "Come up, gentlemen—they've fired all their powder!" someone yelled.

"Hallo, Jerry!" one of the remaining marshals shouted. "You can quell this riot. Get out! Why the devil don't you go?"

"How can I—you've chained me!" Jerry yelled back.

The lawman took hold of Jerry and shoved him through the door and into the hands of his rescuers. The mob in the outer office roared victoriously. Several of the rescuers put their hands under the stunned and bloodied fugitive and carried him downstairs to the street. They were not shy in their triumph. Before they even got Henry's shackles off, they defiantly brandished him before a crowd of local dignitaries who were gathered at the front door of the Syracuse House hotel. Finally someone thought to shove Henry into a waiting carriage, and he was driven by a roundabout route to the home of a black family, the Watkinses, where a blacksmith cut off his chains.

For the next four days, Jerry was concealed in the Genesee Street home of a white butcher named Caleb Davis, a veteran of the War of 1812 and an outspoken proslavery Democrat, to all appearances the last person anyone could imagine sheltering a fugitive slave. But the sight of Henry being dragged in chains through Syracuse had converted him to abolitionism literally overnight. Like many who now found themselves being drawn toward the underground, Davis had no special fondness for blacks, but he did have a bedrock sense of Yankee independence, and he felt visceral outrage at the invasion of his town by slave-hunting Southerners and aggressive federal officials. True to form, while Henry was hidden in his own house, Davis was seen on the streets of Syracuse artfully denouncing abolitionists.

On the evening of October 5, Henry was handed a revolver, hidden under the seat of a carriage (its team lent by a former mayor), and with the brawny Davis riding as bodyguard, driven to the town of Mexico, about twenty-five miles north, where he lived for two weeks in the barn of a church elder, until a ship could be found to take him to Canada. A local tanner delivered him to the nearby lake port of Oswego as a consignment of "boots and shoes," and smuggled him on board under cover of night, virtually beneath the walls of the federal fortress that guarded the entrance to the harbor. He reached Kingston, Ontario, before nightfall the same day.

Twenty-six men, including fourteen whites and twelve blacks, were eventually indicted for their part in the Jerry rescue. Nine others, including Jermain Loguen, who was charged with assault with intent to kill, fled to Canada. The prosecution was a slow-motion fiasco. The trials dragged on into 1852, at a cost to the federal government of fifty thousand dollars. In the end, only one man, a black named Enoch Reed, was found guilty, but he died while his appeal was pending. Every other case ended in either acquittal or a hung jury. Reverend Samuel J. May wrote, "The cases were postponed and adjourned so many times that the expense alone convinced many who supported it that the Fugitive Slave Law was unenforceable." In the spring of 1852 Loguen was quietly permitted to return to Syracuse, where in the ensuing years he turned his home into an Underground Railroad depot so public that he advertised it in the local newspapers. (In the meantime, Gerrit Smith attempted unsuccessfully but with great propaganda effect to have Marshal Harry Allen prosecuted for kidnapping.)

The government fared no better in its attempts to convict the men arrested in the Boston and Lancaster County affairs. Ten men were arrested in connection with the rescue of Shadrach Minkins, including two of the fugitive's lawyers and Lewis Hayden. Their trials continued on into 1853. Although eyewitnesses were able to place Hayden at every stage in the rescue, juries failed to convict him, or any of the other defendants. In Pennsylvania, prosecutors initially charged thirty-eight Christiana men with "levying war" against the United States government, the largest indictment for treason in American history. The only man actually brought to trial, however, in December 1851, was the hapless Castner Hanway, one of the whites who had appeared in the midst of the confrontation. Although he was peripheral to what happened, the federal government felt that it had to convict a white man to avenge Gorsuch's death in the eyes of Southerners. After a brilliant defense directed by Thaddeus Stevens, the jury took only fifteen minutes to return a verdict of not guilty. When it became obvious that the other trials were likely to produce the same result, the government declined to prosecute anyone else, and the charges against them were eventually dropped.

Not surprisingly, there was outrage in the South. After the Christiana "tragedy," as the press dubbed it, a huge public rally in Baltimore called for an end to all commerce with the North, and in the wake of Jerry Henry's rescue, the *Savannah Republican* editorialized, "We warn the press and the people of the North that there is a point, not far distant, when forbearance on our part will cease to be virtuous or honorable, and that they and they alone will be responsible for all the ills that may betide this government." With the administration's failure to convict anyone for breaking the law, Southerners became convinced that the federal government was deliberately failing to enforce the Fugitive Slave Law.

Statistically, they were wrong. During the first fifteen months that the law was in force, eighty-four alleged fugitives were remanded south by commissioners, and only five set free. Although the administration continued to apply the law with vigor throughout the decade, the events of 1851 made it abundantly clear that it was doing so against Northern sentiment. To be effective, the law required the North's acceptance of the authoritarian regime already in place in the South to be extended across the North. And for that there was no Yankee will at all.

4

On May 7, 1852, Isaac Tatum Hopper died in New York City. He was eighty years old. How many fugitives owed their freedom to him, it was impossible to say. He never kept count. Certainly hundreds, very possibly thousands. He had served the abolitionist underground for more than fifty years, from its humble beginnings on the Philadelphia waterfront. Indeed, if any man could be called the father of the Underground Railroad it was he, although, the simplest of men to the last, he would have found such a claim both grandiose and unfair to his now forgotten collaborators. He had caught a cold during a visit to a discharged prisoner, for whom he served as a sort of volunteer counselor and mentor. The cold became an infection. He lingered on for ten weeks. Finally, too weak to rise, he lay in bed gazing at a small China bird that an escaped slave had given to his daughter Abby when she was small, in thanks for his part in her rescue. He remained serene until the end, speaking of death, his biographer Lydia Maria Child, who was by his bedside, recalled, "as if he had been anticipating a trip to Pennsylvania." In keeping with the simplicity that had been a hallmark of his life, he told his family that he wanted to be buried in a bare pine box made by one of his poor neighbors, who was to be paid the same price that he would have received if it were a luxury one. His last words were intended for his fellow Quakers, friends and enemies alike. "Tell them," he said, "I love them *all*."

Hopper's death marked the end of the underground's beginnings. At the turn of the century, the few white men and women (nearly all of them Quakers) who were willing to lend help to the fugitive slave were as gentle and religious as Hopper himself, and as reluctant as he was to break the letter of the law. Radical abolitionism had now become a mighty movement. Public opinion in the North was steadily shifting in favor of the abolitionists, who were seen as the defenders of free speech, free assembly, and personal liberty. The once-ridiculed fringe was now an army of resisters capable of heroism on a mass scale, and the civil disobedience that Thoreau preached in genteel Concord was being dramatically acted out in the streets. Old orthodoxies were boiling away. Public opinion in both North and South was galvanized in ways that made it harder to resolve differences over slavery without violence. As support for the pro-Southern

Democratic Party rose in the South, the political stock of the compromising Whigs in both North and South rapidly waned, never to recover. It was a particularly bad year for Daniel Webster, who saw the support for his presidential ambitions evaporate like spring snows off the hills of Massachusetts. (He too died in 1852, a few months before the election of yet another compliant Northern doughface, President Franklin Pierce of New Hampshire.) Among abolitionists, reasoned moral persuasion seemed increasingly inadequate. It was giving way to the belief that battles ought not to be avoided, but sought and won, if slavery was finally to perish. When William Salmon, who had helped carry the battering ram during Jerry Henry's rescue, was later asked what he would have thought if someone had been killed, he replied truculently, "Why, you talk just like the Tories of the Revolution. I am in for revolution."

The language of abolitionism was becoming the language of warfare and slaughter. In a speech to the National Free Soil Party convention in Pittsburgh, in 1852, pointedly alluding to Edward Gorsuch's killing at Christiana, Frederick Douglass declared, "The only way to make the Fugitive Slave Law a dead letter [is] to make half a dozen or more dead kidnappers." Gorsuch's corpse was a signpost for the future. Marylanders themselves retaliated in early 1852 when proslavery vigilantes cold-bloodedly murdered a Pennsylvania farmer named Joseph Miller, who had traveled to Baltimore to attempt to gain the release of a free black woman who had been kidnapped from his farm. It was only the beginning of a violent decade that would leave a steadily darkening trail of blood through Kansas, Harpers Ferry, and Bull Run.

The events of 1851 also revealed a new generation of remarkably bold, capable, and self-confident black leaders in men such as Lewis Hayden, Jermain Loguen, and William Parker. There were others like them in Philadelphia, Albany, Detroit, and the towns of the Ohio Valley. In the 1830s their forerunner, David Ruggles, had been driven to a nervous breakdown by the unyielding hostility that surrounded him. These men knew instinctively that the tide of history was running in their favor. The Christiana resistance had been planned and carried out entirely by African Americans, who had faced down the federal government and won, showing for all to see that blacks could and would defend themselves on a field of battle, while Hayden and Loguen had shown themselves able to inspire whites not just to lend moral support and money, but also to engage in a physical confrontation against their own government. Blacks had always played an assertive and sometimes dominant role within the clandestine purlieus of the underground, but this was the first time that they had done so in the open, and in the heart of two major cities, no less.

All in all, it was a good year for the Underground Railroad. In Boston and Syracuse the underground had temporarily dropped its veil of secrecy to publicly reveal its efficiency, tactical flexibility, and unflinching willingness to make physical sacrifices for what it believed in. Longtime activists were deluged with idealistic volunteers who were inspired by what they had read, or seen firsthand. They were needed, for the flood of refugees only grew that winter. "This road is doing better business this fall than usual," the African-American journalist Henry Bibb gleefully wrote from Canada, in November 1851. "The Fugitive Slave Law has given it more vitality, more activity, more passengers, and more opposition, which invariably accelerates business. We have been under the necessity of tearing up the old strap rails and putting down the regular T's, so that we can run a lot of slaves through from almost any of the bordering slave states into Canada within 48 hours, and we defy the slave holders and their abettors to beat it if they can . . . We have just received a fresh lot today of hearty-looking men and women on the last train from Virginia, and there is still room."

CHAPTER 16

GENERAL TUBMAN

When that old chariot comes,
I'm going to leave you
I'm boun' for the promised land.

—CODED HYMN, MARYLAND, 1850S

1

Kessiah Bowley—"Kissy," to her owners—her infant daughter, Araminta; and her six-year-old son, James, attracted a crowd when they were put up for sale in front of the doors of the county courthouse in Cambridge, Maryland, on a December morning in 1850. Two blocks down High Street, beyond the Episcopal church and Bradshaw's Hotel, where slave traders stayed, and the pillared homes of the town's elite, the sails of trading sloops and oyster boats could be seen on the Choptank River, the town's outlet to Chesapeake Bay. Slave sales were not to be missed. In small towns, they were like country fairs. Rural people came to watch them as they would to a cattle show. Men with nothing else to do mingled with serious buyers to follow the bidding, friends convivially swapped cigars and good stories, liquor flowed freely, and by the middle of the afternoon streets and stores were usually well speckled with drunks. Bowley was a young, healthy woman, a good investment, though married to a free black man, a possible source of annoyance to an owner who wanted the complete loyalty of his human property. It is impossible to say how much she knew about what was supposed to happen. Perhaps everything, perhaps nothing. But undoubtedly she looked out with trepidation at the arc of white faces, faces that were sizing up her physique and her fitness for labor, and perhaps for sex. She knew that her entire life would be abruptly changed whatever the outcome.

Somewhere in the crowd, Kessiah's husband John Bowley, a ship's carpenter, was bidding. (In Maryland, unlike some slave states, there was no law against a man buying his family out of slavery.) He must have sworn that he would save her somehow. But how could she trust such a promise? There was no way that a black man, free or not, could count on keeping that kind of promise to his slave wife. But John Bowley kept on without hesitation, as if he had a purse full of money, until every other bidder fell silent. He had won. Although the exact figure is now lost, it was probably around five hundred dollars, the equivalent of about eighteen thousand dollars in current dollars, a hefty sum for a seagoing man.

Kessiah was now told to stand aside somewhere while the auctioneer took his dinner. When he returned, John Bowley was nowhere to be found. His bid, it seemed after all, was just a black man's pathetic ploy to keep hold of his wife. The bidding was restarted. "*Serious buyers only this time!*" Again the numbers climbed. There was a whispered word to the auctioneer. The bidding abruptly stopped. The news rippled through the incredulous crowd. Not only John Bowley, but Kessiah and her children had disappeared.

While the agents of Kessiah's owner, and presumably the local constables, scoured the town for her, she and her husband lay hidden in the house of a woman who lived just minutes' walk from the courthouse. That evening the Bowleys made their way under cover of darkness to the Choptank River. There John Bowley, now a criminal liable to arrest for stealing his own wife and children, placed them in a small boat and set out to sail them to Baltimore, seventy-five miles away. The danger was extreme. Down the Choptank he sailed, then north up Chesapeake Bay past Tilghman, Romancoke, Annapolis, Sparrow's Point. Hundreds of African-American fishermen, oystermen, and crab pluckers worked on the bay, but few of them were sailing a woman and children across it in an open boat. The bay could be a treacherous place in winter. The weather and the winds could change suddenly, and without warning. But luck was with them.

In Baltimore the Bowleys faded into the teeming and varied world that was the black community. Baltimore's thirty-six thousand blacks, twenty-nine thousand of them free men and women, enjoyed a considerable amount of independence. By 1850 they supported an alternative universe of churches, schools, and benevolent societies at least partly beyond the prowling eyes of watchful whites. Frederick Douglass, writing of his days as a slave in Maryland, considered Baltimore "the very place, of all others, short of a free state, where I most desired to live." But the Bowleys were still far from safe.

The Bowleys probably found shelter with friends who lived in the black enclave of Fell's Point, where narrow houses jammed together in cobbled lanes that trickled back from the docks. According to plan, they met there with Kessiah's aunt Minty, or Harriet as she had begun calling herself. Harriet and John Bowley had planned the daring rescue together. They must have had a good laugh over its stunning success. It wasn't often that slaves managed to make public fools of their masters, and get away with it. Harriet had herself escaped overland to Pennsylvania in 1849. She could have remained safe in the North, but at great risk to herself, she had slipped back into Maryland when she heard news of Kessiah's impending auction. Her job now was to guide the Bowleys to Philadelphia. It was the beginning of one of the most extraordinary careers in American history.

There were others, almost all of them men except for Harriet, who served as the long distance tentacles of the ever-expanding Underground Railroad, traveling repeatedly into the slave states to pluck away slaves from the belly of the beast. There was John Parker, the black foundry owner by day and conductor by night, who later in the decade worked out of Ripley, Ohio, and Elijah Anderson, the Indiana ironmonger, who was said to have brought twenty or thirty slaves at a time out of Kentucky. There were white men like Seth Concklin, the ill-fated Calvin Fairbank, and the mysterious, gun-toting John Fairfield, who masqueraded as a slave trader, and drove fugitives out of the South in coffles. But there was no one quite like this incredibly single-minded, mystical, diminutive woman (she was barely five feet tall) who defied every antebellum notion about what women were supposed to be.

Although her speech was "uncouth," and she referred to herself casually as merely "a poor nigger," there was a quiet dignity about her that made her indifferent to her surroundings, whether she was dining at Peterboro with Gerrit Smith, or in a kitchen with white help who complained about having to sit down with a black woman. She was strongly muscled from years of hard outdoor physical labor, which had burned her skin a dark chestnut color, and made her look decades older than she was. At thirty, she was mistaken, even by whites who knew her, for a woman twice her age. John Brown, who got to know her only after his bloody days in Kansas, admiringly called her "*General* Tubman," and wrote of her, "He is the most of a man, naturally, that I ever met with." More than that of any other actual participant, her story would shape the legend, and the myth, of the Underground Railroad. She eventually became a kind of metaphor for the entire underground, endowed—a remarkable individual by any measure—with virtually superhuman personal qualities, while her uniquely brilliant work evolved into a template for the entire diverse system. Illiterate her entire life, she kept no record of her many rescue expeditions into Maryland, and had no clear memory of their sequence or dates. Her story survived only in the memories and impressions of others, and can only be assembled from fragments, like a shattered mosaic.

The fifth of at least nine children, Araminta "Minty" Ross was born in 1822, near Tobacco Stick on Maryland's Eastern Shore, a flat, watery country of wide vistas, marshy creeks, sodden woodlands, and lonely stands of lofty loblolly pines. Her childhood on the Brodess plantation had a feral, almost anarchic quality. "I grew up neglected like a weed, ignorant of liberty, having no experience of it," she told the abolitionist Benjamin Drew, who interviewed her in Canada, in 1855. Her hair was never combed and "stood out like a bushel basket" from her head. When she needed to eat, she sometimes fought the hogs for their mash. Discipline was swift and harsh. There were days when she received as many as six or seven beatings. Scars from them remained visible all her life. The threat of sale worried her constantly after she saw two of her sisters taken off in a chain gang. She told Drew, "Every time I saw a white man I was afraid of being carried away."

She was eleven or twelve years old when something happened that permanently marked her not only physically but in some obscure way spiritually, adding a dimension of pronounced strangeness to what had been an otherwise unremarkable girl. She was in a general store when a white overseer ran in, chasing a slave who had walked away from his work. Furious at seeing the man he was searching for, the overseer grabbed a two-pound lead weight from the counter and hurled it at him. He missed the man, but hit Tubman in the head so hard that it drove a piece of the shawl she was wearing into her skull, and knocked her unconscious. Not considered worth a doctor's attention, she was allowed only a day and a half to rest before being sent back to work in the fields, with blood rolling down her face. For the rest of her life, she suffered from what was probably a form of epilepsy that produced headaches, seizures, and "fits of somnolency," causing her to suddenly fall unconscious for minutes at a time, and pushing a mind already fertilized by evangelical religion into a feverish mysticism that awed those who came in contact with her. In a prepsychological age steeped in a culture of spiritualism, middle-class abolitionists were fascinated by her powers that seemed to defy explanation, like the "fluttering" that seemed to foretell imminent danger, and her ability to know what happened around her during her sleeping fits. As one awestruck Yankee friend put it, "There is a whole region of the marvelous in her nature."

Slavery in Maryland was in steady decline during the years of Ross's youth. It was undermined less by any moral revolution than by changing economic conditions which put a higher premium on mobile free labor. Between 1790 and 1850, as Dorchester County's slave population shrunk by almost 20 percent, to just over 4,000, the number of free blacks swelled from 528 to nearly 4,000. Ross adapted readily to the changing environment, revealing a natural independence that would become even more pronounced during her years of clandestine work. While still in her twenties, she negotiated a work-for-hire arrangement with her master that allowed her to rent out her labor as she wished, paying him a set annual fee of fifty or sixty dollars. Despite her size and infirmity, she was a prodigious worker, driving teams, packing and hauling grain on the wharves at Tobacco Stick, dragging heavy sleds laden with produce "like an ox," and hauling timber for her father, who had purchased his freedom in 1840, and who oversaw the cutting and hauling of lumber for the Baltimore shipyards.

In 1844 she married John Tubman, a free man of mixed race. About the same time, she changed her first name to Harriet, perhaps as a gesture of affection for her mother, also named Harriet. In the spring of 1849 she learned that she and several of her brothers were likely to be sold. They had never heard of any free states except New Jersey and Pennsylvania, and they had no clear idea how to get there. But they decided to set off anyway. What Harriet told her husband, and what he might have thought about it, she never confided to anyone. In any event, the attempted escape was a fiasco. The three fugitives tried to follow the north star. They argued about directions, and finally gave up and returned in defeat. If Harriet drew any lesson from this dismal experience, it was that the odds against escaping without help were close to insurmountable. She would not make the same mistake again.

In the months that followed, Tubman's mind was overcharged with prophetic visions. She saw horsemen coming for her, like the riders of the apocalypse; she heard the terrifying screams of women and children. She dreamed of flying over fields and towns, rivers and mountains, and looking down upon them like a bird, until she reached at last a great fence, which she feared she hadn't the power to fly over. But just as she was sinking down, and losing her strength, ladies dressed in white would stretch out their arms and pull her across. She found release only in incessant prayer, praying for her sins to be washed away when she went to the horse trough for a drink, praying for them to be swept away whenever she plied a broom.

Characteristically, she did not leave her salvation to chance. In the late autumn of 1849 she fled on her own. Although she was vague on the details, she later described her hundred-mile overland trek through eastern Maryland, and probably Delaware, as having been accompanied, phantasmagorically, by a pillar of cloud during the day, and a pillar of fire by night. She also sought, and received, concrete help from a white woman, almost certainly a mill owner's wife named Hannah Leverton, who was part of a fragile network that linked Dorchester County Quakers with those farther north in Camden, Delaware, and beyond. The white woman wrote two names on a piece of paper, which she gave to Tubman. That night, the woman's husband carried her concealed in his wagon to the outskirts of a town, where he directed her to the home of one of the people whose names had been given to her. She was passed on in this fashion from hand to hand until she eventually reached Pennsylvania.

Pennsylvania, in Tubman's mind, was not only a physical or political landscape, but a profoundly spiritual one. "When I found I had crossed that line," she said, "I looked at my hands to see if I was the same person. There was such a glory over everything; the sun came like gold through the trees and over the fields, and I felt like I was in Heaven. I had crossed the line." But she felt an utterly unexpected sense of loss and desolation. In Maryland she was a slave, but she had family. She was now alone in a way that she had never been before. "I was *free*, but there was no one to welcome me to the land of freedom. I was a stranger in a strange land." What was she without family? she wondered. "I was free, and *they* should be free," she thought. For the next decade, the rescue of her family became the focus of her life, a private crusade that bordered on obsession. She was convinced that she was a chosen agent of God, who guided her every act, and he was now sending her back to the Eastern Shore. When friends in the underground cautioned her "against too much adventure & peril," she replied, "The Lord who told me to take care of my people meant me to do it just so long as I live, and so I do what he told me to do."

Emboldened by her success in rescuing Kessiah Bowley and her children, she returned to Baltimore a few months later, and brought north her brother Moses and two other men. In the fall of 1851, she returned to Dorchester County to bring out her husband, John. Tubman was a free man and could have left on his own. That he did not might have given Harriet pause. With her customary single-mindedness, however, she saved money from her kitchen work in Philadelphia to finance another trip south, and to buy a new suit of clothes for John. She had not seen him for two years, and she had much to tell him. But bitter disappointment awaited her. From a hiding place somewhere near her old home, she sent John word that she had come. He replied, through an intermediary, that he had taken another wife, a free woman, and had no intention of leaving. In her fury, Harriet's first instinct was to invade John's house and make as much trouble for him as she could. Perhaps it was at this moment, amid rage, hurt, and betrayal, that the indomitable, iron-willed Harriet Tubman of legend was born. If the rescue of family was at the heart of her quest, John Tubman was perhaps its crux, the only person whom she believed had belonged to her alone. How she must now have hated the sight of the clothes that she had brought for him! But a cold instinct for self-preservation, and her growing sense of a greater mission ordained for her by God, won out. If Tubman had ever been a sentimentalist (an almost unimaginable luxury for a slave), she certainly no longer was now. She collected a group of willing fugitives from the neighborhood, gave one of them John's new clothes, and led them north.

Before the year was out, she had brought out eleven additional slaves, including another of her brothers and his wife. These she accompanied all the way to Canada, traveling from Philadelphia to New York City, Albany, and Rochester, where they stayed in Frederick Douglass's barn, the largest number that he ever had in his home at one time. "I had some difficulty in providing so many with food and shelter, but, as may well be imagined, they were not very fastidious in either direction," Douglass remarked, a little snobbishly. In all, in the course of thirteen journeys back to the Eastern Shore, Tubman would lead at least seventy African Americans out of slavery in Maryland, and indirectly enable perhaps fifty others to escape to freedom on their own. (Her first biographer, Sarah Bradford, inflated these numbers for dramatic effect to nineteen trips and three hundred passengers.)

In legend, Tubman typically appears as a solitary figure trekking with her parties of fugitives through dense forests of oak and pine, and across its marshes in lonely isolation. As Kate Clifford Larson has shown in a recent, groundbreaking biography of Tubman, *Bound for the Promised Land*, she was in fact able to draw for assistance not only on the Levertons' small circle of Quakers, but also on a much larger web of African Americans, including both slaves and free men and women linked by marriage, friendship, and work from the Eastern Shore as far north as Pennsylvania and New Jersey. Networks that could efficiently transmit family news, Tubman correctly surmised, could also facilitate the furtive movement of human beings. She most often conducted her passengers on foot by one of two routes across eastern Maryland, either directly east from the Cambridge area or adjoining Caroline County to Seaford, Delaware, and then due north along the line of present-day U.S. Route 13, or else northeast via Denton and Sandtown to join the main New Castle road around Camden, and then north through Wilmington to Philadelphia.

She preferred to do her underground work in the winter, when the long nights provided more hours for travel. She usually collected her passengers somewhere far from their homes, to lessen the chance of someone recognizing her, and often in a cemetery, where groups of apparent "mourners" would go unnoticed. To move around as widely as she did in Maryland and Delaware, Tubman must have carried convincing documentation. She may have acquired forged free papers from certain black market women in Baltimore, who were linked to the Philadelphia underground, and kept a stock of forged free papers that they circulated and renewed at regular intervals. She paid for shelter and transportation for her passengers when it was available; once, when she had no money to give, she paid a helpful family with her underclothing. Thanks to her years of work in lumber camps, she could find her way through the woods as skillfully as any of the old Nanticokes who had once roamed the land. When circumstances called for it, she could also slither through tall grass like a snake, flat on her stomach, using only her arms and the serpentine motion of her body to propel herself forward.

She was a consummate actress. A friend later wrote of her that "she seems to have command over her face, and can banish all expression from her features, and look so stupid that nobody would suspect her of knowing enough to be dangerous." She often disguised herself as an elderly woman or man, or carried a book that, although she was illiterate, she used to deflect the attention of pursuers who were looking for a fugitive field hand. Well aware that blacks were liable at any time to be stopped and questioned by whites, she sometimes carried a pair of chickens as a deliberate ruse, which at least once she was obliged to put into effect. Coming face to face with her own master on a street in Cambridge, she pinched the chickens so that they ran loose, and in the confusion of chasing them, she went unnoticed. She also used familiar hymns to communicate with her passengers in a kind of simple code. She would, for example, pass along the road to see if the coast was clear. If it was, she would sing, in a powerful, full-throated voice

Hail, oh hail, ye happy spirits,
Death no more shall make you fear.

And if there was danger, she would sing, in warning

Oh go down, Moses
Way down into Egypt's land.

Tubman expected her passengers to have nerves as steely as her own. She permitted no "whimpering," and made it clear that she was willing to kill anyone who faltered. "That several who were rather week-kneed and faint-hearted were greatly invigorated by Harriet's blunt and positive manner and threat of extreme measures, there could be no doubt," wrote one of her close collaborators. During one trip, when she was compelled to keep her party hidden in a swamp for a day and a night without food, one of the men declared in disgust that he was going home. Tubman stepped up to him and aimed a revolver at his head, saying, "Move or die." He went on with the rest to Canada. A live runaway could do great harm by going back, she knew, but a dead one could tell no secrets. When there were babies to be carried, she dosed them with paregoric to prevent them from crying, and put them in a bag that she slung around her waist.

Although Tubman must have become aware that there was an abolitionist underground as soon as she reached Philadelphia in 1849, if not before, her first rescue missions appear to have been independent operations. Sometime in 1851 or 1852, however, she met two men who would draw her into the inner mechanism of the Underground Railroad, providing her with money, new connections, and introductions to many of the most influential abolitionists in the country. One of these men was Thomas Garrett, one of the grand old Quakers of the underground, who rivaled Levi Coffin in both the length of his service and the number of fugitives who passed through his brick home on Shipley Street, in Wilmington. A thickset, sandy-haired man with slightly unbalanced blue eyes set in a broad, genial face, which gave "an impression of repose, kindness and strength," Garrett began his underground work in the 1820s, at a time when abolitionists were, he wrote, "like Virgil's ship-wrecked mariners, very few in number and scattered over a vast space." He made no secret of his views. Sheer fearlessness may have disarmed some of his opponents. But good connections also helped: his wife, Rachel, was the daughter of a director of the National Bank of Wilmington, and he received financial contributions from the DuPont family, the wealthiest in the state.

In Delaware, as in Maryland, slavery was in decline, but the punishment for aiding fugitives was still severe, as Garrett found out in 1848. In that year he was tried and convicted of assisting the escape of six slaves, and required to pay a fine of fifteen hundred dollars, about fifty-three thousand dollars in present-day value. (Garbled reports inflated this to forty thousand dollars in 1850 by confusing the fine with business losses, and erroneously asserting that the judgment had included the seizure of Garrett's property.) At his trial, Garrett shocked his listeners by admitting publicly that he had assisted over fourteen hundred slaves to freedom in twenty-five years, an average of fifty-six per year: "[H]ad I believed every one of them to be slaves, I should have done the same thing . . . I should have done violence to my convictions of duty, had I not made use of all the lawful means in my power to liberate those people." He added, "I now consider the penalty imposed might be a license for the rest of my life: but be that as it may, if any of you know any poor slave who needs assistance, send him to me, as I now publicly pledge myself to double my diligence, and never neglect an opportunity to assist a slave to obtain freedom."

Garrett had cut back his underground work somewhat after his 1848 conviction, when he was fifty-nine years old. But by the early 1850s he had sufficiently recovered financially to recommit himself to his true vocation. He was the linchpin, if not the formal director, of a diverse network that reached south at least as far as Camden and Middletown, and included Quakers and Catholics, farmers, whites within the law enforcement establishment, black fishermen and watermen, and, as he called her, "that noble woman," Harriet Tubman. She would appear at his door without warning, a party of fugitives stashed somewhere in the vicinity, asking for cash or some other kind of help that she took for granted would immediately be forthcoming. On one occasion she turned up suddenly and announced, "Mr. Garrett, I am here again, out of money, and with no shoes to my feet, and God has sent me to you for what I need." The Quaker replied, "Harriet, art thou sure thou art not deceived? I cannot find money enough to supply all God's poor. I had five here last week and had to pay 8 dollars to clothe and forward them." Tubman persisted that he must have enough to pay for a pair of shoes and passage for herself and a companion to Philadelphia. Then she added, "I must have 20 dollars more to enable me to go down to Maryland for a woman and three children." That very morning, she told Garrett, she had paid "her last copper" to a driver who had brought her and "a delicate female" thirty miles in his carriage. Garrett thereupon handed her five British pounds that had been sent to him by Quaker donors, more than enough to meet her needs without having to solicit more from her friends in Philadelphia.

Although Garrett boasted at one point, for rhetorical effect, that he would have to build another story onto his three-story house to accommodate more fugitives, most were probably in fact concealed in the homes of his black collaborators elsewhere in Wilmington. Although Garrett sometimes sent fugitives directly to Philadelphia by steamboat, more often they were guided across the Pennsylvania state line, the women and children in carriages and the men by foot, often in the company of a traveling African American grocer, who was able to make frequent journeys, day or night, between Wilmington and the underground stronghold of Chester County, without prompting suspicion. Garrett would sometimes present a fugitive with a scythe, rake, or hoe from his store to carry through town like a workman. Having reached a certain bridge, the man would conceal the tool under it and continue on his way. The tool would be retrieved by one of Garrett's allies, and reused for the same purpose. Other times, he would dress a fugitive in his wife's Quaker clothing, with a deep bonnet and veil, and personally walk her, or him, through the streets, arm in arm to a safer location. Although there were more direct routes from Wilmington to Philadelphia, Garrett usually preferred to send fugitives first northwest to Kennett, where he had close personal connections, preceding them with a tongue-in-cheek note announcing: "I send you three bales of black wool."

2

Most of the fugitives sent north by Garrett were directed to the Anti-Slavery Office on North Fifth Street, in Philadelphia, where they met the other man who would shape Tubman's career in the Underground Railroad, William Still. Although, like Frederick Douglass, Still was embarrassed by Tubman's countrified ways, he was also in awe of her. "Her like it is probable was never known before or since," he would write. "[A] woman of no pretensions, indeed, a more ordinary specimen of humanity could hardly be found among the most unfortunate farmhands of the South. Yet, in point of courage, shrewdness and disinterested exertions to rescue her fellow-men, by making personal visits to Maryland among the slaves, she was without her equal."

Still was born free in 1821, near Medford, in the Pine Barrens of New Jersey, the youngest of eighteen children. His father, Levin, had purchased his freedom and moved north from Maryland in 1807. His mother, Charity, later escaped to join him there, leaving behind their two oldest, enslaved sons. Largely self-taught, William moved to Philadelphia in 1844, where he worked at various menial jobs until, in 1847, he was hired as a clerk and janitor by the Pennsylvania Society for the Abolition of Slavery, at a salary of three dollars and seventy-five cents per week. When the Vigilance Committee was reorganized after the passage of the Fugitive Slave Law, Still was named its chairman. He coordinated escapes with underground activists as least as far away as Norfolk, Virginia and Washington, D.C., where the frugal Yankee lawyer Jacob Bigelow had rebuilt a clandestine network after William Chaplin's arrest. Still's Philadelphia office also served variously as a reception center, a kind of social services agency for needy fugitives, and a clearinghouse for information. He was usually the first person fugitives encountered when they arrived from underground stations in the Pennsylvania hinterland, from the Delaware line, or by sea from the South. Still had greeted William and Ellen Craft after their epic journey from Georgia, and he was on hand to help Henry "Box" Brown out of his packing crate. It was also Still who sent word to William Parker and his men at Christiana that the Maryland slave owner Edward Gorsuch and his party were on their trail.

In the early 1850s Still's office was aiding an average of sixty fugitives per month. He interviewed every one of them in detail, noting down their places of origin, family histories, former names, and the like. (These documents remain the best record of daily underground operations anywhere in the country.) In the spring of 1850, a recently freed slave from Alabama named Peter Friedman walked into Still's office seeking information about his parents, from whom he had been separated as a child. The illiterate Friedman was startled to see a poised and polished young black man sitting at a desk writing letters, something that he had never witnessed in Alabama. Still began to question him at length, in his usual fashion. Both men were wary, Still suspecting that Friedman might be a spy sent by slave masters to hunt down fugitives, and Friedman, knowing nothing about abolitionists, fearing that he was being led into a trap of some kind. Something about Friedman's story seemed eerily familiar to Still. Finally, after learning the names of Friedman's parents, and that they had disappeared from Maryland forty years before, leaving Peter and another brother behind, he looked the stranger in the face, a near mirror of his own, though twenty years older and weather-beaten, and said, "Suppose I should tell you that I am your brother?"

Still explained to the incredulous Friedman that their eighty-year-old mother was still alive, as were ten of her children, and living across the Delaware River in New Jersey. After an emotional family reunion at Charity's farm, Friedman explained that he had left behind his own enslaved wife and three children in Alabama, and was hoping to work diligently to earn the money to buy them himself. Against the Stills' protests, he returned to Alabama, where he spent several months pretending to be a slave-for-hire, saving money, and looking for a way to bring his family north. He began to grasp that it would take years to save the thousands of dollars that it would cost to purchase them. He returned to Philadelphia deeply discouraged.

In the meantime, news of the brothers' reunion, and of Peter's seemingly hopeless quest to recover his family had appeared in the local newspapers. One of the people who read about it was a crusty underground veteran named Seth Concklin, whose life thus far sounds like a Cook's tour of the underside of antebellum America. A small, homely man, often scruffily dressed and taciturn to the point of eccentricity, Concklin was born in upstate New York, in 1802, and endured an appallingly grim childhood that left him with the cocky combativeness of a perpetual survivor, coupled to an indelible affinity for every underdog he ever met. His father died when Concklin was still a boy, leaving him responsible for a large, virtually indigent family. One of his sisters was given away to strangers when she could no longer be fed. To support his remaining siblings, he tramped the roads of rural New York peddling trifles. After living for a time in a pacifist Shaker community near Albany, he enlisted in the small, ill-starred republican force that sought to overthrow the British colonial regime in Canada during the so-called Patriot War of 1838–39. Later he served in Florida as a soldier in the First Seminole War, returning home contemptuous of the government's expansionist propaganda, and with a deep sympathy for the beleaguered Indians. He hated slavery with such a passion that it was said of him that "he was a whole Abolition Society in himself," and he served for a time as an underground conductor in Springfield, Illinois, where he may have known, or at least met, the up-and-coming young lawyer Abraham Lincoln.

Concklin had not long before advanced a plan to break the abolitionist William Chaplin out of prison in Washington, but it was never adopted. Now he offered to personally bring Peter Friedman's family out of Alabama. He was forty-nine, an age when many men were already being described as "old." Perhaps he saw this as his last chance at adventure before he slipped into old age. Since he was poor all his life, money meant nothing to him. He wanted no payment beyond expenses, and in fact pledged to contribute his own savings, a total of twenty-six dollars. Friedman agreed to the proposal, albeit reluctantly, for he recognized the risks for his family if Concklin failed. He gave Concklin a detailed description of the plantation near Florence, Alabama, where his wife, Vina, and their children lived. He then handed Concklin the one hundred dollars that he had raised so far and a cloak belonging to Vina, to show her as an identifying token.

Concklin traveled first to Cincinnati, where he stayed with Levi Coffin, who had moved to the city in 1847. Using the Coffin home as a base, he explored the north bank of the Ohio River as far west as Illinois for the best place to bring Friedman's family ashore, once he got them out of Alabama. That he had to do this on his own suggests both the inherent limitations and the ingrained localism of the underground. Coffin could offer Concklin useful introductions to agents only as far away as southwestern Indiana, while he met outright resistance from western underground men when he tried to raise money for what they told him was "a case properly belonging east of Ohio." Initially, Concklin hoped to land the family in southern Illinois, but he was dismayed to find that region infested with proslavery sentiment and exceptionally strong support for the Fugitive Slave Law. In Indiana, physical attacks against blacks were on the increase, and proslavery vigilantes belonging to the secretive Knights of the Golden Circle were doing their best to disrupt the Underground Railroad. Frustrated but undaunted, Concklin decided that he would have to bring Friedman's family up the Wabash River and well into Indiana before he could deliver them to a secure underground line.

At the end of January 1851, Concklin made a scouting trip up the Tennessee River to Florence, which he found to be a dismal hamlet consisting of twenty white families, a couple of warehouses, and a post office. Calling himself "Miller," he roamed the area, ostensibly seeking work. At the McKiernan plantation, he made contact with an enslaved cobbler, a friend of Peter Friedman, who arranged a rendezvous with Vina. She was unnerved at the prospect of setting off into the unknown with a total stranger. But she put her trust in the cloak that Peter had given Concklin, and agreed to go with him.

Concklin had by now decided against an escape by steamer as far too risky. They would have to row themselves to Indiana instead. He returned to Cincinnati where he purchased a large, six-oared skiff—"a first-rate clipper," he called it in a letter to William Still—and brought it back with him on board a steamboat to Florence. By prearrangement, Vina and her children slipped away in the night to meet Concklin on a deserted stretch of riverbank outside the town. Before them lay more than four hundred miles of rowing. The two boys, Levin and Peter, and Concklin were all strong oarsmen, and before daylight they had passed through Colbert Shoals and Bee Tree Shoals, a treacherous obstacle course of flinty rocks that were the curse of larger craft. By daylight they had reached Eastport, Mississippi, where the river made its great bend north back into Tennessee, forty miles from Florence. Whenever they came within sight of another boat Concklin made sure to stand at the helm like a proper slave master, keeping the two boys at the oars, while Vina and her daughter, Catherine huddled at their feet beneath blankets. They floated through one of the wildest, most defiantly uncivilized regions of the state, past primeval forests of beech, black gum trees, and evergreen magnolias; past cane bottoms and cypress marsh and small clearings where hardscrabble farmers raised a few cattle and hogs in brushy pastures of wild grass; past Shiloh, where barely a decade later one of the bloodiest battles of the Civil War would leave thousands dead; past the towns of Cerro Gordo, Clifton, Reynoldsburg, and Paris Landing; and finally, fifty-one hours after their departure, into the great Ohio River.

Thus far, they had been traveling with the current. Now they had to row upstream. They reached New Harmony, Indiana, fifty miles up the Wabash from the Ohio River, at 10 A.M. on Sunday, March 23, after traveling for seven days without a break, chilled to the bone and utterly exhausted. Concklin now exchanged the boys' shabby Southern clothing for "pants of Kentucky jean and black cloth coats," and clothed the women in plaid shawls such as free Yankee blacks would wear. That night they reached the nearest station of the Underground Railroad, where they were fed, and rested for a day. The next day, another "friend," probably David Stormont of Princeton, arrived to conduct them northward to his own home. After another day's rest there, they continued on foot to an underground station north of Vincennes. Although it was a notoriously proslavery area, Concklin deemed that they were by now so far from the river that it was safe to travel in the daytime. It was his first mistake.

Vina and her children drove northward in a driving rain, while Concklin walked some distance behind, close enough to keep them in view. Just before they reached the next underground station, they were hailed by a group of white men and challenged to explain themselves. Concklin quickly came up and claimed, first, that the four "slaves" were his and then, contradicting himself, that he was merely accompanying them north after they had been emancipated by his "brother in Kentucky." Not surprisingly, perhaps, the whites found all this less than convincing and ordered the party to turn around and head back to Vincennes. Concklin could easily have escaped at this point, but he continued to follow doggedly on foot. After nightfall, he slipped into the wagon and was in the process of untying the fugitives when he was seen. One of the whites pulled out a revolver and told him that he would shoot him if he tried it again.

Vina and her children were placed in the Vincennes jail, while the local authorities decided what to do with them. Since there was no charge against Concklin, a free white man, he was left to his own devices. He still had some hope of rescuing the four, and he brazenly visited them every day, despite Vina's pleas that he save himself and flee. By now, however, the Evansville sheriff's office had received a copy of a circular telegram that had been sent by the fugitives' owner, Bernard McKiernan, to be on the lookout for Vina's family, offering a reward of four hundred dollars for their capture, and one of six hundred dollars for the "thief" who absconded with them. Concklin was now arrested, and McKiernan sent for. When the slave owner arrived a few days later, Concklin and the fugitives were handed over to him without even the formality of a hearing. Fearing a rescue attempt, they were hurried by stagecoach to Evansville, and there placed immediately aboard a southbound steamboat, the *Paul Anderson*, accompanied by McKiernan, his personal agent, and the flamboyant Evansville sheriff, John Smith Gavitt—proslavery man though he was, he would die bravely leading a Union cavalry charge against Confederate troops in 1861—who was there to protect the slave owner under the terms of the Fugitive Slave Law and, doubtless, to collect the reward once they reached Alabama.

Sometime during the downriver trip, as the free state of Illinois slipped by on the port side and the slave state of Kentucky on the starboard, McKiernan told Concklin that he would see him hanged in Alabama "if it cost him $1,500." Concklin replied that he was not at all sorry for what he had done. He was doing his Christian duty, and felt a clear conscience.

The *Paul Anderson* docked for the night at Smithland, at the mouth of the Cumberland River, where many of the passengers disembarked. There were contradictory reports about what happened after that. The only thing that was certain was that the next morning Concklin's corpse was found floating in the muddy, crud-filled water alongside the wharf. His hands were shackled, and his head was crushed.

Sheriff Gavitt later said that he had left McKiernan and the shackled Concklin together on the hurricane deck and gone to bed. When McKiernan was questioned, he said that he too had fallen asleep, and that when he woke Concklin was gone. He suggested that maybe Concklin had tried to escape and jumped overboard and drowned, rather than face trial in Alabama. Then how had his head been staved in? Perhaps he had been hit by the paddle wheel of a passing steamboat, McKiernan supposed. No one bothered to ask much more. His body was taken to a sand bank and buried in his clothes, still chained. Later, when they heard about his death, Concklin's friends assumed that McKiernan had murdered him in cold blood, and thrown his body overboard. Proslavery forces gloated. "There was none of that pretended philanthropy which induces a disregard for the rights of property," the *Vincennes Gazette* smugly editorialized.

In a curious way, Concklin's death helped free Peter Friedman's family after all. Though less well remembered, the apparent murder of Seth Concklin became, like the rescues of Shadrach Minkins and Jerry Henry, and the Christiana prosecutions, one of the most widely discussed events of that tumultuous and pivotal year. For many months thereafter, Friedman traveled profitably among abolitionist gatherings, telling the story of his enslavement and Concklin's martyrdom, and appealing for donations (as he had originally planned) to buy his family out of slavery. By 1855 he had managed to accumulate the five thousand dollars that McKiernan demanded: one thousand for each member of his family, plus one thousand for the expenses he claimed to have incurred tracking down Concklin. Reunited, and changing their family name to Still, they settled on a farm in New Jersey to live out their days in long overdue peace.

Seven months after Concklin's death, another brave man was lost to the underground. On the evening of November 2, 1851, worshippers couldn't help noticing the tall white man dressed in a black broadcloth coat at prayer in the Centre Street Church, in Louisville, Kentucky. The fact that he was white wasn't by itself particularly unusual. Whites came to the church from time to time to hear the Reverend Bird Parker who, though he was as black as the rest of his congregation, was renowned in town for the sonorous gravity of his preaching. Proslavery whites were also keeping a watchful eye on black churches at a time when talk about slave uprisings was on everyone's lips. Although the risings never quite seemed to materialize, fear was nonetheless close to fever pitch. But this white man was a stranger.

At thirty-five, Calvin Fairbank was well-built and clean-shaven, with a high, clear forehead, placid eyes, and the self-contained manner of someone who, if not precisely a gentleman in the nineteenth century's rather lofty sense of the term, had spent a great deal of time alone, in serious thought. This was Fairbank's first trip back to the South since his release in 1849 from the Kentucky State Penitentiary, where he had been incarcerated for helping Lewis Hayden and his family to escape to Ohio. Fairbank had spent a day wandering around the city, a mere tourist to all appearances, observing the comings and goings of steamboats along the earthen levee that served as the city's riverfront, and visiting all four of the slave markets. Louisville was a vibrant, rowdy place, a blend of riverfront roughness and genteel pretensions, barely a generation removed from its frontier origins. The constant river traffic between Pittsburgh to the east, St. Louis, and points south as far as New Orleans, lent the city's atmosphere a certain cosmopolitan phizz.

Almost one-fifth of the city's population was African American. Black slaves worked alongside Irish immigrants on the steamboats and levees. Free blacks operated barbershops and worked as draymen, laborers, and housemaids, while slaves were rented out in considerable numbers by their masters as personal servants, blacksmiths, and iron mongers in the city's foundries, and as cooks and waiters in the city's restaurants. Fairbank was more than a casual tourist in Louisville's black world. In the winter of 1851 he was a deeply conflicted man. At his trial in 1845, he had thrown himself on the mercy of the court, strongly hinting that he would forswear any further assistance to fugitive slaves if he was released. While in prison he had been called a hypocrite, and worse, by fellow abolitionists who had read or heard reports of his recantation. He was free only because bail for his release had been paid by Hayden, now a successful businessman in Boston: Fairbank knew that to visit the South again like this was to invite physical attack. He was well aware of Seth Concklin's fate. But he was bitter at the accusations that had been leveled against him. For an abolitionist who never doubted that he was acting at God's command, to be accused of hypocrisy was deeply shaming and painful.

About one hour after Fairbank was seen at the Centre Street Church, A. L. Shotwell realized that his slave Tamar was missing. The twenty-seven-year-old Tamar was reportedly "as white and fair . . . as most ladies," and of a "lively" temperament. She had once almost escaped from Shotwell on a trip to Boston, but had held back for fear of losing her children, who had remained behind in Kentucky. She was shattered when, on her return to Louisville, she asked to see her youngest child, and was told that the infant had died. Shotwell had recently hired Tamar out as a servant to a Judge Purtle. Sometime after eight o'clock, a little after dinner, Purtle heard a window being raised in the basement, and going downstairs to check, he realized that Tamar was gone.

The meeting between Fairbank and Tamar had been secretly arranged by underground contacts in Louisville and in Indiana. In the course of their conversation, Tamar told him, "I came back for my babe. God has it. It is better off than I am. Now I want freedom." The two walked quickly a few blocks to the riverfront, where at night the spars of dozens of riverboats lined up along the muddy levee resembled a forest of winter-bare trees against the night sky. In spite of the hour, the levee was far from deserted. At almost any time of the day and night, riverboats, the long-distance haulers of their era, were arriving and departing, smokestacks streaming, steam screaming through gauge-cocks, bells ringing, as they maneuvered toward the levee, or backed out into the stream.

With no money to buy or rent a properly equipped boat, Fairbank had earlier in the day identified an apparently abandoned, and as it turned out dangerously leaky, skiff. He never recorded Tamar's feelings, but the trip across the river must have terrified her. Somehow, they shoved off from the bank unnoticed, and using a four-foot plank as a paddle, Fairbank managed to propel the skiff into the river, while Tamar bailed furiously with a cup that she had taken from the judge's home, scooping the water that bubbled around their shoes and threatened continually to swamp them. Once they were away from the shore, they would have been virtually invisible: they must have known that had a riverboat borne down on them, they would have been killed instantly. It is quite possible that neither of them knew how to swim, since swimming had not yet caught on as a popular pastime, and it was not until late in the century that it began to be taught to children as a matter of course. In addition, there was the ever-present danger of discovery. One can only imagine them, rescuer and slave, mumbling rapid prayers beneath their breath, wondering tensely whether even those furtive sounds, like the splash of the paddle, would carry fatally across the water, but praying all the same, the white man with all the fervency of his conviction that God's own great hand was guiding their flimsy craft, and Tamar with desperation, knowing that if she were caught and returned to Kentucky the consequences, most likely being sold for plantation work, would be terrible.

Fairbank steered as best he could toward the town of Jeffersonville, which was hard to discern until they were well out into the river. Even then, all that could be seen was the dim flicker of kerosene lamps in two or three windows. Fairbank kept up a steady pace, trying to compensate for the pull of the current. They landed a short distance downriver from Jeffersonville, and spent most of the rest of the night shivering in a field outside town. At about four o'clock, Fairbank was pounding on the door of a Jeffersonville livery stable. He told the groggy proprietor that he wanted to rent a buggy for the two-day drive to the town of Vienna. His actual destination was Salem, where he was to hand Tamar over to a black barber named Jackson, a local stationmaster on the Underground Railroad. By eight o'clock, Fairbank was driving fast, still thirty miles short of their destination, when the horse was spooked by a barking dog and bolted, and the carriage broke against a stump. He knew by now that Tamar's disappearance would have been discovered, and a search begun, and that slave catchers would soon start scouring the Indiana side of the river. With no time to lose, at the nearest town Fairbank flagged down a passing freight train. Although the trainmen agreed to take Tamar on to Salem, they asked him to wait for the next passenger train, but he forced himself aboard, and then, Methodist minister that he was, annoyed the trainmen by insisting that they suppress their profanity in Tamar's presence.

When the train stopped at Salem, Fairbank sought out Jackson and handed Tamar over to his keeping. Within days, she would be safe in Canada. Fairbank returned to Jeffersonville, intending to cross back over the river to Kentucky, to Lexington, to recover the body of his father, who had died there of cholera while visiting him in prison before his release. With the same transcendental self-confidence that had allowed him to set off across the Ohio River in a leaky rowboat, he assumed that he would be in no immediate danger. In fact, Tamar's owner, A. L. Shotwell, had already reported her disappearance to the United States marshal in Louisville.

While Fairbank was in Salem, the marshal, a man named Ronald, had been hard at work. He had quickly discovered that Tamar had met Fairbank in Louisville, and had found witnesses who gave him reason to think that the pair had escaped to Indiana. Crossing the river, he soon found the owner of the livery stable where Fairbank had rented the carriage. On Sunday, November 9, Fairbank was walking past the stable on his way to church when somebody called to him. Three or four men including Ronald came up to him. "What do you want of me?" Fairbank asked. "I want you in Louisville," Ronald replied. "You have been aiding off some niggers." When Fairbank refused, he later wrote, another man "seized me by my cravat, and twisting so as to confine me . . . rendering it uncomfortable for me to speak or even to breathe." In the struggle that ensued, Fairbank cried aloud for help "to preserve the honor of the law of the State." Although the altercation took place in front of many of the townspeople, no one stepped forward to help him. Within the hour, Fairbank was put in a skiff and rowed back to Kentucky, to a trial, and to a sentence of fifteen years in the state penitentiary, the longest ever imposed on an underground activist. This time there would be no reprieve.

3

Despite their divergent origins, there were striking similarities between the personalities of the rough-hewn ex-slave Harriet Tubman, the soldier-of-fortune Seth Concklin, and the evangelical, middle-class Calvin Fairbank. Apart from their unbreachable commitment to emancipation, all three were extraordinarily courageous individuals, natural risk takers, and had a knack for holding the trust of wary slaves. Fairbank, at least, shared Tubman's intense piety and her sense of divine direction. Concklin was as much adventurer as idealist, but he shared Tubman's capacity for ruthless self-control and her tolerance of extreme physical discomfort. Why, then, did they ultimately fail, while Tubman was able to continue her work without serious interruption for more than ten years? Being white, they were of course unable to blend in with African Americans as Tubman did. On the other hand, their whiteness conferred a privilege of movement and freedom from random interrogation that more than compensated for its limitations. They lacked, however, Tubman's exquisite instinct for danger, her matchless knowledge of the territory through which she traveled, and her gift for theatrics. In addition, while Concklin and Fairbank were essentially loners, Tubman enjoyed the advantage of a personal network in which she could place complete trust.

There was, of course, another difference between Tubman and the others, the most obvious of all: she was a woman. As a physically nondescript black woman with a field hand's manners and speech, she was far less likely to be suspected than was any man, white or black. More to the point, few Southerners even remotely credited blacks with the intelligence and strategic skill to plan complex rescues carried out over long distances and requiring the management of numbers of people. They assumed, even where there was no evidence, that the disappearance of slaves must have been the work of white subversives working in collusion with disloyal blacks within the borders of their own states. While Southern lawmen were ever on the lookout for clones of Concklin and Fairbank, Tubman again and again slipped by them unnoticed.

It is probably not entirely coincidental that Tubman came to prominence just as the women's rights movement was breaking upon Americans' consciousness. Although she was wholly a product of the particular African American culture of the Eastern Shore, she was in her own distinctive way part of a larger, still inchoate force that was reshaping, if not yet American society, then at least the antislavery movement. Abolitionists who very likely would have ignored Tubman a decade or two earlier, by the 1850s were able to recognize in her a heroism that transcended gender. Abolitionism was the threshold through which American women took their first steps into the nation's political life. Back in the 1830s white women were expected to be unobtrusively abolitionist, and then only within their own parlors and sewing circles. Rare exceptions were Quaker activists like Lucretia Mott, and the Grimke sisters, Sarah and Angelina, daughters of a South Carolina slave owner, who repudiated slavery, moved north, and drew large crowds when they lectured on behalf of abolition. The very nature of the struggle against slavery demanded a new willingness to look at the roots of oppression and to confront authority, whether in the form of husband, church leaders, or public opinion. The experience exposed many women to the hypocrisy of abolitionist males who demanded freedom for slaves but insisted that their own womenfolk remain silent. The combative antislavery lecturer Abby Kelley, for example, found church doors closed to her, and was roundly denounced from pulpits as a "jezebel" because she traveled with men other than her husband. And in 1840 William Lloyd Garrison's nomination of her to the business committee of the American Anti-Slavery Society so offended evangelicals that they broke away from the organization entirely, leaving Garrison with little support beyond Boston and a few Quaker communities. Increasingly, however, women began to appear at public antislavery meetings alongside men, and often black men at that, a sight that utterly scandalized Americans outside the movement. Frederick Douglass, however, reported with heartfelt pride (and a trace of astonishment) how at a rally for the fugitive George Latimer, "we were all on a level, everyone took a seat just where they chose, there [was] neither men's side, nor women's side; white pew nor black pew, but all seats were free, and all sides free."

One of the countless women radicalized by the antislavery movement was Gerrit Smith's cherubic first cousin Elizabeth Cady, who spent several languorous but intellectually provocative weeks each summer at his rambling home in Peterboro, absorbing the ceaseless talk of politics and reform. There, for the first time, she found men who were willing to listen to her opinions. She later wrote, "I felt a new inspiration in life and was enthused with new ideas of individual rights and the basic principles of government, for the antislavery platform was the best school the American people ever had on which to learn republican principles and ethics." She also met there the handsome Henry Stanton, one of the most famous abolitionist speakers in the country, and her future husband. Coming from the cosmopolitan salon of Peterboro, Stanton was flabbergasted by the treatment that she and other antislavery women received at the

World's Anti-Slavery Convention, held in London, in 1840. The Americans, among them Lucretia Mott and the usually irrepressible Abby Kelley, comprised a brigade of the most formidable public women in the entire United States at the time. But in keeping with the rigid scriptural notions that permeated the British antislavery movement, not only were they barred from participating as delegates, they were relegated to smoldering silence in a segregated gallery off the convention floor. They were told that the rubric "World's Convention," Mott recorded in her diary, "was a mere poetical license," and that women were "constitutionally unfit for public or business meetings."

The humiliating experience in London gave fiery edge to Stanton's growing recognition of the "oppression I saw everywhere," and which was only intensified by her own experience of motherhood. After the Stantons moved to Seneca Falls, New York in 1847, she was swept by waves of loneliness, depression, and bitterness at women's foreordained "portion as wife, mother, housekeeper, physician, and spiritual guide." Although increasingly impelled toward some kind of action, she could not say what until the redoubtable Lucretia Mott came to visit in the early summer of 1848. To her, and a small group of like-minded women, all of them Quakers except herself, she poured out her discontent.

In contrast to the profoundly frustrated Stanton, who was an Episcopalian, her friends were all vocal, self-reliant, and accustomed to participating in the affairs of their religious community on an equal basis with men. They were also politically astute, having been active for years in the antislavery cause—Mott since at least 1833—and, in some cases, in the work of the Underground Railroad. They already lived the kind of engaged and intellectually liberated life that Stanton felt so painfully denied. What Stanton brought to the parlor table in the home of Quaker abolitionist Elizabeth McClintock was festering outrage at her exclusion from the public world.

Impulsively, the women decided to call a convention just five days thence, on July 19 and 20, "to discuss the social, civil and religious condition and rights of women." Most of those who came were local women, with the exception of Mott and her husband James, who presided over the meeting, no woman having filled such a position before. The only black person present was the Stantons' friend Frederick Douglass, who lent the authority of antislavery to the next great reform cause of the day, declaring that "if that government only is just which governs by the free consent of the governed, there can be no reason in the world for denying to woman the exercise of the elective franchise, or a hand in making and administering the laws of the land. Our doctrine is that 'right is of no sex.' " Stanton, who had never addressed a public meeting before, presented the conference's final document. Declaring that "all men and women are created equal," it protested against man's "usurpations" against woman, the denial of "her inalienable right" to the vote, and her submission to laws in whose formation she had no voice. A few years later, in a speech in New York City, Stanton memorably suggested that only women could truly fathom the helpless suffering of the slave: "Eloquently and earnestly as noble men have denounced slavery . . . they have been able only to take an objective view . . . [because as] a privileged class they can never conceive of those who are born to contempt, to inferiority, to degradation. Herein is woman more fully identified with the slave than man can possibly be. For while the man is born to do whatever he can, for the woman and the Negro there is no such privilege." Despite the occasional attendance at women's conventions of individuals like the evangelist Sojourner Truth, and later in the decade Harriet Tubman herself, the movement as a whole remained a largely white one.

Women had always done much of the Underground Railroad's unsung work of feeding, sheltering, and nursing fugitives. When they arrived travelworn and hungry at the Hayden home in Boston or the Douglass home in Rochester, it was Harriet Hayden and Anna Douglass who made their beds and cooked their meals. Many women did much more than that. In one Michigan community, women were responsible for giving the alarm if slave catchers appeared, and in Cleveland four of the nine members of that city's very active, all-black Vigilance Committee were women. White women as well as black women sometimes served as conductors. Delia Webster, who was arrested with Calvin Fairbank in 1844, later purchased property on the Kentucky side of the Ohio River, in an unsuccessful scheme to run off slaves to Indiana. The Michigan Quaker Laura Haviland frequently escorted fugitives north from Cincinnati to Michigan, where she had founded an interracial school, and made several forays into Kentucky on pretended berry-picking expeditions. When the womenfolk of the Gibbons family arrived for a visit to their Quaker friends the Wrights at Columbia, Pennsylvania, young

Phebe Gibbons reported matter-of-factly in her diary that the family's daughters were "absent, upon on the *underground rail-road*." Almost everywhere, women circulated antislavery petitions and held fairs where they sold homemade products to raise money for fugitives.

Ironically, no one did more to shape the enduring image of slavery and the Underground Railroad than a woman who opposed giving females the vote and harbored a not-so-secret envy for the genteel manners of Southern aristocrats. The daughter of a prominent New England theologian and the wife of a seminary teacher, Harriet Beecher Stowe seemed to see herself as a sort of literary missionary, an amanuensis to God who, she once said, "hath . . . sent me to heal the broken-hearted, to preach deliverance to the captive, to set at liberty those who are bruised." Though often emotionally overwrought and steeped in Victorian sentimentality, her blockbuster novel of 1852, *Uncle Tom's Cabin, or Life Among the Lowly*, distilled the nation's moral crisis over slavery so that it finally and overpoweringly penetrated the hearts of ordinary Americans in a way that a generation of abolitionist lecturing and the provocation of the Compromise of 1850 had not. Stowe canonized kindly, selfless Quakers as the quintessential heroes of the underground, leaving no room for African-American activists, or for working-class whites like Jonathan Walker and Seth Concklin. But she accomplished something truly extraordinary. She made abolitionism not only respectable, but romantic, and turned the underground from a vague rumor into a Homeric endeavor that was part Christian drama of self-sacrifice, part frontier saga ripped from the pages of James Fenimore Cooper.

Uncle Tom's Cabin left readers by the millions seething with anger and shame. A decade later, as armies surged across the farmland of Virginia, Abraham Lincoln welcomed Stowe to the White House, where he is said to have greeted her as "the little lady who wrote the book that made this great war." Although the remark may be apocryphal, the Northern armies were filled with men who as boys had wept over the fate of Uncle Tom. Stowe based her eponymous composite hero partly on Josiah Henson, whose story had appeared in print in 1849. She portrayed Tom as a martyr who believed, as Henson had during his years in slavery, that if he accepted his fate in the spirit of Christ-like martyrdom, his earthly sufferings would be repaid with an eternity of divine love in the hereafter. Tom's character in the novel troubled few if any of the leading African Americans of the day, nearly all of whom shared Stowe's religious beliefs, and recognized the book's importance as propaganda.

The single most memorable passage in the novel, indeed in all nineteenth-century American literature to readers of the day, and one that inspired countless previously neutral Americans to embrace the cause of abolitionism, recounted the flight of the fugitive mother "Eliza" across the frozen Ohio River. Stowe learned the story directly from Reverend John Rankin, to whose home in Ripley, Ohio, just such a mother had come one winter's night in 1838. Although she might never know it, her flight that night was to achieve the dimensions of myth. Rankin's son John was a student of Stowe's husband at Lane Seminary, in Cincinnati, and the families were well acquainted. "One Sunday afternoon," John Rankin Jr. recalled, "father and I called upon Prof. Stowe, in the presence of Harriet. Father told of the flight of the slave mother and child crossing the river on the ice. Stowe was greatly moved by the narrative, exclaiming from time to time, 'Terrible! How terrible!' "

In Stowe's rendering, Eliza races toward the banks of the frozen Ohio with a slave trader and his minions in close pursuit: "Right on behind her they came; and, nerved with strength such as God gives only to the desperate, with one wild cry and flying leap, she vaulted sheer over the turbid current by the shore, onto the raft of ice beyond. It was a desperate leap,—impossible to anything but madness and despair . . . The green fragment of ice on which she originally alighted pitched and creaked as her weight came on it, but she stayed there not a moment. With wild cries and desperate energy she leaped to another and still another cake;—stumbling,—leaping,—slipping,—springing upwards again! Her shoes are gone,—her stockings cut from her feet,—while blood marked every step; but she saw nothing, felt nothing, til dimly, as in a dream, she saw the Ohio side."

Virtually every literate American (and many who weren't literate) knew Eliza's story, if not from reading the novel itself, then from the numerous dramatic versions that remained staples of the popular stage well into the twentieth century. Unlike the stocky, very dark woman who found her way to Rankin's house, Stowe's Eliza was a fine-mannered, light-skinned mulatto and her son a virtually white child, the offspring of a rape by her master—a potent combination of sentimentality, sexuality, racial coding, and moral outrage that was intended to wrench the heartstrings of nineteenth-century readers in the most violent possible way. In her martyred innocence, Eliza epitomized the tragedy of slavery as evangelical abolitionists saw it. Like the other characters in Stowe's book, Eliza crossed the line into cliché, facilitating the degeneration of stage productions of the novel into the Jim Crow melodramas that also tranformed Uncle Tom into the icon of spineless servility that would disgust later generations. Nevertheless, as characters in the novel, Tom and Eliza were radical inventions with powerful ramifications, for they enabled countless white Americans to identify emotionally with African Americans for the first time.

Uncle Tom's Cabin also provided the country's first popular view of the Underground Railroad in action. Following her dramatic escape across the ice, the fictional Eliza Harris is directed to the Hallidays, a couple modeled closely on Levi and Catherine Coffin, whom Stowe also knew. "[T]all, straight, muscular" Simeon quotes scripture incessantly, while upon Rachel's peach-fresh face "time had written no inscription, except peace on earth, good will to men." At their home, Eliza and her son Harry are united with Eliza's husband George, whose "atheistic doubts, and fierce despair, melted away" beneath the sunny rays of the Hallidays' benevolence. When George urges Simeon not to endanger himself on his family's account, Simeon replies, with a loftiness that may have seemed less condescending to Victorian readers, "Fear not, then friend George; it is not for thee, but for God and man, we do it." It may also have been more revealing of many underground activists' real feelings than Stowe intended.

From the Halliday home, the Harrises and two other fugitives are driven north in a covered wagon by a Quaker backwoodsman named Phineas Fletcher. Slave hunters are in hot pursuit, and a spirited chase takes place through the night. The fugitives and their conductor eventually flee up the side of a mountain that rather implausibly appears in the middle of the Indiana plains. There, poised histrionically upon a naked crag, George proclaims, as much to America as to his snarling pursuers below, "I am George Harris. A Mr. Harris of Kentucky did call me his property. But now I'm a free man, standing on God's free soil; and my wife and child I claim as mine." A gun battle ensues. Harris shoots the boldest of the slave catchers, and the others flee pell-mell. In keeping with Stowe's all-encompassing Christian agenda, the fugitives take pity on their erstwhile enemy, scoop him up in their arms, and carry him to an underground safe house where he is nursed back to health. The fugitives, meanwhile, are disguised and delivered to the wharf in Sandusky, where they are escorted aboard a ship under the very noses of slave hunters who are searching for them. Soon, Stowe orotundly concludes, "rose the blessed English shores; shores charmed by a mighty spell,—with one touch to dissolve every incantation of slavery, no matter in what language pronounced."

Harriet Tubman was unimpressed. She could not read the actual book, of course. But she was once invited to attend a stage performance of *Uncle Tom's Cabin* in Philadelphia, where she was working as a domestic, but she declined. "I haint got no heart to go and see the sufferings of my people played out on de stage," she said. "I've seen de *real ting*, and I don't want to see it on no stage or in no teater."

CHAPTER 17

LABORATORIES OF FREEDOM

> The eye of the civilized world is now looking down upon us.
>
> —HENRY BIBB, JOURNALIST AND FUGITIVE SLAVE

1

On Christmas Eve, 1854, Harriet Tubman made her way on foot over low rain-soaked hills toward her parents' cabin near Poplar Neck, on the middle Choptank. The wet night shrouded her diminutive figure from curious eyes as she approached the Thompson plantation, where it occupied a lonely swath of woodland overlooking the river. How she reached Poplar Neck is unknown. Using false papers, she may have taken a steamer from Baltimore to Cambridge, Maryland, or a point farther up the Choptank, or she may have traveled south from Philadelphia by train, and then overland through Delaware. In any event, sometime before dawn, she slipped into a fodder shed that stood near the Rosses' cabin, and waited. She was a different woman from the tough but untried twenty-seven-year-old who had fled north in 1849. She was now a seasoned underground veteran who had made at least three trips back into Maryland since the rescue of Kessiah Bowley. If all went well, before the night was out she would see her three enslaved brothers, and then lead them north to freedom.

Tubman had brought out one brother, Moses Ross, in 1851. She had attempted to bring the others, Ben, Robert, and William Henry, the previous spring, but failed. She returned to Philadelphia, where she worked in kitchens for a dollar a week, until in December she learned that the three were to be sold after Christmas. Tubman had a friend write on her behalf to Jacob Jackson, a free black who lived near her brothers at Tobacco Stick, and must have been one of her secret collaborators in Dorchester County. Encoded in the letter was a cryptic message that she trusted Jackson to pass on to her brothers: "Read my letter to the old folks, and give my love to them, and tell my brothers to be always watching unto prayer, and when the good old ship of Zion comes along, to be ready to step aboard." The letter was signed with the name of Jackson's son. Tubman could only hope the white postmaster, who censored Jackson's mail as a matter of course, would ignore the message as pious gibberish. The risk to Jackson was extreme—he was already suspected of having helped other slaves to escape—but perhaps the urgency of the brothers' situation overcame Tubman's usual scruples about safety. In the end, Jackson claimed that the letter made no sense to him, and refused to even take it out of the post office. But he knew what it meant, because he immediately let the Ross brothers know that Tubman was on her way, and to head for Poplar Neck, thirty miles to the north.

Ben and William Henry Ross set off across country as soon as they could, taking with them two male friends, John Chase and Peter Jackson, and Ben's fiancée Jane, who disguised herself in men's clothing. Robert Ross faced an agonizing dilemma. His wife, Mary, went into labor on Christmas Eve with their third child, and he was torn between the pull of family and the hope of freedom. As Tubman recounted the story to her first biographer, Sarah Bradford, Robert waited until the baby was delivered and then, forced to decide between his family and what might be his last chance for freedom, chose the latter. He told his wife that he was just going to try to hire himself out for the holiday, and left her to join his brother. Mary sensed somehow that he was not coming back. "You're going to leave me," she sobbed. "But wherever you go, remember me and the children."

The brothers and their friends hurried north along the winding route of present-day Highway 16, through East New Market and Preston, past miles of stubbly cornfields, ice-crusted marsh, and gloomy, gray-green phalanxes of loblolly pines gaunt against the iron-colored sky. That was the visible landscape: over it, like a gossamer web, lay a less palpable human landscape of extended families and hidden underground affinities that may not even have been wholly visible to the brothers, and that indeed may have been linked only through the person of Harriet Tubman herself. They passed the house of Samuel Green, a free black man, who was another one of her local contacts, and farther along, near the ford over Hunting Creek, the farm of the Quaker abolitionist Jonah Kelly, and soon after that, prominent at the crest of a gentle hill, the brick home of Hannah Leverton, the white mill owner's wife who had probably arranged Tubman's flight in 1849. (Before the 1850s were out, Green would be jailed for possessing road maps and a copy of *Uncle Tom's Cabin*, and a lynch mob would come looking for the Levertons, and they would be forced to flee for their lives to Indiana.)

By daybreak, Tubman and her brothers had made their rendezvous. Her emotions can only be imagined as they came through the shed's door, exhausted, one by one: Robert, thirty-five and well-built; Ben Jr., the shrewd one, chestnut-colored like herself; and long-legged William Henry, with his handsome oval face, who was also leaving two small children and a wife behind. It was an annual Christmas custom for the sons to gather for dinner at the home of their parents—Ben Sr. and Rit Ross—and the scene that played out that long rainy day is one of the most famous in Tubman's life: Tubman and her brothers in the shed, waiting for the rain to end, and peering through chinks in the walls at their mother, who, ignorant of their presence, appears again and again at her cabin door, distraught and wondering why her children have not come. At some point, one of the brothers' friends, a stranger to the elder Rosses, was sent to tell their father about the group hidden in the corn crib, and he brought them out packets of food. But as much as they wished to bid farewell to their mother—Harriet had not seen her parents for five years—they deemed her love to be their greatest danger, fearing that if they revealed themselves, she would lose control of her emotions, and give them away.

They set out after nightfall, with Ben Sr. walking with them part of the way, wearing a handkerchief tied over his eyes, so that if he was questioned later he could truthfully say that he had not *seen* any of his children that Christmas. Tubman's destination was Wilmington, Delaware, eighty-five miles north, and then Philadelphia, another thirty miles farther on. She knew the route well by now. They traveled along roads that were troughs of red mud, across a soaking land that was intermittently brought to life by flotillas of white gulls and the aerial scrimshaw of Canada geese wheeling high overhead. They somehow sneaked through, or around, the towns of Harmony, Denton, and Greensboro, and then crossed the state line near Sandtown. Given the distance that they had to cover, Tubman may have arranged for wagons to carry them part of the way. But they doubtless walked much of it. When they arrived in Wilmington, Thomas Garrett, the stationmaster there, wrote ahead to the Philadelphia Anti-Slavery office, "Harriet and one of the men had worn the shoes off their feet, and I gave them two dollars to help fit them out, and directed a carriage to be hired at my expense, to help take them out." He added that two more fugitives had just arrived in Wilmington, and that he was assigning "one of our trusty colored men" to conduct the enlarged party, probably via the secluded valley of the Brandywine Creek, to the home of Allen Agnew across the state line in Chester County, Pennsylvania.

Five days after leaving Poplar Neck, Tubman and her companions entered William Still's office, in Philadelphia. Here they were issued fresh clothing and food by Still's assembly-line operation, and in a rite of passage that for countless fugitives symbolized their transformation from enslaved to free people, they relinquished their birth name of Ross, and adopted the new name Stewart which, curiously enough, was the name of one of Dorchester County's most prominent white families. On December 31, after a day's rest, Still gave three dollars to each member of the party except Harriet, to whom he gave four dollars, and forwarded them by railroad to New York City, where they boarded another train for Albany. There, with help from Stephen Myers, the director of the local Vigilance Committee, they were sent, again by train, to either Syracuse or Rochester, and finally across Lake Ontario by steamship to St. Catharines, near the mouth of the Niagara River, in Canada West.

They were welcomed by Tubman's friend, the unctuous missionary Hiram Wilson, who had cofounded the Dawn Institute with Josiah Henson. Fired by the institute for financial incompetence, he was now the head of the St. Catharines Refugee Slaves' Friend Society, the local agency of the Underground Railroad. Neither time nor man had been kind to Wilson. Although enemies sneeringly called him a "designing white man" more interested in dominating refugees than helping them, his devotion to what he pompously liked to term "strangers of the sable hue" was genuine enough. Between 1850 and 1856, he took well over one hundred refugees into his own home, and distributed food, clothing, Bibles, medicine, and advice to many more. However, blacks who had established themselves in Canada no longer wanted to think of themselves as the pathetic objects of charity, but as the engineers of their own liberation, a process in which whites, even the most dedicated abolitionists, played an increasingly ambiguous role, when they played any role at all.

2

For refugees in Canada, the decade of the 1850s was one of striving, and considerable success. In 1855 the Boston educator and sometime journalist Benjamin Drew traveled through refugee communities in Canada, interviewing hundreds of former slaves, many of whom had come north on the Underground Railroad. They spoke with as much eloquence about their experience of freedom as they did of their years in bondage. William Grose, who had been living in Canada for several years, told him that he had been astonished to find blacks who owned farms and stores, and that he had since come to know several who had even become rich. "As a general thing, the colored people are more sober and industrious than in the states; there they feel when they have money, that they cannot make what use they would like of it, they are so kept down, so looked down upon," he observed. "Here they have something to do with their money, and put it to a good purpose." He added that his whole way of thinking about racial differences had changed: "When in the United States, if a white man spoke to me I would feel frightened, whether I was in the right or the wrong. But now it is quite a different thing,—if a white man speaks to me, I can look him right in the eyes—if he were to insult me, I could give him an answer. I have the rights and privileges of any other man . . . I am a true British subject and I have a vote every year as much as any other man."

Some refugees complained of "negrophobia" and discrimination, but the law remained steadfastly unbiased, and blacks enjoyed ready access to work in virtually every field of employment. It was not unusual for newcomers with even modest means to open a boardinghouse or some other small business. Within months of his escape from Boston via the Underground Railroad, Shadrach Minkins was running a restaurant in Montreal. Jerry Henry quickly found work as a barrel maker and, along with a letter promising to live "a purer, better life," he was soon able to send a fine hand-carved hickory cane to the mayor of Syracuse as a gift of thanks for his rescue from the hands of his captors. In the burgeoning town of Chatham, "the great resting place of the fugitives after landing on the Canadian shore," where almost one-third of the population was black, James Bell operated a school on the top floor of his house, grocers Henry and Annie Weaver prospered selling smoked hams, and Monroe Jones was regarded as the best gunsmith in the vicinity: all were escaped slaves. "If any man doubts the genius, enterprise, and fidelity of our people to all the claims of manhood, let him visit the colored population of Chatham," the Syracuse underground agent Jermain Loguen wrote in an open letter after a tour of Canada, in 1856.

Estimates of the total number of refugees in Canada varied wildly, and still remain controversial. Even as the underground fed fugitives across the border at a steady rate, other crosscurrents of migration caused the Canadian black population as a whole to fluctuate greatly. Each time there was a widely publicized recapture of a fugitive in the United States, a wave of free African Americans would uproot themselves and move to Canada for safety. At the same time, others who had settled in Canada returned to the United States, where wages were higher, or to be closer to their families. Still others, like Harriet Tubman, who kept a home in St. Catharines through much of the 1850s, were part-time residents and moved back and forth across the border at will. In 1848 Hiram Wilson estimated there to be slightly under twenty thousand fugitives in Canada. Five years later, after the mass influx generated by the passage of the Fugitive Slave Law, the black journalist Mary Ann Shadd put the figure at thirty-five thousand. Other estimates ranged as high as forty thousand, and beyond. However, a modern scholar who has closely studied census records of the period concluded that in 1861 there were probably only between twenty thousand and twenty-three thousand blacks in all of Canada West, including those born in Canada, even taking into account the likelihood that some fugitives deliberately avoided being counted. The real figure is likely to lie somewhere between those proposed by modern analysis and the unscientific estimates of people on the spot.

By the 1850s Canadian blacks comprised a remarkably diverse range of men and women from different parts of the South and North. One of the most ambitious of them all was the journalist Henry Bibb, whose brief, tumultuous career poignantly suggests the opportunities, and the risks, that were opening up for fugitives in Canada, as they invented new lives in freedom. Bibb's handsome, angular face stares out from period daguerreotypes with an impression of lively spontaneity that was rare in nineteenth-century photography. His eyes—they were gray, and apparently very seductive—still engage a viewer with the magnetic intensity with which they reportedly "enchained" antebellum audiences, as he recounted one of the most heartbreaking of all slave narratives.

Bibb was born in northern Kentucky of a slave mother and a white father, a state senator, in 1815. Although without formal education, he was bright and observant. "All that I heard about liberty and freedom to the slaves I never forgot," he later wrote. "Among other good trades I learned the art of running away to perfection." When he was eighteen, he fell passionately in love with a girl named Malinda, a "dark-eyed, red-cheeked" mulatto who, in Bibb's revealing choice of words, "moved in the highest circle of slaves." She inspired in him a degree of devotion, not to say obsession, that would shape the next thirteen years of his life. They formalized their relationship with a personal commitment, since marriage between slaves was not permitted in Kentucky, and Malinda soon bore Bibb a daughter. Hoping to raise his family in freedom, he searched for a way to escape. One day, instead of going to work, he crossed the river to Indiana and boarded a steamboat for Cincinnati. A black man whom he approached on the street led him to the home of a white abolitionist, who fed him and started him on the way to Canada, with recommendations to "friends" along the way. He spent the winter in the black enclave of Perrysburgh, Ohio, and in the spring traveled on to Detroit, where he bought an assortment of dry goods, intending to peddle them on his way back to Kentucky, determined to retrieve Malinda and his daughter.

From this point on, Bibb's life became an odyssey of epic dimensions. Ignoring the pleading of his friends, he set off for Kentucky wearing false whiskers and a disguise. He succeeded in safely reaching his old home, where he arranged with Malinda to meet him in Ohio. Bibb then returned to Cincinnati, where he appealed to abolitionists for money to pay his family's traveling expenses to Canada. Betrayed by a pair of black informers, he was dragged bodily through the streets and handed over to the authorities, and by them to his owner. Shortly after his return to Kentucky, Bibb escaped again. After a hurried visit to Malinda, he traveled back to Perrysburgh, where he waited in vain almost nine months for her to arrive. Despite what had already happened to him, and again over the protests of friends, he set off once again for Kentucky. He reached Malinda's cabin safely, but a slave go-between betrayed him for a five-dollar reward.

After this episode, Bibb's disgusted owner sold the entire Bibb family to a slave trader who transported them to New Orleans. There they were purchased by a Methodist minister named Whitfield, who owned a plantation in upcountry Louisiana. After an attempted escape with his wife and daughter, Bibb was stripped, staked spreadeagled to the ground, and savagely flogged, first with a bull whip, and then with a flat wooden paddle. For weeks afterward, he was also made to wear a heavy iron collar with prongs extending above his head, on the end of which dangled a small, humiliating bell. Perhaps most painful of all, he was never again allowed to sleep with his family. After yet another failed escape, Whitfield sold Bibb away from his wife and child to a company of itinerant "sportsmen," who took him across the Red River into Texas, where they spent time horse racing and gambling. "Although they were wicked black legs of the basest character, it is but due to them to say, that they used me far better than ever the deacon did," Bibb wrote, paying him a little money almost every day for attending to their horses, and driving the wagon in which they carried their clothing, baggage, and "gambling apparatus." At a horse race in the Indian Territory, present-day Oklahoma, the gamblers sold Bibb to a wealthy Cherokee for nine hundred dollars in gold. When the Indian died suddenly a few months later, Bibb made a great show of grief, and then fled in the night. He followed the Missouri state boundary line due north to Jefferson City, passing in terror through several tribes of Indians, "afraid to enter any of their houses or wigwams," and unnerved by the "implements of death"—bows and arrows, tomahawks, guns, butcher knives—that they invariably carried. At Jefferson City, Missouri, Bibb sneaked aboard a steamboat bound for St. Louis by mingling unobtrusively with the deck passengers. In St. Louis, a black steward arranged passage for him aboard a boat headed to Ohio. After working for a time as a bootblack and porter in the river town of Portsmouth, Ohio, in January 1842, Bibb finally arrived in Detroit, where he would establish the first secure home that he had enjoyed for almost a decade. But his odyssey was not quite ended. Through everything, he never forgot Malinda and their daughter. In 1846 he set off once more for the South. Although he never saw his family again, he got close enough to learn, devastatingly, that Malinda had finally abandoned hope of rescue, and had become the acquiescent concubine of her master. "From that time," he wrote, "I gave her up into the hands of an all-wise Providence."

In Detroit, Bibb was drawn almost immediately into the work of the Underground Railroad, probably by one of its leading local figures, Reverend William Monroe of the Second Baptist Church, with whom Bibb studied grammar and public speaking. (He had already taught himself to write during his years in slavery, by copying words he noticed onto scraps of discarded paper.) Unique within the underground, by the 1850s and perhaps earlier, the Detroit group practiced elaborate rituals of membership that seem to have been roughly modeled on those of the Masons. Induction into what its members called the "African-American Mysteries" was cloaked in what another underground leader, the erudite radical William Lambert, described in an 1886 interview as a "good deal of frummery" in order to "give the deepest impression of the importance of every step." There were three degrees of membership. Any man who attained the first degree, known as "Captive," became eligible to conduct fugitives. Initiations into the "Mysteries" took place in a building near the riverfront, and were filled with grotesque symbols of slavery. First the candidate was told to stand outside a door while certain questions were solemnly put to him.

"What do you seek?"

"Deliverance," he was to answer.

"How do you expect to get it?"

"By my own efforts."

"Have you faith?"

"I have hope."

Next, the candidate was shackled at the wrists, "clad in rough and rugged garments, his head was bowed, his eyes blindfolded, and an iron chain placed about his neck." He was led through the door. Then, kneeling at an altar, he took a vow of secrecy and faith. The blindfold was removed, and he found himself surrounded by all the members of the lodge. He was required to wear the shackles to each meeting thereafter, until he qualified for the second degree, known as "Redeemed," when he was required to submit—symbolically, one presumes—to the whip, the most loathed symbol of slavery, after which the shackles were finally struck off. For men who had worn shackles on Southern plantations, this must have been an incredibly intense, perhaps retraumatizing, experience, as they ritually relived the helpless, claustrophobic darkness of bondage, and were then released by, and into, a brotherhood of men of their own slavery-hardened kind. The highest degree, the "Chosen," was subdivided into five phases: "Rulers," "Judges and Princes," "Chevaliers of Ethiopia," "Sterling Black Knight," and "Knight of St. Domingo." To achieve this last stage, which was probably devised by the intellectual Lambert, the candidate had to memorize a lengthy text "dealing with the principles of freedom and the authorities on revolution, revolt, rebellion, government." Bibb left no record of his own participation in such rituals, although he is known to have escorted many fugitives across the Detroit River to Canada.

However, there is no doubt that in Detroit Bibb underwent another profound experience that changed his life. He discovered his voice, and that with words he could forge the grief and rage that he felt over the loss of Malinda and his daughter into a weapon with which he could strike back publicly at the monolith of slavery. He first began to tell his life story to antislavery audiences in Detroit, then elsewhere in Michigan, and finally as far east as New England. Words were his salvation. He declared, "If I had a thousand tongues, I could find useful employment for them all."

The passage of the Fugitive Slave Act drove Bibb and his new wife, Mary, a well-educated black Quaker, across the Detroit River for greater safety in Canada. Although he physically moved only a few miles to the town of Sandwich, Bibb both emotionally and politically turned his back on the United States, and thereafter became the most eloquent of all fugitive advocates for emigration to Canada. His protest against slavery also took a bold new form. With financing from Gerrit Smith, he established Canada's first black newspaper. Its name trumpeted Bibb's intent: the *Voice of the Fugitive*. In its maiden issue, on January 1, 1851, he declared: "We need a press, that we may be independent of those who have always oppressed us. We need a press that we may hang our banners on the wall, that all who pass by may read why we struggle, and what we struggle for." The *Voice* served as an unofficial organ of the Underground Railroad, and Bibb's handsome, slender figure often could be seen at the Windsor wharf, where the ferry from Detroit docked, interviewing refugees as they stepped ashore. His articles were detailed and explicit. "Four able bodied men have just arrived in the promised land," he announced in a typical notice, on March 26, 1851. "They look well, are in good spirits, rejoicing at the prospect of being rewarded hereafter for their honest labor, in a free country. Two of them are off this morning to chopping cord wood, the others are looking for employment." Other articles announced the arrival of shipments of donated foodstuffs and clothing, advice on where to find work, and news of conditions in the black settlements, informing recent arrivals, for example, that they would find a good school at Colchester, and at Sandwich a temperance society as well as schools, churches, and a black-owned grocery store. The paper also offered fugitives advice on more general subjects, like education, crop prices, free trade, and ladies' fashions.

In 1851, Bibb organized and chaired the landmark North American Convention of Colored People, which brought together in Toronto fifty-three leading black abolitionists, and a few whites, from Canada and the United States. In his keynote address, Bibb posed the central question to which all the labors of the Underground Railroad inexorably led: "What is the future of the black race on the North American continent?" What was ultimately to become of the twenty thousand (or thirty thousand) refugees whom the underground had delivered into the queen's dominions? Was Canada to become the black homeland in North America? Or was it but a way station, where they would mark time until slavery was overthrown in the United States? "[T]he eye of the civilized world is looking down upon us to see whether we can take care of ourselves or not," Bibb told the assembly. "If it should be seen, that under a free Government, where we have all our political and social rights, without regard to our color . . . we should prove ourselves to be incapable of self-government, it would bring down reproach and disgrace upon the whole race with which we are connected, and would be used as an argument against emancipation."

For Bibb, part of the solution was the development of an archipelago of agricultural colonies in Canada and Jamaica, where large numbers of former slaves could learn self-sufficiency and independence, and which, he added, would also "give a new impulse to the Under-ground Railroad." His own contribution, oratory apart, was the founding of the Refugee Home Society, in partnership with white abolitionists, to develop thirty thousand acres of farmland around Sandwich, exclusively for fugitives, to whom the land would be sold at cost. Bibb editorialized in the *Voice of the Fugitive*, "If we would be men and command respect among men, we must strike for something higher than sympathy and perpetual beggary. *We must produce what we consume.*" His ideological debt to Josiah Henson and the founding principles of the Dawn colony was made clear by his choice of the old man as the society's president. Bibb himself would serve as its recording secretary, and its real leader.

Among those who attended the Toronto convention was a woman who would soon upset the entire black cosmos of Canada West. Mary Ann Shadd, at twenty-nine, was also a product of the underground world, although of a very different background from Bibb. Her father, Abraham, an affluent shoemaker, had served as an underground conductor in West Chester, Pennsylvania, throughout her childhood, and she no doubt grew up familiar with the sight of furtive refugees recuperating in the family home. She was, like Bibb, very light-skinned, and her small, often angry eyes burned like coals when she was impassioned. She was a born muckraker: well-educated, unabashedly opinionated, and highly articulate, she had already made a name for herself in African-American circles by publishing a remarkable attack on the influence of "corrupt" and "superstitious" black clergy over black communities. Inspired by what she heard at Toronto, she abandoned her job as a teacher in New York City and moved to Canada. When Bibb invited her to accompany him back to the Detroit River settlements, where there was a desperate need for teachers, she leaped at the chance. She settled at Windsor, opening a school in a drafty barracks left from the War of 1812, and taking on many of her students free of charge. Henry Bibb had no idea what he was in for.

Initially, the two got along well. They shared many of the same qualities: both were young, literary, and emblematic of a rising generation of black leaders who were already looking beyond slavery to a permanent Canadian home for refugee blacks. But their relationship soon soured.

Bibb pragmatically believed that fugitives were most likely to be happy, at least initially, among their own people, and that for the foreseeable future they had to depend on the financial support of friendly whites to survive. Shadd argued that full black equality could only be achieved through complete integration with whites, and she was caustic about segregated communities of any type, no matter what the motivation, believing that they condemned blacks to second-class status. She also denounced outside fundraising as "begging" that "materially compromis[es] our manhood, by representing us as objects of charity." There were also personal differences. Although she lacked Bibb's capacity for personal leadership, Shadd was a type rare in her era, an independent, middle-class woman with a mind entirely her own, self-confident to a fault, unafraid to confront men on their own ground, and set on a professional career.

By 1852 Shadd's relationship with Bibb had disintegrated completely. She came to believe that the Refugee Home Society was nothing less than a scheme to enrich Bibb and his supporters. She claimed that neighbors derided the society lands as "Bibb's plantation," and that the settlers who occupied the land were for the most part "shiftless" whiskey drinkers. She wildly denounced Bibb himself as an out and out fraud who had used donations to buy himself a house, a farm, and a boat, and had ignored the needs of the fugitives for whom he was "begging." She even added, gratuitously, in a letter to a white missionary whom she knew would spread her accusations far and wide, "His chickens have been roosting on good fugitive clothes the entire season," while the needy went about in rags. Although Bibb's manifold talents appear to have stopped at the threshold of financial management, there is no evidence, apart from Shadd's polemics, to prove that he was personally corrupt, or that his white colleagues in the project were anything but sincere. Wounded, he retorted in kind, referring to his nemesis as "Shadd-as-Eve-the-Evil," and asserting dismissively that the only opposition to his projects came from "a set of half cracked, hot headed individuals." In March 1853 Shadd established her own competing newspaper, the *Provincial Freeman*, the first ever in North America to be published by a black woman. Although the black abolitionist Samuel Ringgold Ward was listed as editor, most of the copy was written by Shadd herself, who distinguished its columns with her trademark crackling invective. The controversy between Bibb and Shadd ultimately served no one well, but it did show to fugitive slaves who had never enjoyed political life of any kind just what it meant to exercise the freedoms of speech and the press in a public debate over the *way in which blacks were to be free.* In their polemics, it is possible to see the foreshadowings of debates that would continue through the twentieth century, and beyond: over integration versus self-imposed segregation, over the financial obligations of whites to blacks, over the consequences of dependency on public welfare.

Caught amid the collateral damage of this journalistic warfare were the reputations of the Dawn colony and Josiah Henson, Bibb's friend, whom the *Provincial Freeman* cruelly described as a "nigger driver" doing the bidding of white financial backers. There was no more evidence that Henson was personally dishonest than there was to convict Bibb. However, the old man's limited management ability had finally proved inadequate to the complexities of overseeing a two-hundred-person community, developing a local economy, and operating the manual labor school. Financial records were chaotic, at best. A sawmill long championed by Henson had come to nothing. When the manager to whom Henson had leased it absconded with three boatloads of lumber, the unpaid workers vented their anger on the mill, and tore it down to its foundations. "Thus they ruthlessly destroyed this valuable building, the establishment of which had cost me so many anxious hours," Henson would gloomily recall. "When it was gone, I felt as if I had parted with an old idolized friend." Meanwhile, mounting debts kept him on a treadmill of fund-raising as far afield as Boston and London, precisely the image of "begging" from whites that so incensed Shadd.

Another problem was more subtle. Henson could proudly point out that the institute had educated some five hundred students since it opened in 1841, and that not one of them had been arrested for even a misdemeanor by the local police. But he had idealistically envisioned the colony as a sort of black utopia that would grow steadily more populous over time. What happened, in fact, was that immigrants typically acquired the skills that the institute offered—basic literacy, and a crash course in farming—and then moved on to someplace where they could earn more money. Dawn was a stepping stone to a better life in freedom, but it was rarely a final destination. Management of the institute was eventually taken over by a British abolitionist, John Scoble, who was supposed to reorganize the community's finances, but who, in Henson's words, squandered its meager resources on "the most expensive cattle in the market, at fancy prices," and on "expensive farming utensils." Scoble also pulled down the school buildings, "as they were too primitive to suit his magnificent ideas." They were never rebuilt.

Perhaps Dawn's fatal weakness, however, was Henson himself. The indomitable leader who had carried his children on his back across hundreds of miles of frontier wilderness to freedom, who had returned to Kentucky to lead away fugitive slaves, and who through force of personality had brought into existence one of the most ambitious black settlements in Canada, had in his mid-sixties become an imperious and self-righteous patriarch who could admit no wrong, telling critics simply that his hands were too full "feeding the hungry, clothing the naked, and instructing the ignorant" to bother with carping complaints. He had also grown increasingly vain, boasting of his (probably slight) acquaintanceship with "some of the noblest men and women in England," and dilating at embarrassing length upon his having enjoyed a picnic on the grounds of the prime minister's estate, during one of his fund-raising trips to Britain. While he remained immensely popular as a preacher, in demand by both black and white congregations, Shadd's attacks effectively marked the end of his political influence outside Dawn.

For Henry Bibb, the controversy with Shadd ended in personal catastrophe. In October 1853 fire wiped out the office of the *Voice of the Fugitive*. Bibb was virtually ruined. Arson was assumed. Bibb suspected Shadd's partisans, but the culprits were never found. For a time he managed to put out an occasional single-sheet edition, but the paper never recovered its former influence. Bibb was still only thirty-nine years old, and as charismatic as ever, and for a man who had escaped from slavery seven times, the recovery of his fortunes and reputation might well have proved possible. Much was still expected of him. But in August 1854 he died suddenly from an undetermined illness, at the lowest ebb in his life as a free man, eclipsed by the star of Mary Ann Shadd. Meanwhile, if Shadd's coruscating attacks did not cripple the Refugee Home Society by themselves, they didn't help. In 1855, the touring abolitionist Benjamin Drew, who admired Bibb, found just twenty disappointed families living on the society's lands, complaining about the terms of land purchase, restrictions on the reselling of property, and the ban on alcohol. No more than sixty families would ever settle there.

Shadd too was damaged by their quarrel. Protests against both her abrasive style and the fact that a woman dared even to engage in such public polemics compelled her to relinquish personal control of the *Provincial Freeman* in 1855. Her brother Isaac took over as publisher, and William Newman, a black Baptist minister with long experience in refugee affairs, as editor. A defiant, and well-justified, editorial in the *Freeman* blamed her surrender on a "wrongly developed public sentiment that would crush *a woman* whenever she attempts to do what has hitherto been assigned to men, even though God designed her to do it." However, she continued to write much, if not most, of the paper's copy, and there was no slackening in her diatribes. She attacked long-suffering Hiram Wilson for allegedly enjoying "fine furnishings and valuable real estate," and for distributing clothing and food only to blacks who supported him. She even mocked Frederick Douglass, who believed that blacks should remain in the United States to fight slavery, rather than immigrate to Canada. "Having been permitted so long to remain in our tub," she wrote in 1856, "we would rather the great Frederick Douglass, for whose public career we have the most profound pity, would stay out of our sunlight."

The only planned black settlement that Shadd did not attack was, on its surface, the most paternalistic of all. But it was also the most successful. The origins of the Elgin Settlement, also known as the Buxton Mission, were unique, even romantic. It was the single-handed creation of Reverend William King, a University of Glasgow–trained scholar, with a leonine shock of black hair, a craggy Presbyterian demeanor, and a commitment to abolition hardened by years of ethically troubled residence in the South. After immigrating to the United States from their native Ireland, King's family settled in Ohio, where their farm eventually became a station on the Underground Railroad. King himself, aspiring to a career as an educator, accepted a position as headmaster of a private academy in Louisiana, where he fell in love with and married the daughter of a wealthy slaveholding family. He feared the corrupting atmosphere of slavery on his family for "both the life that is now and that which is to come," and resolved to have nothing to do with "the domestic institutions of the country." However, when his wife, Mary, died suddenly in 1848, he was mortified to find himself, as her heir, the owner of fourteen slaves. By then King had lived long enough in the South to realize that simple manumission, difficult enough in itself in Louisiana, would consign the slaves to lives of poverty and hopeless insecurity. After considerable prayer, he determined to build for them, and with them, their own "City of God," a "haven against social ostracism and legal discrimination," where they could live as fully free men and women, in Canada.

King, in contrast to Henson, Wilson, and Bibb, had a real gift for administration, and never allowed pious hopes to cloud sound judgment. He traveled to Canada, where he enlisted support from the Presbyterian Synod, and acquired an eighteen-square-mile tract of land forested with oak, hickory, beech, and elm, near Chatham. He recruited twenty-four respected businessmen, including Wilson Abbott, Toronto's most successful black entrepreneur, to oversee the settlement's finances, through an incorporated company empowered to raise investment capital, to be called the Elgin Association, in honor of Lord Elgin, the governor general of Canada. Settlers would be required to pay a total of one hundred and twenty-five dollars for fifty acres of land, the standard allotment, either in a lump sum or in yearly installments. Land could neither be rented nor sharecropped until the purchaser had fully paid for it, and if resold within ten years, it had to be transferred only to other blacks. King left nothing to chance. Before a single settler appeared on the land, he wanted to ensure that the community would be a success, and that it would not only match in respectability and aesthetics, but demonstrably surpass, neighboring white towns. Each settler was required to clear at least six acres immediately, and to build a house that had to be a minimum of eighteen feet by twenty-four feet in area, be set back precisely thirty-three feet from the road, and be surrounded by a picket fence and a flower garden.

King personally led his band of settlers by steamer to Cincinnati, where he formally handed them their papers of manumission, and then by canal to Lake Erie, and across it by steamer to Chatham. Waiting for them when they arrived in December 1849, they found the first of many fugitives who would make their home at Elgin, Isaac Riley and his family, who had escaped from slavery in Missouri only a few months before. Another early settler was the notorious William Parker, who was wanted for treason and murder in the United States for his leading role in the Christiana, Pennsylvania, resistance. He was introduced to King by Henry Bibb. "[King] received me very politely," Parker wrote in his 1866 memoir, "and said that, after I should feel rested, I could go out and select a lot. He also offered to kindly give me meals and pork for my family, until I could get work." Many more affluent blacks settled in the surrounding area, including Mary Ann Shadd's father, Abraham, who bought two hundred acres of land nearby, and no doubt helped to soften her view of Reverend King.

From the start, King fostered an atmosphere of shared responsibility. The settlers, with King working alongside them, saw in hand, joined together in logging bees, chopping bees, and house-raising bees. "When we grew tired of the cold and hard work," one settler recalled, "Mr. King would jump upon a stump and swing his axe around, calling out 'Hurrah boys' and set us laughing over some nonsense." King led rather than governed, with a deft touch for the sensitivities of men and women who had only recently slipped from the control of omnipotent white masters. He established a five-member court of arbitration, for which he disqualified himself. The court took over management of industrialization, emergencies, festivals, and general welfare, and handled complaints and disputes. Other committees elected annually saw to it that laws were enforced, and the settlement's strict regulations obeyed. Fugitives were always welcome, and at six o'clock every morning and nine every evening, a five-hundred-pound bell sent as a gift by the black Presbyterians of Pittsburgh rang out its clarion call across the forest, in King's words, "proclaiming liberty to the captive."

Initially, the settlers faced harsh prejudice. Opposition coalesced around the demagogic editor of the *Chatham Journal* and regional power, Edwin Larwill, a deceptively elfin-looking tinsmith with a fringe of curly beard, whose followers collectively called themselves the "Free and Easy Club." Declaring blacks to be "indolent, vicious and ungovernable," Larwill told anyone who would listen that any further influx would destroy property values, lead to racial "amalgamation," and provoke war with the United States. He demanded that a poll tax be imposed on blacks, and that they be barred from voting, and ultimately deported to the United States. To blacks, Larwill was an all-too-familiar type. In the United States, men with views like his filled Congress and state legislatures, mobbed black neighborhoods, and hunted fugitive slaves across the countryside. King maintained a low profile, at least initially, keeping a strict watch over the settlement, and counseling the settlers to give no offense to their white neighbors. At times, armed blacks patrolled the woods around the settlement, making it clear that if they were attacked they would fight back.

But King had a subtler strategy to overcome whites' fears. His trump card was education. He set out to provide Elgin with the best school in the vicinity. He rejected the idea of an industrial school, like Dawn's, reasoning that it would channel blacks into low-skilled trades. Instead, he emphasized academics, beginning with English, arithmetic, and geography, and soon adding Latin and Greek. Within months after the school's opening, white children appeared, asking if they could attend, and then white adults. King welcomed everyone free of charge. Soon there were more white children in the Elgin school than in the district one. "The hard feeling against myself and the coloured people considerably abated," King would recall. "The whites and the blacks mingled freely on the playground, and sat together in the classroom, and stood up in the same class, and they found that the young coloured children were equal to the whites in learning, and some of the coloured children often stood at the head of the class." Indeed, the fugitive Isaac Riley's oldest son, Jerome, who had been among those waiting for King when he arrived in 1849, was often produced for visitors to demonstrate his faultless Latin recitation of Virgil's *Aeneid*. He would go on to become a medical doctor, and establish the first Freedmen's hospital in Washington, D.C., during the Civil War. (Another graduate, William Rapier, would become a Reconstruction era congressman from Alabama.) By the end of the decade, black graduates from Elgin were teaching in district schools throughout the area.

White fears also ebbed as the settlement prospered. Elgin's farmers profitably cultivated wheat, tobacco, corn, and hemp for the burgeoning markets of Canada West, enabling many settlers to pay off their farms in just five or six years. The settlement could soon boast a steam-powered sawmill, a brickyard, and a grist mill, as well as its own post office, temperance hotel, savings bank, and several churches. As early as 1854, Elgin's taxpayers were contributing more to the public coffers than any comparable town in the region, causing land values to actually rise. By 1855 the settlement's population had grown to more than eight hundred. (It would reach one thousand by the 1860s.) A visiting reporter from the *New York Tribune* found industrious inhabitants, tidy whitewashed cabins, and gardens blooming with phlox, poppies, and cornflowers. He wrote warmly of the people he met: "Those of them who have been accustomed to farming and have had some capital to commence with, have done remarkably well, having cleared more land and made greater improvements, than the greater majority of white settlers in the same time and under similar circumstances."

In a sense, Elgin's crowning moment came in 1857, when the racist Edwin Larwill ran for reelection to Parliament. In preparation, King had organized the registration of hundreds of new black voters. On election day, 320 of them joined King in front of St. Andrew's Presbyterian Church, in the heart of the Elgin Settlement, and walked proudly into Chatham, seven miles away, where they cast the first votes of their lives against Larwill, and for an abolitionist candidate for Parliament. When all the votes were counted, Larwill had been defeated by nearly eight hundred votes, many of them from whites, and the biggest margin ever recorded in the district. King wrote laconically, "From that time forward all opposition both to me and the coloured people ceased; they were now clothed with political power."

The Underground Railroad continued to funnel fugitive slaves into Canada up to the eve of the Civil War, and beyond. For a few years more, there would still be gaggles of newcomers at the docks of Windsor and St. Catharines, dressed lumpily in donated clothes, and bewildered by freedom. But by the end of the decade, the homeowners of the Elgin Settlement, the townspeople of Chatham and Toronto, even the disgruntled farmers at the Dawn colony and on the Refugee Home Society's tract, would cease to think of themselves as "fugitives." They were *Canadians.* The underground had done its work well, and delivered them to safety. Now their lives angled away from the United States, and away from the dragging spiritual inertia of slavery, toward the free future, where their successes and failures were their own. Josiah Henson, Henry Bibb, Mary Ann Shadd, William King, even the bedraggled Hiram Wilson, had all in their own ways taught refugees who bore every physical, emotional, and mental injury known to the world of slavery how to begin thinking and acting like free men and women. Problems remained, of course, but they were the problems of ordinary citizens, not of slaves. There was still prejudice to be overcome, and it did not disappear quickly. But there was no second act to Edwin Larwill. There were no mobs, no lynchings. The racists accepted their defeat at the polls. For years to come, in the Chatham area, blacks would hold the balance of power in local elections. In 1859, another watershed was crossed when Abraham Shadd, the old underground veteran, was elected the regional councilor for his district, the first black to be elected to public office in Canada.

3

In the Grecian mansion where he lived in Peterboro, New York, Gerrit Smith was also dreaming of a black utopia. He was morally outraged by the state law which required that each African American prove that he owned at least two hundred and fifty dollars' worth of property before he would be permitted to vote. The law effectively disqualified almost every black voter in the state. (No such property qualification had been imposed on whites.) "[T]his mean and wicked exclusion," Smith wrote, was but another intolerable outrage perpetrated by heartless politicians against "the most deeply wronged class of our citizens." Smith felt spiritually compelled to respond in some way. But how? The plan that God revealed to him—for Smith's understanding of the world allowed for nothing that was not provided by God—was one that only he of all living men could make a reality. The source of Smith's immense wealth was land speculation. He owned at least 750,000 acres (some said a million acres—even Smith may not have known for sure), mostly in New York state. He proposed to donate 40 acres apiece to three thousand black New Yorkers, a total of 120,000 acres, completely free of charge. The scheme had some things in common with the other pioneer black communities in Canada. With the erection of farmsteads and the planting of crops, the assessed value for the property would lift each settler across the infamous two-hundred-and-fifty-dollar threshold. Not only would this plan enable them to become a significant voting bloc, it would also, he hoped, draw them together in a community rooted in the ennobling, spiritually transformative tillage of the soil.

Smith had an almost religious feeling about land: Paradoxically, although he was one of the largest landowners in the United States, he felt an abiding uneasiness with the principle of private property. He believed that the possession of land was "a natural, universal, and inalienable right," and that each man had a right to as much of it as he needed. "Alas that good men should be so slow to see that the acknowledged right of every generation, to the use of the earth, as well as the use of the sea, the light, and the air, is necessarily preliminary to that state of universal comfort, and happiness, for which good men labor and pray!" He enlisted prominent African Americans, including Frederick Douglass, to hold meetings around the state to sign up volunteers. "The sharp axe of the sable-armed pioneer should be at once uplifted over the soil of Franklin and Essex counties, and the noise of falling trees proclaim the glorious dawn of civilization throughout their borders," Douglass proclaimed in the *North Star*. "Let the work commence at once. Companies of tens and twenties should be formed, and the woods at once invaded." By the autumn of 1847, Smith had made out 2,000 deeds: 861 in New York City, 215 in Queens County, 197 in King's County, and so on throughout the state. Although the grants were not specifically allotted to fugitives from slavery, many of the recipients were certainly former slaves.

Apart from his generosity with his land, Smith's philanthropy was legendary. "The tide of benefaction was continuously flowing," as his biographer, Octavius Frothingham, put it. "The small cheques flew about in all directions, carrying in the aggregate thousands of dollars." Frothingham estimated that it "carried away" forty or fifty thousand dollars a year. On his desk, Smith kept a stack of blank checks in varying amounts, waiting only for his signature. Sometimes he gave away tens of thousands of dollars in a single day. He sent donations to destitute Irish, Poles, and Greeks; orphans; indigent old maids; bankrupt farmers; paupers who needed money to send their children to school; as well as untold numbers of beggars and swindlers. Free blacks were frequent recipients of his generosity. One of them, William G. Allen, a talented flautist whom he had sponsored at the Oneida Institute, had gone on to teach at the Dawn colony.

Nothing was dearer to Smith's heart than abolitionism. He was close to the Tappan brothers, Lewis and Arthur, of New York City, and played host to their ideological nemesis William Lloyd Garrison. He corresponded with, among others, the Ohio firebrand John Rankin, former president Martin Van Buren, Harriet Beecher Stowe, and Senator William H. Seward of New York, Lincoln's future secretary of state. He was also a major financial supporter of Oberlin College, in Ohio, the most important racially integrated institution of higher learning in the United States. He counted as personal friends Henry Bibb, Frederick Douglass, Jermain Loguen, and Lewis Hayden of Boston, who had organized the

Shadrach rescue, and he willingly donated money to anyone with an even half-plausible plan to help free slaves. In one instance, when he learned that a slaveholder was willing to emancipate his fifty slaves if they would be taken to a Northern state and provided for, Smith contacted the man and directed that they be sent to him. On another occasion, he had commissioned a friend to travel to Kentucky to purchase on his behalf an entire family of slaves who had once belonged to Smith's wife's family, and to personally escort them back to Peterboro.

The mansion at Peterboro was a welcoming watering hole for every abolitionist lecturer who traveled through Central New York, as well as for fugitives fresh from the South, who found themselves in what must have seemed a bizarre, if friendly environment. On any given day, Elizabeth Cady Stanton recalled, a guest might encounter a party of refined sophisticates from the cities, "a shouting Methodist, a Whig pro-slavery member of Congress, a southern ex-slave holder," three or four local Oneida Indians, a speculator trying to interest Smith in some investment scheme, "a crazy Millerite or two, who, disgusted with the world, thought it destined to be burned up at an early day," and a "sprinkling of Negroes from the sunny South on their way to Canada." In his diary, Smith meticulously recorded the unending parade:

"Mrs. Crampton, a beggar woman, spent last night with us. Charles Johnson, a fugitive slave from Hagerstown, took tea at our house last evening and breakfasted with us this morning.

"Mr. William Corning, a wandering pilgrim, as he styles himself, dines with us. He is peddling his own printed productions.

"Poor Graham, the insane literary colored man, has been with us a day or two.

"Elder Cook and William Haines of Oneida depot arrive this evening. Mr. H. is a 'medium,' and speaks in unknown tongues.

"Dr. Winmer of Washington City, with five deaf mutes and a blind child take supper and spend the evening with us.

"We find Brother Swift and his wife and daughter at our house, where they will remain until they get lodgings. There come this evening an old black man, a young one and his wife and infant. They say they are fugitives from North Carolina.

"A man from _____ brings his mother, six children and her half sister, all fugitives from Virginia.

"An Indian and a fugitive slave spent last night with us. The Indian has gone on, but Tommy McElligott (very drunk) has come to fill his place."

One day, in April 1848, the stream of pilgrims had included a rail-thin man with a shock of graying hair that grew thick and low on his bony brow, and extraordinarily penetrating steel-gray eyes. He introduced himself as a wool merchant from Springfield, Massachusetts, and said that he had read in the newspapers about Smith's generous donations of land in the Adirondacks. Their encounter was one of the great moments in antislavery history, with ramifications that would resonate for many years to come, contributing its small but significant impetus to the nation's acceleration toward civil war. They were a study in contrasts, the humorless guest and the gregarious host, with his broad intellectual face, "deep, flexible, musical voice," and faultless manners. The stranger probably wore his customary crisp white linen shirt and brown woolen coat, and Smith almost certainly a broad collar and black ribbon upon his neck, his invariable costume, whatever the fashion.

It was a bad time for the man from Springfield. He was deeply in debt. (By itself, this hardly distinguished him from a great many of Smith's visitors.) Piles of wool lay unsold in his warehouse. One of his sons was "proclaiming some form of 'idolatry' in Ohio." Another was going blind from "an accumulation of blood on the brain." But at the age of forty-eight, in spite of his personal sufferings and financial reverses, John Brown was convinced that God had chosen him for a special role, and that it was bound up with the abolition of slavery. He told Smith that he trusted utterly in a destiny ordained by God, and that if his maker chose such a fate for him, he would willingly lay down his life for the cause.

The stranger's abolitionist credentials were impeccable. Like Smith, he knew with ferocious certainty that slavery was nothing less than a sin against God. His beliefs were rooted in a granitelike Calvinism that had been chiseled to finished form by the hard experience of a frontier childhood. When he was an infant, his family had carried him west in an ox-drawn wagon from Connecticut to the raw wilderness of frontier Ohio. An early ambition to enter the ministry had fallen prey to a combination of poverty and an eye inflammation that forced him to give up his studies. But there was still much of the minister in him. He despised card playing, dancing, and all forms of entertainment. Church attendance had been compulsory for the workers in the tannery that he once operated, and he had also insisted that they come to his home every day for Bible readings. Convinced that righteous punishment was an instrument of the divine, he flogged his sons for every infraction: eight lashes for disobeying their mother, three for "unfaithfulness at work," eight for telling a lie.

At the age of thirty-seven, Brown had taken a personal vow before God to consecrate his life to the destruction of slavery. He and his abolitionist father, Owen Brown, a trustee of Oberlin College, had proven their commitment by serving as conductors on an underground line near Hudson, Ohio, which was known as "a rabid abolition town." A friend of Brown, interviewed in 1879, said, "I've seen him come in at night with [a] gang of five or six blacks that he had piloted all the way from the river, hide them away in the stables maybe, or the garret, and if anybody was following he would keep them stowed away for weeks." He had never hesitated to publicly denounce racism, even when he found it within his own church, where African Americans were required to sit on separate seats in the rear. Such discrimination made Brown so mad that he defiantly escorted some of the local blacks to his own family pew, an act that struck the rest of the congregation "like a bomb shell." In Springfield, he had met Frederick Douglass, who was very impressed with him, having found him living humbly on a back street "among laboring men and mechanics." Douglass had even mentioned him in his newspaper, the *North Star*, as a man who "though a white gentleman, is in sympathy, a black man, and as deeply interested in our cause, as though his own soul had been pierced with the iron of slavery."

Brown told Smith that he had heard that the settlers in the Adirondacks were having difficulties. Only a handful of black families had taken up residence on the Smith lands. Smith had commissioned Jermain Loguen to inspect the settlement. Loguen reported back that although some of the tracts were "as good land as any man can need," much of the region was poorly fitted for farming. Worse, he found that local men were charging would-be settlers exorbitant fees to guide them to their property, and swindling them out of their deeds. "My best advice to my brethren," he warned, "is not to venture in search of their farms, unless they can read and write, or are in the company of tried friends who can do both." The truth was, much of the land was simply impossible to farm profitably. The core of the settlement, in the township of North Elba, could be reached only by a single difficult road through the spectacular but remote valley of the Ausable River, and there was no market within scores of miles. In addition, even the most willing settlers needed wagons, livestock, tools, and basic supplies just to survive the next year, an investment that was beyond the means of the propertyless urban poor whom Smith had in mind. Brown made Smith an offer. "I will take one of your farms myself, clear it up and plant it, and show my colored neighbors how much work should be done; will give them work as I have occasion; look after them in all needful ways, and be a kind of father to them."

Smith liked Brown's piety, and his determination. He agreed to sell Brown 244 acres for one dollar an acre, on credit. The following May, bankrupt but afire with faith in his destiny, Brown moved his family—less one child, his youngest, who had just died from pneumonia—from Springfield to the deceptively blooming valleys of the Adirondacks. He was undeterred by the rugged boulder-strewn landscape, thickly forested with maple, oak, and spruce. They settled into a four-room farmhouse that looked out over valleys shimmering with goldenrod and four-thousand-foot-high Whiteface Mountain. Like Smith, he believed in the regenerative power of the wilderness. Far from the ruthless marketplace, the Adirondacks, like the hands of omnipotent God, would lift up the suffering black poor, and himself.

His goal was to transform the rag-tag settlement into a self-sufficient community. He hired black workers, sowed crops, helped rationalize confused boundaries, and prepared to take the community's affairs in hand. Visitors occasionally stumbled into Brown's mountain fastness. One of them, the celebrated author of *Two Years Before the Mast*, Richard Henry Dana, was fascinated by this "tall, sinewy, hard-favored, clear-headed, honest-minded man," who had the best cattle and best "farming utensils" for many miles around, as well as a teeming mob of children. Most of all, however, Dana was astonished to find the Browns, including even their daughters, dining equably with their black neighbors, addressing them as "*Mr.* Jefferson" and "*Mrs.* Wait," and so on.

But Smith's dream, and Brown's, would never come to fruition. The problems that Loguen had identified early on only got worse. No more than one hundred people ever managed to make the move to Smith's Adirondack lands, and only thirty-three of them would still be there in 1850. Within a few years, hundreds, if not thousands, of the parcels of land given away by Smith were being sold for taxes. If this left Brown feeling defeated once again, he did not record it. He had other, greater things in mind. Fermenting even now, as he sat in his cabin beneath the high peaks of the Adirondacks, was an apocalyptic plan to liberate slaves in numbers never before attempted. A "Subterranean Pass Way," as he visualized it, would reach deep into the South, through Virginia and Kentucky, Tennessee, North Carolina, even into Georgia. Along the way there would be posts manned by abolitionists and free blacks, all of them armed and ready to fight. It would drain the South of slaves utterly. It would be the apotheosis of the Underground Railroad.

Chapter 18

The Last Train

> I cannot now serve the cause I love so well better than to die for it.
>
> —John Brown

1

One of the saddest incidents in the history of American slavery took place in Cincinnati, on the morning of January 28, 1856. The drama's overture began the previous night, when several dark figures, bundled against the sub-freezing temperature, slipped from the slave quarters of Archibald Gaines's plantation in northern Kentucky, and into a waiting sleigh. The driver, Robert Garner, had stolen it from the plantation where he lived, a few miles away. He sped north through the snowswept hills, flogging the horses until blood flecked their nostrils. Eight lives hung in the balance: Garner, his parents, two young boys and two infant daughters, and their mother, Garner's common-law wife, Margaret, the story's ultimate protagonist, a slight woman with a high forehead, "bright and intelligent" eyes, and scarred cheeks where, she would only say, "White man struck me." Around 3 A.M., they reached the Ohio River at Covington, and slipped and stumbled down the steep bank, past the ghostly shapes of riverboats locked in the ice. Unseen, they crossed safely to Cincinnati, on the northern shore, putting behind them what should have been the most dangerous part of their break for freedom.

Their destination was the home of Margaret's cousin, Elijah Kite, who lived two miles from the river. The waterfront was as silent now as the snow, as they struggled to make their way through the unfamiliar maze of streets, stopping several times to ask directions. They reached Kite's house just before dawn. After building a fire to thaw his frozen guests, Kite hurried off toward the home of Levi Coffin, a mile and a half away, to set the machinery of the Underground Railroad in motion. Although the fugitives did not know it, Margaret's owner, Archibald Gaines, and a posse were in hot pursuit. By the time Kite reached Coffin's house at Sixth and Elm, they were already in Cincinnati.

Coffin had moved to Cincinnati in 1847, to open a "free labor emporium," which sold only goods that had not been produced by slave labor. He brought nearly three decades of experience to the city's underground, and had helped to make it one of the most efficient in the country. His collaborators included stevedores and cartmen, black entrepreneurs like the elite seamstress Kitty Doram, churchmen, businessmen, and a reserve of white abolitionist lawyers who donated their time to the defense of fugitives, among them future President Rutherford B. Hayes. By the time the Civil War brought an end to his work, Coffin would estimate that he had handled some three thousand fugitives since his early underground days in North Carolina. He never knew how many fugitives might appear at his door on any given day. If there were only a few, he hid them in his own attic. Bigger parties were scattered in different parts of the city, until they could be sent north. But Kite found Coffin at a loss. Operatives whom he would normally mobilize to help a party as large as the Garners' were already engaged with another group of fugitives who had crossed the river in the night and, as luck would have it, had reached Coffin earlier. He directed Kite to hurry the Garners for the time being to a safer location on the city's outskirts, promising that by nightfall he would have them aboard a northbound "train" of the Underground Railroad.

It was 8 A.M. when Kite returned home. He may have been followed, or it may have been sheer coincidence, but minutes after his arrival a lookout cried, "They are coming!" The fugitives rushed to bar the doors and windows. A deputy demanded their surrender in the name of the United States government. Robert and Elijah Kite drew guns. Margaret screamed to her mother-in-law, "Before my children shall be taken back to Kentucky, I shall kill every one of them!" Hundreds of blacks had gathered outside, and with decisive leadership they might have rescued the Garners before anything worse happened. But the deputies seized the initiative. Two of them tried to force their way in. Margaret seized a carving knife, and before anyone realized what she was doing she cut the throat of her two-year-old daughter, Mary—newspapers would hint that she was Archibald Gaines's child—nearly decapitating her. Using planks as clubs and battering rams, the deputies broke through the door and windows. Robert shot one of them in the face, but before he could fire again, Gaines yanked the gun from his hand. In the pandemonium, Margaret tried to cut the throats of the two boys, but they scrambled, bleeding but not badly hurt, underneath the bed. She was in the act of swinging a shovel at the head of her ten-month-old infant, Cilla, when the deputies tore it away from her.

The mood of the Garner trial captured a certain shift in the historical wind, pointing like a moral pennant toward the vaster brutality that was soon to come. Guerrilla armies were already on the march in Kansas, as newspapers across the country reported every detail of the case with a prurient fascination that would later be perfected by twentieth-century tabloids. The trial is recounted in poignant detail by Steven Weisenburger in *Modern Medea: A Family Story of Slavery and Child-Murder from the Old South*. Militant abolitionists hardly saw the slaughter of little Mary Garner as a crime at all, but rather as a form of mercy killing, and they embraced Margaret not as a murderess but as a martyr. "If in her deep maternal love she felt the impulse to send her child back to God, to save it from coming woe, who shall say she had no right to do so?" the women's rights advocate Lucy Stone asked in a speech in the courtroom. John Jolliffe, the abolitionist attorney who represented Garner, declared that Garner's dead child was not a victim of her mother's hand at all, but of the Fugitive Slave Law, a law so barbarous "that its execution required human hearts to be wrung and human blood to be spilt." In a provocative and clever move, Jolliffe had state arrest warrants issued against the Garners, charging

Margaret with murder and the others with complicity, to prevent them from being carried back into Kentucky. His aim was not to hang her, but to put the law itself on trial in a free Ohio court. For a time, it seemed that blood might really be spilled on the streets of Cincinnati, as the antislavery city sheriff's office and the proslavery federal commissioner's office fielded rival armed forces. President Franklin Pierce, a proslavery New Hampshire Democrat, even took a role, instructing Secretary of War Jefferson Davis, the future president of the Confederacy, to mobilize federal troops to ensure that order was maintained, and the Fugitive Slave Law enforced.

Through everything, Margaret Garner sat impassively, perhaps in shock, dressed in dark calico, with a yellow handkerchief wound around her head as a turban. As a slave, of course, she was never called upon to testify, either to defend herself or to explain her actions. To no one's real surprise, the judge ruled in favor of the slaves' owners, and on March 7, five weeks after they began their flight, the Garners were returned in chains to Kentucky. Southerners treated the case as a terrific victory. One Kentuckian was heard to remark, "We've got that damned abolition state under foot now, and by God we'll keep it there." In Covington, an Ohio reporter observing the Garners' return was set upon by a mob, who beat him to the ground and threatened to set him afloat on the Ohio River on a cake of ice.

But Margaret Garner's terrible odyssey was not yet over. On March 7, the Garners were loaded onto the steamboat *Henry Lewis*, bound for a cotton plantation the Gaines family owned in Arkansas. At four o'clock the next morning, just above Owensboro, Kentucky, the *Henry Lewis* was struck by a northbound steamboat and split in two, knocking passengers out of their beds, and sending them screaming into the icy river. In the chaos, Margaret Garner was seen standing with Cilla in her arms near the gunwale. What happened next was never clear. She may have thrown the baby into the river and jumped in after it, in hope of swimming to the Indiana shore. Or perhaps she intended for them both to die. A black cook jumped into the water and pulled Margaret to safety. But Cilla's body was never found. According to one newspaper report, Margaret displayed "frantic joy" when she was told that her child was drowned.

The surviving Garners were loaded onto another boat the next day, and delivered to their destination in Arkansas. Margaret would live for two more years, finally dying at the age of about twenty-five, from typhoid fever. Her last words to her husband were, "Never marry again in slavery."

The gruesome tragedy of the Garners reminded underground workers, if they needed reminding, that a failed rescue was often a matter of life and death. It was also further proof to a much broader spectrum of Northerners that complacent lip service to the principles of abolition would not be enough to end slavery's horrors. The passage of the Fugitive Slave Law, in 1850, had awakened whites to the price in personal liberty that they were expected to pay in order to protect slavery in the South. *Uncle Tom's Cabin* had enabled them to grasp the agony of slavery in an emotional way, undoubtedly a factor in the outpouring of sympathy that whites expressed for Margaret Garner's terrible act. Now personal liberty laws that in some states had fallen into disuse were reinstated or strengthened, forbidding the use of state jails to hold fugitives, and barring state judges and officials from helping Southern masters reclaim their lost "property." In Massachusetts, any official who granted a certificate permitting the removal of a fugitive from the state was instantly and permanently disbarred from holding state office. In other states, officials who violated similar statutes were punished with anywhere from five hundred dollars and six months in jail in Pennsylvania, to two thousand dollars' fine and ten years in prison in Vermont. In much of the North, the hated Fugitive Slave Law became a virtual dead letter. Even where antislavery laws were weaker, local authorities increasingly made the recovery of fugitives as expensive and time-consuming as possible. Benoni S. Fuller, for example, the sheriff of Warrick County, Indiana, bluntly replied to proslavery citizens who complained to him that fugitives were coming through the county by the hundreds, "Let 'em!" What made Fuller's statement particularly striking was that he was no evangelical abolitionist, but a Democrat. Old orthodoxies were boiling away.

In January 1854 another act of Congress pushed still more Northerners beyond their last limits of tolerance. Under pressure from the South and its Northern Democratic allies, Congress had opened the western territories to slavery. The Kansas-Nebraska Act left the legality of slavery up to voters in each territory, under the slogan of "popular sovereignty." Northerners who had been willing to leave slavery alone in the

South saw its expansion into the West as an attack on their own interests. Few believed that free labor could compete there with slave labor, any more than it could in the South. Even many deeply racist Yankees were converted into an army of voters committed to the principle of keeping the soil of Kansas and Nebraska free for white immigrants. "[T]his Nebraska business is the great smasher in Syracuse, as elsewhere," Jermain Loguen, who had helped lead the rescue of Jerry Henry, in 1851, gleefully wrote to Frederick Douglass. "It is smashing up platforms and scattering partizans at a fine rate . . . The people are becoming ashamed to have any connection with the ungodly course that many of their Congressmen follow . . . The time is coming when blood is to flow in this cause; and let it come I say."

Nebraska, the more northerly of the two territories, was in no danger of becoming a slave state. In Kansas, however, the situation was fluid and combustible. There pent-up political passions ignited the pistol-point politics of the frontier, and the inherent violence of slave-owning culture, to produce open warfare between Free Soil and proslavery forces. Even before the territory was formally opened to settlement, proslavery men poured across the state line from Missouri, egged on by demagogues and the Missouri Democratic Party, which declared itself "in favor of making Kansas a 'Slave State' if it should require half the population of Missouri, musket in hand, to emigrate there, and even sacrifice their lives [for] so desirable an end."

Free State settlers begged for support, and for guns to defend themselves. Speaking to an assembly in Albany, Gerrit Smith promised the settlers immediate help: "Will we do for them what we can? We will!" Smith's friend, Senator William H. Seward, declared, "We will engage in competition for the virgin soil of Kansas, and God give the victory to the side that is stronger in numbers as it is in right." Emigrant aid committees sprang up from Maine to Illinois.

Among the thousands who left behind farms, workshops, and schools to respond to the Free Staters' call were five abolitionist brothers living in Ohio. Once in Kansas, the Browns found it a country of expansive beauty in which the rough-hewn cabins of scattered settlers seemed adrift like lonely dinghies upon the tidal sweep of grassy, wind-rippled prairie, broken occasionally by meandering streams shaded by gnarled cottonwoods, oak trees, and sycamores. They staked claims near the hamlet of

Osawatomie, thirty-five miles south of the Free State bastion of Lawrence. Along with settlers like the Browns came the Underground Railroad. By the end of the decade, as many as three hundred Missouri slaves would be carried to freedom through Kansas.

Once they were settled, the Brown brothers wrote to their father back East, describing the dire plight of the Free Staters, and urging him to join them: "[W]hile the interest of despotism has secured to its cause hundreds of thousands of the meanest and most desperate of men, armed to the teeth with Revolvers, Bowie Knives, Rifles & Cannon—while they are not only thoroughly organized, but under pay from Slaveholders—the friends of freedom are *not one fourth* of them *half armed*, and as to *military organization* among them *it nowhere exists in this territory*."* Their father, John Brown, had promised his patron Gerrit Smith, as well as his black neighbors, that he would remain to help build their community at North Elba, in the Adirondacks, whose wild beauty spoke so deeply to something in his own unsettled heart. But his wool business had fallen to pieces, and he was plagued by lawsuits from angry creditors. He had already been compelled for financial reasons to lease a farm on more fertile land in Ohio, far from North Elba. Early in 1855, responding to his sons' call, Brown made the fateful decision to join them. He arrived at Osawatomie in early October, driving a wagon loaded with rifles and swords, determined "to help defeat Satan and his legions." Kansas would transform him from a failed businessman into a prophet whose private apocalypse would become a battle plan for guerrilla warfare.

2

While abolitionists armed themselves in Kansas, across the North the Underground Railroad was reaching a level of efficiency and speed that it would maintain until the Civil War changed the landscape of slavery forever. It was aided greatly by the advent of a new national political party,

---

* There was actually a total of about ten thousand white settlers in Kansas at this time.

whose members added a fresh cohort of activists to its work. In 1854 remnants of the old Whig Party, Free Soilers, dissident Democrats, and unaffiliated abolitionists came together in a coalition to challenge the hegemony of the South. Although the Republican Party shunned abolitionist rhetoric, its opposition to the expansion of slavery into the western territories was unequivocal. The rising Illinois railroad lawyer Abraham Lincoln, for one, rejected the South's claim that slavery was based on moral principle, but he also made it clear that he supported neither freeing the slaves nor making them "politically and socially, our equals." In certain areas, especially after 1856, when the party fielded its first presidential candidate, the explorer John C. Frémont, it would transform the underground. Recalled Isaac Beck, a longtime underground conductor in Ohio, "The great Fremont campaign and the organization of the Republican Party diffused anti-slavery sentiments so widely in Northern states that [the Underground Railroad] was necessary no longer or rather every Republican became a 'Railroader.' "

In much of the North, the Underground Railroad was operating with an openness that would have been unimaginable only a few years before. Some sense of the increasing volume of traffic handled by the underground lines may be gleaned from Thomas Garrett, the stationmaster at Wilmington, Delaware, who was one of the few to keep a tally of his passengers over a long span of time. In 1848 Garrett admitted in court to having assisted more than 1,400 slaves to freedom since he began his underground work in 1822, an average of 56 per year. Between 1848 and 1854, he assisted another 450, an average of 75 per year, and by 1860, he claimed to have helped a grand total of 2,750, an average of 225 per year before the Civil War brought an end to his work. Reports from other parts of the country, though fragmentary, also suggest that underground travel was approaching a peak in the middle years of the decade. Between mid-1854 and early 1855, the all-black Committee of Nine, which oversaw underground work in Cleveland, Ohio, forwarded 275 fugitives to Canada, an average of one per day, while the *Syracuse Journal* reported in October 1855 that about 140 fugitives had passed through the city since January, an average of slightly fewer than one every two days. The Detroit Vigilance Committee, possibly the busiest in the United States, reported 1,043 fugitives crossing to Canada from May 1855 to January 1856, an average of 130 per month. By contrast, in Massachusetts, liberty laws had made the state so safe for fugitives that by the last years of the decade, the Underground Railroad was virtually obsolete: despite its financial resources and abundance of volunteers, the Boston Vigilance Committee saw its share of fugitives dwindle from 69 in 1851, its busiest year, to just 9 in 1858.

Technology was also transforming the work of the underground, as the rapid spread of iron railways dramatically accelerated the speed of underground travel across the Free States. Wherever trains were available, the underground used them. The black lumber merchant William Whipper shipped fugitives from Columbia, Pennsylvania, directly to the Canadian border hidden in special compartments in his fleet of freight cars. Travel by rail from Philadelphia to Canada, a journey that had once taken weeks on foot or in the beds of jolting farm wagons, now took as little as two days. In the West, fugitives coming out of Missouri could be put on a train in western Illinois in the morning and be in Canada by nightfall the same day. (Railroads were used so commonly by fugitives passing through Illinois that in March 1855 a bill was proposed in the legislature, calling for blacks to be barred completely from traveling on trains within the state, without first showing a certificate of freedom; significantly, it failed to pass.)

Certain railroad companies were led by antislavery men and facilitated the passage of fugitives as a matter of policy. H. F. Paden, a conductor on the Sandusky, Mansfield & Newark Railroad, was frequently directed by the company's local representatives, who doubled as underground agents, to pick up fugitives at stations along the line, en route to the Lake Erie port of Sandusky, Ohio. In one instance, Paden was informed that nine fugitives would board his train for Sandusky at 10 P.M. They were placed in different cars for most of the journey. Then, about forty miles south of Sandusky, Paden moved them all quietly to the last car, turned out the lights, and locked the doors. At Sandusky, the white passengers got off at the platform, and the train rolled back on a siding. At midnight, Paden unlocked the car and led the fugitives to a safe house owned by an African American, who later packed them into sleighs and drove them thirty miles across the frozen lake to Pelee Island, in Canadian territory.

The fact that fugitives could travel openly with relative safety by train was another indication of the broad shift that was taking place in public opinion. By the middle years of the decade, the "underground" was no longer a clandestine phenomenon at all in much of the North, but an open part of local life. When the Supreme Court issued its infamous Dred Scott decision, in 1857, removing all existing territorial restrictions on slavery, members of the underground, and for that matter most of the North, expressed dismay, but in practice simply ignored it. The *Pennsylvania Freeman* regularly published appeals for donations to be sent to the Philadelphia Vigilance Committee specifically for Underground Railroad work, asking that they be directed by name to William Still. *Frederick Douglass' Paper* (the successor to the *North Star*) regularly published detailed reports on underground activity in articles that were signed by agents themselves. In one of these, on November 5, 1854, George DeBaptiste, one of the underground's leaders in Detroit, reported, "We have had, within the last ten or fifteen days, fifty-three first class passengers landed at this point, by the Express train from the South. We expect ten more tonight." In another, on December 11, George Weir Jr. of Buffalo, New York, wrote that "a train of cars belonging to the *Underground Railroad* had just arrived, bringing eight passengers, six men and two women, all direct from 'Old Kentuck.' Of course the doors of the depot were thrown open, and in they marched, rank and file, led by T. R. Esq., one of the conductors on the road." In December 1855 Douglass himself reported from Syracuse that "three good bouncing fat Negroes stepped aboard the train on the Underground Railroad, and are now safe in the Queen's dominions. It is proposed by the directors of that road, to lay down a double track, as the business is getting to be very large—more than can be done on a single one."

The source for this last information could have been no one else but Jermain Loguen, who advertised his underground work and his address in local papers, and identified himself on his business cards as "Underground Railroad Agent." Loguen handled up to two hundred fugitives annually, and estimated that in the course of the 1850s he helped about fifteen hundred in all, most of them during the last few years of the decade. (Fugitives normally arrived in Syracuse as ordinary passengers by train or via the Erie Canal, although in 1857 he received one woman directly from the South, packed in a box.) In addition to serving as the underground's public face in Syracuse, Loguen lectured on slavery throughout central and western New York, and made several investigative trips to Canada, where he studied the condition of refugees and established a reception center under the supervision of a fugitive slave.

At home, Loguen and his wife Caroline existed in an almost constant state of sleepless exhaustion, tending to refugees who showed up at their rambling clapboard house on suburban East Genesee Street with frostbitten feet, sick children, and "in such conditions of destitution and uncleanness, as subjected her to the most disagreeable inconvenience." One night, Frederick Douglass himself by chance encountered a group of nine fugitives at the Syracuse railway station, who asked if he could direct them to Loguen's home. Douglass led them there himself, and described their reception: "We had scarcely struck the door when the manly voice of Loguen reached our ear. He knew the meaning of the rap, and sung out 'hold on.' A light was struck in a moment, the door opened and the whole company, the writer included, were invited in. Candles were lighted in different parts of the house, fires kindled, and the whole company made perfectly at home. The reception was a whole souled and manly one, worthy of the noble reputation of Brother Loguen, and showed that he remembers his brethren in bonds as bound with them." So committed were the Loguens to their work that they continued to receive fugitives even as their thirteen-year-old daughter Latitia lay dying of tuberculosis.

The only known photograph of Loguen, a formal portrait taken after the Civil War, shows a broad, self-confident, rather light-skinned face whose fleshiness hints at his once powerful body's middle age decline. He had spent several worried months in Canada after the Jerry Rescue, not returning to Syracuse until 1852, when he felt assured that he would not be prosecuted for his part in the affair. In 1856 the local Vigilance Committee formally designated his home as the main reception center for arriving fugitives, replacing that of his friend Reverend Samuel J. May. Loguen had found his historic vocation: his whole life—as a slave, a fugitive, a minister, an agitator—had prepared him perfectly for the role that he now undertook. He wrote to Douglass, "Had I not been terribly wronged, as you and all our race, I think I should have been a very still, quiet man. Oppression has made me mad; it has waked up all my intellectual and physical energies."

Loguen was not alone. He was one of a fraternity of remarkably similar black men, including William Still in Philadelphia, Lewis Hayden in Boston, Henry Bibb in Canada, and the Detroit triumvirate of William

Lambert, George DeBaptiste, and Reverend William Monroe, among others, all roughly the same age, most former slaves, and all of them having come to political maturity as activists in the interracial world of the underground. There had always been teamsters, farmhands, and sailors who had worked hand-in-hand with white underground operatives. But these were different. They were self-made men who had achieved success through native ability: Hayden, Lambert, and DeBaptiste as businessmen, Bibb as a journalist, Loguen and Monroe as ministers, Still as a manager. Outside the churches, few black men like these had existed before in American history.

In contrast to many white agents, for whom their own moral elevation was an end in itself, Loguen and other African Americans regarded emergency aid as only the first step in the liberation of escaped slaves. As a fugitive himself, Loguen knew that to become truly autonomous, former slaves needed good work, and education. In Canada Josiah Henson and his imitators had attempted to address these needs with their ambitious attempts to establish comprehensive training schools, and model communities. Loguen, anticipating the principle of affirmative action, vigorously appealed not just for charitable donations, but for jobs for blacks: "Who, then, in and about Syracuse will take into their shops and on their farms, our colored youth, and discipline and educate them to the industry and arts of life, as white children are educated?" he asked in a widely published letter. "We ask not for them professional employment, but we do ask our white brethren who engross the avenues of laborious industry, to open to our gifted and unfortunate young men the paths of life . . . [L]abor, honest labor, must be connected with the education of our heads and hearts, or we can never come to the natural level of our race."

Loguen could not have carried out his work so openly without the support of influential segments of the white community. Syracuse was now so thoroughly "abolitionized" that the city council voted that if the Central Rail Road, which ran through the middle of town, ever carried a recaptured fugitive back toward slavery, its rails should be physically taken up from the streets. Public fund-raisers for the underground were even held in the council's chambers. For one of them a local band composed a song titled "The Underground Railroad Quickstep," and dedicated it to Loguen. So famous did Loguen become that Syracuse was sometimes referred to as "the Canada of the United States," and in 1860 the *Weekly*

Anglo-African, a journal of the AME Zion Church, went so far as to proclaim him the "Underground Railroad King."

Reports of Loguen's activities eventually reached the ears of his nominal owner in Tennessee, the widow of Manasseth Logue, from whom he had escaped in 1834, taking his master's fleetest horse with him on his flight to Canada. He received an astonishing letter from Sarah Logue, addressed to him by his slave name, "Jarm," a deliberate indignity, certainly, and a reminder that in the state of Tennessee he was still legally a slave. "I write you these lines to let you know the situation we are in—partly as a consequence of your running away and stealing Old Rock, our fine mare," she wrote. "Though we got the mare back, she was never worth much after you took her; and now as I stand in need of some funds, I have determined to sell you; and I have had an offer for you, but I did not see fit to take it. If you will send me one thousand dollars and pay for the old mare, I will give up all claim I have to you. In consequence of your running away, we had to sell Abe and Ann [Loguen's brother and sister] and twelve acres of land; and I want you to send me the money that I may be able to redeem the land that was the cause of our selling, and on receipt of the above sum of money, I will send you your bill of sale. If you do not comply with my request, I will sell you to someone else, and you may rest assured that the time is not far distant when things will be changed with you."

The stunning presumption of the letter was not lost on Loguen. He wrote back: "You are a woman; but had you a woman's heart you could never have insulted a brother by telling him you sold his only remaining brother and sister, because he put himself beyond your power to convert him into money. Now you have the unutterable meanness to ask me to return and be your miserable chattel, or in lieu thereof send you $1,000 to enable you to redeem the *land*, but not to redeem my poor brother and sister!" He added defiantly, "If you or any other speculator on my body and rights, wish to know how I regard my rights, they need but come here and lay their hands on me to enslave me."

Loguen knew that slave catchers, if they dared, might come for him any time. But they never did. The nation went to war instead. Before that happened, however, Loguen would have a role to play in the last great drama of the antebellum era.

3

At fifty-five, John Brown was still, in the words of Frederick Douglass, "lean, strong, and sinewy, built for times of trouble and fitted to grapple with the flintiest hardships." In Kansas, he finally found reality violent enough to fit the cosmic battle between Good and Evil he had always carried in his head. His first taste of warfare came in December 1855, when a proslavery force of two thousand men menaced the Free State town of Lawrence, fifty miles north of the Browns' cabins at Osawatomie. The Browns and their neighbors raced to Lawrence's defense, arriving there in a wagon that bristled like a lethal porcupine with rifles, pikes, and bayonets. Brown was commissioned a captain on the spot, and appointed to command a company of twenty men, his first military commission. From the first moment, he savored the power that weapons and leadership conferred. Although the anticipated attack never materialized, Brown had discovered that men would follow him, and fight for him. In the months and years to come, some would see in him an "imperial egotism." To others, he would reveal a charisma that would draw to him both hard men and naive ones, mesmerized by his towering certainties, and trusting that his icy, sword-sharp gaze truly saw the will of God.

Still, until the spring of 1856, John Brown was not much different from many other scripture-quoting abolitionists in Kansas. Despite the incendiary rhetoric in the air, only six Free Staters had so far been killed. Then, in May, proslavery raiders attacked Lawrence. Brown and a party of his men were on their way to the town's defense when they learned that it had surrendered without even a fight, and had afterward been subjected to an orgy of burning and looting. Almost simultaneously, Brown was informed by a messenger that Charles Sumner of Massachusetts, the most outspoken abolitionist in the United States Senate, had been beaten senseless on the floor of the chamber by a cane-wielding congressman from South Carolina. The news from Lawrence and Washington left Brown "frenzied" at the North's seeming impotence in the face of Southern power. He "went crazy—*crazy*," his son Salmon later recalled. "Something must be done to show these barbarians that we, too, have rights," Brown told his followers. Advised to act with caution, he retorted, "Caution, caution, sir. I am eternally tired of hearing the word caution. It is nothing but the word of cowardice."

Revenge for Lawrence and for the attack on Sumner was on Brown's mind on the night of May 23 as he swept with an armed party that included four of his sons through an isolated settlement on Pottawatomie Creek, thirty miles from Osawatomie. They dragged five men out of their cabins and hacked them to death with cutlasses embossed with the American eagle. The victims were all notorious proslavery men, and had advocated attacks against the Free Staters, but none was guilty of killing anyone. The horrific nature of the murders disgusted even abolitionists. Two of Brown's sons who had not participated in the raid were so distraught that they suffered nervous breakdowns. Brown was unrepentant. "God is my judge," he laconically replied when asked to account for his actions. "We were justified under the circumstances."

The murders ignited a reign of terror. Proslavery "border ruffians" raided Free Staters' homesteads. Abolitionists fought back. Federal troops scoured the prairie in search of Brown and his band. Hamlets were left desolate, farms abandoned. Osawatomie was burned to the ground. Brown's son Frederick, who had participated in the massacre, was shot dead by a proslavery man. Brown himself was almost caught in September, when a troop of dragoons rode up to the cabin where he was hiding, and stayed for refreshment. He lay hidden in the loft, with a revolver in each hand, watching through cracks in the floorboards as his host fed melons to the soldiers. Although he survived many brushes with the enemy, Brown seemed to sense his own fate. He told his son Jason, the quietest of all the Browns, a farmer who dreamed more of raising fruit trees than of vengeance, "I have only a short time to live—only one death to die, and I will die fighting for this cause."

The national elections that autumn solved nothing. Although the Republicans made a strong showing in their first presidential contest, receiving an impressive 33 percent of the vote in a three-way contest, the election was won by yet another doughface Democrat, Pennsylvanian James Buchanan, a man who made a pious virtue of complacency and invoked maintenance of the status quo as a lofty ideal. A Northern man only in terms of geography, he was a lifelong defender of Southern interests. As far back as the 1820s, as a freshman congressman, he had declared that if

Southerners were ever to be threatened by a slave rebellion he would be among the first "to bundle on my knapsack" and march "in defense of their cause." In his inaugural address, he now proclaimed his enthusiasm for popular sovereignty in Kansas. "[E]verything of a practical nature has been decided," he blandly assured the nation. "No other question remains for adjustment, because all agree that under the Constitution slavery in the States is beyond the reach of any human power except that of respective States themselves wherein it exists . . . Most happy will it be for the country when the public mind shall be diverted from this question to others of more pressing and practical importance."

Like his predecessor, Franklin Pierce, Buchanan uncritically embraced the proslavery territorial government of Kansas, based at Lecompton, and dismissed the rival Free State administration at Topeka as "revolutionary." When elections for the territorial legislature were held in October 1857, thousands of Missourians crossed the border to vote illegally, in the most nakedly fraudulent grab for power in American history. In one county, in which only eleven cabins had been erected, 1,828 votes were recorded. In another county, proslavery forces packed the poll lists with names taken verbatim from an old New York City directory. Elsewhere, abolitionists were physically kept from entering the polls by proslavery toughs. Laws enacted by the legislators barred abolitionists from holding office or from serving on juries, and imposed a term of imprisonment for not less than five years on anyone who denied the existence of slavery in Kansas, opposed the right to own slaves, or circulated abolitionist literature. Abolitionists were understandably outraged. In New York, Gerrit Smith denounced the new laws as "the most diabolical and infamous statutes" ever enacted, and pledged more aid to the Free State forces. (He would eventually donate to the cause more than sixteen thousand dollars, the equivalent of four hundred and fifty thousand dollars in present-day terms.)

Meanwhile, a grandiose plan was fermenting in the fertile imagination of John Brown, who had continued to evade punishment for the Pottawatomie massacre. "Railroad Business on a somewhat extended scale is the identical object for which I am trying to get means," he confided to a friend. To his old vision of a "Subterranean Pass Way" that would run the length of the Appalachian chain, he now added the concept of a militarized enclave based in the mountains, which would provide a permanent haven for fugitives from all over the Deep South, and thus bring the entire institution of slavery to its knees. Having eluded his enemies for months on the open prairies of Kansas, he believed that it would be even easier to defy them in the forested fastnesses of the Blue Ridge Mountains. Only "a few resolute men" would be needed at first. Once they had established a chain of defensible positions, recruits could be sent down as they were needed.

In January 1858 Brown left Kansas to seek backing for his plan. His itinerary was a Cook's tour of the leading underground figures in the East. He spent three weeks with Frederick Douglass, in Rochester, where he wrote a forty-eight-article constitution for a "Provisional Government," including a unicameral legislature, president and vice-president, supreme court, a commander-in-chief, all to serve without pay. He told Douglass that his first objective was the capture of the Virginia town of Harpers Ferry, at the confluence of the Potomac and Shenandoah rivers, with its important federal armory and rifle works, which would provide weapons for the thousands of slaves he expected to flock to his cause.

From Rochester, Brown moved on to Gerrit Smith's mansion at Peterboro, where he was introduced to the well-connected abolitionist and educator Franklin Sanborn, for whom Brown enthusiastically sketched plans for his mountain redoubts on a scrap of paper. (Sanborn cautiously labeled the designs "woolen machinery.") Sanborn and Brown then traveled to Boston, where Brown won the support of four more prominent radical abolitionists who had already lent their support to the Free State cause in Kansas, and now agreed to organize financing for Brown's southern strategy.*

After Boston, Brown moved on to Philadelphia to recruit William Still. Then, after a brief visit to his family at North Elba, he journeyed to Syracuse, where he had the ardent support of Jermain Loguen, whose defiant oratory echoed Brown's own. Loguen's part in the plan, like

---

* The four were the educator and journalist Samuel Gridley Howe, whose wife would write the Civil War anthem, "The Battle Hymn of the Republic"; George L. Stearns, a wealthy Massachusetts linseed oil manufacturer who had supplied guns for Kansas; the radical Unitarian minister Thomas Wentworth Higginson, later editor of the *Atlantic Monthly*; and another Unitarian minister, the silver-tongued Theodore Parker. Together with Smith and Sanborn, they would become known as the "Secret Six."

Douglass's, would be to recruit the battalions of black volunteers Brown wanted for his Appalachian army. He also hoped that either Douglass or Loguen would agree to serve as president of his provisional government. Brown and Loguen continued on to St. Catharines, in Canada, where they sought out Harriet Tubman. At her house, Brown told a gathering of her friends that the Day of Judgment was at hand, that it was time for "God's wrath to descend," and that he was the divine instrument ordained to deliver it.

By now, Tubman was a celebrity within the underground. She had made eight trips to the South, and brought out some fifty fugitives, including her parents, who although free had been in danger of imminent arrest because of her father's involvement in the underground. Brown recognized in her a kindred spirit, whose physical courage, boldness, and skill at traveling unnoticed through the South would be invaluable. He took to referring to her as "General Tubman," and wrote to his son John Brown Jr.: "He is the most of a man, naturally, that I have ever met." Tubman, for her part, embraced Brown as one of the few whites she had ever met who understood, as blacks always had, that antislavery work was not just moral uplift but part of a war in which combatants had to be prepared to die.

On May 8, at a secret convention in Chatham, in Canada West, Brown proclaimed the establishment of his provisional government, based on the constitution that he had written at the Douglass home. Of the forty-six men present, the only whites were thirteen of Brown's followers from Kansas. Among the more prominent blacks were Mary Ann Shadd's brother Isaac, publisher of the *Provincial Freeman*, and two leaders of the Detroit underground, William Lambert and Reverend William Monroe, who chaired the convention. However, Tubman, Douglass, and Loguen were all notably absent, a portent, perhaps, that they had second thoughts about Brown's ambitions. None of them ever disowned him. But they may have concluded that if his plan failed they were certain to be arrested, and the Underground Railroad possibly wrecked, as its lines, methods, and membership were revealed. The delegates adopted the constitution that Brown had written with little debate, and unanimously elected Reverend Monroe the provisional government's temporary president, and Brown its commander in chief. Brown left Chatham with the hope that hundreds, if not thousands, of Canadian blacks would eventually join his expedition.

Only one did, Osborne P. Anderson, a printer who worked for the *Provincial Freeman*, and had been elected a member of Brown's provisional congress.

Brown wanted to invade Virginia that summer. But hints of his strategy had leaked out. To draw attention away from his real intentions, he returned to Kansas, where he lay low for the next six months. When he left Kansas in December 1858, his departure was spectacular. A Missouri slave named Jim Daniels had contacted him, and asked for help in liberating the members of his family, who were about to be sold. It was an opportunity to carry out precisely the kind of raid into slave territory that Brown had in mind, on a vaster scale, for Virginia. Brown led a detachment of men ten miles into Missouri to the plantation where Daniels lived. They collected the five members of Daniels's family, and five more slaves from another plantation nearby. A second detachment freed a slave at a third farm, and killed her owner. For the next month, the fugitives were hidden in a cabin across the state line in Kansas. In late January 1859 Brown and the twelve fugitives (a baby having been born in the interim, and christened "John Brown"), set off northward toward Nebraska with the fugitives in an ox-drawn wagon and an armed guard of fifteen abolitionists, dodging proslavery guerrillas, marshals' posses, and at one point fending off a much larger force of United States troops, taking several of them prisoner. One of them later complained that although none of the prisoners had been otherwise mistreated, "It did go a little against the grain to eat with and be guarded by 'damned niggers.' " Near Nebraska City, when thawing ice halted their flight at the Missouri River, Brown's men cut down trees and flung logs from the shore to firmer ice, and dragged their wagons across by hand, just hours ahead of their pursuers. They traveled east along an established underground route through Iowa, via Tabor and Grinnell, where they were welcomed by Josiah Grinnell, the founder of the college that bears his name. Grinnell personally reserved a boxcar for Brown's party at the nearest railhead, to carry them directly to Chicago, which they reached on March 10. Two days later they arrived in Detroit, where, presumably with the assistance of the local underground, they were taken to the wharf and ferried across the Detroit River to Windsor. As he watched them embark, Brown recalled a passage of Scripture: "Lord, now lettest thy servant depart in peace, for my eyes have seen thy salvation." They had covered almost fifteen hundred miles in eighty-two days, proof to scoffers, Brown felt sure, that he was capable of making the Subterranean Pass Way a reality.

Around ten-thirty on the dank night of Sunday, September 17, nineteen shadowy figures led by the man some now called Old Osawatomie slipped down from the brooding bluffs of Maryland overlooking the Potomac River, and with the brisk steps of men who knew that whatever the outcome, they were about to make history, they entered the black tunnel of the covered railroad bridge that spanned the river to Harpers Ferry. Each carried a Sharpes rifle, a brace of pistols, and a knife sheathed at his waist. Twelve of the men were white, five black. Almost all were in their twenties. Some were naive idealists, others veterans of the guerrilla war in Kansas. Among them were Brown's youngest sons Watson and Oliver, two neighbors from North Elba, a Canadian spiritualist, a black graduate of Oberlin College, a pair of Quakers who had abandoned their pacifist beliefs to follow Brown from Iowa, a freed slave hoping to liberate his wife and children, and boys from Maine, Pennsylvania, and Indiana. Three more members of Brown's twenty-two-man "army" remained behind in Maryland to guard the weapons with which he planned to arm battalions of rebellious slaves.

Of all the men on the bridge, Shields Green knew the dehumanizing reality of slavery best, for he had lived it all his life. Millions of other enslaved men and women symbolically walked with him that night: those who prayed hopelessly for freedom that never came, as well as all those who had struck out for Canaan and failed, and were dragged back to auction blocks, or who died unmourned on wilderness trails, or from the gunshots of their pursuers. Less than two years earlier, the uneducated Green had escaped from Charleston, South Carolina, and made his way to the home of Frederick Douglass, in Rochester. A dark-skinned man with sharp, chiseled features and a goatee, Green looked older than his twenty-three years. He had traveled south with Douglass to a secret meeting at a rock quarry on the Conecochequi River, near Chambersburg, Pennsylvania, where Brown assembled his men before the attack. Douglass bluntly told Brown that his plan was hopeless, that he was "going into a steel trap, and that he would not get out alive." Brown responded that the time for peaceful persuasion was long past, and that the nation's complacency needed to be shattered. After two days of discussion, Brown, by no one's account a man given to physical warmth, put his arms around Douglass, and pleaded, "Come with me, Douglass. I will defend you with my life." Douglass, choosing survival over his old friend's assurances, pulled himself away, and bade Brown farewell. He asked Shields Green what he planned to do. Green knew that he could simply return to Rochester. A life of freedom and safety lay before him. He had heard Douglass's warnings. Finally he said, "I b'leve I'll go wid de ole man."

As Brown's men came off the bridge into Harpers Ferry, he dispatched parties to seize the musket factory, the armory, and the fire-engine house, taking several nonplussed watchmen prisoner in the process. Within minutes, the raiders were in control of thousands of rifles and huge stocks of powder and ball. Guards were posted at the bridges over the Potomac and the Shenandoah. Telegraph lines were cut. The railroad station was seized, and a Baltimore-bound express train halted. It was at the station that the raid's first casualty occurred. The baggage master, an enslaved black man named Hayward Shepherd, challenged Brown's men and was shot dead in the dark. Once the key locations had been secured, Brown sent a detachment to arrest several of the area's prominent slave owners as hostages, including Colonel Lewis W. Washington, the great-grandnephew of the first president.

Brown was audacious and extremely brave, but he had seduced himself with his sense of destiny, and he was no strategist. He expected to have fifteen hundred men under his command by midday Monday, and later said that he believed that he would eventually command between two thousand and five thousand. "When I strike, the bees will swarm," he had assured Douglass. His first mistake was to release the Baltimore train, allowing word of the raid to spread quickly up and down the line, and then by telegraph across the nation. The earliest reports were hysterical, claiming that Harpers Ferry had been taken over by a company of first fifty, then one hundred and fifty, then two hundred white "insurrectionists" and "six hundred runaway negroes," evoking the terrifying specter of race war. However, as Brown's band watched dawn break over the rugged ridges that enclosed Harpers Ferry like the walls of a natural amphitheater, militias as far away as Baltimore, Frederick, and Winchester were already hastening to arms. President Buchanan personally dispatched a company of marines from Washington, under Colonel Robert E. Lee, who would one day command the armies of the Confederacy. By mid-afternoon, volunteers were pouring toward Harpers Ferry from every direction, carrying everything from shotguns and old muskets, to squirrel rifles. There was no sign at all of the thousands of slaves who Brown had convinced himself were just waiting to rally to his standard.

At about noon, the Charlestown militia made a dash across the bridge over the Shenandoah, firing shotguns and pistols as they ran, killing the first of Brown's men to die that day, forty-eight-year-old Dangerfield Newby, who had been born into slavery but freed by his white father. Newby had moved North to earn money to buy freedom for his wife and six children, but had not succeeded. In Newby's pocket was found a letter from his wife. She had written: "It is said Master is in want of money. I know not what time he may sell me, and then all my bright hopes of the future are blasted, for their [*sic*] has been one bright hope to cheer me in all my troubles, that is to be with you . . . Come this fall without fail money or no money."

As the number of attackers swelled, Brown's men retreated to the engine house, a formidable brick structure that was windowless on three sides and had three stout oak doors in the front. Three abolitionists, including the provisional government's "congressman," Osborne Anderson, held the armory, and three more men the musket works, half a mile to the west. Acknowledging the precariousness of his predicament, Brown sent out William Thompson of North Elba under a flag of truce, to propose a cease-fire. But Thompson was immediately seized and dragged away to a local hotel, where he was kept under guard. As militiamen worked their way toward the rear of the engine house, Brown then sent his twenty-four-year-old son Watson and one of his best men, the powerfully built ex-cavalryman Aaron Stevens, out under a white flag, but the mob shot them down in the street. Watson, though fatally wounded, managed to drag himself back to the engine house. Stevens, who was shot four times, was taken into custody.

Brandishing a sword that had once belonged to Frederick the Great and that had been taken from Colonel Washington, Brown strode among his remaining men, urging them to stay calm and not to waste their ammunition. Loopholes had been drilled in the doors, and through them Brown's men tried to pick off attackers who came too near. One of their shots killed the popular mayor of Harpers Ferry, Fountain Beckham. Seeking immediate revenge, a mob of townspeople pushed its way into the hotel where William Thompson was being held, dragged him outside, and cold-bloodedly shot him in the head, as he begged for his life.

Realizing that their position was untenable, the three men in the rifle works made a run for the shallow Shenandoah, firing as they ran. Two, John Kagi, the vice president of the provisional government, and a black man named Lewis Leary, were shot down in the rapids. The black Oberlin student, John Copeland, managed to reach a rock in the middle of the river, where he threw down his gun and surrendered. William Leeman, at twenty the youngest of the raiders, broke and ran from the armory, jumped into the Potomac, and swam for his life. But he was trapped on an islet, and shot. Throughout the afternoon, militiamen with nothing else to shoot at used his body for target practice.

Late in the afternoon, Shields Green managed to reach the armory with a message from Brown. The surviving men there, Osborne and Hazlett, had already decided to try to make their escape, and they urged Green to join them. It was obvious that their position was hopeless. Green declined their offer and returned to the engine house. He must have understood that he was going back to certain death. But he had promised Brown that he would do his duty. Soon militia reinforcements arrived and attacked the engine house from the rear, cutting off his last chance of escape.

Frederick Douglass had of course been right. Brown was trapped. There would be no Subterranean Pass Way, no chain of forts, no Appalachian refuge for fugitive slaves. If Brown felt like a defeated man, however, it was not evident. As his son Watson wept with pain, Brown advised him to die "as becomes a man." His twenty-year-old son Oliver already lay dead on the floor. When dawn came, Brown and his four remaining uninjured men looked out through their loopholes into the morning mist to see Robert E. Lee's marines deployed with fixed bayonets, and beyond them a mass of militiamen, spoiling for more blood. Shortly after seven o'clock, Lee's aide, a brash young lieutenant of cavalry, walked toward the engine house, carrying a white flag. He was met at the door by Brown. The soldier demanded immediate and unconditional surrender, and promised only that Brown's men would be tried according to law. Brown asked that they instead be allowed to retreat across the river to Maryland, where they would free their remaining hostages. Suddenly, cutting Brown short, the lieutenant jumped aside, and signaled for the marines to attack. Brown could easily have shot him dead—"just as easily as I could kill a musquito," he said later. Had he done so, the course of the Civil War would undoubtedly have been different in ways that can never be known. The lieutenant was J. E. B. Stuart, who would go on to serve in the war as Robert E. Lee's brilliant commander of cavalry.

Time suddenly speeded up now. The marines rushed forward in two columns. Two of the burliest first tried to batter the door down with sledgehammers. When that failed, another party charged the weakened door, using a forty-foot ladder as a battering ram, breaking through on their second try. The soldiers poured through the breach. Two fell in the melee, one shot through the body and the other in the face. But Brown's men were overwhelmed. A marine impaled Indianan Jeremiah Anderson against a wall. Another bayoneted young Dauphin Thompson of North Elba where he lay under a fire engine. An officer stabbed at Brown with his sword, and with a second stroke actually lifted him off his feet, but failed to kill him. He then knocked the dazed old man to the ground and beat him unconscious with the hilt of his sword. Minutes after it had begun, the battle was over. Only Shields Green and one of the Quaker brothers from Iowa, Edward Coppoc, were captured unwounded. Of the nineteen men who had walked across the bridge into Harpers Ferry barely thirty-six hours before, five were now prisoners, and ten had been killed or fatally injured.

Having witnessed the capture of the engine house, Osborne Anderson and Hazlett slipped out the back of the armory, climbed a wall, and scuttled behind the embankment of the Baltimore & Ohio Railroad to the bank of the Shenandoah, where they found a boat, and, while attention was concentrated on the scene at the engine house, paddled across to the Maryland shore. Two more of the original group, including Brown's son Owen, played no part in the fighting, having been sent back to join the three men in Maryland before the battle commenced. Of the seven who managed to evade the debacle, two would be caught later in Pennsylvania, and eventually executed. Five would escape.

After the attack, panic swept like an electric charge through the network that had provided Brown with logistical and financial support. Hazlett and three men whom Brown had left behind to guard supplies were soon captured in Pennsylvania, and later extradited to Virginia. Jermain Loguen and Frederick Douglass destroyed whatever documents they had that might implicate them in Brown's plot, and fled to Canada, as did several of Brown's secret backers. Gerrit Smith collapsed with a nervous breakdown, becoming so "wild" with guilt and hallucinations that he committed himself to the insane asylum at Utica. William Still stayed at his post to assist the last of Brown's fleeing men, including Osborne Anderson, who appeared at his door in Philadelphia "footsore and powder begrimed," and put them on the Underground Railroad for Canada.

Harriet Tubman was in New York City when she learned that Brown's raid had failed. She remembered a strange dream that she had just before she met Brown for the first time. She was in "a wilderness sort of place, all full of rocks and bushes," when she saw a serpent lift its head among the rocks, and become transformed into the head of an old man with a white beard, gazing at her "wishful like, jes as ef he war gwine to speak to me." Two other heads rose up beside him, younger than he. As she stared back at them, a crowd of men rushed up and struck down first the younger heads and then the old man's. Only now did the dream finally make sense to her. She recognized the two younger serpents as Brown's sons, Watson and Oliver. The third, bearded serpent, looking toward her so hopefully, was John Brown himself.

On October 25, Brown and his six surviving men were charged with treason, first-degree murder, and "conspiring with Negroes to produce insurrection." They were tried at Charlestown, the county seat, ten miles from Harpers Ferry. All the charges carried the death penalty. The outcome was never in doubt. Throughout, Brown remained serene and unapologetic. From the Bible, he told the court, he had early learned to do unto others as he would have done unto himself: "It teaches me further to remember them that are in bonds, as bound with them. I endeavored to act up to that instruction . . . Now, if it is deemed necessary that I should forfeit my life for the furtherance of the ends of justice, and mingle my blood with the blood of millions in this slave country whose rights are disregarded by wicked, cruel, and unjust enactments, I say let it be done."

He met death stoically on the morning of December 2. At eleven o'clock, he was led out of the jail and seated on a small wagon carrying a white pine coffin. He handed a note to one of his guards: "I John Brown am now quite certain that the crimes of this *guilty land: will* never be purged away; but with blood. I had as I now think: vainly flattered myself that without very much bloodshed; it might be done." Escorted by six companies of infantry and a company of cavalry, he was driven to a scaffold that had been built for him in an open field. At about eleven-fifteen, a cloth sack was placed over his head, and the rope adjusted around his neck. Then, while he stood atop the trap door in a pair of bright red slippers, the soldiers marched and countermarched until their officers finally got them into position. Brown told his guard, "Don't keep me waiting longer than necessary." They were his last words. At eleven-thirty, the trap was pulled away, and with "a few slight struggles," he yielded up his life.

Shields Green and John Copeland were hanged two weeks later. Green, born and formerly enslaved in the South, falsely told the authorities that he had been born in Rochester, New York. In a sense, perhaps, he had been. He preferred to die remembered as a free man. The Oberlin graduate went silently to his death. Green engaged in loud and earnest prayer until the moment the trap opened beneath his feet and, as a reporter put it, he was "launched into eternity."

In death, John Brown did more to quicken the mind of America on the subject of slavery than any man of his time. "We shall be a thousand times more Anti-Slavery than we ever dared to think of being before," shouted the *Newburyport (Massachusetts) Herald.* In a deeply pious age, his death was viscerally understood as a martyrdom, a living part of the eternal Christian drama. "Some eighteen hundred years ago Christ was crucified," Henry David Thoreau opined, in a speech in Concord, on the day of Brown's execution. "This morning, perchance, Captain Brown was hung. These are the two ends of a chain which is not without its links. He is not Old Brown any longer; he is an angel of light."

Paranoid rumors of more insurrections raced through the South. Gun sellers made fortunes: in the four weeks after the raid, Baltimore dealers were reported to have sold ten thousand pistols to terrified Virginians. Northern schoolteachers, peddlers, and preachers were subjected to all manner of indignities. Real and apocryphal stories of persecution fed Northern rage. A planter was said to have forced his slaves to execute a Yankee evangelist who was found preaching to them. A peddler was said to have been strung up by the neck six times (but let down before he expired) on suspicion of being an abolitionist. In South Carolina, an Irish stone cutter was allegedly flogged, tarred, and feathered for daring to say that slave labor was degrading to white labor.

Brown, even before his death, was accused by many Americans of sheer madness for undertaking such a hopeless endeavor as the attack on Harpers Ferry. But if any American was seriously detached from reality in these waning years of peace, it was President Buchanan, ever an apologist for slavery. In his annual message to Congress, delivered barely two weeks after Brown's execution, Buchanan sounded a note of delusory optimism. Barely mentioning "the recent sad and bloody occurrences at Harpers Ferry," he implored Americans of North and South to "cultivate the ancient feelings of mutual forbearance and good will toward each other," and to allow agitation over slavery to "give place to other and less threatening controversies." He went on in his inimitable way, smugly reiterating his belief in the inalienable right of any American citizen to own slaves, and to carry them into any territory of the United States, rights which he praised as "so manifestly just in themselves and so well calculated to promote peace and harmony among the States."

Buchanan's words were, in their spineless way, a fitting epitaph for the age of slavery, for the long acquiescence of Northern political interests to the South. They were the last gasp of the "doughfaces," of the temporizers, hypocrites, and opportunists who had for generations helped to protect and preserve American slavery. What followed was Abraham Lincoln, secession, and war.

4

The work of the underground did not end with John Brown's capture and execution. Later in December, Governor Henry A. Wise of Virginia told the state legislature that the underground still posed a greater threat to slavery than John Brown's raid. "It is no solace to me," he said, "that our border slaves are so liberated by this exterior system, by this still, silent stealing system that they have no need to take up arms for their liberation." Slaves continued to flee their masters, and masters continued to hunt them down. Bold rescues still occurred: in April 1860, in Troy, New York, a crowd of thousands that included Harriet Tubman snatched the fugitive Charles Nalle from federal marshals. Federal commissioners would continue to remand recaptured fugitives into the hands of their owners as late as April 1861, just days before the outbreak of the Civil War. Even on the cusp of war, the "trains" of the Underground Railroad continued to run, and new recruits continued to join the clandestine ranks. One of the last was Arnold Gragston, a nineteen-year-old slave living in Mason County, Kentucky. Sometime in 1859, Gragston was "courtin'" on a neighboring plantation when the woman he was visiting told him that she knew a girl who wanted to cross the Ohio River to Ohio, and asked if he would take her. "I was scared and backed out in a hurry," Gragston told an interviewer, later in life. "But then I saw the girl, and she was such a pretty little thing, brown-skinned and kinda rosy, and lookin' as scared as I was feelin', so it wasn't long before I was listenin' to the old woman tell me when to take her and where to leave her on the other side." Gragston finally agreed to row the girl across to Ripley, Ohio, the following night. All the next day, however, his mind tossed back and forth between visions of his master "laying a rawhide across my back, or shootin' me," and of the desperate girl beseeching him with huge eyes.

"I don't know how I ever rowed the boat across the river—the current was strong and I was trembling," Gragston recalled. "I couldn't see a thing there in the dark, but I felt that girl's eyes." Where would he put her out of the boat? he worried. Would there be anyone there to meet them? Would it be a friend or enemy? Gragston had never been to Ohio, and knew nothing about the north bank of the river. "Well, pretty soon I saw a tall light and I remembered what the old lady had told me about looking for that light and rowing to it. I did, and when I got up to it, two men reached down and grabbed her." Gragston's entire body shook with terror. "Then one of the men took my arm and I just felt down inside of me that the Lord had got ready for me. 'You hungry boy?' is what he asked me, and if he hadn't been holdin' me I think I would have fell backward into the river."

Gragston overcame his fear and soon became a regular conductor, crossing the river three or four times a month, always on moonless nights, usually carrying two or three passengers in each load. But apart from his first passenger, the girl with the huge eyes, he never again saw the face of anyone he helped. He was given a password, "Menare," which he supposed was taken from the Bible, and with it he would identify his passengers, who would invariably meet him either in a darkened field or in an unlit house. He usually delivered them to a man whom he knew as "Mister Rankins," in Ripley. Although the Reverend John Rankin was still alive, and his home on the hill above Ripley was still illuminated at night with a light that Gragston "remembered" as a "lighthouse in his yard, about thirty feet high," the slave's contact was more likely one of the old minister's younger sons, who served as conductors in the years before the Civil War. Gragston came to relish the excitement and danger. And, like so many underground agents before him, he discovered that his courage had given him the power to bestow the gift of freedom. "Even though I could have been free any night myself," he said, "I figgered I wasn't getting along so bad so I would stay on Mr. Tabb's place and help the others get free."

Gragston was still a relative beginner in the underground when Abraham Lincoln was elected the first Republican president of the United States, on November 6, 1860. On December 20, South Carolina seceded from the Union, followed six weeks later by Mississippi, Florida, Alabama, Georgia, Louisiana, and Texas. In his inaugural address, Lincoln made clear his determination to preserve the Union, and stated that he neither intended to abolish slavery nor repeal the Fugitive Slave Law. But the time for reconciliation had run out. On April 12, 1861, South Carolina militiamen fired on Fort Sumter, in Charleston harbor. Immediately afterward, four more states—Virginia, Arkansas, North Carolina, and Tennessee—joined the Confederacy. About three hundred sixty thousand Union soldiers and two hundred sixty thousand Confederates would die before the war was over.

No matter what Lincoln said, slaves who had access to any news at all realized that the chaos of war offered their best chance ever to escape. The borderlands began hemorrhaging slaves. On April 9, 1861, three days before the attack on Fort Sumter, the *Detroit Daily Advertiser* reported that 300 fugitives had passed through the city en route to Canada within the previous few days, *190* of them on April 8 alone. Houses and churches in Windsor were filled to overflowing, and it was only with difficulty that sleeping space of any kind could be found for them. Any action that weakened the South became a patriotic cause. Recalled one Cleveland underground man, "the excitement was such that the most radical Democrats would contribute to assist fugitives."

Congress had almost unanimously declared in July 1861 that the purpose of the war was to defend the Constitution, not "overthrowing or interfering with the rights or established institutions" of the states. However, as early as May, General Benjamin Butler, the federal commander at Fortress Monroe, at the mouth of the James River, in Virginia, was forced to confront the problem of fugitives when a Confederate colonel insisted that he return slaves who had fled into Union lines. Butler, a New York lawyer, replied that the Fugitive Slave Law did not apply in "a foreign country, which Virginia claimed to be," and refused to yield them up. The War Department's equivocation on the issue became the most powerful tool of emancipation the nation had yet produced: Butler was ordered not to deliberately interfere with the "servants" of peaceful citizens, but permitted to allow "contraband" slaves into his lines, and to put them to work.

Without quite meaning to do so, the federal government had undertaken the work of the Underground Railroad on a scale that would help destroy the plantation economy of the Confederacy. John Brown's dream of a Subterranean Pass Way became an open highway wherever federal troops marched. Slaves poured by the thousands and tens of thousands into refugee camps behind Union lines. "The war ended the usefulness of the railroad," the Detroit underground leader William Lambert told an interviewer in 1886, adding that the last fugitive he saw passed through that city in April 1862. "The line of freedom crossed the lakes and moved south, keeping step by step with the battle line of the union." On January 1, 1863, Lincoln signed the Emancipation Proclamation, which freed slaves in all areas still in rebellion and not yet in Union hands. (However, it did not apply in slave states, such as Maryland and Kentucky, that had not seceded.) The proclamation was an open invitation to slaves to flee: what had once been treason was now government policy. That May, the Union began arming black troops.

As the lines of the Underground Railroad fell into disuse, its agents, conductors, and stationmasters offered themselves to the war effort. Five of John Rankin's sons and a grandson, all of them underground veterans, would serve in the Union forces. Frederick Douglass, Jermain Loguen, and Mary Ann Shadd Cary (she had married a black Canadian businessman) worked vigorously throughout the war to recruit black volunteers for the Union cause. Harriet Tubman, serving as a spy in Union-occupied South Carolina, would become the first woman in American history to lead a detachment of troops in battle. Josiah Henson's son Tom, who had taught him to read his first words, joined the Union navy, and was never heard from again. Joseph Hayden, who as a child had ridden out of slavery in Kentucky beneath the seat of the carriage driven by Calvin Fairbank, also saw service in the navy, on the Gulf Coast, and would die there in 1865. William Still resigned his job with the Philadelphia Anti-Slavery Office, and formed a company to supply coal to the Union army. Gerrit Smith, who recovered rapidly from his breakdown once the threat of prosecution was past, donated between twenty and twenty-five thousand dollars (between four hundred thousand and five hundred thousand dollars in present-day terms) to the U.S. Sanitary Commission and the Christian Commission, to provide soldiers with medical care and Bibles on the front lines. Levi Coffin and many other Quakers worked heroically to improve living conditions in the often appallingly unsanitary refugee camps where so many "contrabands" lived out the war.

By 1863 the western battlefront had moved deep into Tennessee and Mississippi. But Kentucky remained an anomaly. Since it had never seceded from the Union, the federal government was scrupulous in respecting its laws, including those upholding slavery. Indeed, poor Calvin Fairbank, who had been arrested for "abducting" the slave Tamar, in 1851, was still in the state penitentiary thirteen years later, having endured during that time more than one thousand beatings, and a total of 35,105 stripes from a leather strap (he maintained a record). He was not released until 1864, by special order of the governor.

Bypassed by the war, Arnold Gragston continued his clandestine trips across the Ohio River. Although his nocturnal activities took an obvious toll on his daytime work, his master never asked him what he had been doing. Gragston suspected, in fact, that he might actually be some kind of "secret abolitionist" himself. "Sometimes," he speculated, "I think he did know and wanted me to get the slaves away that way so he wouldn't have to cause hard feelin's by freein' 'em." Although Gragston never kept count, he guessed that he carried hundreds of fugitives across the river during the four years that he served the underground. However, one night in 1863, after rowing a cargo of fugitives to Ohio, he was spotted as he stepped back onto the Kentucky shore and, fearing that he was finally about to be caught, took to a fugitive's life in the fields and woods.

Gragston was his own last passenger. "Finally I saw that I could never do any more good in Mason County, so I decided to take my freedom, too," Gragston recalled. "I had a wife by this time, and one night we quietly slipped across and headed for Mr. Rankins' bell and light. It looked like we had to go almost to China to get across the river; I could hear the bell and see the light on Mr. Rankins' place, but the harder I rowed, the farther away it got, and I knew if I didn't make it I'd get killed. But finally I pulled up by the lighthouse, and went on to my freedom." It is possible that his journey north was the last triumphant escape on the Underground Railroad.

There was, of course, no official termination to the Underground Railroad. But if ever it had a symbolic end, it can be said to have come in April 1870, when blacks throughout the United States celebrated the passage of the Fifteenth Amendment, which extended suffrage to African Americans. At a huge interracial rally in Cincinnati, seventy-three-year-old Levi Coffin publicly relinquished the title of "president" of the Underground Railroad that had been conferred on him thirty years earlier by Southern slave hunters. "Our underground work is done," he declared, "and as we have no more use for the road, I would suggest that the rails be taken up and disposed of, and the proceeds appropriated for the education of the freed slaves."

On the same day, in Detroit, George DeBaptiste placed a sign in his store window that read: "Notice to Stockholders of the Underground Railroad: This office is closed. Hereafter all stockholders will receive dividends according to their merits."

EPILOGUE

On March 10, 1913, Harriet Tubman died from pneumonia in the institution she had founded for aged and indigent African Americans at her home, in Auburn, New York. She had devoted much of the later years of her life to painstakingly raising funds for its establishment, a far less colorful labor than her years as a conductor on the Underground Railroad, but heroic in its own way, and consistent to the end with her lifelong devotion to the welfare of her people. In her ninety-one years, she had endured more privation and danger than almost any of her friends in the underground, yet she had outlived them all.

Thomas Garrett, who had declared after his conviction for harboring fugitives that he would go home and add another story to his house so that he could shelter more, was the first to go, in January 1871, at the age of eighty-one. Former fugitives whom he had helped to freedom were among the fifteen hundred people who crowded the Friends Meeting House in Wilmington, Delaware, for his funeral.

Jermain Loguen was next. After the Civil War, he traveled widely through Kentucky and Tennessee, preaching and setting up schools and churches for newly freed slaves, with the same whirlwind energy that he had brought to his underground work in Syracuse. In 1868 he was appointed a bishop of the AME Zion Church. Four years later, while preparing to set out for the Pacific Coast for a new round of missionary work, he died of tuberculosis, at the mineral springs near Saratoga, New York. He was about fifty-five years old.

Gerrit Smith continued his philanthropy in the years after the postwar period, including large donations to newly founded Howard University, for the education of African Americans. When he died suddenly from a stroke just after Christmas 1874, at the age of seventy-seven, the *New York Times* declared: "The history of the most important half-century of our national life will be imperfectly written if it fails to place Gerrit Smith in the front rank of the men whose influence was most felt in the accomplishment of its results."

George DeBaptiste opened a catering business after the war. In his obituary, the *Detroit Tribune* noted that he "labored zealously for the improvement of the colored people of this city," and especially for the desegregation of Detroit's public schools. He died from cancer of the stomach, in February 1875. He was about sixty years old.

Levi Coffin continued to work for the welfare of former slaves, twice traveling to Europe to raise money for the Freedmen's Aid Commission. After a long illness, he died in September 1877, at the age of seventy-nine. At his funeral, heavily attended by both black and white Cincinnatians, a relative, Charles Coffin, said of him, "The great question with him was not, is it popular, but is it right?"

The hardy Yankee seaman Jonathan Walker, the "Man with the Branded Hand," died almost completely forgotten, in April 1878, at his home in Muskegon, Michigan, where he had eked out a living as a fruit farmer. He was seventy-nine.

Josiah Henson remained popular as a preacher at both black and white camp meetings in Canada. During a visit to England in 1877, he was introduced to Queen Victoria as Harriet Beecher Stowe's "Uncle Tom," a public role that he came to relish in his later years. He preached his final sermon at the age of ninety-four, on the last Sunday of April 1883. Three days later, he collapsed. At dawn on May 5, he lay in bed surrounded by children and grandchildren. He whispered to them before he died, "I couldn't stay if I would, nor I wouldn't if I could."

Reverend John Rankin's last months were spent in agony resulting from a cancer that slowly ate away his face, and entered his brain. He died in March 1886, aged ninety-three. He was buried in Ripley, Ohio, where from his hilltop home he had assisted so many refugees from slavery. A poem was read at his funeral: "Dear hero of our age, thy work is o'er/ Thou canst and needst no more thy warfare wage."

In 1873 Lewis Hayden, the leader of the Shadrach rescue, became one of the first African Americans to be elected to a Northern state legislature, in Massachusetts. He remained an active community leader in Boston until his death in April 1889, when he was about seventy-eight years old.

George DeBaptiste's coleader of the Detroit underground, William Lambert, continued to prosper in the tailoring business, eventually amassing a fortune of seventy thousand dollars. Toward the end of his life he became increasingly irrational, and in newspaper interviews claimed that "nearly 1,000,000 free negroes" had been inducted into the "secret rituals" of the underground, and that he had assisted 40,000 fugitives to freedom through Detroit. In 1890, at the age of seventy-one, he hanged himself.

Mary Ann Shadd Cary remained passionate and confrontational on behalf of civil rights causes for the rest of her life. In 1869 she was the first woman to enroll in the law school of Howard University. Five years later, she was among the first group of suffragettes to attempt, though without success, to vote in the District of Columbia. She was a popular feminist speaker until her death, at the age of seventy, in 1893.

Frederick Douglass lived long enough to see many of the gains that African Americans had made as a result of the Civil War undone by the politics of Jim Crow. An ardent supporter of the Republican Party after the war, he was rewarded with appointment as federal marshal for the District of Columbia by President Rutherford B. Hayes, and he later served as U.S. ambassador to Haiti. At the age of seventy-seven, on February 20, 1895, he returned home from a women's rights convention in Washington, chatted for a while with his wife, then gasped, clapped a hand over his heart, and fell to the floor. Within twenty minutes, he was dead.

William Still's coal business flourished, and he eventually became a prominent figure in Philadelphia business circles, serving as a member of the city's Board of Trade, founding one of the first YMCAs for young African Americans, and lending his support to numerous charitable causes. He died of a heart attack in 1902, aged eighty-one.

With the death of Harriet Tubman, the living memory of the Underground Railroad passed into the realm of legend. But by then its real meaning had already been forgotten, as commitments made to the freed slaves were sacrificed to political expediency, and reconciliation among whites became more important than redress for the damage done to blacks by slavery. Even most abolitionists shared the laissez-faire philosophy of their time, and with it the assumption that slaves, once freed, ought to be able to make their own way in the open market without additional assistance from whites. With the abandonment of Reconstruction in the 1870s, the nation's best chance to create the conditions for black economic and political equality were lost. The idealism of the antebellum era gave way to the revisionist mythology of the South's "Lost Cause," and the heroic role of African Americans in the Underground Railroad (and the Civil War) was consigned to a footnote in the nation's collective memory. By the twentieth century, when the Underground Railroad was remembered at all, it was usually as a kind of national fairy tale, in which the fugitives themselves were cast only as bit players, and abolitionists stripped of their disturbing radicalism. Only in recent years have historians and local researchers, many of them African American, begun to chip away the encrustation of myth that encases the Underground Railroad, to reveal this extraordinary chapter in the nation's history.

Looking back from the perspective of a century and a half, the meanings of the Underground Railroad seem both subtle and varied. Its most important achievement, obviously, was helping tens of thousands of enslaved Americans on their way to freedom. Just how many, however, is still uncertain. Every Southerner who lost a slave tended to blame the Underground Railroad. In the 1850s slave state census records reported about one thousand runaways per year, and on the eve of secession, a New Orleans newspaper asserted that 1,500 slaves had escaped from the South every year for the previous half century, at a cost of at least forty million dollars, more than one billion dollars in present-day terms. Not all slave escapes were recorded, but neither did all fugitives necessarily find their way to the Underground Railroad, or even to the free states. Modern estimates of the number of fugitives assisted by the underground between 1830 and 1860 range from 70,000 to 100,000, of whom perhaps one-third or one-quarter were delivered to Canada. When the often neglected period from 1800 to 1830 is added in, the total must be increased somewhat, but it is unlikely that the underground handled more than 150,000 passengers, at the outside, and 100,000 may be much closer to the mark.

It is similarly difficult to determine just how many Americans participated in the Underground Railroad. Its first historian, Wilbur Siebert, in his 1898 work *The Underground Railroad from Slavery to Freedom*, identified 3,211 individuals by name, nearly all of them white men. But he failed to take into account the large numbers of African Americans—possibly the majority—who risked their lives to help fugitives, or the fact that women who provided refugees with food, clothing, and advice were as much a part of the underground as were their husbands and brothers. There were, in addition, numerous support personnel, such as lawyers, businessmen, and the suppliers of clothing, who may not have harbored or conducted fugitives, but were essential to the system's operation. At a minimum, three or four times the number estimated by Siebert must actually have worked intimately in the Underground Railroad.

But the importance of the underground cannot be judged just by numbers, or even by the inspiring quality of its great saga of dramatic escapes, recaptures, and feats of individual courage. The Underground Railroad came into existence in an America in which democracy was the property of white men alone, and in which free as well as enslaved blacks lived under conditions that had more in common with what we today call totalitarianism than many Americans might care to admit. The nation's founders, as W. E. B. DuBois once wrote, made a Faustian bargain with the evil of slavery, "truckling, and compromising with a moral, political, and economic monstrosity," in the hope that the democracy they invented would never have to pay a price for their accommodations. The abolitionist movement and its driving wedge, the Underground Railroad, forced Americans to think in new ways about that history of compromise, to face its moral consequences, and to realize that *all* Americans were, in some sense, prisoners to slavery, and shackled to the fate of the slave. Without the confrontational activists of the underground, the abolitionist movement might never have become anything more than a vast lecture hall in which right-minded, white Americans could comfortably agree that slavery was evil.

Abolitionism taught the country that the problem of race was not on the margins but at the center of its national story. In the underground, blacks and whites discovered each other for the first time as allies in a common struggle, learning to rely on each other not as master on slave, or child on parent, but as fellow soldiers in a war that most Americans did not yet even know had begun. Apart from the lives saved, the underground's greatest achievement may have been its creation of a truly free zone of interracial activity where blacks not only directed complex logistical and financial operations, but also, in some places, supervised support networks that included white men and women who were accorded no special status owing to their skin color. Perhaps more than any other aspect of our mostly disheartening racial heritage, the story of the Underground Railroad thus stands as an answer to slavery's legacy of hurt and shame, reminding us that our ancestors were not always enemies across an unbridgeable chasm of color, and that even a century and a half ago, we were capable of heroic collaboration.

By understanding how Americans participated in and reacted to the Underground Railroad, we can better understand the difficulties that a society based on law rather than on passions and power has always had in coping with political movements that challenge its most basic assumptions. The underground was the greatest movement of civil disobedience since the American Revolution, engaging thousands of citizens in the active subversion of federal law and the prevailing mores of their communities. Isaac Hopper, David Ruggles, Levi Coffin, Jermain Loguen, and the others were the forerunners of twentieth-century labor organizers, civil rights activists, antiwar protestors of the Vietnam era, and for that matter such contemporary provocateurs as Earth First! and those who take to the streets to protest globalization. Not least, they were also the progenitors of the modern women's movement. As part of the struggle to free the slaves, Northern women began to discover the nature of their own servitude as women, and in speaking out on behalf of enslaved African Americans, they discovered their own voices and began for the first time to challenge the preconceptions and laws that governed their place in society.

While the Underground Railroad and the larger abolitionist movement clearly made a profound contribution to progressive politics by attacking racial discrimination and asserting for the first time that each individual had a personal responsibility for others' human rights, it is less obvious that it was also the seedbed of religious activism in American politics. Most members of the underground uncompromisingly regarded their work as answering only to a law higher and more sacred than those enacted by mere men. In this, they were hardly different from modern activists who today cite the same "higher law" to justify their attacks against abortion clinics. Indeed, as a lawyer representing the "pro-life" organization Project Rescue declared in court a few years ago, asserting his clients' moral responsibility to disobey unjust laws, "The slave-holding industry had the law on its side, just as today the abortion industry has the law on its side." The story of the Underground Railroad thus sheds light on, if it fails to answer, uneasy questions about what happens when revealed religion collides with a secular society that shares neither its politics nor its reading of the Scriptures.

The deeply pious activists of the underground would surely find much to disappoint them in the materialistic, not to say hedonistic, United States of the present-day. But their faith was also balanced by generous idealism, and by an uncompromising devotion to the rights of others. In their hearts and their actions, they were democrats of the deepest sort, for whom the nation's highest ideals were a living spirit that required almost daily personal self-sacrifice in order to be made real. The moral machinery that they set in motion would continue to power the ongoing effort to ensure fairness and equality for all Americans: a century later, their descendants would see the ultimate fruits of the struggle they began, in the triumph of the civil rights movement of the 1950s and 1960s. Though ridiculed, persecuted, and sometimes murdered for their efforts, the men and women of the underground strove always to compel government to take the moral measure of its decisions. Doing do, they set a standard of principle that few governments are able to reach, but nonetheless one that only the cynical and the foolhardy would dare to mock: that temporizing and unprincipled compromise on civil rights can be risked only at the peril of damaging the nation's soul.

NOTES

INTRODUCTION

Page

1 *The barber has done:* Interview with George DeBaptiste, "Underground Railroad: Reminiscences of the Days of Slavery," *Detroit Post*, May 16, 1870.

2 *White vigilantes sometimes attack:* Diane Perrine Coon, "Reconstructing the Underground Railroad Crossings at Madison, Indiana" (unpublished paper, 1998, University of Louisville, copy made available by its author); Drusilla Cravens, "African-Americans in and Around Jefferson County, Ind.," typescript compilation of articles and transcribed notes (Madison, Ind.: Jefferson County Historical Society, n.d.), pp. 31 ff.; and W. W. Woolen, letter to the editor, *Madison* (Indiana) *Weekly Courier*, February 18, 1880.

2 *George DeBaptiste, the man:* Coon, "Reconstructing the Underground Railroad Crossings"; also in Diane Perrine Coon, "Southeastern Indiana's Underground Railroad Routes and Operations" (unpublished study for the Indiana Department of Natural Resources, Indianapolis, 2001); Cravens, scrapbook, pp. 12–13, and interview with George DeBaptiste, "Underground Railroad," *Detroit Post*, May 16, 1870.

3 *"slavery has become a language":* Ira Berlin, "Overcome by Slavery," *New York Times*, July 13, 2001, op-ed page.

5 *The method of operating:* Isaac Beck, interview with Wilbur H. Siebert, December 26, 1892, Wilbur H. Siebert Collection, Ohio Historical Society, Columbus, Ohio.

6 *"Woman [is] more fully identified":* quoted in Geoffrey C. Ward and Ken Burns, *Not for Ourselves Alone: The Story of Elizabeth Cady Stanton and Susan B. Anthony* (New York: Knopf, 1999), p. 92.

Chapter 1: An Evil Without Remedy

Page

11 *Josiah Henson's earliest memory:* The description of Henson's youth is based on Josiah Henson, *The Life of Josiah Henson* (Boston: Arthur D. Phelps, 1849), pp. 1–9, and Josiah Henson, *Uncle Tom's Story of His Life from 1789 to 1879* (Boston: B. B. Russell, 1879), pp. 1–17.

14 *Isaac Riley, who was to shape Josiah:* Henson file, Montgomery County tax records, Montgomery County Historical Society, Rockville, MD.

14 *Like most of Montgomery County:* Ray Eldon Hiebert and Richard K. MacMaster, *A Grateful Remembrance: The Story of Montgomery County* (Rockville, Md.: Montgomery County Historical Society, 1976).

15 *North American slavery was born:* Peter Kolchin, *American Slavery 1619 to 1877* (New York: Hill and Wang, 1995), pp. 8–11.

16 *As tobacco production expanded:* Ibid., pp. 26–27.

16 *black slaves in Connecticut:* "Connecticut as a Slave State," *Connecticut Western News*, May 23, 1916.

16 *"The Negro Business":* Mills Lane, introduction to *A South-Side View of Slavery*, by Nehemiah Adams (Savannah: Beehive Press, 1974), p. x.

16 *Commercial trade in all kinds:* Daniel P. Mannix and Malcolm Cowley, *Black Cargoes: A History of the Atlantic Slave Trade* (New York: Viking Compass, 1965), pp. 56–58, 32–33.

16 *Slaves came in many varieties:* Ibid., pp. 14–19.

17 *Olaudah Equiano:* Olaudah Equiano, "The Life of Olaudah Equiano," in *The Classic Slave Narratives*, Henry Louis Gates, Jr., ed. (New York: Mentor, 1987), p. 33.

17 *The slave trade could be immensely profitable:* Anthony Burton, *The Rise and Fall of King Cotton* (London: British Broadcasting Corporation, 1984), pp. 57–58; and Mannix and Cowley, *Black Cargoes*, p. 74.

17 *By the time of the American Revolution:* John C. Miller, *The Wolf by the Ears: Thomas Jefferson and American Slavery* (Charlottesville: University Press of Virginia, 1991), p. 9.

18 *Slave ships sailing from Charleston:* Mannix and Cowley, *Black Cargoes*, p. 160; Hugh Thomas, *The Slave Trade: The Story of the Atlantic Slave Trade 1440–1870* (New York: Simon & Schuster, 1997), pp. 260–61, 271.

18 *the Brown family of Providence:* Sasha Polakow-Suransky, "Sins of Our Fathers," *Brown Alumni Magazine* (July/August 2003), pp. 36–42; Thomas, *Slave Trade*, p. 261.

18 *"We left Anamaboe":* George Francis Dow, *Slave Ships and Slaving* (Mineola, N.Y.: Dover, 2002), p. 257.

19 *On board ship:* Mannix and Cowley, *Black Cargoes*, p. 106; and Joseph Story, "A Charge Delivered to the Grand Jury of the Circuit of the United States . . . for the Judicial District of Maine, May 8, 1820," in *Against Slavery: An Abolitionist Reader*, Mason Lowance, ed. (New York: Penguin, 2000), pp. 35–36; and Dow, *Slave Ships and Slaving*, p. 206.

19 *Olaudah Equiano, who was transported:* Equiano, "Life of Olaudah Equiano," pp. 34–35.

19 *Normal mortality:* Mannix and Cowley, *Black Cargoes*, p. 123; and Story, "Charge Delivered to the Grand Jury," pp. 35–36.

19 *If there was an emergency:* Mannix and Cawley, *Black Cargoes*, pp. 125–26; and Dow, *Slave Ships and Slaving*, p. 206.

20 *During the entire span:* Kolchin, *American Slavery*, p. 22–23.

20 *"Abraham Seixes":* quoted in Burton, *Rise and Fall of King Cotton*, p. 59.

21 *Part of Brown's job:* William Wells Brown, "Narrative of William W. Brown, a Fugitive Slave," in *I Was Born a Slave: An Anthology of Classic Slave Narratives*, vol. 1, Yuval Taylor, ed. (Chicago: Lawrence Hill, 1999), pp. 693–94.

21 *When demand was high:* Mannix and Cowley, *Black Cargoes*, p. 169.

21 *One auction:* Anonymous travel journal of a New Yorker in the South, Southern History Collection, University of North Carolina, Chapel Hill.

21 *George Whitfield:* Lane, introduction to *South-Side View of Slavery*, by Nehemiah Adams, p. ix.

22 *Philadelphia botanist William Bartram:* William Bartram, *Travels of William Bartram* (New York: Dover, 1955), p. 257.

22 *In 1790:* Mason Lowance, ed., *Against Slavery: An Abolitionist Reader* (New York: Penguin, 2000), p. 8.

22 *Within the common denominator:* Kolchin, *American Slavery*, p. 105; and Charles S. Sydnor, *Slavery in Mississippi* (Baton Rouge: Louisiana State University Press, 1933), p. 120.

22 *In the estuaries:* David S. Cecelski, *The Waterman's Song: Slavery and Freedom in Maritime North Carolina* (Chapel Hill: University of North Carolina Press, 2001), p. 136.

22 *Hired-out slaves:* John Hope Franklin and Loren Schweniger, *Runaway Slaves: Rebels on the Plantation* (New York: Oxford University Press, 1999), p. 35; and Henry Box Brown, *Narrative of the Life of Henry Box Brown* (New York: Oxford University Press, 2002), p. 30.

22 *As far north as New England:* Kolchin, *American Slavery*, pp. 26–27.

23 *Slaves might be property:* Burton, *Rise and Fall of King Cotton*, pp. 60–61.

23 *Disciplining slaves:* Ibid., p. 127; Austin Steward, *Twenty-two Years as a Slave and Forty Years a Freeman* (Syracuse, N.Y.: Syracuse University Press, 2002), p. 9; and Sydnor, *Slavery in Mississippi*, pp. 122–23.

23 *planter William Byrd:* Kolchin, *American Slavery*, pp. 57–59.

23 *Boston King:* Edward Ball, *Slaves in the Family* (New York: Ballantine, 1999), p. 225.

23 *Equiano was terrified:* Equiano, "Life of Olaudah Equiano," p. 39.

23 *a Georgia plantation:* Lane, introduction to *South-Side View of Slavery*, by Nehemiah Adams, p. xvii.

24 *William Dunbar:* Bernard Bailyn, *Voyagers to the West: A Passage in the Peopling of America on the Eve of the Revolution* (New York: Vintage, 1988), p. 491.

24 *flogging was also widely practiced:* Stephen B. Oates, *To Purge This Land with Blood: A Biography of John Brown* (Amherst: University of Massachusetts Press, 1984), pp. 8, 24.

24 *The punishment of slaves:* Kolchin, *American Slavery*, pp. 7, 57–59; Kenneth M. Stampp, *The Peculiar Institution: Slavery in the Ante-Bellum South* (New York: Vintage, 1956), pp. 182–88.

24 *Moses Roper's owner:* Moses Roper, "A Narrative of the Adventures and Escape of Moses Roper, from American Slavery," in *I Was Born a Slave*, pp. 686–87.

24 *The harshest punishments:* Bailyn, *Voyagers to the West*, p. 491.

24 *The French-American farmer and author:* J. Hector St. John de Crèvecoeur, *Letters from an American Farmer* (New York: Oxford University Press, 1997), pp. 163–64.

25 *Late-eighteenth-century advertisements: Virginia Gazette*, Williamsburg, April 17, 1752; June 5, 1752; September 22, 1774; October 10, 1774; May 10, 1776; May 11, 1776; May 18, 1776; May 24, 1776; September 22, 1774; September 29, 1774; November 10, 1774; December 1, 1774; December 8, 1774; "Fugitive Slave Advertisements 1737–1776," compiled by Thomas Costa, University of Virginia at Wise, viewed on-line at http://etext.lib.virginia.edu\subjects\runaways\all-records.

26 *The United States Constitution:* Wilbur H. Siebert, *The Underground Railroad from Slavery to Freedom* (London: Macmillan, 1898), pp. 293–94; and Marion G. McDougall, *Fugitive Slaves (1619–1865)* (Boston: Ginn & Co., 1891), pp. 14, 105.

26 *Slavery in some form:* Lane, introduction to *South-Side View of Slavery*, by Nehemiah Adams, p. x; and Kolchin, *American Slavery*, p. 30.

26 *The story of James Mars:* The Mars family's story is drawn from James Mars, "The Life of James Mars, a Slave Born and Sold in Connecticut," in *I Was Born a Slave: An Anthology of Classic Slave Narratives*, vol. 2, Yuval Taylor, ed. (Chicago: Lawrence Hill, 1999), pp. 726–37; Horatio T. Strother, "The Underground

Railroad in Connecticut" (Middletown, Conn.: Wesleyan University Press, 1962), pp. 14–18, 126; Theron Wilmot Crissey, *History of Norfolk* (Everett: Massachusetts Publishing Co., 1900), pp. 81, 129, 370; and Norfolk town historians Richard Byrne and Kay Fields, interview with the author, Norfolk, Conn., July 23, 2002.

Chapter 2: The Fate of Millions Unborn

Page

29 *Montgomery County's local newspaper: National Intelligencer*, March 2, March 4, and March 6, 1801.

30 *A little before noon:* Alf Mapp, Jr., *Thomas Jefferson: Passionate Pilgrim* (Lanham, Md.: Madison Books, 1991), p. 2; Bernard Mayo, *Jefferson Himself* (Charlottesville: University Press of Virginia, 1942), p. 219; Fawn M. Brodie, *Thomas Jefferson: An Intimate History* (New York: W. W. Norton, 1974), p. 336–37; Samuel Eliot Morison, *The Oxford History of the American People*, vol. 2 (New York: Mentor, 1972), p. 85; and David L. Lewis, *District of Columbia: A Bicentennial History* (New York: W. W. Norton, 1976), pp. 3 ff.

30 *a simple rural nation:* George Dangerfield, *The Awakening of American Nationalism, 1815–1828* (New York: Harper & Row, 1965), p. 17.

30 *the worst defeat:* Allan W. Eckert, *That Dark and Bloody River: Chronicles of the Ohio River Valley* (New York: Bantam, 1995), pp. 567–68.

31 *The prospect of Jefferson's election:* Mayo, *Jefferson Himself*, p. 220; and Morison, *Oxford History*, p. 85.

31 *an "absolute terrorist":* Jean Edward Smith, *John Marshall: Definer of a Nation* (New York: Henry Holt, 1996), p. 19.

31 *When he began to speak:* Brodie, *Thomas Jefferson*, pp. 336–37.

31 *"We are all Republicans":* Thomas Jefferson, "First Inaugural Address," in *Thomas Jefferson: Writings*, Merrill D. Peterson, ed. (New York: Library of America, 1984), pp. 492–94.

32 *"mild and pleasing countenance":* E. M. Halliday, *Understanding Thomas Jefferson* (New York: HarperCollins, 2001), p. 46.

32 *He was an aristocrat:* Miller, *Wolf by the Ears*, p. 2.

32 *Slavery was woven:* Jefferson, "Notes on the State of Virginia," in Peterson, Thomas Jefferson: *Writings*, pp. 264ff; Brodie, *Thomas Jefferson*, pp. 228–34; and Halliday, *Understanding Thomas Jefferson*, pp. 86 ff.

32 *Jefferson's enemies accused:* Miller, *Wolf by the Ears*, p. 162.

32 *"Of all the damsels":* H. W. Brands, "Founders Chic," *Atlantic Monthly*, September 2003, pp. 101–10.

32 *Hemings's descendants cited:* Annette Gordon-Reed, *Thomas Jefferson and Sally Hemings: An American Controversy* (Charlottesville: University Press of Virginia,

1997), pp. 210 ff.; Halliday, *Understanding Thomas Jefferson*, pp. 86 ff, Miller, *Wolf by the Ears*, p. 169; and Lucia Stanton, *Slavery at Monticello* (Monticello, VA: Thomas Jefferson Memorial Foundation, 1996), pp. 21–22.

34 *Jefferson held no illusions:* Miller, *Wolf by the Ears*, p. 95.

34 *"The whole commerce":* Jefferson, "Notes on the State of Virginia," in Peterson, *Thomas Jefferson: Writings*, pp. 289 ff.

34 *an ingrained repugnance:* Ibid., p. 270, 264–67; and Miller, *Wolf by the Ears*, p. 52, 64.

35 *Jefferson was by no means alone:* Henry Steele Commager, *The Empire of Reason: How Europe Imagined and America Realized the Enlightenment* (Garden City, NY: Anchor, 1978), p. 24.

35 *a pseudo-scientific approach:* Leon Polyakov, *The Aryan Myth: A History of Racist and Nationalist Ideas in Europe* (New York: New American Library, 1974), p. 241.

35 *David Hume:* Miller, *Wolf by the Ears*, p. 51.

35 *Even John Locke:* Robert William Fogel and Stanley L. Engerman, *Time on the Cross: The Economics of American Negro Slavery* (New York: W. W. Norton, 1989), p. 31.

36 *"the child can demonstrate":* Polyakov, *Aryan Myth*, p. 145.

36 *James Otis argued:* Bernard Bailyn, *The Ideological Origins of the American Revolution* (Cambridge, Mass.: Harvard University Press, 1992), p. 237.

36 *Tom Paine wrote:* Thomas Paine, *Rights of Man* (New York: Penguin Books, 1982), p. 88.

36 *Alexander Hamilton, who:* Miller, *Wolf by the Ears*, p. 24.

36 *In 1641 Massachusetts:* Mannix and Cowley, *Black Cargoes*, pp. 171–72.

37 *Quakers were beginning:* John M. Moore, ed., *Friends in the Delaware Valley: Philadelphia Yearly Meeting, 1681–1981* (Haverford, Pa.: Friends Historical Association, 1981), pp. 31–32.

37 *Lord Chief Justice Mansfield:* Thomas, *Slave Trade*, p. 476.

37 *British abolitionists:* Ibid., pp. 493–94, 507; Mannix and Cowley, *Black Cargoes*, pp. 176–79; and Eric Williams, *Capitalism and Slavery* (New York: Capricorn Books, 1966), pp. 178–80.

37 *Patrick Henry regarded:* Beverly B. Munford, *Virginia's Attitude Toward Slavery and Secession* (New York: Longmans, Green, 1910), p. 83.

37 *Richard Henry Lee:* Ibid., p. 82.

37 *No man had been more consistent:* Miller, *Wolf by the Ears*, pp. 5, 8.

37 *"We hold these truths":* Declaration of Independence, in *Against Slavery: An Abolitionist Reader*, Mason Lowance, ed. (New York: Penguin, 2000), p. 28.

38 *In 1784 Jefferson:* Thomas Jefferson, "Report of a Plan of Government for the Western Territory," in *The Portable Thomas Jefferson*, Merrill D. Peterson, ed. (New York: Penguin Books, 1975), p. 255.

38 *Had Jefferson's plan:* Miller, *Wolf by the Ears*, pp. 27–28.

38 *Anxiety about slavery:* Merton L. Dillon, *The Abolitionists: The Growth of a Dissenting Minority* (De Kalb: Northern Illinois University Press, 1974), pp. 40–41.

39 *A Vermont judge:* Horatio T. Strother, *The Underground Railroad in Connecticut* (Middletown, Conn.: Wesleyan University Press, Middletown, 1962), p. 22.

39 *By the last decade:* Miller, *Wolf by the Ears*, p. 120.

39 *The president of Yale:* Strother, *Underground Railroad in Connecticut*, p. 22; "Connecticut as a Slave State," *Connecticut Western News*, May 23, 1916.

39 *In New York:* Edwin G. Burrows and Mike Wallace, *Gotham: A History of New York to 1898* (New York: Oxford University Press, 1998), p. 285.

39 *a spate of state legislation:* Kenneth M. Stampp, *The Peculiar Institution: Slavery in the Ante-Bellum South* (New York: Vintage, 1956), p. 25.

40 *most Northern states:* Miller, *Wolf by the Ears*, p. 218; and Kolchin, *American Slavery*, p. 78.

40 *Quaker and Methodist lobbying:* Gary B. Nash, *Forging Freedom: The Formation of Philadelphia's Black Community 1720–1840* (Cambridge, Mass.: Harvard University Press, 1988), p. 138.

40 *In Delaware:* Kolchin, *American Slavery*, p. 241.

40 *"However well disposed":* quoted in McDougall, *Fugitive Slaves*, p. 36.

40 *"The spirit of the master":* Jefferson, "Notes on the State of Virginia," pp. 288–89.

40 *The handiwork of a Yankee:* Material on Eli Whitney is based on David Cohn, *The Life and Times of King Cotton* (New York: Oxford University Press, 1956), pp. 7, 10–11; and Burton, *Rise and Fall of King Cotton*, pp. 61–63.

42 *American cotton exports:* John C. Miller, *The Federalist Era, 1789–1801* (New York: Harper & Row, 1960), p. 177; Dangerfield, *Awakening of American Nationalism*, p. 104; Cohn, *Life and Times of King Cotton*, pp. 44–45; and Sydnor, *Slavery in Mississippi*, pp. 183–84.

42 *Georgia would tally:* Lane, introduction to *South-Side View of Slavery*, by Nehemiah Adams, p. xi.

42 *Slave traders made fortunes:* Kolchin, *American Slavery*, p. 98; Sydnor, *Slavery in Mississippi*, pp. 186–88; and Coleman, *Slavery Times in Kentucky*, pp. 143–45.

42 *"A plantation well stocked":* Sydnor, *Slavery in Mississippi*, p. 186.

43 *a drop in the demographic bucket:* Lowance, *Against Slavery*, p. 8.

43 *As idealism collided:* Miller, *Wolf by the Ears*, p. 37; Kolchin, *American Slavery*, p. 91; Miller, *Federalist Era*, pp. 133, 139; Dillon, *Abolitionists*, pp. 46, 51.

43 *"we shall be the murderers":* quoted in Miller, *Federalist Era*, p. 133.

43 *"brave sons of Africa":* quoted in Dillon, *Abolitionists*, p. 48.

44 *a "Negro war":* Ibid.

44 *the rebels' plan:* Ibid., p. 59.

44 *"Where there is any reason":* Miller, *Wolf by the Ears*, p. 127.

44 *In the aftermath:* Kolchin, *American Slavery*, p. 90.

44 *In North Carolina:* Stephen B. Weeks, *Southern Quakers and Slavery* (Baltimore: Johns Hopkins Press, 1896), p. 222.

44 *also be reenslaved:* Miller, *Wolf by the Ears*, pp. 87–88.

44 *Between 1765 and 1800:* Nash, *Forging Freedom*, pp. 38, 143.

45 *In New York:* Burrows and Wallace, *Gotham*, p. 347.

45 *"on the Pennsylvania road":* Nash, *Forging Freedom*, p. 138.

45 *an unnamed mulatto:* Burrows and Wallace, *Gotham*, pp. 347–48.

Chapter 3: A Gadfly in Philadelphia

Page

46 *A genial New Jersey farm boy:* Lydia Maria Child, *Isaac T. Hopper: A True Life* (Boston: John P. Jewett & Co., 1853), pp. 33–35, 248; and Margaret Hope Bacon, *Lamb's Warrior: The Life of Isaac T. Hopper* (New York: Thomas Y. Crowell, 1970), pp. 7–9.

47 *Nowhere in the United States:* Billy G. Smith, ed., *Life in Early Philadelphia: Documents from the Revolutionary and Early National Periods* (University Park: Pennsylvania State University Press, 1995), pp. 3–11, 34–36; Child, *Isaac T. Hopper*, p. 147; Gary B. Nash, *First City: Philadelphia and the Forging of Historical Memory* (Philadelphia: University of Pennsylvania Press, 2002), pp. 108, 122–29.

47 *C. F. Volney reported:* quoted in Miller, *Wolf by the Ears*, p. 87.

47 *African Americans were excluded:* Kolchin, *American Slavery*, p. 241; and William C. Kashatus, *Just over the Line: Chester County and the Underground Railroad* (West Chester, PA: Chester County Historical Society, 2002), pp. 8–10.

48 *word spread rapidly:* Nash, *Forging Freedom*, pp. 139–42; and Kashatus, *Just over the Line*, p. 25–26.

49 *king of Italy enjoyed:* Child, *Isaac T. Hopper*, p. 248; Christopher Densmore, curator, Friends Historical Library, Swarthmore College, interview with author, Swarthmore, Pa., June 21, 2002.

49 *"had abundant reason to dread":* Ibid., p. 206.

49 *embraced his new faith:* Ibid., pp. 47, 218.

50 *He was appointed:* Bacon, *Lamb's Warrior*, pp. 37–43.

51 *a slave to Pierce Butler:* Child, *Isaac T. Hopper*, pp. 99–103.

52 *a persecuted minority:* Hugh Barbour et al., eds., *Quaker Crosscurrents: Three Hundred Years of Friends in the New York Yearly Meetings* (Syracuse, N.Y.: Syracuse University Press, 1995), pp. 5, 9–10; and Nash, *Forging Freedom*, pp. 24–29.

52 *a "meddlesome Quaker":* Child, *Isaac T. Hopper*, p. 17.

52 *threats of assassination:* Ibid., p. 146.

52 *"We may perform":* Isaac T. Hopper, statement on the requirements of personal duty, dated March 3, 1845, Friends Historical Library, Swarthmore College, Swarthmore, PA.

52 *"It is most certain":* Samuel Sewall, "The Selling of Joseph: A Memorial," in *Against Slavery: An Abolitionist Reader*, Mason Lowance, ed. (New York: Penguin, 2000), pp. 11–13.

53 *Cotton Mather:* Miller, *Wolf by the Ears*, p. 256.

53 *"Who can tell":* Cotton Mather, "The Negro Christianized," in *Against Slavery: An Abolitionist Reader*, Mason Lowance, ed. (New York: Penguin, 2000), pp. 19–20.

53 *Evangelical Methodists and Baptists:* Kolchin, *American Slavery*, pp. 68–69.

53 *Quakers had steadily examined:* Dillon, *Abolitionists*, pp. 8–9; and Burton, *Rise and Fall of King Cotton*, p. 38.

53 *"Now, tho' they are black:* Moore, *Friends in the Delaware Valley*, p. 18.

54 *Quakers generally: A Narrative of Some of the Proceedings of North Carolina Yearly Meeting on the Subject of Slavery within its Limits* (Greensborough, N.C.: Swaim and Sherwood, 1848), preface.

54 *"vain customs":* Kashatus, *Just over the Line*, p. 37.

54 *Quakers most often cited:* Lucretia Mott, "Slavery and the 'Woman Question': Lucretia Mott's Diary of Her Visit to Great Britain to Attend the World's Anti-Slavery Convention of 1840," Frederick B. Tolles, ed., Supplement No. 23 to the *Journal of the Friends Historical Society*, Friends Historical Association, Haverford, PA, 1952; Christopher Densmore, curator, Friends Historical Collection, Swarthmore College, e-mail to the author, June 14, 2004; Barbara Wright, "North Carolina Quakers and Slavery" (unpublished thesis, University of North Carolina, Chapel Hill, 1974), pp. 1 ff.

54 *"The Colour of a Man":* John Woolman, "Some Considerations on the Keeping of Negroes," in *Against Slavery: An Abolitionist Reader*, Mason Lowance, ed. (New York: Penguin, 2000), pp. 22–23.

54 *Samuel Nottingham, a Quaker:* Anthony Benezet, letter, to Moses Brown, May 9, 1774, Quaker Collection, Haverford College, Haverford, Pa.

55 *"How would such a people":* Anthony Benezet, letter to John Fothergill, April 28, 1773, Quaker Collection, Haverford College, Haverford, Pa.

55 *education was the answer:* Nash, *Forging Freedom*, pp. 30–31.

55 *Other meetings soon followed:* Child, *Isaac T. Hopper*, pp. 263–64; and *Narrative of Some of the Proceedings*, p. 5.

55 *"earnestly and affectionately":* Ibid., p. 12.

55 *"labor with such Friends":* Weeks, *Southern Quakers and Slavery*, p. 218.

55 *Nine Partners Meeting:* Christopher Densmore et al., "Slavery and Abolition to 1830," in *Quaker Crosscurrents: Three Hundred Years of Friends in the New York Yearly Meetings*, Hugh Barbour, et al., eds. (Syracuse, N.Y.: Syracuse University Press, 1995), pp. 68–69.

55 *Social pressure within:* Wright, "North Carolina Quakers and Slavery," p. 18.

56 *"In the Christian warfare": Narrative of Some of the Proceedings*, preface.

56 *the Pennsylvania Abolition Society:* Kashatus, *Just Over the Line*, pp. 28, 43; Nash, *Forging Freedom*, p. 103.

56 *man of instinct:* Child, *Isaac T. Hopper*, p. 206.

56 *"I am not willing":* Ibid., p. 187.

56 *preferred a legal attack:* Ibid., pp. 203–04, 150–55.

57 *web of friends:* Ibid., p. 131.

58 *Ben Jackson:* Ibid., pp. 54–55.

58 *snatched a pistol:* Bacon, *Lamb's Warrior*, p. 45.

58 *obtained a horse:* Child, *Isaac T. Hopper*, p. 71.

58 *also perfected ruses:* Ibid., p. 62.

58 *a free man named Samuel Johnson:* Ibid., pp. 97–98.

59 *Hopper's brother-in-law John Tatem:* Ibid., p. 253.

59 *"Verily I say":* Ibid., p. 171.

59 *As early as 1809:* Robert C. Smedley, "History of the Underground Railroad in Chester and the Neighboring Counties of Pennsylvania," *Journal* (Lancaster, Pa.), 1883, pp. 323–25.

60 *the fugitive John Smith:* Child, *Isaac T. Hopper*, pp. 63–64.

60 *Financial problems forced:* Bacon, *Lamb's Warrior*, pp. 82–83.

61 *Timothy Rogers was:* Christopher Densmore and Albert Schrauwers, eds., "The Best Men for Settling New Country: The Journal of Timothy Rogers" (Toronto: Canadian Friends Historical Association, 2000), pp. 3–6, 88–89; Densmore, "Slavery and Abolition to 1830," pp. 71–72.

62 *fewer than one hundred thousand:* Christopher Densmore, e-mail to author, February 7, 2004.

62 *Although their unfashionable dress:* Addison Coffin, "Early Settlement of Friends in North Carolina: Traditions and Reminiscences" (unpublished manuscript, Quaker Collection, Guilford College, Greensboro, N.C.).

62 *Vermont neighbor Joseph Hoag:* Hugh Barbour, et al., "The Orthodox-Hicksite Separation," in *Quaker Crosscurrents: Three Hundred Years of Friends in the New York Yearly Meetings*, Hugh Barbour et al., eds. (Syracuse, N.Y.: Syracuse University Press, 1995), pp. 113–14.

63 *"I was led":* Joseph Hoag, *Journal of the Life of Joseph Hoag* (Philadelphia: Wm. H. Pile's Sons, 1909), p. 182.

63 *He had only contempt:* Ibid., p. 187.

63 *island of Nantucket:* Levi Coffin, *Reminiscences of Levi Coffin* (Cincinnati: Western Tract Society, 1879), pp. 4–7.

63 *By the 1800s:* Weeks, *Southern Quakers and Slavery*, p. 243.

Chapter 4: The Hand of God in North Carolina

Page

64 *"A comfortable living":* N. P. Hairston, letter to John Hairston, December 4, 1821, Peter W. Hairston Papers, Southern History Collection, University of North Carolina, Chapel Hill.

64 *Wherever planters went:* Dangerfield, *Awakening of American Nationalism*, pp. 105–6; Miller, *Wolf by the Ears*, p. 240; Frances D. Pingeon, "An Abominable Business: The New Jersey Slave Trade, 1818," *New Jersey History* (Fall/Winter, 1991): 15–36.

65 *"at least five droves":* H. M. Wagstaff, *Minutes of the North Carolina Manumission Society*, James Sprunt Historical Studies, vol. 22, nos. 1–2 (Chapel Hill: University of North Carolina Press, 1934), p. 51.

65 *an incident otherwise forgotten:* Coffin, *Reminiscences of Levi Coffin*, pp. 12–13.

65 *A second incident:* Ibid., pp. 18–20.

66 *"How terribly we":* Ibid., p. 13.

67 *family farms on the Northern pattern:* Ibid., p. 6.

67 *"All were friends":* Ibid., p. 11.

67 *The North Carolina Yearly Meeting: Narrative of Some of the Proceedings*, p. 12.

67 *Quakers who freed:* Weeks, *Southern Quakers and Slavery*, p. 222.

67 *draconian state laws:* Wright, "North Carolina Quakers and Slavery," p. 5.

67 *"in the care of":* John Howard, letter to Nathan Mendenhall, October 21, 1826, Mendenhall Papers, Letter #66, Friends Historical Collection, Guilford College, Greensboro, N.C.

68 *Quakers attempted to solve:* Weeks, *Southern Quakers and Slavery*, pp. 225–27; *Narrative of Some of the Proceedings*, pp. 27–28; Wright, "North Carolina Quakers and Slavery," pp. 8–11.

68 *groups of Quaker "movers":* Coffin, "Early Settlement of Friends in North Carolina," pp. 139–42.

69 *North Carolina Manumission Society:* Wagstaff, "Minutes of the North Carolina Manumission Society," p. 39; Wright, "North Carolina Quakers and Slavery," pp. 32–33; and Coffin, *Reminiscences*, p. 74.

69 *commitment to gradual emancipation:* Alice Dana Adams, *The Neglected Period of Anti-Slavery in America* (Gloucester, Mass.: Peter Smith, 1964), pp. 127–39.

69 *rancorous internal debate:* Wagstaff, *Minutes of the North Carolina Manumission Society*, pp. 83–85.

70 *Paul Cuffe, a prosperous:* Nash, *Forging Freedom*, p. 184.

70 *Less idealistic members:* Dillon, *Abolitionists*, p. 11; and Wagstaff, "Minutes of the North Carolina Manumission Society," p. 116.

70 *Behind a smokescreen:* Dangerfield, *Awakening of American Nationalism*, p. 138; Miller, *Wolf by the Ears*, pp. 264–66; and Merrill D. Peterson, *The Great Triumvirate: Webster, Clay, and Calhoun* (New York: Oxford University Press, 1987), pp. 284–85.

71 *"Many of us were opposed":* Coffin, *Reminiscences of Levi Coffin*, pp. 75–76; Weeks, *Southern Quakers and Slavery*, p. 237; and Coffin, "Early Settlement of Friends in North Carolina," p. 70.

71 *"long and exciting suit at law":* Coffin, *Reminiscences of Levi Coffin*, p. 22; Weeks, *Southern Quakers and Slavery*, p. 242; Coffin, *Life and Travels of Addison Coffin* (Cleveland: William G. Hubbard, 1897), pp. 19–21.

73 *Ties between North Carolina and Pennsylvania:* Weeks, *Southern Quakers and Slavery*, pp. 227, 233; Wright, "North Carolina Quakers and Slavery," p. 54; *Narrative of Some of the Proceedings*, p. 32; Edward Bettle, letter to Nathan Mendenhall, May 21, 1832, Mendenhall Papers, Letter #185, Quaker Collection, Guilford College, Greensboro, NC; Coffin, *Reminiscences of Levi Coffin*, pp. 65–66.

73 *"The [Benson] case naturally":* Coffin, *Life and Travels of Addison Coffin*, pp. 19–21.

73 *"My sack of corn":* Coffin, *Reminiscences of Levi Coffin*, pp. 20–21.

74 *"took his first lessons":* Coffin, *Life and Travels of Addison Coffin*, pp. 19–21.

74 *Hamilton's Saul:* Coffin, *Reminiscences of Levi Coffin*, p. 21.

75 *fugitive slave named Jack Barnes:* Ibid., pp. 32–66.

79 *slaves belonging to the Yearly Meeting: Narrative of the Proceedings*, p. 28.

79 *"convoys" of blacks:* Ibid., pp. 29–31; Weeks, *Southern Quakers and Slavery*, p. 229.

79 *an Indiana man was hired:* Thomas Kennedy, letter to Nathan Mendenhall, September 11, 1827, Mendenhall Papers, Letter #107, Quaker Collection, Guilford College, Greensboro, NC.

79 *"A gang of ruffians":* Coffin, *Reminiscences of Levi Coffin*, p. 79.

79 *"It seemed as if":* Borden Stanton's letter to Friends in Georgia, in "Friends' Miscellany," vol. 12, no. 5 (May 1839), p. 217, Friends Historical Collection, Guilford College, Greensboro, N.C.

80 *"Gradually the idea prevailed":* Coffin, "Early Settlement of Friends in North Carolina," p. 120.

80 *"If the question is asked":* Ibid., p. 115.

80 *Indelible lines were being drawn:* Quoted in Dangerfield, *Awakening of American Nationalism*, pp. 134 ff.

80 *"Follow that sentiment":* Ibid., p. 135.

81 *Henry Clay proclaimed:* Peterson, *The Great Triumvirate: Webster, Clay, and Calhoun*, pp. 60–61.

81 *If slavery was excluded:* Dangerfield, *Awakening of American Nationalism*, p. 110.

81 *three-fifths of a slave state's population:* Miller, *Wolf by the Ears*, pp. 221 ff.

81 *Southerners rather grudgingly agreed:* Ibid., p. 247.

82 *He was paralyzed:* Thomas Jefferson, letter to Edward Coles, August 25, 1814, in *Thomas Jefferson: Writings*, Merrill D. Peterson, ed. (New York: Library of America, 1984), pp. 1343–46; Miller, *Wolf by the Ears*, pp. 206–7.

82 Reversing his position: Miller, *Wolf by the Ears*, pp. 229, 232.

82 *The federal government was:* Ibid., pp. 125, 217.

83 *"A geographical line":* Thomas Jefferson, letter to John Holmes, April 22, 1820, in *Thomas Jefferson: Writings*, pp. 1433–34.

83 *"Hell is about":* Dillon, *Abolitionists*, p. 23.

Chapter 5: The Spreading Stain

Page

84 *"could run faster":* Henson, *Uncle Tom's Story of his Life*, p. 19.

84 *"autobiography," a work:* Robin Winks, *The Blacks in Canada: A History* (New Haven, Conn.: Yale University Press, 1971), p. 183.

84 *"My vanity became":* Henson, *Uncle Tom's Story*, p. 19.

85 *"jolly Christmas times":* Ibid., p. 20.

86 *Henson's self-liberation:* Ibid., pp. 25–30.

87 *Methodists had vigorously denounced:* Donald G. Mathews, *Slavery and Methodism: A Chapter in American Morality 1780–1845* (Princeton, N.J.: Princeton University Press, 1965), p. 8.

87 *"buying or selling":* quoted in Siebert, *Underground Railroad from Slavery to Freedom*, p. 94.

87 *a time of explosive growth:* Mathews, *Slavery and Methodism*, p. 25; Nash, *Forging Freedom*, p. 111.

87 *no longer subversive outcasts:* Mathews, *Slavery and Methodism*, pp. 18, 41–43.

87 *A similar, cynical process:* Siebert, Wilbur H. Siebert, *The Underground Railroad from Slavery to Freedom*, pp. 95–96; John Rankin, "History of the Free Presbyterian Church in the United States," *Free Presbyterian*, February 11, 1857.

88 *"In Missouri":* Brown, "Narrative of William W. Brown," p. 707.

88 *a Sunday school:* Coffin, *Reminiscences of Levi Coffin*, p. 69.

88 *Henson's status:* Henson, *Uncle Tom's Story*, p. 23.

88 *drivers typically being chosen:* Kolchin, *American Slavery*, p. 103.

88 *doubled the farm's yield:* Henson, *Uncle Tom's Story*, p. 23.

88 *William Grimes:* William Grimes, "Life of William Grimes, the Runaway Slave," in *I Was Born a Slave: An Anthology of Classic Slave Narratives*, vol. 1, Yuval Taylor, ed. (Chicago: Lawrence Hill, 1999), p. 193.

89 *Charles Ball:* Charles Ball, "A Narrative of the Life and Adventures of Charles Ball, a Black Man," in *I Was Born a Slave: An Anthology of Classic Slave Narratives*, vol. 1, Yuval Taylor, ed. (Chicago: Lawrence Hill, 1999), p. 426.

89 *"I had no reason":* Henson, *Uncle Tom's Story*, p. 41.

89 *the tight credit:* Hiebert and MacMaster, *Grateful Remembrance*, p. 152.

89 *"Partly through pride":* Henson, *Uncle Tom's Story*, pp. 44–45.

90 *Henson's wife, Charlotte:* Ibid., p. 42.

90 *"[My] heart and soul became identified":* Ibid., pp. 47 ff.

90 *"No poor man":* R. Carlyle Buley, *The Old Northwest: Pioneer Period, 1815–1840*, vol. 2 (Bloomington: Indiana University Press, 1951), pp. 44–45.

90 *"one-horse tumbrils":* R. Carlyle Buley, *The Old Northwest: Pioneer Period, 1815–1840*, vol. 1 (Bloomington: Indiana University Press, 1951), p. 27.

90 *coffles of slaves shuffling westward:* Cohn, *Life and Times of King Cotton*, pp. 105–6; Dangerfield, *Awakening of American Nationalism*, pp. 105–6.

90 *"droves of a dozen":* Merton L. Dillon, *Benjamin Lundy and the Struggle for Negro Freedom* (Urbana: University of Illinois Press, 1966), p. 6.

91 *the shore of a free state:* Henson, *Uncle Tom's Story*, pp. 51–53.

92 *"Town booming":* Buley, *Old Northwest*, vol. 1, pp. 26–28, 36, 171–72.

92 *few African Americans in Indiana:* Emma Lou Thornbrough, *The Negro in Indiana Before 1900* (Bloomington: Indiana University Press, 1993), pp. 20–21; Weeks, *Southern Quakers and Slavery*, p. 232.

92 *Equality among whites:* Buley, *Old Northwest* vol. 1, pp. 30–31; vol. 2, p. 51.

93 *Coffin spent several weeks:* Coffin, *Reminiscences of Levi Coffin*, pp. 81–84.

93 *de facto slavery continued:* Buley, *Old Northwest*, vol. 2, pp. 53–54.

93 *Whipping was permitted:* Carol Pirtle, *Escape Betwixt Two Suns: A True Tale of the Underground Railroad in Illinois* (Carbondale: Southern Illinois University Press, 2000), pp. 8–10, 101; Dillon, *Abolitionists*, pp. 23–24; Glennette Tilley Turner, *The Underground Railroad in Illinois* (Glen Ellyn, Ill.: Newman Educational Publishing, 2001), p. 108.

94 *Illinois was still raw wilderness:* Buley, *Old Northwest*, vol. 2, pp. 53–54; Buley, *Old Northwest*, vol. 1, p. 48.

94 *"Starvation seemed to stare":* Coffin, *Reminiscences of Levi Coffin*, p. 92.

94 *Hiatt's relatives "asked me":* Ibid., p. 95.

94 *married Benjamin White's sister:* Ibid., p. 103.

95 *settled in Newport:* Ibid., p. 106.

95 *runaway slaves often passed:* Ibid., pp. 107–8.

95 *"I told them":* Ibid., pp. 109–10; Daniel N. Huff, "The Unnamed Anti-Slavery Heroes of Old Newport" (paper presented to the Wayne County, Indiana, Historical Society, September 23, 1905, Friends Collection, Earlham College).

96 *Karl Anton Postl:* Quoted in Harry Caudill, *Night Comes to the Cumberlands* Boston: Atlantic-Little Brown, 1963), pp. 17–18.

97 *Henson's life in Kentucky:* Henson, *Uncle Tom's Story*, pp. 55–57.

97 *Nehemiah Adams:* Nehemiah Adams, *A South-Side View of Slavery* (Savannah: Beehive Press, 1974), pp. 43–45.

97 *the Hensons' security:* Henson, *Uncle Tom's Story*, pp. 58–60.

98 *"a most excellent white man":* Ibid., p. 62.

98 *continued to espouse an antislavery message:* Mathews, *Slavery and Methodism*, pp. 46–53.

99 *The Cincinnati that Josiah Henson found:* Buley, *Old Northwest*, vol. 2, p. 47; Charles F. Goss, *Cincinnati: The Queen City 1788–1912*, vol. 1 (Cincinnati: S. J. Clarke, 1912), pp. 126, 135–36.

99 *the only jobs:* Lyle Kohler, "Cincinnati's Black Peoples: A Chronology and Bibliography, 1787–1982" (unpublished paper prepared for the Cincinnati Arts Consortium, 1986, Cincinnati Public Library), p. 9.

99 *"I found every door":* Ibid., p. 8.

99 *"invaluable friends":* Henson, *Uncle Tom's Story*, p. 64.

99 *By the time he left:* Ibid., p. 66.

100 *an increasingly common practice:* T. Stephen Whitman, *The Price of Freedom: Slavery and Manumission in Baltimore and Early National Maryland* (New York: Routledge, 2000), p. 161.

100 *Riley agreed:* Henson, *Uncle Tom's Story*, p. 72.

100 *Back in Kentucky:* Ibid., pp. 74 ff.

101 *Isaac Riley's widow:* Interview with Matilda Riley, *Rockville (MD) Sentinel*, June 8, 1883.

101 *to New Orleans:* Henson, *Uncle Tom's Story*, pp. 79 ff.

102 *"Nothing was left":* Ibid., p. 93.

Chapter 6: Free as Sure as the Devil

Page

105 *a charismatic Virginia slave:* Nat Turner, "The Confessions of Nat Turner," in *The Rebellious Slave: Nat Turner in American Memory*, by Scot French (Boston: Houghton Mifflin, 2004), pp. 289 ff.

105 *" '[T] was my object":* Ibid., p. 295.

105 *Between one hundred:* Yuval Taylor, ed., *I Was Born a Slave: An Anthology of Classic Slave Narratives*, vol. 1 (Chicago: Lawrence Hill, 1999), p. 236; Scot French, *The Rebellious Slave: Nat Turner in American Memory* (Boston: Houghton Mifflin, 2004), pp. 2, 35–36, 84–85; Harriet A. Jacobs, *Incidents in the Life of a Slave Girl* (Cambridge, Mass.: Harvard University Press, 1987), p. 64; Merton L. Dillon, *Slavery Attacked: Southern Slaves and their Allies 1619–1865* (Baton Rouge: Louisiana State University Press, 1990), pp. 157–58.

106 *Fulfilling the worst fears:* Russel Nye, *Fettered Freedom: Civil Liberties and the Slavery Controversy 1830–1860* (East Lansing: Michigan State University Press, 1949), pp. 122 ff.

106 *In Raleigh:* Louis P. Masur, *1831: Year of Eclipse* (New York: Hill & Wang, 2001), pp. 38–39.

106 *Virginians debated:* Ibid., pp. 57, 62.

106 *"We have, as far":* Nye, *Fettered Freedom*, p. 71.

107 *"I will be as harsh as truth":* Henry Mayer, *All on Fire: William Lloyd Garrison and the Abolition of Slavery* (New York: St. Martin's Press, 1998), p. 112; Masur, *1831*, pp. 23–25.

107 *Tens of thousands:* Franklin and Schweniger, *Runaway Slaves*, p. 282.

107 *Jarm Logue:* Jermain Loguen, *The Rev. J. W. Loguen as a Slave and as a Freeman* (Syracuse, N.Y.: J. G. K. Truair & Co., 1859), p. 124.

107 *Moses Roper:* Roper, "Narrative of the Adventures and Escape of Moses Roper," p. 499.

107 *William Wells Brown:* Brown, "Narrative of William W. Brown," p. 701.

107 *Slaves ran because:* Stampp, *Peculiar Institution*, pp. 110–14; Franklin and Schweniger, *Runaway Slaves*, pp. 17 ff, 50–51.

108 *Occasionally whites enticed:* Mark Twain, *Life on the Mississippi* (New York: Bantam, 1981), p. 144; Franklin and Schweniger, *Runaway Slaves*, p. 30.

108 *most "lurked":* Stampp, *Peculiar Institution*, p. 115; Franklin and Schweniger, *Runaway Slaves*, pp. 58, 67–68, 100–101, 109.

109 *The Tennessee slave:* Loguen, *Rev. J. W. Loguen*, pp. 241, 245.

109 *a Mississippi planter:* Burton, *Rise and Fall of King Cotton*, pp. 159–60.

109 *a system of police control:* Sally E. Hadden, *Slave Patrols: Law and Violence in Virginia and the Carolinas* (Cambridge, Mass.: Harvard University Press, 2001), p. 120; Franklin and Schweniger, *Runaway Slaves*, p. 118.

109 *South Carolina community, Georgetown:* Hadden, *Slave Patrols*, p. 63.

109 *"It was part of my business":* Ibid., 83.

110 *Patrollers typically had:* Franklin and Schweniger, *Runaway Slaves*, pp. 154–55.

110 *"If a slave":* Lewis Clarke, in John W. Blassingame, *Slave Testimony: Two Centuries of Letters, Speeches, Interviews, and Autobiographies* (Baton Rouge: Louisiana State University Press, 1977), p. 157.

110 *Patrollers gathered in a tavern:* John Kendrick, *Horrors of Slavery* (Cambridge, Mass.: Hilliard and Metcalf, 1817), p. 53.

110 *"As I was goin":* Hadden, *Slave Patrols*, p. 119.

111 *tended to run in any direction:* Franklin and Schweniger, *Runaway Slaves*, pp. 100–1, 161; Cecelski, *Waterman's Song*, pp. 128–31; Fergus M. Bordewich, *Killing the White Man's Indian: Reinventing Native Americans at the End of the Twentieth Century* (New York: Anchor, 1996), pp. 74–75.

111 *refuge with Native Americans:* Don E. Fehrenbacher, *The Slaveholding Republic: An Account of the United States Government's Relations to Slavery* (New York: Oxford University Press, 2001), pp. 98–101; Franklin and Schweniger, *Runaway Slaves*, pp. 87–88.

111 *One youngster:* Julie Winch, "Philadelphia and the Other Underground Railroad," *Pennsylvania Magazine of History and Biography* 111, no. 1 (January 1987): 13.

111 *When the Choctaw:* Sydnor, *Slavery in Mississippi*, p. 87.

111 *The Cherokee, in particular:* Franklin and Schweniger, *Runaway Slaves*, pp. 121, 127; Bordewich, *Killing the White Man's Indian*, pp. 40–41; Hadden, *Slave Patrols*, pp. 14–15; William Loren Katz, *Black Indians: A Hidden Heritage* (New York: Atheneum, 1986), pp. 54–55.

112 *"I do think":* Grimes, "Life of William Grimes," pp. 231–32.

112 *Fugitives could count on:* Miller, *Wolf by the Ears*, p. 129; Kashatus, *Just over the Line*, p. 28; Siebert, *Underground Railroad from Slavery to Freedom*, p. 297; Dangerfield, *Awakening of American Nationalism*, p. 130; Franklin and Schweniger, *Runaway Slaves*, pp. 159–60; John Rankin, *Life of Rev. John Rankin, Written by Himself in His Eightieth Year* (ca. 1872), text from a manuscript in the collection of Lobena and Charles Frost, reproduced and copyrighted in 1998 by Arthur W. McGraw.

113 *"The real distance was great":* Frederick Douglass, "Life and Times of Frederick Douglass," in *Douglass: Autobiographies* (New York: Library of America, 1994), pp. 609–10.

113 *Canada in the 1830s:* Winks, *Blacks in Canada*, p. 234; Daniel G. Hill, *The Freedom Seekers: Blacks in Early Canada* (Toronto: Stoddart, 1992), pp. 13–15; Siebert, *Underground Railroad from Slavery to Freedom*, pp. 191–92.

114 *Word slowly spread:* Winks, *Blacks in Canada*, pp. 142 ff; Siebert, *Underground Railroad from Slavery to Freedom*, p. 192.

114 *Lundy described:* Dillon, *Benjamin Lundy*, pp. 171–73; Winks, *Blacks in Canada*, p. 158.

115 *No one really knows:* Michael Wayne, "The Black Population of Canada West on the Eve of the American Civil War: A Reassessment Based on the Manuscript Census of 1861," *Histoire Sociale/Social History* 56, no. 4 (Winter 2000): 284–93; Stampp, *Peculiar Institution*, p. 115; Franklin and Schweniger, *Runaway Slaves*, p. 26; Ball, "Narrative of the Life and Adventures," pp. 438 ff.

115 *A large majority of fugitives:* Stampp, *Peculiar Institution*, p. 111; Franklin and Schweniger, *Runaway Slaves*, pp. 64, 229; Kashatus, *Just over the Line*, p. 15.

115 *The plan terrified Charlotte:* Henson, *Uncle Tom's Story*, pp. 104–9.

118 *very lightly populated:* Diane Perrine Coon, interview with the author, October 10, 2002.

118 *they continued eastward:* Henson, *Uncle Tom's Story*, pp. 110–12.

118 *local constables, slave catchers, informers:* Franklin and Schweniger, *Runaway Slaves*, pp. 119, 157–58, 178; Stampp, *Peculiar Institution*, p. 115; Brown, "Narrative of William W. Brown," p. 704; statement of Alexander Hemsley, in Benjamin Drew, *The Refugee: A Northside View of Slavery* (Reading, Pa.: Addison-Wesley, 1969), pp. 32–25; statement of William A. Hall, in Drew, pp. 220–24.

119 *There was no single prototype:* James W. C. Pennington, "The Fugitive Blacksmith; or, Events in the History of James W. C. Pennington," in *I Was Born a Slave: An Anthology of Classic Slave Narratives*, vol. 2, Yuval Taylor, ed. (Chicago: Lawrence Hill, 1999), p. 120; Hall, in Drew, *Refugee*, pp. 220–24; statement of A. T. Jones, in Drew, *The Refugee*, pp. 106–7.

119 *most fugitives relied on pluck:* Franklin and Schweniger, *Runaway Slaves*, pp. 109–20; Ball, "Narrative of the Life and Adventures," pp. 438–56.

120 *Jim Pembroke, who:* Pennington, "The Fugitive Blacksmith," pp. 115–38.

122 *Since Henson's last visit:* Kohler, "Cincinnati's Black Peoples," p. 9; Thomas E. Wagner, "Cincinnati and Southwestern Ohio: An Abolitionist Training Ground" (thesis, Miami University, 1967), pp. 1–8; Henry Louis Taylor, Jr., *Race and the City: Work, Community, and Protest in Cincinnati, 1820–1970* (Urbana: University of Illinois Press, 1993), pp. 302–4; Winks, *Blacks in Canada*, p. 155.

123 *On their own once again:* Henson, *Uncle Tom's Story*, pp. 115 ff.

123 *vast hardwood forests:* R. Carlyle Buley, *Old Northwest*, vol. 1, p. 51; vol. 2, p. 149.

123 *Benjamin Lundy walked:* Dillon, *Benjamin Lundy*, pp. 174–75.

124 *the Hensons set off:* Henson, *Uncle Tom's Story*, pp. 119 ff.

125 *"I threw myself":* Ibid., p. 126.

Chapter 7: Fanatics, Disorganizers, and Disturbers of the Peace

Page

126 *the damage it suffered:* Loguen, *Rev. J. W. Loguen*, p. 124.

127 *Born around 1813:* Carol M. Hunter, *To Set the Captives Free: Reverend Jermain Wesley Loguen and the Struggle for Freedom in Central New York 1835–1872* (New York: Garland, 1993), p. 33; C. Peter Ripley, ed., *The Black Abolitionist Papers: The United States, 1847–1858*, vol. 4 (Chapel Hill: University of North Carolina Press, 1991), p. 87, note 4.

127 *three slave-owning Logue brothers:* Loguen, *Rev. J. W. Loguen*, p. 14.

127 *treated him as a "pet":* Ibid., p. 23.

127 *Jarm merely fantasized:* Ibid., pp. 227–28.

127 *Ross procured for them:* Ibid., pp. 253, 261.

128 *On Christmas Eve:* Logue's flight to Canada described, Ibid., pp. 275–337.

129 *"a true hearted colored man":* Hunter, *To Set the Captives Free*, p. 42; Diane Perrine Coon, interview with the author, November 11, 2002; Maxine F. Brown, *The Role of Free Blacks in Indiana's Underground Railroad: The Case of Floyd, Harrison, and Washington Counties* (Indianapolis: Indiana Department of Natural Resources, 2001), pp. 2–7.

131 *By 1834, however:* Merton L. Dillon, *The Abolitionists: The Growth of a Dissenting Minority* (De Kalb: Northern Illinois Press, 1974), pp. 62–64.

131 *Many fugitives still:* statement by William H. Hall in Drew, *Refugee*, pp. 220–24; Brown, "Narrative of William W. Brown," pp. 712–13, 715.

132 *"There was no Anti-Slavery Society":* Pennington, "The Fugitive Blacksmith," p. 140.

133 *only in southeastern Pennsylvania:* Child, *Isaac T. Hopper*, pp. 192, 206.

133 *one of his last cases:* Ibid., pp. 189–91.

134 *the deepening rift:* Barbour et al., "Orthodox-Hicksite Separation," pp. 100–30.

134 *"Friends generally seem":* Charles Marriott, letter to Rowland T. Robinson, October 22, 1835, Rokeby Museum, Ferrisburgh, Vt.

134 *his tailoring business suffered:* Child, *Isaac T. Hopper*, p. 295.

134 *vibrant middle class:* Nash, *Forging Freedom*, pp. 130–33, 247–52, 272–73; Julie Winch, "Philadelphia and the Other Underground Railroad," pp. 8–9; Mayer, *All on Fire*, p. 173.

135 *waves of immigrants:* Nash, *Forging Freedom*, p. 251.

135 *New measures had been proposed:* Winch, "Philadelphia and the Other Underground Railroad," pp. 8–9.

135 *Hopper was considered remarkable:* Child, *Isaac T. Hopper*, p. 151.

135 *a white mob gathered:* Nash, *Forging Freedom*, p. 254.

135 *full-scale race riot:* Ibid., p. 275.

135 *Richard Allen, had been seized:* Ibid., 242.

135 *a kidnapping ring:* Winch, "Philadelphia and the Other Underground Railroad," p. 22.

135 *Jarm Logue's mother:* Loguen, *Rev. J. W. Loguen*, pp. 12–14.

136 *repugnance at the kidnapping:* Nash, *Forging Freedom*, p. 243; Winch, "Philadelphia and the Other Underground Railroad," pp. 8–9.

136 *In March 1820:* William R. Leslie, "The Pennsylvania Fugitive Slave Act of 1826," *Journal of Southern History* 13 (1952): 433–35, 445.

136 *In 1826, under pressure:* Ibid., p. 443.

137 *A particularly strong node of activism:* Franklin Ellis and Samuel Evans, *History of Lancaster County, Pennsylvania* (Philadelphia: Everts and Peck, 1883), pp. 73–74; Smedley, "History of the Underground Railroad in Chester," pp. 28 ff.

138 *"We might as well":* Smedley, "History of the Underground Railroad in Chester," p. 148.

138 *African-American abolitionists played:* Smedley, "History of the Underground Railroad in Chester," pp. 27–29, 53–57, 99–100, 143–50, 245–46; Adams, *Neglected Period of Anti-Slavery in America*, pp. 23–24; Siebert, *Underground Railroad from Slavery to Freedom*, pp. 120–21.

138 *the tanner Owen Brown:* James F. Caccamo, *Hudson, Ohio and the Underground Railroad* (Hudson, Ohio: Friends of Hudson Library, 1992), pp. 21–22.

138 *James Adams, the mulatto son:* statement by James Adams in Drew, *Refugee*, pp. 12–19.

139 *whaling port of Nantucket:* Kathryn Grover, *The Fugitive's Gibraltar: Escaping Slaves and Abolitionism in New Bedford, Massachusetts* (Amherst: University of Massachusetts Press, 2001), pp. 95–96; Siebert, *Underground Railroad from Slavery to Freedom*, p. 258.

139 *Some, like David Hudson:* Caccamo, *Hudson, Ohio and the Underground Railroad*, p. 21.

139 *William Jay:* Dillon, *Abolitionists*, pp. 53–54.

140 *"Those who do remain":* quoted in Wright, "North Carolina Quakers and Slavery," pp. 17–18.

140 *underground conductor Calvin Fairbank:* Calvin Fairbank, *Rev. Calvin Fairbank during Slavery Times* (New York: Negro Universities Press, 1969), p. 7.

140 *roving journalist Benjamin Lundy:* Dillon, *Benjamin Lundy*, p. 47.

141 *"immediate and total abolition":* George Bourne, *Picture of Slavery in the United States of America* (Detroit: Negro History Press, 1972), p. 156; Siebert, *Underground Railroad from Slavery to Freedom*, pp. 304–6.

141 *John Rankin of Ohio wrote:* Riley, *Ohio Castigator*, July 24, 1824, and August 31, 1824; Ann Hagedorn, *Beyond the River: The Untold Story of the Heroes of the Underground Railroad* (New York: Simon & Schuster, 2002), pp. 47–50; William Lloyd Garrison, letter to Henry E. Benson, December 10, 1835, Walter M. Merrill, ed., *The Letters of William Lloyd Garrison: I Will Be Heard!*, vol. 1: *1822–1835* (Cambridge, Mass.: Harvard University Press, 1971), pp. 574–75.

141 *Adam Lowry Rankin:* Adam Lowry Rankin, "The Autobiography of Adam Lowry Rankin" (unpublished manuscript, Union Township Library, Ripley, Ohio), pp. 41–45.

143 *The conference was William Lloyd Garrison's idea:* Mayer, *All on Fire*, pp. 170–71; Carleton Mabee, *Black Freedom: The Nonviolent Abolitionists from 1830 through the Civil War* (Toronto: Macmillan, 1970), p. 20.

144 *"we learnt that a goodly number":* Samuel J. May, *Some Recollections of Our Antislavery Conflict* (Miami: Mnemosyne, 1969, p. 82).

144 *The delegates were mostly young:* Mayer, *All on Fire*, pp. 172–74; May, *Some Recollections of Our Antislavery Conflict*, pp. 82–96; Dillon, *Slavery Attacked*, pp. 172–73; Bertram Wyatt-Brown, *Lewis Tappan and the Evangelical War Against Slavery* (New York: Atheneum, 1971), pp. 107–8.

145 *"our Coryphaeus":* May, *Some Recollections of Our Antislavery Conflict*, p. 86.

145 *a ringing proclamation:* William Lloyd Garrison, "Declaration of the National Antislavery Convention," in *Against Slavery: An Abolitionist Reader*, Mason Lowance, ed. (New York: Penguin, 2000), pp. 119–22.

146 *"a holy enthusiasm":* May, *Some Recollections of Our Antislavery Conflict*, p. 96.

Chapter 8: The Grandest Revolution the World Has Ever Seen

Page

147 *That evening, he intended:* Octavius B. Frothingham, *Gerrit Smith: A Biography* (New York: G. P. Putnam's Sons, 1878), pp. 165–66.

148 *Though only thirty-eight years old:* John Stauffer, *The Black Hearts of Men: Radical Abolitionists and the Transformation of Race* (Cambridge, MA: Harvard University Press, 2002), pp. 75–77.

148 *"Boundless was his faith":* Frothingham, *Gerrit Smith*, p. 171.

148 *Smith's moral sensibility:* Whitney R. Cross, *The Burned-Over District: The Social and Intellectual History of Enthusiastic Religion in Western New York, 1800–1850* (New York: Harper Torchbooks, 1965), pp. 3–13.

148 *Smith had thought deeply about slavery:* Alice H. Henderson, "The History of the New York State Anti-Slavery Society" (Ph.D. thesis, University of Michigan, Ann Arbor, 1963), pp. 34 ff.

148 *"By such a concession":* Ibid., p. 36.

149 *But he was not an abolitionist:* Stauffer, *Black Hearts of Men*, pp. 93–94; Gerrit Smith, letter to Lewis Tappan, April 1, 1836, Gerrit Smith Collection, Bird Library, Syracuse University; Gerrit Smith, letter to Joseph Speed, September 7, 1837, Smith Collection, Syracuse University.

149 *The atmosphere in Utica:* May, *Some Recollections of Our Antislavery Conflict*, pp. 163–64; Henderson, "History of the New York State Anti-Slavery Society," pp. 51–57; James Caleb Jackson, unpublished reminiscences, copy in the possession of Milton C. Sernett, Department of African American Studies, Syracuse University, Syracuse, N.Y.

149 *New York Democrats:* Henderson, "History of the New York State Anti-Slavery Society," pp. 49, 127; Monroe Fordham, ed., *The African-American Presence in New York State History* (Albany: State University of New York, 1989), p. 29; James Oliver Horton and Lois E. Horton, *In Hope of Liberty: Culture, Community and Protest Among Northern Free Blacks, 1700–1860* (New York: Oxford University Press, 1997), pp. 167–68.

150 *The convention got under way: Proceedings of the New York Anti-Slavery Convention Held at Utica, October 21, and New York Anti-Slavery State Society Held at Peterboro, October 22, 1835* (Utica: Standard & Democrat Office, 1835), pp. 4–8; May, *Some Recollections of Our Antislavery Conflict*, pp. 168–69; Milton C. Sernett, *North Star Country: Upstate New York and the Crusade for African American Freedom* (Syracuse, N.Y.: Syracuse University Press, 2002), pp. 49–50; Frothingham, *Gerrit Smith*, p. 165; Jackson, unpublished reminiscences.

151 *The delegates made their way:* Henderson, "History of the New York State Anti-Slavery Society," p. 64; Jackson, unpublished reminiscences.

151 *part of a coordinated crackdown:* Henderson, "History of the New York State Anti-Slavery Society," p. 67; David Grimsted, *American Mobbing 1828–1861: Toward Civil War* (New York: Oxford University Press, 1998), pp. 25–26; Dillon, *Abolitionists*, pp. 24–26; Oliver Johnson, letter to Rowland T. Robinson, March 27, 1835, Robinson Family Papers, Rokeby Museum, Ferrisburgh, Vt.

152 *Meanwhile, abandoning his trip:* Frothingham, *Gerrit Smith*, pp. 164–65; Sernett, *North Star Country*, p. 50; Stauffer, *Black Hearts of Men*, pp. 100–101.

152 *the delegates agreed to call for: Proceedings*, p. 16.

152 *Smith himself rose to speak:* Frothingham, *Gerrit Smith*, pp. 165–66; *Proceedings*, pp. 19–22.

153 *had transformed Smith from an intellectual bystander:* Frothingham, *Gerrit Smith*, pp. 166–68; Gerrit Smith, letter to Joseph Speed, September 7, 1837, Gerrit Smith Papers, Bird Library, Syracuse University, Syracuse, N.Y.

154 *when the old Calvinist doctrine:* Judith Wellman, "The Burned-Over District Revisited: Benevolent Reform and Abolitionism in Mexico, Paris, and Ithaca, New York, 1825–1842" (Ph.D. thesis, University of Virginia, Charlottesville, 1974), pp. 441–42; Joseph C. Hathaway, preface to "Narrative of William Wells Brown, A Fugitive Slave," in *I Was Born a Slave: An Anthology of Classic Slave Narratives*, vol. 1, Yuval Taylor, ed. (Chicago: Lawrence Hill, 1999), p. 682.

154 *"This is the carrying out": Friend of Man*, September 6, 1837.

154 *"The abolitionists are wrong": Poughkeepsie Journal*, March 1, 1837.

155 *"My parents and one uncle":* Mary Ellen Graydon Sharpe, *A Family Retrospect* (Indianapolis: Hollenbeck Press, no date), pp. 49–51, 55–56.

155 *a massive national effort:* Nye, *Fettered Freedom*, pp. 51–55.

155 *In the middle of the decade:* William Lee Miller, *Arguing About Slavery: The Great Battle in the United States Congress* (New York: Knopf, 1996), pp. 207–10; Henderson, "History of the New York State Anti-Slavery Society," p. 129.

155 *so many petitions: Friend of Man*, August 8, 1838; Wellman, "Burned-Over District Revisited," pp. 307, 315.

156 *"Jesus Christ has":* Ira V. Brown, "An Anti-Slavery Agent: C.C. Burleigh in Pennsylvania, 1836–1837," *Pennsylvania Magazine of History and Biography* 105 (1981): 70.

156 *"Let the great cities* alone*":* Ibid., p. 74.

156 *"Reformations commence":* Henderson, "History of the New York State Anti-Slavery Society," p. 77.

156 *While the traveling agents:* Brown, *An Anti-Slavery Agent: C.C. Burleigh in Pennsylvania, 1836–1837*, pp. 66, 77–78; Smedley, "History of the Underground Railroad in Chester," pp. 30, 135, 194.

156 *Oliver Johnson:* Mayer, *All on Fire*, p. 128; Merrill, ed., *Letters of William Lloyd Garrison*, vol. 1, p. 85, note 1.

156 *Johnson's remarkable letters:* Oliver Johnson, letter to Rowland T. Robinson, January 27, 1837; March 5, 1837; April 19, 1837; July 6, 1837, Robinson Family Papers, Rokeby Museum, Ferrisburgh, Vt.; Jane Williamson, curator, Rokeby Museum, e-mail to author, May 5, 2004.

157 *Fugitives commonly would work:* Joseph Beale, letter to Rowland T. Robinson, July 12, 1844; Charles Marriott, letter to Rowland T. Robinson, March 14, 1842; Rachel Gilpin Robinson, letter to Ann King, January 9, 1844; James Temple, letter to Rowland T. Robinson, May 11, 1851, Robinson Family Papers, Rokeby Museum, Ferrisburgh, VT; Jane Williamson, Rokeby Museum, interview with the author, August 22, 2002; Raymond Paul Zirblis, *Friends of Freedom: The Vermont Underground Railroad Survey Report* (Montpelier: State of Vermont Department of State Buildings and Division for Historic Preservation), 1996, pp. 26–28.

157 *"I was so well-pleased":* Oliver Johnson, letter to Rowland T. Robinson, January 27, 1837.

158 *"where he will put himself":* Oliver Johnson, letter to Rowland T. Robinson, April 3, 1837.

158 *"Half the moral power":* Sernett, *North Star Country*, p. 111.

158 *"New York is the* Empire State*":* Theodore Weld, letter to Rowland T. Robinson, June 20, 1836, Robinson Family Papers, Rokeby Museum, Ferrisburgh, Vt., letter.

158 *traveling agents were deployed:* Henderson, "History of the New York State Anti-Slavery Society," pp. 71–73, 159; John L. Myers, "The Beginning of Anti-Slavery Agencies in New York State, 1833–1836," *New York History*, April 1962, pp. 175–77.

159 *he debated the novelist:* Henderson, "History of the New York State Anti-Slavery Society," p. 199; James Fenimore Cooper, *The American Democrat* (Baltimore: Penguin Books, 1969), pp. 220–23.

160 *Cooper was far from alone:* Henderson, "History of the New York State Anti-Slavery Society," p. 13; May, *Some Recollections of Our Antislavery Conflict*, p. 163.

160 *to speak at Poughkeepsie:* Amy Pearce Ver Nooy, "The Anti-Slavery Movement in Dutchess County, 1835–1850," *Dutchess County Historical Society Yearbook*, vol. 28, 1943, p. 64.

160 *Henry B. Stanton claimed:* Dillon, *Abolitionists*, p. 76.

160 *Major antiabolition riots:* Grimsted, *American Mobbing*, p. 36; Nash, *Forging Freedom*, p. 277; Hagedorn, *Beyond the River*, pp. 114–15.

160 *its first white martyr:* Dillon, *Abolitionists*, pp. 93–95.

160 *aftermath of Nat Turner's rebellion:* Nye, *Fettered Freedom*, pp. 22–25, 55–58, 122–24; Henderson, "History of the New York State Anti-Slavery Society," pp. 98–99, 174; Masur, *1831*, p. 30.

161 *refused to censure:* David Ruggles, *An Antidote: An Appeal to the Reason and Religion of American Christians*, pamphlet (New York: David Ruggles, 1838), pp. 19–23.

162 *"than is possessed by the INDIVIDUALS":* Wellman, "Burned-Over District Revisited," p. 286.

162 *Every community was advised:* Henderson, "History of the New York State Anti-Slavery Society," pp. 20–22, 132; Wellman, "Burned-Over District Revisited," pp. 286–88.

162 *Children were not forgotten: Slave's Friend* 2, no. 8, 1836.

163 *local antislavery groups typically:* Henderson, "History of the New York State Anti-Slavery Society,", pp. 79–80, 186.

163 *one day in the autumn of 1837: Friend of Man*, February 28, 1838; Wellman, "Burned-Over District Revisited," p. 343.

164 *Clark felt free to report:* Ibid., p. 342.

164 *From a despised fringe group:* Henderson, "History of the New York State Anti-Slavery Society," pp. 100–23, 202, 206; John L. Myers, "The Major Effort of National Anti-Slavery Agents in New York State, 1836–1837," *New York History*, April 1965, pp. 162–63; Brown, "An Anti-Slavery Agent," p. 72.

165 *"My Dear Sir":* Utica, N.Y., *Union-Herald*, December 1, 1838.

Chapter 9: A Whole-Souled Man

Page

166 *A period sketch:* C. Peter Ripley et al., eds., *The Black Abolitionist Papers*, vol. 3 (Chapel Hill: University of North Carolina Press, 1991), p. 170.

166 *Ruggles was born:* Porter, *David Ruggles*, pp. 25–30.

166 *owned a grocery store: Freedom's Journal*, New York, August 22, 1828.

167 *the city had raced:* Hodges, *Root and Branch*, pp. 279–80; Burrows and Wallace, *Gotham*, pp. 478–80.

167 *It was still a low city:* John A. Kouwenhoven, *The Columbia Historical Portrait of New York City* (New York: Harper & Row, 1972), p. 147, 164–66, 171; Burrows and Wallace, *Gotham*, p. 439; Thomas Janvier, *In Old New York* (New York: Harper & Brothers, 1894), pp. 69, 81; Kenneth Holcomb Dunshee, *As You Pass By* (New York: Hastings House, 1952), pp. 193, 201.

167 *The great shaping force:* Burrows and Wallace, *Gotham*, pp. 431, 435, 443, 436–37; Stampp, *Peculiar Institution*, p. 271.

168 *New York's prosperity:* Cohn, *Life and Times of King Cotton*, pp. 83–86; Burrows and Wallace, *Gotham*, p. 336.

168 *Racism was virulent:* Henderson, *History of the New York State Anti-Slavery Society*, pp. 96, 127, 146; Horton and Horton, *In Hope of Liberty*, pp. 163–65, 171; Hodges, *Root and Branch*, pp. 227–28, 232–33.

169 *"IMPORTANT TO THE SOUTH": The First Annual Report of the New York Committee of Vigilance, for the Year 1837 Together with Important Facts Relative to Their Proceedings* (New York: Piercy and Reed, 1837), p. 54.

169 *Fugitives were at the mercy:* Porter, *David Ruggles*, pp. 35–36; Ripley, *The Black Abolitionist Papers*, vol. 3, p. 180, note 21; Lawrence B. Goodheart, "The Chronicles of Kidnaping in New York: Resistance to the Fugitive Slave Law, 1834–1835," *Afro-Americans in New York Life and History*, no. 8 (January 1984): 7–15; *First Annual Report of the New York Committee of Vigilance*, pp. 50 ff.

170 *black inhabitants lived packed:* Hodges, *Root and Branch*, pp. 279–80; Burrows and Wallace, *Gotham*, pp. 478–80; Tyler Anbinder, *Five Points: The New York City Neighborhood that Invented Tap Dance, Stole Elections, and Became the World's Most Notorious Slum* (New York: Free Press, 2001), p. 22; Herbert Asbury, *The Gangs of New York* (New York: Capricorn, 1970), pp. 11–15.

170 *Mob violence was endemic:* Hodges, *Root and Branch*, pp. 227–28; Anbinder, *Five Points*, pp. 8–12; Asbury, *Gangs of New York*, pp. 38–40; Grimsted, *American Mobbing*, pp. 9, 12, 36–38.

171 *a mostly African American group:* Ripley, *The Black Abolitionist Papers*, vol. 3, p. 179, note 14.

171 *"some centre of literary attraction":* David Ruggles, in *Colored American*, June 16, 1838.

171 *envisioned racial separation:* David Ruggles, *The 'Extinguisher' Extinguished: An Address on Slavery*, pamphlet (New York: David Ruggles, 1834), pp. 10–12, 16.

172 *Under Ruggles's leadership:* Porter *David Ruggles*, pp. 31, 37–38; Ripley, *The Black Abolitionist Papers*, vol. 3, p. 179, note 14; Goodheart, "Chronicles of Kidnaping in New York," pp. 12–13.

172 "practical *abolition":* Ripley, *The Black Abolitionist Papers*, vol. 3, p. 172.

172 *The Vigilance Committee consisted: First Annual Report of the New York Committee of Vigilance;* Porter, *David Ruggles*, p. 34.

173 *"We cannot recommend":* David Ruggles, in *Colored American*, December 9, 1837.

173 *"The only 'combination organized' ":* Ruggles, *An Antidote*, pp. 20–22.

173 *"Let parents, and guardians": First Annual Report of the New York Committee of Vigilance*, p. 51.

174 *case of young Edward Watson: Colored American*, September 16, 1837; June 23, 1838; July 21, 1838; July 28, 1838.

174 *"a General Marion sort of man":* Benjamin Quarles, *Black Abolitionists* (New York: Oxford University Press, 1969), p. 151.

174 *boldly pushed his way:* Porter, *David Ruggles,* pp. 32–33; Quarles, *Black Abolitionists,* pp. 150–51.

174 *"Procuring the escape":* Ruggles, *An Antidote,* pp, 20–22.

174 *Ruggles reported in detail:* David Ruggles, *Mirror of Liberty,* August 1838.

175 *first year of operation:* Porter, *David Ruggles,* pp. 32–33.

176 *"sooty scoundrel": Mirror of Liberty,* August 1838.

176 *An attempt to kidnap:* Porter, *David Ruggles,* pp. 37–38.

176 *a model for vigilance committees:* Joseph A. Borome, "The Vigilant Committee of Philadelphia," *Pennsylvania Magazine of History and Biography* 92, no. 1 (January 1968): 323–25.

176 *James Lindsey Smith:* James L. Smith, *Autobiography of James L. Smith* (Norwich, Conn.: Thames Printing Co., 1976), pp. 36–55; Strother, *Underground Railroad in Connecticut,* pp. 52–59.

177 *Other fugitives, probably: Mirror of Liberty,* August 1838.

177 *slower land route:* Frank Hasbrouck, *The History of Dutchess County* (Poughkeepsie, N.Y.: S. A. Matthieu, 1909), p. 490; Vivienne Ratner, "The Underground Railroad in Westchester," *Westchester Historian* 59, no. 2 (Spring 1983); Charles Marriot, letter to Rowland T. Robinson, November 23, 1838, Robinson Family Papers, Rokeby Museum, Ferrisburgh, Vt.

178 *young man named Frederick Bailey:* Frederick Douglass, "Narrative of the Life of Frederick Douglass, An American Slave," in *Douglass: Autobiographies* (New York: Library of America, 1994), pp. 74–86; William S. McFeely, *Frederick Douglass* (New York: W. W. Norton, 1991), p. 63.

179 *Sometime in the summer:* Douglass, "Life and Times," pp. 645–46; McFeely, *Frederick Douglass,* pp. 70–71.

179 *Soon after landing:* Douglass, "Narrative of the Life," pp. 90–91; Douglass, "Life and Times," pp. 648–50; and Douglass, "My Bondage and My Freedom," in *Douglass: Autobiographies* (New York: Library of America, 1994), pp. 350–53.

180 *"The question completely":* Pennington, *The Fugitive Blacksmith,* pp. 138–41.

180 *Bailey now selected:* Douglass, "Narrative of the Life," pp. 90–92.

180 *to New Bedford:* Douglass, "Life and Times," 650–53; McFeely, *Frederick Douglass,* pp. 72–73; Grover, *Fugitive's Gibraltar,* pp. 112, 144–45.

181 *chronically poor health: Colored American,* September 9, 1837; January 20, 1838.

181 *"to retire from": Colored American,* November 10, 1838.

182 *case of a fugitive named Tom Hughes:* Child, *Isaac T. Hopper,* pp. 376–82.

182 *Hopper, at sixty-seven:* Ibid., pp. 316–18.

182 *"I'll do no such thing":* Ibid., pp. 312–14.

183 *his loathing for slavery:* Ibid., pp. 322–27.

183 *his son John:* Charles Marriot, letter to Rowland T. Robinson, February 3, 1837, Robinson Family Papers, Rokeby Museum, Ferrisburgh, Vt.; *Colored American*, May 6, 1837; Nye, *Fettered Freedom*, p. 143.

184 *What now followed:* Isaac Tatum Hopper, *Exposition of the Proceedings of John P. Darg, Henry W. Merritt, and Others, in Relation to the Robbery of Darg, the Elopement of His Aleged Slave, and the Trial of Barney Corse, Who Was Unjustly Charged as an Accessory* (New York: Isaac T. Hopper, 1840), pamphlet, pp. 3–42.

185 *"it behooves us": Colored American*, December 9, 1837.

185 *managed to irritate Lewis Tappan:* Wyatt-Brown, *Lewis Tappan*, p. 180.

185 *a debilitating libel suit:* Porter, *David Ruggles*, pp. 39–42.

185 *"Great in promises": Colored American*, February 23, 1839; July 27, 1839.

186 *"I bleed in silence": Colored American*, January 26, 1839.

186 *"Let not a faithful":* Porter, *David Ruggles*, p. 43.

186 *compelled to plead:* David Ruggles, in *Mirror of Liberty*, January 1839.

186 *Destitute and almost blind:* Porter, *David Ruggles*, p. 44.

186 *"a whole-souled man":* Douglass, "My Bondage and My Freedom," p. 353.

Chapter 10: Across the Ohio

Page

189 *a young seminarian:* Calvin Fairbank, *Rev. Calvin Fairbank during Slavery Times* (New York: Negro Universities Press, 1969), p. 46.

190 *a family of Scotch Presbyterians:* Rankin, *Life of Rev. John Rankin*, pp. 1–5.

190 *tortured by spiritual anxieties:* Ibid., pp. 7–18, 42; Rankin, "History of the Free Presbyterian Church in the United States"; Andrew Ritchie, *The Soldier, the Battle, and the Victory; Being a Brief Account of the Work of the Rev. John Rankin and the Anti-Slavery Cause, 1793–1886* (Cincinnati: Western Tract and Book Society, 1868), pp. 18–19.

191 *Ripley was then:* Rankin, *Life of Rev.* John Rankin, pp. 18–24; Rankin, "Autobiography of Adam Lowry Rankin"; John Rankin Jr., unpublished interviews with Wilbur H. Siebert, Siebert Collection, Ohio Historical Society, Columbus, Ohio, and Frank Gregg, copy in Union Township Library, Ripley, Ohio; R. Carlyle Buley, *Old Northwest*, vol. 1, pp. 530–31; Tiffany Brockway, unpublished diary, copy in Union Township Library, Ripley, Ohio; Carl Westmoreland, National Underground Railroad Freedom Center, interview with the author, Cincinnati, Ohio, March 1, 1999.

192 *In his preaching, Rankin:* Ritchie, *Soldier, the Battle, and the Victory*, pp. 53, 71–72, 111.

192 *The Northwest had changed:* Byron Williams, *History of Clermont and Brown Counties, Ohio* (Milford, Ohio: Hobart Publishing Company, 1913), p. 391; Buley, *Old Northwest*, vol. 1, pp. 353, 528–29; Coffin, "Early Settlement of Friends in North Carolina," p. 58.

193 *color prejudice against blacks:* Wagner, "Cincinnati and Southwestern Ohio," p. 1; Kohler, "Cincinnati's Black Peoples," p. 12; *Philanthropist*, September 8, 1841; Thomas D. Hamm, *The Antislavery Movement in Henry County, Indiana* (New Castle, Ind.: Henry County Historical Society, 1987), p. 11.

193 *"contending, declaiming, denouncing":* Coffin, *Life and Travels of Addison Coffin*, pp. 57–58.

194 *a time of transformation:* Ronald G. Walters, *American Reformers 1815–1860* (New York: Hill & Wang, 1997), pp. 88–93; Mabee, *Black Freedom*, pp. 244–46; Dillon, *Abolitionists*, pp. 116–26; Wyatt-Brown, *Lewis Tappan*, pp. 185–200; Henderson, "History of the New York State Anti-Slavery Society," pp. 329–30.

194 *"THE OVERTHROW OF THIS NATION":* Wyatt-Brown, *Lewis Tappan*, p. 187.

194 *singing at the top of their lungs:* Ibid., p. 198.

194 *the political landscape offered:* Henderson, "History of the New York State Anti-Slavery Society," pp. 316–17; Dillon, *Abolitionists*, pp. 141–45; Mabee, *Black Freedom*, pp. 246–47; Sernett, *North Star Country*, pp. 112–15.

195 *one Samuel Ogden:* Kohler, "Cincinnati's Black Peoples," p. 25.

195 *a staunch Whig:* Rankin, "Autobiography of Adam Lowry Rankin," p. 91.

195 *Rankin believed that the only peaceful way:* Rankin, *Life of Rev. John Rankin*, p. 50.

196 *"If there be human enactments": Friend of Man*, October 9, 1839.

197 *"Our aim was safety":* Interview with Isaac Beck, *Georgetown* (Ohio) *News Democrat*, May 2, 1901; and letter to Wilbur H. Siebert, December 26, 1892, Siebert Collection, Ohio Historical Society, Columbus.

197 *blacks both slave and free lent assistance:* J. Blaine Hudson, *Fugitive Slaves and the Underground Railroad in the Kentucky Borderland* (Jefferson, N.C.: McFarland, 2002), pp. 21–30; Keith P. Griffler, *Front Line of Freedom: African Americans and the Forging of the Underground Railroad in the Ohio Valley* (Lexington: University Press of Kentucky, 2004), pp. 34–35, 42–52; Wilbur H. Siebert, *The Mysteries of Ohio's Underground Railroad* (Columbus, Ohio: Long's College Book Co., 1951), pp. 101–3, 171.

197 *a Kentucky patroller:* Hagedorn, *Beyond the River*, p. 38.

197 *George DeBaptiste:* Interview with George DeBaptiste, "Underground Railroad," *Detroit Post*, May 16, 1870.

198 *antislavery Presbyterian ministers:* Isaac Beck, interview with Wilbur H. Siebert, December 26, 1892, Siebert Collection, Ohio Historical Society, Columbus; Hudson, *Fugitive Slaves and the Underground Railroad*, pp. 123–25.

198 *politicized white abolitionists:* Larry Gene Willey, "The Reverend John Rankin: Early Ohio Anti-Slavery Leader" (Ph.D. thesis, University of Iowa, 1976), p. 173; Rankin, *Life of Rev. John Rankin*, pp. 42–46.

199 *"the cause is going on delightfully":* *Friend of Man*, October 6, 1836.

200 *"a man of good intellect":* Isaac Beck, interview with Wilbur H. Siebert, December 26, 1892, Siebert Collection, Ohio Historical Society, Columbus; Hudson, *Fugitive Slaves and the Underground Railroad*, pp. 123–25.

200 *the Gist settlement:* Hagedorn, *Beyond the River*, pp. 12–13.

200 *"We feel no prejudice":* Samuel S. Cox, *Eight Years in Congress from 1857–1865: Memoirs and Speeches* (New York: D. Appleton and Co., 1865), p. 248.

200 *the recapture of a fugitive couple:* David K. Katzman, *Before the Ghetto: Black Detroit in the Nineteenth Century* (Urbana: University of Illinois Press, 1973), pp. 8–10.

201 *the story of a slave named Ike:* Isaac Beck, interview with Wilbur H. Siebert, December 26, 1892, Siebert Collection, Ohio Historical Society, Columbus; Hudson, *Fugitive Slaves and the Underground Railroad*, pp. 123–25.

202 *In many of the river communities:* Thornbrough, *Negro in Indiana*, p. 44; Griffler, *Front Line of Freedom*, pp. 42–52; John M. Ashley, interview with Wilbur H. Siebert, July 1894, Siebert Collection, Ohio Historical Society, Columbus, OH; Jesse P. Elliott, letter to Wilbur H. Siebert, December 10, 1895, Siebert Collection; J. J. Minor, letter to Wilbur H. Siebert, September 1894, Siebert Collection.

202 *One of the most effective networks:* Interview with George DeBaptiste, "Underground Railroad," *Detroit Post*, May 16, 1870; interview with George DeBaptiste, *Detroit Tribune*, February 23, 1875; Chapman Harris: An Apostle of Freedom, *Indiana Journal*, January 31, 1880; Drusilla Cravens, pp. 2–39; Coon, "Southeastern Indiana's Underground Railroad Routes and Operations," pp. 185–89; "African-Americans in and Around Jefferson County, Ind.," typescript compilation of articles and transcribed notes (Madison, Ind.: Jefferson County Historical Society, n.d.); Diane Perrine Coon, "Great Escapes: The Underground Railroad," *Northern Kentucky Heritage* 9, no. 2 (Spring/Summer 2002): 2–13; Diane Perrine Coon, interview with the author, Madison, IN, October 17, 2002; Jae Breitweiser, interview with the author, Lancaster, IN, October 17, 2002; Hudson, *Fugitive Slaves and the Underground Railroad*, pp. 116–19; Phil Cole, *Historic Madison* (Madison, IN: Three Star Investments, 1995).

205 *"My curiosity, then":* Cravens, "African-Americans in and Around Jefferson County," p. 9.

206 *it stiffened resistance:* Ibid., pp. 19, 24–29; Diane Perrine Coon, interview with the author, Madison, Ind., October 17, 2002; Jae Breitweiser, interview with the author, Lancaster, Ind., October 17, 2002.

206 *like Thomas McCague:* Richard Calvin Rankin, interview with Wilbur H. Siebert, April 8, 1892, Siebert Collection, Ohio Historical Society, Columbus; Hagedorn, *Beyond the River*, pp. 201–2.

207 *Rankin focused his efforts:* Willey, "Reverend John Rankin," p. 236.

207 *At least one of the Rankin boys:* Richard Calvin Rankin, interview with Wilbur H. Siebert, Siebert Collection, Ohio Historical Society, Columbus; Byron Williams, *History of Clermont and Brown Counties, Ohio*, (Milford, Ohio: Hobart Publishing Company, 1913), pp. 399–401; "Emancipationists," *Ripley* (Ohio) *Bee and Times*, April 2, 1884; Hagedom, *Beyond the River*, pp. 81–83.

207 *"The mode of travel:* Isaac Beck, interview with Wilbur H. Siebert, December 26, 1892, Siebert Collection, Ohio Historical Society, Columbus; Hudson, *Fugitive Slaves and the Underground Railroad*, pp. 123–25.

208 *The Rankins' operation was no secret:* Rankin, "Autobiography of Adam Lowry Rankin," pp. 90–91, 78 ff.; Rankin, *Life of Rev. John Rankin*; Richard Calvin Rankin, interview with Wilbur H. Siebert; John Rankin Jr., interview with Wilbur H. Siebert, Rankin Collection, Ohio Historical Society, Columbus.

209 *When Calvin Fairbank landed:* Fairbank, *Rev. Calvin Fairbank during Slavery Times*, pp. 47–48; Randolph Paul Runyon, *Delia Webster and the Underground Railroad* (Lexington: University Press of Kentucky, 1996), p. 10.

209 *Lewis Hayden, who worked at:* Harriet Beecher Stowe, *A Key to Uncle Tom's Cabin; Presenting the Original Facts and Documents Upon Which the Story Is Founded* (Bedford, Mass.: Applewood Books, 1998), pp. 154–55; Runyon, *Delia Webster*, pp. 13–14.

209 *Fairbank's collaborator was:* Fairbank, *Rev. Calvin Fairbank during Slavery Times*, pp. 48–49; Runyon, *Delia Webster*, pp. 14–21; J. Winston Coleman Jr., *Slavery Times in Kentucky* (Chapel Hill: University of North Carolina Press, 1940), p. 143.

211 *Fairbank was tried and convicted:* Fairbank, *Rev. Calvin Fairbank during Slavery Times*, pp. 49–56.

211 *During her imprisonment:* Runyon, *Delia Webster*, pp. 46, 64–66.

211 *This close to the Ohio: Philanthropist*, May 14, 1839, and June 18, 1839; Isaac Beck, interview with Wilbur H. Siebert, December 26, 1892, Siebert Collection, Ohio Historical Society, Columbus; Hudson, *Fugitive Slaves and the Underground Railroad*, pp. 123–25; "Dyer Burgess of Warren, Washington County," biography in *The History of Washington County, Ohio*, pp. 486–87, excerpt in Siebert Collection, Ohio Historical Society, Columbus.

211 *John B. Mahan, a Methodist Minister: Philanthropist*, December 18, 1838; Rankin, "Autobiography of Adam Lowry Rankin," pp. 81ff; Hagedorn, *Beyond the River*, pp. 155 ff.

212 *One Sunday evening:* Rankin, "Autobiography of Adam Lowry Rankin," pp. 105–9; Rankin, *Life of Rev. John Rankin*, p. 49; Hagedorn, *Beyond the River*, pp. 219–22.

214 *rarely more than tantalizing shadows:* Rankin, *Life of Rev. John Rankin*, pp. 47–48.

214 *The most famous single fugitive:* Rankin, *Life of Rev. John Rankin*, pp. 48–49; John Rankin Jr., interviews with Frank Gregg and Wilbur H. Siebert, Rankin Papers,

Ohio Historical Society, Columbus; Rankin, "Autobiography of Adam Lowry Rankin"; interview with Reverend Samuel G. W. Rankin, "The Story of Eliza," *Hartford Daily Courant*, November 23, 1895; Hagedorn, *Beyond the River*, pp. 155 ff.

Chapter 11: The Car of Freedom

Page

217 *the home of Levi and Catherine Coffin:* Levi Coffin, *Reminiscences of Levi Coffin* (Cincinnati: Western Tract Society, 1879), pp. 111–13, 147–50.

218 *a pillar of the local establishment:* Ibid., pp. 106–7; Daniel N. Huff, "Reminiscence of Newport and Fountain City and its Environs from 1830 to 1896" (unpublished manuscript, 1896), Friends Collection, Earlham College, Richmond, Ind.; Huff, "Unnamed Anti-Slavery Heroes" (unpublished manuscript, 1905), Friends Collection, Earlham College, Richmond, Ind.; "How Fugitive Slaves Were Aided," *Richmond Palladium*, January 1, 1931.

218 *a fluid web:* Coffin, *Reminiscences*, pp. 111, 143; Thornbrough, *Negro in Indiana*, pp. 41–43; Hurley C. Goodall, *Underground Railroad: The Invisible Road to Freedom through Indiana as Recorded by the Works Progress Administration Writers Project* (Indianapolis: Indiana Department of Natural Resources, 2000), pp. 43–44.

219 *a new, pivotal kind of figure:* Coffin, *Reminiscences*, pp. 113–18.

220 *Coffin's personal feelings:* Ibid., pp. 159–60, 175, 183.

220 *Coffin's power could be deployed:* Ibid., pp. 195–201; Thornbrough, *Negro in Indiana*, p. 196; Huff, "Reminiscence of Newport and Fountain City."

221 *On another occasion:* Coffin, *Reminiscences*, pp. 193–94.

222 *"Here is where we keep":* Huff, "Unnamed Anti-Slavery Heroes."

222 *As time went on:* Coffin, *Reminiscences*, pp. 224–30; Thornbrough, *Negro in Indiana*, p. 198.

222 *Once Frederick and Anna Douglass:* Douglass, "My Bondage and My Freedom," pp. 359–63; McFeely, *Frederick Douglass*, pp. 81–85, 94; Grover, *Fugitive's Gibraltar*, pp. 287, 143; Stauffer, *Black Hearts of Men*, pp. 47–49.

224 *how he had been taken from his mother in infancy:* Douglass, "My Bondage and My Freedom," pp. 15–18, 21, 43, 74, 89; Robert F. Mooney, *The Advent of Douglass* (Nantucket: Wesco Publishing, 1991).

224 *Garrison followed Douglass:* McFeely, *Frederick Douglass*, p. 88.

225 *benefactor David Ruggles:* Ibid., p. 97.

225 *Douglass was not alone:* Ripley, ed., *Black Abolitionist Papers*, vol. 3, pp. 21, 24; Speech by Peter Paul Simons, delivered before the African Clarkson Association, New York, April 23, 1839, ibid., pp. 289–90.

225 *Douglass knew what:* Douglass, "My Bondage and My Freedom," pp. 364–68; May, *Some Recollections of Our Anti-Slavery Conflict*, pp. 293–94.

226 *an emerging generation:* Ripley, *The Black Abolitionist Papers*, vol. 3, pp. 26–33.

226 *"opportunity to be himself":* Quarles, *Black Abolitionists*, p. 69.

226 *Between 1836 and 1846:* John R. McKivigan, *The War Against Proslavery Religion: Abolitionism and the Northern Churches, 1830–1865* (Ithaca, N.Y.: Cornell University Press, 1984), pp. 107–8; Ripley, *The Black Abolitionist Papers*, vol. 3, pp. 36–39; and 447, n. 1; Quarles, *Black Abolitionists*, p. 84; Mabee, *Black Freedom*, pp. 133 ff.

226 *black newspapers, self-improvement societies:* Quarles, *Black Abolitionists*, pp. 101–4.

227 *"more than a figure of speech":* Ripley, *The Black Abolitionist Papers*, vol. 3, p. 24.

227 *"All the other speakers seemed tame":* McFeely, *Frederick Douglass*, p. 100.

227 *The Douglasses, who:* Ibid., pp. 93–94.

228 *In the Spring of 1843:* Douglass, "Life and Times," pp. 665–75; Coffin, *Reminiscences*, p. 168; Thornbrough, *Negro in Indiana*, pp. 41, 62, 100–3.

228 *"This town is one": Richmond Jeffersonian*, reprinted in *Free Labor Advocate*, January 8, 1842.

229 Palladium *sneeringly blamed: Richmond Palladium*, January 1, 1931.

229 *even racism among Quakers:* Coffin, *Reminiscences*, pp. 230–33; Quarles, *Black Abolitionists*, p. 72; Hamm, *Antislavery Movement in Henry County*, pp. 8, 12, 22; McKivigan, *War Against Proslavery Religion*, pp. 44, 105–6; Barbour et al., eds., *Quaker Crosscurrents*, pp. 185–88; Child, *Isaac T. Hopper*, pp. 389–97.

229 *when Frederick Douglass arrived:* Douglass, "Life and Times," pp. 675–76; McFeely, *Frederick Douglass*, pp. 109–12; Thornbrough, *Negro in Indiana*, p. 129; Coffin, *Reminiscences*, p. 229; Charles Remond, letter to Isaac and Amy Post, September 27, 1843, in Ripley, *The Black Abolitionist Papers*, vol. 3, pp. 416–17.

230 *routes were always in flux:* Siebert, *Mysteries of Ohio's Underground Railroad*, pp. 47, 224, 180–81, 230; Coffin, *Reminiscences*, p. 119; R. S. Miller, letter to Wilbur H. Siebert, April 4, 1892, Siebert Collection, Ohio Historical Society, Columbus; Joseph Patterson, letter to Wilbur H. Siebert, December 19, 1895, Siebert Collection; Isaac Beck, letter to Wilbur H. Siebert, December 26, 1892, Siebert Collection; Hamm, *Antislavery Movement in Henry County*, pp. 25, 47–48; Charles M. Cummings, *Yankee Quaker, Confedederate General: The Curious Career of Bushrod Rust Johnson* (Rutherford, N.J.: Fairleigh Dickinson University Press, 1971), pp. 56–59.

230 *At a reunion: Richmond Palladium*, January 1, 1931; Coffin, *Reminiscences*, p. 113; Huff, "Reminiscence of Newport and Fountain City."

231 *By comparison:* Diane Perrine Coon, interview with the author, Madison, Ind., October 17, 2002; Siebert, "Mysteries of Ohio's Underground Railroad," pp.

226–27; Milton Kennedy, letter to Wilbur H. Siebert, March 10, 1896, Siebert Collection, Ohio Historical Society, Columbus.

231 *David Putnam, an underground man:* Siebert, *Underground Railroad from Slavery to Freedom*, pp. 55–56.

232 *Fugitives remained with station masters:* Coffin, *Reminiscences*, pp. 113, 144, 153, 158, 168; Huff, "Reminiscence of Newport and Fountain City."

232 *For instance, John Todd:* Coon, "Great Escapes," p. 4; Siebert, *Mysteries of Ohio's Underground Railroad*, pp. 50–51, 63, 105, 141, 202.

232 *Although railroads, steamships:* Coon, "Great Escapes," p. 5; "Token Used on the Underground Railroad in Indiana," *Toledo Blade*, undated, Siebert Collection, Ohio Historical Society, Columbus; Joseph Patterson, letter to Wilbur H. Siebert, December 19, 1895, Siebert Collection.

233 *Coffin tried to keep a team harnessed:* Coffin, *Reminiscences*, pp. 111–13; R. C. Hansell, letter to Wilbur H. Siebert, undated, Siebert Collection, Ohio Historical Society, Columbus; I. E. G. Naylor, letter to Wilbur H. Siebert, March 27, 1896, Siebert Collection; Joseph Patterson, letter to Wilbur H. Siebert, December 19, 1895, Siebert Collection.

233 a female fugitive was dressed: Siebert, *Mysteries of Ohio's Underground Railroad*, pp. 141, 158.

233 *"They were very willing:* Coffin, *Reminiscences*, p. 168.

233 *"It often became necessary":* Eber Pettit, *Sketches in the History of the Underground Railroad* (Westfield, N.Y.: Chautauqua Regional Press, 1999), p. 41.

233 *Isaac Beck of Sardinia:* Isaac Beck, letter to Wilbur H. Siebert, December 26, 1892, Siebert Collection, Ohio Historical Society, Columbus.

234 *while Charles Huber:* Siebert, *Mysteries of Ohio's Underground Railroad*, p. 63.

234 *John H. Bond of Randolph:* Thornbrough, *Negro in Indiana*, p. 197; James O. Bond, *Chickamauga and the Underground Railroad: A Tale of Two Grandfathers* (Baltimore: Gateway Press, 1993), pp. 75–78, 83; Coffin, "*Reminiscences*", pp. 178–86.

236 *his new nickname:* Coffin, *Reminiscences*, p. 190.

236 *a brand-new language:* Hagedorn, *Beyond the River*, p. 175; Coon, "Southeastern Indiana's Underground Railroad Routes and Operations," pp. 20, 196; Coon, "Great Escapes," p. 5; "Old Uncle Joe Mayo," *Marysville* (OH) *Tribune*, April 27, 1881.

237 *The country's first practical railroad:* George Rogers Taylor, *The Transportation Revolution, 1815–1860* (New York: Harper Torchbooks, 1968), pp. 77 ff.; Buley, *Old Northwest*, vol. 1, pp. 510–12.

237 *"I saw today":* Mark McCutcheon, *Everyday Life in the 1800s* (Cincinnati: Writer's Digest Books, 1993), pp. 70–71.

237 *almost certainly apocryphal legend:* Siebert, *Underground Railroad from Slavery to Freedom*, pp. 44–45.

237 *Quite possibly:* Elijah Pennypacker, *Phoenixville Messenger*, August 28, 1880; *Village Record*, Kimberton, Pa., February 2, 1831; Emmor Kimber and Elijah Pennypacker files, Chester County Historical Society, West Chester, Pa.; Smedley, "History of the Underground Railroad in Chester," pp. 194, 210–11.

237 *By 1840, about:* Taylor, *The Transportation Revolution*, pp. 79, 346; Buley, *Old Northwest*, vol. 1, pp. 510, 513.

238 *advised "to look around":* Coffin, *Reminiscences*, p. 175.

238 *"Let the ministers and churches":* Sernett, *North Star Country*, p. 54.

238 *"I have never approved":* Douglass, "Narrative of the Life," p. 85.

239 *Coffin made his first trip:* Coffin, *Reminiscences*, pp. 247–53.

CHAPTER 12: OUR WATCHWORD IS ONWARD

Page

241 *The next morning:* Henson, *Uncle Tom's Story of His Life*, pp. 129–30.

243 *Henson began meeting:* Ibid., pp. 140, 171.

243 *The colonial authorities:* Levi Coffin, *Reminiscences of Levi Coffin* (Cincinnati: Western Tract Society, 1879), pp. 252–53; John McLeod, historian at Fort Malden National Historic Park, Amherstburg, Ontario, interview with the author, June 8, 2003; Doris Gaspar, "Fort Malden Historical Study" (unpublished report, Fort Malden National Historic Park, 2000), pp. 16–19, 45; *Colored American*, February 27, 1841.

243 *Henson thrived at Colchester:* Henson, *Uncle Tom's Story*, pp. 165–67.

244 *a grander dream was taking shape:* Ibid., pp. 140–43, 167.

244 *Alexander Hemsley, once a slave:* Statement of Alexander Hemsley, in Benjamin Drew, *The Refugee: A Northside View of Slavery* (Reading, Pa.: Addison-Wesley, 1969), p. 25.

245 *Nowhere in the Northern:* William H. Pease and Jane H. Pease, *Black Utopia: Negro Communal Experiments in America* (Madison: State Historical Society of Wisconsin, 1963), pp. 7, 10–11; Jason H. Silverman, *Unwelcome Guests: Canada West's Response to American Fugitive Slaves* (Millwood, N.Y.: Associated Faculty Press, 1985), p. 53; Winks, *Blacks in Canada*, pp. 154–55; Drew, *Refugee*, pp. 242–43.

245 *"Tell the Republicans":* Hill, *Freedom-Seekers*, p. 67.

246 *"Is not Upper Canada": Colored American*, June 22, 1839.

246 *The law was color-blind:* Hill, *Freedom Seekers*, pp. 50–51, 98, 109; Donald George Simpson, *Negroes in Ontario from Early Times to 1870* (London, Ontario: University of Western Ontario, 1971), p. 396.

247 *In the 1820s:* Siebert, *Underground Railroad from Slavery to Freedom*, pp. 192, 299–300; Winks, *Blacks in Canada*, pp. 149, 170–73; Silverman, *Unwelcome Guests*, pp. 37–40; Michael Power and Nancy Butler, *Slavery and Freedom in Niagara* (Niagara-on-the-Lake, Ontario: Niagara Historical Society, 2000), p. 52.

247 *They were staunch supporters:* John Kevin Farrell, "The History of the Negro Community in Chatham, Ontario" (thesis, University of Ottawa, 1955), pp. 35–36, 40–41, 60–63; John McLeod, interview with the author, June 8, 2003; Winks, *Blacks in Canada*, pp. 151–52; Hill, *Freedom Seekers*, pp. 118–21; John A. Collins, *Monthly Offering*, Anti-Slavery Office, 1840 (otherwise undated), pp. 51–55.

248 *For years afterward:* Victor Lauriston, *Romantic Chatham* (Chatham, Ontario: Shepherd Printing Co., 1952), pp. 163–66.

249 *While living as a farmer:* Henson, *Uncle Tom's Story*, pp. 145–63.

250 *A certain free black man:* Frank H. Severance, *Old Trails on the Niagara Frontier* (Buffalo, 1899), p. 243.

250 *"a bright and determined fellow":* M. C. Buswell, letter to Wilbur H. Siebert, January 6, 1896, Siebert Collection, Ohio Historical Society, Columbus, Ohio.

250 *One day in June 1841:* Eliza's return is recounted in John Rankin Jr., in his interviews with both Wilbur H. Siebert and Frank Gregg, in the Rankin Papers, Ohio Historical Society, Columbus, Ohio; Hagedorn, *Beyond the River*, pp. 213–14.

255 *"We have no means": Free Labor Advocate and Anti-Slavery Standard*, Newport, Ind., March 8, 1841.

255 *Unknown numbers also crossed:* Severance, *Old Trails on the Niagara Frontier*, p. 231; George C. Bragdon, letter to Wilbur H. Siebert, August 15, 1896, Siebert Collection, Ohio Historical Society, Columbus, Ohio; Hildegard Graf, "The Underground Railroad in Erie County," *Niagara Frontier* (Autumn, 1954), pp. 69–71; Rush R. Sloane, "The Underground Railroad of the Firelands" (address delivered to the Firelands Historical Society, Milan, Ohio, February 22, 1888), Siebert Collection, Ohio Historical Society, Columbus, Ohio.

255 *a steamboat captain named Chapman:* Pettit, *Sketches in the History of the Underground Railroad*, pp. 42–43.

256 *relied on trusted captains and crews:* Coffin, *Reminiscences*, p. 264; *Buffalo Daily Republic*, August 19, 1854; Christopher Densmore, curator of the Friends Historical Library, Swarthmore College, email to the author, June 7, 2004; G. T. Stewart, "The Ohio Fugitive Slave Law," *Firelands Pioneer*, July, 1888; Professor Hull, letter to Wilbur H. Siebert, April 2, 1907, Siebert Collection, Ohio Historical Society, Columbus; Horace Ford, interview with Wilbur H. Siebert (undated), Siebert Collection; John McLeod, interview with the author, June 8, 2003; Severance, *Old Trails on the Niagara Frontier*, p. 246.

256 *the lake crossing:* Taylor, *Transportation Revolution*, p. 62; Louis C. Hunter, *Steamboats on the Western Rivers: An Economic and Technical History* (New York: Dover, 1977), pp. 390–91, 400, 271, 278–82; Kathy Warnes, "Across the Lakes to

Liberty: The Liquid Underground Railroad," *Inland Seas: Quarterly Journal of the Great Lakes Historical Society* 56, no. 4 (Winter 2000): 284–93.

257 *the busiest was Detroit:* Anna B. Jameson, *Winter Studies and Summer Rambles in Canada* (Toronto: Thorn Press, 1943), pp. 138–42; Brian Leigh Dunnigan, *Frontier Metropolis* (Detroit: Wayne State University Press, 2001); David Lee Poremba, *Detroit: A Motor City History* (Detroit: Arcadia, 2001), pp. 65–67; Arthur M. Woodford, *This Is Detroit 1701–2001* (Detroit: Wayne State University Press, 2001), pp. 55–65.

257 *black abolitionist William Lambert:* Katherine DuPre Lumpkin, " 'The General Plan Was Freedom': A Negro Secret Order on the Underground Railroad," *Phylon: The Atlanta University Review of Race and Culture* (Spring 1967): 65–67.

258 *nothing if not cosmopolitan:* Jameson, *Winter Studies and Summer Rambles*, pp. 143–45; Power and Butler, *Slavery and Freedom in Niagara*, p. 49; Collins, *Monthly Offering*, pp. 51–55.

259 *Jarm Logue's experience was typical:* Loguen, *Rev. J. W. Loguen*, pp. 338–42.

260 *there may have been as many as: Colored American*, February 6, 1841; Henson, *Uncle Tom's Story*, p. 171; Coffin, *Reminiscences*, p. 251; Winks, *Blacks in Canada*, pp. 144–45; Farrell, "History of the Negro Community in Chatham, Ontario," pp. 34, 52–53; Simpson, *Negroes in Ontario*, p. 306; Silverman, *Unwelcome Guests*, pp. 22–23.

260 *Some refugees, like Logue:* Loguen, *Rev. J. W. Loguen*, pp. 338–42.

260 *In Amherstburg:* Fred Landon, "Amherstburg, Terminus of the Underground Railroad," *Journal of Negro History* 10, no. 1 (January 1925): 1–3; Coffin, *Reminiscences*, p. 251; Farrell, "History of the Negro Community in Chatham, Ontario," p. 53; Winks, *Blacks in Canada*, p. 146; John McLeod, interview with the author, June 8, 2003.

260 *Even Jarm Logue:* Loguen, *Rev. J. W. Loguen*, pp. 341–42.

261 *Isaac J. Rice:* Coffin, *Reminiscences*, p. 249; Winks, *Blacks in Canada*, pp. 145 ff; Simpson, *Negroes in Ontario*, p. 314; *Liberator*, August 23, 1842.

261 *Wilson was also a veteran:* Sernett, *North Star Country*, p. 158; William H. Pease and Jane H. Pease, *Bound with Them in Chains: A Biographical History of the Antislavery Movement* (Westport, Conn.: Greenwood Press, 1972), pp. 137–39; Collins, *Monthly Offering*, pp. 51–55; Winks, *Blacks in Canada*, p. 179; *Colored American*, June 1, 1839, May 23, 1840.

262 *Henson understood this:* Henson, *Uncle Tom's Story*, pp. 133–37.

264 *Hiram Wilson would play:* Ibid., pp. 171–72; Pease and Pease, *Black Utopia*, pp. 66–67; Winks, *Blacks in Canada*, pp. 179–80.

264 *naming their new home Wilberforce:* Pease and Pease, *Black Utopia*, pp. 47–57; Winks, *Blacks in Canada*, pp. 156–60; Hill, *Freedom Seekers*, pp. 67–71; *Colored American*, February 16, 1839.

265 *Dawn's beginnings:* Henson, *Uncle Tom's Story*, pp. 168–70; Judith Wellman and Milton Sernett, *Uncovering the Freedom Trail in Syracuse and Onondaga County* (Syracuse: Preservation Association of Central New York, 2002), pp. 10–11; *Voice of the Fugitive*, May 21, 1851; Lauriston, *Romantic Chatham*, pp. 379–81.

265 *settlers and well-wishers: Friend of Man*, November 1, 1842; *Voice of the Fugitive*, May 21, 1851.

266 *the British-American Institute opened:* Pease and Pease, *Black Utopia*, pp. 64–67; Hill, *Freedom Seekers*, pp. 71–73; Lauriston, *Romantic Chatham*, p. 448; *National Era*, November 18, 1847.

266 *a fugitive named John Brown:* John Brown, "Slave Life in Georgia: A Narrative of the Life, Sufferings, and Escape of John Brown, A Fugitive Slave, Now in England," in *I Was Born a Slave: An Anthology of Classic Slave Narratives*, vol. 2, Yuval Taylor, ed. (Chicago: Lawrence Hill, 1999), p. 381.

267 *"Trusting in the God": National Era*, November 18, 1847.

Chapter 13: The Saltwater Underground

Page

269 *Florida resembled:* Pensacola Beach History: Antebellum Period (1802–1860), viewed online at http://www.pbrla.com/hxarchive_ante_territory, Pensacola Beach Residents & Leaseholders Association.

269 *Walker was an abolitionist:* Jonathan Walker, *The Trial and Imprisonment of Jonathan Walker* (Gainesville: University Presses of Florida, 1974), pp. 22–23, 113–18.

270 *Walker had grown up:* Joe M. Richardson, in introduction to Walker, Ibid., pp. xiii, xxx, also pp. 107–10; Alvin F. Oickle, *Jonathan Walker: The Man with the Branded Hand* (Everett, Mass.: Lorelli Slater, 1998), pp. 2, 9.

270 *Walker first appeared:* Walker, *The Trial and Imprisonment*, pp. 8–9, xviii; Oickle, *Jonathan Walker*, pp. 32–33, 36, 40.

270 *Walker was known to consort:* Walker, *The Trial and Imprisonment*, pp. 63–64, 8–9.

271 *the brig* Creole: Stanley Harrold, *The Abolitionists and the South 1831–1861* (Lexington: University Press of Kentucky, 1995), p. 50; Dillon, *Slavery Attacked*, p. 203.

271 *They would have to traverse:* Walker, *The Trial and Imprisonment*, p. 96.

272 *a commercial extension of the Northern states:* Taylor, *Transportation Revolution*, pp. 106–8, 117, 122–26; Cecelski, *Waterman's Song*, pp. 218–19.

272 *Ashore, they mingled:* Gary Collison, *Shadrach Minkins: From Fugitive Slave to Citizen* (Cambridge, Mass.: Harvard University Press, 1997), p. 47; Cecelski, *Waterman's Song*, p. 136; Jeffrey W. Bolster, *Black Jacks: African American Seamen in the Age of Sail* (Cambridge, Mass.: Harvard University Press, 1997), pp. 214, 194–97.

272 *Escape by sea held:* Merton L. Dillon, *Slavery Attacked: Southern Slaves and Their Allies 1619–1865* (Baton Rouge: Louisiana State University Press, 1990), pp. 185–86; *First Annual Report of the New York Committee of Vigilance*; John M. Taylor, *William Henry Seward: Lincoln's Right Hand* (Washington, D.C.: Brassey's, 1991), p. 47.

272 *"No sooner, indeed":* Daniel Drayton, *Personal Memoir of Daniel Drayton, Four Years and Four Months a Prisoner (for Charity's Sake) in Washington Jail* (New York: Negro Universities Press, 1969), pp. 20–22.

272 *Moses Roper:* Roper, "Narrative of the Adventures and Escape of Moses Roper," p. 515.

273 *William Grimes:* Grimes, "Life of William Grimes," p. 220.

273 *Charles Ball:* Ball, "Narrative of the Life and Adventures," pp. 481–82.

273 *assistance was almost always indispensible:* William Still, *The Underground Railroad* (Chicago: Johnson Publishing, 1970), pp. 162–63.

273 *underground work usually hinged:* Drayton, *Personal Memoir*, pp. 20–22; J. C. Furnas, *Goodbye to Uncle Tom* (New York: William Sloane Associates, 1956), pp. 216–17; Cecelski, *Waterman's Song*, p. 126; McDougall, *Fugitive Slaves*, p. 41.

274 *expected to be paid well:* Still, *Underground Railroad*, pp. 162–63; Collison, *Shadrach Minkins*, pp. 49–50; *Provincial Freeman*, December 22, 1855.

274 *Only around Norfolk:* Cecelski, *Waterman's Song*, pp. 121–24, 135; Collison, *Shadrach Minkins*, pp. 46–50; Smedley, "History of the Underground Railroad in Chester," p. 355; William H. Robinson, *From Log Cabin to Pulpit, or Fifteen Years in Slavery* (Eau Claire, Wis.: James H. Tifft, 1913), pp. 29–35.

275 *Henry Gorham, a fugitive:* Cecelski, *Waterman's Song*, p. 133.

275 *Jacobs spent her entire life:* Jacobs, *Incidents in the Life of a Slave Girl*, pp. 5 ff; John S. Jacobs, "A True Tale of Slavery," *Leisure Hour: A Family Journal of Instruction and Recreation* (London), Stevens and Co., February 7, 1861.

276 *"a sad epoch":* Jacobs, *Incidents in the Life of a Slave Girl*, pp. 27 ff; Jean Fagan Yellin, *Harriet Jacobs: A Life* (Cambridge, Mass.: Basic Civitas Books, 2004), pp. 16–22.

276 *It is hard to understand:* Jacobs, *Incidents in the Life of a Slave Girl*, p. 95; and 265, n. 2.

276 *she chose the single expedient:* Jacobs, *Incidents in the Life of a Slave Girl*, pp. 53 ff, 91; Yellin, *Harriet Jacobs*, pp. 26–28.

277 *On a June night:* Jacobs, "True Tale of Slavery."

277 *When Norcom discovered:* Jacobs, *Incidents in the Life of a Slave Girl*, p. 97; Yellin, *Harriet Jacobs*, p. 45.

277 *they arranged for her to hide:* Jacobs, *Incidents in the Life of a Slave Girl*, pp. 100–3; and 275, n. 3.

278 *Harriet's brother John:* Jacobs, "True Tale of Slavery."

278 *A more permanent hiding place:* Jacobs, *Incidents in the Life of a Slave Girl*, pp. 110–13; and 276, n. 4.

278 *a hiding place in the attic:* Ibid., pp. 114–19; John S. Jacobs, "A True Tale of Slavery," *The Leisure Hour: A Family Journal of Instruction and Recreation* (London), Stevens and Company, February 14, 1861.

279 *Her isolation tested her faith:* Jacobs, *Incidents in the Life of a Slave Girl*, pp. 121–23.

280 *none of this would touch Harriet:* Ibid., pp. 125, 134–35, 141, 280–81; Jacobs, "True Tale of Slavery," February 14, 1861.

280 *"Sir—I have left you":* John S. Jacobs, "A True Tale of Slavery," *The Leisure Hour: A Family Journal of Instruction and Recreation* (London), Stevens and Company, February 21, 1861.

280 *Stowing away was:* Furnas, *Goodbye to Uncle Tom*, pp. 218–20; Bolster, *Black Jacks*, p. 212; *Colored American*, June 12, 1841.

280 *Captain Gilbert Ricketson:* Grover, *Fugitive's Gibraltar*, p. 185.

280 *Frederick Douglass reported: North Star*, March 31, 1848.

281 *It was harder than it had ever been:* Bolster, *Black Jacks*, pp. 194, 200; Collison, *Shadrach Minkins*, p. 50; Cecelski, *Waterman's Song*, p. 134.

281 *Jacobs's friend Peter:* Jacobs, *Incidents in the Life of a Slave Girl*, pp. 148–59.

282 *Jeremiah Durham, a minister:* Ibid., pp. 159–62; Yellin, *Harriet Jacobs*, pp. 65–68.

283 *Jacobs's life in the North:* Jean Fagan Yellin, Introduction to Jacobs, *Incidents in the Life of a Slave Girl*, pp. xvii ff.

283 *on the night of June 19:* Walker, *The Trial and Imprisonment*, pp. 10–14; and introduction, pp. xxviii–xxix; Oickle, *Jonathan Walker*, pp. 47–49.

284 *In 1821 shipwrecked sailors:* Nathan Philbrick, *In the Heart of the Sea: The Tragedy of the Whaleship Essex* (New York: Penguin Books, 2000), pp. 99, 179.

287 *Pensacola was in an uproar:* Oickle, *Jonathan Walker*, p. 52.

288 *The night fell away:* Walker, *The Trial and Imprisonment*, pp. 13, 36–39; Oickle, *Jonathan Walker*, pp. 56–59.

288 *in the* calabozo: Walker, pp. 15–22, 72; and introduction, p. xxi; Oickle, *Jonathan Walker*, p. 70.

289 *Walker's first trial:* Walker, pp. 33 ff.

289 *The three slaves:* Ibid, Introduction, p. lxxxix.

289 *The sentence was carried out:* Ibid., pp. 39–43, 64; Oickle, *Jonathan Walker*, p. 102.

290 *The first notice:* Walker, *The Trial and Imprisonment*, introduction, pp. xlvi–xlix, xxxiv–xxxvix; Oickle, *Jonathan Walker*, p. 77.

290 *The notoriety of Walker's punishment:* Walker, *The Trial and Imprisonment*, pp. 86, 98–99, and introduction, pp. lvii, xlix, lix.

291 *the reaction of the territorial government:* Ibid., pp. 87–92.

291 *Walker was hailed:* Ibid., introduction, lxviii–lxxiii; "The Fair," *North Star*, February 4, 1848; Jonathan Walker and John S. Jacobs, *North Star*, March 31, 1848.

CHAPTER 14: A DISEASE OF THE BODY POLITIC

Page

295 *William Chaplin and Daniel Drayton:* Drayton, *Personal Memoir*, pp. 25–11; Stanley Harrold, *Subversives: Antislavery Community in Washington, D.C., 1828–1865* (Baton Rouge: Louisiana State University Press, 2003), p. 128; *North Star*, August 10, 1848.

296 *one long hard-luck story:* Drayton, *Personal Memoir*, pp. 16–20.

296 *He would be well paid:* Ibid., pp. 24–25, 28.

296 *Much, if not most:* Ibid., pp. 5–11; Harrold, *Subversives*, pp. 127–28; Stowe, *Key to Uncle Tom's Cabin*, pp. 156–59; Grover, *Fugitive's Gibraltar*, pp. 192–93; William Chaplin, letter to Gerrit Smith, March 25, 1848, Smith Papers, Bird Library, Syracuse University; *North Star*, December 8, 1848.

296 *Back in Philadelphia:* Drayton, *Personal Memoir*, pp. 24–27.

297 *Soon after dark:* Ibid., pp. 28–31, 39, 46; Harrold, *Subversives*, pp. 116–21; Hilary Russell, *Final Research Report: The Operation of the Underground Railroad in Washington, D.C., c. 1800–1860* (Washington, DC: Historical Society of Washington and the National Park Service, July 2001); *North Star*, April 28, 1848, May 12, 1848, August 10, 1848.

298 *Just after dawn:* Drayton, *Personal Memoir*, pp. 39–40, 43; Harrold, *Subversives*, pp. 122–23.

299 *Rows of one-story structures:* Charles Dickens, *American Notes for General Circulation* (New York: Harper & Row, 1965), pp. 125–39; David Herbert Duncan, *Lincoln* (New York: Simon & Schuster, 1995), pp. 119–20.

300 *A free African American:* Thomas Smallwood, *A Narrative of Thomas Smallwood (Coloured Man): Giving Account of His Birth—The Period He Was Held in Slavery—His Release—and Removal to Canada, etc. Together with an Account of the Underground Railroad* (Toronto: James Stephens, 1851), p. 16.

300 *Mrs. Ann Sprigg's popular boardinghouse:* Duncan, *Lincoln*, p. 135.

300 *Some of the largest slave-trading establishments:* Frederic Bancroft, *Slave Trading in the Old South* (New York: Frederick Ungar, 1959), pp. 47, 49, 52, 61; Peterson, *Great Triumvirate*, p. 455; Duncan, *Lincoln*, pp. 119–20; Russell, *Final Research Report*, pp. 12, 17.

300 *the Quaker traveler Joseph Sturge:* Joseph Sturge, *A Visit to the United States in 1841* (New York: Augustus M. Kelley, 1969), pp. 74, 78.

300 *a secret ring operated by Charles T. Torrey:* J. C. Lovejoy, *Memoir of Rev. Charles T. Torrey, Who Died in the Penitentiary of Maryland, Where He Was Confined for Showing Mercy to the Poor* (New York: Negro Universities Press, 1969), pp. 105–26; *Narrative of Thomas Smallwood*, pp. 16–21; Harrold, *Subversives*, pp. 82, 90; Ralph Volney Harlow, *Gerrit Smith: Philanthropist and Reformer* (New York: Russell & Russell, 1939), pp. 165, 275.

301 *"We had to pay": Narrative of Thomas Smallwood*, pp. 31, 25–30, 34.

301 *"Did you ever hear":* Lovejoy, *Memoir of Rev. Charles T. Torrey*, p. 127.

301 *That June:* Ibid., pp. 173–86; Harrold, *Subversives*, pp. 86–87.

301 *prison proved an agony:* Lovejoy, *Memoir of Rev. Charles T. Torrey*, pp. 127–28, 276; Quarles, *Black Abolitionists*, p. 164.

301 *Both proslavery forces and abolitionists:* Harrold, *Subversives*, p. 138; Harlow, *Gerrit Smith*, p. 290; William Chaplin, letter to Gerrit Smith, March 25, 1848, Smith Papers, Bird Library, Syracuse University.

302 *Drayton's trial began:* Drayton, *Personal Memoir*, pp. 68–73; Stowe, *Key to Uncle Tom's Cabin*, pp. 159–164; Harrold, *Subversives*, pp. 125–26, 138–39; *North Star*, August 10, 1848.

302 *Key maintained that:* Drayton, *Personal Memoir*, pp. 79–81; *North Star*, August 24, 1848.

303 *Sayres was convicted:* Drayton, *Personal Memoir*, pp. 94–103; Harrold, *Subversives*, pp. 140–41.

304 *John C. Calhoun:* Harrold, *Subversives*, p. 142.

304 *Throughout the South, anxiety:* Morison, *Oxford History*, vol. 2, pp. 265–66; Susan Hubbard, letter to Joseph and Mary, October 13, 1843, Quaker Collection, Guilford College, Greensboro, N.C.; Nye, *Fettered Freedom*, pp. 147–48.

304 *a cache of abolitionist material:* Philip Ashley Fanning, *Mark Twain and Orion Clemens: Brothers, Partners, Strangers* (Tuscaloosa: University of Alabama Press, 2003), pp. 2–3; Shelley Fisher Fisjkin, *Lighting Out for the Territory: Reflections on Mark Twain and American Culture* (New York: Oxford University Press, 1998), p. 54.

304 *Loyalty to the South increasingly:* Cohn, *Life and Times of King Cotton*, p. 82; Miller, *Wolf by the Ears*, p. 249.

305 *praised it, as Calhoun did:* Richard N. Current, *John C. Calhoun* (New York: Washington Square Press, 1963), pp. 20, 23–24, 76–79, 82; Morison, *Oxford History*, p. 267.

305 *"God has made the Negro":* J. H. Van Evrie, *Negroes and Negro Slavery* (New York: Van Evrie, Horton & Co., 1863), pp. 218–21.

305 *Slaveholders pointed triumphantly:* William S. Jenkins, *Proslavery Thought in the Old South* (Gloucester, Mass.: Peter Smith, 1962), pp. 201–6; John Patrick Daly, *When Slavery Was Called Freedom: Evangelicalism, Proslavery, and the Causes of the Civil War* (Lexington: University Press of Kentucky, 2002), p. 95.

306 *scholars such as Louis Agassiz:* Robert E. Bieder, *Science Discovers the Indian, 1820–1880* (Norman: University of Oklahoma Press, 1986), pp. 92–93.

306 *S. A. Cartwright, a prominent:* Stephen Jay Gould, *The Mismeasure of Man* (New York: W. W. Norton, 1981), pp. 70–71; Jenkins, *Proslavery Thought in the Old South*, p. 250.

306 *Similarly, James D. B. DeBow:* Burton, *Rise and Fall of King Cotton*, pp. 56–57.

306 *Meanwhile, the plantation economy continued:* Cohn, *Life and Times of King Cotton*, pp. 86–87, 52, 83, 111, 90–91; Bancroft, *Slave Trading in the Old South*, p. 383.

307 *they credited the underground with a ubiquitousness:* Sydnor, *Slavery in Mississippi*, pp. 88–89, 105, 112.

308 *"The life of anxiety":* Coffin, *Life and Travels of Addison Coffin*, p. 48.

308 *After weeks or months concealed:* Ibid., pp. 15, 35; Weeks, *Southern Quakers and Slavery*, pp. 241, 244; Susan Hubbard, letter to Joseph and Mary, October 13, 1843, Quaker Collection, Guilford College, Greensboro, N.C.; Mendenhall Plantation Historic Site, High Point, N.C., author visits, June 2002.

308 *a vividly detailed account:* Coffin, "Early Settlement of Friends in North Carolina," p. 127.

309 *Addison's brother Alfred:* Ibid., p. 105; Coffin, *Life and Travels of Addison Coffin*, p. 14.

309 *One of the most daring escapes:* William and Ellen Craft, "Running a Thousand Miles for Freedom; or, The Escape of William and Ellen Craft from Slavery," in *I Was Born a Slave: An Anthology of Classic Slave Narratives*, vol. 2, Yuval Taylor, ed. (Chicago: Lawrence Hill, 1999), pp. 487 ff.

309 *a Virginia slave named Henry Brown:* Brown, *Narrative of the Life of Henry Box Brown*, pp. 29 ff, 45 ff, 57–62; Still, *Underground Railroad*, pp. 67–73.

312 *personal liberty laws enacted:* McDougall, *Fugitive Slaves*, pp. 39–40, 65–66; Grover, *Fugitive's Gibraltar*, p. 181.

312 *"Everybody heard of their coming":* Jay P. Smith, "Many Michigan Cities on Underground Railroad in Days of Civil War," *Detroit News*, April 14, 1918.

312 *stationmaster in Wilmington, Thomas Garrett:* Still, *Underground Railroad*, p. 658.

312 *On January 24, 1848:* J. S. Holliday, *The World Rushed In: The California Gold Rush Experience* (New York: Simon & Schuster, 1981), pp. 300–1.

313 *The crisis had been foreshadowed:* Garry Wills, *"Negro President": Jefferson and the Slave Power* (Boston: Houghton Mifflin, 2003), pp. 222–25.

313 *The debate that began in February:* Morison, *Oxford History*, vol. 2, pp. 330–35; Mayer, *All on Fire*, pp. 393–95.

314 *Clay opened the debate:* Peterson, *The Great Triumvirate*, pp. 455–58; Arthur M. Schlesinger, *The Age of Jackson* (New York: Little, Brown, 1945), pp. 82–83.

315 *On March 4:* Peterson, *The Great Triumvirate*, pp. 453, 461; Current, *John C. Calhoun*, p. 32.

315 *Calhoun's complaints were deeply felt:* Garry Wills, *"Negro President": Jefferson and the Slave Power* (Boston: Houghton Mifflin, 2003), pp. 5–12; Nye, *Fettered Freedom*, pp. 226–34; Cohn, *Life and Times of King Cotton*, pp. 97–100; *Philanthropist*, August 30, 1840.

316 *broader demographic trends:* Cohn, *Life and Times of King Cotton*, pp. 46, 49, 83, 88.

316 *But Daniel Webster's speech:* Schlesinger, *Age of Jackson*, pp. 83–84; Daniel Webster, *North Star*, July 18, 1850.

316 *The South loved:* Peterson, *The Great Triumvirate* pp. 463–66; *North Star*, April 12, 1850; *National Era*, May 9, 1850.

317 *The debate continued:* Peterson, *The Great Triumvirate*, p. 471; Siebert, *Underground Railroad from Slavery to Freedom*, p. 341; Harrold, *Subversives*, p. 148.

317 *Chaplin was busy that summer:* Harrold, *Subversives*, p. 147.

317 *charged with larceny:* Ibid., p. 157.

317 *Gerrit Smith wrote:* Harlow, *Gerrit Smith*, pp. 291–93.

317 *abolitionists held:* Sernett, *North Star Country*, pp. 129–32; Harrold, *Subversives*, pp. 158–59; Harlow, *Gerrit Smith*, p. 190.

318 *A Tennessee newspaper: National Anti-Slavery Standard*, September 26, 1850.

318 *Rockville slaveholders:* Harlow, *Gerrit Smith*, pp. 291–93; Harrold, *Subversives*, p. 161.

318 *the new Fugitive Slave Act:* McDougall, *Fugitive Slaves*, pp. 30, 112–14; Nye, *Fettered Freedom*, p. 201.

319 *Webster, with visions:* Peterson, *The Great Triumvirate*, p. 474.

319 *Meetings of condemnation:* Meetings at Canandaigua and Rochester, *North Star*, April 12, 1850.

319 *"Wo to the poor":* Frederick Douglass, *North Star*, October 3, 1850.

Chapter 15: Do We Call This the Land of the Free?

Page

320 *At about 2 P.M.:* Collison, *Shadrach Minkins*, pp. 112–33; Joel Strangis, *Lewis Hayden and the War Against Slavery* (North Haven, Conn.: Linnet Books, 1999), pp. 74–79; Stanley W. Campbell, *The Slave Catchers* (Chapel Hill: University of North Carolina Press, 1970), pp. 148–51; *National Era*, February 20, 1851, February 26, 1851, and February 27, 1851; *Liberator*, February 21, 1851, and February 28, 1851;

Voice of the Fugitive, February 26, 1851; Leonard W. Levy, "The Sims Case: The Fugitive Slave Law in Boston in 1851," *Journal of Negro History* 35 (1950): 39–74.

321 *Minkins, meanwhile:* Collison, *Shadrach Minkins*, pp. 151–58; Strangis, *Lewis Hayden and the War Against Slavery*, p. 86; Record Book of the Boston Vigilance Committee, copy in Siebert Collection, Ohio Historical Society, Columbus.

322 *"Do we call this":* Franklin B. Sanborn, *The Life of Henry David Thoreau* (Boston: Houghton Mifflin, 1917), pp. 469, 480; Van Wyck Brooks, *The Flowering of New England 1815–1865* (New York: Dutton, 1936), pp. 286–87, 434.

322 *Before Thoreau:* Henry David Thoreau, *Walden and Civil Disobedience*, Paul Lauter, ed. (Boston: Houghton Mifflin, 2000), pp. 18, 24–25, 29, 36.

323 *"We must trample":* Jane H. Pease and William H. Pease, "Confrontation and Abolition in the 1850s," *Journal of American History* 58 (1972): 923–37.

323 *"This so-called Fugitive Slave Law": Frederick Douglass' Paper*, December 4, 1851.

323 *That sad honor went:* Siebert, *Underground Railroad from Slavery to Freedom*, p. 269.

323 *There were captures:* Ibid., pp. 317–18; Collison, *Shadrach Minkins*, p. 107; *Voice of the Fugitive*, February 26, 1851; George F. Nagle, "Central Pennsylvania Fugitive Slave Cases," *Bugle (Journal of the Camp Curtin Historical Society and Civil War Round Table)* 12, no. 1 (January 2002), pp. 6–16.

323 *Daniel Webster, promised:* May, *Some Recollections on Our Anti-Slavery Conflict*, pp. 373–74; Hunter, *To Set the Captives Free*, p. 120; *Frederick Douglass' Paper*, December 16, 1851.

323 *Fugitive slaves who had lived:* Douglass, "My Bondage and My Freedom," p. 279; Siebert, *Underground Railroad*, pp. 194, 248–50; Campbell, *Slave Catchers*, pp. 7, 62–63; *Voice of the Fugitive*, January 1, 1851; Levy, "Sims Case."

324 *Columbia, Pennsylvania, one of the largest:* Leroy Hopkins, "Black Eldorado on the Susquehannah: The Emergence of Black Columbia, 1726–1861," *Journal of the Lancaster County Historical Society*, 89, no. 4 (1985), pp. 110–32; Leroy Hopkins, "Bethel African Methodist Church in Lancaster: Prolegomenon to A Social History," *Journal of the Lancaster County Historical Society* 90, no. 4 (1986), pp. 205–31; *Columbia* (Pa.) *Spy*, January 15, 1851, March 8, 1851, and April 26, 1851; *Frederick Douglass' Paper*, November 13, 1851.

324 *Reverend Jermain Loguen of Syracuse:* Loguen, *Rev. J. W. Loguen*, pp. 343–48, 351–52, 391–95; Hunter, *To Set the Captives Free*, pp. 19–21.

325 *Edward Gorsuch was:* Thomas P. Slaughter, *Bloody Dawn: The Christiana Riot and Racial Violence in the Antebellum North* (New York: Oxford University Press, 1991), pp. 4–6, 11, 14, 17–19, 44; Smedley, "History of the Underground Railroad in Chester," p. 120; Charles D. Spotts, "The Pilgrim's Pathway: The Underground Railroad in Lancaster Country," *Community History Annual* 5, Lancaster (1966); *Lancaster Intelligencer and Journal*, September 16, 1851.

326 *Gorsuch did not imagine:* The story of the Christiana riot is based on William Parker, "The Freedman's Story," *Atlantic Monthly*, February 1866, pp. 152–66, and March 1866, pp. 276–88; Smedley, "History of the Underground Railroad in Chester," pp. 108–30; Slaughter, *Bloody Dawn*, pp. 51–74; *Lancaster Intelligencer and Journal*, September 16, 1851, and September 23, 1851; *Voice of the Fugitive*, September 24, 1851; Spotts, "Pilgrim's Pathway"; Nagle, "Central Pennsylvania Fugitive Slave Cases"; Mark C. Ebersole, "Abolition Divides the Meeting House: Quakers and Slavery in Early Lancaster County," *Journal of the Lancaster County Historical Society* 102, no. 1 (Spring 2000), pp. 3–23; Leroy Hopkins, interview with the author, Millersville State College, Millersville, Pa., March 13, 2003.

327 *abolitionist congressman, Thaddeus Stevens:* Hans L. Trefousse, *Thaddeus Stevens: Nineteenth-Century Egalitarian* (Mechanicsburg, Pa.: Stackpole Books, 2001), pp. 14, 73, 25; Fergus M. Bordewich, "Digging into a Historic Rivalry," *Smithsonian Magazine*, February 2004, pp. 96–107.

331 *William Parker had no illusions:* Parker, "Freedman's Story," March 1866, pp. 288–90; Smedley, "History of the Underground Railroad in Chester," pp. 223–24, 247–53, 260–68; Douglass, "Life and Times," pp. 724–26.

332 *If Parker's resistance:* Smedley, "History of the Underground Railroad in Chester," pp. 126–27; Slaughter, *Bloody Dawn*, pp. 72–74, 86–93; Nagle, "Central Pennsylvania Fugitive Slave Cases."

333 *Nevertheless, William Henry:* The story of the Jerry rescue is based on Loguen, *Rev. J. W. Loguen*, pp. 398–429; May, *Some Recollections of Our Antislavery Conflict*, pp. 363, 373–78; Earl Sperry, *The Jerry Rescue* (Syracuse: Onondaga Historical Society, 1924), pp. 41–51; Pettit, *Sketches in the History of the Underground Railroad*, pp. 32–33; Hunter, *To Set the Captives Free*, pp. 114–15, 122–26; Sernett, *North Star Country*, pp. 136–41; *Voice of the Fugitive*, October 8, 1851; *Frederick Douglass' Paper*, October 16, 1851, November 13, 1851, February 4, 1853, February 11, 1853, and February 18, 1853.

339 *Twenty-six men:* Loguen, *Rev. J.W. Loguen*, pp. 427–29, 434–43; May, *Some Recollections of Our Antislavery Conflict*, pp. 379–83; Hunter, *To Set the Captives Free*, pp. 129, 138; Sernett, *North Star Country*, p. 143.

339 *The government fared:* Collison, *Shadrach Minkins*, pp. 147–48, 192–95; Slaughter, *Bloody Dawn*, pp. ix, 86–93, 132–37; Smedley, "History of the Underground Railroad in Chester," pp. 126–27, 129–30; Paul Finkelman, "The Treason Trial of Castner Hanway," in *American Political Trials*, Michael Belknap, ed. (Westport, Conn.: Greenwood Press, 1994), pp. 79–100.

340 *Not surprisingly, there:* Campbell, *Slave Catchers*, pp. 148, 157, 169, 199; Slaughter, *Bloody Dawn*, p, xi.

341 *Isaac Tatum Hopper died:* Child, *Isaac T. Hopper*, pp. 473–77; and Bacon, *Lamb's Warrior*, pp. 182–86.

341 *Public opinion in both North and South:* Nye, *Fettered Freedom*, pp. 175–76; Slaughter, *Bloody Dawn*, pp. 104–5; Pease and Pease, "Confrontation and Abolition," pp. 923–37; Frothingham, *Gerrit Smith*, pp. 118–19; *Frederick Douglass' Paper*, February 11, 1853, and February 18, 1853.

342 *The language of abolitionism:* Campbell, *Slave Catchers*, p. 53; Smedley, "History of the Underground Railroad in Chester," pp. 129–30; Slaughter, *Bloody Dawn*, pp. 132–37.

343 *the flood of refugees only grew: Voice of the Fugitive*, October 8, 1851, November 5, 1851, and December 3, 1851.

Chapter 16: General Tubman

Page

344 *Kessiah Bowley:* Sarah Bradford, *Scenes in the Life of Harriet Tubman* (Auburn, N.Y.: W. J. Moses, 1869), pp. 57–64; John Creighton, historian, interview with the author, Cambridge, MD, February 12, 2004; Kate Clifford Larson, *Bound for the Promised Land* (New York: Random House, 2003), pp. 89 ff, and 324, nn. 11–17; Kate Clifford Larson, e-mail to author, January 21, 2004; Harkless Bowley, letter to Earl Conrad, August 8, 1939, Earl Conrad/Harriet Tubman Collection, Schomburg Center for Research in Black Culture, New York; Barbara Jeanne Fields, *Slavery and Freedom on the Middle Ground: Maryland During the Nineteenth Century* (New Haven, Conn.: Yale University Press, 1985), pp. 45–46; McFeely, *Frederick Douglass*, pp. 27, 59, 68.

346 *There were others:* John P. Parker, *His Promised Land*, Stuart Seely Sprague, ed. (New York: W. W. Norton, 1996), pp. 100 ff; Coon, "Great Escapes," p. 2; Quarles, *Black Abolitionists*, pp. 11, 14; Siebert, *Underground Railroad from Slavery to Freedom*, pp. 153–54.

346 *But there was no one quite like:* Jean M. Humez, *Harriet Tubman: The Life and the Life Stories* (Madison: University of Wisconsin Press, 2003), p. 25; Larson, *Bound for the Promised Land*, pp. 78–79; Lydia Maria Child, letter to John Greenleaf Whittier, January 21, 1862, Earl Conrad/Harriet Tubman Collection, Schomburg Center, New York; Thomas Garrett, letter to Eliza Wigham, December 16, 1855, Quaker Collection, Haverford College, Haverford, PA.

347 *General Tubman:* Oates, *To Purge This Land with Blood*, p. 242.

347 *The fifth of at least nine children:* Statement of Harriet Tubman, in Drew, *Refugee*, p. 20; Harkless Bowley, letter to Earl Conrad, August 8, 1939, Earl Conrad/Harriet Tubman Collection, Schomburg Center, New York; Bradford, *Scenes in the Life of Harriet Tubman*, p. 13; Larson, *Bound for the Promised Land*, pp. 42, 310; Humez, *Harriet Tubman*, pp. 211, 342–48.

348 *She was eleven or twelve:* Franklin B. Sanborn, "Harriet Tubman," *Boston Commonwealth*, July 17, 1863; Mrs. William Tatlock, interview with Earl Conrad, Earl Conrad/Harriet Tubman Collection, Schomburg Center, New York; Bradford, *Scenes in the Life of Harriet Tubman*, pp. 54–56; Sarah Bradford, *Harriet Tubman: The Moses of Her People* (Bedford, Mass.: Applewood Books, 1993), pp. 15–17;

Florence Carter, manuscript, Earl Conrad/Harriet Tubman Collection, Schomburg Center, New York; Larson, *Bound for the Promised Land*, pp. 39, 42–43; Humez, *Harriet Tubman*, pp. 178–79, 210–11.

348 *Slavery in Maryland:* Fields, *Slavery and Freedom on the Middle Ground*, pp. 10–15.

348 *Ross adapted readily:* Bradford, *Scenes in the Life of Harriet Tubman*, pp. 75–76; Mrs. William Tatlock, interview with Earl Conrad, Earl Conrad/Harriet Tubman Collection, Schomburg Center, New York; Harkless Bowley, letter to Earl Conrad, August 8, 1939, Earl Conrad/Harriet Tubman Collection; Larson, *Bound for the Promised Land*, pp. 48, 52, 56, 64, 73–79.

349 *Tubman's mind was overcharged:* Bradford, *Scenes in the Life of Harriet Tubman*, pp. 13–20; Bradford, *Moses of Her People*, pp. 114–15; Sanborn, *Harriet Tubman*; Humez, *Harriet Tubman*, pp. 181–84.

349 *Characteristically, she did not leave:* Bradford, *Scenes in the Life of Harriet Tubman*, p. 76; Mrs. William Tatlock, interview with Earl Conrad, Earl Conrad/Harriet Tubman Collection, Schomburg Center, New York; Humez, *Harriet Tubman*, pp. 216–18; Larson, *Bound for the Promised Land*, pp. 80–83.

350 *"When I found I had crossed":* Bradford, *Scenes in the Life of Harriet Tubman*, pp. 19–20.

350 *For the next decade:* Ibid., pp. 13–20; Humez, *Harriet Tubman*, pp. 25, 260; Thomas Garrett, letter to Eliza Wigham, December 16, 1855, Quaker Collection, Haverford College, Haverford, Pa.

350 *Emboldened by her success:* Bradford, *Moses of Her People*, p. 112; Larson, *Bound for the Promised Land*, pp. 89–90; Humez, *Harriet Tubman*, p. 183; Catherine Clinton, *Harriet Tubman: The Road to Freedom* (Boston: Little, Brown, 2004), pp. 82–83.

351 *Before the year was out:* Larson, *Bound for the Promised Land*, pp. 93–96.

351 *Although, in legend:* Ibid., 65–66; John Creighton, interview with the author, Cambridge, Md., February 12, 2004.

351 *She preferred to do her underground work:* Bradford, *Scenes in the Life of Harriet Tubman*, pp. 21, 25, 50; Larson, *Bound for the Promised Land*, pp. 131–32; Humez, *Harriet Tubman*, p. 138; Siebert, *Underground Railroad from Slavery to Freedom*, p. 68; Robert C. Smedley, "History of the Underground Railroad in Chester," p. 355.

352 *She was a consummate actress:* Mrs. William Tatlock, interview with Earl Conrad, Earl Conrad/Harriet Tubman Collection, Schomburg Center, New York; Harkless Bowley, letter to Earl Conrad, August 8, 1939, Earl Conrad/Harriet Tubman Collection.

352 *"Hail, oh hail, ye happy spirits":* Bradford, *Moses of Her People*, pp. 36–38.

352 *Tubman expected her passengers:* Harkless Bowley, letter to Earl Conrad, August 8, 1939, Earl Conrad/Harriet Tubman Collection, Schomburg Center, New York; Mrs. William Tatlock, interview with Earl Conrad, Earl Conrad/Harriet Tubman Collection; Still, *Underground Railroad*, pp. 305–6; Sanborn, "Harriet Tubman"; Larson, *Bound for the Promised Land*, pp. 100–3.

353 *One of these men was Thomas Garrett:* James McGowan, *Station Master on the Underground Railroad: The Life and Letters of Thomas Garrett* (Moylan, Pa.: Whimsie Press, 1977), pp. 2, 27, 41, 49, 60–64, 70–74, 111, 121, 129–30; Still, *Underground Railroad*, pp. 649, 655, 741–45, 775; Sanborn, "Harriet Tubman," pp. 54–55; Smedley, "History of the Underground Railroad in Chester," pp. 243–44, 249, 256, 270; William C. Kashatus, *Just Over the Line*, pp. 19–20, 51–54; *National Era*, July 13, 1848; Stowe, *Key to Uncle Tom's Cabin*, pp. 54–55.

355 *"Her like it is probable":* Still, *Underground Railroad*, pp. 305–6.

355 *Still was born free:* Linn Washington Jr., "The Chronicle of an American First Family," *Philadelphia Inquirer*, October 11, 1987.

356 *He coordinated escapes:* Stanley Harrold, "Subversives: Antislavery Community in Washington, D.C., 1828–1865," Louisiana State University Press, Baton Rouge, 2003, pp. 162, 212, 214–217; Still, *Underground Railroad*, pp. 161–63, 260–61, 583–89; Siebert, *Underground Railroad*, pp. 81–82; Collison, *Shadrach Minkins*, pp. 46–48.

356 *freed slave from Alabama named Peter Friedman:* Kate E. R. Pickard, *The Kidnapped and the Ransomed, Being the Personal Recollections of Peter Still and His Wife 'Vina,' after Forty Years of Slavery* (Philadelphia: Jewish Publication Society of America, 1970), pp. 245–69; Still, *Underground Railroad*, pp. 18–19; Washington, "Chronicle of an American First Family"; "Slaves Liberated—A Family United," *Provincial Freeman*, January 27, 1854.

357 *a crusty underground veteran named Seth Concklin:* Pickard, *Kidnapped and the Ransomed*, pp. 377–99; Still, *Underground Railroad*, pp. 1–5.

358 *he offered to personally bring Peter Friedman's family:* Pickard, *Kidnapped and the Ransomed*, pp. 279–82.

358 *Initially, Concklin hoped:* Thornbrough, *Negro in Indiana*, pp. 62–63; Stanley W. Campbell, *Slave Catchers*, pp. 148, 157, 169, 199; Slaughter, *Bloody Dawn*, pp. 59–60; James E. Morlock, *Was It Yesterday?* (Evansville, Ind: University of Evansville Press, 1980), p. 124; Coon, "Reconstructing the Underground Railroad Crossings."

358 *Frustrated but undaunted:* Pickard, *Kidnapped and the Ransomed*, pp. 284–85; Still, *Underground Railroad*, pp. 5–7, 13–14.

358 *a secure underground line:* Gil R. Stormont, *History of Gibson County, Indiana* (Indianapolis: B.F. Bowen & Co., 1914), pp. 224–26.

358 *At the end of January:* Pickard, *Kidnapped and the Ransomed*, pp. 286–89; Still, *Underground Railroad*, pp. 7–8; Stormont, *History of Gibson County*, pp. 226–28; Donald Davidson, *The Tennessee*, vol. 1: *The Old River: Frontier to Secession* (Nashville, Tenn.: J. S. Sanders, 1991), pp. 284–85, 299–301.

359 *Thus far, they had been traveling:* Pickard, *Kidnapped and the Ransomed*, pp. 290–98.

360 *the whites found all this less than convincing:* Ibid., pp. 298–300, 404–5; Still, *Underground Railroad*, pp. 9–12; Stormont, *History of Gibson County*, pp. 228–30;

Joseph P. Elliott, *A History of Evansville and Vandenburgh County, Indiana* (Evansville, Ind.: Keler Printing Co., 1897), p. 380.

361 *Sometime during the downriver trip:* Stormont, *History of Gibson County*, pp. 230–31; Still, *Underground Railroad*, pp. 9 ff; *Evansville Daily Journal*, April 15, 1851.

361 *"There was none of that pretended philanthropy":* "Capture of Fugitive Slaves," *Vincennes Gazette*, April 3, 1851.

361 *In a curious way, Concklin's death:* Washington, "Chronicle of an American First Family."

362 *another brave man was lost to the underground:* Fairbank, *Rev. Calvin Fairbank during Slavery Times*, pp. 55–57, 85 ff, 98–103; Runyon, *Delia Webster*, pp. 122–23, 150–54; *Voice of the Fugitive*, December 3, 1851, and April 22, 1852.

366 *There was, of course, another difference:* Julie Roy Jeffrey, *The Great Silent Army of Abolitionism: Ordinary Women in the Anti-Slavery Movement* (Chapel Hill: University of North Carolina Press, 1998), pp. 7, 88–95; Dorothy Sterling, *Ahead of Her Time: Abby Kelley and the Politics of Antislavery* (New York: W.W. Norton, 1991), pp. 2, 281; Keith Melder, "Abby Kelley and the Process of Liberation," in *The Abolitionist Sisterhood: Women's Political Culture in Antebellum America*, Jean Fagan Yellin and John C. Van Horne, eds. (Ithaca, N.Y.: Cornell University Press, 1994), pp. 242–44; Kathryn Kish Sklar, *Women's Rights Emerges within the Antislavery Movement, 1830–1870: A Brief History with Documents* (Boston: Bedford/St. Martin's, 2000), pp. 118ff.

367 *"we were all on a level":* Grover, *Fugitive's Gibraltar*, p. 181.

367 *One of the countless women:* Lucretia Mott, "Slavery and the Woman Question: Lucretia Mott's Diary of her Visit to Great Britain to Attend the World's Anti-Slavery Convention of 1840," Frederick B. Tolles, ed., Supplement no. 23 to the *Journal of the Friends' Historical Society*, Friends' Historical Association, Haverford, PA, 1952, p. 29; Elizabeth Cady Stanton, *Eighty Years and More: Reminiscences 1815–1897* (New York: Schocken Books, 1971), pp. 59, 79–83; Christopher Densmore, curator, Friends Historical Library, Swarthmore College, remarks made at the dedication of the McClintock House national historical site, Waterloo, NY, May 29, 2004.

368 *After the Stantons moved to Seneca Falls:* Stanton, *Eighty Years and More*, pp. 143–50; Nancy A. Hewitt, *Women's Activism and Social Change: Rochester, New York 1822–1872* (Ithaca, N.Y.: Cornell University Press, 1984), pp. 130–32; Ward and Burns, *Not for Ourselves Alone*, pp. 39–41, 58–59; Shirley J. Yee, *Black Women Abolitionists: A Study in Activism, 1828–1860* (Knoxville: University of Tennessee Press, 1992), pp. 140–41; Nell Irvin Painter, "Difference, Slavery, and Memory: Sojourner Truth in Feminist Abolitionism," in *The Abolitionist Sisterhood: Women's Political Culture in Antebellum America*, Jean Fagan Yellin and John C. Van Horne, eds. (Ithaca, N.Y.: Cornell University Press, 1994), pp. 140–47; Larson, *Bound for the Promised Land*, pp. 107–9.

369 *Women had always done:* Yee, *Black Women Abolitionists*, pp. 20–21, 29; Jeffrey, *Great Silent Army of Abolitionism*, pp. 179–84.

369 *White women as well as black women:* Ward and Burns, *Not for Ourselves Alone*, pp. 48–49; Elizabeth Buffum Chace and Lucy Buffum Lovell, *Two Quaker Sisters* (New York: Liveright Publishing, 1937), pp. xxv, 110, 128, 134; Diary of Phebe Earle Gibbons, entry for July 17, 1856, Gibbons Family File, Lancaster Historical Society, Lancaster, Pa.; Yee, *Black Women Abolitionists*, pp. 36, 117; Hewitt, *Women's Activism and Social Change*, p. 150.

370 *Ironically, no one did more:* Furnas, *Goodbye to Uncle Tom*, pp. 5–9, 17, 30–31, 45.

370 *Stowe based her eponymous composite hero partly:* Stowe, *Key to Uncle Tom's Cabin*, pp. 19, 26–27; Winks, *Blacks in Canada*, pp. 185–91.

371 *Stowe learned the story directly:* John Rankin Jr., unpublished interviews with Wilbur H. Siebert, Ohio Historical Society, Columbus, and Frank Gregg, copy in Union Township Library, Ripley, Ohio.

371 *In Stowe's rendering, Eliza:* Harriet Beecher Stowe, *Uncle Tom's Cabin or, Life Among the Lowly* (New York: Signet, 1998), pp. 67–68; Siebert, *Mysteries of Ohio's Underground Railroad*, p. 47; Coon, "Southeastern Indiana's Underground Railroad Routes and Operations," p. 185.

371 *Virtually every literate American:* Furnas, *Goodbye to Uncle Tom*, pp. 11ff; Stowe, *Key to Uncle Tom's Cabin*, pp. 21–23.

372 *Following her dramatic escape across the ice:* Stowe, *Uncle Tom's Cabin*, pp. 147–55, 203–21, 414–19.

373 *Harriet Tubman was unimpressed:* Bradford, *Scenes in the Life of Harriet Tubman*, p. 22.

Chapter 17: Laboratories of Freedom

Page

374 *On Christmas Eve, 1854:* The escape story of Tubman's brothers is based on Sarah Bradford, *Scenes in the Life of Harriet Tubman*, pp. 57–72; John Creighton, historian, interview with the author, Cambridge, Md., February 12, 2004; Larson, *Bound for the Promised Land*, pp. 93–94, 105, 110–17; Humez, *Harriet Tubman*, pp. 23, 351; Still, *Underground Railroad*, pp. 305, 307.

377 *They were welcomed by Tubman's friend: St. Catharines Journal*, April 22, 1852; Humez, *Harriet Tubman*, p. 25; Sernett, *North Star Country*, p. 180; Pease and Pease, *Bound with Them in Chains*, pp. 133–39; Frederick Douglass, *Life and Times*, p. 710; Winks, *Blacks in Canada*, p. 197; *Voice of the Fugitive*, May 21, 1851; *North Star*, November 10, 1848.

378 *sometime journalist Benjamin Drew:* Drew, *Refugee*, pp. 57–60.

378 *Some refugees complained:* Silverman, *Unwelcome Guests*, pp. 73, 128–30, 152.

379 *It was not unusual: Frederick Douglass' Paper*, October 2, 1851; Hunter, *To Set the Captives Free*, pp. 126–27; May, *Some Recollections of Our Antislavery Conflict*, pp. 378–79.

379 *In the burgeoning town of Chatham:* Farrell, "History of the Negro Community in Chatham, Ontario," pp. 65, 138; Jonathan W. Walton, "Blacks in Buxton and Chatham, Ontario, 1830–1890: Did the 49th Parallel Make a Difference?" (Ph.D. thesis, Princeton University, 1979), pp, 62–67; Lauriston, *Romantic Chatham*, p. 458; *Provincial Freeman*, September 9, 1854; *Syracuse Daily Standard*, May 26, 1856.

379 *Estimates of the total number: Liberator*, September 27, 1848; *North Star*, November 10, 1848; *Provincial Freeman*, March 25, 1854, and March 26, 1854; Coffin, *Reminiscences of Levi Coffin* pp. 252–53; Silverman, *Unwelcome Guests*, p. 43; Pease and Pease, *Bound with Them in Chains*, p. 138; Wayne, "Black Population of Canada West," pp. 465–85.

380 *the journalist Henry Bibb:* Henry Bibb, "Narrative of the Life and Adventures of Henry Bibb, An American Slave," in *I Was Born a Slave: An Anthology of Classic Slave Narratives*, vol. 2, Yuval Taylor, ed. (Chicago: Lawrence Hill, 1999), pp. 13–92.

382 *Unique within the underground: Detroit Tribune*, February 23, 1875, and January 11, 1886; interview with George DeBaptiste, "Underground Railroad," *Detroit Post*, May 16, 1870, and February 23, 1875; Lumpkin, "General Plan Was Freedom"; Afua Ave Pamela Cooper, " 'Doing Battle in Freedom's Cause': Henry Bibb, Abolitionism, Race Uplift, and Black Manhood, 1842–1854" (Ph.D. thesis, University of Toronto, 2000), pp. 153–59.

383 *Bibb underwent another profound experience:* Cooper, "Doing Battle in Freedom's Cause," pp. 47 ff; Bibb, "Narrative of the Life and Adventures of Henry Bibb," pp. 86–87.

383 *The passage of the Fugitive Slave Act: Voice of the Fugitive*, January 1, 1851, January 29, 1851, February 17, 1851, March 12, 1851, March 26, 1851, May 21, 1851, October 8, 1851, and April 8, 1852; Cooper, " 'Doing Battle in Freedom's Cause,' " pp. 204, 302, 315, 349, 378.

384 *"What is the future of the black race":* Henry Bibb, "An Address to the Colored Inhabitants of North America," in *The Black Abolitionist Papers*, vol. 2: *Canada, 1830–1865*, C. Peter Ripley, ed. (Chapel Hill: University of North Carolina Press, 1986), pp. 170–75.

385 *For Bibb, part of the solution: Voice of the Fugitive*, March 26, 1851, and December 16, 1852; Jason H. Silverman, " 'We Shall Be Heard!': The Development of the Fugitive Slave Press in Canada, *Canadian Historical Review* 65, no. 1 (March 1984), pp. 54–69; Cooper, " 'Doing Battle in Freedom's Cause,' " pp. 225–27, 241–47.

385 *Among those who attended:* Jane Rhodes, *Mary Ann Shadd Cary: The Black Press and Protest in the Nineteenth Century* (Bloomington: Indiana University Press, 1998), pp. 10–15, 20–22, 32 ff, 110; Smedley, "History of the Underground Railroad in Chester," pp. 33, 337.

385 *Initially, the two got along:* Winks, *Blacks in Canada*, pp. 205–8; Silverman, " 'We Shall Be Heard,' " pp. 54–69; Jason H. Silverman, "Mary Ann Shadd and the Search for Equality," in *Black Leaders of the Nineteenth Century*, eds. Leon Litwack and August Meier (Urbana: University of Illinois Press, 1988); Jeffrey, *Great Silent*

Army of Abolitionism, pp. 191–92; Cooper, " 'Doing Battle in Freedom's Cause,' " pp. 264–68, 282; Rhodes, *Mary Ann Shadd Cary*, pp. 71 ff.

386 *By 1852 Shadd's relationship:* Mary Ann Shadd, letter to George Whipple, December 28, 1852, in Ripley, *Black Abolitionist Papers*, vol. 2, pp. 245–51; Rhodes, *Mary Ann Shadd Cary*, p. 66.

386 *Although Bibb's manifold talents:* Rhodes, *Mary Ann Shadd Cary*, p. 73; Cooper, " 'Doing Battle in Freedom's Cause,' " pp. 251–64, 275; *Provincial Freeman*, March 24, 1853, and March 27, 1853, in Ripley, *Black Abolitionist Papers*, vol. 2, pp. 265–67, 285–87.

387 *Caught amid the collateral damage:* Winks, *Blacks in Canada*, pp. 195–203; *Voice of the Fugitive*, May 21, 1851; Rhodes, *Mary Ann Shadd Cary*, pp. 105–7.

387 *A sawmill long championed:* Henson, *Uncle Tom's Story of His Life*, pp. 137, 164–65, 173–74.

387 *Another problem was more subtle:* Ibid., pp. 165–69; Winks, *Blacks in Canada*, p. 201; Pease and Pease, *Black Utopia*, pp. 75–81.

388 *Perhaps Dawn's fatal weakness:* Henson, *Uncle Tom's Story*, pp. 142, 147, 173–77; *North Star*, January 12, 1849; *Voice of the Fugitive*, January 1, 1854; Joshua Leavitt, letter to John Scoble, March 9, 1843, in Anti-Slavery Papers, Dennis Gannon Collection, Welland Museum, St. Catharine's, Ontario.

388 *For Henry Bibb, the controversy:* William Lloyd Garrison, letter to Helen E. Garrison, October 17, 1853, in *The Letters of William Lloyd Garrison*, vol. 4: *From Disunionism to the Brink of War 1850–1860*, Louis Ruchames, ed. (Cambridge, Mass.: Harvard University Press, 1975), pp. 272–75; Cooper, " 'Doing Battle in Freedom's Cause,' " p. 286; Rhodes, *Mary Ann Shadd Cary*, pp. 74, 81–82.

388 *In 1855, the touring abolitionist:* Drew, *Refugee*, pp. 225 ff.

389 *Shadd too was damaged:* Rhodes, *Mary Ann Shadd Cary*, pp. 102–8; Silverman, " 'We Shall Be Heard!' "

389 *She even mocked Frederick Douglass:* Yee, *Black Women Abolitionists*, p. 127.

389 *The origins of the Elgin Settlement:* Victor Ullman, *Look to the North Star: A Life of William King* (Toronto: Umbrella Press, 1969), pp. 19, 39–62; Bryan Prince, historian and curator of the Buxton National Historic Site and Museum, North Buxton, Ontario, interview with the author, June 7, 2003.

390 *King, in contrast to Henson:* Pease and Pease, *Black Utopia*, pp. 85–95; Winks, *Blacks in Canada*, pp. 210–11; Farrell, "History of the Negro Community in Chatham, Ontario," p. 118; Ullman, *Look to the North Star*, p. 100; Walton, "Blacks in Buxton and Chatham," pp. 90–92.

390 *the first of many fugitives:* William King, unpublished autobiography, manuscript copy in Raleigh Township Centennial Museum, North Buxton, Ontario; Parker, "Freedman's Story," March 1866, p. 291; Ullman, *Look to the North Star*, p. 108; Walton, "Blacks in Buxton and Chatham," p. 94.

391 *"When we grew tired":* Ullman, *Look to the North Star*, p. 106.

391 *King led rather than governed:* King, unpublished autobiography; Ullman, *Look to the North Star*, pp. 141–42; Pease and Pease, *Black Utopia*, pp. 96–99.

391 *Opposition coalesced around: Black Utopia*, pp. 105–6; King, unpublished autobiography; Lauriston, *Romantic Chatham*, pp. 493–94; Ullman, *Look to the North Star*, p. 85; Cooper, " 'Doing Battle in Freedom's Cause,' " p. 308; Silverman, *Unwelcome Guests*, p. 64.

392 *But King had a subtler strategy:* King, unpublished autobiography; Ullman, *Look to the North Star*, pp. 119–23; Pease and Pease, *Black Utopia*, pp. 100–4; Winks, *Blacks in Canada*, pp. 210–11; Silverman, *Unwelcome Guests*, p. 69.

392 *Isaac Riley's oldest son:* Ullman, *Look to the North Star*, pp. 224–26.

392 *White fears also ebbed:* King, unpublished autobiography; Pease and Pease, *Black Utopia*, pp. 85–95: Farrell, "History of the Negro Community in Chatham, Ontario," p. 118; Walton, "Blacks in Buxton and Chatham," pp. 94, 100, 109; Ullman, *Look to the North Star*, pp. 151–53; Silverman, *Unwelcome Guests*, p. 69.

393 *Elgin's crowning moment:* King, unpublished autobiography; Pease and Pease, *Black Utopia*, pp. 96–99; Ullman, *Look to the North Star*, pp. 90, 151–53.

393 *But there was no second act to Edwin Larwill: Provincial Freeman*, May 6, 1854; Walton, "Blacks in Buxton and Chatham," p. 109.

394 *Gerrit Smith was also dreaming:* Harlow, *Gerrit Smith*, pp. 241–58; Frothingham, *Gerrit Smith*, pp. 99–111; Sernett, *North Star Country*, pp. 198–202; Stauffer, *Black Hearts of Men*, pp. 155–56; *Liberator*, March 20, 1846; *North Star*, January 7, 1848, February 18, 1848, February 25, 1848, and December 15, 1848; *Press-Republican*, June 27, 2002.

395 *"The tide of benefaction":* Frothingham, *Gerrit Smith*, p. 98.

395 *One of them, William G. Allen:* Sernett, *North Star Country*, p. 68.

395 *Nothing was dearer to Smith's heart:* Ibid., pp. 169–70; Frothingham, *Gerrit Smith*, pp. 115, 120.

396 *The mansion at Peterboro:* Frothingham, *Gerrit Smith*, pp. 140–42; Stanton, *Eighty Years and More*, pp. 51 ff; Ward and Burns, *Not for Ourselves Alone*, pp. 11–18; *North Star*, July 7, 1848.

397 *a rail-thin man with a shock of graying hair:* Benjamin Quarles, *Allies for Freedom* (New York: Oxford University Press, 1974), p. 23; Otto Scott, *The Secret Six: John Brown and the Abolitionist Movement* (Murphys, Calif.: Uncommon Books, 1979), p. 19; Samuel Ringgold Ward, *Autobiography of a Fugitivie Negro* (Chicago: Johnson Publishing, 1970), p. 42; Caleb Calkins, handwritten deposition, John Brown folder, Gerrit Smith Collection, Bird Library, Syracuse University; Frothingham, *Gerrit Smith*, p. 235.

397 *The stranger's abolitionist credentials:* Oates, *To Purge This Land with Blood*, pp. 8–17, 24.

398 *Brown had taken a personal vow:* Ibid., pp. 41–42; Quarles, *Allies for Freedom*, pp. 18–19; Caccamo, *Hudson, Ohio and the Underground Railroad;* pamphlet, *John Brown Address by Frederick Douglass*, speech delivered at the fourteenth anniversary of Storer College in Harpers Ferry, W.Va., 1881, in *John Brown Pamphlets*, Vol. 5, Boyd B. Stutler Collection, West Virginia State Archives, Charleston, W.Va.

398 *"I've seen him come in:* Merrill D. Peterson, *John Brown: The Legend Revisited* (Charlottesville: University of Virginia Press, 2002), p. 56.

398 *He had never hesitated:* Oates, *To Purge This Land with Blood*, pp. 53, 63; *North Star*, February 11, 1848.

398 *Only a handful of black families: North Star*, March 24, 1848, and March 30, 1849; Stauffer, *Black Hearts of Men*, p. 157; Sernett, *North Star Country*, pp. 201–2; Brendan Mills, National Park Service site manager, interview with the author, John Brown home, North Elba, N.Y., August 11, 2002.

399 *Smith liked Brown's piety:* Stauffer, *Black Hearts of Men*, pp. 149, 169–70; Oates, *To Purge This Land with Blood*, p. 67; Peterson, *John Brown*, p. 51; John Brown, letter to Gerrit Smith, June 20, 1849, John Brown folder, Gerrit Smith Collection, Bird Library, Syracuse University.

399 *Visitors occasionally stumbled:* Scott, *Secret Six*, p. 19; Quarles, *Allies for Freedom*, p. 24.

399 *The problems that Loguen had identified:* Stauffer, *Black Hearts of Men*, p. 157; *Frederick Douglass' Paper*, April 15, 1853; *John Brown Address by Frederick Douglass.*

Chapter 18: The Last Train

Page

401 *One of the saddest incidents:* The story of Margaret Garner is based on Coffin, *Reminiscences of Levi Coffin*, pp. 558–65; Steven Weisenberger, *Modern Medea: A Family Story of Slavery and Child-Murder from the Old South* (New York: Hill & Wang, 1998), pp. 49, 54–65, 71–75; Julius Yanuck, "The Garner Fugitive Slave Case," *Mississippi Valley Historical Review* 40 (1953): 47–66; *Ripley* (Ohio) Bee, February 9, 1856, February 23, 1856, and March 8, 1856; Carl Westmoreland, National Underground Railroad Freedom Center, interview with the author, March 1, 1999.

402 *Coffin had moved:* Coffin, *Reminiscences*, pp. 265–74.

402 *By the time the Civil War:* Ibid., p. 671.

404 *But Margaret Garner's terrible odyssey:* Coffin, *Reminiscences*, p. 567; *Cincinnati Gazette*, March 11, 1856; Weisenberger, *Modern Medea*, pp. 220–25.

404 *The surviving Garners:* Weisenberger, *Modern Medea*, pp. 277–78.

405 *Now personal liberty laws:* McDougall, *Fugitive Slaves*, p. 67; Campbell, *Slave Catchers*, pp. 171–79, 184–85; *Provincial Freeman*, March 24, 1855.

405 *Benoni S. Fuller, for example:* Morlock, *Was It Yesterday?*, p, 125.

405 *In January 1854, another act of Congress:* Morison, *Oxford History*, vol. 2, 1972, pp. 354–60; Louis L. Gould, *Grand Old Party: A History of the Republicans* (New York: Random House, 2003), pp. 11–12; Ross Drake, "The Law That Ripped America in Two," *Smithsonian Magazine*, May 2004, pp. 61–66; Oates, *To Purge This Land with Blood*, pp. 80, 85–86.

406 *"[T]his Nebraska business": Frederick Douglass' Paper*, March 7, 1854.

406 *Free State settlers begged:* Gerrit Smith, speech to the Kansas Meeting, Albany, N.Y., April 6, 1854, Gerrit Smith Collection, Bird Library, Syracuse University; Oates, *To Purge This Land with Blood*, pp. 80, 83; *National Era*, July 10, 1856.

406 *Among the thousands:* John Brown Jr., diary, January 1 to March 11, 1856, copy in possession of the WISH Centre, Chatham, Ontario; Martha J. Parker, *Angels of Freedom* (private printing, Lawrence, Kans., 1999), p. 123; Gunja Sengupta, *For God and Mammon: Evangelicals and Entrepreneurs, Masters and Slaves in Territorial Kansas, 1854–1860* (Athens: University of Georgia Press, 1996), p. 65; Samuel F. Tappan, letter to Thomas Wentwoth Higginson, January 24, 1858, in *Freedom's Crucible: The Underground Railroad in Lawrence and Douglas County, Kansas, 1854–1865: A Reader*, Richard B. Sheridan, ed. (Lawrence: Division of Continuing Education, University of Kansas, 2000), p. 50; Steve Collins, historian, Kansas City Community College, interview with the author, Quindaro, KS, August 13, 2001.

407 *"[W]hile the interest":* Stan Cohen, *John Brown: "The Thundering Voice of Jehovah"* (Missoula, Mont.: Pictorial Histories Publishing Co., 1999), p. 21.

407 *Their father, John Brown, had promised:* Oates, *To Purge This Land with Blood*, pp. 74–75.

407 *There was actually (footnote):* Parker, *Angels of Freedom*, p. 123.

407 *a new national political party:* Gould, *Grand Old Party*, pp. 14–21; Isaac Beck, letter to Wilbur H. Siebert, December 26, 1892, Siebert Collection, Ohio Historical Society, Columbus.

408 *Thomas Garrett, the stationmaster:* McGowan, *Station Master on the Underground Railroad*, pp. 27, 121; Still, *Underground Railroad*, p. 659.

408 *Reports from other parts of the country:* William Still, Journal C of Station 2 of the Underground Railroad, on microfilm, Historical Society of Pennsylvania, Philadelphia; William Still, Still's Underground Railroad Records, William Still, Philadelphia, 1886, Introduction; *Frederick Douglass' Paper*, September 8, 1854, January 26, 1855, and October 12, 1855; C. Peter Ripley, ed., *Black Abolitionist Papers*, vol. 2, pp. 26–27; Wilbur H. Siebert, "The Underground Railroad in Massachusetts," *New England Quarterly* 9 (September 1936): 447–67; Record Book of the Boston Vigilance Committee, copy in Siebert Collection, Ohio Historical Society, Columbus.

409 *Technology was also transforming:* Taylor, *Transportation Revolution*, pp. 84–87, 102–3; Cohn, *Life and Times of King Cotton*, p. 95; John Reed, interviewed by Wilbur H. Siebert, August 2, 1894, Siebert Collection, Ohio Historical Society, Columbus;

Still, *Underground Railroad*, pp. 761–66; Hopkins, "Black Eldorado on the Susquehannah"; William J. Switala, *Underground Railroad in Pennsylvania* (Mechanicsburg, Pa.: Stackpole Books, 2001), pp. 146–47; Charles C. Chapman, *History of Knox County, Illinois* (Chicago: Charles C. Chapman & Co., 1878), p. 211; *North Star*, May 5, 1848; *Frederick Douglass' Paper*, March 9, 1855.

409 *Certain railroad companies:* Furnas, *Goodbye to Uncle Tom*, pp. 223–25; *Firelands Pioneer*, July 1888.

410 *an open part of local life:* Allan Nevins, *Ordeal of the Union*, vol. 2: *The Emergence of Lincoln, Part I, Douglas, Buchanan, and Party Chaos, 1857–1859* (New York: Collier Books, 1992), p. 95; *Provincial Freeman*, July 8, 1854; *Frederick Douglass' Paper*, November 17, 1854, January 4, 1855, and December 14, 1855.

410 *no one else but Jermain Loguen:* Hunter, *To Set the Captives Free*, pp. 162–63, 167; *Syracuse Daily Standard*, November 25, 1854; *National Era*, July 23, 1857; Judith Wellman, historian, interview with the author, October 6, 2002.

411 *At home, Loguen and his wife:* Sernett, *North Star Country*, p. 178; Hunter, *To Set the Captives Free*, pp. 166–68.

411 *"We had scarcely struck": Frederick Douglass' Paper*, November 28, 1857.

411 *He had spent several worried months:* Loguen, *Rev. J. W. Loguen*, pp. 433–43; Hunter, *To Set the Captives Free*, p. 134.

411 *formally designated his home:* Hunter, *To Set the Captives Free*, p. 156; *Liberal Christian*, January 30, 1869; *Voice of the Fugitive*, September 9, 1852; *Frederick Douglass' Paper*, March 7, 1854.

412 *"Who, then, in and about Syracuse": Frederick Douglass' Paper*, June 8, 1855.

412 *Loguen could not have carried: Syracuse Daily Standard*, June 12, 1854; Hunter, *To Set the Captives Free*, pp. 151–54, 161; Sernett, *North Star Country*, p. 179.

413 *Reports of Loguen's activities:* Loguen, *Rev. J. W. Loguen*, pp. 451–55.

414 *At fifty-five, John Brown was still:* The section on John Brown in Kansas is based on Nevins, *Ordeal of the Union*, vol. 2, pp. 133 ff; Oates, *To Purge This Land with Blood*, pp. 106–7, 127–55, 160–61, 171, 264; Quarles, *Allies for Freedom*, pp. 32–36; Scott, *Secret Six*, pp. 32–36, 41–49; Parker, *Angels of Freedom*, pp. 52–53, 58; John Brown, letter to Luther Humphrey, November 19, 1856, copy in possession of the WISH Centre, Chatham, Ontario.

414 *"lean, strong, and sinewy":* Douglass, "Life and Times," pp. 716–17.

415 *The national elections:* W. U. Hensel, "The Attitude of James Buchanan, a Citizen of Lancaster County, towards the Institution of Slavery in the United States," paper presented to the Lancaster County Historical Society, May 5, 1911; Nevins, *Ordeal of the Union*, vol. 2, pp. 64–66; Philip Shriver Klein, *President James Buchanan* (Norwalk, Conn.: Easton Press, 1987), pp. 257–60; Bordewich, "Digging into a Historic Rivalry," pp. 96–107; obituary of James Buchanan, *New York Times*, June 2, 1868.

416 *"[E]verything of a practical nature":* James Buchanan, inaugural address, March 4, 1857, viewed on-line at http://gi.grolier.com/presidents/ea/inaugs/1857buch; Nevins, *Ordeal of the Union*, vol. 2, pp. 60–63, 68 ff.

416 *Like his predecessor:* James Buchanan, Second Annual Message, December 6, 1858, viewed on-line at http://www.pcntv.com/bu_msg58; N. A. Hunt, letter to Wilbur H. Siebert, February 15, 1896, Siebert Collection, Ohio Historical Society, Columbus; Richard B. Sheridan, ed., *Freedom's Crucible: The Underground Railroad in Lawrence and Douglas County, Kansas, 1854–1865: A Reader* (Lawrence: Division of Continuing Education, University of Kansas, 2000), p. xviii; Sidney S. Herd and William E. Connelley, "Quantrill and the U.G.R.R. in Lawrence, Kansas Territory," in *Freedom's Crucible: The Underground Railroad in Lawrence and Douglas County, Kansas, 1854–1865: A Reader*, Richard B. Sheridan, ed. (Lawrence: Division of Continuing Education, University of Kansas, 2000), pp. 14–15; Klein, *President James Buchanan*, pp. 248, 296–99; Oates, *To Purge This Land with Blood*, pp. 89, 100; A. T. Andreas, *History of the State of Kansas* (Chicago: A. T. Andreas, 1883); Parker, *Angles of Freedom*, p. 38.

416 *Abolitionists were understandably outraged:* Caleb Calkins, handwritten deposition, John Brown folder, Gerrit Smith Collection, Bird Library, Syracuse University; Smith, Speech to the Kansas Meeting, Gerrit Smith Collection, Bird Library, Syracuse University.

416 *Meanwhile, a grandiose plan was fermenting:* James Redpath, *Public Life of Capt. John Brown* (Boston: Thayer and Eldridge, 1860), pp. 229–30; Oates, *To Purge This Land with Blood*, pp. 243–46; interview with J. Monroe Jones of Chatham, Ontario, *Cleveland Herald*, date unknown, copy in possession of WISH Centre, Chatham; Sheridan, *Freedom's Crucible*, p. 77.

417 *In January 1858:* Douglass, "Life and Times," p. 756; Cohen, *John Brown*, pp. 159–62.

417 *From Rochester, Brown moved:* Gerrit Smith, letter to John Thomas, August 27, 1859, and John Brown, letter to George L. Searns, via Caleb Calkins, April 4, 1858, both letters Gerrit Smith Collection, Bird Library, Syracuse University.

417 *After Boston, Brown moved:* Oates, *To Purge This Land with Blood*, pp. 240–42; Larson, *Bound for the Promised Land*, pp. 158–60.

418 *On May 8, at a secret convention:* John H. Kagi, Journal of the Provisional Constitutional Convention, May 8, 1858, held at Chatham, Ontario, copy in the possession of the WISH Centre, Chatham; Quarles, *Allies for Freedom*, pp. 45–51; Redpath, *Public Life of Capt. John Brown*, p. 231; Oates, *To Purge This Land with Blood*, p. 248; *National Era*, December 15, 1859.

419 *Brown wanted to invade:* Sheridan, editor's commentary, *Freedom's Crucible*, pp. 132–33; Richard J. Hinton and George B. Gill, "John Brown and the Rescue of Missouri Slaves," in Sheridan, *Freedom's Crucible*, pp. 77–87; Quarles, *Allies for Freedom*, pp. 53–60; Parker, *Angels of Freedom*, p. 71; *Plaindealer*, of Garnett, Kans., June 13, 1879, John Brown File, Watkins Museum, Lawrence, Kans.; *National Era*,

December 15, 1859; Jason Hanway, "Early Reminiscences," *Ossawatomie* (Kans.) *Times*, February 3, 1881, and February 10, 1881.

420 *Around ten-thirty on the dank night:* The story of John Brown's raid draws on Douglass, "Life and Times," pp. 758–60; pamphlet, *John Brown Address by Frederick Douglass,* speech delivered at the fourteenth anniversary of Storer College in Harpers Ferry, W. Va., 1881, in *John Brown Pamphlets,* vol. 5, Boyd B. Stutler Collection, West Virginia State Archives, Charleston, W. Va.; Thomas Drew, *The John Brown Invasion,* pamphlet, in *John Brown Pamphlets,* vol. 1, Boyd B. Stutler Collection, West Virginia State Archives, Charleston, W. Va.; Nevins, *Ordeal of the Union*, vol. 2, pp. 75–84; Oates, *To Purge This Land with Blood*, pp. 290–302; Quarles, *Allies for Freedom*, pp. 92–102; Osborne P. Anderson, *A Narrative of Events at Harper's Ferry* (Boston: Osborne P. Anderson, 1861), pp. 36–51; Redpath, *Public Life of Capt. John Brown*, p. 226; Cohen, *John Brown*, pp. 36–60; *National Era*, October 20, 1859, October 27, 1859, November 3, 1859, November 10, 1859; *New York Herald*, October 17, 1859.

424 *After the attack:* Anderson, *Narrative of Events at Harper's Ferry*, pp. 36–51; Quarles, *Allies for Freedom*, pp. 92–98, 114; Caleb Calkins, handwritten deposition, John Brown folder, Gerrit Smith Collection, Bird Library, Syracuse University, Syracuse, N.Y.; Still, Still's Underground Railroad Records, William Still, Philadelphia, 1886, Introduction.

425 *Harriet Tubman was in New York:* Larson, *Bound for the Promised Land*, pp. 158, 174.

425 *On October 25, Brown:* John Brown, letter to Luther Humphrey, November 19, 1859, copy in possession of the WISH Centre, Chatham, Ontario; *National Era*, October 27, 1859, December 8, 1859; *New York Tribune*, November 10, 1859; Nevins, *Ordeal of the Union*, vol. 2, p. 97; Chace and Chace, *Two Quaker Sisters*, pp. 175 ff; Quarles, *Allies for Freedom*, pp. 109, 124.

426 *The Oberlin graduate went silently: National Era*, December 22, 1859.

426 *"We shall be a thousand times":* Reprinted in *National Era*, December 22, 1859.

426 *"Some eighteen hundred years ago":* Henry David Thoreau, "A Plea for Captain John Brown," in *Slavery Attacked: The Abolitionist Crusade*, John L. Thomas, ed. (Englewood Cliffs, N.J.: Prentice-Hall, 1965), pp. 163–68.

426 *Paranoid rumors of more:* Quarles, *Allies for Freedom*, p. 107; *National Era*, January 12, 1860.

427 *Buchanan, ever an apologist for slavery:* James Buchanan, Fourth Annual Message, December 19, 1859, viewed on-line at http://www.pcntv.com/bu_msg59.

427 *The work of the underground:* Quarles, *Allies for Freedom*, p. 105; Sernett, *North Star Country*, pp. 191–92; Campbell, *Slave Catchers*, p. 188.

428 *One of the last was Arnold Gragston:* Arnold Gragston, quoted *Remembering Slavery: African Americans Talk About Their Personal Experiences of Slavery and Emancipation*, Ira Berlin, Marc Favreau, and Steven F. Miller, eds. (New York: New Press, 1998), pp. 64–70.

429 *In his inaugural address:* Nevins, *Prologue to Civil War* (New York: Collier Books, 1992), pp. 457–59.

429 *The borderlands began hemorrhaging: Detroit Daily News*, April 9, 1861; Horace Ford, interview with Wilbur H. Siebert, undated, Siebert Collection, Ohio Historical Society, Columbus.

430 *as early as May, General Benjamin Butler:* Paul Skeels Peirce, *The Freedman's Bureau: A Chapter in the History of Reconstruction* (New York: Haskell House Publishers, 1971), pp. 1–7.

430 *Without quite meaning to do so:* Campbell, *Slave Catchers*, pp. 189–90, 193.

430 *"The war ended the usefulness": Detroit Tribune*, January 11, 1886.

430 *As the lines of the Underground Railroad:* Rankin, *Life of Rev. John Rankin*, p. 49; Larson, *Bound for the Promised Land*, p. 212; Henson, *Uncle Tom's Story of His Life*, pp. 281–82; Strangis, *Lewis Hayden and the War Against Slavery*, p. 126; *Philadelphia Inquirer*, October 11, 1987; Calkins, deposition; Coffin, *Reminiscences of Levi Coffin*, pp. 620–23.

431 *poor Calvin Fairbank:* Fairbank, *Rev. Calvin Fairbank during Slavery Times*, pp. 149–50.

432 *There was, of course:* Coffin, *Reminiscences*, p. 712.

432 *On the same day:* Woodford, *This Is Detroit*, p. 66.

EPILOGUE

Page

433 *On March 10, 1913:* Larson, *Bound for the Promised Land*, p. 288.

433 *Thomas Garrett, who:* McGowan, *Station Master on the Underground Railroad*, pp. 81–82.

433 *Jermain Loguen was next:* Hunter, *To Set the Captives Free*, pp. 227–28.

434 *Gerrit Smith continued:* Harlow, *Gerrit Smith*, pp. 485, 490.

434 *George DeBaptiste opened: Detroit Tribune*, February 23, 1875.

434 *Levi Coffin continued:* Coffin, *Reminiscences of Levi Coffin*, pp. 711–12, appendix xii–xv; Sandra Jackson, director of the Levi Coffin House historic site, interview with the author, October 15, 2002.

434 *The hardy Yankee seaman:* Jonathan Walker, *The Trial and Imprisonment of Jonathan Walker* (Gainesville: University Presses of Florida, 1974), pp. 1xxviii–1xxx; *North Star*, February 16, 1849.

434 *Josiah Henson remained:* Lauriston, *Romantic Chatham*, pp. 383, 449, 452.

434 *Reverend John Rankin's last months:* Hagedorn, *Beyond the River*, pp. 275–76.

435 *In 1873 Lewis Hayden:* Strangis, *Lewis Hayden and the War Against Slavery*, pp. 128, 131, 136.

435 *George DeBaptiste's coleader:* "Freedom's Railway: Reminiscences of the Brave Old Days of the Famous Underground Line," *Detroit Tribune*, January 11, 1886; "Suicide by Hanging," unidentified Detroit newspaper, April 29, 1890, E & M Scrapbook, Burton Historical Collection, Detroit Public Library, Detroit, Mich.

435 *Mary Ann Shadd Cary:* Rhodes, *Mary Ann Shadd Cary*, p. 222; Silverman, "Mary Ann Shadd and the Search for Equality."

435 *Frederick Douglass lived:* McFeely, *Frederick Douglass*, pp. 289ff, 307, 381.

435 *William Still's coal business: Philadelphia Inquirer*, October 11, 1987; Matthew Pinsker, historian, interview with the author, Dickinson College, February 3, 2003.

436 *Its most important achievement:* Fred Landon, "The Negro Migration to Canada after the Passing of the Fugitive Slave Act," *Journal of Negro History* 5 (January 1920), pp. 22–36; Larry Gara, *The Liberty Line: The Legend of the Underground Railroad* (Lexington: University Press of Kentucky, 1996), pp. 36–38.

437 *It is similarly difficult:* Siebert, *Underground Railroad from Slavery to Freedom*, pp. 403–39.

437 *"truckling, and compromising":* W. E. B. DuBois, quoted by David W. Blight, " 'If You Don't Tell It Like It Was, It Can Never Be as It Ought to Be," keynote talk at Yale conference on "Yale and Slavery," September 26, 2002.

439 *Indeed, as a lawyer:* Randy Alcorn, "February 8, 1991: Lovejoy Surgicenter v. Portland, Oregon ProLifers," closing arguments in trial of rescuers, viewed online at www.epm.org/abcloarg.

Selected Bibliography

A Note About Sources

The decades after the Civil War saw the publication of several books that remain essential reading for anyone wishing to understand the Underground Railroad. The 1877 *Reminiscences* of Levi Coffin is the most detailed, if naturally subjective, rendering of one man's life in the underground. Less exhaustive, but still quite interesting, are Eber Pettit's brief memoir of underground work in western New York State, *Sketches in the History of the Underground Railroad*, published in 1867, and William Cockrum's *History of the Underground Railroad as It Was Conducted by the Anti-Slavery League*, published in 1902, a lively recounting of the activities of the underground cell to which Cockrum's father belonged in southwestern Indiana. Robert Smedley's 1886 *The Underground Railroad in Chester and the Neighboring Counties of Pennsylvania*, though confusingly organized, profiled virtually every known *white* activist in that region, and offers a valuable human roadmap to the interlinked nature of a network in mature form. In many respects, the most important postwar work on the underground is William Still's *The Underground Railroad*, published in 1872, a massive work that culled hundreds of fugitives' stories from the records of the Philadelphia Anti-Slavery Office. The published narratives of fugitive slaves sometimes offer insights into the operation of the underground, though usually only as an episode in the larger trajectory of the author's life. Interesting mentions of underground activity are found, for instance, in the autobiographies of Frederick Douglass, Jermain Loguen, Harriet Jacobs, William Wells Brown, and others. Students of the Underground Railroad owe perhaps the greatest debt to Wilbur H. Siebert of Ohio State University, who in the 1890s began collecting information on the underground at a time when many of its members were still alive. Siebert's primary work, *The Underground Railroad from Slavery to Freedom*, published in 1898, was the first attempt to write an overarching history of the underground as a whole. The vast collection of Siebert's papers at the Ohio Historical Society remains the richest archive of Underground Railroad material in the country, containing hundreds of letters and first-hand interviews with underground veterans, as well as much other well-organized research material on the underground gathered in the course of Siebert's long life.

Serious writing on the underground became very sparse after the turn of the century. Two worthy books appeared around mid-century, *Let My People Go*, by Henrietta Buckmaster, and *Make Free: The Story of the Underground Railroad*, by William A. Breyfogle, published in 1941 and 1958 respectively. Buckmaster's book broke no new ground, however, while Breyfogle's was marred by the inclusion of fictionalized composite stories. Larry Gara's slender but very influential 1961 revisionist work *The Liberty Line: The Legend of the Underground Railroad*, took issue with the then-traditional myth of the Underground Railroad that overemphasized the role of white Northerners. Gara cogently argued that the central figures in the history of the underground were the fugitive slaves themselves. Horatio Strother's masterful 1962 study *The Underground Railroad in Connecticut* is a glowing exception to the blandly conventional quality of most writing on the subject during this period. Beginning in the 1970s, the works of Charles Blockson, including *The Underground Railroad*, an anthology of escape stories, generated a renewed interest in the underground, especially among African Americans, helping to foster a new emphasis on the traces of underground history embedded in family oral history, and local records. More recently, a new generation of historians has begun to bring the tools of modern scholarship to bear on aspects of the Underground Railroad and abolitionism. Among these are Stanley Harrold's superb study of underground activity in Washington, *Subversives: Antislavery Community in Washington, D.C., 1828–1865;* Kate Clifford Larson's trenchant new biography of Harriet Tubman, *Bound for the Promised Land;* Gary Collison's study of the background to one of the most dramatic fugitive rescues of the antebellum period, *Shadrach Minkins: From Fugitive Slave to Citizen;* Steven Weissberger's *Modern Medea: A Family Story of Slavery and Child-Murder from the Old South*, a meticulous reconstruction of the tragic Margaret Garner case; Randolph P. Runyon's fascinating examination of the intricate, interwoven stories of Calvin Fairbank and Delia Webster, in *Delia Webster and The Underground Railroad;* Milton C. Sernett's *North Star Country: Upstate New York and the Crusade for African American Freedom*, a model regional study of abolitionism and its underground component; and Ann Hagedorn's portrait of the Rankin family of Ripley, Ohio, and their collaborators, in *Beyond the River: The Untold Story of the Heroes of the Underground Railroad.*

Much of the most exciting work today is being done by independent local scholars, whose numbers are far too great to cite individually. Among them, however, Judith Wellman's research in Oswego and other parts of central New York, Diane Perrine Coon's work in and around Madison, Indiana, and Christopher Densmore's writings on eastern Quakers and other subjects related to the underground deserve much wider attention.

Books

Adams, Alice Dana. *The Neglected Period of Anti-Slavery in America*. Gloucester, MA: Peter Smith, 1964.

Adams, Nehemiah. *A South-Side View of Slavery*. Savannah: Beehive Press, 1974.

Anbinder, Tyler. *Five Points: The New York City Neighborhood that Invented Tap Dance, Stole Elections, and Became the World's Most Notorious Slum*. New York: Free Press, 2001.

Anderson, Osborne P. *A Narrative of Events at Harper's Ferry*. Boston: Osborne P. Anderson, 1861.

Bacon, Margaret Hope. *Lamb's Warrior: The Life of Isaac T. Hopper*. New York: Thomas Y. Crowell Co., 1970.

———. *Valiant Friend: The Life of Lucretia Mott*. Philadelphia: Friends General Conference, 1999.

Bailyn, Bernard. *The Ideological Origins of the American Revolution*. Cambridge: Harvard University Press, 1992.

———. *Voyagers to the West: A Passage in the Peopling of America on the Eve of the Revolution*. New York: Vintage, 1988.

Ball, Edward. *Slaves in the Family*. New York: Ballantine, 1999.

Bancroft, Frederic. *Slave Trading in the Old South*. New York: Frederick Ungar Publishing Co., 1959.

Barbour, Hugh, Christopher Densmore, Elizabeth H. Moger, Nancy C. Sorel, Alson D. Van Wagner, and Arthur J. Worrall, editors. *Quaker Crosscurrents: Three Hundred Years of Friends in the New York Yearly Meetings*. Syracuse: Syracuse University Press, 1995.

Bartram, William. *Travels of William Bartram*. New York: Dover, 1955.

Berlin, Ira. *Many Thousands Gone: The First Two Centuries of Slavery in America*. Cambridge: Harvard University Press, 1998.

———. *Slaves without Masters: The Free Negro in the Antebellum South*. New York: Vintage, 1976.

———, with Marc Favreau, and Steven F. Miller, editors. *Remembering Slavery: African Americans Talk About Their Personal Experiences of Slavery and Emancipation*. New York: The New Press, 1998.

Bieder, Robert E. *Science Encounters the Indian, 1820-1880*. Norman: University of Oklahoma Press, 1986.

Blassingame, John W. *Slave Testimony: Two Centuries of Letters, Speeches, Interviews, and Testimony*. Baton Rouge: Louisiana State University Press, 1977.

Blockson, Charles L. *Hippocrene Guide to the Underground Railroad*. New York: Hippocrene Books, 1995.

———. *The Underground Railroad: Dramatic Firsthand Accounts of Daring Escapes to Freedom.* New York: Berkley Books, 1994.

Bolster, W. Jeffrey. *Black Jacks: African American Seamen in the Age of Sail.* Cambridge: Harvard University Press, 1997.

Bond, James O. *Chickamauga and the Underground Railroad: A Tale of Two Grandfathers.* Baltimore: Gateway Press, 1993.

Bordewich, Fergus M. *Killing the White Man's Indian: Reinventing Native Americans at the End of the Twentieth Century.* New York: Anchor, 1997.

Bradford, Sarah. *Scenes in the Life of Harriet Tubman.* Auburn, N.Y.: W.J. Moses, 1869.

———. *Harriet Tubman: The Moses of Her People.* Bedford, Mass.: Applewood Books, 1993.

Brandt, Nat. *The Town That Started the Civil War.* New York: Laurel, 1990.

Breyfogle, William. *Make Free: The Story of the Underground Railroad.* Philadelphia: J.B. Lippincott Co., 1958.

Brodie, Fawn M. *Thomas Jefferson: An Intimate History.* New York: 1974.

Brooks, Van Wyck. *The Flowering of New England 1815-1865.* New York: E.P. Dutton & Co., 1936

Brown, Henry Box. *Narrative of the Life of Henry Box Brown.* New York: Oxford University Press, 2002.

Brown, William Wells. *The Travels of William Wells Brown.* New York: Markus Weiner Publishing, 1991.

Buckmaster, Henrietta. *Let My People Go: The Story of the Underground Railroad and the Growth of the Abolition Movement.* New York: Harper & Brothers, 1941.

Buley, R. Carlyle. *The Old Northwest: Pioneer Period, 1815-1840 (Vols. I and II).* Bloomington: Indiana University Press, 1951.

Burrows, Edwin G., and Mike Wallace. *Gotham: A History of New York to 1898.* New York: Oxford University Press, 1998.

Burton, Anthony. *The Rise and Fall of King Cotton.* London: British Boadcasting Corporation, 1984.

Calarco, Tom. *The Underground Railroad in the Adirondack Region.* Jefferson, N.C.: McFarland & Co., 2004.

Campbell, Stanley W. *The Slave Catchers.* Chapel Hill: University of North Carolina Press, 1970.

Cecelski, David S. *The Waterman's Song: Slavery and Freedom in Maritime North Carolina.* Chapel Hill: University of North Carolina Press, 2001.

Chace, Elizabeth Buffum, and Lucy Buffum Lovell. *Two Quaker Sisters.* New York: Liveright Publishing Co., 1937.

Chapman, Charles C. *History of Knox County, Illinois.* Chicago: Charles C. Chapman & Co., 1878

Child, Lydia Maria. *Isaac T. Hopper: A True Life*. Boston: John P. Jewett & Co., 1853

Crissy, Theron Wilmot. *History of Norfolk, 1744–1900.* Everett: Massachusetts Publishing Co., 1900.

Clinton, Catherine. *Harriet Tubman: The Road to Freedom.* New York: Little Brown, and Co., 2004.

Coffin, Addison. *Life and Travels of Addison Coffin*. Cleveland: William G. Hubbard, 1897.

———. *Early Settlement of Friends in North Carolina: Traditions and Reminiscences.* Unpublished manusript, 1894. Friends Historical Library, Guilford College, Greensboro, N.C.

Coffin, Levi. *Reminiscences*. Cincinnati: Western Tract Society, 1879.

Cohn, David. *The Life and Times of King Cotton.* New York: Oxford University Press, 1956.

Cohen, Stan. *John Brown: 'The Thundering Voice of Jehovah'*. Missoula: Pictorial Histories Publishing Co., 1999.

Cole, Phil. *Historic Madison*. Madison, Ind.: Three Star Investments, 1995.

Coleman, J. Winston Jr. *Slavery Times in Kentucky*. Chapel Hill: University of North Carolina Press, 1940.

Collison, Gary. *Shadrach Minkins: From Fugitive Slave to Citizen*. Cambridge: Harvard University Press, 1997.

Commager, Henry Steele. *The Empire of Reason: How Europe Imagined and America Realized the Enlightenment*. Garden City: Anchor, 1978.

Cooper, James Fenimore. *The American Democrat*. Baltimore: Penguin, 1969.

Cox, Samuel S. *Eight Years in Congress from 1857–1865: Memoirs and Speeches*. New York: D. Appleton and Co., 1865.

Crenshaw, Gwendolyn J. *Bury Me in a Free Land: The Abolitionist Movement in Indiana, 1816-1865*. Indianapolis: Indiana Historical Bureau, 1986.

Crèvecoeur, J. Hector St. John. *Letters from an American Farmer*. New York: Oxford University Press, 1997.

Cross, Whitney R. *The Burned-Over District: The Social and Intellectual History of Enthusiasic Religion in Western New York, 1800-1850*. New York: Harper Torchbooks, 1965.

Cummings, Charles M. *Yankee Quaker, Confederate General: The Curious career of Bushrod Rust Johnson*. Rutherford, N.J.: Fairleigh Dickinson University Press, 1971.

Current, Richard N. *John C. Calhoun*. New York: Washington Square Press, 1963.

Daly, John Patrick. *When Slavery Was Called Freedom: Evangelicalism, Proslavery, and the Causes of the Civil War*. Lexington: University Press of Kentucky, 2002.

Dangerfield, George. *The Awakening of American Nationalism, 1815–1828*. New York: Harper & Row, 1965.

Davidson, Donald. *The Tennessee: The Old River: Frontier to Secession*. Nashville: J.S. Sanders & Co., 1991.

Densmore, Christopher, and Albert Schrauwers, editors. *The Best Man for Settling New Country: The Journal of Timothy Rogers*. Toronto: Canadian Friends Historical Association, 2000.

Dickens, Charles. *American Notes for General Circulation*. New York: Penguin, 2000.

Dillon, Merton L. *Benjamin Lundy and the Struggle for Negro Freedom*. Urbana: University of Illinois Press, 1966.

———. *The Abolitionists*. De Kalb: Northern Illinois University Press, 1974.

———. *Slavery Attacked: Southern Slaves and Their Allies 1619–1865*. Baton Rouge: Louisiana State University Press, 1990.

Douglass, Frederick. *Autobiographies*. New York: Literary Classics of the United States, 1994.

Dow, George Francis. *Slave Ships and Slaving*. Mineola: Dover, 2002.

Drayton, Daniel. *Personal Memoir of Daniel Drayton, for Four Years and Four Months a Prisoner (for Charity's Sake) in Washington Jail*. New York: Negro Universities Press, 1969.

Drew, Benjamin. *The Refugee: A Northside View of Slavery*. Reading: Addison-Wesley, 1969.

Duncan, David Herbert. *Lincoln*. New York: Simon & Schuster, 1995.

Dunnigan, Brian Leigh. *Frontier Metropolis*. Detroit: Wayne State University Press, 2001.

Eckert, Allan W. *That Dark and Bloody River: Chronicles of the Ohio River Valley*. New York: Bantam, 1995.

Eleventh Annual Report of the Indiana Colonization Society, Indianapolis, 1846.

Elliott, Joseph P. *A History of Evansville and Vandenburgh County, Indiana*. Evansville: Keller Printing Co., 1897.

Ellis, Franklin, and Samuel Evans. *History of Lancaster Couny, Pennsylvania*. Philadelphia: Everts and Peck, 1883.

Fairbank, Calvin. *Rev. Calvin Fairbank during Slavery Times*. New York: Negro Universities Press, 1969.

Fanning, Philip Ashley. *Mark Twain and Orion Clemens: Brothers, Partners, Strangers*. Tuscaloosa: University of Alabama Press, 2003.

Faust, Drew Gilpin, editor. *The Ideology of Slavery: Proslavery Thought in the Antebellum South, 1830–1860.* Baton Rouge: Louisiana State University Press, 1981.

Fehrenbach, Don E. *The Slaveholding Republic.* New York: Oxford University Press, 2001.

Fields, Barbara Jeanne. *Slavery and Freedom on the Middle Ground: Maryland During the Nineteenth Century.* New Haven: Yale University Press, 1985.

Finkelman, Paul, editor. *Fugitive Slaves.* New York: Garland Publishing, Inc., 1989.

Fishkin, Shelley Fisher. *Lighting Out for the Territory: Reflections on Mark Twain and American Culture.* New York: Oxford University Press, 1998.

Fogel, Robert William, and Stanley L. Engerman. *Time on the Cross: The Economics of American Negro Slavery.* New York: Norton, 1989.

Forbes, Ella. *But We Have No Country: The 1851 Christiana Resistance.* Cherry Hill, N.J.: Africana Homestead Legacy Publishers, 1998.

Franklin, John Hope, and Loren Schweninger. *Runaway Slaves: Rebels on the Plantation.* New York: Oxford University Press, 1999.

French, Scott. *The Rebellious Slave: Nat Turner in American Memory.* Boston: Houghton Mifflin, 2004.

Frothingham, Octavius Brooks. *Gerrit Smith: A Biography.* New York: G.P. Putnam's Sons, 1878.

Furnas, J. C. *Goodbye to Uncle Tom.* New York: William Sloane Associates, 1956.

Gara, Larry. *The Liberty Line: The Legend of the Underground Railroad.* Lexington: University Press of Kentucky, 1996.

Gates, Henry Louis, Jr., editor. *The Classic Slave Narratives.* New York: Mentor, 1987.

Gordon-Reed, Annette. *Thomas Jefferson and Sally Hemings: An American Controversy.* Charlottesville: University of Virginia Press, 1997.

Goss, Charles F. *Cincinnati: The Queen City 1788-1912 (Vol. I).* Cincinnati: S.J. Clarke, 1912.

Gould, Lewis L. *Grand Old Party: A History of The Republicans.* New York: Random House, 2003.

Gould, Stephen Jay. *The Mismeasure of Man.* New York: Norton, 1981.

Greenberg, Kenneth S. *The Confessions of Nat Turner and Related Documents.* Boston: Bedford Books, 1996.

Grimsted, David, *American Mobbing 1828–1861: Toward Civil War.* New York: Oxford University Press, 1998.

Grover, Kathryn. *The Fugitive's Gibraltar: Escaping Slaves and Abolitionism in New Bedford, Massachusetts.* Amherst: University of Massachusetts Press, 2001.

Hadden, Sally E. *Slave Patrols: Law and Violence in Virginia and the Carolinas.* Cambridge: Harvard University Press, 2001.

Hagedorn, Ann. *Beyond the River: The Untold Story of the Heroes of the Underground Railroad*. New York: Simon and Schuster, 2002.

Halliday, E.M. *Understanding Thomas Jefferson*. New York: HarperCollins, 2001.

Harlow, Ralph. *Gerrit Smith: Philanthropist and Reformer*. New York: Russell & Russell, 1939.

Harris, N. Dwight. *The History of Negro Servitude in Illinois*. New York: Haskell House Publishers, 1969.

Harrold, Stanley. *The Abolitionists and the South 1831-1861*. Lexington: University Press of Kentucky, 1995.

———. *Subversives: Antislavery Community in Washington, DC, 1828–1865*. Baton Rouge: Louisiana State University Press, 2003.

Hasbrouck, Frank. *The History of Dutchess County*. Poughkeepsie: S.A. Matthieu, 1909.

Haviland, Laura. *A Woman's Life Work*. Grand Rapids: S.B. Shaw, 1881.

Henson, Josiah. *Uncle Tom's Story of His Life*. Boston: B.B. Russell & Co., 1879.

———. *The Life of Josiah Henson, Formerly a Slave*. Boston: Arthur D. Phelps, 1849.

Hewitt, Nancy A. *Women's Activism and Social Change: Rochester, New York 1822–1872*. Ithaca: Cornell University Press, 1984.

Hicks, Elias. *Observations of the Slavery of the Africans and Their Descendants*. New York: Samuel Wood, 1814.

Hiebert, Ray Eldon, and Richard K. MacMaster. *A Grateful Remembrance: The Story of Montgomery County, Maryland*. Rockville: Montgomery County Historical Society, 1976.

Hill, Daniel G. *The Freedom Seekers: Blacks in Early Canada*. Toronto: Stoddart, 1992.

Hoag, Joseph. *Journal of the Life of Joseph Hoag*. Philadelphia: Wm. H. Pile's Sons, 1909.

Hodges, Graham Russell. *Root & Branch: African Americans in New York & East Jersey*. Chapel Hill: University of North Carolina Press, 1999.

Holliday, J.S. *The World Rushed in: The California Gold Rush Experience*. New York: Simon & Schuster, 1981.

Horsman, Reginald. *Josiah Nott of Mobile: Southerner, Physician, and Racial Theorist*. Baton Rouge: Louisiana State University Press, 1987

Horton, James Oliver. *Free People of Color: Inside the African American Community*. Washington: Smithsonian Institution Press, 1993.

———, and Lois E. Horton. *In Hope of Liberty: Culture, Community and Protest among Northern Free Blacks, 1700–1860*. New York: Oxford University Press, 1997.

Howe, Samuel Gridley. *Report to the Freedmen's Inquiry Commission*. New York: Arno Press, 1969.

Hudson, J. Blaine. *Fugitive Slaves and the Underground Railroad in the Kentucky Borderland.* Jefferson, N.C.: McFarland & Co., 2002.

Humez, Jean M. *Harriet Tubman: The Life and the Life Stories.* Madison: University of Wisconsin Press, 2003.

Hunter, Carol. *To Set the Captives Free: Reverent Jermain Wesley Loguen and the Struggle for Freedom in Central New York 1835–1872.* New York: Garland Publishing, Inc., 1993.

Jacobs, Harriet A. *Incidents in the Life of a Slave Girl.* Cambridge: Harvard University Press, 1987.

Jameson, Anna B. *Winter Studies and Summer Rambles in Canada.* Toronto: Thorn Press, 1943.

Jefferson, Thomas. *Writings.* New York: Viking, 1984.

Jeffrey, Julie Roy. *The Great Sient Army of Abolitionism: Ordinary Women in the Anti-Slavery Movement.* Chapel Hill: University of North Carolina Press, 1998.

Jenkins, William S. *Proslavery Thought in the Old South.* Gloucester: Peter Smith, 1962.

Kashatus, William C. *Just Over the Line: Chester County and the Underground Railroad.* West Chester: Chester County Historical Society, 2002.

Katz, William Loren. *Black Indians: A Hidden Heritage.* New York: Atheneum, 1986.

Katzman, David K. *Before the Ghetto: Black Detroit in the Nineteenth Century.* Urbana: University of Illinois Press, 1973.

Klein, Philip Shriver. *President James Buchanan.* Norwalk, Conn.: The Easton Press, 1987.

Koger, Larry. *Black Slaveowners: Free Black Slave Masters in South Carolina, 1790–1860.* Jefferson, N.C.: McFarland & Co., 1985.

Kolchin, Peter. *American Slavery 1619–1877.* New York: Hill and Wang, 1995.

Kouwenhoven, John A. *The Columbia Historical Portrait of New York City.* New York: Harper & Row, 1972.

Larson, Kate Clifford. *Bound for the Promised Land: Harriet Tubman, Portrait of an American Hero.* New York: Random House, 2003.

Lauriston, Victor. *Romantic Chatham.* Chatham: Shepherd Printing Co., 1952.

Leach, Robert J., and Peter Gow. *Quaker Nantucket: The Religious Community behind the Whaling Empire.* Nantucket: Mill Hill Press, 1999.

The Letters of William Lloyd Garrison, edited by Walter M. Merrill. Vols. I, III, IV. Cambridge: Harvard University Press, 1971.

Litwack, Leon, and August Meier, editors. *Black Leaders of the Nineteenth Century.* Urbana: University of Illinois Press, 1988.

Loguen, Jermain W. *The Rev. J. W. Loguen, as A Slave and as A Freeman.* Syracuse: J.G.K. Truair & Co., 1859.

Lovejoy, J.C. *Memoir of Rev. Charles T. Torrey*. New York: Negro Universities Press, 1969.

Lowance, Mason, editor. *Against Slavery: An Abolitionist Reader*. New York: Penguin, 2000.

Mabee, Carleton. *Black Freedom: The Nonviolent Abolitionists from 1830 through the Civil War*. Toronto: Macmillan, 1970.

Mannix, Daniel P., and Malcolm Cowley. *Black Cargoes: A History of the Atlantic Slave Trade*. New York: Viking Compass, 1965.

Mapp, Alf J., Jr. *Thomas Jefferson: Passionate Pilgrim*. Lanham: Madison Books, 1991.

Masur, Louis P. *1831: Year of Apocalypse*. New York: Hill and Wang, 2001.

May, Samuel J. *Some Recollections on Our Anti-Slavery Conflict*. Miami: Mnemosyne Publishing Co., 1969.

Mayo, Bernard. *Jefferson Himself*. Charlotesville: University Press of Virginia, 1942.

Mayer, Henry, *All on Fire: William Lloyd Garrison and the Abolition of Slavery*. New York: St. Martin's Press, 1998.

McDougall, Marion G. *Fugitive Slaves (1619–1865)*. Boston: Ginn & Co., 1891.

McFeely, William S. *Frederick Douglass*. New York: Norton, 1991.

McGowan, James A. *Station Master on the Underground Railroad: The Life and Letters of Thomas Garrett*. Moylan, Pa.: Whimsie Press, 1977.

McKiever, Charles Fitzgerald. *Slavery and the Emigration of North Carolina Friends*. Murfreesboro: Johnson Publishing Company, 1970.

Miller, Caroline R. *Slavery in Newsprint: Central Ohio River Borderlands*, Vol. 1, *1797–1839*. Augusta, GA: Caroline R. Miller, 2003.

———. *Slavery in Mason County, Kentucky: A Century of Records 1788–1888*. Maysville, Ky.: National Underground Railroad Museum, Inc., 2001.

Miller, John Chester. *The Wolf by the Ears: Thomas Jefferson and Slavery*. Charlottesville: University Press of Virginia, 1991.

———. *The Federalist Era, 1789–1801*. New York: Harper & Row, 1960.

Miller, William Lee. *Arguing about Slavery: The Great Battle in the United States Congress*. New York: Knopf, 1996.

Moore, John M., editor. *Friends in the Delaware Valley: Philadelphia Yearly Meeting 1681–1981*. Haverford, Pa.: Friends Historical Association, 1981.

Morison, Samuel Eliot. *The Oxford History of the American People: 1789 through Reconstruction (Vol 2)*. New York: Mentor: 1972.

Muelder, Herman R. *Fighters for Freedom: A History of Anti-Slavery Activities of Men and Women Associated with Knox College*. New York: Columbia University Press, 1959.

Munford, Beverly B. *Virginia's Attitude Toward Slavery and Secession*. New York: Longmans, Green, and Co., 1910.

A Narrative of Some of the Proceedings of North Carolina Yearly Meeting on the Subject of Slavery within Its Limits. Greensborough: Swaim and Sherwood, 1848.

Nash, Gary B. *Forging Freedom: The Formation of Philadelphia's Black Community 1720–1840*. Cambridge: Harvard University Press, 1988.

———. *First City: Philadelphia and the Forging of Historical Memory*. Philadelphia: University of Pennsylvania Press, 2002.

Nevins, Allan. *Prologue to Civil War*. New York: Collier Books, 1992.

Nye, Russel. *Fettered Freedom: Civil Liberties and the Slavery Controversy 1830–1860*. East Lansing: Michigan State College Press, 1949.

Oates, Stephen B. *To Purge this Land with Blood: A Biography of John Brown*. Amherst: University of Massachusetts Press, 1984.

Oickle, Alvin F. *Jonathan Walker: The Man with the Branded Hand*. Everett: Lorelli Slater, 1998.

Paine, Thomas. *Rights of Man*. 1792; reprint, New York: Penguin, 1982.

Parker, Martha J. *Angels of Freedom*. Lawrence, KS: n.p., 1999.

Paskoff, Paul F., and Daniel J. Wilson, *The Cause of the South: Selections from* DeBow's Review, *1846–1867*. Baton Rouge: Louisiana State University Press, 1982.

Pease, William H., and Jane H. Pease, *Black Utopia: Negro Communal Experiments in America*. Madison: State Historical Society of Wisconsin, 1963

———. *Bound with Them in Chains: A Biographical History of the Antislavery Movement*. Westport, Conn.: Greenwood Press, 1972.

Peirce, Paul Skeels. *The Freedmen's Bureau: A Chapter in the History of Reconstruction*. New York: Haskell House, 1971.

Perry, Mark. *Lift Up Thy Voice: The Grimke Family's Journey from Slaveholders to Civil Rights Leaders*. New York: Viking, 2001.

Peters, Pamela R. *The Underground Railroad in Floyd County, Indiana*. Jefferson, N.C.: McFarland & Co., 2001.

Peterson, Merrill D. *The Great Triumverate:* Webster, Clay, and Calhoun. New York: Oxford University Press, 1987.

———. *John Brown: The Legend Revisited*. Charlottesville: University of Virginia Press, 2002.

Pettit, Eber. *Sketches in the History of the Underground Railroad*. Westfield, N.Y.: Chautauqua Regional Press, 1999.

Pickard, Kate E. R. *The Kidnapped and the Ransomed: The Narrative of Peter and Vina Still after Forty Years of Slavery* Philadelphia: Jewish Publication Society of America, 1970.

Pirtle, Carol. *Escape Betwixt Two Suns: A True Tale of the Underground Railroad in Illinois*. Carbondale: Southern Illinois University Press, 2000.

Polyakov, Leon. *The Aryan Myth: A History of Racist and Nationalist Ideas in Europe.* New York: New American Library, 1974.

Poremba, David Lee. *Detroit: A Motor City History.* Detroit: Arcadia, 2001.

Powell, Aaron M. *Personal Reminiscences of the Anti-Slavery and Other Reforms and Reformers.* New York: Caulon Press, 1899.

Power, Michael, and Nancy Butler. *Slavery and Freedom in Niagara.* Niagara-on-the-Lake, N.Y.: Niagara Historical Society, 2000.

Proceedings of the New York Anti-Slavery Convention Held at Utica, October 21, and New York Anti-Slavery State Society Held at Peterboro', October 22, 1835. Utica: Standard & Democrat Office, 1835.

Quarles, Benjamin. *Black Abolitionists.* New York: Oxford University Press, 1969.

———. *Allies for Freedom.* New York: Da Capo Press, 2001.

Redpath, James. *Public Life of Capt. John Brown.* Boston: Thayer and Eldridge, 1860.

Rhodes, Jane. *Mary Ann Shadd Cary: The Black Press and Protest in the Nineteenth Century.* Bloomington: Indiana University Press, 1998.

Richards, Leonard L. *The Slave Power: The Free North and Southern Domination 1780-1860.* Baton Rouge: Louisiana State University Press, 2000.

Ripley, C. Peter, editor. *The Black Abolitionist Papers (Vols. II, III, and IV).* Chapel Hill: University of North Carolina Press, 1991.

Ritchie, Andrew. *The Soldier, The Battle and the Victory.* Cincinnati: Western Tract and Book Society, 1868.

Robinson, William H. *From Log Cabin to the Pulpit, or Fifteen Years in Slavery.* Eau Claire: James H. Tifft, 1913.

Runyon, Randolph Paul. *Delia Webster and the Underground Railroad.* Lexington: University Press of Kentucky, 1996.

Sanborn, Franklin B. *The Life of Henry David Thoreau.* Boston: Houghton Mifflin, 1917.

Schlesinger, Arthur M., Jr. *The Age of Jackson.* New York: Little, Brown and Co., 1945.

Scott, John Anthony. *Hard Trials on My Way: Slavery and the Struggle Against It 1800-1860.* New York: Mentor, 1974.

Scott, Otto. *The Secret Six: John Brown and the Abolitionist Movement.* Murphys: Uncommon Books, 1979.

Sengupta, Gunja. *For God and Mammon: Evangelicals and Entrepreneurs, Masters and Slaves in Territorial Kansas, 1854–1860.* Athens: University of Georgia Press, 1996.

Sernett, Milton C. *North Star Country: Upstate New York and the Crusade for African American Freedom.* Syracuse: Syracuse University Press, 2002.

———. *Abolition's Axe: Beriah Green, Oneida Institute, and the Black Freedom Struggle.* Syracuse: Syracuse University Press, 1986.

Severance, Frank H. *Old Trails on the Niagara Frontier*. Buffalo: Severance, 1899.

Sharpe, Mary Ellen Graydon. *A Family Retrospect*. Indianapolis: The Hollenbeck Press, private printing, n.d..

Sheridan, Richard B., editor. *Freedom's Crucible: The Underground Railroad in Lawrence and Douglas County, Kansas, 1854–1865: A Reader*. Lawrence: Division of Continuing Education, University of Kansas, 2000.

Siebert, Wilbur H. *The Underground Railroad from Slavery to Freedom*. New York: Macmillan, 1898.

———. *The Mysteries of Ohio's Underground Railroad*. Columbus: Long's College Book Company, 1951.

Silverman, Jason H. *Unwelcome Guests: Canada West's Response to American Fugitive Slaves*. Millwood: Associated Faculty Press, 1985.

Simpson, Donald George. *Negroes in Ontario from Early Times to 1870*. London, ON: University of Western Ontario, 1971.

Sklar, Kathryn Kish. *Women's Rights Emerges within the Antislavery Movement: A Brief History with Documents*. Boston: Bedford/St. Martin's, 2000.

Slaughter, Thomas P. *Bloody Dawn: The Christiana Riot and Racial Violence in the Antebellum North*. New York: Oxford University Press, 1991.

Smallwood, Thomas. *A Narrative of Thomas Smallwood, (Coloured Man): Giving and Account of his Birth—The Period he Was Held in Slavery—His Release—and Removal to Canada, etc. Together with an Account of the Underground Railroad*. Toronto: James Stephens, 1851.

Smedley, Robert C. *History of the Underground Railroad in Chester and the Neighboring Counties of Pennsylvania*. Lancaster: The Journal, 1883.

Smith, James Lindsey. *Autobiography*. Norwich: Thames Printing Company, 1976.

Smith, Jean Edward *John Marshall: Definer of a Nation*. New York: Henry Holt and Co., 1996.

Sperry, Earl. *The Jerry Rescue*. Syracuse, N.Y.: Onondaga Historical Society, 1924.

Sprague, Stuart Seely, editor. *His Promised Land: The Autobiography of John P. Parker, Former Slave and Conductor on the Underground Railroad*. New York: W.W. Norton, 1996.

Stampp, Kenneth M. *The Peculiar Institution: Slavery in the Ante-Bellum South*. New York: Vintage, 1956.

Stanton, Elizabeth Cady. *Eighty Years and More: Reminiscences 1815–1897*. New York: Schocken, 1971.

Stanton, Lucia. *Slavery at Monticello*. Monticello, Va.: Thomas Jefferson Memorial Foundation, 1996.

Stauffer, John. *The Black Hearts of Men: Radical Abolitionists and the Transformation of Race*. Cambridge: Harvard University Press, 2002.

Sterling, Dorothy. *Ahead of Her Time: Abby Kelley and the Politics of Antislavery*. New York: W.W. Norton, 1991.

———. *Turning the World Upside Down: The Anti-Slavery Convention of American Women Held in New York City May 9–12, 1837*. New York: The Feminist Press at the City University of New York, 1987.

Steward, Austin. *Twenty-Two Years a Slave and Forty Years a Freeman*. Syracuse, NY: Syracuse University Press, 2002.

Still, William. *The Underground Railroad*. Chicago: Johnson Publishing Co., 1970.

———. *Still's Underground Railroad Records*. Philadelphia: William Still, 1886.

Stormont, Gil R. *History of Gibson County Indiana*. Indianapolis: B.F. Bowen &Co., 1914.

Stowe, Harriet Beecher. *Uncle Tom's Cabin*. 1852. Reprint, New York: Signet, 1998.

———. *A Key to Uncle Tom's Cabin*. Bedford: Applewood Books, 1998.

Strangis, Joel. *Lewis Hayden and the War Against Slavery*. North Haven, Conn.: Linnet Books, 1999.

Strother, Horatio T. *The Underground Railroad in Connecticut*. Middletown, Conn.: Wesleyan University Press, 1962.

Sturge, Joseph. *A Visit to the United States in 1841*. New York: Augustus M. Kelley, 1969.

Sydnor, Charles S. *Slavery in Mississippi*. Baton Rouge: Louisiana State University Press, 1933.

Switala, William J. *Underground Railroad in Pennsylvania*. Mechanicsburg: Stackpole Books, 2001.

Taylor, George Rogers. *The Transportation Revolution, 1815–1860*. New York: Harper Torchbooks, 1968.

Taylor, John M. *William Henry Seward: Lincoln's Right Hand*. Washington, D.C.: Brassey's, 1991.

Taylor, Yuval, editor. *I Was Born a Slave: An Anthology of Classic Slave Narratives (Vols. I and II)*. Chicago: Lawrence Hill Books, 1999.

Thomas, Hugh. *The Slave Trade: The Story of the Atlantic Slave Trade 1440–1870*. New York: Simon & Schuster, 1997.

Thomas, John L., editor. *Slavery Attacked: The Abolitionist Crusade*. Englewood Cliffs: Prentice-Hall, 1965.

Thoreau, Henry David, *Walden and Civil Disobedience*. Boston: Houghton Mifflin Co., 2000.

Thornbrough, Emma Lou. *The Nego in Indiana Before 1900*. Bloomington: Indiana University Press, 1993.

deTocqueville, Alexis. *Democracy in America*. Chicago: University of Chicago Press, 2000.

Trefousse, Hans L. *Thaddeus Stevens: Nineteenth-Century Egalitarian.* Mechanicsburg, Pa.: Stackpole Books, 2001.

Tucker, E. *History of Randolph County, Indiana.* Chicago: A.L. Kingman, 1882.

Turner, Glennette Tilley. *The Underground Railroad in Illinois.* Glen Ellyn: Newman Educational Publishing, 2001.

Twain, Mark, *Life on the Mississippi.* New York: Bantam, 1981.

Ullman, Victor. *Look to the North Star: A Life of William King.* Toronto: Umbrella Press, 1969.

Van Evrie, J. H. *Negroes and Negro Slavery.* New York: Van Evrie, Hoton & Co., 1863.

Wagstaff, H. M. *Minutes of the N.C. Manumission Society.* The James Sprunt Historical Studies, Vol. 22, Nos. 1-2. Chapel Hill: University of North Carolina Press, 1934.

Walker, Jonathan. *The Trial and Imprisonment of Jonathan Walker.* Gainesville: University Presses of Florida, 1974.

Walters, Ronald G. *American Reformers 1815–1860.* New York: Hill and Wang, 1997.

Ward, Geoffrey C., and Ken Burns. *Not for Ourselves Alone: The Story of Elizabeth Cady Stanton and Susan B. Anthony.* New York: Knopf, 1999.

Ward, Samuel Ringgold. *Autobiography of a Fugitive Negro.* Chicago: Johnson Publishing Co., 1970.

Weeks, Stephen B. *Southern Quakers and Slavery.* Baltimore: Johns Hopkins Press, 1896.

Weisenburger, Steven. *Modern Medea: A Family Story of Slavery and Child-Murder from the Old South.* New York: Hill and Wang, 1998.

Wellman, Judith, and Milton C. Sernett. *Uncovering the Freedom Trail in Syracuse and Onondaga County.* Syracuse: Preservation Association of Central New York, 2002.

Whitman, T. Stephen. *The Price of Freedom: Slavery and Manumission in Baltimore and Early National Maryland.* New York: Routledge, 2000.

Williams, Byron. *History of Clermont and Brown Counties, Ohio.* Milford: Hobart Publishing Co., 1913.

Williams, Eric. *Capitalism and Slavery.* New York: Capricorn Books, 1966.

Wills, Garry. *"Negro President": Jefferson and the Slave Power.* New York: Houghton Mifflin, 2003.

Wilson, Carol. *Freedom at Risk: The Kidnapping of Free Blacks in America 1780–1865.* Lexington: University Press of Kentucky, 1994.

Winks, Robin. *The Blacks in Canada: A History.* New Haven: Yale University Press, 1971.

Woodford, Arthur M. *This Is Detroit.* Detroit: Wayne State University Press, 2001.

Wyatt-Brown, Bertram. *Lewis Tappan and the Evangelical War Against Slavery.* New York: Atheneum, 1971.

Yee, Shirley J. *Black Women Abolitionists: A Study in Activism, 1828–1860*. Knoxville: University of Tennessee Press, 1992.

Yellin, Jean Fagan. *Harriet Jacobs: A Life*. New York: Basic Civitas Books, 2004.

———, and John C. Van Horne, eds. *The Abolitionist Sisterhood: Women's Political Culture in Antebellum America*. Ithaca, NY: Cornell University Press, 1994.

Zirblis, Raymond Paul. *Friends of Freedom: The Vermont Underground Railroad Survey Report*. Montpelier: State of Vermont Department of State Buildings and Division for Historic Preservation, 1996.

Pamphlets, Dissertations, Articles, and Reports

Beal, Gertrude. "The Underground Railroad in Guilford County." *The Southern Friend* 2(1), Spring 1980.

Borome, Joseph A. "The Vigilant Committee of Philadelphia." *The Pennsylvania Magazine of History and Biography* 92(1), 1968.

Brown, Ira V. "An Anti-Slavery Agent: C. C. Burleigh in Pennsylvania, 1836–1837." *Pennsylvania Magazine of History and Biography* 105: 1981.

Brown, Maxine F. *The Role of Free Blacks in Indiana's Underground Railroad: The Case of Floyd, Harrison, and Washington Counties.* Indianapolis: Indiana Department of Natural Resources, 2001.

Caccamo, James F. *Hudson, Ohio, and the Underground Railroad.* Hudson: The Friends of the Hudson Library, Inc., 1992.

"Connecticut as a Slave State." *Connecticut Western News,* May 23, 1916.

Coon, Diane Perrine. "Reconstructing the Underground Railroad Crossings at Madison, Indiana." University of Louisville, 1998.

———. "Indiana's Underground Railroad Routes and Operations." Study for the Indiana Department of Natural Resources, 2001.

———. "Chronicles of Rev. Chapman Harris." Unpublished paper. Copy in possession of the author.

———. "Great Escapes: The Underground Railroad." *Northern Kentucky Heritage* 9, no. 2, spring/summer 2002.

Cooper, Afua Ava Pamela. *"Doing Battle in Freedom's Cause": Henry Bibb, Abolitionism, Race Uplift, and Black Manhood, 1842–1854*. Ph.D. diss., University of Toronto, 2000.

Ebersole, Mark C. "Abolition Divides the Meeting House: Quakers and Slavery in Early Lancaster County." *Journal of the Lancaster County Historical Society* 102 (1), Spring 2000.

Farrell, John Kevin. *The History of the Negro Community in Chatham, Ontario.* Thesis, University of Ottawa, 1955.

Finkelman, Paul. "Prigg v. Pennsylvania and Northern State Courts: Anti-Slavery Use of a Pro-Slavery Decision." *Civil War History* 25: 1979.

Fuller, James. *Letters to the Farmers of Somerset.* Bristol, England: John Wright, 1836.

Gaspar, Doris. *Fort Malden Historical Study.* Report, Library of the Fort Malden National Historical Park, Amherstburg, Ontario.

Goodall, Hurley C. *Underground Railroad: The Invisible Road to Freedom through Indiana as Recorded by the Works Progress Administration Writers Project.* Indianapolis: Indiana Department of Natural Resources, 2000.

Goodheart, Lawrence B. "The Chronicles of Kidnapping in New York: Resistance to the Fugitive Slave Law, 1834–1835." *Afro-Americans in New York Life and History* 8, January 1984.

Graf, Hildegarde. "The Underground Railroad in Erie County." *Niagara Frontier*, autumn 1954.

Hamm, Thomas D. *The Antislavery Movement in Henry County, Indiana.* New Castle: Henry County Historical Society, 1987.

Henderson, Alice. *The History of the New York State Anti-Slavery Society*. Ph.D. diss., University of Michigan, 1963.

Hopkins, Leroy. "Black Eldorado on the Susquehannah: The Emergence of Black Columbia, 1726-1861." *Journal of the Lancaster County Historical Society* 89 (4), 1985.

———. "Bethel African Methodist Church in Lancaster: Prolegomenon to a Social History." *Journal of the Lancaster County Historical Society* 90 (4), 1986.

———. *Among These Hills: African Americans in Lancaster County's Southern End.* Paper presented to the Southern Lancaster County Historical Society, July 6, 2000.

Hopper, Isaac Tatum. *Exposition of the Proceedings of John P. Darg, Henry W. Merritt, and Others, in Relation to the Robbery of Darg, the Elopement of His Alleged Slave, and the Trial of Barney Corse, Who Was Unjustly Charged as an Accessory.* New York: Isaac T. Hopper, 1840.

Huff, Daniel. *Reminiscence of Newport and Fountain City and its Environs from 1830 to 1896.* Manuscript, 1896: Friends Historical Library, Earlham College.

———. *The Unnamed Anti-Slavery Heroes of Old Newport.* Paper presented to the Wayne County (Indiana) Historical Society, September 23, 1905; Friends Historical Library, Earlham College.

Jacobs, John S. "A True Tale of Slavery." *The Leisure Hour: A Family Journal of Instruction and Recreation,* February 7, 14, 21, and 28, 1861 (nos. 476–479).

Kelley, William T. "The Underground Railroad in the Eastern Shore of Maryland and Delaware." *Friends Intelligencer* 55, 1898.

Kenrick, John. *Horrors of Slavery*. Cambridge, England: Hilliard and Metcalf, 1817.

Kohler, Lyle. *Cincinnati's Black Peoples: A Chronology and Bibliography, 1787–1982*. Unpublished paper prepared for the Cincinnati Arts Consortium, 1986: Cincinnati Public Library.

Landon, Fred. "Amherstburg, Terminus of the Underground Railroad." *The Journal of Negro History* 10 (1), 1925.

———. "The Negro Migration to Canada after the Passing of the Fugitive Slave Act." *The Journal of Negro History* 5, January 1920.

Law, Howard. "'Self-Reliance Is the True Road to Independence': Ideology and the Ex-Slaves in Buxton and Chatham." *Ontario History* 77, 2, 1985.

Leslie, William R. "The Pennsylvania Fugitive Slave Act of 1826." *Journal of Southern History* 13, 1952.

Levy, Leonard W. "The Sims Case: The Fugitive Slave Law in Boston in 1851." *Journal of Negro History* 35, 1950.

Lumpkin, Katherine Du Pre. "'The General Plan Was Freedom': A Negro Secret Order on the Underground Railroad." *Phylon: Atlanta University Review of Race and Culture*, Spring 1967.

Mott, Lucretia, *Slavery and 'The Woman Question': Lucretia Mott's Diary of Her Visit to Great Britain to Attend the World's Anti-Slavery Convention of 1840.*" Supplement No. 23 to the *Journal of the Friends' Historical Society*, 1952.

Myers, John L. "The Beginning of Anti-Slavery Agencies in New York State, 1833–1836." *New York History*, April 1962.

———. "The Major Effort of National Anti-Slavery Agents in New York State, 1836-1837." *New York History*, April 1965.

Nagle, George F. "Central Pennsylvania Fugitive Slave Cases." *The Bugle* 12 (1), 2002.

Pease, Jane H., and William H. Pease. "Confrontation and Abolition in the 1850's." *Journal of American History* 58: 1972.

Pingeon, Frances D. "An Abominable Business: The New Jersey Slave Trade, 1818." *New Jersey History* 15–36, Fall/Winter 1991.

Polakow-Suransky, Sasha. "Sins of Our Fathers." *Brown Alumni Magazine* 36–42, July/August 2003.

Porter, Dorothy B. "David Ruggles, an Apostle of Human Rights." *Journal of Negro History* 28 (1), 1943.

Ratner, Vivienne. "The Underground Railroad in Westchester." *Westchester Historian* 59 (2), Spring 1983.

Ruggles, David. *The "Extinguisher" Extinguished: An Address on Slavery*. New York: David Ruggles, 1834.

———. *An Antidote: An Appeal to the Reason and Religion of American Christians*. New York: David Ruggles, 1838.

Russell, Hilary. *Final Research Report: The Operation of the Underground Railroad in Washington, D.C., c. 1800–1860.* Washington, D.C.: Historical Society of Washington and the National Park Service, 2001.

Siebert, Wilbur H. "The Underground Railroad in Massachusetts." *New England Quarterly* 9, September 1936.

Silverman, Jason H. "'We Shall Be Heard!': The Development of the Fugitive Slave Press in Canada." *Canadian Historical Review*, 65 (1), 1984.

Smith, Jay P. "Many Michigan Cities on Underground Route in Days of Civil War." *Detroit Sunday News*, April 14, 1918.

Spotts, Charles D. "The Pilgrim's Pathway: The Underground Railroad in Lancaster County." *Community History Annual* 5, 1966.

Turner, Edward R. "The Underground Railroad in Pennsylvania." *Pennsylvania Magazine of History and Biography* 36, 1912.

"Underground Railroad: Reminiscences of the Days of Slavery." *Detroit Post*, May 16, 1870.

Wagner, Thomas E. "Cincinnati and Southwestern Ohio: An Abolitionist Training Ground." Thesis, Miami University, 1967.

Walton, Jonathan W. "Blacks in Buxton and Chatham, Ontario, 1830-1890: Did the 49th Parallel Make a Difference?" Ph.D. diss., Princeton University, 1979.

Wright, Barbara. "North Carolina Quakers and Slavery." Thesis, University of North Carolina, 1974.

Wayne, Michael. "The Black Population of Canada West on the Eve of the American Civil War: A Reassessment Based on the Manuscript Census of 1861." *Histoire Sociale/Social History*, vol. 28, no. 56, 1995.

Wellman, Judith. "The Burned-Over District Revisited: Benevolence, Reform and Abolitionism in Mexico, Paris, and Ithaca, New York, 1825–1842." Ph.D. diss., University of Virginia, 1974.

Willey, Larry Gene. *The Reverend John Rankin: Early Ohio Antislavery Leader*. Thesis: University of Iowa, 1976.

Winch, Julie. "Philadelphia and the Other Underground Railroad." *The Pennsylvania Magazine of History and Biography* 111 (1), January 1987.

Yanuck, Julius. "The Garner Fugitive Slave Case." *Mississippi Valley Historical Review* 40, 1953.

Zirblis, Raymond Paul. *Friends of Freedom: The Vermont Underground Railroad Survey Report.* Montpelier: State of Vermont Department of State Buildings and Division for Historic Preservation, 1996.

INDEX